The Lawyer's Conscience

The Lawyer's Conscience
A History of American Lawyer Ethics

Michael S. Ariens

University Press of Kansas

Published by the University Press of Kansas (Lawrence, Kansas 66045), which was organized by the Kansas Board of Regents and is operated and funded by Emporia State University, Fort Hays State University, Kansas State University, Pittsburg State University, the University of Kansas, and Wichita State University.

Library of Congress Cataloging-in-Publication Data is available

Names: Ariens, Michael S., 1957– author.
Title: The lawyer's conscience : a history of American lawyer ethics / Michael S. Ariens.
Description: Lawrence : University Press of Kansas, 2023. | Includes index.
Identifiers: LCCN 2022010737
ISBN 9780700634095 (cloth)
ISBN 9780700633838 (paperback)
ISBN 9780700633869 (ebook)
Subjects: LCSH: Legal ethics—United States—History. | Lawyers—United States. | Practice of law—United States. | Honor. | Conscience—Moral and ethical aspects.
Classification: LCC KF306 .A79 2022 | DDC 174/.30973—dc23/eng/20220831
LC record available at https://lccn.loc.gov/2022010737.

British Library Cataloguing-in-Publication Data is available.

Printed in the United States of America

10 9 8 7 6 5 4 3 2 1

The paper used in this publication is acid free and meets the minimum requirements of the American National Standard for Permanence of Paper for Printed Library Materials Z39.48-1992.

CONTENTS

To my mother, Mary "Mimi" Ariens,
and
in memory of my father, Mike

ACKNOWLEDGMENTS

This book was long in the making. I owe a large debt of gratitude to the many persons without whom it would have been longer in the making and poorer in the result. My deepest thanks to Josiah M. Daniel III, Mike Hoeflich, John Leubsdorf, and Keith Swisher, each of whom carefully read the entire manuscript and made crucial suggestions that improved it. My thanks also to my colleagues Vicki Mather, Geary Reamey, and Vincent Johnson, who read parts of several chapters, commented on earlier works, and listened to long-winded arguments as I organized my ideas about the history of lawyer ethics in America. My additional thanks to Tom Morgan and David Skeel, who critically read individual chapters and improved them greatly. I am grateful to all for volunteering their time and sharing their knowledge.

Thanks to St. Mary's law librarian Stacy Fowler, whose assistance was remarkable. She found (and refound) materials that made this work immensely better. Thanks also to St. Mary's law librarian Mike Martinez and former St. Mary's law librarian Brian Detweiler for their assistance in finding sources and anticipating requests. I also thank Maria Vega and Aurora Torres for their superior secretarial assistance. My research assistants over the years—Lauren Valkenaar, Sumner Macdaniel, Dorian Ojemen, Stephanie Green, Mitchell Gonzales, Valerie Sánchez, and Sameer Bhuchar—spent many hours collecting, reviewing, and summarizing material. They represent some of the many wonderful graduates of St. Mary's University School of Law. My research assistant Elise McLaren Villers deserves special mention. She read the entire manuscript several times, contributed incisive memoranda, and uncovered sources of which I was unaware. Elise did an extraordinary job, for which I am grateful.

Thanks to the librarians of Harvard Law School, librarian Richard Tuske of the New York City Bar, the staff of the New York Public Library, archivists of the City of Philadelphia and the American Bar Foundation, and Jason Hiller of the New England area National Archives and Records Administration for correctly interpreting my often unclear requests. Many aided me during the height of the COVID-19 pandemic, for which I am grateful.

At an early stage of this project my wife, Renée, read several chapters and convinced me I was headed in the wrong direction. I am, as always, grateful for her love, her keen insights, and her understanding.

All remaining errors are mine.

This book is dedicated to my parents, a lifelong source of love and support. I have tried to emulate their example in raising our three wonderful children, now parents themselves.

The Lawyer's Conscience

INTRODUCTION

What does it mean to be an American lawyer? In many respects, American lawyers are like lawyers in much of the world: they represent clients in courts and before administrative bodies, advise them how to comply with the law, and counsel them on legal matters both routine and complex. American lawyers are often distinguished from their counterparts elsewhere by their zealous advocacy on behalf of their clients. And Americans live (and have always lived) in a particularly law-saturated society, which affects how lawyers advise and counsel clients. But lawyers zealously advocate for their clients nearly everywhere, and to do so they must master complex legal materials.

Being an American lawyer means exercising power: "In America THE LAW IS KING." Thomas Paine's vision in *Common Sense* proved true after the success of the American Revolution. A government of the people is a government of laws. The law, however, acts only through its agents, the lawyers who possess the knowledge to meet law's demands. Where law is king, lawyers' knowledge makes them especially powerful, placing them "at the crux of the rule of law."[1]

The federal and state constitutions in the new American republic installed a legal framework through which the actions of the people's legislative representatives were judged. Because men are not angels, a temporary majority might adopt legislation hostile to the federal Constitution. In that event, Alexander Hamilton wrote in Federalist 78, the courts possessed a duty to "declare all acts contrary to the manifest tenor of the Constitution void." A court would do so, of course, only at the behest of a lawyer who sued on behalf of a client. A constitutional check on the legislature thus legalized politics. As Alexis de Tocqueville famously wrote, "There is hardly a political question in the United States which does not sooner or later turn into a judicial one."[2]

The American embrace of a capitalist economic system also promoted the power of lawyers. Law in the nineteenth century was "inextricably

1

involved in the growth of our market economy." A major job of the legal system was to "protect and promote the release of individual creative energy to the greatest extent compatible with the opportunity for such expression." The "market revolution" of the early nineteenth century used lawyers, in one critical assessment, as "the shock troops of capitalism." But lawyers played an important role in the ordering of economic life even before the market revolution. Extraordinary economic growth was accompanied by crushing depression. Such dynamic economic and social changes throughout the nineteenth century generated numerous disputes among individuals and between the state and its citizens. Lawyers and judges were central in recognizing, framing, and resolving such disputes. As one historian notes, lawyers were not only "important initiators of the market system, [they] became its engineers, maintenance staff, and garbage collectors." These disputes were increasingly decided according to formal, published, judge-pronounced (and lawyer-inspired) common law, the province of lawyers and judges.[3]

The power of American lawyers increased during the Industrial Revolution, as it generated more work for them. For example, financing railroads and manufacturing concerns became increasingly complex, and both creditors and debtors relied on lawyers to counsel them. The rise of the administrative state, including governmental regulatory bodies such as the Food and Drug Administration, National Labor Relations Board, and Consumer Product Safety Commission, also increased the power of lawyers. The administrative state empowered experts in science and industry; it also made lawyers central to making, interpreting, and enforcing regulatory rules. Though criticized as the "rule of nobody," the rule of the administrative state is rule by lawyers.[4]

American lawyers also accumulated power as they became the principal actors in trials. Sensational trials have always fascinated the American public, and the adversary system highlighted opposing counsel as the trial's protagonists. Further, although Americans have long possessed a jaundiced view of lawyers and the justice system, the nation's cultural reverence for law is long standing, benefiting lawyers.[5]

Power tends to corrupt, and Americans have always feared that lawyers are corrupted vassals of the powerful. Lawyers have defended their exercise of power as a duty undertaken ultimately for the benefit of the public. This duty of fulfilling the needs of the public, lawyers argue, requires them to act as intermediaries between the individual and the state. They also claim they exercise power only within the rule of law, which protects both personal liberty and the public order that allows liberty to thrive. American lawyers have made this public service claim both broadly and modestly. They assert that they are the glue binding a diverse, pluralistic society into one people, allowing *e pluribus unum* to become and remain a reality. The first item of evidence offered to justify this broad claim is usually the predominance of lawyers among the delegates who drafted the Declaration of Independence in 1776 and the Constitution in 1787. Thus, lawyers demonstrated their service to the public by creating the very structure that made the people sovereign and the law king. Lawyers also argue they serve the public by mediating disputes among factions or individuals in accord with the rule of law. The peaceful resolution of disputes protects the liberty and property of the weak from the passions and desires of the strong. Society also benefits because lawyers have made, upheld, and executed the law through their work as legislators, judges, presidents and governors, and, in more recent times, experts populating administrative agencies.[6]

A similar but more modest argument is based on the ideal of the "country lawyer," a wise man (historically, a man) who served all who lived in the community, from the poorest widow to the wealthiest businessman. His professional expertise encompassed the entirety of the law, from writing wills, scrutinizing real property deeds, and drafting corporate bylaws to defending those accused of serious crimes. The country lawyer's wisdom and expertise made him indispensable to the community. The primary example of the country lawyer is Abraham Lincoln.[7]

These justifications for the power of lawyers were joined by the argument that lawyers served two roles, as both a private and a public actor. Lawyers in private practice declared that their primary duty was to serve as loyal, diligent, and competent servants of their clients. Doing so aided the public because protecting the rights of one implicitly protected the rights of others. This was consistent with the goals of a democratic society embracing an adversary system. Critics from the eighteenth century on have chastised lawyers for serving only their clients and not the public. Lawyers have rejected this criticism, pointing to various examples of their dual service. For instance, a 1701 colonial Massachusetts law (based on a much older English law) required an aspiring lawyer to swear an oath to the court, stating in part, "You shall use yourself in the office of an attorney within the court according to the best of your learning and discretion, and with all good fidelity as well to the courts as to your clients." This double fidelity required the lawyer to serve as an "officer of the court" as well as a loyal agent of his clients. As an officer of the court, the lawyer was responsible for facilitating the administration of justice. Though this duty was rarely specifically defined, a lawyer acted properly only when he served both client and society.[8]

Lawyers' dual duties permitted them to tout their position as mediators between court and client and between state and individual. But the colonial oath created a definitional bind. How could a lawyer serve two masters? The Gospel of Matthew, familiar to nearly all eighteenth- and nineteenth-century American lawyers, declared its impossibility: "No man can serve two masters." The bar's failure to define how lawyers could remain true to their oath gave them enormous discretion to decide what constituted the public interest.[9]

Lawyers traveled several paths to fulfill both duties. One approach was to deny the existence of any conflict. In his 1791 lectures on law, Supreme Court justice James Wilson concluded these "obligations are, by no means, incompatible: both will be discharged by uniform candour, and by a decent firmness properly blended with a dignified respect." An early-twentieth-century lawyer concluded, "*A lawyer is not the servant of his client. He is not the servant of the Court.* He is an *officer* of the Court, with all the rights and responsibilities which the character of his office gives and imposes." A second approach was to emphasize that because of the lawyer's greater legal knowledge, the client was dependent on the lawyer, not the other way around. Elite corporate lawyer Elihu Root said, "About half the practice of a decent lawyer consists in telling would-be clients that they are damned fools and should stop." This advantage in knowledge provided lawyers some independence from the demands of paying clients, for only the lawyer was fit to judge how a client should be represented. A third approach was to ostracize those lawyers deemed "unprofessional"—in other words, those who served clients beyond the bounds of the lawyer's duty had broken their oath and should be disbarred.[10]

The lawyers' ideal of a profession, as distinct from a business, also necessitated independence from both paying clients and the public. Independence was essential to professional identity. Early Massachusetts lawyer Theophilus Parsons wrote, "I never lost a case in my life: and the reason I suppose is, I never had one. My clients have lost a great many, but their cases were not mine." The profession's identity also required it to demonstrate its independence from the public for the public's benefit. When a lawyer represented an outcast, a client despised by the community, the lawyer offered a paradigmatic example of public service. Such a decision embraced the ideal that everyone should be tried and punished only according to the law. Lawyers argued that their independence from both client and public was crucial to the success of the republic.[11]

In contrast, a lawyer who was dependent on a client or subservient to the community forfeited this claim. The attachment to independence led an influential part of the profession to claim that service, not income, was their ultimate purpose. A fee was an incidental consequence received after the lawyer had provided competent service. When John Adams was sworn in as an attorney in 1758, his sponsor Jeremiah Gridley advised him, "Pursue the Study of the Law rather than the Gain of it. Pursue the Gain of it enough to keep out of the Briars, but give your main Attention to the study of it." Two centuries later, former Harvard Law School dean Roscoe Pound defined a profession as follows: "Historically, there are three ideas involved in a profession, organization, learning, and a spirit of public service. These are essential. The remaining idea, that of gaining a livelihood, is incidental." One problem with this conception of the practice of law was the public's awareness that lawyers' incomes were higher than those of most Americans. The public perceived that lawyers earned their incomes by aiding clients at the public's expense; thus lawyers' actions, the public concluded, often belied their words. The income premium enjoyed by lawyers has never strayed far from the minds of the profession's critics.[12]

As attorneys, lawyers were agents of their clients. Yet their dual loyalties distinguished them from ordinary agents. A lawyer was required by oath to abide by standards higher than the morals of the marketplace. Lawyers professed allegiance to a duty to obey certain limits on their behavior, even when doing so was contrary to their clients' interests. The American lawyer was ideally *in* the marketplace but not *of* the marketplace. As a corollary, the lawyer was *in* society yet *set apart from* society. These rule-of-law ideals allowed lawyers to argue that they served the public interest when representing any client with a legal claim. Whether that client's cause was good, bad, or unjust was not the lawyer's concern. The lawyer's duty to uphold the rule of law meant that it was ethically proper to take up any cause. In criminal cases, representing the guilty or unpopular client protected civilized society by ensuring the operation of the rule of law. The most commonly cited example regarding such behavior was John Adams's representation of the eight soldiers and one British officer in the Boston Massacre trials (see chapter 1).

American lawyers readily understood the conflict between the ideal of independence and the reality of practicing law. They relied on fees to earn a living. In 1645 the Virginia colonial legislature "expelled" all "mercenary attorneys" from office. Eleven years later, it became clear that the absence of mercenary attorneys meant the absence of nearly all attorneys: "This Assembly findeing many inconveniencies in the act prohibiting mercenary attorneys, do hereby enact, that . . . all other acts against mercenary attorneys to bee totally repealed." American lawyers were always in the market selling their services to private clients. The primacy of lawyers in the legal resolution of disputes demonstrated their power. The necessity of earning a living made them acutely conscious of their clients' interests, as well as sensitive to the community's moods and judgments. Failure to do so might mean the end of a lawyer's practice. These considerations often affected the lawyer's calculus of "independence" when deciding whether to represent an unpopular client.[13]

If the idealized vision of lawyers' independence was often in tension with their need to earn a living, other factors exacerbated that tension. Trials are a zero-sum contest. Lawyers want to win to demonstrate their abilities, but a lawyer who wins an "unjust cause" might be charged with using cunning and tricks. When the ordinary tension between the ideal and the actual arises, the public's tendency is to accuse lawyers of self-interest and public neglect. This common attack has often shifted to the claim that lawyers are amoral, avaricious self-dealers ready to betray clients, the courts, or the public for their own benefit.[14] Ambrose Bierce's *The Devil's Dictionary* defined *lawyer* as "One skilled in circumvention of the law." And a modern joke cleverly accused lawyers of unmitigated greed: "Lawyers' creed: a man is innocent until proven broke."[15]

The powerful are always more feared than loved. The public's recognition of the power of lawyers after American independence gave rise to much antilawyer sentiment, exemplified by a series of essays published in 1786 titled *Observations on the Pernicious Practice of the Law* (see chapter 1). The public's fear of power's corrupting effect on lawyers has resulted in waves of heightened antilawyer sentiment.[16]

In addition to asserting that their work for private clients constitutes public service, lawyers have made several other arguments to defend themselves. First, they claim that most attacks on lawyers are rooted in a lack of understanding of the adversary system, the rule of law, and the needs of the people in a republican form of government. Lawyers zealously represent parties with conflicting claims because such advocacy advances the public good. The lawyer is an advocate, not a judge. James Wilson noted that disputes were "susceptible of no other application, than that they be decided according to the law of the land." In an 1839 speech, Timothy Walker concluded that the lawyer "is not accountable for the moral character of the cause he prosecutes." In a republican government, the better approach is to allow all parties to make their claims in a court of law.[17]

Second, lawyers have blamed a small subset of unprofessional and immoral lawyers for coloring the entire profession. One of John Adams's pet peeves as a young lawyer was the proliferation of *pettifoggers*. The lawyer as *shyster* originated in the 1840s, and the term *ambulance chaser* was coined at the end of the nineteenth century. *Mouthpiece* was commonly applied to lawyers in the early twentieth century, and the appellation *hired gun* arose in the late 1960s. No matter the description, lawyers have argued that these "dirty Dab[b]lers in the Law" are unrepresentative. The good news, according to lawyers, is that, given the minuscule number of outliers, they have caused only limited harm. In 1957 American Bar Association (ABA) president David Maxwell lamented the public's failure to notice the good work lawyers did. Instead, critics harped on "the contumacious conduct of an infinitesimal number of our profession who persist in flouting our canons of ethics."[18]

Third, and related to the pettifogger problem, lawyers have defended themselves by arguing that society would be better served if lawyers controlled entry into the profession. Before Adams left the practice of law in the mid-1770s, sworn attorneys in Massachusetts and other colonies had obtained some success in controlling admission to the bar. By the 1830s, most states had loosened their bar admission standards, a situation that continued for nearly a century. Elite lawyers mused that only a self-governing bar would raise its character, ordinarily by limiting membership. An overcrowded bar led to unseemly and unprofessional behavior.[19]

Finally, lawyers have defended their work by pointing out their ethical duties, which included acting primarily (though never exclusively) for the client's benefit. Even when the client paid the lawyer well, the lawyer's ethical duty to serve the public interest limited the extent to which the lawyer could accommodate a client's desires. Conversely, the lawyer's duty to serve clients diligently and zealously checked the community's passions. The ethical limits applicable to lawyer behavior therefore protected both clients and the public.[20]

If lawyers were held to a higher standard than the morals of the marketplace, what was that standard? One model was the concept of honor. Early-nineteenth-century lawyers were few in number and circumscribed in location. To act honorably, and to be perceived as acting honorably by one's peers, was an important mark of success. Dishonorable behavior was socially shameful and might subject the lawyer to disbarment. Even if not disbarred, the lawyer might be ostracized. Published disbarment cases in the early national era were modest in number, but nearly all referenced the lawyer's dishonorable conduct when striking him from the roll of attorneys. The honor culture, however, slowly lost its authority as a guide to ethical lawyer behavior. This was visible by the 1830s, although honor remained a touchstone through the early twentieth century.[21]

The predominant standard of ethical lawyer behavior from the 1830s through much of the twentieth century was that of individual character and inner conscience. A lawyer's actions were ethical if undertaken in the presence of a well-formed conscience. Unlike honor, conscience is an internal standard. Honor calls to mind reputation, the judgment of the relevant community, and conscience calls to mind a person's moral character. By the mid-nineteenth century, good moral character was considered essential to a good society: "A society is always just what its members make it by their character; nothing more, nothing less." Society needed lawyers and other persons of character to calm the community's passions: "The person of strong character transcended fickle public opinion and fleeting public repute." And reflecting on conscience provided a person of strong character the opportunity to understand what was ethically right.[22]

The emergence of conscience as a standard fit the times, and the idea of honor became anachronistic in much of the United States. In addition to transformative economic change, cultural changes in American society during the early national period—increased democratization of society, rising individualism, and changes in Protestantism—became more pronounced. The standard of honor did not disappear; it was, however, unmoored from its prominent position and later served as either an occasional rallying cry or a fond memory.

A lawyer was supposed to follow high moral principles when assessing conscience, but how was that achieved as a practical matter? A person's instructed conscience corresponded with moral law, making this judgment personal. This inward turn was assisted by broad contours channeling the instructed conscience. General rules prohibited a lawyer from disclosing confidential communications with a client and from having conflicts of interest in representing a client. The specific exceptions to the ethics rules were uncertain, as they lay in the realm of conscience rather than external rule. In addition, the rise of the instructed conscience was accompanied by a more modern use of the words *profession, professional,* and *professionalism*—that is, as nouns rather than adjectives (e.g., a *professional* versus a *professional lawyer*). George Sharswood's 1854 lectures on lawyer ethics were titled in part *On the Aims and Duties of the Profession of the Law.* It was an early effort to name lawyers as members of a profession.[23]

For more than a century, writings on legal ethics emphasized character, conscience, and reflection. Through actual or perceived professional crises in the 1870s, 1890s, 1910s, 1930s, and 1950s, the ethical standard of good conscience remained predominant. The high-water mark emphasizing the lawyer's duty to use conscience to generate ethical, professional behavior was a remarkable joint effort by the ABA and the Association of American Law Schools in the late 1950s. The conference report, largely written by Harvard Law School professor Lon L. Fuller, encouraged lawyers to think more introspectively about the deep connection between conscience and the public work of lawyers in their daily acts of practicing law (see chapter 5). Some important external behavioral limits were developed during the lengthy period in which conscience was the lawyer's guide, such as the (modest) limits related to zealous advocacy at trial, but these rules were relatively few and were largely accounted for by the lawyer's oath of admission to the bar.[24]

The next model resulted from the adoption of codes of legal ethics. This effort began modestly in voluntary state bar associations in the late nineteenth century. Initially, the massive growth of the legal profession from 1870 through 1910 made elite lawyers uncomfortable with the idea of conscience serving as the sole guide to ethical behavior. Those lawyers generated external standards as a general guide informing the lawyer's conscience.[25]

This model has gone through three iterations. The first code of ethics was adopted by the Alabama State Bar Association in 1887. In 1908 the ABA adopted its own canons of professional ethics. These codes were largely exhortations from the elite to the mass of lawyers, urging the latter to practice more conscientiously and professionally. Such codes and canons rarely rose to the standard of enforceable duties.[26]

The second iteration began in 1969 with the ABA's adoption of its Code of Professional Responsibility, consisting of nine canons. Each canon contained ethical considerations that were "aspirational in character . . . toward which every member of the profession should strive," as well as a series of disciplinary rules consisting of enforceable standards below which a lawyer could not fall. The code combined conscience with enforceable external standards, and it was quickly adopted as law by most states.[27]

In the aftermath of the Watergate scandal, the ABA commissioned another project on legal ethics. The Model Rules of Professional Conduct (1983) introduced the third stage in the development of codes of ethics for lawyers. The model rules largely consisted of minimum external behavioral standards that lawyers were legally bound to meet or be "subject to discipline." Even in the model rules, however, some choices of conscience remained. And the freedom to exercise one's conscience includes the freedom to ignore one's conscience.[28]

Several additional projects involving lawyer ethics have been undertaken since 1983, all of which adopted the legalization–external standard model. A more pressing concern for lawyers is the professionalism crisis. That crisis has laid bare the way in which competition for legal work has influenced the ethical ideals lawyers have long claimed to embrace. A principal result of this era of crisis has been a strong sense of the fracturing of the legal profession. The historical promotion of the idea of a single profession of law always papered over the great distinctions among the different types and classes of lawyers. Beginning in the 1970s, efforts to patch those differences became ineffective and increasingly less common.

The first three chapters of this book trace the changing understanding of the ethical duties of American lawyers from the late colonial era through the nineteenth century. Each of the next three chapters is framed by the ABA's three distinct efforts to craft rules of behavior applicable to all practicing lawyers. The last chapter focuses on the professionalism crisis and efforts by American lawyers to understand their roles in a pluralistic, divided, and anxious society. Although the consequences of rapid technological change to the practice of law are mentioned, the ethical issues generated by such change remain a muddled mess and are not discussed.

The American legal profession has always consisted of a disparate group with little in common other than a license to practice law. And for most lawyers, only their actions in representing clients are available to explain their understanding of their professional duties. The chapters that follow often use specific examples of client representation as evidence of what lawyers of that time considered proper (or improper) behavior. The relatively few lawyers who have written about legal ethics are an important subset of the legal profession, and those writings are used as evidence of the profession's ideals. But it is impossible to say these specific examples and writings actually represent the views of this disparate profession. Thus, this book is *a* history of American lawyer ethics.

CHAPTER ONE

Origins, 1760–1830

"I have absolutely heard it used as a Proverb in several Parts of the Province, 'as litigious as Braintree.' And this Multiplicity [of lawsuits] is owing to the Multiplicity of Petty foggers among whom captn. Hollis is one, who has given out that he is a sworn Attorney until 9/10 of this Town really believe it." Twenty-four-year-old John Adams continued his diary entry: "He knows in his Conscience that he never took the Oath of an Attorney, and that he dare not assume the Impudence to ask to be admitted." Adams, unlike Thomas Hollis, was a member of the bar of Suffolk County, Massachusetts. His indignation in this June 18, 1760, entry was an indication, in a draft of a forthcoming court argument, of his view of an "infinitely and contemptible" case. Adams named and criticized "Petty foggers" three times in that draft. Hollis and others generated "strife, Vexation and Immorality" by filing "contemptible" lawsuits against which Adams defended.[1]

Adams's anger may have been stoked by his belief that one or more pettifoggers had "set himself to work to destroy my Reputation and prevent my getting Business." His diary entry a day later brought a cooler but still passionate tone to his argument. He now railed against "dirty Dab[b]lers in the Law." Adams demanded he be allowed to offer "a much greater Veneration for the Law." This contrast would allow the court to "see the Forms and Processes of Law and Justice thus prostituted, (I must say prostituted) to revenge an imaginary Indignity."[2]

Adams's distinction between "dirty Dab[b]lers" or "Petty foggers" and members of the bar was related to the rise of lawyers' status during the late colonial era. Beginning in the 1760s, Suffolk County lawyers undertook a concerted effort to distinguish their calling from the work of unsworn attorneys, in part by creating a bar association. Relatedly, they sought to improve technical proficiency through a deeper knowledge of the common law. In

1771 the Suffolk County bar began such work, based on a 1768 set of "Rules agreed to by the Barristers and Attorneys of the County of Essex." The professionalization of the practice of law accelerated.[3]

The practice of law became increasingly financially attractive to young men during the late colonial period. That made it a viable option for young men like Adams, whose father was a farmer. As lawyers have gloated for more than two centuries, the profession was so important that men trained in law constituted a plurality of those who signed the Declaration of Independence and a majority of delegates at the 1787 Constitutional Convention. Lawyers' perception that they constituted a distinct body increased their attention to membership and the oath of office. Distinctiveness also attracted negative public attention, as lawyers became increasingly powerful. To lessen this concern, lawyers emphasized how they aided the community. An effective republican government was predicated on the rule of law. Lawyers ensured that law was king, thus protecting the sovereignty of the people.[4]

The Boston Massacre trials (1770) demonstrated the legal profession's faithfulness to the law and to the rule of law. Unpopular defendants needed and deserved legal counsel, and lawyers were bound to provide such counsel even when they might suffer a considerable cost. Lawyers have long cited Adams's representation of the defendants in these trials to justify the power they possess. In Philadelphia, over an eighteen-month period at the end of the decade, James Wilson and others represented nearly forty persons accused of treason. Almost all these trials ended in acquittal, in part due to the zeal with which defense counsel represented the unpopular accused. The lawyers were paid well for their work, but they preferred to emphasize their devotion to duty, their willingness to represent the outcast despite public sentiment.

The Philadelphia treason trials ended with a pitched battle at Fort Wilson. A physical confrontation with lawyers was not the only way the public expressed unhappiness with crafty lawyers in the late eighteenth century. Lawyers prospered during these troubled economic times, generating more antilawyer sentiment. Critics denounced lawyers' elevation in wealth and power. The most well-known early American critic of lawyers was Bostonian Benjamin Austin Jr. Under the pseudonym Honestus, Austin wrote a series of essays in 1786 in which he found both law and the work of lawyers wanting. His controversial views were sufficiently popular to be printed as a book, which was edited and republished in 1814 and 1819.[5]

Critics such as Austin found the practice of law corrupting. Lawyers zealously represented their clients while disclaiming any moral responsibility for defending their clients' causes. In New York City, the zeal exercised by the lawyers defending the accused in two closely covered criminal trials angered ordinary citizens. In 1793 Henry Bedlow was acquitted of rape. Seven years later Levi Weeks was found not guilty of murder. Both acquittals were controversial. In Bedlow's case, the public rioted days after he was freed and threatened to burn down his lawyers' houses. Despite news accounts proclaiming the fairness of Weeks's trial, some believed his lawyers had helped him get away with murder.

The defense of Weeks continued the trend of zealous representation found in the Boston Massacre and Philadelphia treason trials. Weeks's lawyers, Alexander Hamilton, Aaron Burr, and Brockholst Livingston, offered "technical" legal arguments regarding the sufficiency of the indictment, questioned the suitability of prospective jurors, objected to "hear-say," and challenged the "pertinence" (relevance) or competence of the evidence. Defense counsel also used effective cross-examination to weaken the prosecution's case. In controversial or sensational trials, the public saw how lawyers worked and both praised and damned them.

The material attractions of the legal profession brought dross as well as gold. Then as now, lawyers defrauded their clients, suborned perjury, and otherwise committed "mal-practices." By the 1810s, and more so during the 1820s, the "mal-practices" of a few lawyers had been discussed in published opinions and other writings. In the modest number of cases that were the subject of extensive reporting, it appeared that only the most pernicious practices of the law subjected a lawyer to disciplinary sanction.

By 1830, the lawyer as zealous advocate was commonplace. Daniel Webster, a famous antebellum lawyer, agreed to serve as a special prosecutor in an infamous murder case. Webster's actions, including some dubious ethical choices, may provide an example of how trial lawyers understood their job.

Practicing Law, 1760–1770

Adams's displeasure with Captain Hollis and other pettifoggers reflected the connection between his reputation and his economic prosperity. As he wrote in an early diary entry, "Reputation ought to be the perpetual subject of my Thoughts, and Aim of my Behaviour. How shall I Spread an Opinion of myself as a Lawyer of distinguished Genius, Learning, and Virtue."

Adams linked learning and oath taking with professional success. He also believed he protected law's virtue more than the "dirty Dab[b]lers."[6]

Adams's interest in separating himself from other, less honorable practitioners of the law was both economic and social. His status as someone who venerated the law helped establish his reputation. Massachusetts was home to several well-regarded lawyers in the mid- and late eighteenth century, but when Adams was admitted to the bar in 1758, it largely lacked a "legal profession."[7]

During Adams's relatively brief career as a lawyer, a profession began to form. When Adams spoke to eminent lawyer Jeremiah Gridley about practicing law in Braintree, Gridley told Adams that he could enjoy an "Introduction to the Practice of Law in [Suffolk] County" once he got sworn. Gridley agreed to recommend Adams if, after consultation, the bar consented. It did. After Lieutenant Governor Thomas Hutchinson was appointed chief justice of the Superior Court of Judicature, he limited appearances in that court to barristers. The distinction between attorneys and solicitors, on the one hand, and barristers, on the other, had not previously existed in the colony. Every attorney who had taken the oath of office was made a barrister, further distinguishing Adams's status.[8]

In early 1765 Adams became a founding member of Solidatis, a club created to study legal history and theory. Adams enthusiastically joined Solidatis because, paraphrasing cofounder Gridley, it would "support the Honour and Dignity of the Bar." In January 1770 thirteen members of the Suffolk bar met and organized themselves into a bar association.[9]

A 1701 Massachusetts law provided the oath of admission to the bar:

> You shall do no falsehood, nor consent to any to be done in the court, and if you know of any to be done you shall give knowledge thereof to the Justices of the Court, or some of them, that it may be reformed. You shall not wittingly and willingly promote, sue or procure to be sued any false or unlawful suit, nor give aid or consent to the same. You shall delay no man for lucre or malice, but you shall use yourself in the office of an attorney within the court according to the best of your learning and discretion, and with all good fidelity as well to the courts as to your clients. So help you God.[10]

This oath was the only formal statement of the ethical duties of sworn lawyers. The first three duties enjoined lawyers from speaking falsely or countenancing false statements from others. The lawyer also served as an administrator of justice by securing justice expeditiously, acting competently, and swearing faithfulness to both courts and clients.[11]

The Boston Massacre Trials

Three years after the Boston Massacre, John Adams wrote in his diary:

> The Part I took in Defence of Cptn. Preston and the Soldiers, procured me Anxiety, and Obloquy enough. It was, however, one of the most gallant, generous, manly and disinterested Actions of my whole Life, and one of the best Pieces of Service I ever rendered my Country. Judgment of Death against those Soldiers would have been as foul a Stain upon this Country as the Executions of the Quakers or Witches, anciently. As the Evidence was, the Verdict of the Jury was exactly right.

Much later, in an unpublished autobiography, he affirmed this judgment. He had acted properly, even though his decision generated "popular Suspicions and prejudices, which are not yet worn out and never will be forgotten as long as History of this Period is read."[12]

On March 5, 1770, British soldiers at the Custom House fired into a restive crowd. Five people died. Captain Thomas Preston and eight soldiers were charged with murder. Preston and the soldiers were tried separately, despite the objections of several soldiers. Preston's trial was first, and he was represented by Robert Auchmuty Jr., Adams, and Josiah Quincy Jr. The trial lasted an extraordinary five days, at the end of which Preston was acquitted, thanks in part to the successful cross-examination of witnesses, which cast doubt on whether Preston had issued an order to shoot, and in part to contrary testimony by defense witnesses. Another advantage was that two of Preston's "close friends" were members of the jury. Adams and Quincy represented the eight soldiers at the second trial beginning in November. The soldiers claimed self-defense. The crowd had pelted them with snowballs, and some carried weapons. This trial took eight days. Six of the eight were acquitted; the others were found guilty of manslaughter and were branded on the thumb instead of being hanged.[13]

The legal profession's understanding of Adams's work (Auchmuty and Quincy usually disappear from view—the former because he was a loyalist, and the latter because, though a patriot, he died in 1775 at age thirty-one) mimics his judgment: representing the unpopular client was the epitome of service to both client and community. Adams honored the nation's embrace of the rule of law, applicable to all. In 2011 President Barack Obama declared May 1 Law Day in honor of "The Legacy of John Adams: From Boston to Guantanamo."[14]

Shortly before Adams died in 1826, the legal profession's interpretation began to take hold. Lawyer and writer William Sullivan praised Adams before the Suffolk County bar for aiding the Boston Massacre defendants: "Considering his devotion to the cause of liberty, at that time, it required no little independence, to appear in defence of the prisoners, when the popular sentiment was so highly adverse to his side of the case." The Boston-based *American Jurist & Law Magazine* offered a similar view in 1841, noting "the degree of moral courage which was then requisite in an advocate, in order to engage in a cause where the popular feeling was so intensely excited as it was on that occasion."[15]

Since then, most legal commentators have agreed. However, a 1937 essay suggested otherwise, based on correspondence during the Boston Massacre trials between Thomas Hutchinson, the loyalist lieutenant governor of Massachusetts, and British army commander Thomas Gage. Hutchinson reported the rumor that "one of the Council [*sic*] is not so faithful as he ought to be" in conducting the soldiers' defense. Hutchinson's report was suspect: the rumor may have represented a "difference of opinion" concerning how much blame to accord the townspeople. The unnamed lawyer, later revealed to be Adams, was a "partisan" (patriot) and might have wished only "to blacken the people as little as may be possible consistent with his Duty to his Clients." Given the increasing divide between loyalists and patriots, Hutchinson had little credibility when speaking of Adams.[16]

In 1969 Hiller Zobel presented a revisionist perspective in two essays. Zobel initially noted the standard story of the Boston Massacre trials representing "the apogee of the American legal profession." But there remained a "mystery, of what might even be called doubt," about its accuracy. Based on Hutchinson's writings, Zobel had an "uncomfortable feeling" about Adams's advocacy for the soldiers. Despite Adams's overall success, Zobel concluded that, "in trying to do what he considered justice to Boston, John Adams came shockingly close to sacrificing his clients for the good of his constituency." (Adams was an elected representative from Boston.) The second essay, coauthored with L. Kinvin Wroth, detailed the history of the trials. The authors noted the absence of evidentiary objections and found "wholly absent . . . slashing cross-examination." This essay also raised the issue of Adams's conflict in representing both Preston and the soldiers. If Preston did not give the order to shoot, he was not guilty. Unfortunately, that also eliminated the soldiers' defense that they were following an officer's order. Wroth and Zobel concluded, at "this distance, we cannot determine whether, as Hutchinson suggested, Adams allowed only the minimum of evidence necessary for acquittal." The "doubt" expressed earlier by Zobel is absent.[17]

Zobel's *The Boston Massacre* (1970) closely analyzes Adams's representation. During Preston's trial, Adams threatened to leave the case if Quincy offered additional evidence of the crowd's intent to drive out the army. Was Adams's threat to withdraw related to excusing Bostonians for the massacre? Zobel concludes that Adams "was not abandoning his client." Adams himself declared his virtue in a note written in the margins of a book alleging his misconduct: "Adams' motive is not here perceived. His Clients [*sic*] lives were hazarded by Quincy's too youthful ardour." Quincy relented, and Adams addressed the jury in his closing argument. Zobel surprisingly writes, "Preston must have wondered whether in his summation the little barrister [Adams] would continue pulling his forensic punches. He need not have worried." Zobel praises Adams's closing argument.[18]

As for the soldiers' trial, Zobel recounts the same disagreement, resolved the same way. That is the extent of his criticism. Of Adams's closing argument, Zobel concludes that it "has never been praised for what it really was, a masterpiece of political tightroping and partisan invective, wrapped in a skillful, effective jury argument." Even Hutchinson found the closing argument praiseworthy: Adams "closed extremely well & with great fidelity to his clients."[19]

The American legal profession celebrates Adams for representing unpopular clients, demonstrating the service a lawyer provides to the community. A fastidious critic might chide Adams for twice threatening to abandon his clients if Quincy disregarded his theory of the case. It is unknown whether Auchmuty, the senior lawyer in the Preston trial, responded in any way to what secondhand gossip considered to be a threat by Adams. Again, Adams's preference won the day. Decades later he offered a rejoinder explaining the disagreement. A lawyer's willingness to abandon the accused in an ongoing trial strikes the modern reader as inconceivable. But no solid evidence exists of such a threat by Adams. The trials were the talk of the town; rumors were rampant among both Preston's supporters and others who saw the possibility of unfaithfulness in every decision made by counsel.

Adams may have been *too* faithful to his clients. In his closing argument to the jury, Adams blamed the dead, claiming they died because they threatened the soldiers. Dr. John Jeffries testified that victim Patrick Carr told him, "He really thought they did fire to defend themselves." Adams used existing prejudices to blame Carr and the other "motley rabble of saucy boys, negroes and molattoes, Irish teagues and out landish jack tarrs" for their own deaths. Carr was a "native of *Ireland*" (that is, he was Roman Catholic, in an anti-Catholic colony) who "had often been concerned in such attacks." Adams repeated these slurs against Carr. The only evidence of Carr's "concern" was that he wore a sword before leaving for the Custom House, but he did not take it with him. No evidence was offered of any mobbish behavior by Carr. Should a lawyer's zeal allow him to use prejudicial and emotional appeals to exonerate his clients?[20]

The Battle of "Fort Wilson" and the Philadelphia Treason Trials

On October 4, 1779, a crowd of militiamen marched through the streets of Philadelphia and eventually past the house of James Wilson. The crowd outside Wilson's house and the crowd inside exchanged words, followed by gunfire. The crowd outside had just breached Wilson's home when Joseph Reed, president of the Supreme Executive Council of Pennsylvania, arrived with a cavalry unit, which ejected the intruders and ended the confrontation. The dead numbered six or seven, and between seventeen and nineteen were injured in the ten-minute battle of "Fort Wilson."[21]

By the time of these events, Pennsylvania courts had presided in thirty-seven cases of high treason. Thirty-two defendants were found not guilty, four were found guilty of treason, and one was found guilty of burglary. Wilson was a well-known lawyer and patriot whose revolutionary politics differed from that of many militiamen, as did the politics of many of the accused.[22]

The treason trials were triggered by the departure of the British from Philadelphia in June 1778 after nine months of occupation. Returning to a devastated city, many revolutionary patriots wanted revenge. Some of those targeted for attack were the pacifist Quakers. About the Quakers and other defendants, Charles Page Smith wrote, "They had rights to defend against the indiscriminate anger of enthusiastic colonials and in many cases good hard money to pay for defending them." Wilson, along with lawyers George Ross and William Lewis, took the "good hard money" of the accused and defended them.[23]

The first Philadelphia-based treason case began on September 25, 1778. The defendant, Abraham Carlisle, was charged with holding a commission with the British army and guarding one of the gates to the city. The lawyers "fought the cases ferociously." Carlisle's lawyers argued the prosecution had to specify which overt acts Carlisle had committed, so he could defend himself. That Carlisle had confessed to accepting a commission, absent other evidence (such as the commission itself), was insufficient to prove treason. The court declined to follow Wilson's arguments. It summarized the law of treason broadly, and the jury convicted Carlisle. His lawyers moved to arrest (halt the entry of) judgment on four separate grounds, all of which demonstrated technical proficiency. The court overruled the motion, and Carlisle was hanged after appeals for leniency were rejected.[24]

Wilson and Ross also represented John Roberts, tried less than a week after Carlisle. Again, they did so ferociously but unsuccessfully. Roberts was convicted and hanged.[25]

From October 3, 1778, through October 2, 1779, twenty-four treason trials took place in Philadelphia. In only one case did the jury convict a defendant of treason. The last of those trials occurred two days before the confrontation at Fort Wilson. Wilson successfully represented the accused traitor.[26]

Some of the public criticized Wilson's work in these trials. Afterward, the Supreme Executive Council indirectly blamed the lawyers for aiding Tories. The history of Fort Wilson was, however, presented as another example in which defense counsel protected the rule of law and the broader public against populist attacks. Fellow Scots Pennsylvanian Arthur St. Clair favorably summarized Wilson's legal efforts, stating, "advocating the causes of the accused persons should certainly not have been considered as a crime, as it is both a part and a consequence of that liberty we have been struggling to establish."[27]

Honestus and Antilawyer Sentiment

In spring 1786 Benjamin Austin Jr., writing as Honestus, authored thirteen essays attacking lawyers and the English common law in Boston's *Independent Chronicle*. The first ten were collected and printed in book form that year. Austin's principal observation was that lawyers were a "USELESS" and "DANGEROUS" body that should be "ANNIHILATED." Lawyers used the law for their own benefit. As a self-proclaimed *profession*, did lawyers aid or endanger the community? Austin concluded the latter. Lawyers were "daily growing rich," collecting "*enormous* FEES" at the expense of the public. Better to abolish them and rely on "gentlemen of fortune" to serve as judges, who "would make the public good their chief object." This was preferable to a "profession as a set of *needy persons*, who meant by chicanery and finesse, to get a living by their practice."[28]

Austin's fourth disquisition touched a nerve: lawyers aided the rich and ignored the poor. Additionally, they lacked moral scruples. They were "like mercenary troops" willing "to support any cause for the consideration of a large reward." Because the poor were unable to pay lawyers' fees, the system of justice tilted in favor of the rich. The profession's quest for fees at the expense of justice demonstrated why it should be abolished.[29]

In response to Austin's attacks, "A Lawyer" wrote three letters published in the *Massachusetts Centinel*. First, the writer admitted misconduct by some: "That there are abuses in the profession, productive of private distress and public uneasiness, I most readily agree." However, these dishonorable lawyers constituted only a modest few engaged in the practice of law. "A Lawyer" also criticized Austin's emotionally laden and generalized arguments. If Austin was unhappy about the public influence of lawyers, why not blame society? The third letter responded to Austin's other proposed reforms, such as using intelligent lay friends to plead a person's case. This would ill serve someone whose entire estate might be lost. Eliminating lawyers, he observed, placed an onerous burden on litigants when just a "small proportion" of the bar's alleged offenses were true. "A Lawyer" suggested, "If a Lawyer is chargeable with malpractices, cease to employ him, and he will soon find it for his interest to correct his conduct, and tread the paths of rectitude and honour." How this market-based approach would work in practice he did not say. Another respondent explained that dishonorable conduct among lawyers was a consequence of an overcrowded profession.[30]

"Zenas," the pen name of lawyer James Sullivan, wrote a three-part defense of lawyers that appeared in the *Independent Chronicle* near Austin's letters. At the time, Sullivan may have been the most highly regarded lawyer in Massachusetts. He made three claims: first, lawyers were necessary to a free government; second, lawyers were particularly necessary in Massachusetts in light of its constitution and laws; and third, "the gentlemen of this profession, in this state have such checks upon their conduct, and are so peculiarly liable to exemplary punishment, for fraud and dishonesty, that the weakest subject of the Commonwealth, has a ready, cheap, and certain remedy against them." Sullivan more fully explained this last point in his third writing, published on May 11, 1786. It was impossible to keep "entirely out of any profession" those "men of bad morals and dishonest hearts." Thus, it was "necessary to regulate the conduct of those who commonly practiced in the Courts." The 1701 oath was one way to do so. The Supreme Judicial Court admitted as a barrister only an individual who would "demean himself so as to do honour to Court and bar." Lawyers usually acted honorably because their "bread as well as the character of the practitioners of the law depends on their integrity and uprightness." Acting dishonorably "must turn him from the bar, and ruin him forever." But Honestus made no specific charges against any lawyer.[31]

Austin's tenth letter responded to Sullivan. He quoted a clause in the oath requiring the lawyer to inform the justices of another lawyer's falsehood. If "A Lawyer" was correct, those lawyers engaged in wrongful conduct needed to be stricken from the roll of attorneys, a duty of the lawyers themselves. Lawyers needed to clean their own house, ejecting pernicious practitioners. Austin then reiterated that lawyers looked to enrich themselves at their clients' expense. They would "pervert" and manipulate the law to do so, threatening the people's liberty. Lawyers, he concluded, were simply untrustworthy.[32]

Antilawyer sentiment in Massachusetts was stoked because lawyers collected debts during "hard times." But the public was also aroused by valid charges of professional misconduct.[33]

Austin's missives generated about 150 letters supporting and challenging his diagnosis and cure. Massachusetts was not the only state in which antilawyer sentiment took hold. Most states saw a rise in such sentiment in the aftermath of the Revolution, and criticisms were sharper and angrier than the antilawyer doggerel commonplace during the Revolution.[34]

Shortly after publication of his thirteenth essay in late June, Austin left for Europe. In late August, farmers in western Massachusetts closed the

Northampton courthouse. Soon Shays's Rebellion was in full swing. Boston newspapers accused Austin of fomenting it. The regulators, as they called themselves, closed some courthouses in western Massachusetts and barred several scheduled sessions of the Supreme Judicial Court. By early February 1787, the rebellion was over. Its rise cannot fairly be placed at Austin's feet. A revisionist understanding of the rebellion casts significant doubt that objections related to debt claims, including litigation, precipitated it.[35]

Observations was republished in 1814 and 1819, and the latter is the enduring edition. In the 1819 edition's "Prefatory Address," Austin no longer called for the annihilation of the legal profession: "The author flatters himself, that the practice within the bar has become more congenial to the happiness of society; and under this impression, acknowledges the utility of the profession." Instead of abolition, he sought "regulation."[36]

In 1806 Benjamin Austin's intemperate feelings about lawyers contributed to the killing of his eighteen-year-old son Charles by an intemperate lawyer named Thomas O. Selfridge. Austin and other Democratic Republican Party leaders organized a Fourth of July celebration. Apparently, a number of celebrants did not purchase tickets to pay for the food they ate. When Eben Eager, who had supplied the food, requested payment, a dispute arose. Eager discussed the matter with Selfridge, a Federalist Party member. Selfridge concluded that Austin and the other organizers were "personally liable" to Eager, and Eager was paid after Selfridge sued on his behalf. Austin accused "a damned Federal lawyer" of stirring up trouble. He "hinted that the suit was brought at the lawyer's instigation." This cast Selfridge as dishonorable because, if he had fomented litigation, he had committed the common-law crime of barratry and was subject to disbarment. When Selfridge learned of the allegations, he demanded a retraction, even though Austin had not named him. Austin seemingly retracted his statement, but Selfridge declared it unsatisfactory. He concluded that his options were "a prosecution, chastisement, or posting," a libel suit, a physical correction, or a public denouncement of Austin as dishonorable. Selfridge chose the last. In the August 4, 1806, issue of the *Boston Gazette*, he declared Austin "A COWARD, A LIAR, AND A SCOUNDREL." The same day, Austin responded in the *Independent Chronicle*, promising to give any inquiring gentlemen the facts. By early afternoon, Charles Austin was dead.[37]

Selfridge, armed with a pistol, met Charles, who was carrying a newly purchased "walking stick," "heavy cane," or "cudgel," at the Market Exchange in downtown Boston. Charles had been conversing with friends for hours at the exchange, which Selfridge was known to frequent at midday. Selfridge was carrying a pistol because he had been warned of threats made against him. At nearly the exact spot of the Boston Massacre, Austin struck Selfridge with his new cane, and Selfridge drew his weapon and shot and mortally wounded Austin. The order of these events was disputed. Selfridge was indicted for manslaughter rather than murder, which angered many. The killing was the subject of intense public interest, and this inspired two shorthand reporters to record and publish an account of the trial.[38]

Republican attorney general James Sullivan ("Zenas") and solicitor general Daniel Davis prosecuted the case. Selfridge was represented by Samuel Dexter, who was nearly as highly regarded as Sullivan, and Christopher Gore, an ambitious Federalist and future governor. After some wrangling about the composition of the jury, the trial began with a significant disagreement about the prosecution's claim that it would prove that Selfridge had murdered Austin. Dexter and Gore objected to the admission of some evidence, and they cross-examined witnesses effectively. Then the case went sideways.[39]

After the defense rested, Sullivan renewed his request to offer evidence of the feud between Benjamin Austin and Selfridge. Gore responded, "I do not exactly know from the course this cause has taken that we ought to object to this motion, because our desire is, if it be consistent with the rules of law, to go into all the anterior circumstances." The motion was granted, and Sullivan called a dozen or so witnesses, several more than once, including Benjamin Austin. The entire sorry mess was recounted in detail.[40]

In his closing argument to the jury, Gore stated, "I therefore leave the Defendant with you, barely stating my own conviction, as a lawyer, a Christian, and a man, that he has committed no offence, either against the law of society, of religion, or of nature." Gore's "vouching" for the innocence of his client would, in less than two generations, be declared unethical. Senior defense counsel Dexter followed and repeatedly urged the jury to acquit Selfridge because Austin's claim of barratry "was fatal to the reputation of a lawyer." It was a "point of honor" that Selfridge had to avenge. (Selfridge repeated this claim in his post-trial pamphlet justifying his actions.) As Sullivan noted in his closing argument, Dexter was arguing that the defense of one's honor allowed one to take the law into one's own hands.[41]

Selfridge was acquitted. On January 3, 1807, a crowd gathered at the Boston Common and hanged in effigy Selfridge and Chief Justice Theophilus Parsons. The disturbances continued for some time. Several weeks later, Selfridge published a pamphlet defending his conduct and disparaging

Benjamin Austin. He showed no remorse regarding this "unfortunate encounter."[42]

Aaron Burr, Alexander Hamilton, and Zealous Representation

Levi Weeks was charged with murdering twenty-two-year-old Gulielma (Elma) Sands, who was boarding at the house of her cousin, Catharine Ring, and Catharine's husband, Elias. In mid-1799 Weeks, a carpenter, also became a boarder in the Ring home. Elma and Weeks began to spend time together. The extent of their romantic relationship was disputed at trial. Shortly before she disappeared on Sunday, December 22, 1799, Elma told several witnesses that she and Weeks were eloping. The prosecution believed that Levi borrowed his brother Ezra's single-horse sleigh, picked up Elma sometime around 8:00 p.m., and killed her within the hour. On January 2, 1800, her body was found in Manhattan Well, a fifteen-minute sleigh ride from the Ring house. Levi Weeks was arrested. Ezra Weeks was building a weekend home for Alexander Hamilton, which explains how he came to represent Levi. Ron Chernow's biography of Hamilton offers another reason why Hamilton, who rarely represented criminal defendants, would do so in this case and without pay: he had an abiding interest in representing the underdog. According to Chernow, Weeks was not just an underdog; "public opinion howled for bloody revenge."[43]

Weeks was also represented by two other very talented lawyers: Aaron Burr and future Supreme Court justice Henry Brockholst Livingston. Burr had done business with Ezra Weeks and was a prominent investor in the Manhattan Well Company. Livingston's involvement is less clear. All three, however, were acutely interested in the outcome of state elections that would soon take place. Defending Weeks in a case that riveted the public's attention would bring publicity. Aligning themselves with a perceived murderer might bring notoriety rather than fame, but the lawyers apparently subscribed to the theory that bad publicity is preferable to no publicity.

The trial began on March 31, and the defense soon demonstrated its tenacity. The lawyers for the defense (the trial report rarely lists who did what) successfully challenged eleven prospective jurors and successfully petitioned the court to take the deposition of an important witness who was ill. Next, they successfully petitioned the court to remove Elias Ring from the courtroom during his wife's testimony, to prevent his testimony from being tainted by hers. When Catharine Ring, the first of dozens of witnesses, stated what Elma Sands had told her, the defense objected to this hearsay evidence. Although the prosecution offered a thoughtful reason why it should be admitted as an exception to the hearsay rule, the court sustained the objection.[44]

Weeks's lawyers continued their vigorous defense. An elderly prosecution witness testified that she had heard Ezra Weeks's sleigh leave at about 8:00 on a Sunday evening, but on cross-examination, she decided this had occurred in January. A second witness said she had heard Elma cry, "Murder, murder. Oh save me!" at about 8:30. On cross-examination, she acknowledged she had not seen Elma's face but only her "form and shape." She had also seen no sleigh.

After a rare adjournment, the following morning defense counsel admonished a witness for offering his opinion: "You are to tell the jury what you saw, not what conclusion you made." On cross-examination, Weeks's lawyers continued to sow doubt about the nature of Elma's injuries and the cause of her death.

Burr opened the case for the defense with praise for the jury's character, including its impartiality, contrary to the "blind and undiscriminating prejudice which had already marked the prisoner for its victim." He then suggested that Elma Sands's character was at issue. She "was in the habit of being frequently out of [sic] evenings, and could give no good account of herself." Additionally, Elma "sometimes appeared melancholy," raising the possibility that she had decided to "destroy herself." Finally, Burr told the jury that the defense would account for the location of Ezra's sleigh and demonstrate Weeks's good character and a demeanor inconsistent with "the idea of guilt."[45]

One defense witness suggested a possible sexual relationship between Elma and Elias Ring when Catharine was away. Witnesses also testified to Elma's evening disappearances. Finally, the defense suggested that a person living at the Ring home the previous December, Richard Croucher, might have killed Elma. It was early on the morning of April 2 when Croucher testified.[46]

To avoid another adjournment, neither side offered a closing argument. The court issued its instructions to the jury, and in commenting on the evidence, said it believed it "insufficient to warrant a verdict against" Weeks. The jury agreed, quickly acquitting him.

In his opening statement in the Weeks trial, Burr had mentioned the 1793 case of "a young man [who] had been charged with the crime of rape." Counsel noted that the "public mind" was so "highly incensed" after the jury rendered a verdict of not guilty that the magistrates were threatened. The crowd also expressed its readiness to "pull down the house of the prisoner's counsel," apparently referring to Brockholst Livingston's house. That defendant was Henry Bedlow, a "rake," and the victim was Lanah Sawyer, a seventeen-year-old seamstress and daughter of a seaman.[47]

Bedlow, ostensibly a gentleman, had convinced Lanah Sawyer to take a walk with him. In her version of events, he then forced her into a house of prostitution (which rented rooms for illicit assignations) and raped her. Rape was a capital crime, and Livingston was one of six lawyers hired to defend Bedlow.[48]

The report of Bedlow's trial haphazardly summarizes the testimony. For the most part, it reprints the lawyers' closing arguments, the first and longest of which was Livingston's. He claimed that Bedlow had gone to great lengths to obtain Sawyer's consent for sex, making him a seducer, not a rapist. Livingston then attacked Sawyer's character. She had spent hours in the late evening walking with Bedlow, and her failure to make an immediate outcry was evidence of her low character and belied her complaint. Three other defense counsel made similar attacks. They claimed that the testimony of three prostitutes (including the madam) regarding the events of that night should be trusted. The prosecutors disagreed. The recorder (judge) instructed the jury that he found Sawyer's character "pure and unblemished" but noted that she might have an incentive to gain revenge. The recorder also mentioned the contradiction between Sawyer's testimony and that of the prostitutes. The trial lasted fifteen hours; the jury deliberated fifteen minutes and returned a verdict of not guilty.[49]

In the middle of his closing argument, Livingston had defended his efforts, including his savaging of Sawyer's character, after spectators hissed him. With a little editing of the particular language, Livingston's statement justifying his role as criminal defense counsel might sound modern: "I stand here in defence of the Prisoner—I will use every means in my power to detect the falshoods [sic] that have been accumulated to deprive him of life; and neither hisses nor clamors shall make me swerve from what I conceive to be the line of my duty." Anger concerning the verdict erupted six days later, when the house of prostitution was destroyed. The mob regrouped the following night and burned several more brothels.

The lawyers were luckier. The threat to "pull down" their homes was not carried out.[50]

Seven years later, defense counsel concluded that zealous representation of their client again required them to put the victim's character on trial. It is unclear whether this was necessary, given the absence of evidence placing Levi Weeks and Elma Sands together on the night she disappeared. The same argument applies to the lawyers' suggestion that Sands might have "destroyed herself." They apparently believed they had a duty to "use every means in [their] power" to defend their client. When in doubt, defense counsel erred on the side of adversarial zeal. Unlike in the aftermath of the Bedlow trial, none of the public's anger was directed toward defense counsel.[51]

Pernicious Practices of the Law

The July 15, 1820, issue of *Niles' Weekly Register* reported that Thomas Bigelow, a Philadelphia lawyer, had been "convicted of a conspiracy, with others, to cheat and defraud Benjamin and Ellis Clark of six gold watches." He was fined $700 and sentenced to three years at hard labor. Although the last docket entry in the Philadelphia Mayor's Court where Bigelow was tried and convicted indicated that his "writ of error [had been] rec'd & allowed," there is no published opinion regarding his case. Bigelow's conviction is referred to only twice in legal proceedings: In an 1822 criminal trial, the prosecutor stated that Bigelow had been "indicted for seducing away the witnesses for the Commonwealth: and for that precise charge, convicted." The second time was in 1824, when a lawyer asked the Supreme Court of New Jersey to disbar a lawyer ("Anonymous") who had been accused of stealing valuable books. "*Bigelow's case*, in the Mayor's Court of Philadelphia, June 1820, session," was favorably cited. The case then disappeared, as did Bigelow.[52]

During much of the antebellum era, a lawyer's disbarment was a local affair, rarely noticed and rarely memorialized. Any applicant with sufficient training who possessed the requisite moral character was added to the local court's roll of attorneys. If the lawyer engaged in "mal-practices," the court had the power to strike the lawyer's name from the roll. When the court witnessed unprofessional conduct, it could disbar a lawyer in a summary proceeding. A lawyer could also be disbarred summarily if convicted of a crime of dishonesty. If the lawyer's professional misconduct occurred outside the court's purview, it could issue a show-cause order demanding that the lawyer justify why his name should not be struck. The court issued its decision after a hearing. Few such proceedings were published in the first half century of the republic. Obtaining appellate review of disbarment was often subject to jurisdictional limitations. Thus, the published record of disbarments is fragmentary.

The record of those who engaged in professional misconduct and avoided any sanction is even more opaque. Some avoided detection; others left town or abandoned the practice of law. In a few cases, stubbornness mixed with effrontery and ego is the only reason a record exists. In 1808, Albany, New York, lawyer John Van Ness Yates filed a matter in the Court of Chancery on behalf of a client. He was not admitted to that court, so he filed the matter using the name of Peter W. Yates, a licensed solicitor in chancery. This was permissible as long as Peter consented, but he claimed he hadn't (although later evidence indicated otherwise). After defense counsel learned about this, they successfully moved to dismiss the matter. John's client, Samuel Bacon, was assessed court costs and complained to John. Finding no satisfaction, Bacon then complained to the chancellor of the Chancery Court, John Lansing, who had John Yates arrested. Instead of solving Bacon's problems or apologizing to Lansing for his misconduct, John Yates began a scorched-earth and ultimately unsuccessful attack on Lansing's authority.[53]

It was uncertain what specific actions, other than a conviction, subjected a lawyer to disbarment. In general, a lawyer's unconvicted misbehavior resulted in disbarment only when the court found proof of a pattern of dishonorable conduct. Even then, courts appeared reluctant to banish a lawyer from the practice of law. Neither the judiciary nor practicing lawyers showed much interest in disbarring venal lawyers to protect either the public or the profession's claim to integrity during this time.

One example of the limits of disbarment for contemptuous behavior is *Strother v. State*, an 1826 Missouri case. After Strother ignored a judge's direction not to interrupt opposing counsel, he was held in contempt. Strother then sarcastically (it appears) asked the court to strike his name from the roll. As he left the courtroom, Strother threatened to resolve his dispute with the judge "out of doors." The court took Strother up on his first request but limited his suspension to six months. The Missouri Supreme Court reversed the decision and held that the trial court's authority was limited to suspending the attorney indefinitely or not at all; if it chose the former, it needed to give written reasons justifying the decision. It did neither.[54]

For acts of unprofessional conduct outside the courtroom, judges were reluctant to confront such behavior due to the uncertainty of their jurisdictional boundaries. Further, unless an inquiry into misconduct outside the courtroom began with a complaint from an engaged (and possibly enraged) lawyer, who made the case for disbarment? Laxity in disciplining lawyers generated a loss of professional honor and prestige. One lawyer advocating disbarment in an 1822 New York case concluded, "The profession has suffered much from the misconduct of unworthy members emboldened by impunity, deriving greater confidence from the indifference of the bar, and a passive community." By the 1810s, however, several disbarment proceedings had been memorialized, including more decisions in which the lawyer's name was struck from the roll.[55]

In January 1822 a grand jury in the city of New York charged lawyer George W. Niven with "practices of a highly dishonourable nature." In particular, Niven had, "by falsehood and misrepresentation," solicited and induced prisoners at Bridewell (a jail) to hire him. Niven promised them the moon. He was the key to their freedom, he said. If they hired him, all would be well, but if they didn't, all would be lost. Three prisoners secured Niven's "services" and had him hold their possessions as security while they tried to obtain the cash to pay his fee. In each case, Niven did little or no work and kept the prisoners' property even after he was paid. The grand jury included affidavits from these former clients in its presentment. Because it concluded that Niven's actions did not constitute crimes of fraud or false pretenses, the grand jury urged the Supreme Court to do the next best thing: strike Niven's name from the roll. The Supreme Court, in turn, decided that the charges should be heard and decided by the Court of Common Pleas (formerly the Mayor's Court).[56] There is no published court opinion explaining Niven's disbarment (or, more accurately, suspension). The case is known only because New York lawyer William Sampson wrote and published a complete report of it.[57]

That disbarment request was the second action taken by a grand jury related to Niven's approach to the practice of law. In late 1819 Niven was indicted on four counts of fraud related to his representation of Robert Latimer, the father of Mary Sarah Holman and the grandfather of Josephine Holman, a child. The widowed Mary Sarah had married Isaac Clason, and at some point before the wedding, she had given her father many of her belongings for the benefit of her daughter, Josephine. The marriage quickly soured, and Clason demanded that Latimer give him Mary Sarah's belongings, as was his legal right as her husband. Latimer refused, and Clason sued him for $10,000. A lawyer named Jeremiah Drake declined to represent Latimer, but he, along with a Dr. Ben Kissam, recommended that Latimer hire Niven. Niven asked for a $10 fee, which Latimer paid. Due to Mary Sarah's ill health, the matter was postponed, and Niven asked for two additional $25 payments. Lacking the money, Latimer gave Niven a gold watch, allegedly worth $100, as security.[58]

Latimer's troubles then worsened. He agreed to Niven's suggestion that he confess judgments related to debts he owed to persons other than Clason. Niven would use the judgment bond to keep "Josephine's" goods out of Clason's hands. The confessed judgment declared that Latimer owed money to two of his actual creditors (though in amounts greater than existed) and that he owed Kissam and Niven $250 each, although Latimer later claimed he owed them nothing. If Latimer confessed to an amount greater than he owed, with the intent to defraud bona fide creditors, he would be guilty of a high misdemeanor. Niven then executed on the (contrived) judgment by auctioning the goods. Niven cheated by arranging for his own agent to win the auction, paying Latimer less than a tenth of the goods' value. Niven thus possessed the goods, was Latimer's continuing judgment creditor, and kept his gold watch. And Latimer's problems with Clason continued.

Niven was represented in his criminal trial by five prominent lawyers. Three of them, Thomas Addis Emmet, John Anthon, and William Price, argued successively that the first count of fraud was not indictable at common law. Anthon and Price specifically (and correctly) argued that the fraud must be of a "public nature" to be indictable. This was a mere "private deception," excluding it from the purview of criminal law. In one report of the case, district attorney Pierre Van Wyck argued that Niven's offense was of a public nature because lawyers are "public officers." When lawyers act in their professional capacity, "in their conduct and demeanor to their client, the public is deeply interested." Lawyers "are the only avenues between the courts in which they practice, and the people; and in the fidelity and integrity of attorneys towards their clients, the whole community is concerned." A second report recorded Van Wyck's argument that the public's interest in the integrity of lawyers "cannot be preserved if their professional malconduct does not subject them to punishment." Fortunately for the public, "the case of fraud on the part of the attorney practised upon his own client seldom occurred." Van Wyck's cocounsel David Ogden joined in that argument. He analogized criminal fraud to a grocer using false scales.

The grocer affects the "public as a whole," making this deception an indictable offense. Here, "an attorney and counsellor, made use of the confidence which those offices are calculated to produce, to get possession of the property of his client, and thus to defraud him. The public then is as subject to be defrauded by the attorney, as by the grocer." Indeed, the lawyer's actions are of greater interest to the public than the grocer's, for the lawyer swears an oath to demean himself honestly in his relations with his clients. There is greater "moral depravity" in the lawyer's actions than the grocer's, and a failure to punish such acts pollutes the "streams of public justice" at its fountainhead.[59]

Emmet responded, "if the defendant had not been an attorney or counsellor, there could have been no pretence for indicting him." He claimed a lawyer is not a public officer. If Niven engaged in "malconduct," he was subject to punishment from the Supreme Court but not criminal sanction. Finally, Emmet explained his forceful representation as intending "to see that [Niven] be dealt with according to the law. This is a matter, sir, in which I speak and act under my own professional responsibility." The idea that lawyers are fiduciaries owing a duty of utmost faithfulness to their clients, not mere private actors, would soon become the standard view. In 1850 the Supreme Court of the United States declared that no duty requires a "higher trust and confidence than that of attorney and client, or, generally speaking, one more honorably and faithfully discharged." That standard was not applied to Niven's actions. The recorder of the Mayor's Court, Peter Jay, agreed with defense counsel: "The office of attorney is not a public office, in the true sense of the term." Niven's acts were therefore an unindictable private fraud.[60]

The case continued under the second and third counts. The defense was, as suggested by Emmet, intent on representing Niven zealously. When Latimer testified to a statement made by Niven, Anthon (futilely) objected on the grounds of attorney-client privilege, claiming the privilege should work reciprocally. Price's cross-examination of Latimer was a model of how to tie the witness in knots. He claimed that Latimer's failed efforts to protect his daughter's assets for his granddaughter's benefit were certain to frustrate his son-in-law Clason and were possibly intended to defraud him. Price, considered the "most prominent criminal practitioner" in New York between 1816 and 1834, kept asking the same question: "Did you intend to defraud your own creditors?" If Latimer said yes, he confessed to committing a crime. If he replied no, why had he confessed a debt of $250 to Kissam and Niven but later declared he owed them nothing? Latimer chose to evade rather than answer, which was also a bad decision. After this exhausting cross-examination, defense counsel noted that the indictment varied from the proof. The recorder used this variance to order the jury to acquit Niven, which it did. The bad news continued. District attorney Van Wyck abandoned the fourth count, that Niven had obtained Latimer's gold watch under false pretenses, because Latimer's testimony made that charge "utterly untenable."[61]

The grand jury's disbarment request came eighteen months later. John T. Irving Sr., brother of the author Washington Irving, was the first judge of the Court of Common Pleas. He tightly controlled its proceedings and was remembered for his "unflinching" and "strict" integrity and his "strong love of justice." The disbarment proceeding began on June 1, at which time district attorney Hugh Maxwell read the affidavits from Niven's three formerly incarcerated clients. Niven's lawyers read several affidavits in response. Apparently because of the nature of Niven's denials, Maxwell moved for the reading of additional affidavits against Niven. John Anthon, "then the most prominent practitioner at the bar," again represented Niven and "strongly opposed" the motion. Irving postponed the matter and ordered that the additional affidavits be given to him; the relevant affidavits would then be served on Niven.[62]

Five additional affidavits from Niven's former clients were read when the case resumed in Irving's court on June 22. Robert Latimer was one of the affiants. He repeated the allegations he made in the criminal trial. A second complaint was quite similar to the three initial complaints. An illiterate prostitute had met Niven in jail and hired him to shorten her six-month sentence in the penitentiary. Niven took her trunk of clothes as security for a $10 fee. He did nothing, she was sent to the penitentiary, and Niven kept the security (worth more than $10). When she returned, a marshal attempted to retrieve the property for her, only to find that Niven had destroyed it rather than return it. Two other former clients rued hiring Niven as their lawyer in civil matters. Both had given him security or money he refused to return. The affidavits demonstrated that Niven was both untrustworthy and disloyal. Indeed, in one case, Niven enticed former client John Davenport to leave the area to which he had been restricted as a debtor ("on the limits"), promising Davenport that nothing bad would happen. He lied. In concert with his brother, Niven had Davenport arrested for escape and sought forfeiture of Davenport's bond. District attorney Maxwell noted that the jury found against Niven and for the surety, impliedly confirming Davenport's assertion that Niven had set up the "escape."

Niven, a "demimonde" lawyer trolling the jails for clients, was absent from the highest ranks of the bar. He was, however, sufficiently supplied with funds and status to continue to hire good lawyers. In addition to Anthon, Niven reemployed William Price and added General Robert Bogardus, from a prominent political family. All were considered "leading practitioners." When the proceeding recommenced, Anthon returned to zealous advocacy. Despite the court's admonition that "counsel should read the [grand jury] presentment and their affidavits without comment," Niven's lawyers interrupted the reading, claiming the presentment was a "nullity." Further, they charged that the manner of the hearing was improper and Niven suffered because he was being "tried not by his peers, but by affidavits of persons not subjected to the test of cross-examination." There was more. Niven had allegedly been "put in jeopardy" by hearsay testimony before the grand jury, which was not evidence. Then came a slippery-slope argument: Niven was wrongly being tried as a "nuisance," which could lead to grave consequences for others. These cascading legal arguments followed the path taken in Niven's criminal trial. Irving was unimpressed. He allowed Maxwell to read the presentment and was committed to deciding the matter based on the evidence, not the presentment.[63]

After the reading, Price made a different jurisdictional argument: Niven was being called "to answer for act[s] not relating to this court." That is, all of Niven's actions had occurred outside the courtroom, as a counselor rather than as an attorney in court. Even if it was proper to hear this matter, what were the charges? Was it soliciting business in jail, receiving an excessive fee from a prostitute, or taking the clothes of a client as security for his fee? Irving remained unimpressed. In summary, he said Niven "has been called upon to answer as a member of the profession, and as officer of this court, for his professional conduct."[64]

As part of Niven's defense, Anthon offered his acquittals on counts two and three of defrauding Latimer. Anthon asked the court to declare that this conclusively established that Niven was not in the wrong. But neither he nor Maxwell correctly stated what had happened at that trial. Maxwell believed the case had never gone to the jury, and Anthon misleadingly stated that Latimer "made himself so ridiculous, that the jury disregarded all he said, and acquitted the defendant." Irving rejected Anthon's request. Niven received another extension to respond to the additional affidavits. The matter resumed on July 20, and Niven offered a host of additional affidavits, including several of his own.[65]

After Niven's defense closed, his counsel offered a certification from other lawyers supporting him. These lawyers stated that they had "never discovered any dishonourable proceedings on his part in his professional practice with us, but on the contrary have found him therein liberal and correct." It was signed by his lawyers Anthon, Price, and Bogardus and forty-three others. It was not signed by two of his lawyers in the criminal case, Thomas Addis Emmet and Josiah Hoffman, or by either of the prosecutors. William Sampson did not sign in support of Niven either.[66]

In closing, Anthon argued that the low-life criminals accusing Niven of dishonorable conduct were unworthy of belief. Every one of the eight witnesses, including those Niven had represented in civil matters, was "without character." This was a tried-and-true tactic going back to the Bedlow and Weeks criminal trials. Even Davenport, whose credibility was vouched for in an affidavit, lacked believability because no evidence was offered showing the good character of his character witness. With a flourish, Anthon rhapsodically compared Niven to the Roman lawyer Cicero, who was enriched by gifts from his grateful clients. Anthon concluded with an appeal to sympathy: Niven might lack in virtue, but poverty awaited him and his family should he spend even one day without his license. No lawyer, he finished, should be "disqualified by rogues and counterfeiters." Bogardus and Price also offered closing arguments. The former reiterated Anthon's attack on the character of the witnesses, sought pity for his client's family, and offered "no apology for the zeal which I may have shown in his defence." Price returned to his earlier argument: Niven was not charged with a specific offense, the evidence came from "secret" accusers, and he was being improperly judged by the court rather than a jury. Price also asked Irving to take pity on Niven's family.[67]

The response advocating disbarment devastated Niven's case. District attorney Maxwell began by remarking that Niven never rebutted any of the three initial affidavits relied on by the grand jury. One of those affidavits indicated that Niven was ready to mislead the court, thus linking Niven's conduct to his status as attorney as well as counselor. Another initial affidavit was from Frederick Stivers, who had confessed to theft and fraud. Other prisoners had urged Stivers to speak with Niven, and when he did, the lawyer told him "he had got several clear that were as guilty as the devil." Niven persuaded Stivers to agree to a fee of $25 secured by goods and then did nothing. The illiterate Stivers had marked his affidavit with an X. Niven responded with another affidavit from Stivers dated January 17, 1822. In it, Stivers declared that he had repeatedly asked Niven to act as his lawyer and had agreed to a $25 fee secured with unwanted goods; further, Niven had protested until Stivers convinced him to take the goods, and Niven voluntarily returned all of Stivers's property. It concluded: "the whole conduct of Mr. Niven was correct and satisfactory." If this seemed too much, that's because it was.

The exculpatory affidavit led to a third affidavit from Stivers in which he claimed he "never meant to contradict his first statement, [and] that if the affidavit procured by Niven did contradict it—that then it had never been read correctly to him." Niven swore that he had "read it twice to [the illiterate] Stivers." Evidence that the second affidavit was false, Maxwell noted, included the fact that it was "the *only* [affidavit] taken in the handwriting of Niven." It was not taken before any "respectable *counsel*, or a judge," but by the partial and biased Niven himself. Additionally, it was the only affidavit read solely in the presence of Niven's brother, who walked under his own cloud of suspicion. Finally, the crucial part of the affidavit exonerating Niven was written not in pen but in pencil in Niven's hand. Either this affidavit was true when read to Stivers and then falsified by the penciled alteration or it was false initially. This invalidated Niven's oath that the second Stivers affidavit was accurately read. Niven interrupted Maxwell, calling it a "malicious insinuation." That it was.[68]

Maxwell also derided the certificate from Niven's fellow lawyers. He recognized its vacuity. It said only "that Niven has never cheated them; that is the amount of it and nothing more." The certificate did not attest to Niven's good character or reputation. Finally, Maxwell exploded the arguments of Niven's lawyers minimizing the import of the four other affidavits. (The fifth had no value.) Niven had cheated and abused his clients, and his technical defenses failed to cover the substance of his actions. Niven was a "professional monster" whose "life and being had been sustained, and invigorated by the injustice which he has inflicted upon misfortune, by moral wounds cankered and inflamed by his fraud, by the tears and misery which his avarice and artifice have aggravated and insulted."[69]

Niven spoke last, for nine hours over two days. He added a lengthy, pitiful written summary. He claimed he was being accused solely because he was a lawyer, not a mere citizen. He was the victim.[70]

Irving found that Niven's practice of accepting goods as security was subject to abuses "too manifest" to countenance its ordinary use. It created, in modern language, a conflict of interest. Better to have the court determine in what circumstances such security could be used when impecunious defendants needed to pay counsel. Irving found it a breach of trust for Niven to refuse to return a client's money held in trust to pay a judgment debt to a third party, which Niven converted to his own use. More generally, the court acknowledged the lawyer's "power and opportunity" to do great evil or great good, and as such, he was held to a higher standard of trust than an ordinary citizen. While the rich could protect themselves against deceitful lawyers, the courts were responsible for protecting the poor. They also possessed the duty to "preserve this fair and honorable character" of most lawyers, who held positions of trust in politics and in the administration of justice. Lawyers owed a duty "to the profession itself, to the learned, the liberal, and the honourable of the bar, whose character and usefulness are in some measure compromited [sic] by permitting these disreputable practices." Irving implicitly adopted Van Wyck's earlier view: a lawyer is a kind of public officer.[71]

Niven's actions showed beyond dispute "a course of professional conduct calling for the severe, and decided reprobation of this court." He was "suspended from further practicing as an attorney or counsel of this court, until the further order of the Supreme Court." The Supreme Court refused to hear Niven's appeal until Irving had issued a final decision, which was: "Mr. George W. Niven [will] be suspended as attorney and counsellor of this court, for the space of one year from this date." Niven's suspension applied only to the Court of Common Pleas. No published Supreme Court opinion was issued.[72]

Niven moved to Long Island and practiced law there. He may even have returned to Manhattan. Historian Sarah Winsberg concluded, "Far from imposing career-defining professional disgrace, Niven's suspension from practice before the court did not merit a mention in a later summary of his career in New York State."[73]

A year later William Cranch, chief judge of the District of Columbia Circuit Court, ordered the disbarment of Levi S. Burr. Burr, a major in the New York militia during the War of 1812, moved to the District of Columbia in 1822. He was admitted to the local bar based on his New York license. His actions quickly excited other lawyers. Francis Scott Key, "counsel of great respectability," accused Burr of "practices unbecoming a practitioner at the bar." Burr denied the accusation and, likely to his regret, invited an investigation into his professional conduct. Judge Cranch asked Key to put his charges in writing, calling this inquiry "important to the character both of the accused and the accusing party as well as to the purity of the administration of justice." Key listed eleven acts, two of which had two parts.[74]

The first complaint concerned Burr's forensic conduct in claiming that a letter he possessed had been written by a person with the same name as a letter offered as evidence in court. This was the only act of Burr's about which Key claimed personal knowledge. The other acts occurred outside of court and were based on information Key had received from others. They included a charge of soliciting business from prisoners in jail (like Niven); soliciting legal business from strangers; filing suits without authority from those Burr claimed to represent; advising a witness in jail "to run away" (which would aid Burr's accused client); filing frivolous complaints, including doing so to "extort money"; abusing the legal process; and having a "general reputation as to your ill-conduct in your profession."

The court issued an order requiring Burr to show cause why he should not be struck from the roll of attorneys. Burr's defense will be recognizable to modern lawyers: He made sensible arguments, such as asking whether Key's first charge made any specific claim of impropriety. He issued blanket rebuttals, such as denying that he told a witness to run away. He offered technical responses, such as claiming that it was impossible to know whether causes were frivolous "until they shall have been tried." He made jurisdictional appeals, claiming that soliciting business was not improper and that the court lacked the authority to strike his name for conduct engaged in "as a private citizen, and not as a member of the bar." Like Niven, he argued that if the court possessed the authority to investigate these claims, he had a right to a jury trial. Burr presented a legalistic argument, stating that the charge of having a bad reputation was "too vague." He appealed for mercy, claiming good faith when erroneously representing persons who had not formally employed him. Burr's written response concluded with a remonstrance offering a smorgasbord of complaints: the process was unfair; Key's complaint was "illiberal, uncharitable, and unbecoming a Christian community"; and the charges were prejudicial, inquisitorial, malignant, intolerant, vague, and entrapping. Burr's lawyer argued the charges were in the nature of a criminal prosecution, and the court lacked the authority to "expel an attorney from the bar."[75]

The court concluded it could expel any lawyer who engaged in "ill practice . . . against the known and obvious rules of justice and common honesty." It could also expel a lawyer for conduct unrelated to the practice of law, such as for "highway robbery, or larceny, or forgery." Overall, "regard to the purity of the administration of justice demands that the bar should be pure and honest, and, if possible, highly honorable."[76]

The court found that Burr had aided himself at his clients' expense, failing to remain loyal to them. One such client was a debtor named Patrick Nicholson. Burr agreed to tell Nicholson's creditor Joseph Johnson how to collect a $20 debt, after which Johnson was supposed to give half to Burr. Burr cautioned Johnson "not to let Nicholson know that he had given him this information." Johnson collected only $9, enraging Burr. The lawyer then claimed the now-runaway Nicholson's goods, in satisfaction of his fee. The court also found that Burr had told a material witness in a murder case to run away, which obstructed justice "in violation of his oath as an attorney of this court." One event not listed by Key but discussed extensively by the court was Burr's writing of a false affidavit signed by his client, a widow who was "little conversant with legal proceedings." The court laid the blame at Burr's feet, concluding that he was, at the very least, "extremely negligent of his duty as counsel."[77]

As Niven did, Burr offered a number of "letters addressed by gentlemen of high standing in society," most of which apparently discussed his good conduct in the War of 1812. Burr also offered evidence of "his general good character previous to his admission to this bar." These were irrelevant. The court owed a duty to those "of high and honorable character for legal science, and for moral and professional integrity," not to require them to "associate with men of an opposite character." Burr was suspended from the practice of law for one year.[78]

A decade later, Burr was in New York's Sing-Sing prison, having been convicted of perjury. While there, Burr wrote about the awfulness of prison. In a note, the publisher mentioned Burr's "unjust" incarceration, related to litigation in which Burr was counsel. In his preface, Burr wrote of his intent to give a "true and faithful history" demonstrating his innocence of perjury. No subsequent work was published.[79]

A third case suggests the difficulty of disbarring a lawyer. In 1824 the New Jersey Supreme Court refused to disbar a lawyer accused of stealing valuable books. A lawyer filed an application with the court, asking that "Anonymous" (from a "highly respectable" but unnamed family) be struck from the roll of attorneys. It was a matter of "public notoriety" that Anonymous had stolen books of great value, and the owners were ready to prove this charge. To maintain its "purity" and "preserve [its] honor and integrity," the bar had to purge itself of thieves. An applicant was admitted to the bar only upon a showing of good moral character, and failure to maintain that character necessitated disbarment.[80]

The court declined to strike Anonymous from the roll. Theft was neither contempt of court nor attorney malpractice. It could disbar Anonymous only after a conviction. One of the two brief opinions reaching this conclusion indicated that *Burr* was "anomalous" in permitting disbarment before conviction for a crime of moral turpitude.[81]

The New Jersey court was correct: *Burr* was anomalous. A lawyer was subject to disbarment if he (1) acted dishonestly "in his office," (2) committed a felony "which would disqualify him as a witness in a Court of Justice" (a public fraud), or (3) committed an unindictable offense "contrary to his oath of office."[82]

In *Burr*, Cranch cited three earlier cases striking a lawyer's name from the roll. In two of them, the lawyer was convicted of a felony involving dishonesty. In the third, the defendant-lawyer Porter defrauded his own client and was convicted. His counsel argued that this was an unindictable private fraud. The court agreed and arrested the judgment but immediately struck Porter's name from the roll. A summary stated, "The court will strike the attorney from the roll, for malpractice, even though it be not indictable."[83]

An 1830 Supreme Court decision underlines the modest effect of disbarment. John L. Tillinghast was a member in good standing of the courts in New York, but in 1829 he was struck from the roll of attorneys in the federal Northern District of New York by Judge Alfred Conkling. Tillinghast asked the Supreme Court to overrule Conkling's decision, which was based on a finding of contempt. It declined, yet it admitted Tillinghast to its own bar.[84] It is unclear whether Conkling's reputation was relevant, as he was not considered an irascible or erratic judge. His decision was final, but its reach was limited to the Northern District. Tillinghast may have sought admission to the Supreme Court to vindicate his honor, but he never represented a party before it.

Tillinghast accurately expressed the state of lawyer discipline in 1830. A lawyer struck from the rolls of a court could not practice there. That was it. Though not inconsequential, the practical effect was slight, as made clear in Niven's case.

Young against Chipman

In early October 1826, in the federal circuit court for Vermont, English-man Alexander Young won a judgment of $8,927.51 (including interest) against Daniel Chipman, his lawyer. Sixty-one-year-old Chipman, a promi-nent Vermonter from Middlebury, was one of the state's leading lawyers. He began collecting debts for Young in 1807, and between 1807 and 1814 he collected at least $6,500 but remitted not one penny. Young sued Chipman in 1824. Shortly after the judgment, Young wrote a lengthy diatribe about the matter.[85]

Young hired Chipman as his agent to collect debts due to Chipman's rep-utation as a "man of true honesty and honourable principles." The relation-ship appears to have been fraught from its inception. Young, who resided in England, periodically wrote to Chipman. These letters, totaling ten, were largely ignored by Chipman, who wrote to Young only twice. In his second letter, dated August 10, 1809, Chipman blamed the Embargo Act of 1807 for his nearly two-year delay in replying. In neither letter did Chipman list what debts, if any, he had collected. Young's letters repeatedly announced his annoyance with Chipman. Inexplicably, Young never terminated his re-lationship with Chipman, nor did he have his correspondents in New York, Philadelphia, or Montreal travel to Vermont to inspect Chipman's work. Then the War of 1812 began.[86]

Young's story skips to December 1820, when he wrote another letter to Chipman after learning that the lawyer "was alive." Young wrote through his Philadelphia correspondent, James Taylor, who forwarded the letter to Chipman. Chipman responded and informed Young that, unfortunately, everything related to his representation of Young had been destroyed in a house fire while Chipman was away. Young noted that every item of value in Chipman's house, other than the legal papers related to Young, had ap-parently been saved.[87]

Young traveled to Vermont in 1824 to collect his due. Chipman ini-tially defended himself on the spurious ground that Young had been paid. He then employed two former Vermont Supreme Court justices, Jonathan Hatch Hubbard and Charles K. Williams, to represent him. They won con-tinuances in October 1825, when Chipman claimed to be "extremely ill," and in May 1826 so his lawyers could obtain the authority to examine wit-nesses in London (no such examinations occurred). They asked for another continuance in October 1826, stating that Hubbard was sick and Williams was unprepared to try the case. Supreme Court justice Smith Thompson, riding circuit, denied the request, although he gave Williams a day's delay to prepare. Chipman did not attend the trial.[88]

Chipman's decision may have been the smart choice. Even accounting for Young's bias, Chipman's case appears not just weak but disprovable. Chipman claimed one debtor's accounts were uncollectible because he was dead, which was, at best, a misstatement, as the debtor was alive and well. Chipman offered no evidence that he had forwarded any collected funds to Young, and the available evidence indicated the opposite. In his charge to the jury, Thompson informed it that the defendant could not plead the statute of limitations due to the "circumstances of this case." Two of those circumstances were the effect of the War of 1812 and Chipman's assertion to Young that little or nothing could be collected, which "appears to have been incorrect." And if the statute of limitations was inapt, so too was Williams's argument that it should be presumed Chipman paid Young. The jury received the case at 10:00 p.m. and returned a verdict in thirty minutes.[89]

Before the jury left to deliberate, Williams offered a bill of exceptions, a requirement before filing a writ of error with the Supreme Court. The bill also delayed the execution of any judgment for ten days. No appeal was made, and Young began the long and frustrating effort to collect. His difficulty in doing so, in addition to his anger at the lack of local condemnation of Chipman, prompted him to write his book on the case.[90]

During his lengthy stay in Vermont, Young corresponded with several of Chipman's acquaintances. He quoted one who commented on the judgment: "I did not expect a public trial, for, as Chipman could not be ignorant of the state of the case, a regard for his own reputation ought to have induced him to avoid exposure." The verdict proved that Chipman must have acted for reasons of "obstinacy, or infatuation, that the matter was not instantly adjusted." But Young concluded that being sued for an unpaid debt in Vermont "little affects either the reputation of the man or the character of the merchant." The published record seconds that view. Chipman was never ordered to show cause why his name should not be struck from the roll. None of the several short biographies of Chipman mentions Young's lawsuit or notes any stain on Chipman's reputation. An 1859 history of Middlebury, whose author was close to Chipman and mentions him often, omits the Young case and any other negative comments.[91]

Also missing from these biographies is a second professional misconduct scandal involving Chipman, which may explain why Chipman kept the money he collected for Young. Chipman was one of three local directors of the Middlebury branch of the Vermont State Bank. This branch made profligate and unsecured loans from its founding in 1807. By late 1811, Chipman had been removed from his directorship, and the branch had effectively failed. A year later, Vermont was ready to sue Chipman for malfeasance. Instead, a commission consisting of members of the Vermont Supreme Court would investigate and make findings, by which the three former bank directors agreed to abide. The commission found that the directors were responsible for $22,826 in branch losses, including $13,750 in missing cash and specie. As the scandal's historian notes, Chipman and his fellow director and former pupil Horatio Seymour had a "conflict of interest at its most brazen." The Middlebury branch was the only one that did not secure its loans by mortgages on real property. Had they been secured, Vermont law offered a simple and efficient way to collect past-due loans. The Middlebury branch eschewed this approach. Instead, it chose to collect money owed by delinquent borrowers through lawsuits, in which Chipman and Seymour represented the branch. Eighteen months after Chipman's removal as director, he was handling seventeen debt-collection cases. The fees generated by these lawsuits were of some help to the two lawyers, each of whom was found to owe the bank $10,000.[92]

"Chipman's gambit" saved the directors from this financial catastrophe. He won election to the Vermont legislature in September 1813 and used his seat to engineer a corrupt Federalist majority and a legislative "reexamination" of the commission's findings. With little evidence and some fantastical reasoning, the legislature found that Chipman and the other directors of the Middlebury branch were not liable, save for a debt of $1,200.[93]

Young continued to complain. Again, silence reigned in Vermont.[94]

Daniel Webster and the Popular Cause

Daniel Webster, another prominent antebellum American lawyer, became a leading legal figure based on his work as an advocate before the Supreme Court. Even before his triumph in the *Dartmouth College* case (1819), wealthy and influential clients sought his legal services. On occasion, he also worked for those lacking both money and influence. In 1817 Webster defended several men accused of robbery and not only gained their acquittal but also proved that the "victim" had invented the robbery, thanks to cunning cross-examination and an insightful closing argument.[95]

Thirteen years later, Webster agreed to serve as special counsel for the prosecution in the sensational murder trials of John Francis "Frank" Knapp and Joseph J. "Joe" Knapp Jr. in Salem, Massachusetts. The victim was eighty-two-year-old Joseph White, a childless widower and wealthy ship owner and merchant. White was brutally bludgeoned and stabbed to death in his bed in early April 1830, but the motive wasn't robbery. The murderer was a paid assassin. Richard "Dick" Crowninshield had been hired by Frank at Joe's behest. Joe was married to White's great-niece, and the Knapp brothers planned to destroy White's will so that (they believed) half of White's estate would go to White's niece, Joe's mother-in-law. The plan came to naught. A will was found, Crowninshield was arrested, and so were the Knapp brothers.

On May 28 Joe confessed his guilt to Henry Colman, the minister who had presided at Joe's wedding. Colman agreed to try to obtain immunity for Joe if he confessed in writing. A third Knapp brother—Phippen, a lawyer—wanted Frank to agree to this offer before Joe accepted it, so Phippen and the minister went to Frank's cell to talk to him. (Later, at Frank's two trials, Phippen and Colman contradicted each other about Frank's response.) The following day, despite agreeing not to proceed until Phippen was present, Colman went back to Joe's cell alone and obtained his written confession. Soon a summary was published in the local papers. In mid-June, Dick Crowninshield killed himself. When the grand jury convened, Joe refused to testify against Frank, vitiating the immunity agreement. Even so, Frank was indicted as a principal, and Joe was indicted as an accessory to murder, as was Dick's brother George Crowninshield.

In murder cases, the Supreme Judicial Court of Massachusetts acted as the trial court. The commonwealth's attorney general and solicitor general prosecuted. Stephen White, a private prosecutor and the murder victim's nephew and heir, and Supreme Court justice Joseph Story, related by marriage to the White family, doubted the prosecutors would succeed. White asked Daniel Webster to serve as a special counsel, and he agreed. He was to be paid $1,000. Frank was tried first because Massachusetts law required the principal to be convicted before trying any accessory.

The defense's opening statement remarked that the entire town of Salem and county of Essex and much of Massachusetts wanted Frank to hang. He was "opposed by the committee of vigilance, opposed by a private prosecutor, Mr. Stephen White, opposed by public opinion, opposed by the whole bar of Essex, and opposed by the learned officers of government." And they were joined by Daniel Webster.[96]

Frank Knapp was a principal only if he was "present" to aid Dick in the murder. Webster sought to prove that Frank was on Brown Street, near White's house, at 10:00 on the night of the murder. Several witnesses testified to the presence of a man wearing a glazed cap and a dark or camlet cloak. They believed it was Frank but either refused to swear to it or otherwise conditioned their identification. Frank typically wore a glazed cap and a camlet cloak, but as the defense showed, so did many other young men. According to Joe's confession, Frank and Dick had met on Brown Street before the murder and again afterward. But Joe's published confession was hearsay and inadmissible against Frank.

On cross-examination, defense counsel teased out testimonial inconsistencies regarding Frank's "presence." The defense called witnesses who contradicted prosecution witnesses, including Joseph Knapp Sr., Frank's father. He testified that Frank came home shortly after 10:00 that night, and no one other than Phippen "moved in the house at night."[97]

Overall, the evidence that Frank was present during the murder was "somewhat shaky." Therefore, just before closing his case, Webster asked the court to reconsider its decision not to admit Colman's statement regarding what Frank had told him after Joe's oral confession on May 28. On the second day of the trial, Colman testified in part that Frank had said something to the effect that it wasn't fair for Joe to get immunity when the crime was committed for his benefit. The court sustained the objection to this testimony after argument. Two days later, given his shaky evidence, Webster argued that Frank's statement to Colman should be admitted because if a higher court determined that Frank's statement was erroneously admitted and he was found guilty, the verdict could be set aside. If it was excluded and Frank was acquitted, the government would have no recourse. Frank's lawyer Franklin Dexter (son of Samuel) correctly noted that because the Supreme Judicial Court heard murder cases as a trial court, no appeal was possible from a decision erroneously admitting incriminating evidence. A divided court upheld its earlier decision.[98]

Webster then immediately offered another reason to admit Frank's out-of-court statement: the government believed Frank had not assented to Joe's confession and immunity deal, so the cloud of a corrupting influence (a possible pardon) generating Frank's confession disappeared. The court allowed Colman to testify. He now stated that Frank had told him the time of the murder, that Dick was alone in the house with the victim, the location of the bludgeon, and, most damningly, that he "went home afterwards," all proving that he was "present" during the murder.

Despite Colman's sudden and astonishing recall, the jurors could not agree on whether Frank was present during the murder, and a mistrial was declared. One newspaper wanted the court to disclose the names of the three jurors voting to acquit. A second claimed defense counsel had offered "technicalities" to avoid conviction. A third decried lawyers and claimed they were "productive of more evil than good." The mistrial was declared on Friday, August 13, and Frank's second trial began the following day.[99]

The second trial was largely a reprise of the first, except the prosecution's witnesses now had their facts in order. Colman repeated his testimony. Those testifying to the presence of a man on Brown Street on the night of the murder were now convinced it was Frank. Dexter's closing argument reminded the jury of its duty to convict only if the evidence proved Frank's guilt beyond a reasonable doubt. This reminder was prompted, Dexter noted, due to the "hostile atmosphere on the testimony." A witness was deemed a "public benefactor" if the testimony convicted Frank and was subject to the "peril of public displeasure and reproach" if it didn't. Dexter noted that the evidence in this trial all moved in the same damning direction. Dexter plausibly criticized the eyewitness testimony and noted, "Whatever the Government cannot otherwise prove, Mr. Colman swears the prisoner has confessed and nothing more."[100]

Webster's closing argument was widely praised, and he quickly edited the best of the closing arguments from both trials and published it to acclaim. In his published reconstruction, he began by asserting he possessed a duty "to bring to light the perpetrators." It was not animosity but safety of the citizenry that led him here. That Stephen White had promised to pay him $1,000 was not mentioned. As for Frank's presence on Brown Street after 10:00, Webster took several liberties with the evidence. According to his argument, the two unidentified men must have been the killers. Why else would they have been there? Of course, others were in the area that night because they testified to their own presence when they testified that others were nearby. But no one testified to seeing any man, much less Frank or the assassin Dick, go near or into White's house. No one saw anyone leave White's house and meet a second man at any time that night. If the jury accepted as true that the men on Brown Street at about 10:00 p.m. were the killers, then Frank was guilty because, Webster claimed, he had been positively identified as one of those men. As Dexter said in his closing argument at the first trial, "Two men were seen in Brown Street at half-past ten, and the murder thus proved to have been committed at that time, the men seen in Brown Street must be the murderers. This is reasoning in a circle."[101]

Based on the doubt expressed by the first jury, Webster emphasized the eyewitnesses' conviction that it was Frank loitering on Brown Street. One of those witnesses, John Southwick, was now certain that the man sitting on the steps of the ropewalk at about 10:30 was Frank. But in his testimony before the grand jury, Southwick had concluded that the person looked like Selman, another suspect at the time. Webster chalked up that misidentification to a bit of confusion. After all, Southwick's wife confirmed that John had identified Frank as the man sitting on the ropewalk steps right after he saw him. After going home and giving his wife this "news," Southwick went back outside and saw a man standing at a post nearby. Neither he nor Daniel Bray, who had joined Southwick, could identify the man. It was not cloudy, and the distance between the witnesses and the unidentified man was modest. Yet Southwick never suggested to Bray or anyone else that he believed this man was Frank Knapp. Bray then took up where Southwick left off, testifying in the second trial that, in his opinion, the man standing at the post was Frank Knapp, even though he had refused to say so at the first trial. In Webster's argument, all doubts were attributable to the "very good reason" that "Frank chose to disguise himself."[102]

Webster also stretched the law in prosecuting Frank. Twice Webster indicated to the jury that Frank needed to prove his alibi for that evening and had failed to do so. But an alibi defense merely negated an element of the crime; it was not an affirmative defense that Frank had to prove. Further, as noted by Howard Bradley and James Winans in their history of the case, until his third effort to have Colman testify about Frank's statements, Webster had either explicitly or implicitly assumed that Frank had agreed to Joe's confessing. Webster then changed his tune, arguing that "the government knew that [Frank] did not assent."[103]

The jury found Frank guilty. Most newspapers found this gratifying. For some part of the community and for most of Webster's earliest biographers, the factual guilt of the Knapp brothers excused the lawyer's conduct. Webster "was ready to adopt every possible legal means to secure their punishments." The end—justice—justified the means. A few papers criticized the trial. One claimed Salem's "street discussion" of the case ensured the verdict, making trial by jury "a solemn mockery," while a second objected to the zealousness with which Webster prosecuted the case. Frank was hanged before Joe's trial began.[104]

At Joe's trial, his lawyers (who had also represented Frank) objected to Webster's appearance on behalf of the prosecution. They correctly argued that Massachusetts law did not allow a private prosecutor (Stephen White) to hire counsel (Webster) to prosecute. Webster "avow[ed]" to the court that he appeared at the request of the attorney general and "without any other consideration." He said he was acting with "a disinterested regard for the public good." He had made a similar argument in Frank's case, declaring that his presence was simply a matter of "duty." But Stephen White had paid him to prosecute both cases, as a written receipt signed by Webster showed.

Joe's chances of acquittal hinged on the exclusion of his written confession. It was admitted, and he was convicted. Joe was hanged on New Year's Eve.[105]

Biographer Maurice Baxter notes that Webster "expertly displayed a lawyer's skills" in prosecuting the Knapps through his examination of witnesses and arguments to the jury. Baxter then turned to the cost of such a display. Had Webster "pressed the law and influenced the jury beyond fair limits?" Baxter answered only that this question "lingered long afterward." What was clear was that Webster sought victory. That goal did not make him different from other trial lawyers. The adversary system was a zero-sum contest, and lawyers were zealous representatives using their skill to win cases.[106]

In 1847 Webster was invited to speak to the Charleston, South Carolina, bar. He gave a tribute to the law and declared, "An eminent lawyer cannot be a dishonest man. Tell me a man is dishonest, and I will answer he is no lawyer. He cannot be, because he is careless and reckless of justice; the law is not in his heart, it is not the standard and rule of his conduct."[107]

Conclusion

A study of criminal trials in Maryland from the late seventeenth century to 1840 found that the presence of defense counsel made all the difference for those accused of committing a crime. Even "lackadaisical" counsel was better than none. Representation by lawyers beginning in the late colonial era correlated with a significant drop in conviction rates. In some cases, lawyers extended the length of criminal trials as they addressed the jury in both opening statements and closing arguments. In "complex" cases, an adversarial spirit carried the day. Lawyers in such cases called more witnesses, made more strenuous efforts to cross-examine witnesses, and were prepared to make more evidentiary objections. These were "radical changes" to which the farmers of western Maryland objected.[108]

Most criminal trials remained "traditional" trials. The average time devoted to traditional trials in western Maryland varied little between 1748 and 1837. Of course, the same dichotomy has existed throughout American legal history. Most criminal matters have been quickly resolved and have received little or no attention from anyone other than the accused. As plea bargaining gained acceptance during the nineteenth century, courts obtained flexibility, allowing lawyers to spend lengthy portions of the courts' limited time on relatively few complex trials. By this time, the public's fascination with violent crimes, and lawyers' roles in prosecuting and defending those cases, drew more attention to how lawyers contributed to the ordering of society and how they performed such work. The adversary system and zealous partisanship were now the norm for professors of the law. Increasingly, and despite recurring complaints, this became the public's view as well.[109]

CHAPTER TWO

Honor and Conscience, 1830–1860

David Hoffman and the Ideal of Honor

David Hoffman was nearly lynched during the 1812 Baltimore riots. He was twenty-seven years old, a lawyer, and a devoted Federalist Party member opposed to the War of 1812. After President James Madison declared war on June 18, the *Baltimore Federal Republican*, "an extreme Federalist journal on almost every count," rejected Madison's administration in extreme invective. An angry mob responded by destroying its printing office. Editor Alexander Contee Hanson Jr. escaped to the District of Columbia and resumed printing his attacks.[1]

Hanson returned to Baltimore on July 26, joined by Hoffman and others. He announced his return in the paper. Unsurprisingly, the mob also returned. By early July 28, two men had been killed by Hanson's defenders. Hanson agreed to surrender, but others, including Hoffman, escaped. He was soon captured but was saved from hanging by "the providential interference of a stranger, who satisfied the murderers that they had got hold of the wrong man." Another supporter was not as lucky. Revolutionary War general James Lingan was beaten to death when a mob attacked the jail. Others were badly injured. The 1812 riots made Hoffman a more steadfast Federalist and opponent of "THE RABBLE." He had been raised as part of Baltimore's mercantile elite, which had, until recently, controlled Baltimore politics. By the time of the riots, Federalists were a decided minority in the city. Deference to educated gentlemen like Hoffman was in decline, never to return.[2]

Two years later, Hoffman was appointed professor of law at the University of Maryland. He married, and he and his wife Mary soon had a son. His book for beginning law students, *A Course of Legal Study*, was published in 1817 and praised by Supreme Court justice Joseph Story, among others. Hoffman prospered, and he claimed to earn $9,000 per year from the practice of law between 1818 and 1823. If true, this made him one of the distinguished Baltimore bar's most successful lawyers. In late 1822 he began presenting his law lectures at the University of Maryland. During the next ten years, he published several lectures while continuing to practice law.[3]

In 1833 Hoffman's professional and personal life unraveled. His legal work diminished; he had earlier announced his decision to close his Law Institute at the university, and he was mired in a bitter dispute with its trustees. His son Frederick died, an event made worse by his efforts to keep the news of Frederick's impending death from Mary. Hoffman also moved to New York around this time. More broadly, Andrew Jackson won a second term in the 1832 presidential election. Hoffman despised Jackson and detested even more the leveling of society. In 1835 Baltimore, known as Mob City, was engulfed in a bank riot caused by bank fraud aided by prominent Baltimore lawyers. Hoffman was a beleaguered aristocrat in a despotic democratic age.[4]

The publication of the second edition of *A Course of Legal Study* in 1836 announced Hoffman's return to public intellectual life. Despite criticism of the first edition's length (334 pages), the second consisted of two volumes comprising 876 pages. The first edition contained a brief appendix concerning the professional deportment of lawyers, and Hoffman noted that, "on the peculiar duties and conduct of the lawyer, little that is valuable, has been written." He attempted to remedy this failure by offering readers of the 1817 edition a list of eleven readings, including commentary on several. This totaled ten pages. His most important statement about professional deportment was to acknowledge that much of the reason for the public's derision of law and lawyers was self-inflicted: "While we may admire and emulate the portraiture which the votaries of law have been fond to appropriate to its professors, we must be content to see its dignity often debased by the ignorant, and its liberality by the mercenary." Much like John Adams, Hoffman worried that those duty-bound to venerate the law were among its greatest violators.[5]

Hoffman's 1836 *Course of Legal Study* enlarged his list to twenty-one readings. He added an introductory essay, notes on the readings, observations on professional behavior, and fifty "Resolutions in Regard to Professional Deportment." These ruminations were located at the end of the book, a lagniappe offered to students completing their studies.[6] He began this section by stating, "Every one echoes the sentiment of lord Bacon, that 'knowledge is power.'" This adage should be joined by the phrase "virtue is power," he opined, for those two principles offered the "only true and solid basis of the 'art of rising in life.'" Hoffman's thesis was as follows: "The knowledge of and strict adherence to professional deportment, are altogether essential to [the lawyer's] honourable and permanent success." He knew that eminence in the profession was not always attributable to professional work done honestly and honorably. However, Hoffman argued that the acquisition of knowledge produced "more *honourable* views," thus elevating the lawyer's status among the elite of the community.[7]

How did lawyers serve clients as their representatives? Through the assiduous study of the moral sciences, a lawyer learned to act virtuously, as one who sought knowledge; embraced labor; pursued justice; aided the "widow, the fatherless and the oppressed" without compensation; "cultivate[d] rectitude, for the more useful exercise of his powers"; and "seem[ed] peculiarly bound to the observance of the most honourable and refined moral deportment." Quoting the Stoic philosopher Seneca, Hoffman proposed as the lawyer's practical motto: *Id facere laus est quod decet, non quod licet* (He is deserving of praise who considers not what he may do, but what it becomes him to do).[8]

The lawyer's accumulation of knowledge and virtue was necessary because "it will often be found that the *practice* of our profession is peculiarly calculated to suppress their influence." Lawyers too often became attached to their clients' interests, and this identification with one's client "is often of such a nature as to generate the seeds of moral evil." Passion displaced virtue, which invited the lawyer to act as an amoral and partisan zealot. Such a lawyer learned "the most dangerous of all lessons, viz: the vast power, conferred by intellectual superiority, over the rights and possessions of the ignorant, or the necessitous." Popular sovereignty made legal knowledge more powerful than it was in other societies. That power was a tool available to aid the just and unjust alike, if lawyers lacked virtue.[9]

To avoid exercising power for evil, the young lawyer should turn to "those principles emphatically denominated *honourable*," which required acknowledgment "in most cases [that] one of the disputants is *knowingly* in the wrong." Though a practicing lawyer might represent a client seeking an ill-gotten or unjust reward, the lawyer should try to avoid representing such clients and thus degrading himself. The young lawyer could claim honor by refusing to take on a "bad cause," a claim or defense that was "knowingly in the wrong."[10]

Alexis de Tocqueville traveled through much of the United States in

1831–1832. He spent a week in Baltimore, where he spoke with lawyer John H. B. Latrobe, among others. (He did not speak with Hoffman.) In *Democracy in America*, Tocqueville wrote, "hidden at the bottom of a lawyer's soul one finds some of the tastes and habits of an aristocracy." This was a compliment, for Tocqueville believed an aristocracy was necessary to check the excesses of the tyranny of the majority. American lawyers possessed power because they knew the law, making them "a somewhat privileged intellectual class." And because Tocqueville believed lawyers were "the only enlightened class not distrusted by the people," the power they exercised was significant.[11]

Hoffman was a fervent aristocrat writing at a time of democratic fervor. Under the pseudonym Anthony Grumbler, Hoffman published *Miscellaneous Thoughts on Men, Manners and Things* in 1837. He despised the leveling age and held out hope that lawyers would retain their elevated social position: "If there be still remaining among us any elements that can be called aristocratic, they will be found no where so certainly, as among gentleman of the legal profession." He divided all Americans into two classes of people: "the one selfish, crude, and mainly unprincipled, the other patriotic, enlightened, and mainly virtuous." The former belonged to "the *earthy*, or *democratic* party," and the latter to "the *intellectual* or *aristocratic* party." His fifty resolutions were designed to inculcate honor in young lawyers, natural aristocrats who, Hoffman believed, were best equipped to exercise the significant power spoken of by Tocqueville.[12]

A man was accorded honor if he met three criteria: he believed in his own worthiness; he publicly announced his claim to honor; and he received a positive "assessment of the claim by the public, a judgment based upon the behavior of the claimant." As defined by historian Joanne Freeman, "Honor was reputation with a moral dimension and an elite cast." The honorable lawyer, in Hoffman's view, behaved morally by acting not merely to benefit his client's interest but also to do what was morally right for society. Ideally, a lawyer was a gentleman. A gentleman acted honorably not to receive public adulation or to obtain wealth but to demonstrate an understanding of his duty to act with the power properly accorded him by society. The concept of honor was fading in urbanizing Baltimore and in much of Jacksonian America, but its power to shape men's behavior was understood by Tocqueville: "Honor, in times of the zenith of its power directs men's wills more than their beliefs." Honor was the lens through which Hoffman viewed professional deportment.[13]

This focus on honor provides clarity to Hoffman's fifty resolutions. For example, a lawyer acted honorably by avoiding a conflict of interest with a client. Resolution XXIV explained why a lawyer should be prohibited from purchasing an interest in a client's cause. It first distinguished a lawyer's purchase of the cause and a contingent fee: the latter was an "independent contract" made between lawyer and client in the absence of undue influence. When lawyer and client agreed to a contingent fee contract, that arrangement permitted a poor client to obtain counsel to prosecute or defend a claim. Ordinarily, a lawyer purchased a client's claim well after the establishment of the lawyer-client relationship, "after the strength of [the client's] case has become known to [the lawyer]." A lawyer who purchased a client's claim after learning of its value enriched himself at the expense of his client, a dishonorable act.[14]

An honorable lawyer refused to adopt the morals of the marketplace. He charged a fee informed by his "judgment and conscience . . . and nothing more." The practice of discounting fees (which Hoffman called "half fees") was dishonorable, for honorable lawyers did not compete for clients. Refusing to bargain with a client was not a conflict of interest because, by definition, a fee based on conscience appropriately considered the interests of both client and lawyer. Additionally, the honorable lawyer promptly returned the client's papers and money, avoided commingling his funds with those of his client, and never switched sides or testified as a witness when acting as counsel. To act honorably also required the lawyer not to engage in invective against others, even when his opponents or the judge demonstrated a lack of "character and deportment."[15]

Honor played a prominent role in other resolutions as well. If a client's reputation was at stake in a dispute, no compromise was possible; the case had to go to a verdict. This was necessary even when the opposing party possessed an "elevated standing," because the "great and wealthy" were required to declare their wrongs publicly and openly, particularly when one was who "ignoble and poor" suffered harm to his reputation by the actions of those possessing power.[16]

Most important, honor defined the lawyer's duties to his clients. A lawyer who promoted a hopeless cause "at my client's expense, and to my own profit, must be dishonourable." A lawyer who failed to understand his client's case possessed a duty to confess his incomprehension and refer the client to a more knowledgeable lawyer. The lawyer exerted the same diligence and effort on all legitimate matters, small or large, as each was important to the client. Retainers for services the lawyer had not completed were to be refunded before any such request was made by the client.[17]

A lawyer was also required to act as a client's "zealous and industrious" representative. Hoffman's ideal of honor offered a particular understanding of this requirement. An honorable lawyer never made a "vexatious and frivolous defence." A client who insisted that a lawyer do so "shall have the option to select other counsel." Hoffman expanded on this concept. In Resolution XI he concluded that when a lawyer was persuaded that the client's claim or defense "ought not, to be sustained," the lawyer's duty was to advise the client to abandon such a claim or defense. Aiding a client in such an event "would be lending myself to a dishonourable use of legal means," for the lawyer generated some benefit for the client by pursuing a claim "which I have reason to believe would be denied to him both by law and justice."[18]

Hoffman made similar statements that ran contrary to actual practice. In Resolutions XII and XIII he announced that the honorable lawyer "will never plead" the statute of limitations or the defense of infancy. Resolution XIV gave the lawyer in civil matters the "privilege" of deciding whether to make arguments in "doubtful cases" of facts or principles, "which may be neither one nor the other." The lawyer enjoyed the authority to decide "to what extent to go." When the claimed legal principle was "wholly at variance with sound law," it was "dishonourable folly" to add it to the common law. Finally, when defending persons charged "with crimes of the deepest dye" (Resolution XV), the lawyer's zeal was limited if there existed "no just doubt of their guilt." The lawyer was neither required nor permitted to "use my endeavours to arrest, or to impede the course of justice, by special resorts to ingenuity." In an honorable profession, the lawyer's duty in such cases was "securing to them a fair and dispassionate investigation of the *facts* of their cause, and the due application of the law: all that goes beyond this, either in manner or substance, is unprofessional."[19]

Honor required the lawyer to draft honest, accurate legal opinions, even if it disappointed the client and led to the loss of a large fee. The lawyer never met low and vexatious conduct with similar behavior. The lawyer passionately and diligently studied the science of the law and argued through "the medium of logical and just reasoning," not impassioned appeals. His duty was to execute this trust "faithfully and honourably."[20]

Hoffman's ideal lawyer cared little for money or fame. However, he cared greatly for posthumous reputation, striving "to leave this world with the merited reputation of having lived [as] an honest lawyer."[21]

Hoffman used the word *honor*, its cognates, and antonyms eleven times in the resolutions and another thirteen times in his introductory essay. Acting honorably merited a reputation as an honest lawyer, and such a lawyer refused to engage in morally damning conduct: "What is morally wrong, cannot be professionally right, however it may be sanctioned by time or custom." This ethical claim was fading as conscience began to supplant honor.[22]

Hoffman understood he was fighting a losing battle. He acknowledged that it was lawful to plead the statute of limitations or infancy. And he recorded in favorable language the policy reasons why these laws existed. But in deciding whether to use these defenses, "*I shall claim to be the sole judge.*" His resolutions were an ideal, offered to counteract the fact that the practice of law was "peculiarly calculated" to suppress virtuous and moral behavior.[23]

The best evidence that Hoffman was speaking of an ideal and not a present reality or a future possibility was the critical reaction to the 1836 edition of *A Course of Legal Study*: almost none. Just two reviews were published. The Boston-based *American Jurist and Law Magazine* published a lengthy review that mentioned the fifty resolutions only in its final paragraph. The second review was largely dedicated to the value of study for those training for the ministry. Its reviewer praised the resolutions, particularly the limits on zealous advocacy for those of "atrocious character" or those who wished to disclaim a debt by the defense of the statute of limitations. The 1836 *Course of Legal Study* had no impact.[24]

When Hoffman's *Miscellaneous Thoughts* was published in 1837, the *North American Review* ostensibly reviewed it, but the article was largely an assessment of *A Course of Legal Study*, and it ignored the resolutions. Hoffman later blamed the absence of reviews on his Baltimore printer, Joseph Neal, claiming that the book "was only very partially *published.*"[25]

In 1846 *A Course of Legal Study* was reprinted in Philadelphia, where Hoffman had moved. He claimed a reprinting was necessary to correct Neal's faulty publication. Three months later, Hoffman published *Hints on the Professional Deportment of Lawyers* through the same Philadelphia printer. *Hints* consisted of the material on professional deportment found in *A Course of Legal Study* and a short essay from *Miscellaneous Thoughts*. *Hints* was published separately, Hoffman wrote, due to a "deep conviction that the high tone of the Bar has suffered some impairment, consequent upon its immense increase in this country within the last ten years." The need for *Hints* was so great that its price was "intentionally placed at its *minimum.*"[26]

Between the 1836 and 1846 printings of *A Course of Legal Study*, several older, higher-minded law magazines folded. More practical publications took their place. None mentioned either of Hoffman's 1846 books.[27]

Michael Hoeflich charted the price of *A Course of Legal Study* from the 1840s through 1860. He found it slightly declined over time, even in remote areas. One reason was its "lost popularity." Both *A Popular and Practical Introduction to Law Studies* (1836) by Englishman Samuel Warren and Timothy Walker's *Introduction to American Law* (1837) were more popular. Both went through second and third editions before the end of the Civil War. The 1846 printing of *A Course of Legal Study* was its last.[28]

Hints had no impact on the American legal profession. It was neither reviewed nor cited. It was not traced by Hoeflich. It simply disappeared. In 1849 Warren published an American edition of *The Moral, Social, and Professional Duties of Attornies and Solicitors*. It was sufficiently popular to be reprinted in America in 1855, ensuring the irrelevance of Hoffman's *Hints*.[29]

The fate of *Hints* foreshadowed Hoffman's. He left America for England in 1847 and returned in 1854, the year he died. Hoffman was listed in the extensive 1879 *Biographical Cyclopedia of Representative Men of Maryland and District of Columbia*, but he was not mentioned in a history of the Maryland bar and was omitted from the eight-volume *Great American Lawyers* series (1907–1909). Neither a recent nor a much older biography of contemporaneous Baltimore lawyers mentions Hoffman.[30]

Honor among Lawyers in the 1830s

Hoffman was not alone in his efforts. In lectures in the 1830s, lawyers exhorted members of the bar to act honorably, as if doing so would return them to their former privileged place in society. Most betrayed anxiety about their status. John M. Scott, speaking to the Law Academy of Philadelphia in 1830, declared that if a lawyer pursued his profession "by an upright and honourable mind, it frowns upon crime—it spurns at baseness—it abhors fraud—it advocates pure morality—it upholds truth—it illustrates virtue." Conversely, a lawyer possessing "a depraved heart" joined the company of evil. Though the profession was "manly and honourable," it "has suffered deeply from the unworthiness of individuals who have worn its garb without adopting its principles." Two years later, James C. Biddle of Philadelphia made a similar plea: "Cherish those feelings of high honor which you have here imbibed." Those who acted with "gentlemanly propriety" would receive respect even from those lawyers who practiced for base (monetary) motives. Massachusetts lawyer Emory Washburn also responded to attacks on the aristocracy of the bar. The choice, he said, was whether the bar was to consist of "an enlightened, educated, independent body of men" or "self-constituted, noisy and narrow-minded pettifoggers."[31]

In 1830 the Philadelphia-based *Journal of Law* made a brief appearance. It published an essay titled "The Good Advocate." A good advocate was defined as "one who will not plead the cause wherein his tongue must be confuted by his conscience." Nor would the good advocate pursue a bad cause. The *Journal of Law* did not inform its readers that the essay was quoting *The Holy State*, a 1642 English book. And its applicability to the practice of law in Philadelphia was unstated. The essay's advice, however, was consonant with Hoffman's ideals.[32]

By 1840, Tocqueville's conclusion that lawyers were "a somewhat privileged intellectual class" no longer seemed true to elite lawyers. Philadelphia lawyer Job Tyson began his speech to the Law Academy by stating, "while the study of the law is highly esteemed as an elevated science, there, perhaps, [are] few objects against which popular prejudice has been so unsparingly direct, as the legal profession." This was due to the presence of too many pettifoggers who turned the profession "into a pernicious and *driving trade*." Public condemnation of lawyers was in some respects reasonable, for "many bad men, wearing the panoply of the profession, have been enabled to perpetrate their deeds under its sanction." Better lawyers had to live by those "moral sentiments and professional deportment . . . free from reproach" and confront the pettifoggers. They also needed to aid those lawyers subjected to "popular indignation" for undertaking the "fearless and independent discharge of [their] functions" by championing "professional integrity" and the importance of "an enlightened, virtuous and independent bar." Such lawyers remained independent of both "bad men" and the community.[33]

Hoffman agreed. An honorable lawyer exercised power knowledgeably and virtuously, and he abjured both the pursuit of wealth and the public's praise. These arguments were commonplace at the time. Lawyers who tied themselves to wealth or fame lacked the independence necessary to maintain a republic's prosperity.[34]

The Lawyer-Advocate, 1830–1845

In both editions of his *Course of Legal Study*, Hoffman emphasized the importance of skillfully examining witnesses. A skillful examiner neither demeaned witnesses nor ignored their feelings. The lawyer was a gentleman possessed of a duty to act honorably, including in cross-examination.[35]

Interest in zealously cross-examining witnesses grew along with greater adversariness. In contrast to Hoffman's writings, many publications about professional deportment emphasized the lawyer's duty to vindicate the client's interests, even at the expense of the lawyer's honor. However, some limits in advocating for the client remained, found largely in the lawyer's conscience. A lawyer was defined less often as a gentleman and more often as a "professional." A professional acted according to his knowledge and his public role, in the light of his conscience.[36]

Timothy Walker's *Introduction to American Law* was popular with law students. In section 7 of the first edition, "Dignity of the Profession," he distinguished between the "successful pettifogger" and the "high-minded jurist." The former "prowls in courts of law for human prey," making them "among the most detestable of their species." A successful pettifogger might gain wealth but remained an object of scorn. The high-minded jurist acted with "clean hands and a pure heart" and never mistook the "shouts of a fickle mob, for the loud clear trumpet of fame."[37]

These sentiments were echoed by Walker's elite contemporaries. All acknowledged and bemoaned the fact that pettifoggers constituted a significant body of the legal profession. Like Hoffman and others, Walker urged his readers to avoid dishonorable means in the practice of law. Like Hoffman, Walker emphasized the hard work of attaining knowledge of the law. Only hard work in search of the "gladsome light of jurisprudence" would pave the way to success. Though Walker wrote of honor, his understanding of the concept differed from Hoffman's. Walker was less concerned about honor in practice than about integrity and dignity. Integrity and dignity allowed a greater range of client representation than that envisioned by Hoffman.

If a lawyer acted honorably by representing the most miserable criminal, what did that portend when representing the "bad cause"? Walker gave the valedictory address to the 1839 law graduates of Cincinnati College. The Panic of 1837 had generated massive numbers of lawsuits related to the collection of debts. These lawsuits put a spotlight on the actions of lawyers, especially those representing creditors. Walker bluntly asserted that the legal profession was "not reputed to have a very high standard of professional ethics." He encouraged his listeners to foster their integrity and create a path toward professional success. Walker then pondered whether a lawyer could maintain his integrity: "When a client has a bad cause, shall we prosecute it for him?" Hoffman had concluded that such an act was generally dishonorable, but Walker disagreed. He relied on individual conscience: "[A] lawyer is not accountable for the moral character of the cause he prosecutes, but only for the manner in which he conducts it." To mandate otherwise made lawyers "their clients' conscience-keepers." Further, refusing to prosecute a bad cause required the lawyer to prejudge the case.[38]

The second edition of Walker's *Introduction to American Law* expanded his thoughts on the lawyer's moral duties. The "bad cause" consisted of "two classes of cases." In one, the law was against the client; in the other, "though the law may be with him, the abstract justice of the case appears to be against him." In both cases, "no principle of moral obligation prohibits me from prosecuting his cause." First, prejudging might lead to error; second, a lawyer was not his client's "conscience keeper"; and third, "Every man . . . has a right to have his case fairly presented before the court." Although the lawyer did not keep his client's conscience, he kept his own: not "every thing is fair in litigation."[39]

Peleg W. Chandler, a young Boston lawyer and legal writer, agreed. In an 1843 essay he asked whether a lawyer must "first settle in his own mind, beyond the possibility of mistake, precisely where the truth and equity of the cause lies?" The answer was no. The lawyer was permitted to represent clients "in a cause of doubtful justice." He was also "bound fairly and fully to present to the court and jury whatever of law or fact there may be favorable to his client." Chandler defended the work of the criminal defense lawyer and rejected the view that pleading the statute of limitations was a "technical rule of law." He asked, "what right has a lawyer to set up his own scruples of conscience by denying to a citizen the protection of one of these laws?" Chandler subsequently reaffirmed his position: "The place to try causes is before the properly constituted tribunals."[40]

The Zeal of David Paul Brown

The successful antebellum courtroom lawyer represented clients by mastering oratory and expertly cross-examining witnesses. One prominent practitioner was David Paul Brown, a Philadelphia lawyer from 1816 until his death in 1872. Brown's renown was due in part to his work as a criminal defense lawyer. He exemplifies how American lawyer-advocates altered the understanding of lawyer ethics.[41]

A part-time dramatist, Brown saw trials as shows in which he played the lead. Writing decades after Brown's death, elite lawyer John Dos Passos (the novelist's father) recalled how Brown drew the jury's attention to him alone: "After many minutes of clever preliminary acting, he bowed gravely to the Court, and began his classic, ornate, address to the 'gentlemen of the jury.'" Brown considered oratory a "magnificent temple" vital to imparting knowledge.[42]

A lawyer who excelled at oratory also excelled in rhetoric, the art of persuasion. That skill might endanger the cause of truth in an adversarial trial and allow civil litigants with a "bad cause" and criminal defendants who had "violated the laws of God and man" to escape justice. In theory, Brown claimed adherence to an ethic similar to Hoffman's. In practice, Brown ignored Hoffman's limits on advocacy. Brown's legal work illuminates changes in the professional deportment of lawyers between 1830 and 1860. He presented himself as both a gentleman and a fast friend to his clients. He spoke of the lawyer's search for the truth and was accused of bending it to assist his clients. He praised the lawyer's cultivation of virtue but sought fame and the wealth that accompanied it.[43]

Brown was professionally admired for his skill in examining witnesses. In 1835 he circulated his rules for examining witnesses to friends. In 1843 Brown formally published his "Golden Rules for the Examination of Witnesses." The original version offered eleven rules for direct examination and seven for cross-examination. Brown enjoined the lawyer from calling a witness that his opponent was "compelled to call." This allowed the lawyer to ask leading questions on cross-examination and to impeach the witness, neither of which was permitted on direct examination. On cross-examination, Brown urged that different witnesses be treated differently: "Be mild with the mild—shrewd with the crafty—confiding with the honest—merciful to the young, the frail or the fearful—rough to the ruffian, and a thunderbolt to the liar." And "in all this, never be unmindful of your own dignity. ... Bear all the powers of your mind—not that *you* may shine, but that *virtue* may triumph, and your *cause* may prosper." Brown collates several ideas in tension: the importance of lawyerly dignity, the subordination of popular acclaim to the community's interest in the triumph of virtue, the lawyer's goal in obtaining a prosperous cause, and the connection of that cause not to the client alone but also to the lawyer ("your cause"). In contrast, Hoffman argued that virtue was the lawyer's primary goal, even at the expense of the client's cause. Brown attempted to marry those ideas within the ideal of lawyerly dignity in cross-examination. Brown also offered advice that has been given to young lawyers ever since: especially in a criminal case, never ask a question "the answer to which, if against you, may destroy your client, unless you know the witness *perfectly* well, and know that his answer will be favourable *equally* well."[44]

When Brown's "Golden Rules" was reprinted in 1848, he added two rules for cross-examination. The more important was Rule VIII: "Never undervalue your adversary—but stand steadily upon your guard." This clarified two aspects of the trial: it was a contest between adversaries, and the witness was an afterthought.[45]

Brown recognized that it was the prosecution's duty to prove each element of a crime beyond a reasonable doubt; the correlative duty of defense counsel was to ensure that this was done. In addition, defense counsel used any applicable law for the client's benefit. Brown's "Golden Rules" was reprinted in a number of books for trial lawyers for more than sixty years. In his memoir, he claimed to serve truth and justice; however, his practice suggests that, if necessary, he chose his clients over contradictory claims of truth and justice.[46]

Hoffman disapproved of a lawyer who used the "artifices of eloquence" to persuade the jury to render a favorable verdict if it perpetuated an unjust result. This perverted the lawyer's talents for the benefit of a guilty defendant. This did not serve "truth and justice, and the substantial interests of the community."[47]

Yet Brown was celebrated for his "artifices of eloquence." His appeals to passion were famous. He was ready to cry perjury and to intimidate damning witnesses. He wanted foremost to win, and by winning, he found fame and wealth. Yet he believed his "honorable elevation at the Bar" was because he adhered to standards of "Ethics and Etiquette."[48]

Brown's 1856 memoir *The Forum* accepted propositions related to ethics that were consonant with Hoffman's rules. For example, a lawyer was prohibited from delaying a client's cause for lucre or malice and was "not to delay *for* his client" unless it was necessary to do justice. Brown rejected the ideal of zeal offered by British lawyer Henry Brougham in 1820, concluding that Brougham's claim to care for "THAT CLIENT AND NONE OTHER" was anathema and "can certainly never be approved by any just or reasonable man." He agreed with Lord Hale that no lawyer should prostitute his eloquence or rhetoric "to make any thing look worse or better than it deserves." A lawyer was "bound to refuse a case that he believes to be dishonest, or to retire from it, the moment he discovers it to be so," including debt cases defended by the statute of limitations. And the lawyer never gratified his client's "malignant passions." He was "no man's man" but an independent lawyer who was neither "the slave [n]or serf of his client."[49]

Brown distinguished between representing a client knowing that the client had a bad cause and possessing a "mere impression and opinion" that this was the case. Only the former was condemnatory; a lawyer was permitted, when he possessed doubts about the matter, to "fairly incline in favor of the party he represents." Like Walker, Brown believed the lawyer was not "morally responsible for the act or motive of a party, in maintaining an unjust cause." Again, this came with a caveat: the lawyer "*is* morally responsible, if he does it knowingly, however he may 'plate sin with gold.'"[50]

In 1852 John Livingston's *United States Monthly Law Magazine* published a lengthy memoir of David Paul Brown that portrayed him as a zealous advocate. One appraising commentator concluded, "As an advocate he has few superiors. He enters thoroughly into his case—identifies himself with his client—and his warmth and energy always secure attention." But Brown claimed to support the view that lawyers should not identify with their clients. His "impassioned" declamations also belied his own statements about proper oratory. Livingston quoted an unnamed Philadelphia lawyer's private journal from 1836, which praised both Brown's "gift of oratory" and his "art of making the most of his case, and the worst of his adversary's." The diarist also noted the view of Brown's critics: "I am not unaware of objections to his style—it may be that he is sometimes over zealous." Even so, Brown's overzealousness was a "quality the noblest of any that an advocate can possess, and which this gentleman eminently possesses," and it served "the 'sacred duty' which Brougham so eloquently described and enforced . . . , the sacred duty he owes his CLIENT." Analogizing Brown's ethics to Lord Henry Brougham's seems more accurate than Brown's later contrary protestations.[51]

The maxims about lawyerly zeal offered in *The Forum* did not match reality. Brown's most sensational case, the murder trial of Lucretia Chapman, provides an example. In late 1831 Chapman was charged with murdering her husband William by poisoning him with arsenic. The case gained national notoriety. The trial, which took place near Philadelphia, drew thousands, and the reporter for the trial crowed about his sales. Brown's successful defense of Chapman was grounded in his zealous representation.[52]

Lucretia was accused of having an affair with grifter and confidence man Lino Espos y Mina and plotting with him to kill her husband, William. William's death was originally attributed to cholera. Eight days after he died, Lucretia and Lino married. He soon deserted her. After suspicions arose in the community, William's body was exhumed. Several doctors concluded he had died of arsenic poisoning, although there was no reliable test for arsenic at the time. Lino had purchased arsenic the day before William first became ill. Although Lucretia had accompanied Lino to town that day, she was not tied to the arsenic purchase. Lino was arrested in Boston, and Lucretia fled, abandoning her children and the school she had founded. She was arrested 500 miles from home.[53]

Brown's work as defense counsel in a capital case would be familiar to modern lawyers. First, he obtained a two-month postponement. He subsequently argued the defendants be tried separately because their defenses were inconsistent. The court agreed; the public should believe "that the prisoners have had a full, fair, and impartial trial."[54] Defense counsel objected to questioning potential jurors about their "conscientious scruples" regarding capital punishment. The court agreed. Chapman's lawyers made cascading, albeit unsuccessful, evidentiary objections to testimony that Lino had purchased arsenic. Defense counsel also made other objections during the lengthy trial. Most of them were overruled, but all were strategically designed to hamper the prosecution's case.

Prosecutor John Ross made the trial's fourth and final closing argument. He criticized Brown's "zeal to defend his client," claiming that it led Brown to initiate "an attack upon the prosecution as unjustifiable as it was ungenerous." Ross denounced Brown's "rude assault" and "abusive epithets" while attacking the credibility of several prosecution witnesses. He reminded the jury that this "mode of attack has . . . been too often resorted to throughout this case to make any impression upon your minds." In its instructions to the jury, the court also criticized defense counsel's conduct. Although defense counsel in capital cases "frequently deem it their duty, not only to scan the evidence with the closest scrutiny, but also to comment upon the character, the motives, and the conduct, of the witnesses, with a freedom that would not be tolerated" if done by the prosecution, no evidence existed that any prosecution witness had lied. Brown's attacks on two witnesses had been "entirely without reason."[55]

These responses were the result of Brown's clever and passionate arguments. He began with a romantic appeal, noting he was happy to offer a speech "in the just defence of an oppressed fellow creature—a woman—hapless, helpless, friendless, and forlorn." He used knowledge of forensic medicine to challenge the conclusion that William had been poisoned. He used the lawyer's art to argue, in the alternative, that even if William had been poisoned, Chapman did not do it. Brown challenged the prosecution's experts who had testified about poisoning by arsenic and attacked the prosecutor for impugning the credibility of the defense's expert, an "unoffending individual" testifying in the cause of "justice." Brown called a prosecution witness a "female Iago" who possessed only "malevolence" toward Lucretia. He pointed out that the poison was allegedly put in William's soup, which was later available for the children to eat. No mother would place her children at such risk. After several hours, Brown concluded with another appeal to passion.[56]

Brown won. Lucretia was found not guilty. Lino was not as fortunate. He was tried, found guilty, and hanged in quick succession.

Henry Brougham in the United States, 1840–1860

In 1820 the House of Lords heard what is commonly called the Trial of Queen Caroline. Soon-to-be King George IV sought a divorce from his wife Caroline on the grounds of adultery. One of Caroline's legal advocates was Henry Brougham, who detested George IV. At the opening of the queen's defense, Brougham reiterated his view of the advocate's duty: "An advocate, by the sacred duty of his connection with his client, knows, in the discharge of that office, but one person in the world, that client and none other. To save that client by all expedient means—to protect that client at all hazards and costs to all others, and among others to himself—is the highest and most unquestioned of his duties."[57] Brougham's declaration is the strongest version of an advocate's duty: to save "that client and none other . . . by all expedient means," the consequences be damned. American lawyers largely ignored Brougham's definition of zealous advocacy for twenty years, after which it was a frequent topic of legal writings.[58]

In 1839 Brougham's *Opinions of Lord Brougham* was published in the United States, followed two years later by his *Speeches*. Both included his famous oration defending Queen Caroline. This initiated the American legal profession's adverse reaction to Brougham. In 1843 the Philadelphia-based *Pennsylvania Law Journal* became the first American magazine to criticize Brougham's definition of the advocate's ethical duties. It was odd that the journal did so at all, and that it did so in such an odd way. The *Pennsylvania Law Journal* was a biweekly publication that ordinarily printed bankruptcy decisions and summaries of new statutes. The criticism of Brougham was a reprint of a book review for *Dublin University Magazine* by an anonymous author. The subject of the review was an English book, *The Lawyer, His Character, and the Rule of Holy Life*, recently printed in Philadelphia by Carey & Hart. The journal may have reprinted the review to offer some publicity to a local printer, but in any event, the reviewer's criticism of Brougham was thorough.[59]

It began: "The great principle of Mr. O'Brien's book is the obligation of governing legal practice by strict reference to the supreme Law of Conscience, in despite of the evil prescription that so strongly countenances oblique and dishonest courses." Brougham ignored the law of conscience in favor of a singular duty to save his client. Brougham's defense was a "popular theory" of advocacy, which "only evinces how easily a principle of false honour may assume the dignity of self-sacrificing virtue." The reviewer offered a clever modification of Brougham. In England, barristers followed a "cab rank" approach to taking cases: "An advocate was bound to accept all briefs, irrespective of his opinions of the merits of the client's case." If the conscientious barrister refused too many briefs, this harmed the operation of the system of justice. The reviewer suggested modifying Brougham "by impressing upon the conscientious advocate the danger of overstrained scrupulosity in the refusal of cliencies."[60]

Though not yet forty years old, David Dudley Field was already a prominent New York lawyer. In 1844 he was the first American lawyer to criticize Brougham in print. Field's essay offered a clear-eyed view of the problems of the New York legal profession. Even so, he noted that American lawyers helped shape an "index of civilisation." Field was confused about the details of Brougham's speech (he thought it had been "within a year or two," not 1820), but he was adamant in dismissing it: "Now to our view a more revolting doctrine scarcely ever fell from any man's lips. We think it unsound in theory and pernicious in practice." One false assumption about the legal profession was that a client "may rightfully avail himself of every defect in an adversary's proof which the rules of evidence, or accident, or time, may have caused."[61]

Field rejected Brougham, but he could not embrace Hoffman. A lawyer was ethically permitted to represent a client he knew was guilty. He could not, however, "show him to be innocent." This was the antebellum consensus.[62]

A few favorable references to Brougham's ethic of advocacy were published before the Civil War. In the July 1847 issue of the *Pennsylvania Law Journal*, which had initiated the criticism of Brougham, an anonymous author concluded, "However open to animadversion as a social principle, [Brougham's position] is, and will continue to be, the motive power by which most trials are conducted. In the heat of the contest all other considerations recede." A Pennsylvania Court of Common Pleas judge agreed in 1849: Brougham's ethic, "although unsound in professional morality, is, and will continue to be in *practice*, the ruling principle by which trials will generally be conducted."[63]

The Butler Did It

A second case from England also generated discussion of legal ethics among American lawyers. In 1840 butler Benjamin Courvoisier was accused of murdering his employer, Lord William Russell. Noted barrister Charles Phillips was hired to defend Courvoisier. Shortly before beginning the second day of a three-day trial, Courvoisier informed Phillips that he was guilty of either theft or murder—there was disagreement over which crime he confessed to—but he refused to plead guilty. When Phillips broke this news to one of the presiding judges, he was told to continue to defend Courvoisier using "all fair arguments arising on the evidence." During his closing argument, Phillips said he hoped Courvoisier was "innocent," but "where the truth is not clear," as Phillips claimed, he should be exiled, not hanged.[64]

Courvoisier was found guilty. He then confessed publicly, although what he confessed to remained unclear. He was hanged a little more than two weeks later. The initial reaction to Phillips's advocacy varied. One commentator commended Phillips's "honourable zeal"; another stated that a lawyer "who defends the guilty, knowing him to be so, forgets alike honour and honesty."[65]

This controversy landed in the United States in 1850. Two Boston-based publications printed articles variously praising and condemning Phillips's actions. The January 26, 1850, issue of *Littell's Living Age* reprinted the attacks on Phillips initially published in England. It also reprinted other articles from the British press attacking Phillips in its February 2 and February 16 issues. The January 1850 issue of the *Monthly Law Reporter* indicated its approval of Phillips's actions, but by the next issue it had changed its mind; even so, it offered a lengthy study and suggested that readers make up their own minds. In particular, the *Monthly Law Reporter* reprinted an English paper's accusation that Phillips had justified his conduct in part by citing Brougham's ethic of "that client and none other." This justification was inculpatory, not exculpatory.[66]

The *Monthly Law Reporter* returned to Phillips again in its March issue but found it impossible to publish all that had been written. It was no coincidence that these two Boston publications were training such lavish attention on a decade-old murder trial in the Old Bailey. At the time, a Harvard Medical School professor was on trial for murdering one of Boston's richest and most prominent citizens.[67]

Murder at Harvard

On Friday, November 23, 1849, George Parkman disappeared. That day, he had visited chemistry professor Dr. John Webster at Harvard Medical College to demand payment of an eight-year-old debt. Webster owed Parkman over $2,000, more than his yearly salary at Harvard. After Parkman disappeared, his family offered a large reward. A week later, the college's janitor, Ephraim Littlefield, broke into a vault, found human bones, and informed the authorities. They found dismembered body parts in the vault and false teeth and bits of bone in Webster's laboratory. More human remains were found the following day in a room next to the lab. Webster was arrested and charged with Parkman's murder. The case was notorious; some 60,000 spectators watched the trial proceedings, rotating in and out of the courtroom in ten-minute increments. It was covered by newspapers and magazines in much of the country. A number of pamphlets recording the trial or criticizing the conduct of the attorneys and the court were published, including a compilation totaling more than 500 pages by special prosecutor George Bemis.[68]

Webster's legal counselor, Franklin Dexter, began looking for a lawyer to defend him. Daniel Webster, Rufus Choate, Charles Loring, future Supreme

Court justice Benjamin Curtis, and Charles Sumner all declined the opportunity. From a list of attorneys drawn by the court, Webster chose Pliny Merrick, a former judge, and Edward Sohier to represent him.[69]

The prosecution offered expert evidence that the victim's skull had been violently fractured and presented evidence of other injuries to the remains. This suggested murder. Parkman's dentist testified that the false teeth found in Webster's rooms were Parkman's. If the dead person was murdered, and if the murder victim was Parkman, the question was, did Webster commit this murder?

On the fourth day of the trial, janitor Littlefield took the stand. By then, defense counsel surely knew that their best and possibly only defense was to attack Littlefield's credibility. Historian Robert Sullivan notes that attorney general John Clifford understood that "if Dr. Parkman was killed in the college and his body never carried out but subsequently conveyed into Webster's rooms for concealment or consumption, then Webster or Littlefield must have been in [on] the secret."[70] A thorough cross-examination of Littlefield's actions, intentions, and incentives was crucial, especially because his testimony on direct examination was damning.

The reward for information concerning Parkman's disappearance was $3,000, and Littlefield was poorly paid. As part of his compensation, he was provided living space at the college. Littlefield had access to most of the rooms in the college, possibly including Webster's rooms (although this was disputed). Finally, it was generally known that Littlefield was engaged in a second job as a "resurrectionist" (body snatcher). On cross-examination, Sohier suggested Littlefield was prejudiced against Webster because the professor had learned that the janitor was "in the habit of using [Webster's] rooms for gambling." Littlefield declined to answer, stating only that he had not used Webster's rooms for card games that winter. Littlefield also denied thinking about the reward and claimed his actions were simply a result of his suspicions of Webster. He admitted getting a date wrong when testifying about a conversation with Webster, but otherwise, Sohier's cross-examination was a feeble attack. Sohier's questions allowed Littlefield to repeat his claim that Webster had "tried to lead [authorities] away from the privy," as well as much of the rest of his story implicating Webster. Littlefield's work as a resurrectionist and his knowledge of human dissection were never raised on cross-examination. Sohier also failed to press Littlefield on his access to Webster's rooms. Webster's lawyers ignored possible holes in Littlefield's timeline of when Parkman disappeared and the week that followed. Robert

Sullivan discovered 194 pages of notes Webster gave to his lawyers for use in his defense. For example, Webster claimed Littlefield lied about seeing him on the evening of Parkman's disappearance and spoke falsely on other occasions. Sullivan created a timeline listing more than a dozen discrepancies between Littlefield's testimony and Webster's notes, none of which were raised by Sohier.[71]

Sohier compounded his error in his opening statement for the accused, given after the close of the prosecution's case. His introduction was engaging (he asked the jury "to become in one sense the counsel for the prisoner—to watch over and protect his rights"), and he requested that the jurors focus on the evidence, not public opinion. Sohier then shifted to a lengthy discussion of the legal difference between murder and manslaughter and the equally abstract issues of reasonable doubt and circumstantial evidence. He concluded by reasserting Webster's claim to "know nothing about" the murder and urged the jury to consider the professor's good character when deliberating. The defense cited evidence that Parkman had been seen after meeting with Webster the day he disappeared; further, Webster did not exhibit any signs of guilt before his arrest. This was the slender mass of counsel's claim of Webster's innocence. These claims were overwhelmed by Sohier's implicit acceptance that Webster had likely done something to Parkman. Sohier's opening statement, coming after his cross-examination of Littlefield premised on Webster's lack of involvement with Parkman's disappearance, was a model of inconsistent advocacy. As New York lawyer A. Oakey Hall wrote immediately after the verdict, "From the moment we understood that Mr. Sohier was talking to the jury about manslaughter, we gave over Dr. Webster's chance of acquittal. So suicidal a policy was never known in a criminal case."[72]

After closing arguments, Webster was invited to make an unsworn statement. He charged his counsel with failing to offer evidence he had gathered that "firmly established" his innocence. But, he said, counsel "have not seen fit to bring forward the evidence on a great variety of subjects, which, therefore, have been brought to bear, with consummate ingenuity, against me." Much of the remainder of his statement haphazardly contested minor points of evidence.[73]

The jury quickly found Webster guilty. Before he was hanged, the *Monthly Law Reporter*'s editor, Stephen Phillips, decried the verdict and the actions of the court, the prosecution, and defense counsel. Phillips argued that the prosecutors, though "display[ing] the very highest degree of professional ability," went beyond their duty to present the government's case by alluding to material designed to inflame the public's prejudice against Webster. This was not legal evidence but a naked emotional appeal. Phillips had harsher words for Merrick and Sohier: "The counsel for the defence manifested great embarrassment in the management of their case." They acted honorably and did not resort to the tricks of Charles Phillips in *Courvoisier*, which "might have saved their client." They also acted like "gentlemen of eminent reputation for professional learning and skill." Unfortunately, their manner of representing Webster allowed the jury to conclude that the defendant's lawyers "were satisfied their client was guilty." Phillips believed the verdict was a miscarriage of justice (Webster subsequently confessed to killing Parkman but denied murdering him) caused by the influence of public opinion on the lawyers and the court. Though duty-bound to ignore the public's conviction of Webster's guilt, participants in the trial believed him guilty before the proceedings began, "which affected, to an unfortunate extent, the medium through which the evidence was viewed."[74]

Stephen Phillips sought a type of professional disinterestedness in legal advocacy. This appeared to be a middle ground between the excessive zeal of Henry Brougham and Charles Phillips and an abstract representation of the accused that protected the defendant's right to due process but evinced little concern for the accused as a person. On the one hand, independence of mind required the lawyer to exercise sufficient zeal to ensure that even the outcast received a fair trial, with a verdict based on evidence, not community conviction. On the other, appropriate zeal did not include using the artifices of eloquence and passionate appeals on behalf of the accused.

Phillips's lamentations on the *Webster* case suggested David Hoffman's definition of zeal and industry had been cast aside. Some contemporaneous evidence indicates that Phillips's middle ground was not a stable compromise but was itself rejected as insufficiently zealous. Lawyers like A. Oakey Hall seemed ready to declare a greater attachment to the needs and interests of the client, even at the expense of the community. In this view, "artifices of eloquence" was an incoherent phrase. Eloquence in the defense of someone accused of a crime was an essential aspect of zealous representation, as long as the lawyer did not lie to the jury. Lawyers should engage in reason when arguing a client's case, but passion had its place of honor in oratory as well. No American lawyer writing before the Civil War offered an unequivocal defense of Brougham's ethic in the Trial of Queen Caroline or Charles Phillips's behavior in *Courvoisier*. But they began to qualify their criticisms of these two lawyers, either by exaggerating the circumstances of the queen's case or by raising the stakes, listing cases in which an innocent person had nearly been executed due to a lack of zealous representation.

The Field Code, the Oath of Attorneys, and the Meaning of Zeal

In 1847 David Dudley Field was named to a seat on the New York Commission on Practice and Pleadings. Though appointed only after the resignation of one of the original commissioners, his contribution was such that the 1850 Code of Civil Procedure is known as the Field Code. In Title V the commission defined attorneys and counselors, their duties and authority, and standards for admission to practice. Section 511 of the code declared eight particular duties of lawyers: a lawyer supported the Constitution and laws; respected judges; maintained client confidences; avoided despoiling the "honor or reputation" of a party or witness, unless required by the justice of the cause; and never denied aid to the "defenceless" and "oppressed" for mere personal reasons. In addition, a lawyer was "to counsel or maintain such actions, proceedings or defenses, only, as appear to him legal and just, except the defense of a person charged with a public offense." A lawyer used "means only as are consistent with truth, and never [sought] to mislead the judges by any artifice or false statement of fact or law." Field appended a lengthy note explaining those duties. Part of it was taken from his 1844 essay "The Study and Practice of the Law." Though vouching for the moral scrupulousness of most lawyers, Field reminded them that scrupulousness did not permit them to advocate a bad cause. Thus, when offering a client an opinion regarding the law, the lawyer was to state the law as it existed. If a client asked how he should act in light of the law as it existed, the lawyer was to "advise justice" and "to throw his influence upon the side of integrity." "To assent to the bad scheme of an unjust client, is to become equally guilty with him." In litigation, Field rejected Brougham's definition of zeal. The advocate owed "duties to society," not merely to his client. It was immoral to use "reason and eloquence, to sustain a bad cause, to support the guilty, or . . . more revolting, to persecute innocence." The advocate was permitted, however, to represent a "man whom he believes to be guilty." In civil cases, the lawyer was allowed to take any lawful defense permitted by law, even if he disapproved of it. "But here the advocate should stop." The lawyer "who, in his zeal for the means, forgets the ends, betrays not only an unsound heart, but an unsound understanding." The *American Law Journal* editorialized in support of Field's section 511 duties, maintaining that a lawyer may make all arguments "which he believes to be fair" but was unjustified "in any known unfairness."[75]

Field avoided explaining the duty to use only those defenses "as appear to him legal and just, except the defense of a person charged with a public offense." He appeared to distinguish between representing a person accused of a crime and having actual knowledge of that client's guilt and representing a client "whom he believes to be guilty." However, he discussed only the latter instance, in which case the lawyer could not use "reason and eloquence . . . to support the guilty." Supporting the guilty was different from attacking the prosecution's proof. The question remained: was Brougham's idea that the lawyer owed a duty of loyalty to "that client and none other," that he had an obligation to use "all expedient means" to save the client, no matter its cost, sound? Field offered no answers. Even so, section 511.3 suggested that Field had changed his mind since 1844. The lawyer's duty to a client was broadened and the duty to society narrowed. The appended note was conflicted, but Field remedied that conflict in favor of his clients involved in the post–Civil War Erie "wars" (see chapter 3).

Defending Rufus Choate's Zeal

Another example of change in the legal profession's understanding of its duties to client and community is found in the praise accorded elite Boston lawyer Rufus Choate (1799–1859) after his death. Choate was the best-known lawyer in New England at the time, and biographer Claude Fuess collected a number of quotes from New Englanders lauding Choate as "the greatest lawyer" of the era, "at the head of his profession," in "first place," and "the most eminent American lawyer not only of his own time but of any time."[76]

Like his contemporary David Paul Brown, Choate was a brilliant orator and actor, a keen observer of juries, a skilled cross-examiner, a devoted reader of Shakespeare, and an admirer of the Roman orator and lawyer Cicero. As an orator, Choate was considered second only to Daniel Webster. As an advocate, he took "every just and proper advantage" permitted in an adversary system. His closing arguments were imaginative, describing scenes easily pictured by listeners and suggesting possibilities that traveled well beyond the evidence. Choate, like Brown, also understood the promise and peril of cross-examination: "If you don't break your witness, he breaks you; for he only repeats over in stronger language to the jury his story."[77]

Choate's eminence was attributable not only to his brilliance but also to his sole interest in "victory," in using all his "resources to *win*" his client's case. George Minns was a young lawyer when Choate was practicing, and in 1876 Minns declared, "I think he felt but little interest in the client, who was forgotten almost as soon as the case ended: his interest was in the trial,—the game,—and in winning it." Choate's biographer Edward Parker, whom Choate mentored, praised him for his zeal in representing clients: "Mr. Choate accepted and acted in the doctrine with no qualification whatsoever; he carried it practically as far as Lord Brougham, and carried it to the extremest verge of honor." To soften this hard praise, Parker justified Choate's behavior by stating, "yet he was scrupulously careful not to do any thing which would be false to his attorney's oath, . . . to be true to the court as well as the client." To Choate, winning meant using any tactic, and he regularly attacked witnesses whose testimony harmed his clients' cases. Destroying a person's reputation was a standard aspect of Choate's advocacy. In the infamous 1857 Dalton divorce trial, in which his client was accused of adultery, Choate attacked the character of a female witness by accusing her of having a child out of wedlock, even though its relevance was "almost nil."[78]

His contemporary Theophilus Parsons Jr. noted that Choate's zealousness was due to the "dangerous power" of a mind that saw things only through his clients' eyes. Yet Choate did not use his gifts for evil. Certainly, the desire to win made him ready to argue conflicting legal positions and to "broaden or narrow, as the interests of his client dictated," the meaning of the law. But Choate was a loyal and faithful advocate who wanted only to serve his clients' interests. He left to the adversary system the heavy lifting of determining whether partisan zeal served a public interest and if so, how.[79]

Most elite Boston lawyers justified Choate's ethic of advocacy on rule-of-law grounds. Both Parker's biography and Joseph Neilson's 1884 biography justified Choate's advocacy as demonstrating "his independence as a member of the bar." Neilson acknowledged that Choate's approach to the defense of persons accused of crimes was, "at times, unfavorably mentioned" due to his astonishing ability to obtain acquittals. And Choate's "sympathies [toward his client] were not always under his control, and . . . he was liable to be carried beyond the line of logical argument." However, "no one has suggested that he ever practiced any artifice or evasion to enable the guilty to escape." Indeed, every action undertaken by Choate in defending those accused of a crime was ethically appropriate, for his zeal protected the rights of the accused. To act otherwise would make him "guilty of a moral offense deserving the severest reprobation." It was "more just and humane to err, if at all, by excess of zeal than by want of it."[80]

Choate's reputation was that, as a lawyer, he was an untrustworthy public servant. Early on, the people of Essex County wondered how it was possible that none of Choate's clients were convicted. The conclusion: Choate was willing to pervert the cause of truth and justice to save his client. That willingness was apparently widely known. In one of his few unsuccessful cross-examinations, a witness admitted to conspiring with the captain of the *Missouri* to steal from the ship's owners. The *Missouri* was scuttled, and the two captains stole a significant sum. The witness, Captain Pitman, claimed that the conspiracy had been initiated by Captain Maxey. Choate fatefully asked, "What did he say? Tell us *how* and *what* he spoke to you?" Pitman replied, "Why he told us there was a man in Boston named Choate and he'd get us off if they caught us *with the money in our boots*." On this occasion, he didn't.[81]

This anecdote was written by Choate's sympathetic and earliest biographer, a lawyer who had spent his career working with and for Choate. An antagonist, the abolitionist Wendell Phillips, remarked with venom just months after Choate died, "This is Choate, who made it safe to murder, and of whose health thieves inquired before they began to steal." Massachusetts newspaper editor Samuel Bowles (see chapter 3) condemned Choate's advocacy in the *Springfield Republican*: Choate's "disregard of truth and justice in the undertaking and trial of causes" was "notorious" in the profession. Another obituary noted: "the lightnings of his genius were brandished with little regard to consequences, and that it was comparatively a matter of indifference to the great actor of the scene whether they purified the moral atmosphere by vindicating the cause of truth and justice, or struck down the fair fabrics of public virtue and public integrity."[82]

Public criticism of Choate peaked after his successful defenses of Albert J. Tirrell in 1846–1847. Tirrell was charged first with murdering his mistress, Maria Bickford, and then, after acquittal, he was charged with arson for setting a fire in the room where her body lay. Twenty-two-year-old Tirrell was married but living in a brothel with the also-married twenty-one-year-old

Bickford. Tirrell and Bickford were in the same room at nine o'clock on the night of October 26, 1845. At four the following morning, a resident heard a noise from the room and then heard someone leaving it thirty minutes later. Soon thereafter, someone cried "Fire!" When the blaze was extinguished, Bickford's body was found—her throat cut from ear to ear. Tirrell was gone. He had hired a vehicle to take him to his family's home. From there he left for (or escaped to) New Orleans. Choate, as usual, attacked the character of the prosecution's witnesses, most of whom were associated with the brothel. He offered two possible but contradictory defenses: either Bickford killed herself, as "suicide is the natural death of her class," or if Tirrell killed Bickford, he did it while sleepwalking and thus was not responsible.[83]

Choate's defense of Tirrell is justified by all his biographers. Most interesting is the 1860 assessment by Edward Parker: "It was this Tirrell case from which the idea chiefly took rise that Mr. Choate was somewhat unscrupulous in his defense of criminals. But there was never a greater misapprehension." Choate simply did what all lawyers are duty-bound to do: offer every available defense, demand that the jury apply the proper burden of proof, and leave to the adversary system the job of ascertaining the truth. More specifically, Parker claims Choate's sleepwalking defense was based on statements from friends and family, who "*upon that ground* wished him defended," and the declaration of junior counsel Amos B. Merrill that he had found Tirrell's somnambulism "a *fact.*" Choate, who "never saw Tirrell, except in the court house," simply adopted the defense prepared by Merrill. The public was not amused. An unnamed obituarist accused Choate of exercising genius without care for consequences and pointed out the "preposterous" Tirrell defense, one of several "efforts of a similar kind."[84]

According to Parker, the mature Choate was careful when deciding whether to defend an accused because "he felt his responsibility to the public." For example, "*he refused the case*" of Harvard professor John Webster. Yet that decision may offer a specific example of his broad understanding of zeal. Choate declined a proposed $2,000 fee for defending Webster. Choate's friends told biographer Neilson that the lawyer believed Webster's only defense was to admit that the remains were Parkman's. "But, assuming that Dr. Parkman came to his death within the laboratory on that day, we desire the Government to show whether it was by visitation of God, or whether, in an attack made by the deceased upon the prisoner, the act was done in self-defense, or whether it was the result of a violent altercation." Choate suggested this defense without talking to Webster, which he acknowledged the defendant would not countenance, even if it shifted the case from murder to one of manslaughter or self-defense. In Neilson's telling, this showed not Choate's impressive imagination and strategic insight but his unwillingness "to assert what he did not believe to be true." This interpretation is plausible but unconvincing. Choate was a "master technician." He arranged his clients' defenses based on his knowledge of the law, his oratory, his skill in cross-examination, and the prosecution's burden of proof. He was at his best when defending a hopeless cause, which is exactly how he would have defended Webster.[85]

Choate's defenders also claimed that he was a true lawyer, independent of the community's passions; he was a defender of unpopular clients and a protector of their rights from state depredation. According to insiders, Wendell Phillips's acerbic statement about Choate got it all wrong. He was just doing his duty.[86]

And yet something about Choate's understanding of zealous representation made other lawyers uneasy. He was "of New England, in every habit and thought and affection, and even in his personal appearance," Peleg Chandler wrote. But he was "a 'strange product of New England'; there was something about him of Oriental magnificence." Richard Henry Dana Jr.'s most recent biographer notes that Choate "combined his extraordinary courtroom skill with an equal capacity to rationalize its exercise on behalf of only those who could afford his fees." Reconciling Choate's notion of partisan zeal with the belief that the trial remained a search for truth and justice may have allowed Choate's colleagues to justify their own partisanship.[87]

Theophilus Parsons Jr. spoke to Harvard Law School students several months after Choate's death. He cautioned them not to believe Choate won his cases with mere words. He possessed a logical mind and a linguistic facility to provide a chain of reasoning understandable to all. Parsons then contrasted Choate's "forensic mind" with Daniel Webster's "judicial mind." Judicial minds answer a legal question "in their own minds." Forensic minds "see only what offers itself to them as their own side." Such lawyers used "all their resources and ability . . . to establish that [perspective] as right and triumphant." Webster's judicial mind meant that "if he had a bad case, he was very apt to make a feeble argument." This was not true of Choate, who could make "a hostile reality look . . . dim and dark, next to the seductive appearance he offered in its stead." Though this was a "dangerous power," Choate was a rare lawyer who could resist using this "enormous temptation."[88]

Parsons contrasted two general theories of the lawyer's duty. The first was that "an honest lawyer will remember that he should be devoted to the service of truth and of justice." The opposing view was that "it is always the duty of a lawyer to be faithful and true to the client who places his interests, perhaps his life, in his hands." These were "extremes" between which "lies the difficult and narrow path which the lawyer should pursue." Possibly unintentionally, Parsons suggests how difficult it is to ascertain a morality in advocacy.[89]

Every person charged with a crime has a right to be tried according to the law. This is a fundamental tenet of civilization. The law is imperfect, but it is better for the community to be ruled by law than by whim (like others, Parsons referenced the Cadi of Turkey). It was a mistake to think otherwise, and a corollary of this mistake was to assume that an "honest lawyer will not engage in a case which, as it seems to him morally, should not prevail." Lawyers themselves made two errors in deciding whether to represent a client: to "ignore the right and wrong of any case that comes before him," and to "save his conscience by the sacrifice of his judgment." The lawyer who threaded the needle by neither ignoring the morality of the cause nor sacrificing personal moral judgment was then duty-bound to exercise his professional skill "with all his strength" to protect his client's legal rights. Successfully doing so served both the lawyer's client and society. Parsons offered several examples. Assume a man commits murder and is observed by two unimpeachable witnesses, who tell friends what they saw. The witnesses testify to the coroner and the grand jury identically in all important particulars. Both witnesses then die before trial, and the prosecution offers hearsay evidence consisting of what they told their friends. Defense counsel is required to object as part of "his duty to law and society." The murderer goes free, but "the law will not perish." Hang the murderer solely upon inadmissible evidence, and the law dies as well. Parsons listed historical examples of horrific errors, including the Salem witch trials, and heroic efforts, such as John Adams's defense of the soldiers in the Boston Massacre trial.[90]

One problem with this hypothetical example is its fantastical construction. Parsons elevated the stakes by assuming the systemic costs (the death of law) are greater than the particular costs (a murderer escapes punishment). This was a common view held by William Blackstone ("better that ten guilty persons escape, than that one innocent suffer") and others. But hanging a man without admissible evidence of his guilt is not a hard case. A harder case is suggesting that a woman committed suicide by slitting her throat from ear to ear because she was a prostitute. A harder case is when counsel makes things up (or, more prosaically, speculates). A witness called by Choate first denied and then admitted having a child out of wedlock. To restore her credibility, Choate argued, "*I solemnly assert there is not the shadow of a shade of doubt on that evidence or on her character.*" She bore a child out of wedlock, he claimed, because the father "*was suddenly struck dead at her feet* by a stroke of lightning" the day before they were to be married! Likewise, Parsons rigged the examples. This justified the practice of other elite lawyers.[91]

Benjamin Curtis used Choate's death to reflect on a lawyer's duty to clients. Curtis is most famous for his 1857 dissent in the slavery case of *Dred Scott v. Sandford*, after which he resigned from the Supreme Court. He and his brother George Ticknor Curtis zealously represented wealthy clients and grew fabulously wealthy themselves. Curtis addressed the Supreme Judicial Court and presented the bar's resolutions on Choate. Curtis spent most of his energy defending lawyers against charges from the "thoughtless or inexperienced." He did so in both traditional and very modern ways. Choate followed the advocate's duty to "manifest and enforce all the elements of justice, truth, and law which exist on one side, and to take care that no false appearances are exhibited on the other." The "zealous discharge of this duty" was consistent with "the most devoted loyalty to truth and justice." Choate never showed "any want of loyalty to truth, or any deference to wrong." And like all good lawyers, he was no "brawler for hire." Aggression, "irritating captiousness," and "wrangling" were absent from Choate's formidable arsenal. Curtis then made a quite modern argument: "In nearly all cases there is truth and justice and law on both sides; that it is for the tribunal to discover how much of these belongs to each, and to balance these, and ascertain which preponderates." This relativistic understanding of law and truth suggested a new approach to justifying adversarial zeal. The zealous advocate was not shackled by claims of morality. His role was amoral, representing the autonomous interests of his client. This was an important but limited role, as the exertions of one's adversary and the trial judge steered the lawyer's zeal on his client's behalf.[92]

John Clifford, coprosecutor of John Webster, echoed Curtis's sentiments in a letter to Choate's biographer Samuel Gilman Brown. Choate adopted a "true theory of advocacy," and shouts of the "'unscrupulousness of his advocacy' are the merest cant." He wrote, "I believe that a conscientious conviction of his duty led him, at times, to accept retainers . . . when the service to be performed was utterly repugnant and distasteful to him." Precisely to "escape . . . the defence of criminal cases," Choate agreed to serve as attorney

general in 1853. He took repugnant cases only because he viewed "the profession . . . as an *office*, and not as a *trade*." It was a public service to represent
the outcast. Parker similarly defended Choate's advocacy in criminal cases
as consonant with public service. He claimed Choate showed consciousness
of the public interest by refusing to represent John Webster. Earlier, Parker
cited Choate's service to the public and to the "true idea of the Law" by noting he never made "any distinction in accepting cases" but took "every case
that came." Parker did not reconcile those contradictory claims.[93]

Clifford wrote to Brown after Wendell Phillips's excoriation of Choate
as a friend to murderers and thieves. Clifford, Curtis, and Parker all urged
an ideal of duty in which the lawyer representing an atrocious criminal did
his utmost for his client not because the client had bought the lawyer's conscience but because the lawyer's conscience demanded that he do his best
for his client as a service to the public. Choate was an extreme example, only
in the sense that his learnedness, industry, and abilities were of the highest
quality. He performed the duty asked of every lawyer: to protect the rights
of one's client and thus protect the republic. Elevating the stakes of ordinary
legal work made lawyers more central to the democratic experiment; it also
shielded them from criticisms that they were mere brawlers for hire.

Individual Conscience and Remnants of Honor

In 1831 Timothy Walker wrote "Letters from Ohio" for the first issue of *New
England Magazine*. Walker had moved to Cincinnati from Massachusetts a
year earlier and sang its praises. He emphasized the spirit of equality among
men. Cincinnati was a city of trade and bustling markets, and its residents
pursued their private economic interests: "To use the homely but significant
phrase, every man stands upon his own bottom. . . . Standing thus alone,
and unallied, our motto in action is 'each for himself, and heaven for us all.'"
Shortly thereafter, Alexis de Tocqueville arrived in Cincinnati, where he
conversed at some length with Walker.[94]

One of Tocqueville's insights was his exploration of individualism.
Though popularized by him, the term *individualism* was already in common
use in the 1820s. In both his essay and his conversations with Tocqueville,
Walker acknowledged that democracy emphasized equality among white
men, and Jacksonian democracy elevated public demands for equality. One
consequence, Tocqueville concluded, was that "every man finds his beliefs

within himself, and . . . all his feelings are turned in on himself." An American "had come to locate the standard of judgment in himself alone."[95]

Ralph Waldo Emerson wrote in his diary in 1827 that it "is the age of the first person singular." The market revolution prompted greater choices in work and goods. Antebellum religious awakenings offered the individual vast choices. The individual moved to an "inner-directed character type." Of course, a person's wide range of choices was not a license to flout all social and Protestant religious norms. The values that supported individual choices in religion and commerce also demanded that individuals choose to improve their intellect and character. Merchants were urged to follow their conscience, particularly their religious conscience, and by doing right they would oblige the ungodly to "conform to your standard." As Daniel Walker Howe notes, the rise of the individual in the nineteenth century led to "the substitution of *personal* discipline for *community* discipline."[96]

Engaging in self-discipline required one to commit to developing one's conscience and thus forming one's moral character. Properly formed, a person's conscience reflected "the law of God written in his heart" and harmonized that person's actions with God's moral law. A series of choices made through an instructed conscience demonstrated good moral character. And a person's good moral character "meant integrity, the perfect and harmonious interaction of all one's mental and moral powers." Even in a democratizing age, American society asked its elite, including lawyers, to model good moral character for all: "A society is always just what its members make it by their character; nothing more, nothing less." Elite lawyers were confident they possessed the character necessary to play an important moral role in channeling society's passions. "Upon the character of the bar in these United States, depends the character of the country, its peace, its safety, its liberty, its everything." Law's sovereignty was the antidote to the mob's (or king's) passions. In the battle between reason and passion, between law and mob rule, lawyers believed they were essential.[97]

By the late 1840s, the lawyer's duty to represent the atrocious criminal or bad cause was justified on three related grounds: First, the rule of law required that even the most wretched receive due process. Second, lawyers took an individual's case to protect the rights of both the client and society, and they necessarily took on matters in the absence of actual knowledge that the cause was bad. Third, the lawyer's exercise of conscience in taking any case was morally proper. The conscientious lawyer protected the outcast, despite public condemnation: "The person of strong character transcended fickle public opinion and fleeting public repute." Emory Washburn told his Harvard Law School students, "People are not always accurate or wise in their discriminations." Because the people's passions might be tamed by recourse to reason, lawyers were necessary if democratic self-government was to survive. If short-term public opinion was wrong, as Washburn and others argued, the lawyer protected the community by remaining independent of its whims. This protected all members of the community, for anyone might come under suspicion.[98]

The second definition of *integrity* in Noah Webster's 1828 *American Dictionary* was, "The entire, unimpaired state of any thing, particularly of the mind, moral soundness or purity." Timothy Walker was an early proponent of linking a lawyer's integrity to professional success. Integrity was one of the profession's three pillars, he said in 1839. The libel that the legal profession was "not reputed to have a very high standard of professional ethics" led Walker to consider more deeply the importance of integrity. Could a lawyer act with integrity when aligned with a bad cause? If the lawyer acted honestly, without "artifice and indirection," Walker believed, "I stand justified at the bar of my own conscience, whatever others may think of my conduct." Walker reaffirmed this view in the 1846 edition of *Introduction to American Law*. Professional integrity was the "greatest of all" criteria for success. Though some pettifoggers allowed their conscience to be "bought and sold," no lawyer with integrity acted contrary to the bar of his conscience. Pennsylvania chief justice John Bannister Gibson, in *Rush v. Cavenaugh* (1845), declared a lawyer was not a "mercenary." It was "a popular, but gross mistake, [to] suppose that a lawyer owes no fidelity to any one except his client, and that the latter is the keeper of his professional conscience." A lawyer who acted with integrity ignored the opinions of others, even other lawyers. Both the lawyer's instructed conscience and the legal profession's duty to protect society by protecting the rule of law justified representing the reviled.[99]

Perry Miller argued that American lawyers of the 1850s engaged in a concerted "effort to vindicate the ethical conduct of lawyers . . . , as though to show that while the political situation was deteriorating the lawyers needed some renewed assurances that they were respectable." Miller simply found the same situation that had prevailed for decades: lawyers attempting to allay the public's suspicions that they used their power for private benefit. Elite lawyers looked to persuade the public that a few pettifoggers misused their power and subverted the public interest. Although some "base advocates and base attorneys" were untrustworthy, "the true profession" was noble, and the frailties of a few should not be used to excoriate the many. Lawyers in the 1850s presented a sharp distinction between the true lawyer and the pettifogger. Of course, "the educated man is necessarily a man of power either for good or evil." Lawyers exercised power for good through an instructed conscience, generating ethical behavior.[100]

One significant difficulty of using a standard of honor in the legal profession was its sheer size in 1850. In a nation of about twenty-three million people, the Census Bureau counted nearly twenty-four thousand lawyers. The Panic of 1837 generated a massive amount of business for lawyers for a decade, enticing many to become lawyers. A second difficulty was a consequence of Jacksonian egalitarianism, as more lawyers meant more lawyers from the emerging middle class. David Paul Brown memorialized great Philadelphia lawyers in his 1856 book and lamented their passing, for they were "gentleman [who] acted in accordance with the title, and in conformity with its obligations." They were unlike the plain lawyers of the 1850s. For Brown, the profession was in decline and might fall.[101]

Honor might have served as a touchstone at one time, but legal elites looked for behavioral constraints in conscience. A review of Brown's *The Forum* in the *Southern Literary Messenger* promoted the idea that even the most vicious criminal deserved a defense of his legal rights. A lawyer owed a duty to prevent judicial murder. For a Christian lawyer to "undertake the cause of the culprit" was, admittedly, an "extreme case." To accept the defense of the outcast was "a test of [the lawyer's] conscience" and was not subject to interference from the community. Parsons made a similar argument about Choate: zeal in defending the vilest person was necessary to protect all in society, even and especially when society cried out for blood. The decision to defend the accused was the lawyer's alone. Doing so signaled the lawyer's independence from the mob and his ascension to the highest ranks of the profession. When no rule dictated the lawyer's duty, Parsons urged his students to "call upon your conscience."[102]

Richard Henry Dana Jr. and the Unpopular Practice of the Law

In his first four years of practicing law (1840–1844), Richard Henry Dana Jr. appeared in fifty-three cases in Massachusetts federal district court. He represented plaintiffs forty-eight times and won forty-five; many of his clients were seamen claiming back wages. By 1846, Dana was recognized for his expertise in maritime law and was hired in cases with large amounts of money at stake. Three years later, after forming a partnership with Frank Parker, he was retained to handle all legal matters for several members of the wealthy Lawrence family.

Congress adopted the Fugitive Slave Act in September 1850, and the following February an alleged fugitive slave named Shadrach Minkins (or Frederick Jenkins) was apprehended in Boston pursuant to the act. Dana went to Chief Justice Lemuel Shaw seeking a writ to free Minkins. When Dana found Shaw in the lobby of the courthouse, the justice refused to hear his plea. At one point, he suggested that Dana was acting unethically in claiming to represent Minkins. Dana demanded that Shaw tell him what legal authority he desired. Shaw evaded the issue. Dana returned to his office to amend his claim and saw Minkins being escorted from the courthouse to freedom.[103]

Daniel Webster persuaded—or, more accurately, told—George Lunt, the United States attorney in Massachusetts, to enforce the Fugitive Slave Act. Lunt indicted ten men for aiding and abetting Minkins's escape, including two of his lawyers, George Davis and Robert Morris. Morris was the only Black lawyer in Boston. Dana represented all four of the defendants tried in the "rescue cases." The government proceeded first against Davis. Dana showed the government's evidence was a shambles, and the case was dismissed before trial. By November, Dana and John Hale (then also a senator from New Hampshire) obtained a not-guilty verdict in Morris's trial. The two other trials resulted in hung juries. Dana gained another acquittal in 1852. None were convicted.[104]

Webster wanted enforcement of the act, and so did Cotton Whigs. Dana, once an admirer of Webster, attacked him in a speech in April 1851. Webster had entered into a corrupt bargain with Boston's elite, Dana charged, keeping him "in a state of endless servitude." Whig Party newspapers retaliated by attacking Dana. In May "proper" Bostonian George Ticknor ended his social relationship with Dana. In early June the *Boston Daily Advertiser* suggested a boycott of Dana. This was the unsigned work of lawyer George S. Hillard, who catered to the Boston Brahmins who wanted Dana punished. In July Choate attacked Dana at a social dinner. Dana was called one of the "babblers against the Law" who should consider the fate of Socrates. Thirty-five-year-old Dana, a husband and father of five, was responsible for supporting them and other family members. He may have exaggerated later in life when he claimed this dispute cost him "professional success in Boston for the next six or eight years," but cost him it did. Charles Francis Adams Jr., who "began his legal career in Dana's office," concluded that the boycott "not only retarded [Dana's] professional advancement, but seriously injured his income." Dana represented alleged fugitives for free and charged just $400 for all the rescue cases, significantly less than his ordinary fee of $2,500. And in 1854 his involvement in fugitive slave cases almost cost him his life.[105]

Dana was walking past the courthouse on May 25, 1854, when he was informed that a fugitive slave was in custody. He asked the prisoner whether he wanted legal representation, but Anthony Burns seemed uncertain. He told Dana, "It is of no use." Dana observed in his diary that Burns appeared "entirely helpless, & could not say what he wished to do." Burns feared injury or death if he created any delay or expense for his "owner." Dana "would not press a defense on him" but sought a delay because Burns "was in no condition to determine whether he would have counsel or not." Dana asked the rendition commissioner to give Burns time to consider whether to accept legal representation. He agreed. Burns eventually decided he wanted counsel, and Burns's agents chose Dana.[106]

Dana tried but failed to keep Burns from returning to slavery. One biographer called it "extraordinary trial advocacy." After Burns was marched to the wharf to board a ship, Dana returned to his office. Late in the evening, as he was walking home, Dana was struck just above the eye by a man wielding an iron bar. The rendition of Burns, the attempt to kill Dana, and, most importantly, the adoption of the Kansas-Nebraska Act transformed Boston into a city of abolitionists. It also effectively ended the boycott against Dana.[107]

Dana's intervention in the Burns case—asking Burns whether he wanted a lawyer and interposing as a friend of the court during the initial rendition proceeding—has been criticized as ignoring Burns's "refusal of aid." That conclusion seems inaccurate. Burns was unable to immediately make a knowing and intelligent decision whether to request counsel. Given his apprehension and the quick effort to return Burns to slavery, Dana's conclusion was plausible, if uncertain. Burns was returned to slavery and was treated inhumanely. Burns's fate had Dana not chanced upon the rendition proceeding is speculation.[108]

At the 1853 Massachusetts constitutional convention, George S. Hillard criticized Dana for ignoring the fact that "the bread that he & I eat is drawn from the business community of Boston." Dana should support that community, he said, which wanted nothing to do with the abolitionist cause. Dana immediately responded: "The hand that feeds us! The hand that feeds us! Sir, no hand feeds me that has any right to control my opinions!" Dana expressed the ideal of the lawyer as independent of both clients and the community, an advocate who aided the unpopular client no matter the cost.[109]

George Sharswood and the Lawyer's Conscience

George Sharswood was a devoted Democrat and a devout Presbyterian. He was a Philadelphia judge when he was appointed the sole professor of law at the University of Pennsylvania's revived Law Department in 1850. His first lecture, on the legal profession, emphasized the role of lawyers in protecting individual liberty. When civil liberty existed, a government formed a civil society that recognized "each individual has the power to pursue his own happiness according to his own views of his interests and the dictates of his own conscience, unrestrained except by equal, impartial, and just laws."[110]

In 1854 Sharswood gave lectures on the ethical duties of American lawyers. As published, they reflected the emerging understanding of the lawyer's dual role as advocate and officer of the court. A client had a right to demand that his lawyer make all lawful arguments favorable to him and to argue for the most favorable interpretation of the evidence. Lawyers used all available legal arguments because courts were bound by law. If courts used "mere notions of justice" to decide cases, this would lead to "the most appalling of despotisms." All laws, even bad ones, had to be obeyed. Sharswood desired peace and order in a violent, disorderly age.[111]

Sharswood's positivism made it easy for him to accept that a lawyer's decision to defend a claim on statute of limitations or infancy grounds was moral. As a matter of moral sensitivity, the defendant, *in foro conscientiae*, should not instruct his lawyer to plead such a defense. But the realm of client conscience was not the realm of law; the sound policy of these defenses made them impartial and just laws that could be used. Unlike Hoffman, Sharswood called for the lawyer's "entire devotion to the interest of the client, warm zeal in the maintenance and defence of his rights, and the exertion of his utmost learning and ability." Sharswood rejected Brougham's definition of zeal. He did, however, defend Charles Phillips's conduct in

Courvoisier and agreed the advocate could "use all fair arguments arising on the evidence." He also concluded that the extent of a lawyer's zeal in a criminal case was broader than in a civil case, as the former was more central to effectuating the rule of law. The lawyer was "not morally responsible for the act of the party in maintaining an unjust cause"; the lawyer took cases the public believed unjust because to refuse to do so "usurps the function of both judge and jury." Agreeing with Walker, he believed the successful lawyer was one who excelled in "learning, industry, and integrity." Sharswood blamed pettifoggers for much of the poor reputation of lawyers. Those lawyers intent on financial self-interest were anathema to society and were distinct from the larger, "high-minded, honorable bar," which focused on duty, not wealth. Additionally, a lawyer was "not merely the agent of the party" but "an officer of the court."[112]

Sharswood and Hoffman embraced different views of lawyer ethics. Sharswood was willing to countenance a lawyer's identification with his client as an aspect of his fidelity, with conditions. Hoffman strongly disagreed.[113]

Both agreed that, unlike the cab rank system for English barristers, the American lawyer was not required to take all causes "indiscriminately." They also agreed that no lawyer should take cases "with a view to one single end, *success.*" They differed on how to assess the discretionary judgments involved in lawyers' decisions to take or decline certain matters. Sharswood urged discretion "be wisely and justly exercised." Whether to take a case depended on its peculiar and particular circumstances. Because the particulars were "known, peradventure, to the counsel alone," those not privy to the matter should rarely "condemn either client or counsel upon what appears only." Some rules "assist[ed] the mind in coming to a safe conclusion *in foro conscientiae,* in the discharge of professional duty." If the lawyer sought to effectuate "high moral principle," his conscience was unassailable. Hoffman, of course, was ready to condemn those who defended the guilty criminal and the bad cause.

Although Sharswood concentrated on honing the lawyer's conscience, he did not ignore the lawyer's interest in remaining honorable. Throughout his 1854 *Compend of Lectures,* Sharswood suggested his readers act honorably. He declared, "Nothing is more certain, than that the practitioner will find in the long run, the good opinion of his professional brethren of more importance, than that of what is commonly called the public." Obtaining the good opinion of one's peers required the lawyer to act with "the strictest integrity and honor." He reiterated this point twice more.[114]

Sharswood believed combining honor and conscience made it more likely to meet high moral principles. His unwillingness to look to conscience alone, contrary to Walker, may reflect his politics and religion. Broadly speaking, Democrats were less likely than Whigs to embrace inner-directed individualism, and they were more likely than Whigs to embrace positive law and banish references to "higher law." Sharswood rejected any link between conscience and a duty or right to flout positive law, including the Fugitive Slave Act. The duty to obey lawfully made positive law was also emphasized by Presbyterian ministers in the 1850s. Walker was never an abolitionist, but in 1855 he acted as cocounsel in two cases challenging the Fugitive Slave Act and the Kansas-Nebraska Act.[115]

However, in weighing conscience and honor, the former predominated. The second edition of Sharswood's work, retitled *An Essay on Professional Ethics*, was published in 1860. It is the only edition that significantly edited the previous edition. Sharswood deleted his warning that a lawyer's professional reputation was more important than public acclaim. He continued to reject the contingent fee because relying on the lawyer's honor to treat poor clients fairly was unworkable: "A high sense of honor may prevent counsel from abusing his position and knowledge; but all have not such high and nice sense of honor." Individual conscience, shaped by a few moral principles and several rules of action, was the stronger basis for ethical behavior than honor. Sharswood sprinkled mentions of "integrity and honor" throughout the 1860 *Essay*, but within the framework of conscience.[116]

Sharswood's *Essay* went through two more editions before his death in 1887 and another after he died. It was a source for thinking about American lawyer ethics through the early twentieth century.[117]

Conclusion

During the three decades before the Civil War, the public routinely criticized lawyers for abusing their power. By zealously representing their clients, members of the public believed, lawyers failed to serve them.

Lawyers deflected this criticism. Acknowledging their poor reputation, they blamed pettifoggers. These untrained, self-interested pretenders ruined the reputation of lawyers. But what about representing the bad cause? The true lawyer did so not because he was immoral or greedy but to effectuate the rule of law. In criminal matters, defending the outcast was an act of high moral principle. Zealously representing the accused protected the community from itself and the individual from the state. Ignoring the mob was the epitome of professional behavior.

Justifications of the legal profession's power shifted significantly from 1830 to 1860. The consensus was that the factually guilty criminal defendant deserved a defense based on the law and the evidence. Additionally, clients in civil matters could demand that their lawyers use all lawful claims and defenses. No lawyer was required to take every prospective client who importuned him, but any lawyer who did so was not subject to censure by the courts or the bar, so long as the lawyer acted in light of his own conscience. Finally, lawyerly zeal in all cases was both necessary and limited. Each of these justifications was contrary to Hoffman's fifty resolutions.

CHAPTER THREE

Clients, Zeal, and Conscience, 1868–1905

"Brains were the cheapest meat in the market," said Jay Gould (allegedly), the Gilded Age Wall Street speculator, financier, and (to some) robber baron, near the end of his life. Gould's declaration seemed to target elite lawyers, who unhappily concluded he was more right than wrong. Lawyers sold their expertise, but they did so conditionally. They practiced law within certain ethical constraints, encompassed by the phrase "officer of the court." An officer of the court was faithful to the court as well as to his clients. As professionals, lawyers were supposed to resist any devolution from "an honorable office to a money-making trade." In the decades between the Civil War and the turn of the century, some elite lawyers were accused of flouting these limitations. Instead of serving as officers of the court, they were mercenaries.[1]

The United States underwent extraordinary economic, demographic, and cultural changes during the last third of the nineteenth century. One minor consequence was a considerable growth in the practice of law. Corporation counsel and personal injury work were but two expanding fields. The number of lawyers nearly tripled between 1870 and 1900, while the American population doubled. Lawyers blamed this burgeoning supply for turning independent professionals into highly paid servants.[2]

Several crises of professionalism roiled the elite bar. The first involved the well-known New York lawyer David Dudley Field. For several years beginning in 1868, Field and the firm Field & Shearman represented Jay Gould, Gould's partner James Fisk Jr., and the Erie Railway in a number of legal proceedings, most famously involving the Erie "wars."[3] Field's actions were criticized as dishonorable and unethical by lawyer-critics and defended by others. The root of this crisis was a dispute concerning the breadth of the lawyer's duty to represent a client zealously. Zeal sold in the marketplace. It was also celebrated in newspaper accounts of sensational trials. But lawyerly zeal was tempered by the lawyer's duty to the courts and the public. Critics argued that Field and other lawyers had exceeded the ethical bounds constraining zealous representation.[4]

A second crisis was related to the rise in personal injury litigation. A lawyer representing an injured client was paid only if the plaintiff won monetary damages, called a contingent fee. The lawyer's contingent fee was often 50 percent of the monetary damages the injured plaintiff was awarded. As the United States industrialized, the number of personal injury cases exploded. So too did the size of the monetary awards. The elite bar blamed pettifoggers who filed dubious cases based on dubious principles and who used dubious tactics to win. These pettifoggers, also called shysters and ambulance chasers, allegedly constituted the "practitioners who most largely discredit the profession." Legal elites who defended the companies sued by personal injury lawyers unsuccessfully argued that the contingent fee should be abolished. They couched their argument in professional and ethical terms: They wanted a more creditable profession. They were not protecting their clients' economic interests, they protested.[5]

Finally, elite lawyers perceived a crisis of professional identity: Had enormous fees been gained at the cost of individual independence? That is, had a profession been exchanged for a trade?[6]

At the first meeting of the voluntary Alabama State Bar Association, Thomas Goode Jones suggested that it agree to adopt a code of ethics. Jones worked on a proposed code in fits and starts for six years, and the association adopted Jones's code of ethics in 1887. By 1907, eleven other voluntary bar associations had adopted ethics codes, usually modeled on Alabama's. The elite American Bar Association (founded in 1878) generated a statement about lawyer ethics the following year. This chapter offers several explanations why the legal elite believed it was necessary to establish canons of professional ethics.[7]

David Dudley Field and the Limits of Advocacy

"As to the Fields (*pere et fils*), [Edwin W.] Stoughton, [William] Fullerton, and that blatant beast John Graham, they would take retainers from Satan himself. As between Michael and Satan disputing for the body (or the assets) of Moses, they would prefer to be concerned for the latter." Elite New

York lawyer George Templeton Strong wrote this in his diary in December 1871 on the day William ("Boss") Tweed, the Tammany Hall chief who controlled New York City government, was indicted. The named lawyers, including Field and his son Dudley, had agreed to serve as Tweed's defense counsel. To Strong and other elite lawyers, this was another in a series of occasions when David Dudley Field perverted his immense legal talents to his shame and the shame of the respectable New York legal profession.[8]

From early 1868 through early 1872, the law firm Field & Shearman represented Jay Gould, Jim Fisk, and the Erie Railway in a multitude of cases, including railroad takeovers and other litigation. The initial Erie wars litigation ended in May 1868, but a second war occurred in the fall. Another railroad takeover raged in mid-1869, and in 1870 Field & Shearman was counsel in the Heath and Raphael affair, which ended in March 1872 with Gould's ouster; by then, Fisk was dead.

In late December 1870, more than two years after these events began, David Dudley Field was first publicly accused of unethical behavior. These attacks, which were several and somewhat connected, flared in April 1871 and then subsided. At some point, Field offered to prosecute Tweed, but his offer was rejected by members of the newly formed Association of the Bar of the City of New York (ABCNY), which drove Tweed's prosecution. Field then accepted Tweed's long-standing request that Field's firm defend him. This provoked Strong's reaction, quoted earlier. Attacks on Field's professional conduct were renewed in the latter half of 1872, after the removal of corrupt judges whose orders had often benefited the Erie.[9]

Field's apparent manipulation of the law on behalf of Gould, Fisk, and the Erie were the product, critics claimed, of excessive zeal. In his April 9, 1868, diary entry, Strong wrote, "Bench and bar settle deeper in the mud every year and every month. They must be near the bottom now. Witness the indecencies done and suffered by Dudley Field, [Judge George] Barnard, [James T.] Brady, [John B.] Haskin, etc." Strong and other lawyers uninvolved in the first Erie war could have turned their attention to any of the forty or so lawyers representing the railroad, including the elite Thomas G. Shearman (Field's partner), William Evarts, and Clarence A. Seward. Instead, critics focused on David Dudley Field.[10]

Critics attacked Field due to his renown. He was justly lauded (though occasionally assailed) as a legal reformer, most importantly for drafting New York's 1850 Code of Civil Procedure, which revolutionized the law. This code included a section on the ethical duties of the lawyer (see chapter 2). Among other provisions, lawyers were to maintain only "legal and just" proceedings and defenses and "use such means only as are consistent with the truth." Two decades later, Field was accused of violating this duty.[11]

Field's work on matters involving the Erie Railway was well rewarded. Critics suggested that he devoted himself to the Erie for monetary gain, at the expense of the public. According to these lawyer-critics, Field transgressed the limits applicable to a lawyer's professional conduct.

In early 1868 Fisk became a client of Field & Shearman. Field was vacationing in Europe when his son Dudley agreed to represent Fisk. Fisk had purchased shares of stock of the Rock Island Railroad, believing it would increase in price ("going long"). Unfortunately for Fisk, several members of Rock Island's board of directors illegally issued nearly $5 million (in nominal terms) in additional shares, causing the stock price to fall ("going short"), as the directors intended. Field & Shearman succeeded in limiting Fisk's losses.[12]

At about the same time, Cornelius "Commodore" Vanderbilt, probably America's wealthiest person, suggested that the railroads serving New York City cooperate rather than compete for business. To his surprise, the directors of the Erie Railway declined. In response, Vanderbilt decided to buy it, and his lawyers obtained an injunction against the Erie's directors to constrain their ability to foil Vanderbilt's plan. The injunction was issued after an ex parte hearing—that is, the Erie's directors were not notified of the hearing and were thus absent from court. Such injunctions were permitted by law, but this particular injunction had been issued by the corrupt and incompetent judge George G. Barnard, reputed to be in Vanderbilt's pocket. Two days later, Vanderbilt's lawyers returned to Barnard seeking additional constraints on the Erie's directors. Barnard again did the Commodore's bidding.[13]

David Dudley Field made his first appearance on behalf of the Erie Railway and its directors in late February. Initially, little happened. On March 3 Barnard issued a third injunction against the Erie's directors and others. On March 5 the Erie's lawyers traveled to rural Broome County and got their own contrary injunction, also at an ex parte hearing. The Erie's counterinjunction was disputed by Vanderbilt's lawyers. When Judge Barnard postponed a hearing on the matter, Field went to Brooklyn and obtained an injunction against the judge himself. Again, this injunction was issued after an ex parte hearing. Field claimed, without evidence, that Barnard and Vanderbilt were conspiring unlawfully to control the Erie Railway. Barnard was enjoined from aiding this "conspiracy," and the Erie's directors were ordered to do what Barnard had forbidden. That afternoon, Judge Albert Cardozo (father of Benjamin) issued an injunction in favor of Vanderbilt, contrary to the Brooklyn injunction. On and on it went, with judges of the state supreme court issuing contradictory injunctions. In one instance, Field obtained an injunction that prohibited the clerks of the court to record another injunction contrary to his clients' interests.[14]

Counsel's actions in these proceedings reflected poorly on all lawyers, but they conformed to the law. Supreme court judges in New York were trial judges. Though elected locally, they possessed statewide equity jurisdiction. They were not required to abide by another judge's injunction.

At one point, Field asked Barnard, "only in the discharge of my duty," to recuse himself because the judge had become a defendant. "Whether he be or be not interested, is another thing," Field said; "that is not for me to decide at all." Of course, Field had made Barnard a defendant, which made him "interested" in the matter. The lawyer's concern was duplicitous, but it benefited his clients, as delay strengthened their practical position against Vanderbilt. Barnard was corrupt. Unfortunately, the Erie's witnesses alleging Barnard's corruption lacked knowledge of it, and the Erie's lawyers made no effort to find such evidence before seeking an injunction against Barnard. At best, Field was willfully ignorant in making his charges; at worst, he presented false evidence to the court. Field evaded his duty to account for "moral aspects of the cause," for which he had criticized others in 1850. Barnard declined to recuse himself. More injunctions flew.[15]

Disrepute among bench and bar was demonstrated in four courtroom exchanges between counsel for Vanderbilt and counsel for the Erie Railway in April 1868. First, though enjoined, Barnard continued to act. He appointed his friend John B. Haskin as referee to take testimony. The Erie's counsel objected, with good reason. Haskin served as a conduit for bribing Barnard. Haskin's reputation, delicately put, was that he had "been connected not with all that is purest and best even in New York City politics." Second, well-regarded lawyer James T. Brady engaged in an extraordinary confrontation with Haskin, with Barnard presiding. Haskin surprisingly testified that Dudley Field had offered him a retainer to work for Gould. If Haskin persuaded Barnard to sign a modified injunction, Haskin would receive $5,000, and Dudley would protect Barnard from legislative reprisal. Haskin declined and testified that Barnard had said, "Dudley Field must be a dirty fellow."[16] Brady warned that "he was not responsible for what was to follow." He then effectively accused both men of corruption while cross-examining Haskin. The following day, Barnard halted the proceedings. Remarkably, the judge reacted not with horror but adopted a "business-like manner." This extraordinary proceeding led George Templeton Strong to write about bench and bar sinking further into the mud.[17]

Third, David Dudley Field and Horace F. Clark argued the bounds of adversarial advocacy. Field objected to a question Clark had asked an Erie director. Clark demanded that Field "rise and act like a gentleman" when objecting. Field sarcastically applauded Clark for his manners and did the same the following day. Clark responded in kind. Clark subsequently accused Dudley Field of attempting but failing to suborn perjury in one witness but succeeding with another. Field defended his son's honor, but the damage was done.[18]

Finally, Field and Clark closed another "prolonged" debate by mocking each other. As Charles Francis Adams Jr. wrote, counsel "would indulge in personal wrangling, and accuse each other of the grossest malpractice."[19]

Sharp exchanges between opposing lawyers were nothing new. What the Field-Clark and Brady-Haskin exchanges marked was the end of gentlemanly decorum in New York courts. This tradition differentiated elite lawyers from pettifoggers. Pettifoggers relied on passionate appeals; the elite bar claimed reason was its guide. Elite lawyers preached gentlemanly behavior, but they practiced nearly unbridled adversarial behavior. Opposing counsel repeatedly brought the court's attention to their adversary's ungentlemanly behavior, noting the mote in their opponent's eye but not the beam in their own. What Clark and Field demanded was honor. Civil and decorous behavior toward one's adversary demonstrated that each was honorable. Thus, one never attacked an adversary's character.

Charles Francis Adams Jr., trained as a lawyer, lamented, "The magnates of Wall Street and the great corporations of New York treated the law and the judge with equal contempt." Law was simply a tool to attain wealth, and lawyers were necessary to use that tool effectively. For Gould, Fisk, Vanderbilt, and the Erie claimants, law possessed no intrinsic value. The amount charged by the more than forty "brains" representing the Erie Railway in early 1868 was "more than a third of a million of dollars." Adams noted that Peter Sweeny, part of the Tweed ring, was paid $150,000, even though "he had nothing to do, as there was nothing to be done." Yet that extravagant cost was cheap when control of the Erie would bring so much more.[20]

The parties settled. Gould and Fisk maintained control of the Erie

Railway. Vanderbilt received nearly $5 million. Others involved received $429,250 for their troubles. Boston investors who joined Gould received $4 million. Soon a second Erie war began.[21]

British investors sought and received an injunction against the Erie's directors for fleecing the corporation. But it was too late. Barnard had switched allegiances and named Gould receiver of the Erie two hours earlier. (The Erie had formally cleared Barnard of the previous charges of conspiracy and corruption.) More suits followed. The only change was the substitution of Judge Cardozo to do Gould's bidding. Gould ended up $10 million richer.[22]

Field & Shearman represented Fisk in other lawsuits. One was a defamation suit against Samuel Bowles, editor of the Springfield, Massachusetts, *Republican*. He had editorialized that Fisk was a swindler, fat, and the son of a lunatic. The suit was refiled in New York but was not pursued. When Bowles visited New York City just before Christmas 1868, a Fisk-friendly judge issued a warrant for his arrest. Bowles spent a night in jail for criminal libel. That experience caused Bowles to join the attacks on Field's ethics.[23]

The third Erie war involved its attempted takeover of the Albany & Susquehanna Railroad (A&S) in 1869. Fisk and Gould adopted the same modus operandi: use the courts, especially Barnard, to your advantage, and use force when the law is unhelpful. One of the most astonishing aspects of the A&S raid was the arrest of several of its executives, including lawyer Henry Smith, at its annual meeting. Barnard issued the arrest warrant at the request of Field & Shearman. In the legal aftermath, New York Supreme Court judge E. Darwin Smith concluded that Erie's lawyers had "fraudulently procured an order for [their] arrest." The takeover failed. Several critics concluded that some of the firm's tactics were unethical.[24]

Finally, the Heath and Raphael matter also concerned control of the Erie. In March 1872 English investors ousted Gould from the Erie's presidency after two years. The Erie's ledgers showed that lawyers (and possibly judges) had cost the railroad $489,909.30 in September 1869 and $898,054.86 the following year.[25]

The first published criticism of Field's ethical behavior appeared in late 1870. A small commentary in the December 16, 1870, issue of the *New York Times* discussed the report that Field & Shearman had accepted a general retainer from Fisk. The firm defended its decision on the grounds that "it was the duty of the advocate to accept all cases offered him." This, the *Times* noted, was untrue. Ten days later, the *Times* reprinted two short items from other newspapers. One repeated the information from the December 16 article, which offered another opportunity to state that no advocate was required "to accept all cases offered to him." It cited George Sharswood's *Essay on Professional Ethics* to the contrary. The second item involved correspondence from the December 7, 1870, issue of Bowles's *Republican*. The *Republican* had received a letter from a young, unnamed New York lawyer originally from Massachusetts who claimed that Field had received more than $200,000 from Erie alone, "and his regular income is enormous." But his connection with Gould and Fisk and his association with Barnard have "destroyed his reputation as a high-toned lawyer with the public, while the Bar lawyers disliked him for his avarice and meanness." The correspondent then cut more deeply: "His reputation as a lawyer is based upon his knowledge of legal technicality, and once during a legal controversy with the late James T. Brady, the latter dubbed him 'the king of the pettifoggers,' which title has stuck to Field ever since."[26]

Brady died in February 1869 and was universally lauded by the elite New York bar. To be called the king of the pettifoggers was the worst insult one elite lawyer could make about another. For Brady to be its author surely intensified Field's discomfort. And for that appellation to be made public by Bowles was a low blow. Lawyers were well aware of the difference between an honorable lawyer and a pettifogger. Field's contemporary Timothy Walker told his students, "Were I to concentrate in a single word whatever I can conceive of despicable in our profession, it would be pettifogging." The insult was compounded by citing Field's "avarice and meanness." Field lacked the virtues of a gentleman; he was driven not by honor but by the base desire to acquire wealth. He failed to demonstrate the courtesy a gentleman was honor-bound to offer others, particularly those below him, by his mean temperament.[27]

Field immediately responded, not to the impertinent *New York Times* but to Samuel Bowles. His December 27, 1870, letter to Bowles asked the editor to publicly disavow the published statements. Bowles refused. As a fellow native of western Massachusetts, Bowles told Field, the "one feeling of your old friends" was "one of mingled sorrow and indignation at your professional association with Fisk and Gould and their desperate schemes." Dudley Field refuted the claims about his father's income from the Erie and justified the firm's decision to take the railroad's cases by listing the other elite lawyers who had served it. His father was not avaricious and mean, as he gave money to his alma mater and made other charitable contributions.

Finally, James T. Brady was a friend of both Fields, and despite a "warm contest" years earlier, Dudley was sure Brady had not so insulted his father.

Bowles urged Field to reject immoral clients and immoral claims. Field resorted to the legal profession's ordinary defense for representing the "bad cause": a lawyer cannot know beforehand that his client's case is wrong. But Field added two interesting twists to this doctrine: First, the "general rule" was, he declared, that "the lawyer, being intrusted by the Government with the exclusive function of representing litigants before the Courts, is bound to represent any person who has any rights to be asserted or defended." Second, Field used the defamation case made by Fisk against Bowles. Field asserted that Bowles was "guilty of a gross libel" against one of Field's clients. Should Bowles not receive legal representation?

As the *New York Times* noted, Field's general rule was not a rule followed by the American legal profession. American lawyers were free to accept or reject the cause of any prospective client. Only English barristers were so bound. Field had rejected that proposition in his 1844 essay on the legal profession. More interestingly, Field's specific example of the defamation lawsuit indicates his belief that, at or before the filing of the complaint against Bowles, Bowles had a bad cause. In other words, Field's caution that a lawyer cannot predict the moral worth of a client's case was inapt when he represented Fisk against Bowles. Therefore, one *can* know whether a cause is good or bad at its inception. In the same letter, Field declared, "I do not assent to the theory of Brougham, that the lawyer should know nobody but his client. I insist that he should defend his client *per fas*, and not *per nefas*" (by right and not by wrong).[28]

Bowles's biographer believed his subject got the better of the argument; most lawyers, even those critical of Field, disagreed. The correspondence was, however, widely published.[29]

Bowles was merely Field's first public critic. E. L. Godkin, editor of the *Nation*, agreed to publish three unsigned articles by New York lawyer Francis C. Barlow, all criticizing Field's behavior. Barlow then went public. The *New York Tribune* published a lengthy article on January 31, 1871, on the Erie lawsuits, followed by the inevitable response from Field. Barlow wrote three very long letters to the editor, published successively on March 7–9. Field responded with an ad hominem attack (calling Barlow "this person"; refusing to address him as "General," his Civil War rank; and denigrating his legal abilities and stature). Field selectively responded to Barlow's substantive charges. Barlow published a pamphlet of his letters and Field's response, as well as other material, in *Facts for Mr. Field*. The April 1871 issue of the *North American Review* included two articles about Field's legal ethics in the A&S raid. One was authored by Albert Stickney, who, like Field, was raised in Massachusetts and moved to New York to practice law. The other, written by Charles Francis Adams Jr. (great-grandson of John Adams), specifically responded to Field's unanswered question to Bowles: What specific act of professional misconduct did I, Field, take?[30]

Barlow detailed Field's work on the A&S raid. His most important accusations of professional misconduct were (1) Field & Shearman's routine reliance on Barnard for orders favorable to its client ("let it not be said that Judge Barnard was not the favorite judge of these litigants"), despite earlier allegations (made by Shearman, among others) that Barnard was corrupt, and (2) Judge E. Darwin Smith's finding that some of the Erie proceedings were fraudulent. Field's actions were not those of a "fair and honorable lawyer." Barlow also repeatedly claimed that Field had acted dishonorably: Field "conducts [the Erie's] litigations in defiance of all rules of professional honor and common honesty." Lawyers, "if they care for the dignity and honorable name of their profession," must help it "purify itself," for "there is no profession or guild in the world which would have permitted the professional misconduct of leading members (on the bench and at the bar) to go unrebuked, as has the legal profession in this city."[31]

Stickney's ostensible review of the Field-Bowles correspondence further specified Field's misconduct. Stickney agreed with Field on at least two points: "Sinners do have rights and must have justice. They cannot have justice without counsel." Further, a "lawyer is at perfect liberty to take any client that he chooses, with blame from no one." The crucial question was, what limits are placed on the lawyer when representing a client? Stickney praised Field's "acuteness of mind" and knowledge of both the law and "the most honorable traditions of the profession." Thus, Field knew what "the honor of his profession demands of him." Stickney offered more specifics than Barlow did. In one A&S suit, the plaintiff, represented by Field & Shearman, lacked authority to sue, yet Judge Barnard granted an injunction at an ex parte hearing. He listed other examples of Barnard's acquiescence at the merest whisper from Thomas Shearman. Stickney criticized the firm for initiating a suit in Barnard's court rather than in Albany, where A&S was headquartered. More importantly, Field & Shearman sued on A&S's behalf, even though it was not a client. It did so under the pretense that it had been asked to sue by A&S's new operators. Barnard's order to arrest A&S

president Joseph Ramsey, its counsel Henry Smith, and Ramsey's preferred receiver Robert Pruyn was "unauthorized" and "in aid of the fraudulent purposes of Mr. Fisk and his associates," as declared by Judge Smith. Despite the availability of Albany-based judges, Field & Shearman returned again and again to Barnard, who issued injunctions under suspicious circumstances. Stickney evaluated Field's conduct and asked, "Is there not danger lest, if such practice obtain, the delicate courtesies of the profession be lost?" Stickney recalled the bar during Field's youth, when "counsel showed one another the knightly courtesy of a Bayard."[32]

Charles Francis Adams Jr. wrote of Field's willingness to accommodate any interest of his client in the A&S raid. Field was willing to go beyond even the bounds set by Henry Brougham:

> Certainly no counsel could have acted more fully up to both the letter and spirit of this famous rule, than did Messrs. David Dudley Field and Thomas G. Shearman, of counsel for the Erie Railway Company, on this notable occasion. They even "cast to the wind" the single faint limitation conveyed by Lord Brougham in the words "to *save*" and "to *protect*" by all "expedient means"; and, in the intense fervor of their devotion to their clients, had recourse in aggressive proceedings to processes of law which were subsequently judicially characterized as procured "in aid of fraudulent purposes." . . . The ingenious device, also, of arresting one's opposing counsel and holding him to $25,000 bail, at the moment when his professional services are likely to become peculiarly necessary, is a feature in legal amenities with which [Brougham] could not have been expected to be familiar. A high authority has now, however, established these as part of the duties of the American advocate. Instances of similar devotion will, therefore, unless the now obsolete practice of disbarring should chance to be revived, probably hereafter become more common than they hitherto have been.[33]

These accusations led the Boston-based *American Law Review* to opine that the ABCNY "must immediately examine the charges of unprofessional conduct, fraud, and perhaps crime, made in the most respectable quarters, against one of its members, Mr. David Dudley Field." This case was a matter of interest not merely to New York lawyers but to "the profession throughout the country," and only the ABCNY could resolve it. The *Review* noted that a disbarment proceeding against Field was "out of the question, because the machinery is hopelessly rotten." Its young, reform-minded lawyer-editors were Arthur Sedgwick and Oliver Wendell Holmes Jr. An unsigned article in the *Review* urged the bar, including the ABCNY, to inculcate a "faith in something nobler than success." Society needed to understand that "wealth does not signify honor, nor notoriety mean fame . . . and that the most precious possession in life, when all is said, is character."[34]

Field and his defenders responded to every criticism. One routine tactic was to list other eminent lawyers who had received Erie retainers. A second was to appeal to expertise. The sympathetic *Albany Law Journal* printed a letter to Field from legal ethics writer George Sharswood, who affirmed that a lawyer was free to decide whether to represent any client. More professional discretion existed whether to prosecute "bad causes" than to defend them. Sharswood's generalities were irrelevant, yet they were offered as proof. Shearman responded to Barlow's attacks, and Field objected to the assertion that he "had a silken halter round the neck of Judge Barnard and a hempen one round that of Cardozo."[35]

Field asked Boston lawyer George Ticknor Curtis (see chapter 2) to evaluate his conduct regarding A&S. In a long, turgid response (its length and tone may have been part of the point), Curtis (who was paid by someone) absolved Field and the firm: This controversy was about the mysterious ways of lawyers, the details of which were unintelligible to the common man. Its value was in the simple conclusion that lawyers disagreed. That was where the matter should lay. Curtis first concluded that no evidence (but much speculative gossip) existed of Barnard's corruption. Thus, the firm's requests for injunctions specifically from Barnard raised no issues of professional misconduct. Second, the arrest of A&S lawyer Henry Smith at its 1869 annual meeting was simply an "accident," as Field had declared in responding to Barlow. Because experienced lawyers "do not commonly allow zeal for their clients to carry them into acts, and to pursue objects, which would be irrational because they could not possibly be successful, even if there were no higher restraint operating to prevent them," and because Smith's arrest was irrational because unhelpful, Field could not have meant to have Smith arrested. Curtis assumed a great deal in this syllogism. Third, Field was attacked because of his clients' poor reputations. But a lawyer's independence required that he "be allowed to do everything for his client that he can honestly do." The "bad motives" of a client should not be imputed to his lawyer, who is "to assume it to be right to do for any man what the law allows to be done." This also echoed previous statements by Field.[36]

The *American Law Review* and the *Albany Law Journal* offered predictably contrary views of Curtis's defense. The former dismissed Curtis, concluding his exoneration was an example par excellence of technical, legalistic reasoning, of assuming, "for purposes of argument, a condition of affairs which every man, who knows any thing at all of the subject knows does not exist." It found Curtis's method of arguing so false that "sophistry is no name for it." The *Albany Law Journal* appealed to its readers to defer to Curtis's expertise. It called Curtis "one of the most eminent lawyers of the country," possessed of a "high personal and professional character," who presented a "careful examination" of the "real merits" of the litigation.[37]

Field may have believed the attacks were now behind him, but anticorruption forces were ascendant in New York. In late June 1871 papers documenting municipal corruption were given to the *New York Times*. Tweed's fall from power was under way. Francis Barlow won election to the office of attorney general in the November elections, and Tweed was indicted on felony charges in December. Field was not publicly impugned at this time, but an article by Albert Stickney recounted a "juridical farce" involving the Erie Railway. He accused Barnard of becoming the first Anglo-American judge who "has openly professed his willingness to sell the process of his court to thieves." Stickney never mentioned Field.[38]

In early 1872 an ABCNY committee urged the removal of certain unnamed judges from office. The judiciary committee of the New York State Assembly began to investigate Barnard, Cardozo, and Fisk's friend Judge John McCunn. Stickney aided the Assembly's investigation, and over a two-month period, he and two other lawyers examined 239 witnesses, including Field. Field complained vigorously of Stickney's pointed and sharp examination. In April the committee recommended that all three be impeached.[39]

Cardozo resigned from office in May. McCunn was convicted, went home, and died three days later. Barnard, initially represented by Curtis (who had apparently urged him to resign), retained new counsel and went to trial on July 22. Half of the thirty-eight articles of impeachment concerned his actions in the Erie wars. He was convicted in August of twenty-five, including all those related to Erie.[40]

Field was among the defense witnesses in Barnard's impeachment trial. He denied any corrupt association with Barnard and again lashed out at the prosecutors. Barnard's conviction reinvigorated Field's accusers.[41]

In late 1871 Field decided he needed an additional letter of exoneration from an eminent lawyer, and he chose Jeremiah S. Black, former

Pennsylvania Supreme Court judge and United States attorney general. Black's exoneration of Field was published in March 1872. Black ignored Barlow and Stickney, praised Curtis for his "spirit of perfect fairness," and echoed Curtis that the firm had been accused because it was "retained by a bad client."[42]

A bitter colloquy between Stickney and Field related to the Barnard investigation and impeachment in the spring of 1872 may have led Stickney to revive his condemnation of Field. Stickney replied to Black and skewered Curtis, defender of both Field and (briefly) Barnard. Curtis "delivered his 'opinion' that Judge Barnard was an upright judge, and Mr. Field an upright lawyer," he wrote. After Barnard's impeachment conviction, what did that imply for Field? Stickney also claimed that when Field obtained an order from Barnard, he was "acting all the time knowing that the writ was granted without a shadow of authority in law, by a corrupt judge, for his client, from corrupt motives, Mr. Field himself being paid by his client for his services in that very matter." Stickney then reprised Judge Smith's conclusion that Erie's counsel, including Field, had engaged in a conspiracy to abuse the legal process in the arrest of A&S lawyer Henry Smith and others.[43]

Before Stickney's rejoinder was published, he, fellow Barnard prosecutor Joshua Van Cott, and Wheeler Peckham, brother and son of a lawyer and judge involved in the A&S raid, attacked Field by proposing that the ABCNY judiciary committee report its recommendations regarding the lawyers implicated in the Barnard-Cardozo impeachments. The implicated lawyers were the Fields and Thomas Shearman, among others. Nothing happened until an extraordinary meeting of the ABCNY on December 10, 1872. Presiding was its president, William Evarts, recently returned from nearly a year in Europe. After Peckham, the judiciary committee chairman, asked for another extension, Field rose and objected.[44]

Field demanded that he be immediately tried and either expelled or cleared. Though ABCNY members raised a clamor that prevented Field from finishing his prepared speech, he provided his entire complaint to the *New York Herald*, which published it in full the following day. He belittled his accusers for their lack of honor, both for impugning him in the newspapers and for expecting to judge him despite their own prejudice. He demeaned Barlow, Van Cott, and Stickney, the first two for their alleged "disreputable practices," of which Field claimed to possess evidence, and Stickney for seeking "the little newspaper notoriety that he has coveted, begged and earned." His persecutors, including Peckham, were his "personal enemies" and terrible lawyers, making it presumptuous of them to accuse him of unprofessional behavior. Field searched for a telling criticism of Stickney but was left with the claim that Stickney had taken fifteen lawsuits involving Jay Gould's failed effort to corner the gold market "on speculation"—that is, on a contingent fee. And Field had the duty to defend these suits brought by this speculator! In addition to being incompetent and venal, these complainants were "interlopers," Field claimed, and lacked any justification to accuse him, as they were not involved in the lawsuits in which Field had allegedly acted badly. Finally, Field made another appeal to authority, providing letters from twelve prominent lawyers and judges who defended his conduct.[45]

These letters offer some insight into Field's understanding of his ethical duties in contrast to that of his critics. The letters consist of two distinct batches. The first five were sent to Field between March and May 1871, when Field's ethics were first assailed by lawyers Barlow and Stickney. All concerned Field's behavior in the A&S litigation. Each was relatively short, and all found Field's behavior honorable and professionally proper. None specifically discussed Barnard's order for the arrest of A&S lawyer Henry Smith. None mentioned the more general topic of Field's obtaining orders from Barnard, who was still in good standing yet still generally known to be corrupt. The other seven letters were written in reply to Field's request of November 9, 1872, after publication of Stickney's attack in the *Galaxy*. Field asked the recipients to give their opinion of his behavior relative to three orders he obtained in the Union Pacific case, including an order to break into the railroad's safe. This was in response to a specific accusation in Stickney's *Galaxy* article. Field asked whether "it was in any respect unprofessional or improper for attorneys or counsel to apply for those orders or any of them?" All seven found "nothing unprofessional." Four of the seven letters adopted the specific language ("unprofessional or improper") used by Field. A few took the same approach as Curtis, making legalistic arguments to reach their conclusions, and a few resorted to the language of professional honor. Several discussed the importance of the principle that a lawyer remain independent of society by "assert[ing] the legal rights of obnoxious individuals." Judge Thomas W. Clerke, who had presided over some aspects of the Erie litigation, concluded that if Field did not know allegations in the complaint were false, "I am of the opinion that it was in no respect unprofessional or improper" to request the injunctions.[46]

Neither Field nor his accusers left the meeting satisfied. No action was taken; Field's demand was delayed until late January 1873. The judiciary committee's report, which the membership adopted, neither moved to expel Field from the ABCNY nor recommended that he be referred to the court for disbarment proceedings. Although the report itself has disappeared, a few of its conclusions can be found in the *Albany Law Journal*. For example, the committee's initial suggestion to refer "certain members" for disbarment proceedings was found impractical and dismissed. Expulsion was also inapt because the ABCNY's constitution assumed "so high an estimate" of every member's "professional character" that the "practice of his profession cannot be impeached in a summary way." Only the grievance committee could look impartially at a member's actions and decide whether to expel him. Unfortunately, Field's extraordinary speech made impartiality impossible in his case. The *Albany Law Journal* scoffed at the judiciary committee's reasoning and likened Field to English barrister Charles Phillips, who represented the confessed murderer Courvoisier (see chapter 2). Both had been the subject of "groundless" accusations.[47]

Legal Ethics in the Aftermath of the Field Debate

The *Albany Law Journal* noted that Stickney, Van Cott, and Peckham all signed the report of the ABCNY's judiciary committee, dismissing the request to expel Field. This proved that their "appeals to passion and prejudice" had been overridden by the "intelligent and unbiased portion of the community."[48] But the lessons in legal ethics resulting from the Erie wars make this conclusion both simplistic and unhelpful.

First, both Field and Curtis argued that Field lacked knowledge of Barnard's corruption and thus was not culpable for obtaining injunctions from him. As a rule, willful ignorance is rarely an effective defense, and that holds true here. Field's partner Thomas Shearman publicly wrote about Barnard's corruption in 1867. James T. Brady said as much in Barnard's court, and Dudley Field made private accusations. Field himself publicly stated that Barnard had unreservedly supported Vanderbilt's interests when Field initially represented the Gould-Fisk interests. (Field refused to acknowledge this during the Barnard impeachment investigation.) Other eminent lawyers defending Field assumed his ignorance exonerated him. Barnard acted based on allegations made by Field's clients. Those allegations were false, but Field was not responsible because he claimed he did not know this. Field's supporters gave him the benefit of the doubt in judging his actions. They judged Field's critics much more stringently. Field's supporters argued that the burden was on his critics to present evidence that Field either knew Barnard was corrupt or knew his clients gave him false evidence. Until such evidence was produced, Field's name was clear. This was a near impossible task.

Field's demand for proof of his knowledge of judicial corruption created a bind for his critics, who premised most of their criticisms on the concept of honor. An honorable lawyer would not seek orders from a judge well known to be corrupt (though not yet formally accused) when that lawyer's partner, son, and cocounsel had all said so. Field also ignored this injunction from his own 1844 essay: "An unscrupulous bar could not exist among an upright, high-minded community; and if you find anywhere a corrupt legal profession, you find it in the midst of a corrupt and corrupting people." The attention to honor led Field's detractors to de-emphasize the question of whether Field had obtained orders from Barnard or Cardozo in violation of the law. The contestants argued using incommensurable premises. In Field's view, no one could conclude his actions were "unprofessional or improper." But Field's detractors found him dishonorable.[49]

Field's defenders were all his contemporaries. Most were Democrats, most disliked Lincoln, and most supported Democratic Party candidate George McClellan in the 1864 presidential race. Most were too old to serve in the military during the Civil War, and most strongly disagreed with congressional Reconstruction. The reformers, in contrast, all fought for the Union. Albert Stickney, Oliver Wendell Holmes, and Charles Francis Adams Jr. were all raised in the Boston area, and Arthur Sedgwick, though raised in New York City, had many family members there. All but Adams graduated from Harvard Law School, and all graduated from Harvard College. They were all a generation younger than Field. They largely believed in good government and the importance of lawyers in creating good government. They took seriously the ideal of public service and believed, along with Field in 1844, that lawyers should not do whatever their clients demanded.

Field rejected Lord Brougham's view that a lawyer must use "all expedient means" to satisfy the desires of "that client and none other." Field admitted using all lawful means (*per fas*) to obtain a client's desired lawful ends, but he did not and would not use unlawful means (*per nefas*). A lawyer owed some unarticulated duties to society, Field acknowledged, but he apparently no longer believed a lawyer owed a duty to "a society whose welfare the advocate is bound by the highest sanctions to promote." Field never reconciled his earlier and later understandings of the lawyer's duties to both client and public.

He was, however, aware of this conflict. In 1884 the seventy-nine-year-old Field's speeches and writings were published. The reprinted "Study and Practice of the Law" (1844) omitted two parts of the original essay. Field deleted the statement, "No dishonest or dishonorable man could retain the confidence of honest and honorable men," as well as several statements proclaiming that the lawyer was bound to obey moral law. Most tellingly, Field deleted his conclusion: "To assent to the bad scheme of an unjust client is to become equally guilty with him, and the two are as much conspirators to effect a wrong, as if they had originally concocted a plan of iniquity with the view of sharing in the plunder."[50]

The standards by which a lawyer's conduct was judged were changing during this period. Horace Clark's 1868 fulminations concerned Field's dishonor. When Field asked his peers for their opinion in late 1872, he asked them to determine whether his actions were "unprofessional or improper," not whether they were dishonorable. That was also the approach taken by the ABCNY's judiciary committee. A lawyer could do whatever was lawful to do.

The concept of honor was not extinct, however, even in Field. This may partly explain his anger at the impertinence of young lawyers questioning his behavior, and it suggests why he obtained letters of support from his peers. But that was only a secondary front. The main battle was whether to characterize his actions as unprofessional. This was a standard of lawfulness, not propriety. Field used lawful means, which made his actions professional. His critics might be gentlemen well acquainted with the ideals of honor, but that standard was largely irrelevant.[51]

During the 1880s, elite lawyers writing about the profession toggled between conscience and honor as the better generator of moral rectitude among lawyers. They feared lawyers had lost their way. For example, in 1886 a bar admission committee in South Carolina lauded lawyers of learning and character "who recognize their responsibility as officers of justice, [who] pursue their profession as something different and higher than a mere money-making vocation." Even so, the South Carolina bar had been invaded by quacks who used tricks and improper means to obtain verdicts. One part of the solution to the bar's degradation was to ensure that the licensed "lawyer should not only have a conscience, but an enlightened conscience." That was achieved by requiring greater educational attainment before eligibility for admission to the bar. New York's *Columbia Jurist* argued that the "true lawyer" was a "gentleman—courteous, well bred, refined and manly." The true lawyer's "single purpose" was to assist courts in the administration of justice rather than to pursue wealth. The good news was that lawyers were largely "pure and honorable men" whose conscience prevented them from becoming tools of dishonest clients.[52]

The Ideal and the Actual in the Late Nineteenth Century

Columbia Law School professor Theodore Dwight gave the commencement address to the graduating class of 1870. He urged the graduates to "follow their profession not as a trade for money making, but as a high, lofty and honorable cause." The public, unfortunately, regarded the profession as a nuisance. He "condemned . . . in strong language" Brougham's claim that a lawyer owed a duty to "that client and none other." With Field on the stage, Dwight "warned against the practice of improvident injunctions." In a series of early 1871 lectures later published in book form, prominent New York lawyer William Allen Butler also rejected Brougham's ethic. Brougham's idea was "a high and somewhat rapid flight of oratory, far beyond any justifiable limit of duty or privilege."[53]

A decade later, Dorman B. Eaton made a similar statement in an address at Yale Law School: "No language can too strongly reprobate so detestable and barbarous a code of professional ethics, more becoming a ban of pirates or brigands than a Christian office of justice." Eaton, a founding member of the ABCNY, had nearly been beaten to death for opposing Fisk. Other elite lawyers agreed with his statement. The earliest treatises on legal ethics either avoided discussing the limits of advocacy or followed the view of elite lawyers. The only lawyer publicly embracing Brougham's ethic was A. Oakey Hall, who was mayor of New York at the height of the Tweed ring's reign. As a young man, Hall had criticized the lack of zeal by the lawyers representing John Webster in his 1850 murder trial (see chapter 2).[54]

Though Hall was singular in his published praise of Brougham, the actions of courtroom lawyers indicated that he was not alone. The adversarial zeal demonstrated in the Erie wars was the rule. When Charles Guiteau was tried for assassinating President James Garfield, his principal lawyer was George Scoville, who ordinarily practiced patent law and "knew almost nothing about the criminal justice system." Even so, Scoville was a mighty advocate who skillfully argued that Guiteau was insane. The trial took nearly two months; the transcript consisted of nearly three thousand pages. The adversaries forced the court to issue a number of rulings, many concerning the admissibility of expert testimony. Cross-examination was extensive and incisive. Evidentiary objections were often made and contested.[55]

In notorious criminal cases of the 1880s and 1890s, lawyers practicing in different regions of the United States acted as zealous advocates for their clients. An Iowa murder trial in late 1897 is emblematic of this embrace of zeal. In general, the criminal defense lawyer believed that the proper ethic of advocacy required constant action. To prevent the state's star witness from offering damning testimony, defense counsel "repeatedly objected during his testimony." On cross-examination of this witness, defense counsel attacked his credibility, because he was eligible to receive a reward; made legal arguments only tangentially related to factual disputes (arguing that the witness's arrest of the accused in Canada was unlawful); and ended one day of cross-examination with the caution, "We will see on Monday whether you are telling the truth." Zealous advocacy meant "objecting to every single prosecution point, no matter how small."[56]

Courtroom advocates became more technically proficient during the Gilded Age, one mark of modern professional behavior. But technical proficiency married to zeal led judges and others to criticize lawyers for serving only their clients' interests. In *Commonwealth v. Hill* (1898), the Pennsylvania Supreme Court admonished a convicted murderer's counsel for excessive zeal:

> The errors assigned are of the most formal and perfunctory kind, and are sufficiently answered in the opinion of the learned judge below refusing a new trial. There is nothing in the case to justify bringing it here, and, indeed, there is considerable ground for belief that it was never intended in good faith to reach a hearing in this court. It is a flagrant example of the perverted standard of professional ethics which assumes that counsel should help his client to escape the proper consequences of his act by any move or device, short, perhaps, of actual fraud or imposition. This is a very serious error, and apparently becoming more widespread, especially in cases involving life. The boundaries of professional privilege and professional obligation are clearly defined, and in no way doubtful. Counsel represents the prisoner to defend his rights. In so doing he is bound to exercise competent learning, and to be faithful,

vigilant, resolute. But he is at the same time an officer of the court, part of the system which the law provides for the preservation of individual rights in the administration of justice, and bound by his official oath to fidelity as well to the court as to the client. . . . The duty of the counsel is to see that his client is tried with proper observance of his legal rights, and not convicted except in strict accordance with law. His duty to his client requires him to do this much. His duty to the court forbids him to do more. An independent and fearless bar is a necessary part of the heritage of a people free by the standards of Anglo-Saxon freedom, and courts must allow a large latitude to the individual judgment of counsel in determining his action; but it must never be lost sight of that there is a corresponding obligation to the court, which is violated by excessive zeal or perverted ingenuity that seeks to delay or evade the due course of legal justice.[57]

The *American Lawyer*, a monthly New York–based magazine for business lawyers, regularly bemoaned the moral and professional failures of lawyers. In its first issue it decried the "reprehensible" behavior of many lawyers and urged the better part of the profession to renew efforts to disbar them. "In their advocacy of their clients['] claims, lawyers have neither moral nor legal rights to pervert testimony, distort or conceal facts, or seek to circumvent the law." It agreed that a lawyer could "take measures" for a client that he would not take personally, but "the lawyer should never so absorb the [client] as to induce him to either seek legal ends by illegal means or illegal ends by legal means." In contrast, it excoriated the prosecutor in the Lizzie Borden murder case for "professional negligence," claiming he ignored his duty "to learn from his witnesses before they came into court the story they each would tell." The challenge to lawyers was to act zealously on behalf of their clients and remain loyal officers of the court.[58]

One significant difficulty for courtroom advocates was the zero-sum nature of trials. Winning was the measure of professional skill and accomplishment. Skillful personal injury lawyers offered arguably inadmissible evidence to stir the jury's passion; defense lawyers hedged against defeat by generating evidentiary errors by the trial court in the hope of winning a new trial on appeal. Wealthy financier Russell Sage was sued in 1891 by William Laidlaw Jr. for personal injuries. Sage was accosted by Henry Norcross, who was carrying a bomb concealed in a bag. He threatened to kill Sage unless he was given over a million dollars. Sage allegedly placed Laidlaw between himself and Norcross during this conversation. When Norcross dropped the bag, the bomb exploded, killing Norcross, injuring Laidlaw, and killing another of Sage's employees. Sage was largely uninjured. The case was dismissed before trial, and Laidlaw appealed. The New York Appellate Division reversed the dismissal, and after a trial, Laidlaw obtained a favorable verdict and damages. Sage appealed, and the judgment was reversed. At the second trial, a mistrial was declared. Laidlaw won again at the third trial, but Sage appealed and won. Laidlaw demanded another opportunity, but it never occurred. His lawyer was Joseph Choate, then ambassador to Great Britain. A personal injury case in Chicago was tried at least five times. Trial lawyers knew that appellate courts reversed judgments if the trial court made evidentiary or other "technical" errors.[59]

Nan Patterson was tried for the murder of her married lover in 1904. The prosecution alleged in closing argument, "I don't want to make any charges about my brothers in the profession, but I will say that there are those among her defense who are capable of manufacturing testimony which they know to be false." This was sometimes true of defense counsel, as demonstrated in the 1905 trial of lawyer Abe Hummel for conspiracy to obstruct justice by suborning perjury. But in Patterson's case, this remarkable attack lacked evidentiary support. Patterson's first trial ended in a hung jury, and she was retried. New York district attorney William Travers Jerome appeared in court on every day of both trials, and after the second hung jury, he complained of "a miscarriage of justice." The *New York Times* responded in a searing editorial: "If the theory that it is the duty of the District Attorney and his assistants to pursue with ferocious hatred every person under indictment for murder, to employ every available method and device to secure conviction, and to piece out unconvincing evidence . . . be the true one, then the District Attorney would have been called, not the public prosecutor, but the public hyena."[60]

By 1890, the legal profession's modus vivendi with regard to zealous representation of clients included two legal fictions: First, Lord Brougham's claim that the lawyer's only duty was to "that client and none other" was formally rejected though practically embraced. Second, although the ethical duty of the prosecutor was to seek justice, once an indictment was issued, the prosecutor's entire effort was focused on winning.

Thomas Goode Jones and the Alabama Bar's
1887 Code of Ethics

In 1881 thirty-seven-year-old Thomas Goode Jones suggested that the Alabama State Bar Association create a code of legal ethics. His timing was propitious. The association's committee on legal education castigated the presence of unscrupulous lawyers, or "shysters." Alabama's was one of many bar associations founded in the 1870s and 1880s to "uphold the honor of the profession of the law." First, this required an acknowledgment of its decline. In 1879 the *Southern Law Journal* approvingly reprinted an article from Pennsylvania arguing that lawyers were unpopular because the public believed they were tricksters and shysters. Myra Bradwell, famously denied admission to the Illinois bar in 1872, wrote of her joy upon the creation of the Chicago Bar Association, which might bring about the end of "the disreputable shysters who now disgrace the profession." Elite lawyers who were perceived as shysters were a threat to the profession. Unlike the dull and often incompetent pettifogger, the unethical shyster was technically proficient. He used his talents to beguile both clients and juries to gain wealth, an objective inconsistent with the elite claim that the profession's foundations were "altruism and personal sacrifice." The attention paid to shysters suggests an increasing anxiety among legal elites about the profession's status.[61]

The motion by Jones went nowhere, but the Alabama State Bar Association agreed to create a three-person committee to create a code of ethics the following year. Jones was one of only a few Alabama lawyers who owned a copy of Sharswood's *Essay*, and he did the committee's work, completing the code in 1886. The manuscript was then lost, which delayed its adoption until 1887. The code consisted of two parts—an oath and a set of general rules. Violating the oath, which set out "duties specifically enjoined upon attorneys by law," subjected a lawyer to disbarment. The general rules, fifty-seven in number, were applicable, depending on the "peculiar facts, in the light of conscience, and the conduct of honorable and distinguished attorneys in similar cases." Violating a rule led to disbarment if doing so also violated an analogous duty imposed by the oath.[62]

Jones was among many elite lawyers interested in using ethical standards to elevate the status of lawyers and benefit the country; he was unusual in crafting such a code. Printed addresses, essays, and articles of the 1880s promoted the belief that improved lawyer ethics aided governance and thus the people. These publications were almost uniformly exhortations to do good, and the decade was good for reformers. For example, federal judge George W. McCrary, speaking to the Iowa Bar Association, argued that lawyers' ethics "reflect about the average of public sentiment." Improving lawyer ethics would generate "wise legislation and faithful administration." One important ethical standard was that a lawyer "should never permit himself to be made the tool of an unscrupulous client." This was not difficult, for most lawyers were "pure and honorable men." McCrary contrasted the honorable, "true lawyer" with "the counterfeit, the shyster, the pettifogger, the quack, the charlatan, the fomenter of suits, the man of tricks, stratagems and chicanery." The true lawyer was a "man of character . . . who never loses sight of the great interests of society." The true lawyer was loyal to clients and met "his duty to the community in which he lives." Other elite lawyers wrote in a similar vein. Massachusetts lawyer and politician George F. Hoar reiterated the claim that an honorable lawyer must "abandon the pursuit of wealth as a principal . . . object of life" for the benefit of the republic.[63]

Alfred Z. Reed later concluded that the "impulse behind the new organization of the profession was primarily ethical." That conclusion is sound, once one understands the ethical vision of the organizers. Lawyers regularly spoke of protecting the honor of the profession. They also believed a code was useful to remind lawyers to consider their consciences before acting. Bar leaders were unconcerned with enhancing the standards of lawyer discipline. In general, the ethical concerns of bar association members lay in heightening the standards for licensure, not disbarment.

Lawyers in seven cities followed New York City in creating a bar association in the 1870s. The first state bar association was formed in New Hampshire in 1873. By 1878, when the American Bar Association (ABA) was organized, ten others existed, including Alabama's. Only Alabama created a code of ethics. By 1890, only Georgia and Virginia had embraced a code of ethics, and they simply adopted Alabama's.[64]

As a member of Alabama's aristocratic elite, Jones pursued the vindication of honor. During the 1870s and 1880s he represented railroads, which demanded unswerving (and broadly defined) loyalty. Railroad work paid well but threatened the lawyer's traditional claims of independence from clients. Jones's biography explains the origins of the Alabama code of ethics, which reflects the views of legal elites. It is based on honor, conscience, and the emerging concept of the lawyer as a professional.[65]

The Alabama code begins by emphasizing the importance of lawyer ethics to democratic governance. Judicial administration "is largely government itself," and its "purity and efficiency" depend in significant part on the "character, conduct, and demeanor of attorneys." The lawyer's only safe guide is "high moral principle," quoting Sharswood. It then cites the seven duties an Alabama lawyer is sworn "not to violate." However, rules do not ordinarily determine a lawyer's duty. What a lawyer should do depends on the particular facts, the exercise of the lawyer's conscience, and the example set by honorable lawyers of the past. The code ignores any possible conflict between a lawyer's internal light of conscience and past examples of honorable lawyers.[66]

The fifty-seven general rules are guidelines, not standards. They are divided into two categories: the "duty of Attorneys to Courts and Judicial Officers" and the "duty of Attorneys to each other, to Clients and to the Public." This order and the order in which the specific rules are listed are revealing. Rule 1 indicates the elite bar's deep displeasure with Alabama judges, stating that even if a judge issued a "bad opinion," the lawyer must respect the office. The duties of lawyers to "each other" came before those owed to clients or the public. This structure demonstrates the importance of the lawyer's honor and dignity. An attack on a lawyer's honor harms the profession and the administration of justice.

The rules interweave the interests of honor and conscience with calls for professional behavior. For example, Rule 3 declares "disreputable" any effort by a lawyer to obtain the special attention of the judge, while Rule 5 calls it "unprofessional" for a lawyer to conceal his legal positions in his opening statement "in order that opposite counsel may not discuss them." Rule 5 also denounces deceitful behavior, such as knowingly offering inadmissible evidence, and it demands fairness and candor to others. Rule 27 states, "The client can not be made the keeper of the attorney's conscience in professional matters." Rule 28 deems it "unprofessional" for lawyers to embrace their clients' antipathy to the opposing party, and Rule 33 requires competent and diligent representation. Only the lawyer can decide whether to accommodate opposing counsel in incidental matters before trial. Relatedly, a client may not "do anything therein repugnant to [the lawyer's] own sense of honor and propriety." Honor requires the lawyer to inform prospective clients of any information relevant to their hiring of the lawyer (Rule 34). Rule 40 combines professional and honorable behavior: a lawyer should put in writing any important agreement affecting a client's rights, but it is dishonorable to avoid performing an oral agreement, even when the court requires that the agreement be in writing. The guiding principle of the seven rules concerning fees is that "the profession is a branch of the administration of justice and not a mere money-getting trade."

The code embraced both Hoffman and Sharswood. The lawyer "should always be a friend to the defenceless and oppressed" and never commingle his funds with those of his clients. A prosecutor acted criminally when seeking to convict a person the prosecutor believed innocent. A lawyer should refuse to represent a civil plaintiff whose goal was to harass or oppress the defendant and should not "hunt up defects in titles" to generate litigation. The code followed Hoffman in permitting contingent fees, but it followed Sharswood by cautioning that such arrangements were subject to abuse.[67]

More generally, the code promoted a vision of adversary ethics contrary to practice but consonant with Sharswood's ideals. The code used the word *zeal* only once, in Rule 10. It quoted without attribution Sharswood's statement that the lawyer's duty was to exercise "warm zeal," but zeal did not permit the lawyer to "do everything to succeed in his client's cause." Once again, Brougham's ethic was rejected (see chapter 2). However, Rule 10 echoed Brougham in part: "No sacrifice or peril, even to loss of life itself, can absolve from the fearless discharge of this duty." A criminal defense lawyer who "knows or believes" his client is guilty still owes the accused all "fair and lawful means" to ensure due process of law (Rule 13). This is straight from Sharswood. That these ideals did not mirror practice is suggested by Rule 10's closing sentence. The lawyer was reminded of his "accountability to his Creator," his duty to obey the law, and his obligations to his neighbor. These additional behavioral constraints were offered in light of the code's demand that the lawyer act within the law and avoid "any manner of fraud or chicanery." Rule 13 also suggests a diminution in the ideal of honor, for the phrase "fair and lawful" suggests that professional behavior involves acting within the limits of the law. If honorable behavior and professional behavior conflict, the latter triumphs.[68]

The eleven other state bar associations that adopted a code of ethics between 1889 and 1907 made only modest alterations to the Alabama code. But some of those amendments reflected changing views of ethical lawyer behavior. Alabama's Rule 10 began by bemoaning the popular prejudice against lawyers owing to the false claim that a lawyer will do anything for a client. All eleven adopted this first paragraph. The second paragraph quoted Sharswood regarding the duty to use all "fair and lawful means." Most states adopted this language, although Wisconsin substantially amended it and Missouri omitted it. When the ABA looked at this language, it misquoted it as "fair and *honorable* means." This confusion may suggest that state bar associations were more comfortable than the ABA with the idea that a standard of professional behavior had largely replaced a standard of honorable behavior.[69]

Anxious Lawyers and a Transformed Profession

As Alabama prepared to adopt its code of lawyer ethics, the pseudonymous Valmaer, a St. Louis lawyer, published *Lawyer's Code of Ethics: A Satire*. Valmaer begins by noting the first goal of the young lawyer is to obtain a client, and once that is accomplished, to demand a retainer. The lawyer is then instructed to delay the case in order to look up the law and increase his fee. Most importantly, the lawyer must "strictly *adhere* to the retainer, and the adding of items to your bill." Once in court, "object to everything, no matter whether your objection is good in your own mind or not." After all, the court might agree. To the jury, praise your client, "even though it be notoriously false." "Abuse" your opponent. Your duty is to do whatever your client desires: "You had better let it be generally known that you will resort to anything to win your cases," for then business will increase dramatically. As a member of a profession, "you are practicing law for the money there is in it." Others may be interested in dignity or morality, but "success is measured by the amount of wealth a person accumulates." Of shysters, Valmaer suggests that both the word and the individual have "become obsolete." Certainly, some lawyers practice law for their own benefit at the expense of clients and the public, but to proclaim such persons shysters is inapt, for they could not possibly be. The implication, of course, is that all lawyers are shysters.[70]

Valmaer encapsulates all the fears of those protecting the standing of American lawyers. They overbill and underserve their clients, and when they serve them faithfully, they do so at the expense of the opposing party, the court, and the public. The sole reward sought by every lawyer is monetary success.[71]

A January 1889 letter to *Century* magazine made the same arguments, but more soberly. John D. Works, a California Supreme Court justice, responded to an 1884 article criticizing lawyer ethics. Works made several standard arguments: a lawyer ethically represents a party who possesses a legal case but not a moral one, such as invoking the statute of limitations. A lawyer also acts ethically in representing the "criminal whom he knows to be guilty." If the public believes these two actions are ethically wrong, they need to be more fully informed of the importance of due process and of following the law. Too often, clients ask not whether the lawyer is honest and trustworthy but "is he smart, can he win my case?" Honesty and moral stature have "but little to do with his success in getting business from the great mass of litigants," including "many of the very best and most upright business men." In sum, as long as "lawyers are employed because they are regarded as being dishonest, so long will the profession be subject to reproach because it has bad men in its ranks."[72]

Whether a lawyer could be both successful and honest was increasingly in doubt. In the *North American Review*, Homer Greene asked, "Can Lawyers Be Honest?" In answering this question, Greene reframed it: "Can an attorney be successful in his calling if he follows the lines of integrity and the promptings of conscience with unvarying strictness?" Because clients, including "respectable persons," believe they "are capable of being their own custodians of morals" and believe their causes just, they expect their lawyers to serve their interests. Clients demand that their lawyers ignore a "too tender conscience" or "over-scrupulous sense of honesty." Client demands are the "secret" of moral decadence in the legal profession. Unfortunately, no bar's written code of ethics would ever change things. A lawyer "must be his own censor and guide." Greene ended plaintively: "Who will rescue a most honorable calling from its present unfortunate environment?"[73]

Instability in the legal profession was a result of both a weakened culture and economic fears. One study of late-nineteenth-century Boston lawyers found that the average income of a young lawyer was barely sufficient to make ends meet. While elite lawyers did remarkably well during this period, ordinary lawyers faced much greater competition. From 1870 to 1880, the lawyer population rose 54 percent. In the following decade, it rose another 40 percent, substantially exceeding overall population growth. The increase in the number of lawyers may have caught some by surprise. In an 1883 address to the ABA, New Hampshire lawyer John M. Shirley discussed "The Future of the Legal Profession." Although the number of lawyers had always been "weaker numerically than" ministers or doctors, lawyers were more potent because of their social role. Shirley noted that there were fewer lawyers than doctors or clergymen in 1880, and just one out of sixteen lawyers had been born outside the United States, compared with one in five clergymen and one in nine doctors, and few were from eastern or southern Europe. He concluded that the profession's prospects were favorable.[74]

A measured assessment of the profession's growth, composition, and financial opportunities was rare thereafter. Even before the Panic of 1893, the increase in lawyers led to complaints about the bar's composition and overcrowding. The number of lawyers who were first-generation Americans increased tremendously in the last decade of the nineteenth century. The *American Lawyer* claimed that these lawyers were a "discredit" to the profession. Overcrowding resulted in a debased competition for clients and a degradation of the profession. Overcrowding also led bar associations to raise standards of admission. In 1892 the ABA called for the highest court of each state to regulate admission to the bar and provide "supervision of their professional conduct." More than three-fourths of the states responded over the next quarter century by creating statewide bar examining boards. Several state appellate courts eased disbarment proceedings by rejecting the claim that they were equivalent to criminal matters.[75]

These efforts failed to stem the apparent flood of "bad men" in the law. Melville Davisson Post, a twenty-seven-year-old lawyer and author, exploited this state of affairs in his 1896 book *The Strange Schemes of Randolph Mason*. Mason was an antihero, a quintessential lawyer-villain who used his knowledge of the law to help his clients commit murder and other crimes with impunity. The book was sufficiently popular and disturbing that a second set of short stories involving Mason, *Man of Last Resort*, was published the following year. At the close of the nineteenth century, the editors of the *American Law Review* answered a Cincinnati lawyer's question about prospects at the New York City bar: "Its bar, while possessing many worthy members, swarms with touters, shysters, grafters, rascals who practice law with a political pull, and other species of professional vermin." Too often "the cheap lawyer outruns the good one." In the same publication, a South Carolina lawyer touted the continued high tone of the legal profession in the South, except for the arrival of "shyster attorneys."[76]

The presence of pettifoggers, shysters, and ambulance chasers in the legal profession was often discussed after the Panic of 1893. In an 1894 speech to members of the Illinois State Bar Association, Isaac Miller Hamilton called shysters a "monstrosity." The shyster was evil because he knew his actions were immoral. Three years later, lawyers speaking to the Tennessee and Alabama bar associations raised the stakes for the legal profession. In Tennessee, H. M. Wiltse argued that the number of shysters was "rapidly increasing," leading to reputational decline. Robert L. Harmon told the Alabama bar the shyster had "an abundance of shrewdness and cunning," promoted perjured testimony, bribed juries, and invented evidence. Lawyers were under greater attack than at any other time in American history. The public viewed lawyers with "suspicious distrust." Harmon's most damning criticism was that the "shyster, in his worst form, is a greater menace to society than the socialist." The profession's duty was to weed out shysters by reviving disbarment.[77]

The ambulance chaser was another professional threat. The term was coined in 1896, suggesting a concern about the rise in personal injury cases. The ambulance chaser was no pettifogger. He dressed well and knew "by style and volume all the accident case-law of his State." He made a living by taking half the damages awarded to his client, thus bleeding the injured party a second time. By the mid-1890s, fraudulent tort and insurance claims had been well publicized. In New York a group set fires to buildings to obtain insurance payouts; fraudulent "banana peel" slip-and-fall cases had been uncovered there too, as well as in Chicago and Boston. Life insurance scams were sufficiently numerous by 1896 that the authors of an 1878 book on life insurance fraud published a second edition. Like the shyster, the number of ambulance chasers was increasing, and their existence was a warning sign to the legal profession. An additional warning sign was the ambulance chaser's first cousin, the "corporation trickster." Lawyers for transportation companies were charged with acting unethically and unlawfully, suborning perjury, paying witnesses, and communicating and settling cases with injured persons in the absence of their lawyers.[78]

The rise of the corporation trickster was considered a result of lawyers' subservience to their railroad clients. In 1886 several railroads bureaucratized their legal work, creating a hierarchical structure that channeled decision-making authority toward the railroad's general solicitor and away from the local lawyer defending the case and the regional lawyer supervising the litigation. Senator William Breckinridge of Kentucky gave a talk to the members of the Virginia Bar Association in 1891, condemning this change. He praised the unknown lawyer who served the poor, challenged the lynch mob, and remained independent of the "clamors of public opinion." Like everyone else writing on the topic, Breckinridge chastised the legal profession for failing to police its own ranks and removing "the men who dishonor the name of lawyer." More tellingly, Breckinridge also went after the railroad lawyer who acted as his client's "servant" rather than its "counsellor." Too often, railroads wanted a lawyer "not to give advice but to obey; not to counsel, guide, inform, protect, but to carry out plans . . .

to make legal that which is devious, to devise means for ends which are doubtful." Such a lawyer lacked independence from his client. Writing in 1914 about changes in the practice of law since the 1870s, New York lawyer Theron G. Strong concluded that a lawyer working for "important business interests" had become "little more than a paid employee, bound hand and foot to the service of his employer." Such a lawyer was "virtually owned and controlled by the client he serves." Near the end of his life, prominent Texas lawyer William Pitt Ballinger experienced this change. In the early 1880s he had helped Jay Gould expand his railroad holdings in Texas. Ballinger was handsomely paid and maintained a law office that was a counterpoint to the "cold and impersonal" law offices of Shearman & Sterling and other large New York firms. Although he found his railroad clients "a troublesome lot," through the mid-1880s he was able to exercise significant autonomy in handling legal matters. This changed after the merger of the Santa Fe and the Atchison, Topeka & Santa Fe Railroads in 1886. Ballinger continued to serve as general counsel in Texas, with division and local attorneys reporting to him, and he continued to report to national counsel. But his autonomy had ended. Soon after the merger, the railroad's general lawyer informed him that he would make the final decisions, not Ballinger. Though Ballinger "felt very affronted by the new policies," he concluded that "times have changed, my dear friend—the practice of law is going forward at such a rate that those who do not accept these changes will be left behind."[79]

The Contingent Fee

The contingent fee was subjected to searching criticism in the early 1880s, as personal injury litigation increased. Critics charged that contingent fees fomented lawsuits and diminished the profession's honor. This was something of a shift. Hoffman wholly approved of contingent fees, but Sharswood was much more circumspect. He found contingent fee contracts lawful but immoral in all editions of his *Essay*, from 1854 through 1876. In 1881 the *Albany Law Journal* asked judges, including Supreme Court justice Joseph Bradley, their opinion of contingent fees. They uniformly condemned such fees, one judge calling them "derogatory to the honor of the profession." New York's Field Code allowed lawyers and clients to make any contract regarding the lawyer's compensation. Even so, New York State Bar Association president Samuel Hand criticized contingent fee abuses in 1879 and urged that creating "limits of professional decency and decorum" with regard to such fees would elevate the profession's honor. At the same 1879 meeting, lawyer Tracy Becker attacked the contingent fee as unethical, asserting that it transformed the "ancient standards of professional honor . . . [into] the modern one of 'honor to whom' money (not honor) 'is due.'" The US Supreme Court held such fees permissible.[80]

Except for Maryland, all state ethics codes followed Alabama's, permitting lawyers to earn contingent fees. By the early twentieth century, elite lawyers renewed the charge that the contingent fee was unethical. By then, the alarm had been sounded by the rise in damages awarded in railroad and other tort cases. Texas railroad lawyer Edwin Parker wrote of an explosion in personal injury litigation in the 1890s. Everything was bigger in Texas, including damage awards in railroad cases. But even Parker understood that railroads had induced this response by their earlier intransigence in litigation.[81]

The Revival of Ethics Codes

The renewed effort by state bar associations to adopt codes of ethics beginning in the late 1890s suggests an increased anxiety in the legal profession. When Alabama adopted its code of ethics in December 1887, lawyers in approximately thirty states and territories had formed voluntary state bar associations. By the end of 1899, lawyers in nearly all states and territories had created statewide bar associations. Yet only three state bars, Alabama, Georgia, and Virginia, had adopted ethics codes before 1897, and all of them had done so before 1890. The ABA did not even consider adopting a code until 1905, and a first draft of its canons of ethics was published in 1908. At the state level, ethics code activity was nil until the Michigan State Bar Association adopted a code of ethics in 1897. Colorado followed in 1898. Five more state associations—North Carolina, Wisconsin, West Virginia, Maryland, and Kentucky—adopted codes between 1900 and 1903. Missouri adopted its code in 1906, and the following year Mississippi became the final state to do so before the existence of the ABA code.[82]

Relatively little connects these twelve states. Alabama, Virginia, Georgia, and Mississippi were former Confederate states. Eight were former slave states, although three remained in the Union during the Civil War. Wisconsin and Michigan were both subject to the 1787 Northwest Ordinance, which famously banned slavery. Although West Virginia was carved from Virginia during the Civil War, it is unlikely that the latter bar influenced the former to adopt an ethics code. The West Virginia bar was created in 1886, two years before the Virginia Bar Association, but it didn't adopt an ethics code until 1902. The Michigan State Bar Association adopted a code in the aftermath of its success in convincing the legislature to adopt more stringent admission standards, including the creation of a Board of Law Examiners. Michigan apparently misread a recommendation by the ABA's Committee on Legal Education and Admissions to the Bar that the Alabama and Virginia (but not Georgia) codes be used as the basis for lectures to law students. Michigan read this as recommending that other state bars follow those states and adopt a code. The Colorado Bar Association adopted its code within a year of forming, and it was an outlier in several respects. First, it adopted Alabama's code because its leaders were serious about cleansing the local profession. Colorado considered thirty-one complaints and began fifteen disbarment actions in its first two and a half years. Further, "50 or 60 fellows took the hint, and got out before the proceedings were started." Second, Colorado was the only mountain state and the only state admitted to the union after the Civil War to adopt a code of ethics. The importance of honor in the South may explain the predominance of ethics codes in former slave states. Honor does not explain why other states adopted codes, nor does it explain the delay in adoption by state bars after 1889. Additionally, the revival of ethics codes occurred in Michigan and Colorado, which were not former slave states. It is possible that the Panic of 1893 lessened the interest in legal ethics among most lawyers and intensified their interest in economic survival. However, most elite lawyers were relatively unaffected by the panic. It is also possible that when the economy improved in late 1897, lawyers turned their attention back to codes of ethics. Even so, the elite lawyers who dominated the ABA did not do so for nearly a decade.[83]

The most likely reason for bar associations to adopt ethics codes in the late 1890s was a crisis of professional identity. In addition to the twelve bar associations that adopted ethics codes by 1907, nine more were preparing such codes, including New York, Ohio, and Pennsylvania. All were either northeastern states or states organized after the Civil War. Further, several bar associations in Field Code states, including California, Oregon, and Washington, interpreted its provisions relating to a lawyer's duties as an ethics code established as law. In nearly all these states, the concept of gentlemanly honor was not central to a lawyer's status, even though most bar associations were organized in part to preserve the "honor and integrity" of the profession. However, reputational honor was rarely a core aspect of a lawyer's identity outside the South. Most lawyers embraced "personal honor," or the individual's belief in self. Yale Law School dean Henry Wade Rogers wrote, "[A lawyer] must live in rectitude and cherish his personal honor, not forgetting that personal honor is the distinguishing badge of the legal profession."[84]

When ABA president Henry St. George Tucker suggested that it consider a code of ethics, the specific trigger was President Theodore Roosevelt's June 28, 1905, address to the graduating class at Harvard University. Tucker referred to Roosevelt's charge that "many of the most influential and most highly remunerated members of the Bar in every centre of wealth make it their special task to work out bold and ingenious schemes by which their very wealthy clients, individual or corporate, can evade the laws which are made to regulate in the interest of the public the use of great wealth." Tucker believed the only response to such a charge was to demonstrate that the legal profession maintained its "high standard which its position of influence in the country demands." But Roosevelt's speech did not dwell on the moral debasement of lawyers (he ended by acknowledging the "great profession of the law, whose members are so potent in shaping the growth of the national soul"). Tucker's proposal was also made in light of the momentum among the state bar associations. If there was to be an ethics parade, the ABA wanted to step in front and lead it. The longer-term concern of elite lawyers was whether any lofty ideals remained.[85]

Conclusion

Tucker knew his audience. ABA members agreed to draft a code of ethics. But as this work began, lawyer Charles F. Chamberlayne published an essay, "The Soul of the Profession," attacking its lack of fundamental ideals. Like many contemporaries, Chamberlayne mourned that "the client's money too largely dominates professional *morale*." More importantly, "system has replaced society." Possibly alluding to the organization of railroad lawyers or the corporation law firm, Chamberlayne noted that many lawyers were simply part of "bureaus and departments" whose heads were good at "hustling" and "getting there." And all the bar associations and grievance committees working to remove "gross offenders" were "as powerless to prevent professional degeneration as our criminal codes prove to be in eradicating crime." More savagely, Chamberlayne excoriated the lawyer possessed of intellectual gifts. Those "smart" lawyers who bet on clients' "loyalty, zeal, sagacity, or the like," in pursuit of the clients' "perverted uses," were not smart enough to understand the instrumental role they played. Once their value was squeezed out of them, smart lawyers who sold their souls would be repaid with "contempt." American lawyers would remain lost until they agreed that the practice of law was "a fundamentally ethical calling."[86]

As a young lawyer, Elihu Root, along with David Dudley Field and a number of others, represented Boss Tweed in his 1873 criminal trials. The jury was deadlocked at the first trial, and a second was scheduled for November 1873. As it began, Field, Root, and six others acting as counsel for Tweed signed a note asking trial judge Noah Davis to recuse himself for reasons of prejudice. Davis was displeased and declined. Afterward, Davis cited most of the signatories for contempt of court (Field was in France and was not cited). Davis imposed no fine on Root and another junior lawyer. Instead, he offered advice: "I ask you, young gentlemen, to remember that good faith to a client never can justify or require bad faith to your own consciences, and that however good a thing it may be, to be known as successful and great lawyers, it is even a better thing to be known as honest men."[87]

Root would become one the most successful American lawyers during his long life. Early evidence of his legal aptitude is found in the preceding story: Root and William Bartlett, the two young lawyers to whom Judge Davis spoke, were responsible for drafting the note and persuading their co-counsel to sign it. Nearly half a century later, progressive journalist Burton J. Hendrick wrote an essay discussing the lawyer's ethical duties. He began by discussing Root's behavior in the Tweed trial and quoted Davis's excoriation. Hendrick concluded that one reason for Root's failure to be selected as the Republican nominee for president in 1916 was the difficulty in explaining Root's behavior to the voting public. Root's answer, made years later, was that, "no matter how vile the criminal," he was entitled to counsel and to the protection of every constitutional right he enjoyed. That, of course, evaded the issue. Davis did not chastise Root for representing Tweed; the reprimand was for the manner in which he did so.[88]

Field too lived a long life. The treasurer of the ABCNY notified its executive committee of Field's death in 1894. Normally, this would have begun the process of writing and printing Field's memorial, but the committee decided not to undertake a memorial of Field nor mention his death "in any way."[89]

In the twenty-first century, a calling can be a vocation, a profession, or a trade. But an earlier definition, taken from its religious roots, focused on one's duty to serve others. A calling required one to aid the community, even if doing so was contrary to self-interest. Chamberlayne's essay makes several references to a decline in religious belief generating professional drift. What he does not refer to explicitly, but what some lawyers reading him may have understood, is the Gospel according to Matthew in the Christian Bible: "For what is a man profited, if he shall gain the whole world, and lose his own soul?" If lawyers were the "cheapest meat in the market," had they already lost their souls?[90]

CHAPTER FOUR

Legal Ethics, Legal Elites, and the Business of Law, 1905–1945

In 1906 lawyer Charles F. Chamberlayne marveled at the increasingly frequent "warnings" by lawyers "that the client's money too largely dominates professional *morale*; that rising tides of commercialism stifle the cry of its outraged conscience." He rattled off a list of eminent and "authoritative" sources endorsing this assertion. Others unnamed by Chamberlayne made the same argument, and more were soon to come.[1]

Henry St. George Tucker was mentioned by Chamberlayne. Speaking at the annual meeting of the American Bar Association (ABA) in 1905, Tucker used this criticism to ask members to consider the current state of lawyer ethics. Like many elite lawyers, Tucker believed the profession's honor was tarnished, and the ABA's adoption of a code of ethics might improve its reputation. A number of states were in the process of writing ethics codes. President Theodore Roosevelt's speech at Harvard provided the national, elitist ABA an opportunity to take the lead in ethics reform.[2]

It adopted a code of ethics in 1908, consisting of an oath and Canons of Professional Ethics. The following year, Chamberlayne assessed what it had wrought. He was underwhelmed. The code was a missed opportunity: "To the fervent cry for the bread of moral life a stone of formalism and negation, admirable in itself, has been given." The "thou-shalt-nots" of the canons failed to express any worthy ideal in the practice of law (and "ideals of some kind, lawyers, like other men, necessarily must have"). Instead, law was "a trade, a business, a money-getting, power-procuring, success-securing occupation." As other lawyers urged throughout American history, Chamberlayne concluded that a better proposition was that "social service, not personal profit, is the aim of your profession."[3]

In spite of this criticism, state and local bar associations quickly adopted

126

the ABA Canons. The ABA's rather disorganized count found that twenty-four state bar associations and several local bars had adopted the canons by 1910. The newly formed ABA Committee on Professional Ethics reported thirty-one state bar associations had done so by 1914. "Almost all" had adopted it by 1924.[4]

The impact was modest. The Texas Bar Association adopted the ABA Canons in 1909. This made so slight an impression that in 1923 association president W. A. Wright had to remind members seeking approval of an ethics code that they had "overlooked" the 1909 resolution. Wright's reminder itself was so unmemorable that the association readopted the ABA Canons in 1926. Texas was not an outlier. The ABA Canons were not law; they constituted statements of professional behavior crafted by an elite, voluntary bar association. Every state bar association was a voluntary organization through 1920; nearly all lacked the authority to enforce any code of ethics. On occasion, courts positively referred to the ABA Canons, but they rarely influenced the erratic and chaotic approach to lawyer discipline.[5]

The 1908 ABA Canons remained the only widespread statement of American lawyer ethics until 1969. On the occasions when the ABA supplemented and amended the canons, it focused narrowly on declaring unethical nearly all types of "client-getting." Lawyers practiced law to earn a living. Constricting the formation of a lawyer-client relationship, particularly for nonelite lawyers, belied a core aspect of practicing law: lawyers needed clients. Supreme Court justice Harlan Fiske Stone spoke in 1934 for many critics: "Our canons of ethics for the most part are generalizations designed for an earlier era." Revisions of the 1908 code in the 1920s and 1930s constituted a long struggle about professional behavior based on past, not present, realities.[6]

From the late nineteenth century until the early 1940s, elite lawyers argued that "overcrowding" of the legal profession ensured a drift from profession to business. Higher standards of admission to the bar was one approach elite lawyers believed would slow this drift. Other options included persuading law schools to offer a course on legal ethics and requiring bar applicants to pass an exam on ethics to gain admission.[7]

Legal elites bemoaned the business of law for two other reasons. First, they asked, had they become mere servants aiding their wealthy and powerful clients? A lawyer working for "important business interests" was "little more than a paid employee, bound hand and foot to the service of his employer," wrote Theron Strong in his 1914 memoir. Second, legal elites regularly condemned the business-getting practices of nonelite lawyers, in part to distract attention from their actions. Some nonelite lawyers obtained clients in an underhanded way. Legal elites worked to ban almost anything that smacked of client-seeking. Otherwise, "the shyster, the barratrously inclined, the ambulance chaser, the member of the Bar with a system of runners, pursue their nefarious methods with no check save the rope of sand of moral suasion." Elite lawyers turned "sharp corners" to assist "the money-getter." But that was a mere sideshow. The main attraction, elite lawyers argued, was the ethically impaired nonelite lawyer.[8]

The foremost effort attacking commercialism in the 1908 ABA Canons was to declare improper any form of "advertising, direct or indirect" (Canon 27). Eventually, this was expanded to include law lists, published lists of commercial lawyers who collected debts. For most lawyers, the ABA's position constricting communications with prospective clients was unrealistic. Those complaints had no impact.

As the Great Depression took hold, the ABA renewed its commitment to preventing commercialization of the legal profession. That meant guarding the boundaries of the practice of law and trying (and failing) to reduce the supply of licensed lawyers. It did not include rethinking the ideals of the legal profession in light of significant changes in the American economy.[9]

Lawyers employed by large law firms did well financially during the Great Depression. They did not do so well in terms of reputation. Critics attacked "law factories" for disregarding the ethical standards they imposed on their struggling fellow lawyers.[10]

The 1908 Canons of Ethics

The ABA approved the Tucker Committee's 1906 proposal to begin work on a code of ethics. The following year, Thomas Hubbard reported on its progress. He quoted a letter from Supreme Court justice David Brewer, who suggested a two-part code. The first should consist of "a body of rules to be given operative and binding force" in the states. A lawyer who "willfully" violated the rules would be disbarred. The second was "a canon of ethics, which shall discuss the duties of lawyers under the various conditions of professional action." The canons were "ethical considerations which should ever control the action of the profession." The committee adopted Brewer's suggestion: it eventually drafted a distinct set of thirty-two canons covering Brewer's "ethical considerations," followed by an oath of admission listing seven "rules." This was similar (though in reverse order) to the division made by Thomas Goode Jones when drafting the 1887 Alabama Code of Ethics (see chapter 3).[11]

In addition to Brewer, the Tucker Committee added Jones and several other members in 1907. The ABA's proposed canons were based on the Alabama code, which in turn used George Sharswood's *Essay on Professional Ethics* as its template (see chapter 2). The committee compiled a list of seventy foundational provisions. Hubbard, who funded a series of lectures on ethics at Albany Law School, paid for the cost of printing and distributing Sharswood's *Essay*, which was sent to every ABA member and to the secretary of every state bar association, along with the ABA's 1907 report. Recipients were asked for comments. Member Lucien Alexander compiled the comments, which were printed in March 1908 as the *Red Book*. The committee met for three days at the end of March to shape the code, and it received more than a thousand comments on its May draft. Based on those comments, the draft was modified and served as the committee's proposal.[12]

Of the thirty-two proposed canons, only Canon 13, on contingent fees, was amended by ABA members (with approximately 115 voting) at the August 1908 annual meeting. That the ABA declared contingent fees ethical was no surprise. Of the eleven states that had followed Alabama's ethics code by 1906, only Maryland disallowed contingent fee contracts. But many commenters disagreed. This was the ABA code's most controversial item, and it was the focus of 20 percent of all comments. The final draft took a halfway position: "Contingent fees may be contracted for, but they lead to many abuses and should be under the supervision of the court." Future Montana senator Thomas Walsh defended the contingent fee in a long written speech read to ABA members. Others looked to amend Canon 13 to acknowledge both the propriety of contingent fees and the danger of harming the poor through their abuse. Cutting through the general confusion, ABA president Jacob Dickinson successfully offered the following: "Contingent fees, where sanctioned by law, should be under the supervision of the court, in order that clients may be protected from unjust charges."[13]

This was a pragmatic solution, premised on existing ethical standards. Elite lawyers who railed against contingent fees were in the minority. Nearly all bar associations and state courts permitted contingent fees, and many ABA members used them. Backing a minority position would have hindered the ABA's goal of drafting an authoritative statement of lawyer ethics.

For some ABA members, this debate was about broadly framing the ABA's interest in stamping out commercialism. Elite lawyers had paired calling and trade, profession and business, and professionalism and commercialism as opposites. The ABA Canons broadened what constituted commercial—that is, unprofessional—behavior by lawyers. But most bar associations would not have adopted a rule banning contingent fee contracts.[14]

The *Red Book* grouped the foundational canons into thirteen categories. Four canons were categorized as "Solicitation and Advertising, Direct and Indirect." Stirring up litigation was condemned in a canon significantly longer than its Alabama code counterpart. This was due to a perception that "agents or runners" generated personal injury litigation, which the Alabama code did not address. Canon 28 linked those agents to "what are called, for convenience, 'shysters,' 'calaboose lawyers' and 'ambulance chasers.'"[15]

Canon 27 also aimed to stamp out commercialism by banning advertising. A lawyer could circulate an "ordinary" business card, for doing so was not "*per se* improper." Everything else was. "Solicitation" included advertisements, circulars, personal communications, and interviews. All were considered "unprofessional," as were "indirect" advertisements through "touters of any kind." Comparable Alabama Rule 16 was more modest: "Newspaper advertisements, circulars and business cards, tendering professional services to the general public, are proper." What "ought to be avoided" was personally soliciting possible clients and "self-laudation"; the latter was limited to "indirect advertisement for business" through news publications. ABA Canon 27 included this provision because self-praise lowered "the tone of our high calling."

Unlike the contingent fee standard, the ABA intended Canon 27 to alter lawyer behavior. All the states with pre-ABA ethics codes, with the exception of Kentucky, adopted Alabama's view that newspaper advertisements and circulars were proper. Even Kentucky did not ban such activity; it simply stated that such advertisements "while not improper are to be dealt in sparingly." In spring 1908 Nebraska Law School dean George Costigan wrote, "on this question of advertising there is growing dissent." The dissenters favored more advertising, a result of a "growing feeling at the bar in America that a legitimate solicitation of business may be made by self-respecting and high-minded lawyers." Costigan believed this view was dangerous, apparently because it altered the bar from "a noble and inspiring calling" to "a money-getting trade." Even the conservative Boston Bar Association opposed a ban on advertisements, finding them "matters of personal taste" that "do not involve any question of professional ethics." What was unprofessional was lawyers engaging in the personal solicitation of strangers. The ABA disagreed.[16]

The ABA Canons largely ignored the issue of adversarial zeal. In 1906 ABA members heard a speech from Roscoe Pound on the failings of the administration of civil justice. It was so well received that many members demanded (but failed to convince) a recalcitrant ABA leadership to reprint it. Pound attributed the public's dissatisfaction with the civil justice system to its embrace of the "sporting theory of justice." Opposing counsel tended to "forget that they are officers of the court." Instead, they sought only to win or, failing that, to "get error into the record" so the appellate court would grant their client a new trial. Pound was right, but he was ignored.[17]

Others remarked on the adversary system's encouragement of lawyerly zeal long after Pound spoke. In a 1932 book detailing the reasons for wrongful convictions in sixty-five cases, Professor Edwin Borchard categorized thirteen cases, or 20 percent, as resulting from overzealousness by the prosecution: "It is common knowledge that the prosecuting technique in the United States is to regard a conviction as a personal victory calculated to enhance the prestige of the prosecutor." Former New York City assistant district attorney Francis L. Wellman, in a 1931 book written for the general public, agreed: "A lawyer always strives to win his cases. He in that way obtains his professional advancement and reputation. His one wish is to smash the other fellow, and he often does not care what means he uses." Wellman's fellow New York City prosecutor Arthur Train, later a successful novelist, noted the same in 1912. As one plaintive cry put it, "And in some far off golden age, we may even expect that the unnecessary brow-beating of witnesses, marked discourtesy to opposing counsel and petty and mean tricks of advocacy may take their place among offenses" calling for judicial rebuke.[18]

The word *zeal* is found only once in the ABA Canons. Canon 15, "How Far a Lawyer May Go in Supporting a Client's Cause," rejects Brougham's claim that the lawyer cares for "that client and none other" (see chapter 2). After prohibiting a lawyer from personally vouching for the client's cause, Canon 15 declares the lawyer's duty to exercise "warm zeal" on the client's behalf, quoting Sharswood's 1854 *Compend of Lectures on the Aims and Duties of the Profession of the Law* (see chapter 2). Sharswood, in turn, was quoting the 1840 *Courvoisier* case. Sharswood included a study of *Courvoisier* in his 1860 *Essay*, so ABA members presumably were aware of this distant controversy. Warm zeal included the right of the lawyer possessing knowledge of the defendant's guilt to "assert every such remedy and defense."[19]

Canon 15 and Alabama Rule 10 differed in a few respects. First, Rule 10 romantically declared: "No sacrifice or peril, even to loss of life itself, can absolve from the fearless discharge of this duty." Canon 15 was more prosaic: "No fear of judicial disfavor or public unpopularity should restrain him from the full discharge of his duty." Defending the unpopular client, of course, was considered a grave duty owed to the community. Second, Canon 15 stated explicitly what Rule 10 implied: A lawyer "must obey his own conscience and not that of his client."[20]

Canon 15, joined by Canon 5's demand that counsel for the accused use "all fair and honorable means, to present every defense that the law of the land permits," stated the required duties and formal limits of adversarial zeal in relatively clear fashion, as formulated by Sharswood before the Civil War. The actual work of trial lawyers, particularly criminal trial lawyers, remained a type of entertainment. In practice, it was difficult to discern whether zeal could be excessive. The desire to win, for the client's sake as well as the lawyer's, justified using any means necessary. Clarence Darrow, the most famous lawyer in the United States in the early twentieth century, was a passionate opponent of capital punishment. In late 1911 he was indicted for attempting to bribe two jurors (through an intermediary) in the capital murder trial of the McNamara brothers. California was seeking the death penalty and had the evidence to obtain it. Though Darrow was not fully acquitted of bribery and was likely factually guilty, his friends excused his conduct as justified by the dangers facing the McNamaras.[21]

The structure, organization, and specificity of the 1908 ABA Canons were uninspiring and often unhelpful. As already discussed, a lawyer had to read Canons 5 and 15 to understand the duties of the criminal defense lawyer. Canon 19 couldn't quite decide how to answer the question: may a lawyer testify as a witness for his client? Yes, as to formal matters, "such as the attestation or custody of an instrument and the like." But maybe not because, in other instances, "he should leave the trial of the case to other counsel." And, "except when essential to the ends of justice, a lawyer should avoid testifying." Canon 30 offered five disparate ideas under the heading "Upholding the Honor of the Profession," including exposing corrupt conduct, informing prosecutors of any perjury in a case in which the lawyer was representing a party (a confused concept on several levels), and ensuring that applicants to the bar possessed the correct "moral character or education."

The most trenchant criticism of the ABA Canons came from New York City lawyer Charles A. Boston, who objected to their failure to reference the proper principles of lawyer ethics. Boston was one of the most prolific correspondents to the committee drafting the canons. The *Red Book* noted comments from him on all seventy proposed canons. Few were adopted. In his general comments, Boston concluded the canons were ill framed. He believed "a Code of Ethics should be a statement of principles rather than specific illustrations of the application of those principles." Boston doubled down in a May 1908 essay. He proposed a set of ethical statements, nine of which were applicable to lawyers, one to judges, and one that created reciprocal duties between lawyer and judge. These broad statements suggested a lawyer should act honorably and with integrity, avoid "sharp" practices, and, following Sharswood, accept that acting with "high moral principle is essential to the practitioner of the law." A lawyer should never "mislead judge or jury . . . by artifices or false statement of the law or facts" (Item 3). A lawyer should maintain only "legal and just actions," except when defending a person accused of a crime (Item 8). Boston proposed a creed, rather than a code or a catalog. Neither his general *Red Book* comments nor his proposed code went anywhere.[22]

Boston's second important suggestion was also ignored. An ethics code meant nothing to the scofflaw; it was only as good as the disciplinary system that enforced its provisions. In light of New York's unusual disciplinary system, Boston suggested creating a panel to hear and decide such cases. By 1908, the Association of the Bar of the City of New York (ABCNY) had successfully claimed authority to present and prosecute grievances against lawyers. Given its elite membership, this was a significant claim of authority, and it applied to ABCNY members and nonmembers alike. The ABA Canons assumed the usual disciplinary system, which was not a system at all. In 1909 one critic noted, "in most, if not all, of the jurisdictions the [disciplinary] machinery is too cumbersome and too difficult to set in motion to accomplish adequately the purposes for which it is designed."[23]

Although most bar associations adopted the ABA Canons, the San Francisco Bar Association did not. It adopted a set of principles starkly different. Connecticut borrowed some of the code, but its structure and approach differed significantly. Some wondered whether a code of ethics was worth the trouble. One Illinois lawyer concluded, "Those canons of ethics recently adopted by the American Bar Association are merely platitudes, and no lawyer under them could be deprived of his professional emoluments." This was fine by lawyers, for "I fear, [they] do not pine for too strict codes of ethics."[24]

The New York County Lawyers' Association, Charles A. Boston, and Julius Henry Cohen

The New York County Lawyers' Association (NYCLA), formed in late 1907, took its time adopting an ethics code, despite a supreme effort by Charles A. Boston. Though he failed here, Boston was one of the most influential lawyers on the topic of American lawyer ethics until his death in 1935.

In 1908 Boston and the NYCLA's Committee on Professional Ethics began drafting a code of ethics. Late that year he published an annotated proposed ethics code and reiterated the greatest failings of the ABA Canons: neither the canons nor the oath was "a comprehensive statement of the whole duty of a lawyer, nor of the principles which he should apply." Boston's proposed code of ethical principles was concise, and he claimed it better separated enforceable duties from aspirational ideals.[25]

Boston's proposed code consisted of four statements of a lawyer's legal (and thus enforceable) duty, which included representing a client using all means "consistent with truth," keeping inviolate the client's confidences and secrets, and "observ[ing] the strictest integrity" in practicing law. A list of five professional ideals followed. This proposal included suggestions from another committee member, Henry W. Jessup, who prepared ten "Professional Ideals of the Lawyer." Boston's proposed code clarified which duties a lawyer was bound to obey and which sought to inculcate virtuous behavior. The committee did not act.[26]

Undaunted, Boston soldiered on. By the end of 1909, the committee agreed to a drafted code of ethics. It was sent to the board of directors for consideration in mid-1910 but delayed until October. The 1910 version consisted of nineteen propositions, including the duties and ideals from the 1908 NYCLA draft code, most of Jessup's professional ideals, and three provisions from Boston's initial 1908 proposal. It encouraged lawyers to act with "moral principle" and to uphold the "dignity, honor and integrity of the profession." Compared with earlier versions, it paid greater attention to the lawyer's duty to serve clients faithfully and loyally. What it did not do was clearly distinguish between enforceable duties and professional ideals.[27]

Boston's published address also included proposed legislation creating a board of lawyer discipline, as well as a preliminary statement explaining his rejection of the ABA Canons. After hearing Boston, the board again postponed discussion.

Canons 10 and 12 were the two controversial propositions Boston defended from criticism within the NYCLA. Canon 10 declared it was ethically permissible to represent at trial a person the lawyer believed to be guilty of the crime charged. Canon 12 declared a lawyer "should not make a practice of soliciting." Both caused a significant division among committee members. Canon 10 was not new and was consonant with Sharswood's antebellum view. The 1887 Alabama Code and, arguably, the ABA Canons agreed. Canon 10's detractors argued that it paid too little attention to the defects of the sporting theory of justice. This was true but unenlightening.

In addition to the caution regarding soliciting, Canon 12 barred any division of fees other than between lawyers. Boston's address noted three interpretive limits: the practice of soliciting did not mean every act of solicitation, advertising was outside the practice of soliciting, and a commercial debt lawyer could share commissions with nonlawyers. The first two interpretive limits were contrary to ABA Canon 27. The third would become the subject of repeated ABA attention in the 1930s.[28]

Boston interpreted the board's October 1910 delay as a minor impediment and again urged the adoption of an ethics code. The NYCLA board agreed in principle but rejected Boston's proposal. He regularly raised the issue, and the board regularly avoided considering it. He then stopped bringing it up, and the NYCLA stopped considering it. As Boston mused in a 1912 speech, "the proposed [NYCLA] code now sleeps in a state of innocuous desuetude." Boston was successful in enlarging the jurisdiction of the professional ethics committee to answer "questions of proper professional conduct," and it started to offer ethics opinions in January 1912. In an era of nicknames, the committee became known as the Legal Ethics Clinic. It was so successful that West Publishing, Martindale's *Legal Directory*, and scattered law journals reprinted the committee's questions and answers. Similar committees were later created by other bar associations, eventually including the ABA.[29]

The Legal Ethics Clinic's first opinion was about advertising. Was it unethical for a lawyer to insert in a trade journal a business card with the lawyer's name, profession, address, and telephone number? The committee's brief answer was that this was not "unprofessional," as this concerned the lawyer's sense of propriety, but it did not approve of the practice. By the end of 1919, the committee had answered 179 questions, 33 of which concerned advertising or soliciting business. Even so, Boston wrote, "In respect to advertising, [the committee] has announced no general policy." Boston served as chairman of the committee until 1932, and although he was a thoughtful and articulate expert, the committee did not simply apply Boston's proposals when answering questions. Many of its early advertising opinions applied a standard closer to the more stringent Canon 27 than Boston's looser proposed Canon 12.[30]

The committee's most important opinion may have been Opinion 47 (1914), which answered a series of questions from other NYCLA committees looking to raise "the professional standards of practice of commercial law." The committee was "guided by its view that the practice of law is a profession and not a trade or a business." Thus, lawyers existed "for the public good, and not primarily for private advantage." It condemned direct or indirect solicitation of claims; advertisements or cards "in publications" must be confined to the requirements of Canon 27. (Both Boston and fellow member Julius Henry Cohen had published articles in *American Legal News* in 1912 and 1913, a journal for commercial lawyers that was festooned with advertisements.) Overall, the answers in Opinion 47 distinguished personal or indirect solicitation of business (impermissible) from truthful advertising (permissible).[31]

After ending his quixotic quest for an ethics code, Boston suggested the NYCLA board authorize the committee to investigate the practice of law by nonlawyers, including notaries public, collection agencies, and corporations. Julius Henry Cohen, a member of the ethics committee, presented a resolution to create a special committee dedicated to that subject. The NYCLA board agreed. During the last half of 1913, the board was urged to make the committee permanent and to hire a lawyer to prosecute cases of unlawful practice, and it amended its bylaws to do so. The lawyer the NYCLA employed handled both discipline and unlawful practice cases, and Cohen was named chairman of the unauthorized practice committee. At the July 1913 meeting of the Commercial Law League of America, Boston spoke about lawyer ethics and the NYCLA's recent efforts to discipline lawyers. Cohen, using Boston's speech as momentum, argued "that the unprofessional conduct of the bar on the part of our weaker brethren, can be attributed in my personal judgment more to the temptations occasioned by the competition with the unlawful practice of law by laymen than to any other cause." The next day the Commercial Law League voted unanimously to create a committee to help prosecute unlawful practice of law. Cohen was named its chairman.[32]

Cohen's *The Law—Business or Profession?* was published in 1916. He divided his study into three "books": "Business," "Profession," and "Which?" In "Business" Cohen offered disciplinary information, discussed the lawyer's role as an "officer of the court" throughout the world, and summarized American lawyers in history. It concluded with the rise of codes of ethics for lawyers. Cohen explained Dr. Felix Adler's idea of service in life and its use by a group of lawyers (including him) to apply principles of ethics to actual problems in the practice of law. "Profession" considered the business aspects of the practice of law, such as advertising, fees, "business enterprise" (e.g., stirring up litigation, collection matters), the rise in commercialism, and the unauthorized practice of law. All these things tended to "kill its professional ideal at birth, to destroy its sense of fealty to court, to client and to community," to place "*profits first.*" The section titled "Which?" examined the choice lawyers faced. Cohen believed "the quality of trustworthiness is as important as the quality of celerity, and that loyalty to the ideals of the profession is quite as much a requisite as business acumen." Cohen hoped businesses would seek lawyers of skill and integrity.[33]

Cohen acknowledged the influence of Charles Boston and Felix Adler on his thinking. Adler, whom Cohen later credited with improving lawyer ethics, founded the Society for Ethical Culture in 1876. Adler encouraged lawyers to "solve their own ethical problems out of their own experiences." In December 1908 Cohen invited a number of lawyers to join a group seeking practical solutions to practical ethics problems. Among the two dozen or so who joined were Boston and Henry Jessup. Also joining the group was Everett Abbot, one of Cohen's mentors, a writer on legal ethics, and a correspondent who rivaled Boston in commenting on the proposed ABA Canons in 1908. They met monthly to discuss the "conscientious expression of their own views," subject to "unlimited criticism from each of the others." Like Cohen, Boston acknowledged and channeled the group's approach. He noted that members commonly disagreed on "the proper application of recognized principles." The key to overcoming this difficulty was for lawyers to begin with ethical principles, not illustrations.[34]

The ABA Committee on Professional Ethics
and Grievances, 1913–1920

Boston's ethics work made him a sought-after speaker. At the ABA's 1912 meeting he renewed his pleas that it draft a set of "principles of conduct for the judiciary" and create a committee on professional ethics with the same authority to issue opinions as the NYCLA's. It took more than a decade and a judicial scandal for the ABA to adopt Boston's first suggestion; it took just a year for the ABA to create an ethics committee but a decade for it to give the committee any work. Boston and Cohen served as members of the ethics committee for the first three years. After those two left the committee in 1916, Jessup served until 1920.[35]

The committee's jurisdiction was initially limited to collecting information on bar association activity related "to the ethics of the legal profession" and to "make recommendations on the subject." Despite these constraints, its first report, heavily influenced by Boston and Cohen, performed several useful services. First, it tallied the number of state bar associations that had adopted the ABA Canons. Only two jurisdictions, California (using the Field Code oath) and Connecticut, had chosen different codes. Second, it found that, with the exception of the ABCNY, the NYCLA, and the Boston Bar Association, bars did not discipline lawyers. Third, it discussed the unauthorized practice of law and referenced the creation of committees by the NYCLA and the Commercial Law League of America to suppress it. Fourth, it noted the value of the NYCLA's Legal Ethics Clinic.[36]

In November 1915 the executive secretary of the National Association of Credit Men (NACM), J. H. Tregoe, sent a letter to Charles Boston. The NACM membership largely comprised unsecured creditors. The letter complained about bankruptcy lawyers. Tregoe, who was trained in law, charged that much "bad debt waste may be attributed to the advice and guidance of conscienceless Attorneys." The greater the waste, of course, the less debt recovered by unsecured creditors. He concluded by asking, "what is the [ABA] going to do with these units of the profession?" Two months earlier, at its annual meeting, the NACM had issued a two-part resolution: (1) that the ABA and local bar associations should aid the authorities in "prosecuting dishonest attorneys," and (2) that bar associations should help legislatures draft reasonable state laws to disbar lawyers. Tregoe sent a second letter in January 1916 and, after again quoting the resolution, wrote, "we have been led after an impartial and unprejudiced observation, to locate a large

proportion of our bad debt waste to unfairness and fraud, originated or encouraged by commercial lawyers." The ABA committee's (i.e., Boston's) 1916
report shrugged. It opined that bar associations should "promote the proper
performance of professional duty" but did not specifically respond to the
NACM resolution. Its limited authority made anything else impossible.[37]

The NACM vastly overestimated the ABA's power. It could draft an ethics code and educate some lawyers about it, but it lacked any enforcement
power and possessed little persuasive authority in the legal profession.

Cohen and Boston left the ABA ethics committee to serve as chairman
and member, respectively, of the Committee on Co-operation among Bar
Associations. That committee had been created to find ways to enforce the
ABA's code of ethics. Jessup replaced Boston as chairman of the ethics committee, and in its 1917 report he wrote, "The Canon against advertising and
soliciting seems still to be the chief stumbling block in the matter of general
acceptance of the standards." The report also included a significant discussion of *In re Schwarz*. The NYCLA had charged Adolph Schwarz, a commercial lawyer, with three instances of malpractice and unprofessional conduct:
for soliciting creditors in a pending bankruptcy proceeding to hire him on
a 10 percent contingent fee ("No collection, no charge"); for sending letters
to individuals "inciting and urging" them to hire him "for the purpose of
collection by suit or other professional service"; and for "widely circulating,
in circulars and public prints, advertisements of himself and his methods,
. . . with the purpose and intent of procuring parties unknown to him to
employ him as attorney at law." The court held that Schwarz had violated
ABA Canon 27, which barred advertising and the soliciting of clients, as adopted by the voluntary New York State Bar Association. Schwarz's defense
was twofold: the advertisements did not "lower the tone of the legal profession," and his debt collection work was more a business than a professional
endeavor. In his counsel's words, Schwarz's "activities are more along business than along professional lines. His work is the collection of commercial
claims, without any legal proceedings, if that be possible. He resorts to legal
proceedings only when other means of obtaining payment have been ex-
hausted without success, and only when specifically directed to do so." The
court rejected both arguments. Advertising by its very nature lowered the
honor of the profession. The court analogized one of Schwarz's advertisements to "the advance bills of the late P. T. Barnum in heralding the approach of the Greatest Show on Earth." After determining that Schwarz was
advertising his legal acumen, the court relied on a 1915 case, *In re Neuman*.

Neuman had been suspended from the practice of law for violating ABA Canon 27. The New York Appellate Division censured rather than disbarred Schwarz because it believed his assertion that he had no intent to violate either the letter or the spirit of Canon 27 and because he promised to stop his activities if so ordered by the court.[38]

Schwarz did not stop, at least not entirely. He "continued to solicit business by means of circular letters sent out in large quantities" to former clients. Schwarz stopped using "extravagant, crude, and flashy advertising addressed to the public at large." In 1921 the Appellate Division disbarred Schwarz on the grounds that his circulars were misleading, but more so because he had broken his promise. The judgment was affirmed by a bare majority (four to three) of the New York Court of Appeals. The dissent found "no precedent for disbarment for conduct that does not indicate some lack of respect for truth and honor or some interference with or contempt for the administration of justice or some violation of law on the part of the attorney." The circulars distributed by Schwarz, the dissenters concluded, were not grounds for disbarment, "even to the extent of disregard of the order of the court on the former proceeding."[39]

The Appellate Division's decisions in *Neuman* and *Schwarz*, and Schwarz's eventual disbarment, did not lead to a flood of disciplinary hearings for violating Canon 27. This was in part a result of the profession's resistance to the demands of Canon 27, as noted by Jessup, and in part a result of the United States entering World War I in the spring of 1917. The most significant reason, however, was disclosed in the committee's 1920 report to the ABA: "Judges in many localities are ignorant of the fact that canons have been adopted in their states," and grievance committees are generally "very inactive." Few associations possessed the financial resources to initiate disbarment proceedings, and no public outcry spurred judges and grievance committees to become informed and take action.[40]

In 1919 the ABA's energetic but constrained Committee on Professional Ethics and its somnolent Committee on Grievances merged. Three years later, committee chairman Thomas Francis Howe proposed that the ABA amend its bylaws to permit the committee to issue ethics opinions. Howe justified his proposal by stating, "The ever increasing complexities of modern business, the rapid changes in its methods, and the relations of lawyers thereto, are constantly raising questions concerning proper professional conduct that were not contemplated—or even dreamed of—when the canons were prepared." Additionally, because most bar associations had adopted the ABA Canons, the committee would provide uniformity in interpretation. ABA members agreed.[41]

The Canons of Judicial Ethics

In 1913 the ABA created a Judicial Section to make policy recommendations. Each section elected its own officers, voted on its own bylaws, and ran its own program schedule. Any judge who was an ABA member was eligible to join. The Judicial Section did little, and it ignored a suggestion by the Committee on Professional Ethics to consider a code of ethics for judges. Then the Black Sox scandal erupted.[42]

The American League champion Chicago White Sox were heavily favored to win the 1919 World Series, played against the National League champion Cincinnati Reds. When the White Sox lost, rumors swirled that some of the team's best players had taken bribes to throw the series. A year later, a grand jury investigating the bribery scandal heard several White Sox players confess their involvement.[43]

The two leagues were as much rivals as oligopolists. In the scandal's aftermath, how would the owners proceed? They eventually offered Kenesaw Mountain Landis, a Chicago-based federal district court judge, the job of commissioner of baseball. Landis accepted, provided he could remain a judge. They agreed. This double-dipping annoyed ABA members as well as some congressmen. A desultory effort was made to impeach Landis in early 1921. It failed, as did an effort to pass legislation banning federal judges from receiving outside salaries.[44]

The ABA executive committee trained its sights on Landis. His $42,500 salary (and $7,500 expense account) from major league baseball was widely reported and apparently offended the ABA leadership. It proposed that Landis be condemned, and a resolution doing so was adopted. Landis was the only person condemned by the ABA in its first half century. The only effect of this condemnation was to reinvigorate the effort to craft canons of judicial ethics.[45]

A month later, Charles Boston wrote to the executive committee, reminding it that the ABA leadership had delayed writing a code of judicial ethics to blunt the "agitation for a recall of the judiciary and the recall of judicial decisions." That cause had now dissipated. "The time is now ripe" for a judicial ethics code, he wrote. The executive committee, using a 1909 resolution, appointed recently confirmed chief justice William Howard Taft as chairman of the judicial ethics committee and Boston as secretary. Boston was the code's principal draftsman. As two of the other three judges on the committee agreed, "You and I will have to put the work on to Boston." A draft code was printed in the February 1923 *ABA Journal*. These canons were based on Boston's philosophy and set out "those principles which should govern the personal practice of members of the judiciary in the administration of their office."[46]

The committee received "a host of suggestions." Most were rejected. The final report and revised draft were published in the July 1923 *ABA Journal*. Taft's introductory letter, which mimicked Boston, stated the committee's position: the ABA "should supplement the canons of ethics adopted in 1908, . . . and, to do this completely, it is necessary to state many universally recognized principles."[47]

The proposal was delayed for a year to give the Judicial Section an opportunity to voice its opinions.[48] It made only one recommendation: amend Canon 13. Canon 13 declared in part, "if such a course can reasonably be avoided, [the judge] should not sit in litigation where a near relative appears before him as counsel." Taft received pushback from a Massachusetts Supreme Judicial Court justice, who noted that Canon 13 would affect five justices on that court. As far as that court's members recalled, no justice had ever recused himself when a near relative was counsel for one of the parties. Taft wrote to Boston and concluded that Canon 13 was unnecessary because it focused on only "a few abuses." Boston disagreed. Just before making its presentation at the 1924 ABA meeting, a committee of the Judicial Section met in Boston's room with the Taft Committee, absent Taft. As Taft Committee member and Pennsylvania Supreme Court justice Robert von Moschzisker wrote, "Our friend Boston died a little hard, but die he did, and we have eliminated the part that should go out." Boston, despite his reticence, spoke for the committee in Taft's absence and argued that the ABA should acquiescence and amend Canon 13.[49]

Boston worked hard to present amended Canon 13 as ethically permissible, but he also told members it denounced the practice without using "the particular words." As amended, it stated that the judge "should not suffer his conduct to justify the impression that any person can improperly influence him or unduly enjoy his favor, or that he is affected by the kinship, rank, position or influence of any party or other person." Upon a close reading of this provision, "other person" included counsel as well as witnesses and jury members. As amended, the ABA adopted the Canons of Judicial Ethics.[50]

Taft's introductory letter to the 1923 proposal provided clear insight into the committee's goals. They were educative, not disciplinary. Although some critics argued that the canons would be "inefficacious without a sanction," the committee concluded that the code was "not intended to have the force of law." Boston agreed. The foremost role of any ethics code was educative. Boston encouraged judges to not only avoid improper behavior but also avoid even the "appearance of impropriety."[51]

The judicial canons had little immediate impact. By 1945, just eleven states or state bar associations had adopted the 1924 canons. As Taft and Boston urged, they were viewed as hortatory. The canons remained the ABA's official statement of judicial ethics until another judicial scandal led it to draft a Code of Judicial Conduct (see chapter 6).[52]

Boston was immediately appointed chairman of the ABA Special Committee on Supplements to Canons of Professional Ethics.[53]

Supplementing the 1908 Code, 1924–1928

In 1919 Henry Jessup received permission from the ABA to send a questionnaire to judges to determine "their views of abuses and violations of the canons of professional ethics." He sent out more than thirty-five hundred questionnaires and received enough helpful responses to state that knowledge of the canons and enforcement of discipline for misconduct were spotty at best and often nonexistent. In 1922 the ABA expanded the ethics committee's jurisdiction, justified in part by the "rapid change" in the legal profession. Its chairman, Thomas Howe, quoted Boston: "I think that comparatively few of the questions submitted to our [NYCLA ethics] committee could be answered by any provision of the canons." Howe implicitly suggested the need for a revision of the 1908 ABA Canons. The 1923 ABA meeting indirectly led to approval of that implicit request.[54]

Nothing had happened when the NACM's J. H. Tregoe complained to the ABA about bankruptcy lawyers in November 1915. In 1922 Tregoe revisited the problem. He wrote an essay listing twelve canons of commercial ethics the NACM had adopted. The first two implicated lawyers. Canon 1 declared "improper" any act of a lawyer and a businessman if that act would be unethical for a lawyer alone to do. Canon 2 stated, "It undermines the integrity of business for business men to support lawyers who indulge in unprofessional practices. The lawyer who will do wrong things for ONE business man injures ALL business men."[55]

A few months later, Tregoe distributed a circular letter to NACM members and to the press titled "The Profession of Law Needs a Good Housecleaning." He pointedly ignored the ABA, which ensured its attention. The *New York Times* printed an article on September 1, 1922, extensively quoting Tregoe's circular. It claimed "a large proportion of indecent bankruptcies . . . are urged by members of the bar." Further, a "small company of legal representatives" worked with debtors to file defective petitions "so that the debtors may get away with a large part of the assets." Though Tregoe was addressing NACM members, few of whom were lawyers, he appealed to the ethics of the legal profession: "The credit waste of the nation, resulting from bad debts, would be in large measure reduced if all legal practitioners were faithful to their trust and held constantly in mind the fact that they are officers of the State, sworn to defend the law and maintain good order." Tregoe then wrote, "We appeal strongly to the leaders of the bar to clean house." Tregoe kept the claim of "bankruptcy rings" alive through the end of the year. News regarding the "dishonest merchant and unscrupulous lawyer" was catnip to the public.[56]

Bankruptcy lawyers and creditors had long known the former could take advantage of bankruptcy law for their personal benefit. In a 1902 article Everett V. Abbot (who later discussed legal ethics with Cohen, Boston, and Jessup at the Society for Ethical Culture) examined several practical ethical problems, one of which concerned bankruptcy. When a lawyer is appointed trustee of a bankrupt's estate, the lawyer often (and properly so) hires "counsel to advise" the lawyer-trustee. The lawyer-trustee's choice of counsel is subject to abuse. How counsel advises the lawyer-trustee and what he charges for that advice are also subject to abuse. The lawyer-trustee and counsel for the trustee may abuse their fiduciary duties by making decisions contrary to the best interests of the creditors or in favor of some creditors to the detriment of others. A specific practical problem Abbot envisioned was how to divide the counsel's fees when counsel and lawyer-trustee were law partners. Abbot found no easy answers. In 1912 a committee of the Commercial Law League issued a report recognizing abuses in the practice of bankruptcy law and sought ways to limit or eliminate them. Its chairman was Julius Henry Cohen.[57]

By the time the ABA met in late August 1923, its ethics committee was already working with NACM members on bankruptcy abuse by lawyers. In offering the ethics committee's report to the ABA, Howe referred to the wide distribution of Tregoe's circular letter. He attributed Tregoe's claims to a "misunderstanding" of bar associations but admitted that the committee was out of touch regarding bankruptcy practice and noted that its members were "greatly astonished" at lawyer misconduct. The committee recommended appointing a special committee to work with the NACM. Chief Justice Taft successfully moved to join this special committee with an existing committee on bankruptcy of the Federal Judicial Council.[58]

Boston immediately moved that the ethics committee decide whether to recommend an additional canon on a particular conflict of interest and "whether any further amendment or supplement to said canons is desirable, and if so, to make its recommendations in respect thereto."[59] Boston's motion was referred to the committee, which reached eight conclusions. The second conclusion considered desirable but not feasible the idea that "the Canons consist of a statement of fundamental principles that should govern a lawyer's conduct rather than of definite rules applied to specific items of conduct." This placed out of bounds Boston's favored approach to lawyer ethics. The last conclusion was that a special committee should be created to supplement the canons; this committee's jurisdiction was explicitly limited to recommending the adoption of "such supplements to the present Canons of Ethics as they [sic] may determine to be desirable." The ABA agreed. Thus, the special committee would decide only whether to recommend additional canons. No one mentioned supplementing the oath.

All five members of the ethics committee were named ex officio members of the special committee, joined by ten others. Boston was named chairman of the Special Committee on Supplements to Canons of Professional Ethics (the Boston Committee). Between 1924 and 1926, this unwieldy committee consisted of twenty-four persons, making the chairman's influence both great and small. A committee that large needed a leader to take on most of the work, which suited Boston, but it also meant a small number of dissidents or resisters (those who would "prefer not to") could wreak havoc.[60]

The original committee included Henry Jessup and another New Yorker, Walter Taylor (a dissenter). According to its 1925 report, one issue was whether to draft a canon that stated "in generic terms the essential elements of adequate Canons." That task would be assigned to a subcommittee including Jessup and Taylor.[61]

The report also mentioned that a special committee of the Commercial

Law League was interested in learning the Boston Committee's views on lawyer ethics as they applied to commercial lawyers. The rise of the NACM (1896) and the Commercial Law League (1895), along with estimates that up to 20 percent of all lawyers were engaged in debt collection work, suggested its importance in the economy and in the legal profession. One specific issue was whether a lawyer who collected a debt absent litigation was engaged in the practice of law. A related problem was whether it was ethically proper for a lawyer to give part of the collected proceeds to the collection agency that had forwarded the matter to the lawyer. The Commercial Law League's position was that collecting a debt without going to court was a "business matter," so lawyer ethics were inapplicable. On the second issue, the league's nuanced position was that the collection agency that forwarded the matter to the lawyer, not the creditor, was the "principal client." Thus, a lawyer was not sharing fees with a nonlawyer—the lawyer was instead returning part of the debt to the principal client. The Commercial Law League offered to share its views with the Boston Committee on any proposed canons involving these and related issues, including advertising and solicitation. Boston created a subcommittee to meet with league representatives.[62]

The Committee on Professional Ethics and Grievances did not officially take a stand on the Commercial Law League's propositions, although it called the league's claims "extreme" and noted with satisfaction that it had "appeared to recede" from them. In the revolving door of Boston Committee membership, the 1925–1926 ABA president, a member of the Commercial Law League, added two league members to the Boston Committee.[63]

League representatives on ethics issues then "await[ed] developments." They were invited to the Boston Committee's April 1926 meeting. Boston had proposed twenty-nine additional canons, and Jessup had suggested a thirtieth on the "essential elements" of a code of ethics. The foundation for these supplements was Boston's compilation of annotated canons, a copy of which was given to each committee member. Walter Taylor wrote a critical, detailed response to the proposed additional canons that was "fully discussed."[64]

The committee also discussed the Commercial Law League's concerns. Five topics of interest to the league were on the committee's agenda, but the three most important were a ban on bonding (insuring) the integrity of lawyers, the division of collected funds with nonlawyers, and the use of lay intermediaries between lawyer and client. A league representative at this meeting reported his optimism, citing the addition of two league members to the Boston Committee and his belief that the committee had listened to the league. The Commercial Law League argued that its lawyer-members sought to act professionally in collecting debts, even though the business had changed markedly over time. The prediction was that additional canons would be shaped by "practical men animated by a high regard for professional ideals," and "neither the view of the doctrinaire nor the go-getter will prevail." A "just right" solution awaited.[65]

In January 1927 the Boston Committee met for the last time. It again invited the Commercial Law League, and Boston sent it a copy of the committee's tentative conclusions. The committee and the league were deadlocked on several issues. First, what were the rules regarding the relationship between a lawyer and a lay intermediary? The tentative conclusion was that a lawyer's professional services should not be controlled or exploited by a lay intermediary, such as a collection agency. Second, why was the issuing of a bond to insure good performance by a lawyer against the public interest? The proposed canon declared that lawyers "should not" give or secure a "bond to insure the faithful performance of their professional obligations." The league, noting human frailty, believed a bond made sound business sense and was not contrary to public policy. The league's third concern, a proposed canon on the division of fees, inclined toward its 1925 position. In part it declared, "But the custom of the usual sharing of commissions upon collection of commercial claims between forwarder and receiver, though one be a lawyer and the other not, is not condemned thereby." That was similar to Boston's interpretation of proposed NYCLA Canon 12 in 1910. Last, a modest part of Jessup's summary canon urged lawyers not to solicit professional employment, divide fees with nonlawyers, or self-advertise, as it was "commercial in spirit and tends to lower the sense of professional dignity." As these statements affected the league's three substantive concerns, it urged that the summary be amended. It did not object in principle to Jessup's summary.[66]

League representative J. Purdon Wright was permitted to speak first at that final meeting, as he had a train to catch. The Commercial Law League supported the language of the canon on the division of fees. Wright knew that Thomas Howe, an ABA member working with the league, was going to propose deleting part of that canon, but he had to leave before any decision was made on Howe's motion. The league remained in the dark until the Boston Committee's fifteen proposed supplemental canons were published in the May 1927 issue of the *ABA Journal*.[67]

The Boston Committee did not listen to Wright and thus actively harmed the interests of commercial lawyers. It adopted Howe's motion and eliminated the exception allowing lawyers and nonlawyers to share commissions for collecting commercial debts. It also left untouched the bonding and lay intermediary canons. As written, both were contrary to the interests of league members because they lessened lawyers' value to businesses forwarding collection matters. What rankled the league was that these proposed supplements did not make commercial lawyers better professionals; they seemed designed to attack the business model long in place among commercial lawyers.

Maurice Davidson, Commercial Law League president, roused members to object. The league's annual meeting began August 22, 1927, in Atlantic City. The ABA's meeting began August 31 in Buffalo. Wright wrote a supplemental report on August 10 explaining the league's opposition to the proposed canons on the division of fees, lay intermediaries, and bonding of lawyers. Each was closely tied to the work of lawyers who collected debts locally and nationally. Of these, the Howe amendment to the canon on the division of fees was most critical. A canon condemning the sharing of commissions between lawyers and nonlawyers who forwarded the debt claim posed an existential threat to the league's lawyer-members. If the supplemental canons barred the regular practices of commercial lawyers, the league was in the unenviable position of either rejecting the ABA's approach to preserve the work of many of its members or adopting it and calling those who acted contrary to the canon outlaws. Neither made sense. League leaders believed they needed to avoid both horns of this dilemma.[68]

The league agreed on August 23 to Wright's resolution that it voice its opposition to the ABA. Shortly before approval and immediately after Wright's peroration, Charles Boston was given the privilege (and burden) of speaking in defense of the controversial proposed canons. A league memorial in opposition to the supplemental canons was approved the following day and delivered to the ABA.[69] Boston met with Davidson and Wright and proposed a delay to consider suggestions from the league and others. Davidson and Wright agreed, and so did the ABA.[70]

In addition to the concerns from the eight thousand or so members of the Commercial Law League, Boston faced internal dissent. Committee member Frank W. Grinnell dissented in part from the 1927 proposal. He disagreed with the partnerships canon and considered it wrong to condemn a lawyer for representing both a trade association and its members in their "individual affairs." But mostly he fulminated about the final canon, Jessup's summary of professional ideals.[71]

Jessup had pursued a decalogue of ideals for two decades. He was now in a position to make those ideals part of the ABA's code of ethics.[72] When the Boston Committee first met, Jessup, Grinnell, and Taylor were the subcommittee members charged with drafting a summary of essential principles of lawyer ethics. Jessup offered his professional ideals, slightly revised from his 1925 book. Grinnell disagreed, and Taylor died (although Grinnell notes Taylor's published criticisms of the summary). The Boston Committee sided with Jessup. His summary consisted of general statements about lawyers' behavior in relation to the Constitution, courts, clients, the public, other lawyers, and the community; in public office; and as a judge. He also offered some illustrations. For example, Jessup's third ideal concerned the lawyer's "relation to clients." A lawyer's duty of loyalty to clients included the duty to decline a matter if accepting it would betray the confidences of a former client.[73]

Grinnell first praised Jessup then attacked the summary. Jessup's expertise in legal ethics was second only to Boston's, and his crafting of the summary showed thoughtfulness and dedication. But Grinnell was "skeptical . . . as to the advisability of various canons of a dogmatic character containing sweeping prohibitions." Instead, he favored "explanatory canons setting forth or reflecting the better standards of practice." This, of course, was how the 1908 ABA Canons were framed, through illustrations rather than principles.

The distinction between Grinnell and Jessup may have been less than meets the eye. Both accepted the view that the canons were educative, and both agreed that ideals and practical considerations often diverged. The issue was whether Jessup's summary was practically helpful. A lawyer looking for general guidance could turn to the summary for an overarching statement about appropriate behavior. But the summary's length and repetitiveness (it mimicked the language of several supplemental canons) might put off those lawyers most in need of its ideals.

The yearlong delay gave the Commercial Law League and Boston an opportunity to reach an agreement. By April 1928, the Boston Committee had agreed to two amendments proposed by the league's ethics committee. First, it agreed to restore the exception to the proposed canon on the division of fees ("But the established custom of sharing the commissions . . . upon collections of commercial claims between forwarder and receiver, though one be a lawyer and the other not . . . is not condemned hereby"). That had been the Boston Committee's tentative view before Howe's motion deleted it. Second, it added league language to the canon on lay intermediaries: "The established custom of receiving and forwarding collections through lay agencies is not condemned hereby." No agreement was reached on the proposed canon banning the bonding of lawyers.[74]

When the revised supplements were published in the May 1928 issue of the *ABA Journal,* Jessup's summary of professional ideals was missing. So were Jessup and Grinnell, neither of whom was reappointed to the Boston Committee. League president J. Purdon Wright was added to the committee, and he alone dissented to the proposed canon on bonding. For tactical reasons, Boston moved that canon to the top of the list. The committee vote was otherwise unanimous.[75]

Wright urged league members to write letters to the ABA executive committee objecting to the bonding canon and, if possible, to do so in person too. The stakes were high. Failure to eliminate the bonding canon would "seriously interfere with and affect the interests of all lawyers engaged in commercial practice, as it will result in the preemption and absorption of practically all the commercial collection business by lay agencies and corporations." League members voted and resolved their disapproval, and a week later, the ABA met.[76]

According to the league historian, "Hundreds of letters protesting against adoption of the proposed canons were sent" to the ABA president and executive committee. Further, "many members . . . came to Seattle to take the floor and voice their opposition." The meeting was so contentious that the executive committee, of which Boston was an incoming member, suggested deferral. Instead, Boston simply excised the bonding canon from the committee's proposal. The other canons, Boston said, had been widely distributed and had resulted in no unfavorable comments or criticisms.

The first interlocutor during the lengthy debate was Julius Henry Cohen. He had written skeptically about the legal ethics of the debt collection business. Specifically, Cohen was concerned with the division of collected funds and with the possibility that collection agencies forwarding debt claims might unlawfully practice law by controlling the lawyer's work. He asked for clarification on the first sentence of the division of fees canon: "No division of fees for legal services is proper, except with another lawyer, based upon a division of service or responsibility." Did this mean that commissions (which were divided between the collection lawyer and the lay forwarder) constituted a division of fees when a lawsuit was filed? Boston elliptically responded, "I think it speaks for itself." He interpreted the canon as distinguishing "legal" fees from other (nonlegal) services. Boston also acknowledged that this "exception" was not part of the 1927 proposal. The committee had listened to objections and changed its mind. Cohen underscored his disagreement with the canon's text. What part of a lawyer's debt collection work was the practice of law, the fee for which was not divisible with a nonlawyer? Boston eventually fell back on the committee's conclusion that it was "not here to undo the work of state and local [bar] Associations." These unnamed associations had not sanctioned commercial lawyers who shared commissions with lay collection and referral agencies. Thus, a lawyer dividing a recovered debt was implicitly permitted to share part of that recovery with a nonlawyer, usually the lay forwarding collection agency. Without naming the Commercial Law League, Boston reported, "One committee in particular formulated this exception." The Boston Committee "could not properly go to the American Bar Association and ask it to disregard the views of those men." Cohen moved to defer consideration of this canon. Wright supported the interests of commercial lawyers. After further debate, Cohen's motion failed by a vote of 61–112. The supplemental canons were then adopted.[77]

The league may have believed this victory ended the war against commercial lawyers. Unfortunately, this was merely the first of many battles that continued through 1937. The Boston Committee was ordered to make a recommendation on bonding. Boston remained its chairman.

The thirteen supplemental canons approved by the ABA were largely unrelated. The duty of confidentiality was part of the oath in the 1908 ABA Canons, which made it an enforceable injunction, not merely an ethical consideration. Even so, the 1928 supplements added Canon 37, a statement of the duty to keep the confidences of a client. This decision suggests the abandonment of the dual structure of the 1908 ABA Canons. Lawyers were to consider the canons foremost when facing an ethical problem. Another canon of interest to commercial lawyers was Canon 43, which permitted a lawyer to insert a simple professional card in a "reputable law list." On that list, but not on the professional card, a lawyer was permitted to include the names of references and clients. Soon, a pressing question became: what is a reputable law list?

Same Terrain, Same Battles: Amending the Canons, 1929–1933

Trust is a necessity in many commercial interactions. In the interwar period, distance increased distrust. An unpaid creditor looking to collect from a distant debtor often turned to a collection agency to recoup the debt. The agency was paid a commission, or a percentage of what it recovered. The agency often forwarded the debt collection matter to a lawyer located near the debtor. The lawyer was thus an agent of the collection agency, which made the agency legally responsible to the creditor if the lawyer stole the recovered debt. To protect themselves against this risk of loss, agencies either hired known, trustworthy lawyers or purchased bonds (a type of insurance) that compensated the agency for any financial loss caused by the lawyer. Purchasing a bond meant the agency needed to verify only the trustworthiness of the bonding company. It then became the job of the bonding company to determine which lawyers were trustworthy. The bonding company or similar entity compiled a list of trustworthy lawyers, called a law list. Creating a valid list cost money, so the law list owner had to generate income. One income stream came from the collection agencies that used the list. Some law list publishers also received a second income stream from lawyers who paid a fee to join the list. In the latter case, the law list owner had a conflict of interest, as it might add any paying lawyer to the list, including untrustworthy lawyers. Julius Henry Cohen discussed and criticized this conflict of interest in 1916.[78]

The Commercial Law League was responsible for the ABA's 1928 decision to defer consideration of the bonding canon. In Boston's view, this meant the league was responsible for resolving the issue and carried "the burden of promptly solving the 'Law List Problem.'" Wright accepted this responsibility on the league's behalf. In addition to continuing its special ethics committee, the league created a new committee to learn about the business of bonding the lawyers on those law lists.[79]

This new committee reported that nineteen of twenty-three law lists "guarantee forwarders who use these lists against loss on the part of the lawyer listed." The bond was "practically the same." The forwarding collection agency was reimbursed "against loss by embezzlement and fraudulent failure to account." Some law list publishers provided a bond from a third-party surety company; others gave a personal guarantee to the forwarding collection agency, separately indemnifying themselves.[80]

The Boston Committee made no decision on a bonding canon for two years. In 1929 Boston's absence due to illness paralyzed the committee. The following year it didn't even file a written report. Boston then left the committee to serve as ABA president after the death of its elected president. This quiet soon ended, as the Great Depression began to take its economic toll.[81]

In 1930 both the Illinois State Bar Association and the Chicago Bar Association considered adopting the 1928 supplements to the Canons of Professional Ethics. Largely at the urging of Francis X. Busch, president of the Chicago Bar, both declined to adopt as written the canons on the division of fees (Canon 34) and lay intermediaries (Canon 35). Busch argued that they were unprofessional, and the two associations resolved that the "Canons as heretofore adopted be amended by omitting the reference to the custom of sharing of commissions with lay agencies."[82]

The ABA committee's authority was limited to deciding whether to add a canon prohibiting lawyer bonding. But in May 1931 chairman Edward Harriman called a meeting to discuss Canons 34 and 35. League leaders supported the canons, and Harriman stated that no action would be taken that year. However, he also declared that "members of his committee strongly favored the position of the Chicago and Illinois Bar Associations." Harriman then asked for additional authority, including the ability to amend the existing Canons of Professional Ethics. President Boston and the ABA executive committee agreed but cautioned the committee "in its consideration of amendments to the existing canons." The committee also replaced Harriman as chairman.[83]

The Commercial Law League met in advance of the ABA's 1932 annual meeting. Wright, its most perceptive analyst, saw the writing on the wall. The Chicago Bar Association had argued to the ABA that "law lists, lay agencies and attorneys had engaged in improper practice." Such claims raised serious concerns within the ABA, which created an unlawful practice committee in 1930. Taking advantage of this concern, the Chicago Bar urged the ABA to ban lawyers from putting their names on "a bonded law list." Wright acknowledged that some collection agencies were wrongly "importuning lawyers to divide legal fees" and agreed this needed to stop. The league's initial solution was to create a committee on interrelations, through which commercial lawyers, law list publishers, and commercial collection agencies could "work out those problems that vex us, vex them, and vex all of us." Wright was named its chairman. The committee quickly attacked this vexing problem and reported its progress to the ABA, which commended its initial work. It is unclear, though plausible, that the league was aware Charles Boston was to resume chairmanship of the special committee in 1932.[84]

No canon on bonding was proposed in 1932. But the ABA special committee's disparagement of the earlier work of the Boston Committee portended significant changes. It admitted, "Many bar associations have unhesitatingly approved [the supplemental canons] as presented." But some did so "reluctantly, . . . because of opposition to the last sentence in Canons 34, 35, and 43." (Canon 43 allowed lawyers to be on law lists.) The special committee did not name any associations that fit this description, but it was applicable only to the two Illinois associations that refused to approve Canons 34 and 35. That claim led the ABA special committee on supplements to the canons to consider the entire ethics code, which meant it needed more time. It noted complaints against law lists and lay forwarders attempting to cow lawyers "by threats and intimidation." Such attacks threatened lawyer compensation and independence. This too required investigation.[85]

The Commercial Law League's committee on interrelations proposed several resolutions adopted at the league's 1933 meeting. First, Canon 34, barring a division of fees with nonlawyers, was to be "strictly enforced." Second, commercial agencies forwarding a matter to a lawyer would receive an improved commission split. Third, no law list would "advertise" the bonding of a lawyer, which might "traduce the reputation of the legal profession." Fourth, the committee created an eight-point plan to regulate law lists. For the second time in six years, the lack of communication between the league and the ABA created a crisis. The Boston Committee proposed amending Canons 34 and 35 without league input.[86]

Boston's 1933 report proposed one supplement (Canon 46, "Notice of Specialized Legal Service") and five amendments. He frankly stated, "There is no general agreement in the profession as to some of the declarations which we have advised you to adopt."[87]

The adopted amendments to both Canon 11 (prohibiting the commingling of a client's money with the lawyer's) and Canon 13 (requiring that a contingent fee be reasonable) better protected clients during "the present period of economic difficulty." Canon 43 (professional cards) and new Canon 46 were adopted without debate. As expected, an intense, involved debate arose on amending Canon 34, "Division of Fees."[88]

Boston introduced this amendment by asserting that it generated "the second greatest controversy and difference of opinion." (The greatest controversy was unnamed.) Amended Canon 34 initially permitted lawyers and collection agencies to share any collection, "without suit, of liquidated" debts. The league objected. A predebate agreement deleted the phrase "without suit." Thus, the issue was the one raised by Cohen in 1928: was a lawyer's effort to collect a debt without filing a lawsuit the practice of law? Boston divided the debaters into commercial lawyers and their opponents, "the theorists among our profession who are perfectly logical, in my judgment, in their attitude." Boston agreed with the latter, "but we are confronted not with a theory, but with a fact." In the depths of the Great Depression, Boston accepted the league's argument. Many rural lawyers relied on debt collection to earn a living. Thus, "lawyers cannot destroy that business no matter how theoretically correct they are in their attitude toward it." Only lawyers would suffer if the ABA upended the debt collection business model. Would they obey this directive?[89]

Boston spoke highly of the Commercial Law League's efforts to protect lawyers against abuse from lay forwarders. He praised its recent work to protect the independence of lawyers as greater "than anything that the American Bar Association has ever conceived in these pious injunctions to its members." John G. Jackson, chairman of the Committee on Unauthorized Practice of Law, proposed, with "reluctance," an amendment essentially to revive the phrase "without suit." Boston objected. League leaders agreed with Boston, as did the ABA membership.[90]

Again, league leaders understood that victory was temporary. League president William Henderson noted, "local bar associations and state bar associations are not fully satisfied that the present Canons 34 and 35 are right." The ABA continued the committee's existence, Boston remained chairman, and Henderson would be proved right.[91]

The Great Depression and the Business of Regulating Legal Business

In a 1954 study of American lawyers, the authors noted a correlation between complaints of unethical lawyer conduct and economic conditions. Using Chicago Bar Association data, they found that complaints rose from an average of 375 in the 1920s to a high of 952 during 1933–1934. Complaints fell dramatically during and after World War II, averaging 174 a year from 1942 through 1948.[92]

Nearly two decades after the Commercial Law League and the NYCLA created unauthorized practice of law committees, the ABA joined in, proclaiming this was not a reaction to the economic struggles of many lawyers. Only in 1930 had the ethics committee's duties become so great that an unauthorized practice committee was necessary. The ABA also created the National Conference of Bar Examiners to reduce "overcrowding" in the profession by raising admission standards. Again, this was not about limiting competition; it was about ensuring professionalism.[93]

The ABA protested too much. As the Great Depression worsened, state bar associations policed more vigilantly the boundaries of the practice of law. They also looked to discipline unprofessional lawyers and raise bar admission standards. Missouri's efforts to regulate the practice of law during the Great Depression provide a useful example. In 1933 the St. Louis and Missouri Bar Associations sued to disbar Paul Richards, recently acquitted of conspiracy to commit kidnapping. Richards correctly argued that prior cases prohibited disbarment based on acts for which an individual had been acquitted. The Missouri Supreme Court overruled precedent and disbarred Richards. *Richards* was the catalyst for greater regulation.[94]

In *State ex inf. Miller v. St. Louis Union Trust Co.* (1934), the issue was whether a corporation was practicing law. It was a test case defining the practice of law. The Missouri Supreme Court held that corporation employees who wrote wills and drafted trust documents were engaged in the unlawful practice of law. The ABA cheered the ruling.[95]

Miller was published in July 1934. A week later the Missouri Supreme Court adopted the ABA Canons as applicable to all Missouri lawyers. In November it promulgated rules "integrating" the Missouri bar. *Richards* was cited as authority for the court to regulate admission to the bar, discipline lawyers for unprofessional conduct, and regulate the unauthorized practice of law. The court appointed Boyle G. Clark general chairman to oversee four regional committees policing the business of law.[96]

Clark broadly interpreted his jurisdiction. In a 1935 speech to the Commercial Law League, he claimed the "means for the rehabilitation of the legal profession," returning it to its former glory as independent of government and lay control. He thus needed to challenge the league's "status." Lawyers were independent only if they possessed "economic security" and were "unimpeded by exploitation and encroachment" from corporations. The league had failed to provide economic security, requiring Missouri to take on this duty. One step was to amend Canon 43 on law lists. By September,

Clark was lauding the state's (or his) efforts to make lawyers obey the ethics rules, "suppress control" of the law business by laypersons, and reduce unauthorized practice. Clark also cited lawsuits against corporations allegedly engaged in the practice of law.[97]

Shortly after Clark's September speech, Missouri amended Canon 43, going far beyond its ABA counterpart. The Missouri canon defined "law list" and "law directory" and specified when each was "reputable." A list that bonded lawyers was, by definition, not reputable, and a lawyer who "places his name" on such a list was guilty of professional misconduct. An advisory committee to the court decided which lists were reputable. This caused much consternation among league members.[98]

The ABA and the league were working on resolving the "law list problem" at the same time. Two years later, this culminated in amending ABA Canon 43.[99]

In March 1936 Clark announced detailed rules regarding published law lists and directories. Lawyers could be listed in any law directory; in law lists, names were listed alphabetically, and any lawyer rejected from a list could appeal to the advisory committee. Subscription prices could not exceed the committee's maximum rate. All publications had to be approved by the committee, and they would be evaluated only after the publishers applied for "reputable" status. A lawyer could not "permit his name to be published" in an unapproved list. If a lawyer later learned of such publication, he had to tell the publisher to remove his name. A Kansas City commercial lawyer coincidentally wrote an apt riposte that same month: "The lawyer who causes the words, 'Law Office,' 'Attorney at Law,' or similar descriptive title, after his name to be placed on his office door, window, stationery, or business cards, is seeking business." Missouri's law list rule had nothing to do with professionalism or independence from clients or the government. It was a power grab by Clark and a confused response to questions of professional identity. Businesses employing lawyers were allowed to advertise that fact, but circulating a law list to creditors was condemned. Any critical difference between the two was not explained.[100]

Clark's efforts to prosecute those engaged in the unauthorized practice of law was initially successful. In *Clark v. Austin* (1937), the Missouri Supreme Court held that the unlicensed respondents practiced law by representing third parties before the Public Service Commission.[101] That same month, the court held in *State ex rel. McKittrick v. C. S. Dudley & Co., Inc.* that the collection agency illegally practiced law by selecting the attorneys, declaring the fee it collected, and acting as the client by communicating directly with the lawyer. The court then reached an extraordinary conclusion:

> If collections cannot be made without the services of an attorney, the [collection agency] should return the claim to the creditor who should be free to select and employ his own attorney. The respondent should not engage directly or indirectly, in the business of employing an attorney for others to collect claims or to prosecute suits therefor, nor have any interest in the fee earned by the attorney for his work.[102]

Its approach was impractical. Creditors used collection agencies because they didn't know any local lawyers. Intermediaries such as collection agencies were useful because they possessed or had access to local knowledge. Missouri even criticized law lists, which contained the names of competent commercial lawyers, as impermissible intermediaries. What was a creditor to do? The court did not deign to explain.

Clark went too far when he claimed casualty insurance companies were practicing law by having adjusters investigate claims, negotiate settlements, and participate in informal conferences with the Workmen's Compensation Commission. Clark's "aggressive action" led six casualty insurers to sue for declaratory relief. When it reached the state supreme court, Clark was no longer general chairman, and the court tempered its enthusiasm for policing the boundaries of law practice. It held that the adjusters' activities were not the practice of law.[103]

In 1939 the chairman of the Missouri bar's ethics committee wrote a romantic and realistic assessment of lawyer ethics in the state. Things were looking up. Grievance committees were much more effective than earlier, lawyers were articulating the public harm of unauthorized practice, "snitches" (Missourian for "runners") were in less plentiful supply, and scandalous behavior was less common. However, lawyers needed to understand that "the public is entitled to better and more efficient service." If lawyers failed to provide it, nonlawyers would fill the vacuum. "Undoubtedly," although lawyers had made "progress in professional ethics," more work was necessary to restore "public confidence" in them.[104]

Amending the Canons (Again), 1934–1937

The ABA's 1933 amendments to Canons 34 and 35, which permitted commercial lawyers to divide commissions but not fees with collection agencies, continued to rankle some elite lawyers. Charles Boston's 1934 report acknowledged the "persistent controversies respecting the terms of these two canons." The New York State Bar Association, for example, had declined to adopt them. On January 10, 1935, Boston wrote to the ABA executive committee, expressing his views that the committee had no specific duties and "that some time in the near future the American Bar Association should face the fact that some of the more fundamental problems of the profession should be grappled with." It agreed with his first view and expressed no opinion on the second. Two months later, Boston died. Although the committee did not meet, Boston's successor noted a number of tasks. Critics and defenders of these canons continued to chime in.[105]

The ABA switched to a federalized constitution in 1936. It created a House of Delegates to pass on proposals, displacing the Assembly of members. It also killed the special committee on canons of ethics. The professional ethics and grievances committee was authorized to propose amendments and supplements to the canons.[106]

At the 1937 meeting this committee recommended eleven changes. Many tried to disguise the fact that lawyers were paid money for legal services. Several replaced the word *business* with *employment*, as the latter was apparently less suggestive of a mere economic transaction. Canon 27, which banned direct or indirect advertising, was "completely redrafted." It became a bloated statement damning nearly all communications with prospective clients. It also became the primary canon informally regulating law lists. Solicitation was permitted only when "warranted by personal relations." This incongruous addition made no effort to define the "personal relations" exception. The House of Delegates then adopted rules and standards for law list approval to which collection agencies agreed to be bound.[107]

This was an extraordinary and successful power grab by the ABA. It "nationalized" law lists, crowding out the Commercial Law League. The law list agreement was the first in a series of agreements with other entities allegedly traipsing on the practice of law. The ABA and the American Bankers Association Trust Division agreed in 1941 on the "principles" regarding the proper work of each. It also entered into agreements with adjusters (1939), publishers of law books (1941), realtors (1942), and accountants (1944).[108]

The discussion of the 1937 amendments was appallingly brief. No one spoke, and the changes were adopted.[109]

A new law list committee was empowered to implement the law list approval process. However, there was still a problem with law lists. In 1942 the committee suggested slimming down Canon 27, and the chairman noted the simmering division regarding Canon 43's statement on law lists: "As to Canon 43, there are three schools of thought: One school is that the Canon as it reads ought to be repealed; another school of thought is that it ought to be left alone. A third school of thought is that it ought not to be repealed as too backward a step." Action was delayed until 1943, when the relevant committees agreed on the third option. Canon 43 was ignored; modest changes were made to Canon 27, allowing a lawyer to list business references in law lists.[110]

Ambulance Chasing

In early 1926 the Lawyers' Club of Milwaukee began quizzing lawyers about ambulance chasing. The inquisitors found evidence of client fraud and deceit. A well-organized system of "runners" or "chasers" sometimes signed clients and settled their cases without involving a lawyer. Sometimes the runner was the lawyer's agent. In any case, relatively few lawsuits were filed, and settlement benefited the agents, not the injured. The investigation also found that insurance companies and other defendants behaved abominably, soliciting injured persons and often deceiving them. This scandal became significant news in 1927. The Lawyers' Club successfully petitioned the presiding judge of a circuit (trial) court in Milwaukee County to initiate a formal investigation. Some witnesses spoke frankly and apologized for their actions. Others left town. One, William Rubin, the first Russian Jewish lawyer in Milwaukee, fought back. The circuit court was less interested in disbarring or disciplining lawyers than in purging frivolous cases from the docket and ending ambulance chasing by nonlawyers. It was somewhat successful. The Supreme Court of Wisconsin upheld the circuit court's investigative authority and a contempt citation of Rubin. It declined to disbar him.[111]

Wisconsin's success led ABCNY president Charles Evans Hughes to petition the First Department of the Appellate Division to investigate ambulance chasing. In February 1928 it agreed. Isidor J. Kresel led the investigation under the formal supervision of Justice Isidor Wasservogel. Kresel and his staff interviewed eleven hundred witnesses in roughly six months. They found a practice of ambulance chasing controlled by "relatively few lawyers, some of whom have conducted their practice purely as a business, to the detriment of the public and the profession." As in Wisconsin, Kresel found a number of lawyers who had no intention of taking their clients' cases to court. Some clients were defrauded by their lawyers; some cases were brought for nuisance value only; and many lawyers settled their clients' cases in amounts "which are grossly inadequate." The conduct of casualty insurance companies was also condemned as "reprehensible." Wasservogel recommended seventy-four lawyers for disciplinary proceedings. Six resigned, fourteen were disbarred, and thirty-one others were censured or suspended for up to two years.[112]

The Philadelphia bar, with Hughes's encouragement, began a probe a month after New York's. It named names, but only some names. Elite lawyer Henry Drinker, a once and future member of the ABA's professional ethics and grievances committee (see chapter 5), was chairman of the Philadelphia bar's grievance committee, and his conclusion was bigoted, extreme, and unforgiving. Apparently expressing a lack of surprise at the results, Drinker noted that a number of "Russian Jew boys" mentioned in the report had been the subject of complaints. The *ABA Journal* praised these investigations and discussed similar investigations in Ohio, Minnesota, San Francisco, and St. Louis.[113]

Ambulance chasing was not stamped out. Philadelphia undertook two additional investigations, one in the mid-1930s and a second in the early 1940s. In 1936 New York district attorney William Dodge opened an investigation into an accident fraud ring. Assistant district attorney Bernard Botein led the investigation. The accident ring was not about improperly soliciting or defrauding injured clients; it was about faking personal injuries to defraud companies. Some lawyers scrutinized in the 1928 investigation were involved, and a small number were convicted.[114]

Bankruptcy Ethics

Uncovering misbehavior by bankruptcy attorneys in New York (and elsewhere) occurred between the first and second ambulance chasing investigations. In early 1929 the judges of the Southern District of New York in Manhattan ordered a federal grand jury to investigate alleged abuses. It looked into five thousand bankruptcy cases, after which "two prominent attorneys" pleaded guilty to embezzlement, a third resigned from the practice of law, and a fourth, before committing suicide, informed the United States attorney how this illicit behavior flourished. Bankruptcy practice had been corrupted by "serious abuses and malpractices upon the part of attorneys, receivers, trustees," and others. The ABCNY, the NYCLA, and the Bronx Bar Association were asked to assist, and they agreed to pay for the investigation. Judge Thomas Thacher oversaw the probe. As suggested by the associations, he appointed William J. Donovan to lead it.[115]

Donovan interviewed more than four thousand witnesses and studied more than a thousand bankruptcy cases. His May 1930 report found fierce competition among bankruptcy firms, such that "attorneys frequently adopted unethical methods" to gain and keep business. The circumstances made "corruption on the part of attorneys" easy. Twelve lawyers were indicted, four resigned from the bar, another four were disbarred, and two were subjected to lesser discipline. The ABA concluded that practices in the Southern District were the outlier. Thacher disagreed. He resigned from the district court to serve as solicitor general of the United States and convinced President Herbert Hoover that an investigation of the nation's bankruptcy courts, modeled on the Donovan investigation, would be valuable in assessing whether bankruptcy "malpractices" were systemic or isolated. His report reminded readers that lawyers "are frail human creatures and the temptation is too great where there is an estate out of which fees can be paid to trump up opposition to discharge, thereby earning fees . . . all to no purpose."[116]

If the Donovan report uncovered an isolated problem, the ABA could stereotype it much like Drinker did in Philadelphia. Thacher's report warned against this thinking, as did Cohen, who noted that bankruptcy and ambulance chasing scandals were more likely to be uncovered in New York than in smaller towns. Lawyers who regularly rubbed elbows were less likely to criticize one another's misbehavior. Virtue and vice were found everywhere. These "scandals" were not about the "low character of the men now involved" but about conditions "conducive" to those "who care little or nothing about professional standards."[117]

Bribing Judges

Attorney General Homer Cummings charged that lawyers were "on trial before the public." As far as the public understood it, the "uncurtailed activities of unscrupulous lawyers" were condoned by the bar because it condemned them only "in pious resolutions."[118]

In mid-1933 Cummings announced a public investigation of a "receivership racket" in the United States District Court for the Middle District of Pennsylvania. One lawyer was indicted for embezzling funds in bankruptcy matters. The trustee in sixteen of the thirty-seven cases was the son-in-law of Albert W. Johnson, the district's federal judge. A year later, one of Johnson's three lawyer-sons was indicted for misappropriating funds as a bankruptcy trustee. Despite this smoke, the investigation was closed, leaving Johnson untouched. Ten years later, the extent of Johnson's corruption became public knowledge.

Albert W. Johnson was a flagrantly corrupt federal district court judge for two decades. Lawyers in the Middle District knew he was corrupt, but none of them spoke publicly, too fearful of Johnson's retaliatory power. In 1945 both a federal grand jury, managed by Department of Justice lawyer Max Goldschein, and a House Judiciary Subcommittee unveiled his corrupt behavior. An indictment in the fall charged Johnson, his three sons, and six other lawyers with conspiring to obstruct justice. By far, the most extraordinary indication of Judge Johnson's corruption was the bankruptcy case of Williamsport Wire Rope Company. Hoyt Moore was a partner in the elite New York law firm now known as Cravath, Swaine & Moore. He was also general counsel to Bethlehem Steel, which was the major creditor and a minority shareholder in Williamsport Wire. Williamsport had filed for bankruptcy due to a cash squeeze.

In September 1932 the assets of Williamsport Wire exceeded its liabilities by more than $4.8 million. Even so, its value steadily declined even after business picked up, for it remained in bankruptcy. Bethlehem Steel wanted all of Williamsport Wire, and it wanted it as cheaply as possible. Johnson was presiding over the bankruptcy, and he saw a chance for a large payout. His sons and another lawyer believed they could make a "killing" by selling Williamsport Wire to Bethlehem Steel. They did. Stockholders objected, but in 1937 Bethlehem Steel bought Williamsport Wire for $3.3 million, $1.2 million less than it was willing to pay. Bethlehem Steel got this bargain because Hoyt Moore agreed to a plan to funnel a $250,000 bribe to Johnson.

Goldschein eventually questioned Moore and dragged out of him exactly how this $250,000 in "administrative expenses" was divvied up. Proving again that there is no honor among thieves, John Memolo, a lawyer central to the conspiracy, told Johnson the bribe was $150,000, not $250,000, and he never forwarded any of the bribe money to Johnson.

Moore and two others who were indicted successfully pleaded the statute of limitations. Moore was not the subject of any disciplinary proceeding by the ABCNY. A history of Cravath, Swaine & Moore by partner Robert Swaine recounted Moore's representation of Bethlehem Steel in its purchase of Williamsport Wire, but it omitted the bribe, the congressional hearings, the indictment, and Moore's plea. About Moore, Swaine wrote, "No lawyer ever unreservedly gave more of himself to a client."[119]

Law Factories

Cravath, Swaine & Moore is one of the best-known large corporate law firms in the United States. It and many other New York–based law firms specializing in corporate practice went through a period of change and growth in the late 1910s and early 1920s. Similar growth occurred in major law firms in other large American cities between 1915 and 1924.[120]

As they grew, they became more powerful. In 1927 lawyer Newman Levy suggested their power overshadowed their ethical failings. The elite bar professed its adherence to "higher standards" than the morals of the marketplace but acted in whatever way their clients desired. "Flagrantly anti-social" bar leaders sought to "purge the bar of shysters" while declaring similar behavior by elites admirable.[121]

The muckraking journalist Ferdinand Lundberg wrote a trio of essays on lawyers at the end of the 1930s. He criticized law factories as "brains of the status quo," enabling the powerful. The law factory lawyer was "in reality a business man rather than a professional man." Lundberg was bemused by the profession's claim that it was independent from society because it served the needs of the powerful. His doleful conclusion was that, despite being essential to democratic government, the legal profession had "negated its ideals." "The legal profession, instead of working for justice as an end, has been invoking it as a means toward the retention and attainment of power by special groups."[122]

Conclusion

In a 1934 speech Justice Harlan Fiske Stone noted that "factory" lawyers were "the obsequious servant[s] of business." His criticism was not new; a year earlier, another critic called the corporation lawyer the "greatest enemy of human society, not excepting the gangster."[123]

But Stone also noted that this "servant" maintained the "ideal" of loyalty to clients, demonstrating that lawyers were not without ideals. Both Stone and Charles Chamberlayne believed the practice of law should be about service rather than personal profit. Both understood that too often it was practiced as a moneymaking business. They differed in their skepticism. For Chamberlayne, writing in 1909, the profession had lost its soul. A quarter century later, Stone remained a romantic. Just as lawyers led the way in shaping new ideals in a new nation, lawyers in this modern age could do the same. Ideals still mattered, and it was possible for lawyers to refashion their ideals.[124]

CHAPTER FIVE

Prosperity, Professionalism, and Prejudice, 1945–1969

During World War II, nearly every cover of the monthly *American Bar Association (ABA) Journal* portrayed a legal figure, ordinarily in military uniform. The portraits had no rhyme or reason; Union and Confederate Civil War lawyer-officers were intermingled, and twice Abraham Lincoln graced its cover. The *ABA Journal* changed course beginning in April 1945, when it featured the World Court in The Hague. Succeeding covers were of legal or political institutions. The editors helpfully explained that their choices marked the beginning of a continuing effort among the American elite to build a lasting postwar world peace. Building such a peace required the creation of effective multinational legal and political organizations, such as the Permanent Court of International Justice. Lawyers were particularly qualified for this work because this was a peace created not by force but by justice. "And to lawyers at any rate that peace is possible only if justice can be administered according to law."[1]

The hallmark of the rule of law is the administration of justice, and lawyers had a duty to preserve the rule of law, through which liberty and order flourished. Lawyers had been, in "every movement," leaders of the fight "to gain and retain liberty under law." ABA president David Simmons's April 1945 column was a plea to American lawyers to recognize this momentous time. Simmons reported that 87 percent of ABA House of Delegates members agreed the ABA should take "a broad view of its obligation of national leadership." The most famous example of administering justice to fashion a just, secure world was the prosecution of war criminals. Shortly before Supreme Court justice Robert H. Jackson was appointed to serve as chief American prosecutor in the Nuremberg trials, he encouraged the trial of any alleged war criminal as long as the prosecution was "prepared to establish his personal guilt." A show trial was worse than no trial.[2]

For most Americans, World War II was a "good war." Afterward, bar leaders embraced the burden to help "solve the critical problems of this age." Approximately 170,000 American lawyers had served their country, 40,000 of them in uniform in all ranks and services, yet "not more than five per cent are doing law work." Another 27,000 civilian lawyers had volunteered their services to aid the war effort. Now lawyers were ready to do even more.[3]

Victory generated optimism, despite economic fears. In the late 1940s the United States "possessed 42 percent of the world's income and accounted for half of the world's manufacturing output." It produced a majority of the world's steel, oil, and automobiles and 43 percent of all electricity. Per capita income was almost twice that of any other economically advanced nation. Economically, the quarter century following the end of World War II was "an extraordinary time," a "golden age." A booming economy benefited most Americans, including lawyers. Although the number of lawyers increased at a rate slightly faster than population growth, the demand for legal services outstripped the supply. This remained the general trend through the 1960s.[4]

The quarter century after World War II was a golden age for most but not all lawyers. Demand for legal services led to an increase in real median income (i.e., after inflation and stated in 1983 dollars) from $25,415 in 1947 to $37,300 in 1959 to $47,638 in 1969. Their median income nearly doubled, and lawyers found themselves gaining influence in government and politics. Economic prosperity, however, did not reach all lawyers. The vast majority of American lawyers who benefited from these economic gains were white and male. Black lawyers constituted less than 1 percent of the lawyer population in 1950, and an infinitesimal number worked for large law firms serving large corporations. The ABA itself did not lift its ban on Black members until 1943, and for the next decade it made little effort to encourage Black lawyers to join. Women accounted for just 3 percent of the lawyer population in 1950 (and less than 5 percent in 1970); they rarely worked at large law firms or at private firms at all, often due to discrimination. As the civil rights movement gained momentum in the early 1960s, American lawyers were challenged to meet the ideals of the profession by representing civil rights demonstrators and others. This echoed a plea from a decade earlier, when many lawyers refused to represent admitted or alleged communists for reasons of fear, prejudice, and economic worry. Idealists induced some recalcitrant lawyers to meet their obligations to serve unpopular clients by appealing to their professionalism.[5]

Survey of the Legal Profession

In 1946 the ABA expanded a two-year-old project analyzing legal education and the admission of new lawyers to practice. In light of the needs of the postwar United States, ABA leaders concluded that a project to study "the functioning of lawyers in a free society" was crucial. This became the Survey of the Legal Profession.[6]

Although the ABA contributed financially to the survey and its president chose the initial members of the Survey Council, the survey itself was officially independent of the ABA. The council was a self-perpetuating group of influential and well-positioned members; it was aided by an Advisory Committee of Laymen. The survey's first director (chosen by the council) was Arthur T. Vanderbilt. In a 1947 speech, Vanderbilt noted that the survey was divided into five parts: the professional services of lawyers, the public service of lawyers, judicial service, professional competence and integrity in the bar, and economic security of the profession. The survey intended to "determine what are the proper standards of conduct and how well they are maintained." A related issue was whether the profession protected the "public interest" against the practice of law by laymen.[7]

Vanderbilt's successor, Reginald Heber Smith, wrote annual survey updates for the *ABA Journal*. His initial report asserted the important role of American lawyers: "Everywhere [lawyers] exert influence and exercise power." Smith described professional responsibility as a subject both "vast" and "vital" and of such importance and depth that those progress reports would "require the longest time."[8]

The completed survey consisted of about 175 separate reports. Fewer than a dozen concerned the professional responsibility of lawyers. One report by Robert McCracken, a former ABA ethics committee chairman, evaluated survey responses regarding adherence to the Canons of Ethics. Lawyers from just twenty-five states answered these questions. McCracken's initial conclusion was, "Most of the Canons here dealt with seem to be observed by an overwhelming majority of the lawyers in the United States." The two modest exceptions involved the continuing existence of unrealistic canons and a few lawyers who disregarded the canons "for reasons of gain or in their zeal to win cases." Although these violations were "prevalent with a limited section of the Bar in most communities," they were less prevalent than "a half century, or even a quarter of a century, ago." Overall, the bar "maintains a strict observance of the ethical standards set forth in the Canons."[9]

The authors of *The American Lawyer* (1954), a summary volume of the manifold survey reports, dug a bit deeper into these responses. One issue they highlighted was the profession's failure to represent "the cause of the defenseless or oppressed," with lawyers in more than half the states reporting that it was not unethical to refuse to defend a person accused of a crime. Lawyers in nine states reported this was a common practice. A second issue was unethical trial behavior, including presenting "evidence known to be false." This was a sufficiently "common practice" to raise "grave concern" about whether lawyers were fulfilling their duty as officers of the court. The authors also noted the profession's "failure to take appropriate action where fraud or deception is intended or has been perpetrated by the client," as well as prosecutorial abuse and excessive fees. They urged amending the ABA's Canons of Professional Ethics and made specific proposals, including the recommendation that some actions deemed unethical should be permitted, such as allowing labor unions and other associations to hire lawyers to represent members.[10]

Henry S. Drinker, a longtime ABA ethics committee member, reported survey responses by laymen on the integrity and competence of lawyers. He quoted several critical responses, and his overall assessment pointed in different directions. The public believed lawyers failed to enforce standards of ethical behavior, yet laymen viewed lawyers favorably compared with other professionals.[11]

Conduct of Judges and Lawyers (1952) compiled the published survey reports on lawyer ethics. Its authors, federal judge Orie L. Phillips and California judge Philbrick McCoy, had also served on the ABA ethics committee. Their conclusions were mixed. They agreed lawyers largely adhered to the canons, although the profession had a problem with repeat ethics offenders because the courts were too forgiving and thus failed to protect the public. The public expected lawyers to serve as "disciples" of the law and to provide "active leadership" in administering and protecting the rule of law. Unfortunately, too many lawyers failed these standards, demonstrating a need for improvement in the profession. They concluded that the average American lawyer's public standing was "'well—but not well enough!'"

Another reason for a lack of public respect was the Canons of Professional Ethics, which were "demonstrably inadequate" and not a sufficiently "authoritative statement of the standards of professional conduct to which all lawyers should adhere." Further, many canons were paid "lip-service, while others are more honored in the breach than in the observance." The need for reform was clear, but on the particulars, the authors declined to opine. They were confident, however, that a "Restatement of Professional Standards" would better serve everyone by shifting the emphasis from "professional 'ethics'" to "ideals and standards."[12]

Phillips and McCoy were the first to suggest replacing the canons. Like others, they understood that the canons were too often framed in terms of etiquette rather than standards and as wishes rather than authoritative statements. Their efforts were initially stymied.

The Adversarial Ethic

In an October 1952 addendum to *Conduct of Judges and Lawyers*, McCoy noted that he and Phillips had concluded their research in 1951, after which several important essays were published. The first was by elite Boston lawyer Charles Curtis. Curtis, whose duty was to read every draft report about the survey, presented a bracing vision in "The Ethics of Advocacy." Elite lawyer Henry Drinker responded critically.[13]

Curtis stated, "A lawyer handles other people's troubles"—a task that required the lawyer to serve clients loyally. Loyalty was specific; it ran to the client alone, for courts demanded that the lawyer "devote himself to the client." Curtis praised and quoted Brougham's 1820 defense of Queen Caroline (see chapter 2): lawyers should know "but one person in the world—that client and no other." Loyalty thus required the lawyer "to lie for his client" to anyone other than the court; to the court, a strategic silence that redounded to the client's benefit was ethical. Such loyalty was countenanced because the advocate's morals differed from society's. The lawyer-advocate's work created a paradox: "I don't know of any other career that offers ampler opportunity for both the enjoyment of virtue and the exercise of vice, or, if you will, the exercise of virtue and the enjoyment of vice." That paradox existed in fulfilling the advocate's duty to give his "entire devotion" to the client. A lawyer who followed that command necessarily failed to do so. Devotion to a client required detachment. Such lawyers, "by not putting up their emotions as well as their minds for hire," better served their clients. Further, devotion was not love. Detachment was a Stoic conception, not a Christian one. To be detached from the client's case required the lawyer to approach advocacy in one of two ways: either "to treat the whole thing as a game" or to possess "a sense of craftsmanship." The lawyer either embraced his job as a role to be performed well or made his craft an "art." The lawyer's craft as art form allowed the lawyer to enjoy "the intense pleasure of doing a job as well as you can irrespective of usefulness or even of its purpose."[14]

Drinker was having none of Curtis's perverse opinions. Paradox was not the practicing lawyer's fate. Instead, "no man can be either too honest, too truthful, or too upright to be a thoroughly good lawyer, and an eminently successful one." By treating "vice and virtue on such equal terms," how could Curtis love his profession? Curtis's cynical suggestion that "leaders of the Bar actually practice the kind of chicanery in which he pretends to believe" harmed lawyers, especially young lawyers. Drinker was well aware of the "unique difficulties" lawyers faced. They were "constantly confronted with conflicting loyalties" that must be reconciled. Unlike Drinker, Curtis simply did not believe reconciliation was possible. Drinker concluded that a lawyer could zealously represent a client and remain "honest" and "truthful."[15]

Did lawyers owe a duty to disclose to a court "decisions" adverse to their clients' interest? In 1935 the ABA's professional ethics committee answered "yes" in Opinion 146. It concluded that a lawyer's obligation "to the public is no less significant than his obligation to his client." Fourteen years later, a lawyer wrote urging the ethics committee to revise its opinion. In his view, the duty should be limited to notifying the court only if asked and only if the adverse decision was a "controlling authority." In Opinion 280 (1949), Drinker wrote an opinion for the committee that did so. It agreed that a lawyer "is not an umpire, but an advocate." The lawyer had to disclose "a decision directly adverse" to the client if the lawyer expressly relied on a contrary proposition of law and if it "would reasonably be considered important" in the judge's decision. These two conditions created significant ambiguity. First, "directly adverse" was broader than "controlling authority." Second, an objective reasonableness standard was restated, "which the court should clearly consider." The noun *court* and the adverb *clearly* simply muddied the waters.[16]

Curtis noted that Opinion 146 failed to "distinguish a lawyer's loyalties." The "somewhat bigamous" lawyer owed a higher duty to the court than to the client regarding matters of law. Drinker chastised Curtis for not mentioning Opinion 280, which Drinker assured the reader returned the lawyer to monogamy.[17]

The lawyer's duty to represent clients zealously, and to represent those most desperately in need of counsel, those despised by the community, were rising in importance by 1952.[18]

The Unpopular Client and Systemic Interests

In late 1949 Eugene Dennis and ten other members of the Communist Party were found guilty of conspiracy. It was then the longest trial in American history. After the verdict, Judge Harold Medina "turn[ed] to some unfinished business": criminal contempt specifications for the five lawyers and Dennis, who had represented himself. Medina listed forty specifications and held the lawyers in contempt without any opportunity to be heard, as was then permitted by law. The contemnors were sentenced to between thirty days and six months in custody. The appellate panel consisted of three extraordinary judges: Augustus Hand, Jerome Frank, and Charles Clark. Hand concluded that all the contempt certifications should be affirmed, Clark concluded the opposite, and Frank affirmed all but three specifications.[19]

In its January 1948 issue, the *ABA Journal* reprinted a December 2, 1947, letter from Supreme Court justice Felix Frankfurter memorializing Boston lawyer Arthur D. Hill. Hill had agreed to represent Nicola Sacco and Bartolomeo Vanzetti twenty years earlier in a last-ditch effort to avoid their execution. He did so at Frankfurter's request, after William G. Thompson could no longer give them the energy they deserved. Hill agreed it was "a perfectly honorable thing" to look at the record to determine whether any legal issue remained. That the defendants, "against whom the feeling of the community is strong," could not pay was irrelevant. As portrayed by Frankfurter, Hill was thus the epitome of the zealous, independent lawyer whose defense of the outcast was essential to the protection of a democratic society. According to the authors of *The Legacy of Sacco & Vanzetti* (1948), the "fragmentary" record indicates that Hill spoke "with great force" to the trial judge, Webster Thayer, in support of a motion that Thayer's prejudice required a new trial; the motion failed. The authors also concluded that Hill was paid "proper money compensation" for his work.[20]

In an unpublished February 1949 report to the survey's Advisory

Committee of Laymen, director Reginald Heber Smith discussed reasons for the public's dissatisfaction with lawyers as a group. One reason was the adversary system, or, as he stated more colloquially, "lawyers are liars" who will, for the right price, "tell the best lies and you will be acquitted." Smith then repeated Frankfurter's story about Hill to contradict this. Hill demonstrated how to fulfill "the lawyer's *duty* to say everything for his client that can be said."[21]

Curtis knew Arthur Hill and used him to explain why society should make it "as easy as possible" for a lawyer "to take a case that other people regard as bad." It was important for the community to have its speculative conclusion tested by the accused's advocate. A society that acted on an untested belief that the defendant's cause was bad harmed itself. Curtis departed from Frankfurter's opinion in a crucial respect and emphasized that Hill had been paid. Hill's representation of Sacco and Vanzetti was thus "a case, not a cause. He was not the partisan, he was the advocate." However, the Sacco-Vanzetti case was a cause for Frankfurter and others. By the time Hill agreed to represent them, the case "had become the premier cause célèbre of its day." That cause had costs. Thompson had asked to withdraw because representing the alleged anarchists was a "catastrophe" to his firm. Hill's detached, professional, paid devotion to his role as advocate was exactly what society needed. Curtis added a story about his only personal interaction with Judge Thayer: He was in Thayer's chambers settling an accident case when he suddenly realized Thayer "was no longer talking about our case, but strutting up and down and boasting that he had been fortunate enough to be on the bench when those sons of bitches [Sacco and Vanzetti] were convicted." Curtis's "chill" at this comment was "warmed" by "thoughts of Arthur Hill." Drinker did not respond to these arguments.[22]

The lawyers held in contempt by Judge Medina "came under hostile scrutiny by professional associations in their home states." Two, Harry Sacher and Abraham Isserman, were disbarred; another was publicly reprimanded. Both Sacher and Isserman were reinstated to the practice of law, but the latter was not fully reinstated until 1961.[23]

In the Supreme Court's decision upholding the contempt specifications in *Sacher* (1952), Justice Robert H. Jackson made clear the court's interest in protecting "persons identified with unpopular causes" and wrote, "that there may be no misunderstanding, we make clear that this Court . . . will unhesitatingly protect counsel in fearless, vigorous and effective performance" as an "advocate on behalf of any person whatsoever." Jackson was echoing the statements of Judge Jerome Frank, who had rejected the argument that af-firming the contempt specifications would mean that "unpopular persons will . . . be intimidated or throttled." Lawyers would not be subject to pun-ishment "because they courageously defended their client, or because those clients were Communists." It was their own "outrageous conduct . . . which no lawyer owes his client," that led to their punishment for contempt.[24]

The Unpopular Client and the Cold War

Despite these reassurances, when the Supreme Court issued *Sacher*, unpop-ular clients found willing lawyers scarce. They increasingly feared economic reprisal. Like Thompson in the 1920s, they worried that representing com-munists would result in economic catastrophe.

In late 1951 Harvard Law–trained Philip Graham spoke at the Associa-tion of the Bar of the City of New York (ABCNY) and reminded lawyers that they were crucial in protecting individual liberty, such as defending those accused of being a communist or having communist associations. Unfortunately, "the legal profession has substantially failed to meet its proper obligations of supporting individual freedom." The bar's tepid re-sponse in defending alleged communists might be a result of "the sub-servience of many lawyers to their client's points of view, of the growing tendency to consider a lawyer a part of his client rather than a part of the law, and in general of the growing commercialization of the profession." If so, lawyers could no longer "pretend to be guided by a sense of public responsibility higher than the ordinary self-interest of the business men and merchants."[25]

"In a sense Graham's indictment of the legal profession was fair." This was the milieu in which Curtis was writing. As the Red Scare metastasized, the ABA adopted a resolution in September 1950 demanding that lawyers demonstrate their loyalty by swearing an "anti-Communist oath." Its pro-ponents claimed this met the profession's "high tradition of service to the public" and protected Americans from "the threat to individual liberty."[26]

The resolution was unanimously adopted. Soon, however, a number of elite lawyers published their opposition in the *ABA Journal*. They explained that swearing falsely would be simple for true believers in the communist cause. Further, disbarment should be based on unprofessional miscon-duct proved at an adversarial hearing. Finally, the resolution put an entire profession under suspicion to snare "a few random delinquents." No state licensing board adopted it.[27]

The problem of finding counsel remained. As attorney general, Tom Clark had twice indicated his view that lawyers who "carry out Communist missions" might be unfit to practice law. This chilled the ardor of many, although a few elite lawyers agreed to represent alleged communists. But as prominent lawyer John P. Frank wrote in 1952, "It is now, as I can personally vouch from some observation, almost impossible to obtain 'respectable counsel' in the political cases." Frank's assertion was indirectly supported by a union lawyer who found "his law practice vanished" after he agreed to represent an alleged communist. Despite Hill's reminder that the lawyer represented a client, not the client's political or economic views, guilt by association was common. Several courts tried to remedy this ill by shaming bar associations into helping the accused find counsel.[28]

The ABA formed a Special Committee on Communist Tactics, Strategy, and Objectives in 1950. Its first task was to encourage state bar associations to implement the anticommunist oath, which utterly failed. Next, in February 1951 it proposed that the ABA expel any "member of the Communist Party or [one] who advocates Marxism-Leninism." That proposal was successful, but not without cost. First, the debate on the issue was contentious, and a number of moderating amendments were accepted. Second, wrapped inside its report was the oath's propriety. Its defenders won the battle but lost the war. Third, the ABA created a Special Committee on Individual Rights as Affected by National Security.[29] This special committee was led by Whitney North Seymour, a partner in the Wall Street firm of Simpson Thacher and Bartlett, which opposed the loyalty oath. Seymour was a Republican, president of the ABCNY (he led its rejection of the oath), and a longtime proponent of civil rights. His committee began working on proposed solutions to balance individual rights with national security. The committee offered the ABA three resolutions in 1953, the most important of which "*reaffirms the principles*" that the right to counsel generates a correlative duty among lawyers to "aid even the most unpopular defendants." Other parts of that resolution made it ABA policy to defend a lawyer who represented an unpopular client if that lawyer acted in accord with the standards of the bar. Other bar associations were asked to promote "these *declarations of principles*."[30]

These declarations had already been adopted in the 1908 ABA Canons, which was not mentioned by Seymour's committee. Canon 15 stated, "No fear of judicial disfavor or public unpopularity should restrain him from the full discharge of his duty." Canon 5 permitted a lawyer to represent a person "regardless of his personal opinion as to the guilt of the accused." All was not well, however, for guilt by association continued. For example, "counsel of outstanding reputations, well known for their anti-Communist views, in several recent cases involving Communists, or persons accused of being Communists, which they took out of sense of public duty, have been subjected to severe personal vilification and abuse." Similarly, in a late 1953 speech, Judge Irving R. Kaufman, who had presided over the 1951 espionage trial of Julius and Ethel Rosenberg, lamented the threat to the right to counsel. Kaufman declared that the "increasing reluctance of attorneys to defend" those accused of "crimes related to Communism" was "a serious threat to the integrity of our system of criminal justice."[31]

Despite this stuttering effort, the initial success of Seymour's committee took the wind out of the sails of the Special Committee on Communist Tactics. The latter stressed that anyone who invoked the Fifth Amendment privilege against self-incrimination was unfit to practice law; beyond that, it was uncertain how to proceed. The attorney general had not responded to the committee's urgings to ban unfit attorneys from federal practice, and only the Maryland Bar Association (where its chairman practiced) had agreed to investigate whether communists were practicing law. Most importantly, it reluctantly acknowledged its duty to protect Americans from "unjust and unfair accusation." Thus, it expressed "the hope that legal representation of the highest order will be available upon request to any accused person, even one alleged to be a Communist." As reported to the House of Delegates, the committee knew its first duty was "to be sure that no innocent lawyer or citizen is subjected to ill-considered charges."[32]

An *ABA Journal* editorial tried to bolster the position of the Special Committee on Communist Tactics. The House of Delegates had agreed that "grave doubt" existed about a lawyer's fitness to practice law after invoking the Fifth Amendment. A lawyer's place "of public trust and honor" was at risk in such cases. To invoke the privilege raised "the strongest sort of inference that he has been guilty of some reprehensible action from the consequences of which he would take shelter." It subsequently published a dissent, explaining that it offered "as good a case as we can imagine for resolving [the issue] in favor of the lawyer who invokes the shield of the Fifth Amendment." A year later, Harvard Law School dean Erwin Griswold published a small book explaining how and why an innocent person would invoke the privilege. Elite lawyer Telford Taylor also explained in a 1955 book why the phrase "Fifth Amendment Communists" was a non sequitur.[33]

In early 1954 Senator Joseph McCarthy was interviewed by *Newsweek* magazine. At the time, McCarthy was still powerful though was soon to fall. The article concentrated on McCarthy's responses to criticisms by Telford Taylor, a Nuremberg trials prosecutor. McCarthy suggested, in vague yet unsubtle terms, that Taylor's criticisms were influenced by his work "defending Communists." Taylor had represented labor leader Harry Bridges, whom the government was attempting to deport for allegedly lying about his Communist Party membership. ABCNY president Bethuel M. Webster defended Taylor, who was simply representing "unpopular clients" or "unpopular causes," quintessential professional actions of a lawyer. In fact, it was ABCNY policy to defend a lawyer's right to represent unpopular clients free from the public's assumption that the lawyer agreed with the client's views, character, or reputation.[34]

The Special Committee on Communist Tactics reiterated its views in 1954. A lawyer who invoked his Fifth Amendment privilege "as to possible communist affiliation or other subversive activities, thereby automatically disqualifies himself from the practice of the profession." This stance imploded in part because McCarthy's power abruptly ended.[35] McCarthy was condemned by the Senate in December 1954, and in early 1955 Telford Taylor's book *Grand Inquest* was published. It was a scathing attack on congressional efforts to claim that invoking the privilege against self-incrimination signaled criminality. As the Red Scare ebbed, unpopular clients found it easier to hire counsel.[36]

Income and Ethics

Though the Red Scare continued in reduced form through the early 1960s, its impact on lawyers was slight. For example, ABA president David Maxwell's 1957 address reframed the discussion of communism and American lawyers. Maxwell first praised the profession's "dedication to the public interest." He then criticized Supreme Court decisions that declared unconstitutional state efforts to use the requirement of "good moral character" to refuse to license bar applicants with communist ties. He was relatively dispassionate, for his address served as a critique rather than a "hysterical attack."[37]

A second example was incoming ABA president Charles S. Rhyne's speech. Rhyne bowed, promising to create a mandatory pledge for lawyers emphasizing the differences between communist and American ideals. He also promoted recognition of May 1 as Law Day, which symbolized those differences. Law Day was recognized, but the promise of a pledge was unkept.[38]

Most lawyers were worried about their economic prospects, not communism. The net income of lawyers and doctors was approximately the same in 1929. A 1953 study found that lawyers' income increased by 46 percent from 1929 to 1949, but this was dwarfed by the 125 percent increase enjoyed by doctors. Between 1953 and 1957, a drive increased ABA membership by 68 percent, from 52,624 to 88,396. Many of these new members desired assistance in building successful practices, which required both a steady clientele and, to a lesser extent, economic protection from nonlawyer competitors. From the 1930s, the Standing Committee on the Unauthorized Practice of Law had facilitated agreements with bankers, accountants, and others. These agreements protected the lawyer's economic territory, but they were always written with a nod to the profession's duty to protect the public interest. That committee, the self-appointed guardian of the boundaries of legal practice, supported this broader economic effort of the ABA. In 1957 it concluded, absent empirical evidence, "The biggest and most important problem facing the American Bar as a profession today is that of the unauthorized practice of law by laymen and by corporations." This problem put the public in harm's way, but if resolved, it had the knock-on effect of reducing competition for legal services. Rhyne's 1957 speech emphasized the need to help new ABA members, the "'grass roots' lawyers of the country." He recognized that pocketbook issues were primary and proposed a Special Committee on Economics of Law Practice, with "the duty of laying the groundwork for the development of practical suggestions to lawyers designed to improve their economic status." (A brief but sharp recession had just begun.) Future ABA president John C. Satterfield was named its chairman.[39]

The Special Committee on Economics investigated how to improve the profession's economic status. "Operation Check-up" consisted of four elements (ABA, state and local bar associations, individual lawyers, and clients) to increase the income of lawyers. It also demanded that states enforce their bans on laypersons practicing law. This was intended not to increase lawyers' income but to protect the interests of clients. The special committee's most important action was publication of *The 1958 Lawyer and His 1938 Dollar*.[40] More than 200,000 copies were printed the first year. Because the American lawyer population was about 262,000, this meant the pamphlet was available to nearly every lawyer in the country. The pamphlet's goal was "to ascertain the causes which have resulted in the failure of lawyers to maintain an economic status comparable to that of persons in other professions." In part, that failure was a product of the profession's "high ideals of ethics and of devotion to the public interest." Because of their devotion to others, lawyers failed to pay "sufficient regard to the mundane matters of business."[41]

The pamphlet's success led the committee to initiate an Economics of Law Practice series. The second pamphlet suggested that lawyers "should never permit the making of money to become paramount to the rendition of [public] service" and that "ethical standards of the profession should never . . . become subservient to selfish monetary motives." However, lawyers needed to take "drastic" action to increase their incomes. The pamphlet discussed pricing, including minimum fee schedules. And what should a bar association do if a lawyer consistently set fees below that schedule? It could charge the lawyer with violating Canon 12, which reminded members that they needed to make a living and therefore should avoid either overestimating or undervaluing their services. This solution assumed, without evidence, that the minimum fee correctly valued the lawyer's work. No one objected to this assertion, and minimum fees largely remained in place until they were held unconstitutional in 1975 (see chapter 6).[42]

These pamphlets renewed the ABA's interest in nonlawyer "encroachments" into the practice of law. In early 1961 the ethics committee issued Opinion 297, which concluded that a lawyer-accountant had violated Canon 27 on advertising. By accurately describing himself as both a lawyer and an accountant, he had engaged in unethical indirect advertising. Even though it was a significant stretch, the ABA reiterated this conclusion the following year. If a lawyer-accountant held himself out only as an accountant, he was permitted to engage in legal activities. This hair-splitting caused some consternation. What was the authority for this conclusion? In a subsequent informal opinion, the committee both stood its ground and refused to cite any legal authority, likely because none existed. The ABA reversed its dual practice ban in 1972.[43]

These beggar-thy-neighbor policies became less defensible as lawyers' annual income steadily increased—by 14 percent in 1961 and 10 percent in

1965. The ABA linked higher incomes with protecting the public interest. Future Supreme Court justice Lewis F. Powell Jr. declared, "It is plainly in the public interest that the economic health of the profession be safeguarded." The reason was self-evident: only an independent lawyer could protect an individual from the government, and only an economically secure lawyer could act as an independent lawyer.[44]

Legal Ethics in the Mid-1950s

In 1955, upholding the tradition that no good deed goes unpunished, the suggestion by McCoy and Phillips that the canons were out of date led to the creation of a special committee of the American Bar Foundation (ABF) to review them (the McCoy Committee, named for its chairman). The ABF was created in 1952 as a nonprofit entity and owned the building that housed the ABA and other legal organizations. After the Survey of the Legal Profession, the ABA outsourced some projects to special committees of the ABF, whose members were "appointed to supervise major research activities." One activity was "to determine first whether the American Bar Association's Canons of Ethics and Canons of Judicial Ethics required revision or restatement in the light of new conditions and, if so, the cost of a long-range, detailed report." The answer to the first question was affirmative. Powerful dissents were almost immediate. Drinker's ethics committee concluded that "no general revision of the Canons is now necessary or advisable." Drinker reiterated that conclusion in a 1958 letter to the ABF's board of directors. Philadelphia lawyer Robert McCracken made the same dissenting argument in the *ABA Journal*. The McCoy Committee persuasively argued that changes in the practice of law since 1908 necessitated a revision of the canons. It argued, "The problems discussed . . . demonstrate beyond any reasonable doubt that the Canons do not meet those standards." The dissenters claimed the practice of law was largely unchanged since 1937, when the ABA last amended the canons (see chapter 4). Drinker also argued that revising the canons would lessen the value of ABA ethics opinions by creating "obvious confusion." This was surely putting the cart before the horse. More importantly, surveyed lawyers desired continuity. Finally, the "basic ethical principles embodied in the Canons have not materially changed." This was an insufficient intellectual response to the McCoy Committee's findings. Both Drinker and McCracken were in their mid-seventies, and their backgrounds suggested more than an affinity for the status quo. Yet they got their way.[45]

The ABF's board of directors, all high-level ABA leaders, found the cost of revision too dear. The McCoy Committee produced a report after this decision in which it extensively discussed specific problems and explained the necessity for ethics reform. The report then largely disappeared. It was not published in book form and was not widely distributed in typed form; nor was it mentioned in the *ABA Journal* or in the ABA's *Annual Reports*.[46]

A December 31, 1959, letter by ABA insider James L. Shepherd Jr. suggested another reason the study was scrubbed. He claimed that its abandonment was a result of the committee's inability to agree on reforming Canon 35.[47]

Canon 35, "Intermediaries," had the laudable goal of protecting clients by barring the lawyer from taking orders from a lay intermediary instead of the client. But the canon's history was fraught with controversy, owing to its effect of undermining the work of commercial lawyers collecting debts (see chapter 4). By the 1950s, the canon was contentious due to its expansive reach. The ethics committee construed any intermediary as a threat to professional ideals. For example, Formal Opinion 270 declared that Canon 35 was violated if an anonymous lawyer wrote a newspaper column answering legal questions of general interest, even if the lawyer cautioned readers that the answers provided did not constitute legal advice and they should consult a lawyer should any legal problem arise. The newspaper was an intermediary that interfered with the personal relationship between an unknown lawyer and an unknown future client. A greater threat was group legal services plans. Some unions hired or recommended lawyers for its members, such as when a member needed assistance in making a workers' compensation claim. Many lawyers believed Canon 35 should permit group legal services plans, and the politically conservative Henry Drinker agreed. Unions "finding lawyers to advise their members" was part of a "modern trend." The "real reason" Canon 35 was applied was lawyer self-interest, a "loss of income to the lawyers." As Drinker drily noted, "These features do not commend the profession to the public." The McCoy Committee's 1958 report agreed. Still, the ABA opposed group legal services plans even after state bans on such plans were held unconstitutional in 1964.[48]

Drinker's view of the lawyer's duties was traditional and tradition minded. The primary "characteristics" distinguishing the practice of law from a business were duty of public service, duty to serve as an officer of the court, a fiduciary relationship with clients "in the highest degree," and a relationship with colleagues at the bar that made the lawyer unwilling "to resort to current business methods of advertising and encroachment on their practice." In this ordering of duties, Drinker announced the commonly stated view of elite practitioners. Earning an income was a secondary concern of lawyers, well behind the lawyer's duty to serve the public and the court. That extended to a type of noncompete agreement among lawyers: no poaching the clients of others. "Getting" and "keeping" clients, an essential activity of private-practice lawyers, was not discussed. Lawyers simply "had" clients. In their writings, elite lawyers ignored the pressure a client might exert on a lawyer to keep the client's business. The idea that duty to client and duty to court were sometimes irreconcilable was rarely contemplated, which may be at the root of Drinker's response. Drinker also believed a lawyer's ethical formation began and ended in a kind of will to rectitude, the tendency to follow what is "right," "irrespective" of any "law" on legal ethics.[49]

Another statement on ethics during the 1950s was made by the Joint Conference on Professional Responsibility. Published just two weeks after the McCoy Committee's report, this 1958 statement took a very different approach to matters of professional responsibility. It was a joint effort by the ABA and the Association of American Law Schools to assess professional responsibility through the lens of the nature of the lawyer's calling.

The ABA had asked its unauthorized practice committee to create a rule that states could adopt listing those eligible to practice law. This task proved too great, so the committee decided to pivot to the broader issue of professional responsibility. Why it did so, and why the ABA ethics committee did not object to this invasion of its territory, remain a mystery. The committee proposed a joint conference with the Association of American Law Schools. The conference was not connected with the ongoing survey and predated the ABF's McCoy Committee. The ABA may have thought it valuable to foster better relations with law professors, but the more likely explanation is that its prime proponents, John D. Randall Sr. and A. James Casner, were well-regarded ABA insiders.[50]

Randall served in a number of ABA roles, including Iowa's delegate in the House of Delegates and member or chairman of the unauthorized practice committee from 1946. Randall was elected 1959–1960 ABA president, when personal popularity was crucial to success. Harvard Law School professor A. James Casner had also been a member of the unauthorized practice committee, and he was appointed a member of the joint conference. Randall was named cochair of the Joint Conference, along with Joseph F. Rarick. Rarick was replaced by Harvard Law School professor Lon L. Fuller in 1955.[51]

The initial draft of the statement was written in 1953 by Columbia Law School professor Elliott Cheatham, a legal ethics scholar who was not a member of the Joint Conference. Fuller wrote the "second revised draft" in mid-1954, which created the framework for the published version. It was written during and in the aftermath of the Army-McCarthy hearings and included Fuller's assessment of why lawyers needed to represent "unpopular causes."[52]

Fuller argued that lawyers' willingness to represent the unpopular cause was always important, but it was most important when the public was right. Advocacy by a competent counsel gave the unpopular cause "its full day in court." That sense of fair play allayed any later suspicions about the court's decision and helped maintain the public's confidence in the "fundamental processes of government." The statement followed the traditional path by recognizing that the lawyer's duty to represent unpopular causes was one of "individual conscience"; the legal profession, in contrast, possessed a "clear moral obligation" to ensure that competent counsel represented unpopular defendants.[53]

After receiving comments, Fuller sent the May 2, 1955, "final" draft to the Joint Conference. This was the first draft to mention the canons, but it was only to remind lawyers that "a letter-bound observance" of the canons "is not equivalent to the practice of professional responsibility." Fuller amended this draft by expanding the explanation of "The Lawyer's Role as Advocate in Open Court" in the second, October 1, 1957, final draft. That draft was published in 1958.[54]

What distinguished the Joint Conference statement from other declarations of the lawyer's ethical duties were its approach and tone. The statement asserts that a lawyer's "work must find its direction within a larger frame." Joined by a "dedication" to the "ideals of his vocation," this allows the lawyer to learn how to "reconcile a fidelity to those he serves along with an equal fidelity to an office" that demands the lawyer act beyond self-interest. "When the lawyer fully understands the nature of his office," he becomes aware of the important social role he plays. As a result, the lawyer looks at the reasons that lie behind the lawyer's ethical "restraints," rather than at the restraints themselves.[55]

Fuller's level of generality in connecting the work of lawyers with its purposes and goals was unusual for this time. It avoided both mere platitudes and specific disagreements. It was not a framework for an ethics code. It did, however, examine the social and political purposes of the legal profession. By doing so, the statement offered a fresh starting point to reconsider the justifications of American lawyer ethics.

Two months after sending the 1955 draft to Joint Conference members, Fuller spoke to the American Institute of Electrical Engineers on the philosophy of ethics codes. He reflected on the necessity that a code of ethics take into account "general principles of social organization" and the "peculiar function which the profession in question performs in the total processes of society." The code had to have a broad "sense of mission" and had to "detail those conditions—including social arrangements and standards of individual behavior—that must be respected" to achieve that mission.[56]

The statement listed three broad roles the lawyer played in modern American society: (1) serving the administration and development of the law, (2) designing a framework giving direction and form to collaborative effort, and (3) generating opportunities and obligations of public service. Within those broad roles the statement then discussed specific activities, including the lawyer's work as an advocate in open court, as a counselor, and as a guardian of due process. Regarding the first, the statement explained the limits of zeal: in a positive sense, zealous representation "promotes a wise and informed decision of the case." The zealous lawyer plays this role badly "when his desire to win leads him to muddy the headwaters of decision."[57]

Much of the talk about reforming the canons focused on the particular. The statement reoriented that debate. Instead of endless discussions of Canon 35, society would be better served if lawyers reconsidered their mission. Most lawyers agreed their work had changed in the last twenty years. Change created an impetus to reshape a code of lawyer ethics in light of society's needs.

Despite Fuller's objection, Randall presented the statement for review in 1958, and it was adopted as official ABA policy the following February. Fuller never again wrote on lawyer ethics. Even so, the statement exerted a strong influence on the ABA's 1969 Code of Professional Responsibility.[58]

Civil Rights and the Duty of Representation

ABA president John C. Satterfield's 1962 farewell address was a long-winded excoriation of the Supreme Court. Its title, "*Law and Lawyers in a Changing World*," might more appropriately be changed to "The Destruction of the United States of America." Satterfield's denunciation of the Supreme Court was bolstered by a report of the Special Committee on Individual Rights as Affected by National Security, which he had packed. It attacked the Supreme Court through Satterfield's fellow Mississippian, the segregationist senator James Eastland.[59]

Taking a different tack was a report of the Standing Committee on the Bill of Rights. It noted the relationship between the profession's public responsibilities and the burgeoning civil rights movement. One aspect of this relationship was the ongoing difficulty of finding counsel to represent unpopular clients. Yale Law School dean Eugene Rostow's September 1961 talk to California lawyers triggered the committee's interest. Rostow encouraged his audience to "strengthen the professional independence of the Bar." One way to demonstrate such independence was for the legal profession to embrace (again) the principle that lawyers are duty-bound to represent unpopular causes and persons. Rostow noted not only cases against alleged communists but also "the cycle of cases asserting the rights of Negroes under the Fourteenth Amendment." The lawyer's duty to represent the unpopular cause was official ABA policy, adopted at the height of the Cold War.[60]

Just as Rostow's talk prompted the 1962 bill of rights committee's interest in defending the unpopular cause, that talk was prompted by the committee's 1961 report. It stated, "Complaints have come from different areas where accused persons have been deprived of right to counsel because of the refusal of members of the bar to represent discredited defendants or become involved in unpopular cases." It concluded, "persons under criminal charges in certain sections of the South have been deprived of their right to effective counsel because of the refusal of lawyers of the Caucasian race to appear in the defense of colored [*sic*] defendants." It also noted the likelihood that more "segregation problem" cases would arise. The 1961 report reiterated the ABA's "standing policy governing the responsibility of its members to which the lawyers in every community should adhere," and it reprinted the 1953 resolution.[61]

Rostow concluded, "A visible and effective program for carrying out the principle, as it was expressed in the American Bar Association's 1953

Resolution, could do more than any other single act to clarify public thought on the role of law and lawyers in society." He suggested adding this duty to the canons to keep "the problem more firmly in the foreground, both for lawyers and for bar associations."[62]

In spite of Rostow's talk, the committee offered only a modest affirmation of his proposals. It quoted the 1953 resolution and the ABA's recommended oath of admission, which obligated lawyers to represent the "cause of the defenseless and oppressed" no matter the personal cost. But its less than full-throated concern may have been revealed by another quotation at the beginning of the report: Canon 31 gave every lawyer "the right to decline employment." Further, the 1953 resolution provided limited value: It "recognizes the *group responsibility* of the profession, 'the duty of the bar,' to provide such aid, and the 'right' of the lawyer to defend in such causes without being penalized by public opinion." The report also discussed the results of a two-day meeting with representatives from the National Bar Association (created by African American lawyers after the ABA banned them from membership) and the National Lawyers Guild (lawyers on the political Left) about representing unpopular persons and causes. The conferees issued six findings, the first of which reemphasized the bar's group responsibility to "see to it that defendants in unpopular causes obtain competent counsel . . . [who] are not prejudiced or damaged by undertaking such representation when requested."[63]

Talk of representing the unpopular cause was common at the time. In 1961 Houston lawyer Leon Jaworski wrote a paean to five great lawyers who represented the unpopular cause. One oddity was the absence of any connection between past and present. A second oddity was that every lawyer gained prestige from representing the unpopular cause. Nothing bad happened. Jaworski's conclusion offered the old refrain: the lawyer's reward "is not measured by wealth or social position or popularity" but by the "inner satisfaction" of meeting one's "faithful discharge of duty." The point was so banal that even FBI director J. Edgar Hoover could endorse it.[64]

In March 1963 the Supreme Court held in *Gideon v. Wainwright* that everyone charged with a felony had a constitutional right to counsel, including the indigent. Two months earlier, the court had found that Virginia's laws regulating the practice of law and the solicitation of legal business were unconstitutional as applied to the NAACP. In the *Button* case, the solicitation of clients by the NAACP and the hiring of lawyers through its litigation arm, the Legal Defense and Education Fund Inc., were constitutionally protected.

These political entities were exercising First Amendment freedoms. Among other arguments, the court rejected Virginia's claim that school desegregation litigation violated Canon 35 because the NAACP might interfere with the relationship between lawyer and client. The court was more concerned with the fact that antidiscrimination lawsuits "are not an object of general competition among Virginia lawyers; the problem is rather one of an apparent dearth of lawyers who are willing to undertake such litigation." *Gideon* meant that every Black civil rights protester charged with a felony was entitled to legal representation. *Button* meant that some civil antidiscrimination lawsuits could be taken by lawyers without fear of disbarment for violating Canon 35. However, finding lawyers willing to participate in these matters was proving difficult, if not impossible, in some southern states.[65]

On June 21, 1963, President John F. Kennedy met with bar leaders, elite lawyers, and lawyers who worked in the civil rights field. Immediately afterward, Philadelphia lawyers Bernard J. Segal and Jerome Shestak, both future ABA presidents, organized many of the attendees and others into the Lawyers' Committee for Civil Rights under Law. The Lawyers' Committee's historian notes that ABA president Sylvester C. Smith Jr. was "wary of Kennedy's intentions." The ABA board of governors gave Smith permission to create a Special Committee on Civil Rights and Racial Unrest to respond to the public service responsibilities and challenges created by the civil rights movement. Smith named Walter Schweppe its chairman. Schweppe's appointment suggested ABA "resistance to [Kennedy's] civil rights legislation," but even so, the committee successfully proposed *another* reaffirmation of the lawyer's duty to represent unpopular causes and clients.[66]

Lawyers' duty to represent the unpopular cause did little, if any, good in 1963. In Mississippi that summer, "hundreds of activists who attempted to exercise their rights of free speech and association" were "unjustly" arrested, and "local lawyers refused to represent black activists." Schweppe's 1963 report stated, "No complaints have reached the Committee." How this could be possible was a mystery. Perhaps the committee made no inquiries and thus received no complaints. Plenty of evidence existed.[67]

The 1963 report of the bill of rights committee made no mention of the costs borne by lawyers who represented unpopular clients, particularly civil rights clients. These costs could be substantial. The legal practices of some lawyers withered, while others were subjected to campaigns to disbar them or to hold them in contempt for piffling reasons. Still others, along with their families, were threatened with violence. As a result, "the white southern lawyer acknowledges this hazard by backing out of the situation."[68]

During Freedom Summer in Mississippi in 1964 (an effort to register Black voters), members of the Lawyers' Committee met with Mississippi bar representatives concerning representation. (In 1964, of the more than two thousand practicing lawyers in Mississippi, only three or four were Black. This number tripled to twelve in 1968, and they faced the same challenge.) The two groups reached an agreement in mid-July. The board of commissioners of the Mississippi bar resolved that practicing Mississippi lawyers "will continue to be faithful and true to their duties and oaths in according to every person . . . , popular or unpopular, respected or despised, and regardless of race, color, creed or national origin, a fair and impartial trial, with assistance and protection, where sought, of competent counsel."[69]

A ten-year retrospective of the Lawyers' Committee's work concluded that the resolution was "an empty gesture." One volunteer in Mississippi privately offered examples of local lawyers avoiding or ignoring it. Members of the Lawyers' Committee had not accurately assessed the depth of the negative reaction of white Mississippians to the civil rights movement; nor had they fully understood "the threat of economic and physical reprisals against white lawyers who might consider stepping forward to help." On two occasions in 1964, in light of the resolution, white lawyers agreed to represent civil rights defendants. In one case, the "mere announcement that a respected attorney would represent a Black minister resulted in an end to the prosecution." This result was an outlier. Neither the Mississippi resolution nor the ABA's reaffirmation inclined lawyers to take on unpopular causes. Overall, an investigation by the United States Civil Rights Commission concluded, "there are no white lawyers in Mississippi who will ordinarily handle a civil rights case."[70]

In January 1965 the Lawyers' Committee decided to open a permanent office in Jackson, Mississippi. It would be staffed by at least two permanent lawyers, with volunteers moving in and out. They would represent civil rights defendants in criminal cases and initiate civil rights cases. The office's success depended largely on the acquiescence of the local bar because few, if any, of the Lawyers' Committee lawyers were licensed in Mississippi. The Lawyers' Committee agreed not to take cases generating attorneys' fees and to take the cases of unpopular clients. With these commitments, the Mississippi bar's board agreed that those lawyers could practice in the state.[71]

The Lawyers' Committee joined the NAACP Legal Defense and

Education Fund and the Lawyers Constitutional Defense Committee in representing Black Mississippians. On one occasion, all three organizations defended individuals arrested after a voting rights protest. White Mississippi lawyers provided no aid. Likely because the Lawyers' Committee included many elite lawyers with strong ABA ties, its presence nettled the Mississippi Bar Association. In late 1966 the bar complained that the Jackson office had violated the agreement on the practice of law and withdrew its consent allowing unlicensed lawyers to practice. The Lawyers' Committee continued on its own, often using large law firms to handle *pro bono publico* (for the public good) matters and using the federal courts (thus avoiding most licensure restrictions) to make its cases.[72]

Baltimore lawyer William Marbury complained in the *ABA Journal* that lawyers had not "lived up to what we nobly profess." He gave several examples in which no lawyer could be found to represent the unpopular cause. One reason the ordinary lawyer declined such cases was fear. And he concluded that it was too much to ask lawyers "to run the risk of social and professional ostracism the representation of the unpopular cause sometimes brings." Instead of exhortations or a return to the safety of the womb of platitudes, Marbury proposed an active bar association effort to fulfill this duty.[73]

Tactically, "massive resistance" may have succeeded for a time. Strategically, it was largely unsuccessful. White lawyers' refusal to represent civil rights activists neither ended the movement nor halted litigation implementing the Civil Rights Act (1964) and the Voting Rights Act (1965). Arguably, lawyer resistance simply redirected civil rights claims to public-interest law firms and, to a lesser extent, to the federal government's program of legal services for the poor created in 1965 by the Office of Economic Opportunity (see chapter 6).[74]

As massive resistance crumbled, the Great Society rose. It seems more than coincidental that ABA president Lewis F. Powell Jr., a Virginian, persuaded the House of Delegates to support the creation of a federal program of legal services for the poor. He linked support to the bar's commitment to public-spirited (thus professional) behavior. In return, the Office of Economic Opportunity committed to "maintaining traditional professional standards in providing legal services to the poor."[75]

Too Much and Not Enough: Zeal in Defense
of the Criminally Accused

In 1950 California lawyer Emil Gumpert created the American College of Trial Lawyers. Membership was limited, and it is unclear whether this was intended to be anything more than a drinking society. Eventually, it grew in stature and influence among civil defense lawyers, in part by recruiting ABA insiders. In 1956 the college adopted its *Code of Trial Conduct*. The preface noted that members "have a particular interest in maintaining high standards of professional conduct and deportment in the courtroom and hearing room." It congratulated itself on putting in print the first code of ethics for trial lawyers.[76]

The code began with the usual statements about the lawyer's duties to the client, opposing counsel, the court, and the administration of justice. The lawyer was exhorted to represent persons without fear of "public un-popularity" and to avoid "zeal." The code consisted of twenty-one manda-tory rules. Rules 3 and 4 specifically concerned the criminal defense lawyer. Both followed the pieties of the ABA Canons.

The lawyer was not permitted to offer knowingly false "testimony" and must avoid offering evidence "inconsistent" with the facts as stated by the confessedly guilty client. Additionally, the lawyer was not to present irrel-evant legal authorities. The code ignored the duty to disclose controlling legal authority unknown to the court and opposing counsel and harmful to one's client. It also ignored the duty of the lawyer when cross-examining a truthful witness. Overall, the standards reflected a complacent elite.[77]

One problem with this code was that it appeared to require criminal defense lawyers to judge their clients' credibility when making confidential disclosures. Even if not a confession, the lawyer had to determine whether the disclosure "clearly and credibly show[ed] guilt." If so, no evidence "in-consistent with those facts" should be offered. The proposed limits on crim-inal defense advocacy appeared to be more stringent than those proposed by George Sharswood in the mid-nineteenth century (see chapter 2).[78]

The "respectable bar" largely shunned the practice of criminal defense during the 1950s. University of Chicago Law School dean Edward Levi noted in 1952 that the workings of criminal law "have been insulated away from a large part of the bar." ABA president Robert Storey explained why: The "bar has never given sufficient attention to the problem of criminal jus-tice in America," and this is "because most of our lawyers practice civil law exclusively." In 1958 the National Association of Defense Lawyers in Criminal Cases was created largely to "meet the need for improving the image of the criminal defense lawyer and to upgrade the practice of criminal law." This need for improvement may have been because criminal law entailed desultory work too often occurring in a corrupt or corruptible environment. It paid poorly relative to other legal fields. And if few desired entry, the respectable bar feared those few were incompetent or venal.[79]

One criminal case offers some evidence of an absence of zealous representation. In 1952 two defendants were charged in Indiana with assault and battery with an intent to commit robbery. They were eventually provided one court-appointed attorney. The unnamed lawyer "advised them that if they pleaded guilty he could probably get" them a sentence of less than life. The defendants claimed they were innocent. Nevertheless, their attorney said that "unless they pleaded guilty there was nothing he could or would do for them." Despite his duty to represent them, "he had no intention of pursuing their interests any further." He kept his word and never appeared at the trial. Even so, the court insisted on proceeding. An unnamed Ohio attorney who had successfully represented a third defendant unwisely volunteered to represent the remaining defendants. The lawyer was game but ineffective. As the Seventh Circuit noted in issuing the writ of habeas corpus and granting them a new trial, "counsel, who was not admitted to practice before the courts of Indiana and who was apparently wholly unversed in Indiana law and practice, proceeded, without any preparation, to conduct petitioners' defense." The lawyer compounded his error when, after his clients' conviction, he "attempted to prosecute an appeal, but because of his ignorance of Indiana appellate procedure he failed to perfect the appeal and finally gave up." The convictions were eventually affirmed on direct appeal. The Seventh Circuit subsequently opined: "The record made by Ohio counsel in his defense of petitioners irrefutably demonstrates that he was so ignorant of Indiana law and procedure that it was virtually impossible for him to protect or even to assert petitioners' rights."[80]

This was not a straightforward case. A criminally accused defendant had no federal constitutional right to counsel. A 1960 study of lawyer incompetency found the result "unusual" and called it a rare instance in which "the representation afforded an accused by an attorney of his own choice may be so inadequate that his conviction should be set aside." The defendants had the choice of no lawyer or an unlicensed, incompetent lawyer. The Indiana courts had decided that this was sufficient, an unexceptionable conclusion.[81]

Arthur Wood was a sociologist who studied criminal defense lawyers beginning in 1951. His unpublished report was filed with the Survey of the Legal Profession in 1955 and updated and published in 1967. Wood found two distinct types of criminal defense lawyers: those who were largely unsuccessful in the practice of law and took criminal cases out of necessity, and those who found success in the drama of the trial and in "the intense satisfaction which comes from promoting" justice for the accused. Criminal law lacked both prestige and pay, and such lawyers were suspected of being unethical. Wood's survey found that about a third of the criminal defense lawyers he interviewed were concerned about the unethical behavior of lawyers, a higher proportion than all other lawyer types. Wood's most important conclusion was that both civil and criminal lawyers lacked concern about the unethical behavior of other lawyers. "It would seem that there is an element in the legal profession who deviate rather seriously from these [ethical] standards."[82]

A survey of Tulane Law School students in the aftermath of *Gideon v. Wainwright* found that many heeded these negative messages. They planned to avoid criminal defense for reasons of low pay and low status. Another reason, possibly peculiar to the South, was the possibility of "social ostracism" if one "vigorously defends Negroes charged with certain crimes."[83]

Although Judge J. Skelly Wright proclaimed "a return to acceptability" in criminal law practice in 1965, this was inaccurate. One law professor accused criminal defense lawyers of engaging in work "rife with unethical or dubious practices." A second argued that criminal defense work was less about professional behavior and more about "extralegal know-how that consists of jockeying cases before the right judge, copping a plea or making a deal." A medical doctor wrote about improving the "low status of the criminal bar." The cruelest conclusion was from a sociologist, who claimed that criminal defense lawyers practiced law as a "confidence game." They barely represented their clients at all, much less with zeal. Criminal defense lawyers were part of a bureaucracy; both prosecutors and defense counsel shared an interest in reaching a plea agreement to keep an overburdened criminal justice system from falling apart. This led the defense lawyer often to act as a "double agent," betraying the client's interests to protect the bureaucracy. The author found few visible examples of the traditional adversary system in criminal courts, and even those were largely for show: "The adversary features which are manifest are for the most part muted and exist even in their attenuated form largely for external consumption."[84]

The ABA initiated a massive project on minimum standards for criminal justice in 1964. The decade-long project offered a series of what are now called "best practices," including standards created in 1971 for prosecutors and defense counsel. In 1970 the Supreme Court clarified its interpretation of *Gideon* and the Sixth Amendment right to counsel: such counsel was required to be "effective." In the meantime, the Supreme Court's ongoing constitutional criminal procedure revolution made knowledge of constitutional law imperative for every criminal defense lawyer. The court's decisions necessitated not only more professionally knowledgeable criminal lawyers but also many more of them. According to a report of the 1966 Airlie Conference on Legal Manpower Needs of Criminal Law, at a minimum, an additional four thousand to six thousand criminal defense lawyers were needed. With the oldest baby boomers still in college, it was unclear where those lawyers would come from.[85]

Greater competence implicitly suggested greater zeal in representing the accused. How far did that zeal extend? Monroe Freedman, a professor of law at George Washington University, concluded that it extended quite far. In 1966 he posed the "three hardest questions" of criminal defense ethics, each of which challenged the perceived limits of adversarial zeal. First, was it ethically permissible to cross-examine a witness to discredit that witness when the defense lawyer knew the witness was testifying truthfully? Second, was it proper to put a witness on the stand when the lawyer knew the witness would commit perjury? Third, was it ethically permissible to give the accused legal advice when the lawyer believed that advice would tempt the accused to commit perjury? Freedman answered yes to each of these questions.[86]

Freedman believed the lawyer's special responsibility lay in achieving the aims of the adversary system. A lawyer could best represent a client when that client spoke truthfully to the lawyer about the facts of the case. If a lawyer failed to test the credibility of a witness known to be truthful, the lawyer was acting contrary to the aims of the adversary system. The hardest question was whether to offer the testimony of a witness, including the accused, if the lawyer knew (or predicted) the witness would commit perjury. The lawyer's duty to keep confidences inviolate required him to allow such testimony, for a client-centered approach meant that the client made the final decision regarding who testified, not the lawyer. This question was "most difficult" because it suggested the lawyer was "encouraging and condoning perjury." This was not true: the lawyer was merely giving legal information to a client, who "is entitled to" it, and allowing the client "to make his own decision as to whether to act upon it." Freedman offered an ethic of advocacy similar to that proposed by Charles Curtis, although he mentions Curtis only glancingly. Freedman explicitly rejected Lon Fuller's understanding of the adversary system as declared in the 1958 statement of the Joint Conference. He did not discuss Fuller's 1961 essay on the adversary system, which concluded, "Obviously, [the lawyer] may not participate in the fabrication of testimony."[87]

The immediate response to Freedman's argument was an effort by several judges (including future chief justice Warren Burger) to disbar him or suspend his license. After an onerous number of proceedings, the effort failed. As an intellectual matter, an immediate response by John Noonan used the statement of the Joint Conference to reject Freedman's conclusions. Noonan first contended that, given the effort to make the modern trial a "rational" process, attacking the credibility of a truthful witness exhibited a kind of paternalism with regard to the jury's ability to reach the correct verdict. Second, if a trial was both rational and intended to reach a "wise and informed decision," offering perjurious testimony was "to mock impartiality, to mislead rather than to inform, and to stultify the decision process." Third, the lawyer's "belief" assumed a future action by the client, and again, the lawyer should avoid such paternalistic behavior toward the client. Noonan noted that both the Joint Conference's statement and Freedman's own analysis urged lawyers not to act paternalistically toward their clients, which made Freedman's argument contradictory. Finally, attorney-client confidentiality was not an absolute. Freedman's decision to make it so, and to elevate it above all other values, was wrong. The premise was that absolute confidentiality was a necessary aspect of the adversary system. Noonan argued that this proposition was untrue as a legal-historical matter and as a jurisprudential matter. Historically, if a client informed his lawyer he intended to commit a future crime, the lawyer could be forced to testify about that conversation. Jurisprudentially, both client confidences and the adversary system existed pragmatically in the service of particular "social needs," not as absolutes. These pragmatic instruments were intended to aid in the "formulation of wise and informed decisions," decisions based on rational reasons. A second rejoinder noted that Freedman actually never answered his second question but only a subset of that question: what if the lawyer knows the accused is going to testify falsely?[88]

Freedman's views on offering false testimony were an outlier; his views on cross-examining the truthful witness and providing legal advice that might lead to perjury, much less so. At a 1966 panel discussion about how to defend a man accused of rape when counsel either knew or suspected he was guilty, most of the panelists considered Freedman's views and largely limited them. For the most part, they adopted the need for zealous advocacy that Freedman embraced. Among the panelists was Warren Burger, who was the least inclined to define zeal broadly, and he neither cited nor explicitly referred to Freedman. Burger rejected the presentation of "false testimony," based on a centuries-old rule. On attacking the credibility of a truthful witness, Burger resorted to both the "private conscience" of the lawyer and the view that an officer of the court should not "pervert or prostitute his powers." The District of Columbia Legal Aid director believed it was improper but defensible to advise a client about the law before learning the facts (citing Freedman) and approved of cross-examining a truthful witness because doing so is "one means of putting the government to its proof." That panelist said he would attempt to withdraw if his client did not take his advice and planned to perjure himself on the witness stand. But if the client took the stand and withdrawal was not possible, he would examine the client as usual and would not disclose the perjury to the court. He also answered Freedman's second question: other than the defendant, he would not call a witness he knew intended to commit perjury.[89]

Burger led the ABA Advisory Committee on the Prosecution and Defense Function until he became chief justice in 1969. By then, most of its work was finished. The ABA formally approved the 1970 draft "Prosecution and Defense Function Standards" in early 1971. The introduction to the "Defense Standards" began, "Few subjects in the administration of criminal justice are more in need of clarification than the role of the defense lawyer in a criminal case." It then implicitly rejected Freedman's perjury argument, noting it has been "universally rejected by the legal profession, that a lawyer may be excused for acquiescing in the use of known perjured testimony on the transparently spurious thesis that the principle of confidentiality requires this." It followed up with Rule 7.5(a), which characterized a lawyer's knowing offer of false evidence as disciplinary misconduct. Rule 7.6(b) declared that the lawyer should not "discredit or undermine a witness" on cross-examination if the lawyer "knows the witness is testifying truthfully." The phrase "should not" indicated that such action was not the subject of discipline but a matter of professional discretion. Finally, the lawyer was prohibited from counseling a client to engage in illegal conduct but duty-bound to inform the client of "the meaning, scope and validity of a law." As the ABA revised the standards, the turn toward Freedman's positions became more pronounced (see chapter 6).[90]

The standards emphasized that the "primary role of [defense] counsel is to act as champion for his client," and a champion needed to exercise both "courage and zeal." The emphasis on zeal occurred as the role of criminal defense lawyers was challenged on the political Left. Ideas such as lawyerly "detachment" were denounced by self-styled radical lawyers as "a hoax and as the graveyard of any hope of social transformation." Instead of defending the case, the radical lawyer argued the cause. The client's "politics should be [the lawyer's] prime concern."[91]

This was anathema to most lawyers. The mainstream counterargument was that a detached but zealous advocacy was the paradigmatic example of demonstrating client loyalty. This argument both rejected the claims of radical lawyers and urged greater professionalism by criminal defense lawyers. These lawyers were essential when they zealously guarded their clients' rights, for protecting clients' rights protected all from the Leviathan state.[92]

Sociological Investigations into the Practice of Law

Arthur Wood's 1951 study was the first sociological investigation of the American legal profession. Others followed. During the 1960s a number of published studies concluded that more than an "infinitesimal number" of lawyers ignored or violated the ABA Canons.

Lawyer-sociologist Jerome Carlin's study of sole practitioners in Chicago included a chapter on the "ethical dilemmas of individual practice." He noted the "sharp conflict" between the canons and the "practical demands" of practice. The sharpest conflict involved getting clients. It was nearly impossible to survive as a sole practitioner without violating the canons proscribing the solicitation of work. A second problem was the bureaucracy of the justice system. Carlin reported that more than "two out of three lawyers interviewed" admitted purchasing "favors from clerks." Others paid administrative officials to resolve disputes on tax assessments, zoning issues, and the like. A third issue was lawyers' failure to act as their clients' fiduciaries. In personal injury, tax and collections, divorce, and criminal law, lawyers viewed clients as "expendable," particularly when they were obtained through referral. It was not the client but the referring party the

lawyer wanted to please. Sole practitioners also faced the opposite problem: the client as partner. The lawyer who joined his client in business deals
and investments often lacked detached independence. Carlin concluded,
"There are some very unpleasant facts about the way in which the practice
of law is being carried on today . . . and there are some hard decisions to be
made as to what should be done about these problems." The review in the
ABA Journal found Carlin's critique "devastating," "eye-opening," and "soul-
searching." The reviewer wondered whether lawyers at large firm "as freely
skirted and broke" the canons as sole practitioners did.[93]

Erwin Smigel's answer in *The Wall Street Lawyer* (1964) was "no." Informal, external professional rules framed the lawyer-client relationship. A
lawyer had to remain emotionally detached from the client to make decisions that were not "based on the self-interest of the professional" and to
perform work with professional excellence. The author later noted some
lawyers' concern that law was becoming a business and quoted one experienced lawyer who attributed this situation to "a drive for money not
just among the lawyers but among their business clients." This led clients
to "pressure the lawyer." This pressure meant the difference between lawyer and client was simply that one had "a special degree." Otherwise, both
were "businessmen." Smigel's answer might have surprised elite lawyer Hoyt
Moore's prosecutors (see chapter 4) and Wall Street lawyer and author Louis
Auchincloss, whose 1956 novel *The Great World and Timothy Colt* showed
exactly how lawyers at large firms could cut ethical corners. One review was
skeptical of Smigel's implicit conclusion that such firms "have higher ethical
standards than those with fewer members."[94]

Carlin returned in 1966 to study the ethical behavior of New York City
lawyers. He interviewed 801 lawyers in Manhattan and the Bronx. He found
that 22 percent of small-firm lawyers and 26 percent of sole practitioners
accepted neither the ethical norms of the bar nor any higher norms, compared with just 5 percent of large-firm and 18 percent of medium-firm lawyers. Carlin then studied whether these lawyers adhered to ethical norms
(regardless of whether they said they accepted such norms). On thirteen
items, adherence ranged from 25 to 89 percent. Professional status, including type of clientele and type of court or agency in which the lawyer usually appeared, differentiated the lawyer's acceptance of, and adherence to,
ethical norms. Lawyers with low-status clients had more competition for
clients and thus less secure legal practices. These factors, Carlin concluded,
were why such lawyers were most likely to violate ethical norms. Low-status

lawyers exploited their clients more often, and were exploited by their clients more often, than high-status lawyers. The reason was opportunity.[95]

"An unscrupulous lawyer can burn his client alive," reported one interview subject. Carlin found that a lawyer's inner ethical disposition "makes a considerable difference in his response to situational pressures, and consequently in his capacity to conform to ethical standards." When an internal disposition was combined with external pressure to adhere to ethical standards, the lawyer, whether high or low status, was much less likely to violate those standards. As noted in the foreword by Geoffrey C. Hazard Jr., Carlin offered "persuasive evidence that many lawyers do not consistently adhere to the standards of ordinary honesty, still less to the special professional rules in the canons of legal ethics." Though not "all lawyers are crooks," the bar's assessment that "the overwhelming majority" of lawyers are "ethical in the strict sense" was "not true." Carlin's was not among the more than 130 books reviewed in the *ABA Journal* that year.[96]

Three sociolegal studies of the legal profession were published in 1967. Wood's *Criminal Lawyer* was not reviewed in the *ABA Journal*, but another book that evaluated the work of American and English lawyers was reviewed. Among the authors' many conclusions was a list of recommendations to improve the ABA Canons and thus the behavior of lawyers. The reviewer paid no attention to those recommendations and instead criticized the authors for not understanding the ABA's limits as a volunteer organization. This criticism occurred as an ABA special committee was working on a new code of professional responsibility designed to serve as law once it was adopted by the states.[97]

The third study, *The Lawyer and His Community*, evaluated lawyers in a middle-sized city in the Midwest. Joel Handler used the same ethics examples and questionnaire as Carlin. The good news for the profession was that the so-called Prairie City lawyers were much more likely to accept and adhere to rules of ethical conduct than were New York City lawyers. However, because Prairie City lawyers had much less opportunity than New York City lawyers to engage in ethical misconduct, it was unclear whether the Prairie City lawyers were actually more ethical than their metropolitan counterparts or whether they simply had fewer occasions to test their ethical boundaries. In one example, a lawyer learns from the district attorney that the prosecution's evidence is so weak that the lawyer's client is unlikely to be convicted in an assault case. The lawyer withholds this information from the client for fear that the client will stop paying installments on the fee he owes the lawyer. In that situation, more Prairie City lawyers (36 percent) than New York City lawyers (30 percent) said they would not disclose the information to the client (i.e., act unethically). Three times more Prairie City lawyers than New York City lawyers had been exposed to that situation (20 percent versus 7 percent). On this issue Prairie City lawyers were more likely than New York lawyers to engage in such unethical conduct but not three times more likely to act unethically. Unanswered was whether the profession's local culture or the local culture of the community made any difference in whether the lawyer adhered to ethical standards. Overall, Handler concluded that the conditions in Prairie City were "optimum" in terms of allowing lawyers to place "service and fiduciary obligations to clients, colleagues, and the administration of justice above economic self-interest." The *ABA Journal* reviewer panned the book.[98]

The Code of Professional Responsibility

In 1964 ABA president Lewis Powell proposed the creation of a Special Committee on Evaluation of Ethical Standards. Why he did so is unknown. He was aware of the failed 1957 effort.[99]

It may have been the zeitgeist: Drinker was no longer a threat to reform, the State Bar of Texas had started to amend its canons, and the American College of Trial Lawyers had amended its Code of Trial Conduct in 1963. Melvin Belli called the 1964 trial and guilty verdict of Jack Ruby (killer of Kennedy assassin Lee Harvey Oswald) the "biggest kangaroo-court disgrace in the history of American law." Belli's comments to the press throughout the case were criticized by lawyers as unethical and as harmful to the constitutionally based fair trial standards. This may have been the lever to renew the debate.[100]

Additionally, in the insular world of bar leaders, a consensus existed that something must be done. John Randall had considered ethics reform during his 1959–1960 term as ABA president. Both Randall and Powell were members of the American College of Trial Lawyers when it amended its code, and the former was on its code committee. Sherman Welpton was prominent in writing both the initial and amended college codes. He worked in the same law firm as Homer Crotty, who was on Randall and Fuller's Joint Conference statement committee.[101]

Another possibility was hubris. ABA president Walter Craig's 1964 address made grand claims. He argued that lawyers were not just leaders in society; they were the true leaders of the United States. The nation's survival did not rest solely on the military or technology but "equally" on the people. And in society, no entity was "better equipped . . . than the members of the legal profession to assert the leadership required to instill among our people that moral and intellectual courage necessary to the survival of the philosophy of the rule of law and freedom under law." But because even lawyers were not angels, this power given to lawyer-leaders might be channeled by an updated ethics code.[102]

A more prosaic reason may have been the Supreme Court's recent decisions affecting the legal profession. In addition to the *Gideon* and *Button* cases in 1963, it decided *Brotherhood of Railroad Trainmen* in April 1964, holding unconstitutional on First Amendment grounds the Virginia bar's claim that the union was engaged in the unlawful solicitation of litigation and the unauthorized practice of law. The decision threatened Canon 35, which attacked lay intermediaries such as unions. Powell was an elite Virginia lawyer.[103]

The initial jurisdiction of the Special Committee on Evaluation of Ethical Standards was narrow: "There is certainly no thought of starting out to rewrite *de novo* the ethical standards of the legal profession." Powell then contradicted Drinker's 1958 claim, arguing that, "in view of the changed conditions since 1908 and the experience of the past half-century, the time has surely come for the American Bar Association to take a careful look at this critical area of our responsibility." The House of Delegates made only one slight amendment, calling for the drafting of a code "to encourage and maintain *the highest level* of ethical standards by the legal profession."[104]

The twelve members of the Wright Committee, named after chairman Edward L. Wright of Little Rock, Arkansas, first met on October 15, 1964. Michigan lawyer Glenn Coulter, Sherman Welpton, and A. James Casner each offered lengthy and detailed suggestions. At its second meeting, the Wright Committee realized it needed "professional help" and reached out to Professor John F. Sutton Jr., who agreed to serve as its reporter. Sutton had served as chairman of the 1962 committee that proposed amendments to the Texas Canons of Ethics. Geoffrey C. Hazard Jr. sent a letter to Wright explaining the committee's job. Hazard was executive director of the American Bar Foundation and would become a leader in legal ethics thinking. Drafting the code was the reporter's job. The committee was "to provide commentary and guide lines for his research effort."[105]

Even after this admonishment, the committee pushed a proposal limiting group legal services. Casner worried about the consequences of *Brotherhood of Railroad Trainmen*. He believed in a broad ethical ban on soliciting business, which both *Brotherhood* and *Button* threatened. His efforts eventually resulted in the adoption of Canon 3, "A Lawyer Should Assist in Preventing the Unauthorized Practice of Law." Canon 3 would generate a host of problems for the ABA in the early 1970s (see chapter 6).[106]

Casner also shaped the code's structure. He organized the forty-seven canons into ten categories and suggested reframing the canons from "thou-shalt-nots" to positive statements. Sutton's "second draft" was sent to the committee in October 1965. At the first meeting he attended, Sutton had suggested a tripartite structure, and in his letter to the committee he urged that it begin with the "indicative principles" of lawyer ethics, which was the "truly ethical level" lawyers should seek. This approach avoided the error of stressing "peremptory rules." The second draft began with twelve canons, after each of which Sutton listed "what is now labeled the ethical considerations." In 1967 the committee voted to eliminate ethical considerations from the code but allowed Sutton to continue working on them, as they would be printed separately.[107]

Wright insisted that the committee work out of sight until it was ready to publish a preliminary draft. The committee tantalized the House of Delegates by filing a report in 1966 indicating that a draft was only a year away. This promise was not kept, possibly due to the disagreement concerning the role of ethical considerations in the code.[108]

The October 1968 tentative draft was sent to 550 lawyers. It consisted of two parts: The canons followed by disciplinary rules, and the canons followed by "Ethical Considerations Underlying the Code of Professional Responsibility." Its preamble made a case for the ethical considerations as the heart of the code: to fulfill his professional responsibilities, a lawyer "should be guided by these Ethical Considerations." Further, lawyers should understand that the ethical considerations "are not nine unrelated discourses but are nine chapters in a single statement." Several found this division "awkward" and suggested merging them. The committee unanimously agreed.[109]

The January 15, 1969, preliminary draft was sent to twenty thousand lawyers. Its preface explained why a revision was insufficient. The canons were outdated, often poorly written, and omitted important issues of lawyer conduct. After receiving hundreds of comments, a final draft, altered in some important respects from the preliminary draft, was presented to the

House of Delegates. It adopted the proposed Code of Professional Responsibility without amendment at its 1969 annual meeting.[110]

Both the preliminary draft and the adopted code presented nine canons as "axiomatic principles." Each canon was followed by ethical considerations that were "aspirational in character and represent the objectives toward which every member of the profession should strive." Finally, the code listed disciplinary rules for each canon. The rules, unlike the ethical considerations, were "mandatory in character."[111]

Lon Fuller played no known role in the code's creation, but he influenced its structure and substance. Structurally, Fuller's influence is visible "in the Code's differentiation of duties and aspirations." Sutton took Fuller's view of law as comprising two moralities—one of aspiration and one of duty—and used them to create the ethical considerations and disciplinary rules. The aspirational ethical considerations came before the mandatory disciplinary rules, which were stated in terms of what Casner called "thou-shalt-nots." Fuller's two moralities were the subject of his 1963 Storrs lectures at Yale, published as *The Morality of Law*. Sutton said that book was one of the two most influential writings in his drafting of the code, and he hoped adopting Fuller's distinction would "eliminate the confusion between moral exhortation and enforceable obligation." Substantively, the code reflected a number of ideas from the statement of the Joint Conference. For example, Ethical Consideration (EC) 8–1 of Canon 8 stated that lawyers should work to improve the system "without regard to the general interests or desires of clients or former clients." The preamble cited the Joint Conference statement for its adoption of ethical considerations as both "objectives toward which every" lawyer should strive and principles on which a lawyer could rely. The statement was cited eight times in Canon 7, concerning the zealous representation of clients, and more than twenty times throughout the code, more than any other source. Sutton said, "The upper echelon of the ABA was extremely proud of the *Joint Conference Report* and wanted it referred to."[112]

EC 7–1 quoted the statement: if "the man with an unpopular cause is unable to find a competent lawyer courageous enough to represent him," a government of laws is at risk. More broadly, the code connected the rule of law with the actions of lawyers, supporting this assertion by citing the quoted statement. One important change between the preliminary and final drafts was the addition of Disciplinary Rule (DR) 7–102(B). In spirit, it followed the statement quoted in EC 7–1, but in practice, it was an exception to the duty to keep client confidences. If the lawyer "receives information clearly establishing" the client has "perpetrated a fraud," the lawyer must tell the client to rectify the harm caused by the fraud, and if the client refuses to do so, the lawyer "shall reveal the fraud." This exception was premised on the belief that the adversary system was perverted if a lawyer kept secret a client's fraud. It was attacked in the 1970s, as the profession's formal statements of zealous advocacy changed (see chapter 6).[113]

After just three years, forty-three states and the District of Columbia had adopted most or all of the code as law. A mere half decade later, ABA president William B. Spann Jr. created a new special committee on lawyer ethics, which scrapped the tripartite division and replaced it with disciplinary rules. Sutton's reflections on the code's brief life noted that its adoption "was essentially a political one." To win approval in the House of Delegates, the Wright Committee bent to tradition. The code was adopted without amendment because no one wanted to rock the boat.[114]

Sutton highlighted a number of examples of this traditional bias, which made the code "at worst obstreperous and obstructionistic." One example was group legal services. Traditionalists perceived *Brotherhood of Railroad Trainmen* and its progeny as both an economic and an ideological threat to lawyers. The one amendment proposed in the House of Delegates was about moving on from this hidebound view. It failed. The limits on group legal services were in Canon 2, "A Lawyer Should Assist the Legal Profession [in] Fulfilling Its Duty to Make Legal Counsel Available." EC 2–16 noted the lawyer's duty to serve the poor, EC 2–26 suggested that a lawyer not decline employment "which may be unattractive to him and the bar generally," and EC 2–27 favorably recalled lawyers "who have represented unpopular clients and causes" and urged that their example be followed. The disciplinary rules, in contrast, followed tradition and condemned all advertising. Judith Maute wrote, "In ironic contrast to Canon 2's titular focus on access to counsel, most of its disciplinary rules restricted permissible communications between lawyers and their prospective clients and group legal services."[115]

The code was qualitatively better than the canons, making it easy for states to switch. It was also easier to do so during economic good times, as lawyers' median real income kept rising—faster than the economy as a whole. This golden age was, however, at an end. During harder times, critics more closely examined the imperfections and self-interested provisions of the code. It was an easy target. The Wright Committee sought to maintain the highest standards of ethical conduct, but the code did not meet this nearly impossible standard, as a rueful Sutton knew.

Conclusion

Two weeks before his eightieth birthday, John D. Randall Sr., coauthor of the Joint Statement on Professional Responsibility with Lon Fuller, became the only former ABA president to be disbarred. The Iowa Committee on Professional Ethics and Conduct charged Randall with violating the Iowa Code of Professional Responsibility for Lawyers by writing a will naming himself as the sole beneficiary of another's estate and by representing that same client in litigation in which he and the client had a conflict of interest. The board recommended Randall's disbarment with no opportunity for reinstatement. The Iowa Supreme Court agreed. Randall unsuccessfully petitioned the Supreme Court of the United States to review his disbarment.[116]

The facts were complicated and the law ambiguous, but Randall was an unsympathetic defendant. His fall from grace was a warning to Iowa lawyers: not even a former ABA president was untouchable.

In disbarring Randall, the Iowa Supreme Court declared that a violation of the ethical considerations subjected him to discipline, for the considerations were "part and parcel" of the law. Had it not listened to Sutton? Iowa's Code repeated verbatim the ABA Code's preliminary statement. It ignored the intentional distinction between duties and aspirations.[117]

The Eighth Circuit's opinion disbarring Randall in federal court was less coherent. Randall offered evidence that, being a past ABA president, he was a target. The opinion noted and dismissed this contention, seemingly because Randall was unrepentant concerning his misconduct. The Eighth Circuit also incorrectly stated the law. It adopted Iowa's ethics code, then confused the duties demanded by the canons with the aspirations of the ethical considerations, calling them ethical *canons*.[118]

Lawyers claimed an outsized role in leading society in the aftermath of World War II. That claim was an important justification for creating the Code of Professional Responsibility. Americans needed lawyers to act as society's guardians and protect the rule of law, which "makes justice possible." To fulfill these roles, lawyers needed to reach for the "highest standards" of ethical conduct. Serving as guardian of the law was a moral undertaking, and that meant drafting a code that grappled with moral issues in the practice of law. The ethical considerations were intended to prompt lawyers to question their "relationship with and function in our legal system." A system in which lawyers bore such great responsibility required every lawyer to "find within his own conscience the touchstone

against which to test the extent to which his actions should rise above minimum standards."[119]

On December 28, 1983, Randall died. His obituary in the local paper
called him a "retired lawyer." It may be true that in Cedar Rapids, where
John Randall spent his professional life, disbarment wasn't the cruelest
blow. As the code's preamble declared, "The possible loss of that respect
and confidence [in the community] is the ultimate sanction." Randall's heirs
urged well-wishers to donate money to the Presbyterian Church or to the
American Bar Endowment. Randall's love for the ABA remained, but it was
unrequited. The ABA memorialized important members who had died the
previous year. Randall was not among them.[120]

CHAPTER SIX

Beginning and Ending, 1970–1983

On May 1, 1970, the Association of the Bar of the City of New York (ABCNY) continued its centennial celebration with a symposium titled "Is Law Dead?" ABCNY members accepted the "vibrancy of law," but others "all over America" disagreed. Symposium speakers asked whether the ABCNY's "premise, faith in law and in the value of trying to mold it and its institutions to fit the needs of a changing society, was still valid." Most speakers proclaimed their continued membership in the church of law.[1]

May 1 is Law Day in the United States. It was created by the American Bar Association (ABA) in 1958 (and subsequently enacted into law) to distinguish democratic governance based on the rule of law from totalitarian governments such as the Soviet Union's. The ABCNY's May 1 defense of a faith in law was symbolically significant.[2]

Friday, May 1, 1970, was the day after President Richard Nixon publicly announced an American ground invasion of Cambodia. This news sparked large and continuing May Day protests, including one that, three days later, ended with National Guardsmen killing four students at Kent State University in Ohio.[3]

One of those many protests involved a group of lawyers denouncing the "Amerikan" system of justice in New York City. This was a reprise of the May 1, 1969, protests in Manhattan, where nearly two hundred lawyers gathered to counter "the platitudes about this 'reaffirmation' of the concept of justice." The 1970 lawyer protests mushroomed to eight cities, "despite the failure of the mass media to publicize" them. The following May Day, "over two thousand lawyers amassed again in New York, protesting the war and ... demanding changes in the legal system."[4]

Other lawyers perceived this deep-seated criticism of the American legal system by movement, New Left, and other lawyers as an attack on them.

This attack threatened a foundational plank of the profession: lawyers were accorded power to ensure that justice was done. The public was protected from abuse of that power by ethics codes. Lawyer behavior was channeled for the public's benefit to preserve a faith in law. If that premise was false, ethics rules harmed the public.

For most lawyers, the beginning of the decade was an optimistic time. Median lawyer income, adjusted for inflation, was higher than it had ever been, and lawyer income inequality was low. Lawyers earned substantially more than ordinary workers. Demand outstripped supply, and the need for legal services expanded. A modest few of the oldest baby boomers had entered the profession by 1970, and it appeared largely united and self-congratulatory regarding its important public service. By mid-1972, most states had adopted the ABA's 1969 Code as enforceable law, ordinarily with few substantive changes. The profession responded to remedy the "scandalous situation" of an abysmal lawyer disciplinary system, and all but a handful of states had adopted a more stringent disciplinary system by mid-1973. The ABA's Criminal Justice Standards Relating to the Prosecution Function and Standards Relating to the Defense Function (1971) were well received as best ethical and professional practices. An impotent judicial discipline system was also reformed through the states' adoption of the ABA Code of Judicial Conduct (1972). Finally, Congress created the Legal Services Corporation (LSC) in mid-1974, funding legal services for the poor.

The New Left's challenge was a relatively minor threat to most American lawyers. But a major threat soon followed: the income of nonelite lawyers representing individuals began a long fall. Although legal services increased as a percentage of gross domestic product throughout the 1970s, most of that growth was fueled by business organizations. Income inequality among lawyers rose, and the income premium lawyers enjoyed fell sharply. One September 1972 prediction was that "the outlook for lawyers is grim." The supply of lawyers ballooned, increasing by 75 percent from 1970 to 1983. In 1972–1973 the number of law students exceeded 100,000 for the first time and continued to grow through the early 1980s. Nonelite lawyers competed for work in unfavorable conditions. Another blow was the public's declining trust in lawyers caused by widely publicized scandals, the most prominent of which was Watergate. The states' widespread adoption of the ABA Code of Professional Responsibility failed to assuage public concern. In late 1977 the ABA decided to "evaluate" the code, essentially abandoning it less than a decade after its adoption. The ABA's six-year effort to draft model rules of professional conduct laid bare a fractured profession. When the ABA adopted new rules in 1983, lawyers agreed only that they disagreed about their profession.[5]

In 1981 ABA president David R. Brink wrote of the profession's "change and challenge." He concluded, "The practice of law changed more in [the 1970s] than in the entire preceding century." One overriding reason was that lawyers were now "operating in a more free market for legal services." Another writer noted that the provision of legal services had gone from a "bar-regulated delivery system to a market-regulated one." This shift generated tension between claims of ethical constraints and earning a living in a buyer's market.[6]

At the time of Brink's article, the brutal debate on the model rules was well under way. It offered a clear sign of the unraveling of a unified profession. ABA membership began its long decline, a harbinger of things to come.[7]

The "Hired Gun" and "I Am Not a Lawyer for Hire. I Only Defend Those I Love"

The concept of the lawyer as a client's "hired gun" was first expressed in a legal publication in January 1970. Professor John Griffiths noted this "common aspersion" of criminal defense lawyers. It soon became a popular characterization of a certain type of courtroom lawyer. In a 1973 case involving Griffiths's wife, Fre Le Poole, Chief Justice Warren Burger wrote of the "erosion" of the lawyer as officer of the court and the adoption of metaphors such as "hired gun" and "mouthpiece." In an influential 1974 speech to the ABCNY, Judge Marvin Frankel concluded, "We should face the fact that the quality of 'hired gun' is close to the heart and substance of the litigating lawyer's role."[8]

Burger's juxtaposition of the "officer of the court" and "hired gun" models revived the perennial question of the lawyer's competing duties to clients and the public. An officer of the court owed some amorphous duties to the court that trumped his duties to the client. Burger believed the erosion of this model "at the hands of cynics" resulted in a "bleak view of the profession." Lawyers who served only as instruments of their clients' legal demands would be led, eventually, to do their clients' "bidding, lawful or not, ethical or not."[9]

William Kunstler may have been America's best-known lawyer in 1970. He was the subject of a favorable portrayal in the July 25, 1969, issue of *Life* magazine, which included a cover story on the successful moon landing. He then defended the Chicago Eight (later Seven) in a widely covered trial lasting from September 1969 to February 1970. Soon thereafter he said, "I am not a lawyer for hire. I only defend those I love."[10]

Kunstler rejected the ideal that the independent lawyer facilitated the rule of law by representing clients even while rejecting their views and values. This ideal had been tested in both the early 1950s and the early 1960s, and the ostensible lesson was not to repeat earlier errors. Lawyers considered themselves "guardians of the law" who "play a vital role in the preservation of society." Kunstler demurred.[11]

The *ABA Journal* called Kunstler's statement "anti-professional," for the "ideal is to provide competent counsel for any person with a legitimate cause." This ideal could be met only when lawyers understood that it was "a badge of honor" to represent the "unpopular" client, "the bad and the ugly, the scorned and outcast." Limiting one's work only to those one loved undermined that ideal. Echoing Charles Curtis (see chapter 5), the *ABA Journal* stated that only an "emotional detachment" from the client allowed one to become a "truly professional advocate": "When the lawyer loses that detachment by too closely identifying with his client, a large measure of the lawyer's value is lost."[12]

The ABA editorial generated a host of published letters. The disparate views implied a professional division about this claim. One writer noted, "Most lawyers admit unequivocally that they will not represent unpopular or impecunious clients." A second critic suggested the lawyer for hire was a hired gun: "Money talks louder than the written law when it comes to the 'this gun for hire' school of advocacy." Society would be better off if lawyers "worried more about the public good they are supposed to represent, rather than the selfish immediate interest of whoever pays the biggest fee."[13]

Movement lawyers and Kunstler believed the system was unjust. Lawyers for hire sold themselves to clients who were often invested in the current system. The unwillingness of lawyers for hire to challenge the legal system exemplified all that was wrong with the legal profession.[14]

The trial of the Chicago Eight highlighted this divide. Even critics of Kunstler's behavior during the trial acknowledged his zealous efforts. The question was whether this zeal had tipped over to obstruction of justice. Had Kunstler failed to serve as an officer of the court by "disrupting" the trial proceedings? The answer depended on whether one thought this was a political trial. Even some who were disinclined to accept Kunstler's tactics criticized the behavior of Judge Julius Hoffman. Hoffman found twenty-four specifications of contempt by Kunstler and subjected him to more than four years in custody.

On appeal, the Seventh Circuit reversed some and remanded other contempt specifications. The test on remand was whether zeal had become an "actual and material obstruction" of justice. Was the causal agent an intemperate judge or Kunstler? This question made sense only if one assumed the trial was essentially fair. At the contempt rehearing before a different judge, Kunstler was found guilty of two specifications.[15]

Most establishment lawyers remained faithful to their belief in the justness of the American legal system. Thus, Kunstler was ethically required to act within the bounds of ordinary zealous advocacy. In the summer of 1970, in response to the trial, the elite American College of Trial Lawyers adopted and published its twelve Principles as to Disruption of the Judicial Process. The college focused on trial decorum as essential to a fair trial, which was itself essential to the rule of law. In Principle XI, it proposed that a lawyer whose contempt conviction was sustained should be subject to possible disbarment. Both the ABA and well-known trial lawyer Louis Nizer publicly agreed.[16]

Who owned the ethical high ground? Both movement and elite and mainstream lawyers claimed they best represented the independent lawyer ideal. The former argued they represented "outcasts" that mainstream lawyers "would shun like the plague." The latter claimed they made "legal advice and counsel available to all." Each accused the other of acting as "hired guns," although their reasoning differed (filthy lucre in one case; willingness to do the client's "bidding," "ethical or not," in the other). Both agreed that lawyers should represent clients "zealously," as mandated by Canon 7 of the 1969 Code. And both rejected the hired gun model of representing clients, again for different reasons (a lawyer representing one he loves is willing to "take a bullet" for the client, not merely expend one; an independent lawyer gives the client her best "independent professional judgment").[17]

If elite and movement lawyers both agreed the hired gun model was wrongheaded, how did it become commonplace? Both the American economy and the legal profession went through several dislocations, making the economic position of many lawyers more precarious. The American economy was moving toward a largely service-based economy. More broadly, beginning in late 1973, economic stasis settled in. The October 1973 Arab oil embargo led to recession and then high inflation, or "stagflation." Though the recession ended in 1975 and several years of growth followed, the rates of inflation and unemployment did not reflect a booming economy. Efforts to curb high inflation in 1979 led to another recession. Professionally, the march toward legal specialization continued. This both enhanced lawyer competence and narrowed the number of possible clients in need of such services. Specialization cleaved the lawyer to the interests of existing clients. The 53 percent increase in lawyers from 1970 to 1980 flattened lawyer income. In a decade, the median income of lawyers fell 21 percent, in constant 1983 dollars, to $36,716.[18]

Just days after Richard Nixon resigned in August 1974, Archibald Cox asked his ABA audience to consider how to mediate the "conflicting duties of 'hired gun' and 'servant of the law.'" The conflict was that work for one's clients "does not *always* serve the general public or build confidence in the law." Cox had been the Watergate special prosecutor before Nixon ordered his firing in October 1973. He concluded that a lawyer was both the client's hired gun and a servant of the legal system, a tension that allowed no simple answers. One mitigating approach was to dub lawyers social trustees who owed a duty to the public as well as to private clients. This broader duty was implicitly based on the license to practice law and often explicitly based on the lawyer's oath of office. Social trustee professionalism in law began a long, slow decline during the 1970s. In addition to economic pressures, this decline was due to a rethinking of the relationship between client and lawyer. As the client's agent, the lawyer's job was to effectuate the client's stated goals. This limited the "independent judgment" of the lawyer to tactics and (maybe) strategies. The client determined the overall mission. This understanding eased a lawyer's responsibilities in an economically stressful environment. The duty to represent clients zealously allowed lawyers to collapse service to clients with public service. In an adversarial legal system in a market-based economy, more lawyers equated zealous representation of clients with public service.[19]

In *Griffiths*, Burger concluded that most lawyers rejected the idea of an advocate being "a lackey to the client." There was little published disagreement with his 1973 conclusion. That quiet did not last long.[20]

The Clark Report and Lawyer Discipline

Few states enjoyed a "system" of lawyer discipline in the 1960s. Some lawyers managed to get disbarred, but that ordinarily took a great deal of effort by the lawyer. Lawyer discipline was haphazard and disorganized, if not wholly unorganized. The ABA created a Special Committee on Evaluation of Disciplinary Enforcement in 1967. Former Supreme Court justice Tom Clark was its chairman, and the Clark Report was issued in 1970. More than two hundred pages long, it was both brutally honest about lawyer shortcomings and insistent on offering solutions.[21]

The Clark Report dolefully noted "the existence of a scandalous situation that requires the immediate attention of the profession." Lawyers' attitudes ranged from "apathy to outright hostility" in matters concerning the discipline of other lawyers. Thus, enforcement was "practically nonexistent in many jurisdictions." Where lawyer disciplinary agencies existed, most lacked any effective power, and nearly all used "antiquated" processes.

The report found cases in which lawyers had been disbarred and subsequently permitted to "practice in another locale." Some convicted lawyers were not disciplined, and disbarred lawyers were "reinstated as a matter of course." Lawyers refused to help investigate fellow lawyers, much less disclose their misconduct. If this weren't enough, the Clark Report issued an existential warning: If drastic measures weren't taken, lawyer self-regulation was at an end. "Public dissatisfaction with the bar and the courts is much more intense than is generally believed within the profession." The public appeared ready to take over this dysfunctional process.[22]

No data existed regarding public dissatisfaction with either the profession or its discipline system. There was some evidence of ethical breaches by lawyers, but the depth of the problem was uncertain, and the ABA had not made any effort to learn more. Even so, the Clark Report could reasonably conclude that the "present enforcement structure is failing to rid the profession of a substantial number of malefactors."

ABA president David Maxwell's 1957 speech had lamented the failure of bar associations and state courts to discipline "ethics-busters." The good news, Maxwell reported, was that these lawyers constituted an "infinitesimal" portion of the profession. The Clark Report contradicted Maxwell.[23]

The upshot was a need for prompt and "radical reforms." The Clark Report offered procedural (better communication and reporting), financial (more funding), structural (centralization of the disciplinary system), definitional (excluding lawyers suffering from mental illness or drug dependency not charged with professional misconduct from disciplinary proceedings), and substantive (adding gradations of discipline to make the reinstatement of disbarred lawyers more difficult) reforms. It listed thirty-six "problems" of disciplinary enforcement and proposed a solution for each. It did not craft rules regarding discipline.[24]

A subsequent ABA special committee found that ten states had implemented sound disciplinary processes and another twenty-five had taken steps toward the "examination and revision of their grievances procedures." By mid-1972, just four states had done nothing. New Jersey was the only state where a committee drafted a report "inconsistent with some of the major recommendations of the Clark Committee," and the New Jersey State Bar Association filed a "critique" of those conclusions with the New Jersey Supreme Court. About a third of all jurisdictions had either changed their system of lawyer discipline to follow the Clark Report's recommendations or already had such a system in place. Most states issued reports adopting most or all of the Clark Report's recommendations and were awaiting approval by the state supreme court.[25]

A year later, "all but a few have made or are making significant progress in reorganizing and strengthening their disciplinary programs and procedures." The ABA created a Standing Committee on Professional Discipline that year.[26] The committee authored Recommended Rules for Disciplinary Enforcement (1974), later renamed Suggested Guidelines for Rules of Disciplinary Enforcement. It sent nine hundred copies to interested parties. These guidelines were a more concrete effort than the Clark Report. States that took seriously the process of disciplining lawyers needed to implement rules by which that discipline was applied. The ABA in 1979 updated the suggested guidelines in Standards Relating to Lawyer Discipline and Disability Proceedings.[27]

The standards were in part a response to the Watergate scandal. Secrecy was out, and transparency was in. The pre-Watergate Clark Report had terrorized lawyers by mentioning public takeover of lawyer discipline. The standards invited the public to participate, proposing that three of the nine members of a state's disciplinary board be nonlawyers. At least one nonlawyer was to serve on each three-person hearing committee, which made the initial findings of fact and conclusions of law. Section 3.16, "Informing the Public," stressed the disciplinary board's duty to publish each matter of public discipline, including the reinstatement of disbarred lawyers. It also encouraged boards to publish information regarding the discipline process. And once formal disciplinary charges were filed, the "proceedings should be public."[28]

The standards were broadly adopted, despite some early resistance. By 1982, thirty-two jurisdictions included public members on their disciplinary boards.[29]

Even though most states quickly adopted a modernized lawyer discipline system, the Clark Report apparently had little substantive effect. A 1984 ABA report indicated that disciplinary data had been collected from every jurisdiction except North Carolina. It reported 2,100 public disciplinary sanctions for fiscal year 1982–1983. Just 0.35 percent of all lawyers had been publicly disciplined. A separate compilation (with some states not reporting) covering 1974–1983 found that annual public disciplinary sanctions ranged from a high of 977 (1983) to a low of 353 (1974). This was not a "substantial number of malefactors." The consumer advocacy group Public Citizen investigated the lawyer disciplinary process in six states as of the mid-1970s and found that disciplinary systems continued to reflect poorly on the legal profession. The authors cited a number of instances in which apparently valid complaints had been dismissed "solely on the basis of the unsworn, written response of the attorney contradicting the allegation." The disciplinary system neglected and ignored some complaints and delayed the investigation of others. Little had been done to eliminate egregious lawyer behavior. A damning empirical study from the early 1970s clarified how little the disciplinary system mattered: "We found little evidence that lawyers found either their performance or conduct was being systematically reviewed." The disciplinary system failed to protect clients from incompetent lawyers. The system "lends itself nicely to the issues of moral fitness and deviance. But it does not easily or usually apply to issues of performance."[30]

Lawyer Ethics and Criminal Justice

Violent crime in the United States increased tremendously during the 1960s. So did prosecutions. But the number of lawyers did not keep up, so what happened to all those cases? Plea bargains. This gave defense lawyers an incentive to trim ethical corners. One sociologist concluded that defense lawyers served as "double agents," not zealous representatives. Two studies —one from Texas and one from Los Angeles County—confirmed that pressure to cooperate made zealous advocacy the exception, not the rule. As one Los Angeles assistant district attorney put it, defense counsel has "got to be willing to become a part of the community he's working in." More than 90 percent of cases there resulted in a guilty plea after a plea bargain.[31]

And what about prosecutors? The 1908 Canons declared the "primary duty" of a prosecutor was "not to convict, but to see that justice is done." The 1969 Code advanced this proposition only slightly. It made the prosecutor's primary duty to seek justice aspirational (ethical considerations), and it made a prosecutor subject to the disciplinary rules only if charges were initiated without probable cause or if the prosecutor failed to disclose evidence that negated guilt or mitigated punishment. What might have confused prosecutors was that these provisions were in Canon 7, "A Lawyer Should Represent a Client Zealously within the Bounds of the Law." Zealous representation coexisted uneasily with the nebulous duty to seek justice. And prosecutors wanted to win, or, as one observer phrased it, there existed "the prosecutor's interest in non-defeat."[32]

As part of a comprehensive series of standards on criminal justice, in early 1971 the ABA adopted Standards Relating to the Prosecution Function and Standards Relating to the Defense Function. Unlike the 1969 Code, these standards provided a much more thorough ethical grounding. This was purposeful, for the "bar has long been woefully lax in enforcing its professed ethical standards, especially those which apply to the quality of representation rather than to the financial dealings with clients or relations among lawyers."[33]

The Prosecution Standards reflected the prosecutor's interest in both winning and seeking justice. Prosecutors were permitted to cross-examine a truthful witness "appropriate[ly]." The prosecutor was to avoid "misuse [of] the power of cross-examination or impeachment to discredit or undermine a witness if he knows the witness is testifying truthfully." The introduction to the Defense Standards began, "Few subjects in the administration of criminal justice are more in need of clarification than the role of the defense lawyer in a criminal case." It lamented the "noisome [criminal defense] lawyers" who "pridefully" spoke of "tactics which at best were pettifoggery and at worst grounds for disbarment." Such tactics were linked to the "universally rejected" argument that "a lawyer may be excused for acquiescing in the use of known perjured testimony."[34]

One major premise of the Defense Standards was that the lawyer's expertise put him or her in charge of how the client was represented. "Defense counsel [never] serves with any moderation of an advocate's zeal," but "in areas of professional judgment and decision, as distinguished from the limited decisions reserved to his client, the lawyer must have control of the case commensurate with his responsibility as a professional advocate." A defense lawyer never became a "mere 'mouthpiece' for or alter ego of his client."[35]

Control of the case meant that defense counsel decided what witnesses were called at trial and "how to conduct cross-examination." But cross-examination was limited in the Defense Standards in the same manner applicable to prosecutors. It was ethically wrong for a defense lawyer to attempt to "discredit or undermine a witness" if the lawyer knew the witness was "testifying truthfully." The commentary to Standard 7.6(b) declared that the purpose of cross-examination was to show "falsehood, not to destroy truth or the reputation of a known truthful witness." It continued, "it is not proper to use those tools to destroy the truth, or to seek to confuse or embarrass the witness under these circumstances." Such action effectively "undermines the administration of justice" and "should be avoided." Bowing to reality, the commentary concluded that, although it could appeal to the "conscience and honor" of lawyers, its admonitions in this regard were largely unenforceable.[36]

The Defense Standards also specified the lawyer's duty when the accused expressed an intention to testify falsely. Counsel should try to dissuade the client, but if that failed, counsel could not directly examine the accused. Instead, counsel should introduce the defendant, who would then give a narrative statement. Defense counsel was also prohibited from presenting "the defendant's known false version of facts to the jury as worthy of belief."[37]

The Criminal Justice Standards were quickly implemented in twenty states and had been relied on as authority in more than two thousand opinions by the end of 1974. Specific standards defined some actions by counsel as "unprofessional conduct," but the standards did not serve as disciplinary rules.[38]

A 1972 joint national study by the National Legal Aid and Defender Association and the ABA found that indigent defendants were poorly represented by "overburdened, undertrained and underpaid" counsel who were allocated "grossly deficient" resources. Both assigned and privately retained defense lawyers faced conflicts of interest in client representation. As zealous advocates, they were bound to serve their clients' interests. But a client's interest in avoiding a criminal record or in pleading guilty only if the sentence was time served might conflict with a lawyer's interest in minimizing the time spent on the case or enhancing his reputation. The flat fee charged by most defense lawyers was the same whether the case went to trial or not. The lawyer therefore had a financial incentive to favor a plea bargain. And as repeat players in the criminal justice system, all defense lawyers wanted to appear to grease the criminal justice machinery. A 1975 study of plea bargaining found that "effective representation" was "a problem that cannot be resolved satisfactorily." The conflicts of interest between client and lawyer were simply "unavoidable."[39]

In 1979 the ABA adopted a slightly revised set of Standards Relating to the Prosecution Function and the Defense Function. The ABA noted that its Prosecution Standards had become the "basic ethical guidelines" for many public prosecutors, and those "standards remain[ed] sound."[40]

The Defense Standards had also "weathered well the test of time." The ABA made two significant decisions about cross-examining truthful witnesses and the lawyer's duty when the accused planned to give (or did give) known false testimony. The ABA deleted the admonition that the lawyer "not misuse the power of cross-examination . . . to discredit or undermine a witness" if he knows the witness is testifying truthfully. The commentary concluded that the lawyer was not required to attack a truthful witness's credibility, as long as the lawyer otherwise provided an effective defense. However, if the client admitted guilt and did not plan to testify, counsel's decision "to forgo vigorous cross-examination of the prosecution's witnesses would violate the clear duty of zealous representation that is owed to the client."[41]

On false testimony by the accused, the ABA decided to keep Standard 7.7. Despite some contrary law, if the lawyer failed to discourage false testimony and an attempt to withdraw from representation failed, direct examination was impermissible, as was any reliance on known false testimony.[42]

By 1980, the standards were divided on whether to embrace the hired gun model. An earlier reference to the defense lawyer's conscience and honor was displaced by a duty to represent the client zealously through the cross-examination of truthful witnesses. A witness's interest in retaining dignity or in avoiding public shame or embarrassment was irrelevant under the revised standards. But some limits to zealous advocacy remained: the lawyer still owed a duty to the court not to aid a client's known false testimony. Overall, the revised standards tied the lawyer more tightly to the client's interests, as defined by the client.

Code of Judicial Conduct

Like the 1924 Canons of Judicial Ethics (see chapter 4), their 1972 successor was fast-tracked after a judicial scandal. In June 1968 lame-duck president Lyndon Baines Johnson nominated Justice Abe Fortas to replace Chief Justice Earl Warren. Fortas's confirmation was slowed and then stopped by a successful Senate filibuster. Johnson withdrew Fortas's nomination.[43]

Fortas had agreed in 1965 to serve as a consultant to the family foundation of a former client, Louis Wolfson, while also serving on the Supreme Court. He was to be paid $20,000 annually for life, which would then continue to be paid to his widow. Fortas's government salary was $39,500. He received the initial $20,000 in January 1966, which he returned in December, after Wolfson was indicted. In late 1967 the law school at American University agreed to pay Fortas $15,000 to teach a summer course. Fortas's former partner, Paul Porter, raised the $15,000 from outside donors, largely former clients and friends. This became public news in September 1968. There was no evidence that Fortas was aware of the donors' identity, but this disclosure helped quash his nomination.[44]

Life magazine published a story in May 1969 questioning Fortas's ethics. It publicized his arrangement with Wolfson and intimated the appearance of impropriety. Days later, Fortas resigned from the Supreme Court. The ABA piled on. Four days after his resignation, in just the second formal opinion issued in nine months, the Standing Committee on Professional Ethics chastised judges whose personal, social, and business relationships had the appearance of impropriety. The committee's unnamed target was Fortas.[45]

President Nixon nominated Judge Clement Haynsworth Jr. to replace Fortas in August 1969. Haynsworth was opposed by civil rights and labor organizations, and they lodged ethics complaints against him. They claimed Haynsworth had twice failed to recuse himself when he had a financial conflict of interest. He was cleared of any impropriety in both cases, although the second was unseemly. In September, Haynsworth's unknowing involvement in a real estate deal years earlier with convicted political "fixer" Bobby Baker killed his nomination.[46]

Fortas's case led the ABA to create a committee to revise the 1924 Canons of Judicial Ethics, and Haynsworth's case encouraged the committee to complete its work quickly. It issued its initial conclusions in less than a year. Some resolved specific concerns related to Fortas and Haynsworth.

Another recommended that the standards of recusal or disqualification be made more robust.[47]

In 1971 the special committee sent a tentative draft to more than fifteen thousand persons. It quoted ABA president Edward Wright regarding the necessity of reform: "Confidence in the courts is vital to the stability of our society. The public's confidence has been shaken in recent years by occasional widely publicized examples of questionable conduct." A final draft was adopted by the ABA with two minor amendments in August 1972.[48]

The Code of Judicial Conduct consisted of seven canons intended to "establish mandatory standards." Most provisions offered bare descriptions of proper or improper conduct, with little or no commentary. Judges were to "uphold the integrity and independence of the judiciary" (Canon 1) and "avoid impropriety and the appearance of impropriety" (Canon 2). They were permitted to "improve the law, the legal system, and the administration of justice" (Canon 4). Only Canons 3 and 5 included significant rules and commentary. Canon 5 required the judge to "regulate his extra-judicial activities to minimize the risk of conflict with his judicial duties." This reflected the concerns raised by the Fortas and Haynsworth scandals.[49]

The ABA created a special committee to implement the code in the states. Three years later, thirty-nine states, the District of Columbia, and the Judicial Conference (making the code applicable to all federal judges other than Supreme Court justices) had adopted it in whole or in part. Another two adopted a small portion of the code, and five more were engaged in "active studies of the ABA Code."[50]

The 1972 Code turned earlier aspirational statements into enforceable legal standards. If a judge failed to "avoid . . . the appearance of impropriety in all his activities," voluntary recusal or disqualification was the judge's only option. What this meant was unclear.[51] Little was offered in terms of defining the appearance of impropriety in the code, particularly Canon 2, or in the published reporter's notes.[52]

Canon 3(C)(1) listed four specific examples in which a judge should disqualify himself "in a proceeding in which his impartiality might reasonably be questioned." The standard could also be met in other ways, although how was not stated. Generally, a judge's impartiality might reasonably be questioned based on a claim of an appearance of impropriety. How would this work? Reporter E. Wayne Thode explained the link between disqualification and the appearance of impropriety: "An impropriety or the appearance of impropriety in violation of Canon 2 that would reasonably lead one to question the judge's impartiality in a given proceeding clearly falls within the scope of the general standard." Thus, an appearance of impropriety "officially became, and would continue to be, the heart of judicial ethics." This was so even though both the meaning of "an appearance of impropriety" and whether it "might reasonably" affect the judge's impartiality were uncertain.[53]

The "appearance of impropriety" standard was initially couched in the ethos of judicial conscience and honor. A judge was to search his mind and heart to determine whether his judicial and nonjudicial actions, even if undertaken honestly and in good faith, would appear improper to others. Enfolding that subjective standard into Canon 3(C)(1)'s "objective reasonable person" standard generated confusion, for the latter ignored the judge's state of mind. Conscience was irrelevant to Canon 3(C)(1).

When the ABA adopted its 1972 Code, the Watergate scandal was just beginning. The Judicial Conference became an early adopter of the code in April 1973, as the scandal took on the character of "high level government dishonesty." By late 1974, when Congress adopted a bill expanding judicial disqualification, President Nixon had resigned, lawyers' fingerprints were all over the scandal, and public trust in government was in short supply. A congressional effort to use the cudgel of "trustworthiness" in federal judging by broadening "partiality" was a winner.[54]

The statute mimicked the 1972 Code by adopting the "might reasonably be questioned" standard of impartiality. At congressional hearings, Thode was asked whether a judge should be disqualified if an attorney was a "distant cousin" the judge had not seen in thirty years and to whom he was not close. As one critic noted, the specific answer was clearly no. But the broad "appearance of impropriety" standard required a broader assessment. Thode's answer: it depends. Recusal was necessary if the judge "decided that his impartiality might reasonably be questioned under those circumstances." Interpreting the standard simply meant repeating its language. That was no rule at all.[55]

Did adoption of the appearance of impropriety standard generate greater public confidence in the judiciary? Little positive empirical evidence exists. Even so, the ABA retained the standard in its 1990 and 2007 revisions of the code, and states have done so as well. As one critic wrote, "There is no evidence that public trust in the judiciary has improved since the ABA's adoption of the new recusal standard in 1972."[56]

Promoting Competence

The Code of Professional Responsibility listed "competence" as an ethical duty in Canon 6. It urged the lawyer to "strive to become and remain proficient in his practice." The only disciplinary admonition involved handling a matter when the lawyer "knows or should know that he is not competent to handle" it. Otherwise, Canon 6 provided little guidance.[57]

Competence became an increasingly important issue in the 1970s. In *McMann v. Richardson* (1970), the Supreme Court held that the Sixth Amendment right to the assistance of counsel meant *effective* assistance. Two years later, the right was extended to anyone possibly subject to incarceration. These decisions required a large increase in the number of competent criminal defense lawyers, but evidence of competence seemed lacking. In a December 1972 speech, well-known chief judge David L. Bazelon spoke witheringly about the "defective assistance of counsel" in criminal cases. He concluded that "a great many—if not most—of indigent defendants do not receive the effective assistance of counsel." How many was unknown because, in Bazelon's view, "the criminal justice system goes to great lengths to bury the problem."[58]

When Bazelon spoke, courts were in disarray when it came to assessing whether defense counsel was ineffective. Proffered standards included a "sham and a mockery of justice," "gross incompetence," "community standards," "genuine and effective representation," "reasonably likely to render and rendering reasonably effective assistance," and standards linked to malpractice.[59]

A decade later, the federal circuit courts had largely agreed on "reasonably competent assistance." That standard, however, was quite malleable. In *Strickland v. Washington* (1984), the Supreme Court declared, "the proper standard for attorney performance is that of reasonably effective assistance." If counsel failed this standard, a court was required to determine whether "deficient performance prejudiced the defense." It justified its first conclusion by approvingly noting the 1979 Standards Relating to the Defense Function. However, these standards were "guides," not a "set of rules," and "judicial scrutiny of counsel's performance must be highly deferential." Deference required a "strong presumption that counsel's conduct falls within the wide range of reasonable professional assistance." Apart from conflicts of interest, the defendant had the burden of proving prejudice. After all, "representation is an art," not a set of "mechanical rules."[60]

Did *Strickland* improve lawyer competence? It appears not. One critic complained, "Even after endorsing the standard of 'reasonable competence' in *Strickland v. Washington*, the Supreme Court framed the standard in such unforgiving terms, and applied it so strictly, that the new standard did little to actualize—and, indeed, *undermined*—the ideal of effective representation." If defending an accused is an "art," then the wide range of professional discretion becomes wider, as deference takes primacy over consequence. One study of pre-*Strickland* ineffectiveness claims found that just 3.9 percent of about four thousand claims were meritorious. After *Strickland*, courts "rarely reverse[d] convictions for ineffective assistance of counsel, even if the defendant's lawyer was asleep, drunk, unprepared, or unknowledgeable."[61]

Concerns about incompetent lawyering extended beyond criminal defense. In a 1973 speech, Chief Justice Warren Burger speculated that anywhere between one-third and one-half of all lawyers "who appear in serious cases are not really qualified to render fully adequate representation." He "observed as many miscarriages of justice in civil cases from inadequacy of counsel as in criminal cases." Burger's anecdotal view was not an outlier. His solution was a "system of certification for trial advocates." Texas and California had just implemented specialization certifications, and he urged other states to do the same.[62]

Lawyer specialization picked up speed in the post–World War II era. By 1970, lawyers largely agreed that specialization was the epitome of professionalism. The twin goals of the California and Texas specialization certificates were "to increase lawyer competency" and to inform the public "who the specially competent attorneys are in the particular field."[63]

Specialization certification programs were explicitly marketed to lawyers who served individuals. "The most direct action a bar can take to protect the small practitioner is to propose and secure adoption of a specialization plan in that state." In a time of falling lawyer incomes, specialization certificates were touted as an economic lifesaver. They were also praised as efficient for clients: "Some degree of specialization is a necessity of modern law practice. The law that applies to our complex society is such that no single lawyer can perform all legal tasks required."[64]

Specialization allegedly generated two additional benefits: enhanced lawyer reputation due to greater competence, and efficiency in obtaining clients. One critic argued that these claims had a "certain plausibility" but masked the profession's effort to use specialization to increase lawyer income. The specialist's advantage in client development ended in 1977, after the Supreme Court held that bans on lawyer advertising were unconstitutional. Although certified lawyers could now market their specialties to the general public, there was no empirical evidence that the certificates made any difference in choosing a lawyer. Consequently, although most states studied whether to adopt such a plan, only seventeen had done so by 1993.[65]

Lawyers also promoted competence through continuing legal education (CLE) programs. In 1971 Minnesota become the first state to consider making CLE mandatory, and it did so in 1975. It was soon joined by neighboring states Wisconsin and Iowa. Six others made completion of mandatory CLE a condition of continued licensure by 1980, and thirty-seven states had some form of mandatory CLE by the early 1990s. CLE was traceable to the 1930s New York–based Practising Law Courses and to joint American Law Institute and ABA programs in the late 1940s, which promoted expertise, not mere competence. Lawyers assumed that mandatory CLE promoted greater professional competence, but no empirical evidence confirmed that assumption.[66]

The federal judiciary took seriously Burger's support for trial advocacy certification. In 1974 the Second Circuit's Clare Committee concluded there was "a lack of competency in trial advocacy in the Federal Courts." It proposed that admission to practice in federal district court be limited to those with some experience in court hearings. The Judicial Conference of the United States followed up by creating the Devitt Committee to improve advocacy in all federal courts. Its tentative recommendations began by stating, "All agree that there is a need for improvement [in advocacy], but what is the extent of this need and how best can it be met?" It looked at the empirical evidence and proposed that admission to try federal cases be conditioned on having "four trial experiences, including two actual trials."[67]

Were federal trial (or appellate) lawyers incompetent in sufficient numbers to alter the rules of admission to practice? Several surveys attempted to answer that question. The Clare Committee surveyed federal judges in the Second Circuit and found that, overall, judges believed 7.1 percent of lawyers were incompetent. Two other studies of judicial perception of competence in advocacy were published. One, by the Federal Judicial Center, surveyed all federal trial and appellate judges and found that the problem of incompetence was less than generally claimed. Of the 81 percent of federal trial judges who responded to the question "Do you believe that there is, overall, a serious problem of inadequate trial advocacy by lawyers with cases in your court?" 41.3 percent answered yes. On closer inspection, negative assessments suggested confirmation bias. A total of 248 judges were asked to rate 1,969 lawyers in 848 trials. The judges concluded that 8.6 percent of the performances were inadequate ("very poor," "poor," or "not quite adequate"). The second survey, by the American Bar Foundation, was sent to 5,399 federal and state trial judges, of whom 26 percent replied. The judges rated 87 percent of lawyers competent; the others were partially or substantially incompetent. The more recent the trial, the higher the percentage deemed competent (90 percent), which suggests a recency bias.[68]

The authors of the Federal Judicial Center study concluded, "On the whole, the ratings present a very favorable picture of the quality of advocacy in the district courts." That study also found that judges perceived federal appellate lawyers to be more competent than trial lawyers. The conclusion of the American Bar Foundation researcher was similar: "Our survey results present a considerably more positive picture of attorneys' courtroom performance than might have been expected in view of recent criticism."[69]

This did not derail the competency train. Warren Burger returned to the fray in 1980, claiming the existence of "a broad consensus" about trial lawyer deficiencies. ABA president David Brink declared, "There is a single word to characterize the single dominant issue in the 1980s. . . . That word is competence."[70]

Despite Brink's prediction, claims of lawyer incompetence in civil cases soon faded. The Conference of Chief Justices' Task Force on Lawyer Competence issued a report in 1982 after a three-year study and stated, "Current information is inadequate to support firm conclusions about the extent of incompetence" among lawyers. An ABA task force tried to keep the idea alive in a 1983 report, but both were quickly forgotten. The ABA engineered the Consortium on Professional Competence, but it did relatively little and was abolished in 1987. These studies may have had little impact because the bar was slowly recognizing the inverse correlation between demands of competence and accessibility to legal services. That is, it may have dawned on bar leaders that the economic realities of providing legal services to individuals were sometimes incompatible with the expectations of competence in law firms serving organizational clients with large budgets.[71]

Another crisis in the 1970s was the increase in legal malpractice claims. This crisis was less about lawyer competence than about finding professional liability insurance. An ABA task force reported an unstable market

due to "high-risk specialties of law practice and in certain geographic lo-
cales." Additionally, "litigation consciousness" resulting from "changes in
the 'social climate'" contributed to this problem.[72]

Public-Interest Law, the Legal Services Corporation, and Mandatory Pro Bono

Sargent Shriver, the first director of President Johnson's War on Poverty,
said he was proudest of the federal government's creation of a civil legal
services program because "it had the greatest potential for changing the
system under which people's lives were being exploited." A lawyer involved
in the program agreed: "Legal aid will have more impact on . . . our social,
economic, and political structures than anything else" in American domestic affairs. This near-messianic belief in the transformative possibilities of
law motivated establishment lawyers to lobby for the program. Soon after
Shriver became director of the Office of Economic Opportunity in 1964, it
housed a federal legal services program. The ABA defended the program's
continued existence starting in 1965 and supported a permanent program.
In early 1971 President Nixon urged Congress to create the Legal Services
Corporation. Nixon signed the law establishing the LSC three years later,
less than a month before he resigned from office.[73]

   The faith in law was not limited to developing legal aid programs. Using
the legal system to effect change led to the existence of at least eighty-six
liberal public-interest law firms by the mid-1970s. Conservative firms soon
organized in response.[74]

   The ABA and other bar associations strongly supported pro bono work.
Many in need of legal services were unable to afford them, and lawyers
could alleviate this immense problem by providing their services for free
as their contribution to society. As the Watergate scandal infiltrated public
consciousness, ABA president Chesterfield Smith urged lawyers to consider
whether they should create "an affirmative duty" to "devote some portion
of [their] services to public interest endeavors." A 1974 ABA committee
report answered affirmatively, and in 1975 the ABA resolved that it was "a
basic responsibility of each lawyer engaged in the practice of law to provide
public interest services."[75]

   Though it was framed as a "basic responsibility," the ABA did not believe public-interest service should be a condition of maintaining one's law

license. The resolution did, however, explain why this was a basic duty, noting that the "duty has been expressly stated as deriving (among other things) from the professional status of a lawyer." The ABA then created a committee to implement this basic responsibility nationally. The committee recommended specific, quantifiable, required guidelines. "Some commentators have urged every lawyer to budget a flat 5 per cent of client-related time for public interest legal service, yielding 40 to 100 hours per year," wrote the committee. Others doubled those numbers. For lawyers with modest incomes, the "principal point" was that "quantitative public interest legal service guidelines by the organized bar . . . should be part" of implementing the 1975 ABA resolution.[76]

The ABA decided to reevaluate the Code of Professional Responsibility in 1977, and it created what is known as the Kutak Commission to do so. Several Kutak Commission members raised the idea of making pro bono work mandatory, reflecting their long-standing interest in the subject. Two members, Robert Kutak and Samuel Thurman, were original LSC board members, and the LSC's first president was commission member Thomas Ehrlich. But other unnamed commission members feared making pro bono work mandatory because it could harm "economically marginal practitioners." As the working draft was prepared in 1979, the Kutak Commission "felt [it] necessary to create some mechanism for more fairly distributing the burden of *pro bono* representation throughout the bar." A proposed pro bono practice was debated, and although no formal vote was taken, one reporter claimed it was disfavored. Still, the pro bono provision was included in the August 1979 working draft, mandating "forty hours per year to such service, or the equivalent thereof."[77]

Lawyers reacted negatively and vociferously. The Kutak Commission's initial response was to expand the definition of *pro bono*, substitute a reporting requirement for the eliminated forty-hour measure, and create a "buy-out" provision.[78] The revised proposal remained in the commission's January 1980 discussion draft. Individual commentators on the draft were nearly unanimous in rejecting a mandate to perform public-interest work as a condition of licensure. Lawyer institutions offered both objections and wholehearted approvals.[79]

The 1981 proposed final draft eliminated mandatory pro bono work. A rule stating that lawyers should aspire to dedicate time to public-interest service was retained when the ABA approved the Model Rules of Professional Conduct (MRPC) in 1983. That rule was an oddity, as the MRPC otherwise avoided aspirational statements, as a matter of policy. It existed to remind lawyers of their duty to serve society and their clients. But during hard times, it was daunting to give forty or fifty hours of free legal services, much less the one hundred to two hundred hours some suggested. Though the profession's division regarding mandatory pro bono work was partly ideological, the greater part was economic.[80]

Watergate

On June 26, 1973, a gripping piece of political theater was shown on the three national television networks. John Dean, the disgraced former counsel to President Nixon, was answering questions from a Senate Select Committee on the Watergate scandal. Dean had been cooperating with the committee even before Nixon fired him. Senator Herman Talmadge (D-GA) asked Dean about a piece of paper on which he had jotted down some names. This was a list of the people Dean "thought had violated the law." Dean then explained why ten of the names were highlighted with an asterisk: these were the lawyers. He testified, "My first reaction was there certainly are an awful lot of lawyers involved here." He continued, "How in God's name could so many lawyers get involved in something like this?"[81]

What the official record does not disclose is the audience's reaction— laughter. This was not a surprise. A 1973 Harris poll found that just 24 percent of the public had confidence in lawyers, and a Gallup poll three years later released similar findings.[82]

The Watergate scandal came to the public's attention when five men were arrested at the Watergate complex in Washington, DC, early on June 17, 1972. They were attempting to enter the offices of the Democratic National Committee. It was later learned that this was their second effort, necessitated by a defective wiretap. Dean's job was to give Nixon legal advice on a host of issues, and he decided this included covering up the connection between the Watergate burglars and the Committee to Re-elect the President (CREEP, to Nixon's opponents).[83]

The burglars pleaded guilty. Coconspirators G. Gordon Liddy and James McCord were found guilty at trial. On March 19 McCord sent a letter to presiding judge John Sirica indicating that the burglary involved government officials and that perjured testimony had been given. Sirica gave the Watergate conspirators lengthy sentences (the stick) and encouraged them to cooperate with the Select Committee (the carrot). McCord cooperated and spoke to the committee about former attorney general John Mitchell's involvement; he also implicated Dean and others. Jeb Magruder informed Nixon's advisers that he too would implicate Mitchell and Dean. Dean hired a criminal defense lawyer and began speaking with prosecutors. Three weeks later, after the public learned Dean had implicated Nixon, he was fired.[84]

Attorney General Richard Kleindienst resigned the same day, and Elliot Richardson was nominated to replace him. Nixon and Richardson agreed to the Senate's demand that they appoint a special prosecutor to investigate the Watergate break-in. Richardson persuaded Harvard Law School professor Archibald Cox to serve. The Select Committee eventually learned of the existence of tapes of conversations that had taken place in the Oval Office and asked Nixon to produce them. He refused the committee's request and ignored its subpoena. When Cox's request for the tapes was also refused, he issued a subpoena demanding them.

October 1973 was the best and worst of times for American lawyers. Law schools were full, and overall, it was a good time to practice law. Affirming Judge Sirica's ruling, the court of appeals ordered Nixon to turn over the tapes for in camera (private) review. Nixon again refused (although he eventually released some tapes to the committee, one of which had a crucial eighteen-minute gap). Meanwhile, Vice President Spiro T. Agnew, trained as a lawyer, resigned after pleading no contest to tax evasion. Dean pleaded guilty to one count of conspiracy to obstruct justice. Then, in what came to be known as the Saturday Night Massacre, President Nixon (a name partner in a large New York City law firm before his 1969 inauguration) ordered the firing of special prosecutor Archibald Cox on October 20, 1973. Attorney General Richardson and his deputy, William Ruckelshaus, both resigned rather than fire Cox. The firing so outraged the public that within two weeks a second special prosecutor, Leon Jaworski, had been appointed. The House of Representatives began impeachment proceedings in early 1974, and a grand jury privately named Nixon as an unindicted coconspirator. After losing a battle with Jaworski to keep other subpoenaed tapes secret, Nixon resigned.[85]

The National Organization of Bar Counsel reported that twenty-nine lawyers were subject to disciplinary proceedings related to Watergate. Seven were disbarred, including Nixon; eleven others were publicly disciplined. Twenty-seven of the twenty-nine lawyers linked to Watergate were either indicted or unindicted coconspirators. As one ABA president put it, it was "a lawyers' scandal."[86]

In response, the ABA took only one action involving legal ethics: students at all ABA-approved law schools were required to take a legal ethics course. Law schools seek ABA approval because every graduate of an ABA-approved law school is eligible to take the bar examination of any state. No evidence was offered that law schools had avoided teaching legal ethics before 1973, and no evidence was offered that such instruction had a positive impact on lawyer ethics. Indeed, John Dean had taken a course in legal ethics as a law student in the early 1960s, and he "liked to boast that he got the highest grade in ethics at Georgetown University."[87]

The Public Interest and the Lawyer's Duty to Keep Confidences and Secrets

Canon 4 of the 1969 Code of Professional Responsibility required a lawyer to keep a client's confidences and secrets. It included just one disciplinary rule, which defined "confidence" and "secret," declared the general rule, and listed four discretionary (not mandatory) exceptions. Canon 7, on zealous representation, also included an exception to the confidentiality rule: A lawyer "who receives information clearly establishing that . . . his client has . . . perpetrated a fraud upon a person or tribunal shall promptly call upon his client to rectify the same, and if his client refuses or is unable to do so, he shall reveal the fraud to the affected person or tribunal." This mandatory rule, DR 7–102(B)(1), was first included in the final draft. To resolve these Janus-like provisions, in 1974 the ABA added, without debate, what was called a "housekeeping" amendment to DR 7–102(B)(1): "except when the information is protected as a privileged communication."[88]

This was no mere housekeeping amendment. It was adopted in response to the National Student Marketing Corporation (NSM) scandal. On October 31, 1969, NSM was about to merge with Interstate National Corporation (INC)—both publicly traded companies. NSM's accountant did not sign a "comfort letter" to investors and shareholders, giving them confidence about NSM's financial condition. Instead, the accountant dictated an unsigned statement suggesting three material adjustments to NSM's claim that it had earned $700,000 in profits in the nine months ending on May 31. Those material adjustments suggested that NSM had actually lost $180,000. INC officers saw the unsigned statement before closing the deal. After the merger agreement, a signed comfort letter was sent to INC officers and directors making two additional material changes. No one informed the public or shareholders of these material changes. Eventually, NSM's stock price collapsed, investors sued, and the Securities and Exchange Commission (SEC) investigated and filed suit on February 3, 1972, claiming a violation of the antifraud provisions of securities law.[89]

The SEC argued that the law firms representing NSM and INC had a duty to disclose the fraud if the directors refused to do so. By the time the district court issued its final opinion six years later, NSM's counsel, the large law firm White and Case, had settled for $1.95 million. The court concluded that "the attorneys' responsibilities to their corporate client required them to take steps to ensure that the information would be disclosed to the shareholders." Whatever the precise nature of their duty, the lawyers "were required to speak out at the closing concerning the obvious materiality of the information." Their "silence was not only a breach of this duty to speak, but in addition lent the appearance of legitimacy to the closing."[90]

Private-practice lawyers widely criticized this view. An ABA committee investigated "the implications of the National Student Marketing case and similar cases from a broader viewpoint." Its report and the larger ABA offered a ringing endorsement of nearly absolute client confidences. The "housekeeping" amendment clarified the ABA's view that, between a paying client and the public, the ABA would protect the former.[91]

After much turbulence, the ABA Committee on Ethics and Professional Responsibility (CEPR) issued Formal Opinion 341 (1975). Its interpretation of this housekeeping amendment expanded the exception's reach even further: "The tradition (which is backed by substantial policy considerations) that permits a lawyer to assure a client that information (whether a confidence or a secret) given to him will not be revealed to third parties is so important that it should take precedence, in all but the most serious cases, over the duty imposed by DR 7–102(B)." The problems with this conclusion were manifold. First, the code's definition of "secret" was, in part, "other information gained in the professional relationship that the client has requested be held inviolate." Only a "confidence" was a communication between lawyer and client. In its haste the previous year, the exception added to DR 7–102(B)(1) was limited to instances in which the information was learned through a "privileged communication." Simply put, a secret was not a privileged communication. This interpretive difficulty was a mere trifle. Any state adopting this amendment required its lawyers not to disclose "secrets" when they learned a client was defrauding someone. Second, CEPR claimed the existence of a "tradition" of a nearly absolute duty to keep confidences. This tradition was modest, contrary to CEPR's bald assertion. Third, the "substantial policy reasons" that joined tradition were unstated. Fourth, CEPR failed to explain the exception to the exception ("in all but the most serious cases"). What did that mean, and who judged it? Fifth, CEPR suggested that a mandatory disclosure rule made lawyers victims rather than counselors: "It is not reasonable to put a lawyer at peril of discipline if, after determining that he has information that 'clearly' establishes fraud (a difficult task in itself), he must also determine the relevant rule of attorney-client privilege, in order to determine whether he must reveal the client's confidences and secrets." But every lawyer had a duty to know the limits of the attorney-client privilege. After all, the client might find it valuable to understand the limits of communicating with counsel as a matter of evidence law. Further, there existed a long tradition that communications from client to lawyer that met the "crime-fraud" exception were not privileged. CEPR understood the perils facing the lawyer in these cases but ignored the peril facing the defrauded victim. Like a trade organization, CEPR protected its members.[92]

The ABA was not especially persuasive. New York amended its rules to create an exception for "confidences and secrets," which is what CEPR should have done. Three years after the 1974 amendment, just nine states agreed with the ABA. But federal courts, which ordinarily lacked a code of legal ethics, often used the ABA Code to define federal legal ethics law. And securities lawyers practiced federal law.[93]

In 1973, in Syracuse, New York, lawyers Frank Armani and Francis Belge were appointed to defend Robert Garrow, charged with murdering Philip Domblewski. Garrow was also suspected of murdering Daniel Porter and was believed to be responsible for the disappearance (and presumed murder) of Susan Petz and Alicia Hauck. Armani and Belge decided on an insanity defense for Garrow. They asked him what he knew about Porter, Petz, and Hauck, and he eventually gave his lawyers directions to the bodies of Petz and Hauck. Neither lawyer disclosed the women's deaths, even after Petz's father vainly asked Armani for information. Before Garrow's trial, the bodies were found by others. After Garrow testified about all these murders, his lawyers held a press conference admitting their knowledge. Why they did this is unclear. Garrow was convicted.[94]

In 1975 Belge was charged with violating a New York public health law because he had failed to report the location of the missing women's bodies.

After a press conference, "public indignation reached the fever pitch." The trial court dismissed Belge's case on grounds of attorney-client privilege. It accepted the slippery slope argument: "No attorney will be able to listen to those facts without being faced with the Hobson's choice of violating the law or violating his professional code of Ethics." The Appellate Division affirmed the trial court's decision but rejected an absolute claim of attorney-client privilege: "We believe that an attorney must protect his client's interests, but also must observe basic human standards of decency, having due regard to the need that the legal system accord justice to the interests of society and its individual members."[95]

The lawyers "became pariahs in their own city." They lost friends and received death threats. Their legal practices shriveled. Their actions became the public's poster child for lawyers serving injustice in the name of justice, not the less defensible actions of the ABA reacting to the NSM controversy.[96]

The Marketing of Legal Services

In 1974 Department of Justice (DOJ) officials threatened to charge the ABA with violating the Sherman Antitrust Act. The ABA's Code of Professional Responsibility, they alleged, included anticompetitive group legal services rules designed to boost lawyers' income. The ABA quickly acquiesced. That year, a Senate Judiciary Committee attacked lawyers for serving themselves at the public's expense. In 1976 the DOJ sued the ABA, alleging its ban on lawyer advertising violated antitrust law. The ABA again acquiesced. In between these events, a unanimous Supreme Court held in *Goldfarb v. Virginia State Bar* (1975) that minimum fee schedules violated federal antitrust laws. The court concluded that the practice of law was a trade subject to the Sherman Act, and "it is no disparagement of the practice of law as a profession to acknowledge that it has this business aspect." In 1977 the Supreme Court held Arizona's ban on lawyer advertising unconstitutional on free speech grounds. The Arizona ban followed the ABA Code's language. Then the Federal Trade Commission (FTC) joined in, investigating whether it should regulate the legal profession.[97]

Group legal services was a longtime ABA bugbear. The traditional argument was that it would lead to a decline in professional independence and an embrace of the "morals of the marketplace." But beginning in the early 1960s, several Supreme Court opinions held that the First Amendment protected union members using a group legal services plan. It reiterated its view in *United Transportation Union v. State Bar of Michigan* (1971). The ABA refused to hear the message; it barely acknowledged a place for group legal services and narrowly amended the code. These so-called Houston amendments, DOJ officials warned, raised the specter of ethics "rules designed to enhance only the economic well-being of lawyers." The ABA got the message and repealed them.[98]

The DOJ filed its antitrust complaint in June 1976. It accused the ABA of restraining trade because the code "prohibit[s] lawyers from engaging in price advertising and other advertising about the availability and cost of legal services." ABA members were accused of agreeing to "abide by" and "police said provisions of the Code." The ABA barely modified its ban on lawyer advertising at its February 1976 meeting. This was deemed unsatisfactory, and the lawsuit followed.[99]

The ABA slightly modified its lawyer advertising rules in August. It also began calling the code a "model," to avoid the "policing" allegation. In its answer to the lawsuit, the ABA defended itself on First Amendment grounds. States independently chose whether to adopt the code, and if so, how. Its answer to the lawsuit modified "Code" with "model" four times. The ABA board of governors called the code a "recommendation." ABA president Lawrence E. Walsh's annual report concluded, "The Association promulgates a model code of professional conduct for consideration by the appropriate state bodies."[100]

This was technically accurate but misleading. The ABA had always prided itself on drafting rules that were adopted as law by states. Its pride and power manifested in the special committees promoting state implementation of the code. It was wildly successful in this endeavor in the early 1970s. Within three years, the Code of Professional Responsibility was law in forty-three states and the District of Columbia. Four additional bar associations adopted it for their members. Other than the group legal services provision, most states adopted the code with just slight modifications. Most states also adopted the Clark Report on lawyer discipline and the 1972 Code of Judicial Conduct.[101]

This dustup ended when the Supreme Court issued *Bates v. State Bar of Arizona* (1977). Remarkably, the court issued its opinion less than eighteen months after Bates placed his first legal services ad.

Even though dismissal was a foregone conclusion once *Bates* was issued, the DOJ did not do so for a year. It fairly criticized as too narrow the ABA's

1977 changes to its rules on lawyer advertising. Once the ABA amended its amended advertising rules in 1978 (though again narrowly), the DOJ let the issue drop. By then, the ABA no longer required its members to swear to obey the "model" code and no longer claimed to regulate its members' professional conduct. It publicly reiterated that the code was a "model." Comparing the indexes of the ABA's 1977 and 1978 *Annual Reports* shows that only in the latter year was the Code of Professional Responsibility listed under *M*, not *C*.[102]

The FTC did not back off. It announced in December 1977 an investigation into the legal profession. Six months later, two FTC officials suggested that "restrictions on the delivery of legal services limit the support . . . and inhibit 'opportunities for price competition.'" This eventually proved an empty threat.[103]

Were restrictions on marketing legal services a crucial or essential aspect of professionalism? No, concluded the *Bates* court. Were bar associations trade or professional associations? Yes, concluded one DOJ antitrust lawyer. Speaking to an ABA group, he concluded that, while many lawyers "honestly believe that much of the activity of the bar association is public service activity," a look at what the bar association had recently done suggested "many of its actions had nothing at all to do with public interest, but were instead the kinds of actions that would have been expected by a trade association." Bar associations had to decide "either to represent the interests of the lawyers . . . [or] disclaim interest or involvement in those issues which relate only or primarily to the economic concerns of lawyers."[104]

Since 1945, the ABA had worked to be both. It fully embraced efforts to link professionalism with higher incomes by the late 1950s (see chapter 5). It enticed ordinary lawyers to join the ABA in large part by teasing economic rewards. In the 1960s the *ABA Journal* ran an annual column on lawyer income; in the 1970s it offered an annual economic forecast.[105]

The ABA also marched resolutely toward becoming a public service organization. In 1975 future ABA president David Brink wrote an essay about lawyer regulation after Watergate. He wrote of the ABA's transformation: "In the last seven years [1968–1975] the Association has evolved rapidly, under my eyes, from a trade organization to one that is a public interest group first and a lawyer interest group second."[106]

As competition for clients increased and income declined, it became more difficult for ordinary lawyers to accept that their needs were not the bar's foremost interest. This was increasingly the case both for lawyers representing individuals and for those learning that "partner" meant little if one wasn't also a "rainmaker" who brought clients to the firm.

"A Dog-Eat-Dog World"

In a posthumously published essay, Robert Kutak, chairman of the commission responsible for the ABA's 1983 Model Rules of Professional Conduct, defended ethical limits on attorney-client confidentiality: "It may be a dog-eat-dog world, but one dog may eat another only according to the rules." The adversary system's rules were based on the premise that "open and relatively unrestrained competition among individuals produces the maximum collective good." The adversary system was also "in most respects Darwinian." Private-practice lawyers engaged in social Darwinian behavior could console themselves with the knowledge that they were doing some collective good. Consolation, however, did not mean reconciliation of the lawyer's duties to client and public.[107]

At a 1976 Pound Conference on public dissatisfaction with the administration of justice, Chief Justice Burger listed nine causes of concern. None included unethical or uncivil behavior by lawyers. Ten other speeches were published, and not one discussed lawyers behaving badly. Only two mentioned excessive conduct by lawyers. One declared, "Abuse in the use of discovery was a major concern" of the conference. But this was untrue. No one inveighed against litigation abuse (the phrase wasn't even used). And even that one author limited abuse to a very small number of cases. Finally, his conclusion was modest: discovery abuse was "an exceptional occurrence." Judge Milton Pollack agreed: "Few, if any, abuses of discovery exist in connection with ordinary litigation."[108]

Yet, from the end of that year through 1983 (and later; see chapter 7), claims of unethical and uncivil behavior among lawyer-litigators bloomed. Just between the Pound Conference and 1980, a number of judges and lawyers concluded that discovery abuse by lawyers had infected ordinary civil cases. The ABA created a Committee for the Study of Discovery Abuse that urged reforming the Federal Rules of Civil Procedure to "curb discovery abuse." Attorney General Griffin Bell agreed. ABA president William Spann followed up by claiming that court congestion was a result of discovery abuse. Federal judge John Grady rested the blame on lawyers, who acted "primarily for the purpose of generating fees." The ABA committee issued a second report, calling discovery abuse "serious and widespread." A lawyer opened a 1981 essay by writing, "Discovery has become an instrument of abuse and oppression" caused by lawyers. In open court in April 1980, Judge Grady excoriated the lawyers representing AT&T for their egregious and unethical behavior. Their conduct in obstructing the case was "disgraceful ... the worst possible example that one could find of all the things that we all decry so much about what the so-called litigators are doing to the court system of this country." He wasn't finished: "Every time I look at something that AT&T has done in this case by way of pretrial discover[y] ... I come away with a feeling of depression that I find difficult to describe to you and I hope that you have some sense of shame for what you have done in this case." Grady's shaming may reflect lawyers' absence of guilt or remorse. Lawyers appeared to align themselves with clients rather than the professional community or the court, suspiciously so when the client paid well. This episode was emblematic of a broader problem. Some lawyers either lacked an ethical compass (or conscience) or were willing to ignore their conscience if their clients so desired. Acquiescence to the "morals of the marketplace" was the rule. Grady's hope that the lawyers felt shame worked only if the ideal of honor existed. Shame is reserved for those who fail to act honorably. But what was shameful behavior in the legal community? What values did lawyers declare?[109]

Upheaval in the Large Law Firm

In 1973 Paul Hoffman optimistically concluded his study of New York's largest law firms. He noted how well placed they were to assist the public interest and urged this elite caste to serve "less as a lackey and more of an 'expert,' more detached, more independent, someone paid by the client but responsible to the general public." A decade later, Hoffman published a sequel. His tone was pessimistic: "The legal powerhouses on Wall Street and in midtown Manhattan exist, not to chase the elusive butterflies of abstract ideals, but to make money."[110]

This bottom-line ethos was commonplace among large law firms by the late 1970s. When Los Angeles lawyer Marshall Manley was profiled in the May 1978 issue of *Esquire*, he was hurriedly building a large corporate law firm: "I have no qualms about stealing away lawyers and clients from other firms. It's the keystone of our program." The profile's author, Steven Brill, published the first issue of *American Lawyer* nine months later; its focus was "the money that partners at big law firms made." *Chicago* magazine published "The Pinstripe Revolution" in July 1979. The "revolution" was the movement of lawyers among large firms in Chicago—a merry-go-round tied to compensation. "These days any partner worth his salt at a major Chicago law firm is earning at least $100,000 a year." What clients apparently wanted for the fees they paid was not a "gentlemanly style of counsel" but a "more aggressive firm."[111]

The largest law firms in 1971 ranged from 110 and 240 lawyers. By 1979, the median number of lawyers in the twenty largest firms was 235; by 1985, that median number was 395. Between 1977 and 1982, the receipts of private-practice lawyers doubled to $34 billion. From 1972 to 1987, receipts for large law firms "increased, in real dollars, an average of ten percent per year . . . more than double the rate of growth in the legal services field generally." Though some complained of "profit pressures," the fifty largest law firms doubled their share of the legal services market between 1972 and 1986.[112]

These were large businesses operated as businesses. The next step was inevitable. A Chicago lawyer said of his partners, "There's a lot of deadwood here. We should get rid of them, but I don't want to be the one to fire them." Soon enough, large law firms found lawyers willing to execute that task. If law firms were to "survive," concluded the new managing partners of New York's Cadwalader, Wickersham & Taft in March 1982, partners deemed "deadwood" had to be cleared out.[113]

Model Rules of Professional Conduct

Dean L. Ray Patterson attacked the Model Code of Professional Responsibility in the May 1977 *ABA Journal*. The code was "a transitional document, representing a middle stage in the development of a law for lawyers." A "defect common" to transitional documents was that they were "rigid and simplistic, complex and contradictory, and difficult to read." The model code should be replaced by a mature code in which lawyers discarded "the fiction that ethical problems for lawyers are matters of ethics rather than law."[114]

Patterson's criticism was among the most prominent in a series of critiques from all political perspectives. It was also a setup. Incoming ABA president William B. Spann Jr., like Patterson, lived in Atlanta. The DOJ had already indicated its dismay with the code's anticompetition rules, and the

Supreme Court's decision in *Bates* was imminent. The code's structure and substance made it an inviting target. Patterson's criticism allowed Spann to call for a new ethics code, publicly announced later that year. Omaha lawyer Robert J. Kutak, an ABA insider, was named to lead the commission; its task was to "take a complete look at all facets of legal ethics." Spann suggested a particular approach: "It would be far more helpful if the code were written as a restatement of law." Patterson was named the Kutak Commission's reporter.[115]

When the ABA approved the Model Rules of Professional Conduct in August 1983, it took a step toward translating ethics rules into statements of law. But it did so while rejecting much of the Kutak Commission's original vision: the lawyer as a trustee of the public interest. This lawyer served both as a loyal representative of clients and as a devoted public servant. As the Kutak Commission's various proposals were drafted, the MRPC diminished the latter role in favor of the former. The lawyer's ethical duties were best understood in light of private markets: the lawyer served as the client's agent, completing legal tasks as directed by the client.[116]

The ten lawyers and judges initially on the commission possessed a significant record of (and interest in) public service. At the time the commission was formed, ABA leaders and legal academics emphasized the lawyer's duties as a public servant. The lawyer's duty as a social trustee was taken seriously by commission members, even though many lawyers dismissed it.

When the Kutak Commission first met in September 1977, it agreed to adopt a restatement-like approach, jettisoning the tripartite structure of the model code. The ethics code needed to restore public trust in American lawyers, so the commission decided to start afresh. Doing so might require it to propose unpopular rules, but as one unidentified commission member commented, "our Committee ought not to hesitate to promulgate statements of ethics it believes to be correct but which may not meet with the general approval of the Bar."[117]

The Kutak Commission also emphasized the lawyer's duty as social trustee. A code of ethics should require lawyers to take into account "a determinable public interest" when representing their private clients. The commission was both realistic and romantic. Even though "invocation of the 'public interest' will not solve the question . . . it must certainly become a part of the equation leading to the solution." The commission's "mission" was "to confront a 'new law' and 'new ethics' of today and tomorrow."[118]

This approach responded directly to the model code's weakness.

Reporter Geoffrey C. Hazard Jr. characterized the code as adopting the "basic posture of 'my client, first, last and always,' [which] allowed little room for development of the attorney's role as an officer of the court." Hazard had replaced Patterson after it became clear that Patterson and Kutak worked poorly together. The change in reporter had no effect on the commission's ethos. Patterson's preliminary working draft declared, as a black-letter rule, "The Code of Professional Standards is based on the policy of fairness in the practice of law on the part of both the private and public lawyers." Its "rationale" was based on a lawyer's duty to assist clients "in a manner consistent with 'Equal Justice Under Law.'"[119]

The commission's early "theme" was "lawyer autonomy." Autonomy meant the lawful discretion to choose "*not* to do what should not be done," which implicitly included acting contrary to the client's desires. What should the commission tell the public about its work? Two members privately said it should be described as "an authoritative statement that lawyers are responsible to demands beyond those of their immediate clients" and "regulation of a private profession in the public interest." Relatedly, the lawyer's status as an "officer of the court" should be understood as making the lawyer "something more than a paid partisan, something more than a mouthpiece, but how much more?" Additionally, the commission sought to ban the words *zeal* and *zealous* from its rules. "'Zealous,' it seems, has curiously come to mean 'overzealous,' [and] strong sentiment was found around the table for dropping 'zeal' altogether as a descriptive term with ethical consequences. It simply has too much baggage."[120]

These comments were challenged by some members. For example, should a lawyer be required to disclose client perjury to the court? Was a lawyer required to tell the client that if the client lied on the witness stand, the lawyer was bound to disclose this to the court?

The commission's working draft was sent to some interested members for discussion at the August 1979 ABA meeting. Kutak believed this wasn't even an actual draft; the commission had not voted, and the document included "portions with which a majority disagree." Despite his effort to lower expectations, critics attacked. The commission was assailed for not releasing the draft broadly (a standard post-Watergate criticism). That issue was "remedied" when the draft was leaked to *Legal Times* and *Daily Report for Executives*. It was also substantively criticized. Monroe Freedman called the working draft "a failure," both "radical and radically wrong." The American Trial Lawyers Association (ATLA), whose members largely represented injured persons, dismissed the working draft and engaged Freedman to write a competing code.[121]

What appeared most grating to critics was what commission members considered the working draft's greatest achievement: reframing the lawyer's duties. For example, Rule 1.4 in the working draft was titled "Representing client with zeal," but it focused on zeal's limits. The rule detailed when a lawyer "may decline to pursue a course of action on behalf of a client that the lawyer considers unjust although in conformity with the law." Rule 1.5 listed several instances when a lawyer was required to disclose a confidence. Rule 3.2(a)(4) required a lawyer to "rectify the consequences" resulting when the lawyer offered false or fabricated evidence, including a client's perjury.[122]

Still, the commission was cautiously optimistic at its post-ABA meeting. "Zeal" continued to bedevil it, however, until it was replaced by "diligence."[123]

A discussion draft was released in early 1980. Again, and more forcefully, critics attacked; they included ATLA's president and the *Wall Street Journal*. The *National Law Journal* editorialized that the draft's "proposals are likely to generate controversy and heated debate within the legal profession." It was right. The commission's draft reemphasized that "lawyers are responsible to demands beyond those of their immediate clients."[124]

Several controversial proposals were dropped. Additionally, this draft listed fewer instances in which a lawyer was required to disclose a client's confidence. But it maintained the prohibition on offering "evidence that the lawyer is convinced beyond a reasonable doubt is false."[125]

Kutak reiterated the commission's interest in starting afresh, noting it had "soon realized that more than a series of amendments or a general restatement of the Model Code of Professional Responsibility was in order. The Commission determined that a comprehensive reformulation was required." The fear of an ethics revolution was so great that the National Organization of Bar Counsel (NOBC) misread Kutak's statement as urging a "comprehensive *reformation*" of ethics, not a "comprehensive *reformulation*." This misreading symbolized growing opposition to the commission's work.[126]

Kutak's cover letter inviting comments on the discussion draft stated, "We plan to submit a final version of the Rules to the House of Delegates at its February, 1981 meeting." Critics had to act promptly, and they produced an "enormous response." One comment summarizes the uneasiness within the profession: "The Model Rules depart from the approach taken in earlier efforts to define the ethical basis for lawyers' actions. The draft represents a comprehensive and far reaching effort to revise both the conceptual framework and much of the content by which the profession is to regulate its conduct." The draft went too far. It was "likely to have a substantial adverse impact on the nature of the attorney-client relationship and on the ability to provide clients with effective assistance of counsel."[127]

Some argued the shift from a "basic posture" to considering the public's needs was wrong. The preamble "marks a significant departure from the traditional concept that the 'duty of the lawyer to his client and his duty to the legal system are the same.'" The lawyer "need not act as a 'mouthpiece' or as a 'hired gun.'" Even so, the discussion draft got the balance all wrong. Another association agreed, noting its "difficulty with the concept of the lawyer as a protector of the public interest especially at the expense of client confidences." On and on they went. Several organizations supported mandatory disclosures, but more were opposed.[128]

ATLA published a draft ethics code in mid-1980, as did the NOBC. They did not agree. ATLA promoted a code premised on client autonomy. For example, a lawyer who disclosed the location of a victim's remains to the victim's parents should be disciplined. NOBC rejected ATLA's approach. It concluded that lawyers were social trustees, and as such, they were required to disclose client confidences in significantly more situations than ATLA believed ethically proper. NOBC believed its proposed limits on the lawyer's duty to keep secret client confidences benefited the public. These conflicting criticisms led Kutak to ask for and receive a tactical yearlong delay.[129]

The proposed final draft (May 1981) bowed to the commenters. It broadened the rule of confidentiality and further narrowed its exceptions. Proposed rules concerning "fairness" disappeared. A lawyer was required to disclose "a client's surprise perjury," but the duty to disclose a client's deception was limited to cases in which rectification was "necessary."[130]

The Kutak Commission largely stood its ground regarding the lawyer's dual loyalties. The lawyer remained "a representative of a client but also an officer of the court." Kutak's introduction framed five questions concerning the limits of a lawyer's duty to a client. This allowed him to argue against the impoverished "basic posture" of my client first, last, and always. He preferred an invigorated role for the lawyer as an officer of the court.

The commission's report on the final draft (1982) portrayed its proposed model rules as a relatively modest reform, avoiding all radical positions. For example, "Nothing in the final draft produced more comment than the three Rules addressing client-lawyer confidentiality." The commission heard and responded: "No fundamental professional value assumed larger importance in the Commission's work than that of client-lawyer confidentiality." The "*only* mandatory [disclosure] provisions" concerned candor to the tribunal (Rule 3.3) and a duty of truthfulness to third parties (Rule 4.1). Even these were more limited than in earlier versions. Two other "broad principles" were listed: "the duty of loyalty to clients, and the requirement that lawyers conform their conduct to law." The lawyer's role as an "officer of the court" was found only in the preamble, and it was mentioned only after declaring the lawyer's role as "a representative of clients." The lawyer's duty to the public largely disappeared. "Zeal" made a triumphant return at the behest of several bar organizations. The report listed each rule change it had made in the past year and which bar groups had caused the change. This was a naked appeal for support. The final draft also listed proposals not adopted, to show transparency and to meet the Goldilocks position.[131]

The final draft continued the drift toward the existing consensus. It hoped to soothe its critics by declaring that its rules were not "an attack on the adversary system [nor did they] tilt away from a concern for clients toward a concern for third parties and society at large." In fact, the rules "work[ed] no such shift in the profession's values." The basic posture, considering the client's interests first, last, and always, was enshrined in the final draft. Still, that wasn't enough.[132]

At the ABA's annual meeting in August 1982, just one rule, Rule 1.5 (fees), was adopted. The House of Delegates did so only after a lengthy, digressive discussion peppered with frequent amendments, including one after approval. When the discussion moved to Rule 1.6 on confidences, things fell apart. More amendments were offered, and a motion was made to discharge the Kutak Commission and appoint another committee for a "fresh approach." Instead, the ABA deferred consideration.[133]

By the time the ABA met in February 1983, Robert Kutak had died of a heart attack and a fraud scandal involving lawyers had been widely publicized in the *New York Times*. The delay "gave the opposition time to organize, which it did very effectively." "Thirty-eight organizations and individuals submitted 216 proposed amendments" to the rules. The sclerotic fix was in. Over the course of five sessions during two long days, the model rules were the subject of extraordinary disagreement.[134]

For example, Rule 1.6(b), which listed the exceptions to the lawyer's duty to keep client confidences, was the subject of ten amendments. Seven were withdrawn, two were defeated, and one was approved. The approved amendment narrowed even further a lawyer's discretion to disclose a client confidence. It prohibited disclosure of a confidence to prevent the client from defrauding another. For example, if a client told the lawyer he was planning to defraud someone of their life savings, the lawyer could not disclose this unless the communication was unrelated to their professional relationship. It also barred a lawyer from disclosing a client confidence to "rectify the consequences of a client's criminal or fraudulent act in the furtherance of which the lawyer's services had been used." This had been the subject of an extensive report in the *New York Times* a month earlier. OPM Leasing Services Inc. (OPM stood for "other people's money") collapsed in 1981 in what was then the largest fraud in American history. "OPM's lawyers knew about [its owners'] criminal ways for years" and said nothing. Some viewed the amendment as "vindication" of those lawyers, but it was not. The law firm "paid out millions of dollars to settle civil litigation brought against it for willfully or recklessly aiding its client's fraud." When the dust finally settled, the ABA took a nearly polar opposite position from the 1979 working draft. As adopted, the model rules spoke to private interest almost exclusively.[135]

The debate ground on. Once the discussion ended, the ABA needed to reconcile the amendments with the rules. After a May 23, 1983, meeting and some additional amendments, the MRPC was approved.[136]

Conclusion

Americans were poorer at the end of the 1970s than at the beginning. Ordinary lawyers joined their fellow Americans, but lawyers working for large firms earned more money and obtained greater professional prestige. Prestige was correlated with whether clients were individuals or organizations; it was "negatively correlated" with pro bono work. Lawyers respected other lawyers for not serving the public.[137]

When finalizing the MRPC's adoption, one delegate proposed striking this sentence: "Thus, when an opposing party is well represented, a lawyer can be a zealous advocate on behalf of a client and at the same time assume that justice is being done." This quote from the preamble created no enforceable duties. The motion failed. What the dissenting delegate feared was the duty to consider anything beyond the client's interest. Given the reshaping of the MRPC, he needn't have worried.

He also expressed the legal profession's inward turn. The commission accepted one amendment to the preamble. It declared: "However, a lawyer is guided by personal conscience and the approbation of professional peers." Somehow, bar leaders were stunned when, post adoption, lawyers looked "at nothing but the rules."[138]

CHAPTER SEVEN

The Professionalism Crisis and Legal Ethics in a Time of Rapid Change, 1983–2015

Professionalism and the Lawyer's Role

Black's Law Dictionary first defined *professionalism* in its eighth edition, published in 2004. By then, lawyers had been worrying for two decades about the decline in "the practice of a learned art in a characteristically methodical, courteous, and ethical manner."[1]

The ABA's adoption of the Model Rules of Professional Conduct (1983) had not clarified how to practice law professionally and ethically. Instead, it revealed fissures in the broader legal profession. Some lawyers argued that those cracks were caused by abandoning the ideal of lawyer independence and professionalism. The issue of threats and challenges to lawyers' professional independence was also a topic at the ABA's annual meeting in 1983. Its importance to ABA leaders was indicated by its assignment to "presidential showcase" status.[2]

The twofold premise of the Tort and Insurance Practice Section (TIPS) program at the 1983 meeting was that the lawyer's professional independence from government, society, and client was crucial to the proper functioning of a democratic society, but that independence had cratered. Lawyer-critics usually argued that this decline was a result of the drive to maximize income even at the expense of serving the public's interests. One speaker was elite New York lawyer Peter Megargee Brown. In March 1982, after twenty-seven years at Cadwalader, Wickersham & Taft, Brown's partners demanded and received his resignation. As Brown delicately put it, he and the firm's five managing partners had "a difference of opinion about the nature and conduct of a professional law firm." Brown billed the dispute as one between professionalism and profits. He believed a law firm existed for reasons beyond measures of profitability, and his former partners strongly disagreed.[3]

His speech struck a professional nerve. It was republished in at least five state bar journals. The ABA published his talk and those of the other TIPS program participants in a 1984 book. Outgoing ABA president Morris Harrell echoed Brown's lament and urged lawyers to maintain their status as professionals. Professionalism, wrote Harrell, "involves acceptance of high ethical standards, which generally include a dedication to public services for the benefit and protection of society that looks beyond the mere earning of a livelihood." TIPS offered a second program on professionalism at the 1984 ABA meeting, which also received presidential showcase status.[4]

Between the two showcases, Chief Justice Warren Burger spoke at the ABA's February 1984 meeting. He agreed with Brown that lawyer professionalism had declined. In response to these charges, the ABA created a Commission on Professionalism, for it feared "the Bar might be moving away from the principles of professionalism and that it was so perceived by the public." The commission agreed with Brown, Burger, and others in its 1986 final report, known as the Stanley Report.[5]

The ABA pressed the issue of lawyer professionalism. It created a committee to promote the Stanley Report's conclusions. More than four thousand copies of the report were distributed in the first year after its publication. The committee also created *The Professional Lawyer*, a publication featuring "issues on professionalism and ethics." In 1992 the ABA made the committee monitoring professionalism issues a standing committee.[6]

The Stanley Report generated a frenzy of published commentary on professionalism. The American Bar Foundation and a bevy of law schools hosted conferences and published essays on the decline and fall of the profession. Others wrote books for the more pessimistically minded. But nearly all held out some hope for the future. Because the emphasis was on recovering from a "loss" of professionalism, some sought to mine the past to uncover the keys to a possible return. The problem with this approach was twofold: First, no golden age of American lawyers had ever existed. Second, it is almost always true that different eras are incommensurable. The 1980s were sufficiently different from earlier times of crisis to make comparisons of the work, status, and role of lawyers nearly impossible.[7]

In 1988 TIPS and the ABA urged other lawyer organizations to advance the cause of professionalism and invited them to adopt "a Lawyer's 'Creed of Professionalism.'" TIPS offered a sample creed, one proposition of which required the lawyer to "remember that, in addition to commitment to my client's cause, my responsibilities as a lawyer include a devotion to the public good." What constituted the public good was undefined. More importantly, the language of this provision highlighted the inevitable bias found in the private practice of the law: the lawyer's duty to the (paying) client was a "commitment" involving action, rigor, and substance, but the lawyer's responsibility to the public good was to serve it with "devotion," which involved faith, not works. The sample creed also warned lawyers to guard against abuses such as "excessive zeal, a 'win at any cost' mentality, 'scorched earth' tactics and apotheosizing of 'playing hard ball.'" The sample creed implicitly asked lawyers to fine-tune the modifier: the lawyer was bound to act zealously, but not in a manner that constituted excessively zealous behavior. The creed defined professionalism modestly, in light of specifically listed behaviors toward clients, opposing parties and lawyers, the courts, and the public. Many provisions in the Model Rules channeled lawyer behavior the same way, backstopping demands with the threat of disciplinary sanction. A creed of professionalism asked lawyers to go beyond the minimum required to keep their law licenses. But "beyond" led to professional fracture. The bare injunctions in the sample creed were intended to bring together a group lacking cohesion by highlighting a purpose other than profit maximization.[8]

At that same meeting, the ABA agreed that a "Lawyers' Pledge of Professionalism" should be sent to members. It included a pledge to "subordinate business concerns to professionalism concerns," and it acknowledged lawyers' "responsibilities" as officers of the court. The twelfth and final pledge was to "honor the spirit and intent, as well as the requirements," of professional ethics. Like the creed, the pledge was "aspirational," having no legal effect. Its sponsor, the Young Lawyers Division, recognized the economic pressures facing lawyers but concluded that "such interests can never be allowed to be predominant and that the practice of law is first and foremost a profession." Practicing lawyers owed a "broader duty of protecting the system of justice."[9]

Professionalism advocates encouraged legal organizations to adopt the creed by noting its de minimis cost and significant reputational benefits. Lawyers might perceive some greater sense of public purpose after reading the creed, and organizational adoption might offer comfort to a broader public suspicious of the significant power wielded by lawyers. At the time this pitch was made, lawyers' reputation was worse than in the aftermath of Watergate. Embracing professionalism appeared to offer a considerable upside and little or no downside risk.[10]

Bar associations and state appellate courts adopted the TIPS sample creed, a variation of it, or their own creed. One early creed adopter was the Illinois State Bar Association (1988). The Georgia Supreme Court created the first statewide Commission on Professionalism in 1989, and by 1990, "forty-five states ha[d] undertaken studies on the professionalism and ethical standards of their bars and ten ha[d] issued formal reports." By 2015, at least 123 courts and lawyer organizations and more than forty states had adopted a professionalism or civility creed.[11]

The intense desire by courts, bar associations, and other legal organizations to do something about the decline in professionalism continued through the 1990s. One such organization was the Conference of Chief Justices (CCJ). In 1996, "in response to concerns about a perceived decline in lawyer professionalism and its effect on public confidence in the legal profession and the justice system," the CCJ began working on a "national action plan" to counteract this decline. It adopted the consensus view that a problem existed and offered a raft of recommendations. It also encouraged the adoption of many recommendations already proposed, including proposals to improve lawyer competence, to teach professionalism in law schools, to implement a more effective lawyer disciplinary process, and to reduce abusive litigation tactics.[12]

Retired chief justice Warren Burger returned to the fray with a more pessimistic view of the profession. His pessimism extended to all members of the learned professions, as well as "those who serve in the 'money markets.'" Incivility, excessive adversarial zeal, and "huckster-shyster" advertising were all culprits. And the rules of ethics offered little or no guidance about how a professional lawyer should act.[13]

One reason for the demand that lawyers repent and turn away from unprofessional behavior was a decade of bad economic news. Although some thrived during the 1970s and 1980s, the economic premium the ordinary lawyer enjoyed dropped from 1.85 in 1970 to 1.35 in 1980. A wrenching recession from mid-1981 through most of 1982 harmed the incomes of lawyers representing small businesses and middle-class individuals. Even so, the supply of lawyers increased significantly during the 1980s, exacerbating the fall in their median income. The number of lawyers rose from 542,205 in 1980 to more than 755,000 by 1990. This increased supply placed greater economic pressure on lawyers serving individuals, accounting for the largest segment of private practitioners. That type of work grew much slower than did work for organizational clients.[14]

A second reason for the call for a (re)turn to professionalism was a desire to repair the damage caused by a rapid change in the practice of law. Diagnosticians of professional decline often linked the loss of lawyer independence and professionalism to dramatic shifts in both American society and the economy. Chief Justice Burger's February 1984 speech concluded, "We are living in a period of dramatic, spectacular and rapid change." Robert Kutak believed "these times of rapid change" required lawyers to "contemplate how changes in our profession and in the law will influence our concepts of professional duty."[15]

Burger's list of complaints in an era of rapid change overlapped the concerns of other critics, most importantly on the issue of discovery abuse. Discovery abuse represented a possible "breakdown in the professional standards of the entire profession," indicating the need for some "basic institutional reform in the legal profession."[16]

A third reason for the call for professionalism involved structural changes in the work and role of American lawyers. By the mid-1980s, an accelerated sorting of lawyers had taken place. Private-practice lawyers largely served either individuals or organizations. Within each of these hemispheres, lawyers further sorted themselves into specialized practices. Prominent lawyers such as Robert H. Jackson had argued a generation earlier that specialization was inimical to professionalism. A sustained effort to link specialization with professionalism had succeeded by the late 1970s. Its consequences became more pronounced a decade later.[17]

Professionalism meant specialization, as stated in both the Model Rules and the 1988 TIPS creed. The former encouraged specialists to communicate their expertise publicly. One of the duties asserted in the latter was for the lawyer to "endeavor to keep myself current in the areas in which I practice."[18]

Proponents of specialization argued that official recognition acceptably merged the commercial and professional aspects of the private practice of law. These advocates did not challenge the standard view that lawyers owed a duty to the public as well as to their clients. Superior private-practice lawyers provided an outstanding example of public service through private representation. Improving lawyer competence was a staple recommendation in the TIPS model creed, the CCJ's national action plan, ABA reports, and the Model Rules of Professional Conduct. For example, Model Rule 7.4

demonstrated the ethical importance of legal specialization. Merging client service with public service obviated the problem of the lawyer as a Janus-like figure, vainly attempting to serve private clients and the public interest.

Lawyers' commitment to competence was also shown by the requirement that practicing lawyers complete fifteen hours of continuing legal education each year, including one or more hours dedicated to legal ethics. In addition, lawyers were encouraged to take courses in specialized areas. By 1990, three-quarters of state bar associations had adopted mandatory continuing legal education programs.[19]

The sorting of lawyers included a cost they rarely recognized: it frayed professional bonds. Lawyers serving corporate clients enjoyed higher incomes from the 1980s on. The revenue of large law firms grew in real dollars by an average of 10 percent a year from 1972 to 1987. Receipts from corporate clients first exceeded individual client revenue by 1980 and accelerated during the next quarter century.[20]

Large law firms focused on increasing profits per partner during this time. Managing partners extended the time it took for a lawyer to make partner, created classes of partnership (equity and nonequity), hired rainmakers from other firms, and fired partners who failed to meet their expectations, such as Peter Megargee Brown. One sign of success was the salary paid new associates at large law firms. By 1986, they received a salary of $65,000 (plus bonuses), greater than the income earned by the average sole practitioner.[21]

Two mid-1980s additions to the American lawyer's lexicon offer some insight into the professionalism crisis. In 1985 *American Lawyer* magazine began publishing its annual AmLaw 100, surveying the hundred most profitable large law firms based on several metrics, including profits per equity partner.[22] As one perceptive critic noted, this "managed to compare (envy) lawyers and law firms (pride) on the metric of money (greed)." The Am-Law 100 survey accelerated (but didn't cause) the disintegration of "lockstep" partner compensation. It was replaced at nearly all large law firms with "eat what you kill" compensation, disproportionately rewarding those who brought in profitable clients. The word *rainmaker* also took hold in the mid-1980s. A rainmaker was a lawyer whose roster of clients generated legal work for many, making "rain" (money) for the firm. The term was sufficiently new in 1984 that an *ABA Journal* article explained what it meant and why all lawyers should strive to become one.[23]

The income disparity among lawyers representing different types of clients "increased substantially" between 1975 and 1995. Additionally, attorney prestige was linked to income. In a 1975 survey, John Heinz and Edward Laumann found a "lack of a strong relationship between income and prestige." Twenty years later, they noted that, among Chicago lawyers, income "distribution corresponds to the distribution of prestige."[24]

The increased supply of lawyers in all fields intensified the competition for work, which made the status of any nonrainmaking lawyer less secure. Specialization brought financial rewards to lawyers with desired skill sets, but demand often ebbed and flowed. Even when feasting, the possibility of famine remained, for a significant percentage of lawyers at large law firms "typically devote[d] a third or more of their billable hours to a single client." Client dependence generated anxiety, as professional status was tied to pay. The call for a renewed professionalism responded to this anxiety.[25]

Client dependence was exacerbated by a change in the role of corporate clients. Such clients had become more amenable to leaving their longtime private counsel. In part, this was because they no longer believed outside lawyers offered a "superior work product." Clients "simply assumed they would find those attributes in any major law firm they hired." Lawyer integrity mattered little to them. Lawyer specialization created economic incentives to please a dwindling number of clients. Rainmakers began taking larger shares of their firms' profits. Consequently, the hired gun ethic became more firmly entrenched in private practice.[26]

The hired gun had transformed into the "*Rambo* litigator." The ABA's 1986 Stanley Report criticized the unprofessionalism of lawyers who sought to "'win at any cost.'" One early effort to punish such behavior was the amendment of Federal Rule of Civil Procedure 11 in 1983 to expand what constituted a frivolous claim. A lawyer filing a frivolous claim might be liable for the costs associated with defending against it. Though designed to dissuade lawyers from engaging in a particular form of unprofessional behavior, the rule change generated "a deleterious effect on lawyer relations."[27]

As competition for clients increased, the surplus value many lawyers had once enjoyed returned to their clients. For those promoting the professionalism crusade, the question was how to shape its meaning in a profit-driven era. The ABA Sample Creed of Professionalism (1988) opened one avenue to private-practice lawyers: "I will be a vigorous and zealous advocate on behalf of my client, while recognizing, as an officer of the court, that excessive zeal may be detrimental to my client's interests as well as to the proper functioning of our system of justice."[28] "May be detrimental" implied that, on some occasions, excessive zeal might benefit the client.

After a fifteen-year professionalism crisis, the ABA Section of Legal Education and Admissions to the Bar finally offered a new definition of professionalism. It spoke of expert service to private clients and nodded to an undefined public good: "A professional lawyer is an expert in law pursuing a learned art in service to clients and in the spirit of public service; and engaging in these pursuits as part of a common calling to promote justice and public good." A professional possessed six "essential characteristics": knowledge, analytical skill, preparedness, practical wisdom, ethical conduct and integrity, and dedication to justice and the public good. The first three were technical skills; practical wisdom included the exercise of good judgment; and the last two bundled internal character traits with external standards. A professional lawyer's strong moral character made it possible to adhere to external standards of ethical conduct, and such lawyers served the public good by dedicating themselves to justice.[29]

The cause of professionalism was lost during the Great Recession of 2008. The ongoing adoption of creeds and civility standards cannot mask the disintegration of the model of the lawyer as social trustee and promoter of justice and public good. To do good was immensely difficult when relatively few were doing well. The market model triumphed.

Disciplining Lawyers

The ABA's efforts to encourage professionalism were joined by a renewed attempt to sanction lawyers through disciplinary enforcement. "Times have changed," intoned the Commission on Evaluation of Disciplinary Enforcement in the McKay Report (1992). Twenty years after the Clark Report (see chapter 6), "revolutionary changes" in lawyer discipline had taken place, but more needed to be done. The McKay Report blamed the ABA—its emphasis on ethics *rules* had led to disciplinary myopia: "The existing system of regulating the profession is narrowly focused on violations of professional ethics. It provides no mechanisms to handle other types of clients' complaints." The result was a pinched and ineffective system in which the complaints of "tens of thousands of clients alleging legitimate grounds for dissatisfaction" were routinely dismissed. The emphasis on rules was supposed to create a more mature document. But the National Organization of Bar Counsel had rejected the 1980 discussion draft of the Model Rules for this very reason: A restatement-like approach to legal ethics "would seriously impair the acceptability and effectiveness of a Model Code."[30]

The conclusion of the McKay Report was brutally forthright: "The profession's attempts to deal with substandard practice have not worked." The sample creed was "valuable only to those predisposed to improve their practice." Unbelievers simply ignored it, which was understandable, given its unenforceability.[31]

The McKay Report made twenty-two recommendations, most of which the ABA accepted. In 1989 the ABA adopted Model Rules for Lawyer Disciplinary Enforcement. The McKay Report's accepted recommendations found their way into these rules, and they were particularly valuable in shifting the disciplinary enforcement debate. Clients' major complaints concerned lawyer ineptness, not intentional misconduct. Lawyers failed to communicate sufficiently and effectively, failed to act promptly and intelligibly, and failed to explain what legal services accompanied which fees. These were features of "lawyer incompetence and neglect." Because most states failed to sufficiently fund lawyer disciplinary entities, delays and unarticulated dismissals of complaints dominated the system: "In 1988, over forty-four thousand disciplinary complaints were summarily dismissed." There was a mismatch between the disciplinary system design (focused on the violation of ethics rules) and most client complaints (related to incompetence and fee disputes).[32]

Additional changes were made to the Model Rules for Lawyer Disciplinary Enforcement in 1995 and 1996. The latter amendments attempted to tackle the problem of "lesser misconduct" (Rule 9B) by creating an Alternatives to Discipline Program. With one exception, these rules have remained unchanged.[33]

Whether lawyer disciplinary systems effectively expel lawyers engaged in misconduct is unclear, although the sparse data indicate they do not. A Florida study (1988–2002) found that approximately 0.3 percent of licensed Florida lawyers were publicly disciplined each year. That percentage fell during the study period. A similar trend was found in Texas. In the year before Texas implemented its Disciplinary Rules of Professional Conduct, 228 lawyers were disciplined. In the next two years, those numbers rose to 354 and 655, a near tripling of public disciplinary decisions between 1991–1992 and 1993–1994. By 2006–2007, just 320 Texas lawyers were publicly disciplined, a decline of greater than 50 percent, even as the number of licensed

Texas lawyers increased 27 percent. Just thirty lawyers were disbarred, or 0.04 percent of Texas lawyers. It seems unlikely that Texas lawyers behaved more ethically in 2007 than in 1994 or that Florida lawyers behaved better in 2002 than in 1988. The greatest unknown is how many incidents of lawyer misconduct occurred for every disciplinary action.[34]

A preliminary empirical study of lawyer misconduct concluded that lawyers behaved no differently in 2010 than in 1990. It found that 5 percent of lawyers had some record of misconduct during their careers. A majority were repeat offenders, reaffirming some prior data indicating a significant recidivism rate among disciplined lawyers.[35]

Another method of disciplining lawyers is the legal malpractice lawsuit. Two indicators of the frequency of legal malpractice claims are the number of liability insurance claims and the cost of lawyers' professional liability insurance. One study, based on data from the Attorneys' Liability Assurance Society (ALAS), found the number of claims per thousand lawyers increased from 1983 to a peak in 1991 and then fell through 2013. In the 1991 peak year there were 11.4 real claims per thousand lawyers; this dropped to 7.5 in 2013, a 34 percent decline. ALAS data are largely relevant to sole practitioners and law firms with ten or fewer lawyers. Using additional data sets, Herbert Kritzer and Neil Vidmar found higher claim rates, ranging from 9.7 to 120 per thousand lawyers; however, they also found that claim rates declined over the long term. For example, professional liability claims fell in Florida between 1985 and 1995 and in Missouri from 1995 to 2005. As for professional liability insurance costs, an insurance crisis in the mid-1980s created an incentive for the ABA to take a closer look at legal malpractice claims. Once that crisis eased, premiums leveled off.[36]

The increase in legal malpractice claims in the 1970s was joined by a professional liability insurance crisis. This led the ABA to create a task force in 1975, which later became the Committee on Lawyers' Professional Liability. Since the early 1980s, the committee has gathered and published data on professional liability claims in seven (largely) quadrennial reports. The initial report (1986) was based on nearly thirty thousand attorney liability claims. Almost half (45 percent) concerned substantive errors, such as failure to know or apply the correct law. The practice area with the most complaints was plaintiffs' personal injury, followed by real estate.[37]

Substantive errors continued to constitute the largest category of allegations in subsequent iterations, as high as 56.3 percent (1999). This finding was replicated in both Missouri and Oregon. In every study except one, plaintiffs' personal injury was the practice area subject to the highest percentage of professional liability claims. Real estate was second, except for taking first place in the 2008–2011 study. Kritzer and Vidmar found slightly different results. For example, the Oregon Professional Liability Fund listed family law and plaintiffs' personal injury as the two areas with the highest percentage of claims, with real estate fourth. (Oregon is the only state that requires lawyers to carry liability insurance.)[38]

The data collected from the 1980s through 2015 also demonstrated that sole practitioners were underrepresented in professional liability cases, and law firms with two to ten lawyers were the most overrepresented group of private-practice lawyers. Minnesota lawyers who had been in practice from eleven to twenty years were significantly overrepresented in professional liability cases.[39]

The existence of two hemispheres in the private practice of law is replicated in professional liability claims. Most claims are made against lawyers in small firms or in solo practice who represent individuals. Additionally, the types of errors correlate with the hemisphere in which the lawyer practices. The relative paucity of lawyers who sue other lawyers is one significant problem in making malpractice claims an effective method of disciplining lawyers. A second significant issue is damages. An unknown amount of lawyer misconduct is never the subject of a lawsuit. Finally, many lawyers in small firms lack malpractice insurance, making at least some of them judgment proof.[40]

In 2000 American Law Institute (ALI) director Geoffrey C. Hazard Jr., then one of the foremost legal ethics scholars in the United States, wrote, "The remedy of malpractice liability and remedy of disqualification are of greater importance in most law practice than the risk of disciplinary proceedings." The empirical data do not support these assertions. The 2012–2015 *Profile of Malpractice Claims* noted a significant drop in the percentage of claims abandoned without any payment—from 67 percent in 2008–2011 to 52 percent in 2012–2015. Lawyers paid nothing in more than 70 percent of all claims, including the claims dismissed after an unfavorable judgment.[41]

Based on an assessment of all seven quadrennial studies, the percentage of claims in which some payment was received by the plaintiff ranged from 20 to 43 percent, with most studies showing some payment in about 33 percent of claims. Data from Missouri and Oregon showed a slightly higher percentage. Overall, the long-range trend is fewer successful claims. Additionally, in most cases in which some payment is made, the amount is small. Professional liability claims are an insufficient threat to influence lawyer behavior, and they are unimportant in the private practice of law, even when "important" simply means "paying attention to."[42]

A third approach to the discipline of lawyers involved the Supreme Court's 1983 amendments to Federal Rule of Civil Procedure 11. Although Rule 11 originally permitted federal district courts to discipline lawyers who appeared before them, there were few efforts to do so. In response to a claimed litigation explosion and increasingly fractious behavior by litigators, the Supreme Court's Advisory Committee suggested that something be done. Amended Rule 11 was crafted in part "to deal with the abuses that undermined civility and professionalism." By signing a pleading, motion, or other paper, the lawyer certified that, after a reasonable inquiry well grounded in fact and warranted by law (or with a "good faith" claim to alter existing law), the filing was not being made for an improper purpose. If the lawyer violated Rule 11, "the court upon motion or upon its own initiative, shall impose upon the person who signed it, a represented party, or both, an appropriate sanction." The amendment was intended to conserve limited judicial resources, reduce the number of frivolous claims and motions filed in federal district courts, and curb litigation abuse. It would have a largely contrary effect.[43]

The amendment immediately fostered substantial "satellite litigation" alleging bad lawyer behavior. Federal district and circuit courts published nearly seven hundred Rule 11 opinions between August 1, 1983, and December 15, 1987; in just under a decade of its existence, a search in the LEXIS database listed 6,947 cases of Rule 11 sanctions. Although formal Rule 11 litigation took relatively little attorney time, informally reacting to Rule 11 was much more time-consuming. Of course, minding the contours of Rule 11 was one of its intended purposes.[44]

The consensus was that Rule 11 significantly affected the private practice of federal court litigators. The benefits of mindfulness and culling some claims and defenses, scholars concluded, were outweighed by its costs. The number of cases alone indicated the value some lawyers attributed to seeking Rule 11 monetary sanctions. However, the breadth of the demands for sanctions seemed to cause a disintegration of professional cordiality. One writer argued that "Rule 11 contributed significantly to the further decline in civility." In addition, although Rule 11 is framed as applicable to all parties, it disproportionately affected lawyers representing plaintiffs.[45]

Although Civil Procedure Rules 11 and 26(g) (mandating sanctions against lawyers who violate discovery rules) apparently had no measurable effect in curbing "litigation abuse," there may have been some positive results. Georgene Vairo concluded that federal courts' willingness to sanction lawyers had a greater impact on lawyer discipline than ethics rules did. Rule 11 "created a vehicle for punishing certain kinds of conduct that were largely unreachable or untouched before." Such sanctions, however, rarely resulted in public discipline. Under Rule 26(g), sanctions for violating discovery rules were mandatory, but monetary sanctions were discretionary. It therefore had little impact, though some complained about a "broken" discovery system.[46]

The outsized, disparate effects of Rule 11 eventually led to a kinder, gentler Rule 11 in 1993. The Advisory Committee concluded that the 1983 amendment had failed to promote more ethical behavior among civil litigators, so the 1993 amendments focused on a modified deterrence: lawyers (or parties) who filed claims or motions that met the conditions of the amended rule would be sanctioned to prevent them from repeating such action. Nonmonetary sanctions were highlighted, and sanctions could be issued only in the court's discretion.[47]

The 1993 rule had some effect on litigators' conduct. One study of its first decade found that federal district courts issued Rule 11 sanctions against lawyers (or lawyers and parties jointly) in 274 cases. Although most sanctions were upheld, the reversal rate on appeal was greater than the overall reversal rate.[48]

In *The Judicial Response to Lawyer Misconduct* (1984), the ABA blamed judges in part for lawyer misconduct. They were unaware of the size of the problem and needed to be encouraged to confront it. When the ABA revised its Model Code of Judicial Conduct in 1990, it included a provision requiring a judge to "inform the appropriate authority" if the judge possessed "knowledge . . . that a lawyer has committed a violation of the Rules of Professional Conduct that raises a substantial question as to the lawyer's honesty, trustworthiness or fitness as a lawyer." Judges have almost universally ignored this injunction. The requirement that the judge possess "knowledge"—defined as "actual knowledge"—may partly explain this state of affairs. Even so, the ABA continued this mandatory duty in its 2007 revision of the Model Code. Nearly all the states that adopted the 2007 Model Code of Judicial Conduct included a mandatory reporting rule, yet judges continue to ignore it. Judicial reticence may be related to lawyers' general unwillingness to report other lawyers to bar disciplinary authorities; it also may have to do with the fact that judges in many states are elected to office.[49]

Anecdotally, it appears that lawyers pay little attention to, and evince little understanding of, the rules of professional conduct, even as courts assume the opposite to be true. Lawyers may pay slightly more attention to the possibility of malpractice claims than they do to disciplinary rules, but even that possibility seems far-fetched. For some litigators, the possibility of monetary sanctions, either loss of a paying client due to disqualification or punishment for filing a pleading for an improper purpose, may be worrisome. But for the vast majority of lawyers, none of these possible disciplinary actions represent a real threat. Even as most states give increased attention and resources to the lawyer disciplinary system, and even with the end of a "conspiracy of silence" among lawyers, regulatory authorities have a de minimis effect on lawyer conduct.[50]

Lawyer Disqualification

"The motion for a judicial order disqualifying a lawyer in pending litigation because of conflict is a traditional remedy that has come into prominence in recent years." Professor Charles Wolfram's 1986 assessment gently explained a feared tool used by lawyers in civil (and occasionally criminal) litigation: one party seeking to sever another's lawyer-client relationship. Incomplete empirical data suggested a rapid increase in motions to disqualify during the 1980s. Courts and commentators perceived "exponential growth"; even though some courts responded disdainfully to such motions, characterizing them as "extreme," "drastic," "severe," and "draconian," their use seemed to increase. In the mid-1990s Kenneth Penegar speculated that up to two-thirds of federal civil cases included a motion to disqualify counsel. He concluded that the number of motions to disqualify exhibited a "sharper rise than the gradual increases in civil filings." This disproportional increase was especially evident when Penegar looked at filings from 1986 to 1990. Relatedly, state appellate courts heard and decided more appeals of lawyer disqualification orders in the 1980s than in the previous four decades combined.[51]

A study of published federal disqualification decisions showed a significant decline in such cases from 2003 to 2012, falling from forty in 2004 to fewer than twenty in 2012. Keith Swisher concluded that the ethics rules leading to lawyer disqualification were "generally justified," and disqualification was both "a unique and effective remedy" for ethics violations.[52]

Swisher noted two other phenomena regarding lawyer disqualification motions: First, such motions were rarely the subject of deep investigation. Second, the absence of any thorough assessment was related to the way many judges characterized disqualification motions: they were ordinarily tagged as "tactical," an effort to distract the opposing party and the court from the substantive legal dispute and to increase the cost and time associated with the lawsuit. Swisher concluded that this characterization was largely untrue. However, the general belief that disqualification motions were tactical "soon translated into a judicial rebellion." That rebellion may have generated the decline in motions to disqualify opposing counsel.[53]

The Model Rules, 1983–1999

Only New Jersey implemented a version of the Model Rules in the year following the ABA's approval of them. The pace then picked up: twenty-six states and the District of Columbia adopted them by the end of 1988. A decade later, some variation of the Model Rules had been adopted in forty jurisdictions.[54]

States were much slower to adopt the Model Rules than the 1969 Code of Professional Responsibility because American lawyers were more divided about their role in society. A significant number of the Model Rules were adopted (or amended on the floor) by a closely divided House of Delegates (see chapter 6). One crucial issue was the breadth of the lawyer-client relationship. Did lawyers owe any enforceable duties to anyone other than their clients? The signal debate within this broader topic was whether a lawyer could disclose client confidences. A bare majority of the ABA House of Delegates answered: hardly any. This disagreement foretold a wider disagreement among and within state bar associations. Discomfort with the ABA's answer to this and related questions led lawyers to assume a position of critical assessment rather than immediate acceptance. The result was an ethics code honored both in the breach and in the observance.

The ABA, through its Committee on Ethics and Professional Responsibility (CEPR), regularly tinkered with the Model Rules over the next fifteen years, making at least thirty changes. For example, in 1987 the CEPR proposed amendments to two rules (Rules 7.2 and 7.3) on written communications with prospective clients. The proposals gave lawyers greater leeway to advertise by mail to persons in need of legal services. They were withdrawn before any ABA vote. The following year the Supreme Court, in *Shapero v. Kentucky Bar Association*, held that Kentucky's ban on direct mail solicitation by lawyers violated the First Amendment. After *Shapero*, the CEPR amendments were revived and adopted.[55]

The ABA also modified Rule 7.4, which permitted lawyers to inform prospective clients that they limited the fields in which they practiced. Although specialization was commonplace, declaring oneself a "specialist" was another matter, and Rule 7.4 barred any such public claim. In 1989 the CEPR proposed amending a comment to Rule 7.4 to declare any such statement "misleading." The ABA approved. Shortly thereafter the Supreme Court held unconstitutional a ban on a similar statement.[56]

Lawyer Gary Peel publicly declared himself a certified "civil trial specialist." Illinois did not recognize the certification organization's authority. The Illinois Supreme Court relied on the ABA's amended comment to hold Peel's declaration misleading. The Supreme Court reversed. The ABA's response to *Peel* was modest at best and begrudging at worst. It amended Model Rule 7.4 to permit Peel and others to advertise specialty certification only if they included a disclaimer that the certifying organization was unapproved.[57]

The ABA was not finished. In 1994 it approved another amendment that benefited neither consumers nor lawyers but did aid itself. If the ABA "accredited" an organization with the power to certify specialists, and if the state did not have a certifying authority, the lawyer was not required to issue a disclaimer. As one might guess, the ABA had a new certification program by which it accredited other entities with the power to certify specialists. One such entity was the National Board of Trial Advocacy (NBTA), which had certified Gary Peel years earlier; only now did the ABA consider the NBTA sufficiently reliable for lawyers to publicly announce their NBTA certification. The ABA's disclaimer exemption seemed tied to a rather confused understanding of what was "misleading" to legal services consumers. The CEPR's recommendation noted, "many lawyers" would forgo communicating their specialty if a disclaimer was mandatory. This, in turn, might "considerably diminish" the "value" of ABA accreditation. Thus, a disclaimer exception should be made because, "given the thoroughness of the procedures established . . . , there would appear to be no valid reason for suggesting to the public that the ABA accreditation is in some way inferior simply because a particular state has not established its own accrediting procedure." The ABA left unstated the market benefits it received, with only the barest evidence that its certification plan helped consumers. Indeed, the ABA's accreditation of the NBTA tacitly conceded that it was not "inferior." This was pure self-interest on the part of the ABA.[58]

Another recurring ethics issue was related to the meaning of professionalism. In 1990 several ABA groups were asked to consider a rule of professional conduct regarding the ownership of ancillary businesses by lawyers. They reached largely contrary conclusions: The Section on Litigation urged a broad ban on the ownership of ancillary businesses by lawyers and law firms. The CEPR urged a regulatory approach, permitting law firms to own ancillary businesses within strictly defined limits. The contending parties spoke past one another. Those supporting a ban argued that any other rule would transform law from a profession to a business. Those proposing a regulatory approach claimed there was no evidence of lawyer misconduct in the operation of traditional ancillary businesses (e.g., a title business). The prohibitionists won, 197–186. The following year the regulators urged withdrawal of Model Rule 5.7 and won by a vote of 190–183.[59]

The House of Delegates then created its own Committee on Ancillary Business. That committee recommended a rule subjecting lawyers who owned ancillary businesses to the rules of professional conduct unless they informed clients of the status of the ancillary business. If a lawyer failed to explain that providing "law-related services" was not the same as providing legal services, or if a lawyer-controlled ancillary business did not take "reasonable measures" to ensure that the recipient of law-related services knew those services were not legal services, the lawyer was subject to discipline. The same professionalism arguments were made against this proposal. It was adopted by a vote of 237–183.[60]

In 1991 the CEPR returned to the issue that had most divided the ABA in 1983: what are the exceptions to the duty to maintain client confidences? The CEPR proposed permitting a lawyer to reveal a client confidence when the lawyer believed it was reasonably necessary "to rectify the consequences of a client's criminal or fraudulent act in the commission of which the lawyer's services had been used." This had been proposed by the Kutak Commission in its 1982 final revised draft and rejected after a contentious debate. It was rejected again.[61]

In 1997 ABA president Jerome Shestak called for another look at the rules of lawyer ethics. He noted that rapid changes in the legal profession required a deeper assessment of how lawyers' conduct should be regulated.

His call was made just as the ALI's *Restatement (Third) of the Law Governing Lawyers* was being readied for member approval.

Restatement of the Law Governing Lawyers

In 1984 Geoffrey C. Hazard Jr. replaced Herbert Wechsler and became the ALI's fourth director. Created in 1923, the ALI constituted a small, elite sliver of the profession. Its membership in 1984 was limited to two thousand American lawyers, judges, and academics, or about 0.3 percent of the lawyer population. The ALI's restatements of the law were heavily cited, and even when criticized, courts and practitioners regularly relied on them.[62]

Immediately before becoming ALI director, Hazard had served as the reporter of the proposed Model Rules and was their principal defender before the ABA. The encounter was an unpleasant one (see chapter 6). In 1986 the ALI Program Committee recommended that its council consider drafting a *Restatement (Third) of the Law Governing Lawyers*. The council agreed. (This would be the third iteration of the restatements but the first covering lawyer ethics.) This was the first restatement project undertaken by the ALI during Hazard's directorship. Charles Wolfram, author of the comprehensive treatise *Modern Legal Ethics* (1986) and a proponent of a restatement, was named reporter.[63]

One oddity of a proposed restatement on lawyering was captured by ALI director emeritus Hazard in his 2000 foreword to the completed work: "The subject matter represents something of a departure in the Institute's agenda, focusing as it does on a specific vocation."[64]

A second oddity was that little law existed to restate. Hazard and Wolfram initially proposed a "mini-restatement" on attorney-client confidentiality. And on this particular subject, much was unclear. Were lawyers permitted to disclose a client confidence to prevent a client from committing any crime? To prevent a fraud? To prevent a crime leading to a person's "substantial bodily harm" or "imminent death"? To prove that another had been wrongly convicted? In any or all of these situations, was the lawyer *required* to disclose the client confidence?

The ALI had found itself in a similar position in the late 1930s. When ALI director William Draper Lewis considered a restatement of the law of evidence, the council demurred and concluded, in Lewis's words, "however much the law needs clarification in order to produce reasonable certainty

in its application, the rules themselves in numerous and important instances are so defective that instead of being the means of developing truth,
they operate to suppress it." The ALI instead looked to revise evidence law
through a model code.[65]

A half century later, the ALI chose a different route. It decided not to
draft a model code (possibly to avoid stepping on ABA toes) and instead
chose to draft a complete restatement. This reflected a shift in the purpose of
the restatement projects—to pave the path of the law rather than to merely
reflect it. As Wolfram stated, "If courts in different states follow conflicting
rules, the restatements seek to divine the better path, which is not necessarily the path more frequently trod." Additionally, a full restatement treatment
responded to perceived problems with the ABA's Model Rules. It also may
have been an attempt to bolster public faith in the ethics of lawyers.[66]

Wolfram's early assessment was the restatement would be completed in
five or six years. Final approval was given in 1998, twelve years later. The
reporters produced fourteen preliminary drafts, sixteen council drafts, eight
tentative drafts, and two proposed final drafts. After the second proposed
final draft and the eighth tentative draft were approved, it took another
year to prepare the "updated, integrated" text of the restatement, which
was finally published in 2000. It was an immense accomplishment. Hazard
stepped down as director soon after the final approval.[67]

The many iterations of the restatement included considerable debate and
criticism over several perennially contentious issues. One concerned when
a lawyer was permitted to disclose a client confidence. In council draft number 2 (September 15, 1988) and council draft number 2A (November 15,
1988), section 117A permitted a lawyer to disclose a client confidence when
necessary to prevent the commission of an illegal act that would cause physical harm or substantial financial loss to another. Disclosure was also permitted if the act had occurred but the consequences had not yet happened.
This essentially revived two exceptions offered by the Kutak Commission
and rejected by the ABA in 1983. These exceptions remained in subsequent
drafts, and their parameters were fixed in 1996. Section 67(1) permitted
disclosure by the lawyer when a client intended to commit a crime or fraud
that would cause a "substantial financial loss" to another and the lawyer's
services were used in committing that crime or fraud. The restatement was
also more permissive in allowing a lawyer to disclose a past crime that could
have future consequences. Neither the Model Rules nor the Model Code
included any such provision. Section 67(2) permitted disclosure to rectify

past frauds causing such loss. This cleaved the restatement from the Model Rules.[68]

Writing in 1993, Fred Zacharias noted that the proposed exceptions to the duty of confidentiality, though more permissive than Model Rule 1.6, were less permissive than the rules in thirty-seven jurisdictions. In thirty jurisdictions, *all* future crimes could be disclosed, following the "law" of the 1969 Model Code.[69]

A second controversial conclusion was the adoption of nonconsensual "screening." A lawyer was not permitted to represent a client if the lawyer had a conflict of interest. One such conflict was representing a client in a matter against a former client when the lawyer's duties to the former client affected his representation of the current client. An individual lawyer's conflict of interest was imputed to the entire firm with which the lawyer was associated. As a business matter, the disqualification of the entire firm had significant negative consequences.

Screening was a work-around of the imputation rule. The former client's lawyer remained personally disqualified from representing the current client; however, no other member of the law firm was disqualified unless that lawyer also had a personal conflict of interest. The disqualified lawyer and the lawyers representing the current client were screened from one another, so the disqualified lawyer did not inadvertently disclose a confidence from the former client to the lawyers representing the current client. Nor was the disqualified lawyer given any share of the revenue or profit generated from the current client. Proponents concluded that this work-around sensibly resolved the problem.

Large law firms disproportionately benefited from screening due to their large roster of former and current clients. Lawyers who were hired from other law firms, especially rainmaker partners, also had many former and current clients. The traditional imputation rule, argued many large-firm lawyers, diminished their ability to hire rainmaker-partners and thus hampered lawyer mobility. The only traditional exception to the imputation rule was consent of the former client. Unsurprisingly, former clients were often reluctant to waive the imputed disqualification rule, for reasons both sound (fear that confidences would be revealed) and unsound (to gain a tactical advantage in litigation or deal making). Proper screening allowed the firm plausibly to claim no conflict of interest existed because the personally disqualified lawyer had kept the former client's confidences, leaving the work of other lawyers untainted. Thus, even absent consent, the former client had no justification to complain.[70]

The 1983 Model Rules permitted the nonconsensual screening of lawyers moving from government positions to private law firms, but not when lawyers switched law firms. In 1991 the ALI concluded that the screening of lawyers moving between law firms was ethically permissible. Seven years later, just fifteen federal and state jurisdictions allowed for such screening. This included eight states that authorized screening through their lawyer ethics rules, joined by decisions in four federal and three state appellate courts. Eight state appellate courts had explicitly prohibited screening.[71]

The reporters first proposed the traditional rule: screens were banned when the lawyer moved between law firms. This led to a significant division among the restatement's advisers (about twenty), the director, the reporters, and the council (about sixty). The advisers were divided between the "pragmatic realists" (joined by Director Hazard) who supported screens and the "purist minority" (including Thomas Morgan, the associate reporter responsible for the conflict-of-interest provisions, and, initially, Wolfram) who opposed them. The realists pointed out several court decisions (the relevance of which was much debated) that permitted the screening of lawyers moving between law firms. The council, which officially governs the ALI, supported the expansion of screening. The reporters then revised their approach.[72]

Preliminary draft number 4A (June 1, 1989) and council draft number 3 (September 14, 1989) permitted screening when "confidential information of the former client has not been communicated to the lawyer." It also permitted screening when the "basis" for disqualification was "not substantially related to protection of confidential client information," the disqualified lawyer was adequately screened, the lawyer's compensation "will not be materially affected by the outcome of the matter," and "written notice" of screening was given to "each affected client." Tentative draft number 3 modified this language to permit the broader use of screening. If the lawyer possessed no confidential information of the former client that was "material to the matter," no imputation arose. In addition, no imputed firm disqualification existed when "material risk of misuse of confidential client information has been avoided." The factors that determined this were the "significance of the confidential client information," the adequacy of the screening measures, the "degree of continued financial benefit" to the disqualified lawyer, and "timely and complete notice of the screening" (not necessarily written notice).[73]

As reporter Thomas Morgan noted, the debate at the 1990 annual meeting demonstrated "two differences in philosophy." Members rejected this four-factor test by a vote of 106–98 and seemed nearly equally divided on the concept of screening lawyers who moved between law firms. The discussion was continued to 1991.[74]

Despite this apparent division, tentative draft number 4 (April 10, 1991) loosened the conditions: screening was permissible if there was "no reasonable prospect" that the disqualified lawyer's knowledge of client confidences would have a "material adverse effect on the former client." That standard was met in part if the lawyer's knowledge was "not likely to be significant in the later case." How one assessed the likelihood of the disqualified lawyer's knowledge being significant was unclear. Additionally, the black-letter rule eliminated the provision concerning the financial incentives of the disqualified lawyer.[75]

The members were again in "substantial disagreement." A motion to reject screening for lawyers moving between law firms failed by a voice vote. A motion to expand screening was also "clearly defeated." After discussion of the reasons for requiring the adverse effect on the former client to be "material" to impute disqualification, a motion to adopt the screening provision "clearly carried."[76]

A major argument was whether lawyers could be trusted to keep former clients' confidences when it might cost them money. This reflected competing definitions of professionalism. The successful pragmatic realists concluded that screening should be permitted because lawyers, as professionals, could be trusted. Lawyers were trustworthy for reasons of training, ethical propriety, and market necessity. The losing purists claimed nonconsensual screening was another tool to maximize lawyer profits, demonstrating that "money increasingly rules the profession, especially in the large firms." For the purists, professionalism was not merely about keeping client confidences. Professionalism meant representing private clients while also serving as a social trustee, a servant of the public. If keeping the confidences of a former client required the disqualification of the lawyer's law firm, that was a small price to pay. To yield on this issue was to embrace the "profit-centered" vision of the practice of law at the expense of public service. The choice, in the purists' view, harked back to the dilemma of elite lawyers at the beginning of the twentieth century: was the practice of law a profession or merely a business?[77]

Lost in this particular debate were empirical claims that neither side considered it necessary to prove. Neither the realists nor the purists advanced any evidence that lawyers had (or had not) demonstrated trustworthiness in keeping former clients' secrets. Nor had they examined whether the imputation rule affected lawyer mobility, and if so, to what extent. Finally, when the lawyer mobility issue (linked to profit maximization) was transformed into one of individual rights (the client's right to choose a lawyer), no evidence was presented of the impact of imputation.[78]

This suggested the contestants' agreement that screening was an issue of principle rather than policy. The problem was, whose principles? The director disagreed with some of the reporters; the advisers disagreed; the members of the council disagreed; and the voting members (less than 10 percent of the total) were nearly evenly divided. Despite this, the imprimatur of ALI approval would make it much easier for the legal profession to embrace screens as ethical.

The ALI returned to the screening issue in 1996. Lawrence J. Fox, a partner in a large Philadelphia law firm, had opposed screening in 1991. In discussing proposed final draft number 1, he moved to delete the provision permitting screens for lawyers moving between firms. Fox stated it was time "to refocus on what is good for clients." That excluded screening. He noted, "no one, no jurisdiction, has the rule that is proposed, . . . and the vast majority, virtually all jurisdictions, do not permit the screening of the lawyer who is switching sides." Legal ethics expert Monroe Freedman spoke in favor of Fox's motion, concluding that the most likely way for a former client to prove screening was impermissible was for the client to disclose the confidence—a "bizarre" standard. Fox's motion failed.[79]

Another oddity of the restatement was the concern that the fox was guarding the henhouse. The ALI consisted of lawyers who had decided to declare what constituted ethical lawyer behavior. Ordinary Americans distrusted lawyers—more so in 1990 than in the aftermath of Watergate. Restatement critics argued that lawyer self-interest made this project self-defeating. Wolfram himself acknowledged lawyers might have the same difficulty as any other "self-interested group" in "achieving objectivity in this exercise in self-scrutiny."[80]

The dissenters' unease was amplified by the ALI's controversial drafting of Principles of Corporate Governance from 1978 to 1992. The path taken in the principles led to rumors that business organizations "were trying to protect their interests both by *hiring* members of the ALI to represent their interests in that body's deliberations and by *firing* law firms that strongly supported the ALI's efforts to transform American corporate law." That caused ALI president Roswell Perkins to remind members in 1991, "the precept of leaving one's clients at the door must be honored if we are to preserve our integrity as an organization."[81]

A 1995 study of the ALI and the National Conference of Commissioners on Uniform State Laws concluded that such entities were often subject to status quo bias and to "capture" by powerful interests. Yet the ALI continued to claim authority due to its commitment to disinterested expertise, joined by its (unenforceable) custom that members leave their clients at the door. Other critics chimed in, concluding the ALI "can hardly be considered disinterested or unbiased."[82]

As if to dispel such fears, ALI members reacted strongly to a significant 1996 lobbying effort regarding the restatement's position on the triangular relationship among insured, insurer, and insurance defense counsel. Wolfram decided the effort of insurance companies and their agents "was not unprecedented"; it was, however, "uncharacteristically audacious" and may have backfired. Lobbying ALI members "produced a dogged determination" at the May 1996 meeting "not to let the [insurance] industry have its way." The negotiated amendment to the restatement's proposal was recommitted to the reporters for further work. The ALI council formally responded by adopting a rule requiring members to "exercise independent judgment" and asking them to "leave client interests at the door."[83]

Monroe Freedman criticized the ALI's "conflict" concerning the Principles of Corporate Governance in 1992. He broadened his assessment in 1998. Freedman criticized the ALI's bias by cheekily using the definition of conflict of interest in the restatement to accuse the ALI of a conflict of interest. One of his three examples of an ALI conflict was screening. Like the purist minority, Freedman concluded that screening "mocks the claim that the law is a profession and not a business." A former client would be hard-pressed to prove a disqualified lawyer had impermissibly disclosed confidential information. Freedman cited recent events in the news as evidence of the problem. A lawyer at the large law firm Sullivan and Cromwell sent a reporter a complaint that had been ordered sealed by the court. The lawyer had not worked on the case and did not know about the court's order. Freedman noted that this lawyer's action was more consequential than the ordinary case to which the imputation rule applied, for Sullivan and Cromwell was subject to sanctions and contempt of court for the disclosure.[84]

The screening rule, of course, disrupted the status quo. This seemed to suggest a spirit of reform in the ALI. But this reform, in the eyes of its critics, was about self-interest. The ALI altered the traditional rule for material reasons benefiting many of those that supported it.

Freedman's conclusion was sweeping: The restatements generally could not be relied on as "the objective judgment of members, unaffected by the partisanship of advocates." They should instead be viewed as the product of lawyers writing rules that served the needs of their clients and themselves. Despite this judgment, the *Restatement (Third) of the Law Governing Lawyers* has been successful. The printed cumulative case citations as of 2015 totaled more than two hundred pages, the vast majority of them approving of the *Restatement*.[85]

The nonconsensual screening rule assumed lawyer mobility would continue to increase and large law firms would become much larger. These assumptions proved correct. Other issues were implicated. For example, what, if any, duty did mobile lawyers owe the firms they left? More important, would multidisciplinary firms be recognized? *Restatement* section 9(3) defined the rule regarding the ethics of taking and grabbing clients. Section 10 answered the latter question. Both took the traditional approach. Before leaving the law firm, a lawyer was permitted to solicit only those clients on whose matters the lawyer was "actively and substantially working," and only after "adequately and timely" notifying the firm of the lawyer's decision to leave. Lawyers were prohibited from providing legal services in a multidisciplinary firm.[86]

The Practice of Law in a Multidisciplinary Organization

In the late 1990s three of the ten largest "law firms" in the world were "Big Five" accounting firms. One count listed 6,362 lawyers, *excluding* tax lawyers, working in Big Five firms. Accounting firms were owned by their partners, including some lawyers and many others not licensed to practice law. Accounting firms offered clients legal services, accounting services, tax services, and consulting services. Like section 10 of the *Restatement*, Model Rule 5.4 banned any lawyer from sharing legal fees with a non-lawyer or practicing law in an entity owned in whole or in part by a person unlicensed to practice law. The long-stated justification for these bans was to protect the lawyer's "professional independence of judgment." A nonlawyer-owner might seek to control the lawyer's work, to the client's detriment.[87]

In the hunt for more business, lawyers serving organizational clients engaged in territorial disputes with Big Five firms over whether the latter were engaged in the practice of law. This dispute, like a similar one in the late 1950s (see chapter 5), threatened the economic model of some business lawyers. One solution was definitional: redefine the practice of law. It could be defined to encompass or exclude the work undertaken by lawyers in accounting firms. One difficulty with this solution was its applicability to some work performed in law firms. That would pressure lawyers to reconsider the breadth of the attorney-client privilege and the duty of client confidentiality. Further, a redefinition might be perceived as intended to benefit the financial position of lawyers, with little or no evidence that clients were harmed by the "legal" work performed by accounting firm employees and partners. A second solution was for law firms to accept this change and alter the ethics rules to allow lawyers to join nonlawyers in entities in which the practice of law and other services, such as accounting, occurred. This would allow large law firms to increase their rate of growth, and it would allow small-firm lawyers to serve individuals with a variety of legal and other needs. A third solution was to reinforce the status quo, even as laws in Europe and Australia allowed lawyers to practice law in multidisciplinary firms. In August 1998 the ABA created a Commission on Multidisciplinary Practice to advise it.[88]

The commission completed its work in less than a year. It recommended that a "lawyer should be permitted to deliver legal services through a multi-disciplinary practice." After some pushback, the ABA and the commission agreed to a year's delay, at which time the commission reaffirmed its recommendation, with the proviso that any specific changes be implemented to protect the public and preserve the "core values of the legal profession." The ABA rejected the recommendation. It urged states to recognize that sharing legal fees with nonlawyers and allowing nonlawyers to "control" the practice of law were "inconsistent with the core values of the legal profession."[89]

Even so, bar associations in forty-four states and the District of Columbia created commissions to evaluate the issue. By July 2001, twelve committees had recommended changes allowing nonlawyer ownership of legal services entities in some fashion.[90]

This effort then collapsed. In early December 2001, after months of alarming stories in the *Wall Street Journal*, *Fortune*, and other publications,

Enron filed for bankruptcy. Enron's fall was linked in part to its auditor, the Big Five accounting firm Arthur Andersen. Critics alleged that Andersen had failed to protect the public by inaccurately auditing Enron's financial statements, and it had done so because it earned extraordinary profits from its consulting work for Enron. How could Andersen and, by extension, other accounting firms be trusted to allow its lawyers to retain their professional independence of judgment if that meant lower profits? In 2002 Andersen was indicted, convicted, and all but dissolved. Other scandals involving public corporations embracing unusual accounting practices generated greater alarm about multidisciplinary practices among state bar associations. Until very recently, only the District of Columbia permitted a lawyer to join nonlawyers in owning a multidisciplinary firm in which legal and other nonlegal services are provided.[91]

Rapid Change and Ethics 2000

Through the 1990s bar leaders regularly intoned that rapid changes in society were transforming the work of lawyers. Some argued that this rapid change had structurally altered the relationship of lawyer and client. Others focused on technological change. Whatever their basis, ABA leaders considered these shifts sufficiently momentous to require lawyers to consider institutional responses. One such response was the ABA's reconsideration of the Model Rules.[92]

Though it was presented as novel, the theme of rapid change was a constant in lawyers' writings about the practice of law. Another constant within the legal profession was to link such change with a reevaluation of ethics rules. One apparent difference between lamentations in the early and mid-twentieth century and those at the end of the century was the emphasis on the velocity of change in the latter.[93]

Whatever the reason for this claimed transformation in the practice of law, it necessitated changes in the training and retraining of lawyers. Rapid change in the practice of law, ABA leaders argued, also required a review and revision of the Model Rules, which were less than fifteen years old. To heighten the importance of this project, created just as society was facing the specter of the Y2K or Millennium Bug, the entity charged with reviewing the rules became known as the Ethics 2000 Commission.[94]

Although the Model Rules had generally served lawyers well, ABA president Shestack concluded that "rapid changes in the profession and technology make a comprehensive study and review necessary to take the legal profession into the next century." Delaware chief justice E. Norman Veasey agreed to serve as the commission's chair. He cited drastic changes to the profession caused by technological, economic, and structural transformations. He also noted that "continuing concerns about the image and standing of lawyers" bolstered the case for the commission's creation.[95]

The Ethics 2000 Commission's final report was discussed at the ABA's August 2001 meeting. It proposed amending rather than supplanting the Model Rules, for it found "much to be valued in the concepts and articulation of the[m]." Veasey's introduction suggested several reasons why the reevaluation had been valuable. First, there existed "an undesirable lack of uniformity" among the states. Veasey did not initially explain why this was so, nor did he explain the value of uniformity in a federal system. He returned to this issue near the end of his introduction, but unfortunately, Veasey simply offered the commission's "fervent hope that the goal of uniformity will be the guiding beacon." Second, the commission's report should be adopted to acknowledge and confront the professionalism crisis. Veasey wrote, "We have been constantly mindful of substantial and high-velocity changes in the legal profession, particularly over the past decade." Those changes resulted in "increased public scrutiny of lawyers"; "persistent concerns about lawyer honesty, candor and civility"; and issues related to law firm size, specialization, and lawyer mobility. A third and related reason was the "explosive dynamics of modern law practice." Veasey concluded that the commission's recommendations were "a balanced blend of traditional precepts and forward-looking provisions that are responsive to modern developments."[96]

Veasey acknowledged that the proposals were merely the agreement of a majority. One proposal was to permit the nonconsensual screening of lawyers moving between law firms, following the *Restatement*. Four members of the commission had also been involved in the *Restatement*: Geoffrey C. Hazard Jr., W. Loeber Landau, Lawrence Fox, and Susan Martyn (commission reporter Nancy J. Moore, like the last three, had served as an adviser to the *Restatement*). In the ALI debates, Hazard and Landau had supported nonconsensual screening; Fox and Martyn had not. The second battle over imputation of disqualification had now begun. Fox again argued that nonconsensual screening protected the interests of lawyers to the detriment of former clients. Veasey implicitly responded to Fox in his introduction:

"The Commission understands that there have been few significant complaints regarding screening in the seven jurisdictions whose rules currently permit it." Commission member Margaret Love made a similar statement in the *ABA Journal*. These conclusions, of course, were not based on empirical evidence; indeed, Love called it a "leap of faith." Fox cited Professor Andrew Kaufman for a contrary view: the commission made a judgment based on the idea that "screening has become the desirable norm." Kaufman criticized both the commission's lack of empirical evidence and its decision to place the burden of proof on opponents to nonconsensual screening, though few states permitted it.[97]

The commission's screening proposal was unusual for other reasons. First, if uniformity was the guiding beacon, proposing a rule adopted by just seven states seemed contrary to that goal. Second, the screening rule, though applicable to transactional as well as litigation matters, was rarely the subject of attorney discipline. Such alleged conflicts were ordinarily resolved by disqualification motions in court. Yet the commission proposed this change while it emphasized its adherence to the "primary disciplinary function of the Model Rules."

Fox won the battle. Echoing claims made the previous year concerning the threat to professional independence caused by multidisciplinary firms, Fox's supporters focused on the importance of adhering to the profession's "core values," one of which was loyalty to clients, both past and present. Fox successfully tagged proposed screening Rule 1.10(c) as a "side-switching" rule, allowing a lawyer to represent a client and then move to a new firm that represented the opponent of that lawyer's former client. Fox's victory was undone in 2009 when the ABA adopted a virtually identical screening rule, despite his opposition.[98]

The commission proposed adding four exceptions and one modification to the rule requiring lawyers to keep their clients' confidences. Most were controversial when proposed and became more controversial over the next two years. And the debate on these exceptions seemed to be déjà vu all over again. As had occurred in 1983 (see chapter 6), the discussion illuminated the extent to which the legal profession was fractured. In 2001 the ABA adopted two minor exceptions. It also agreed to modify the exception to prevent a third party's death or physical harm by adopting *Restatement* section 66, but only after an effort to strike it failed by a vote of 207–213. The vote's narrowness encouraged some opponents to consider reviving the issue.[99]

The two major exceptions were not adopted. Both concerned fraud and financial harms suffered by third parties. The difference was temporal—one focused on the future and the other on the past and present. The *Restatement* had adopted both. Fox moved to delete the future financial crime or fraud exception. For Fox, "confidentiality is the second leg of the tripod of core values that support our professional ethics." He claimed that these exceptions created "whole new categories of disclosure." He tied his amendment to lawyer self-protection and stated that adding this exception "creates more likelihood for lawyers to be held liable than if the rule were permitted to remain as it is." (He had made the same argument to the ALI.) Now Fox was taking a leap of faith. Contradicting his earlier argument, he acknowledged that of the states adopting the Model Rules, more than half had included an exception to client confidentiality statements concerning future financial crimes or fraud. And Fox offered no case law or empirical evidence showing greater lawyer liability in those states with such an exception. He then returned to principle: adopting this change would have an "incalculable" effect on the client-lawyer relationship. Fox won again. The House of Delegates adopted his amendment to delete the future crime or fraud exception. The commission then withdrew consideration of the exception for past or ongoing fraud.[100]

Some protested, claiming that ABA Model Rule 1.6 was "out of step with public policy and the values of the legal profession as reflected in the rules currently in force in most jurisdictions." In 1991 the CEPR had failed to add a client confidences exception to situations in which fraud caused substantial financial loss, in the midst of the savings and loan scandal that implicated some lawyer misconduct. Reporter Nancy Moore pointed out that just nine states had adopted Model Rule 1.6 as written. The public policy reason was simple: Model Rule 1.6 recognized no discretionary duty on the part of a lawyer to prevent a client from harming the financial interests of another, and only a modest (again, discretionary) duty to prevent a client from having someone killed. Most states rejected the ABA's "core values," which held that the duty to keep a client's confidence that he was going to have someone killed outweighed the value of that person's life. In a few instances, the duty of zealous representation might be subordinated to the lawyer's duty to the public interest. "Might" was the operative word, for states differed greatly on where to draw the line.[101]

Speakers debating the ethics of multidisciplinary firms in 2000 and the Ethics 2000 proposals in 2001 relied on the rhetoric of core values to persuade. It is doubtful they agreed on its meaning. In the 2001 debate on exceptions to the duty to keep client communications confidential, both sides claimed the mantle of core values. Fox declared confidentiality was one of the profession's three core values. A delegate who supported additional exceptions asserted a lawyer's personal integrity was a core value. The delegates seemed to be implicitly referring to the list of values in the 1992 MacCrate Report, produced during the professionalism crisis. Former ABA president Robert MacCrate successfully led the 2000 charge against multidisciplinary firms in the House of Delegates by claiming such entities were contrary to the profession's core values. The MacCrate Report listed six core values: maintaining undivided client loyalty, exercising "independent legal judgment," keeping client confidences, avoiding client conflicts of interest, serving as an officer of the legal system and as a "public citizen having special responsibilities for the quality of justice," and promoting access to justice.[102]

The core value of serving as a public citizen was taken nearly verbatim from the first paragraph of the preamble to the Model Rules. But the preamble lacked bite. It was aspirational, imploring lawyers to consider interests beyond those of their clients (or themselves). The other core values were just as compromised or unhelpful. As noted by a perceptive critic writing contemporaneously, a lawyer's loyalty was always divided by the rules themselves. The extent to which lawyers had a duty to keep client confidences varied greatly, and conflicts of interest weren't even mentioned in the 1908 Canons. The rhetoric of core values highlighted its thinness and thus its malleability. Lawyers kept returning to the concept as a last-gasp measure to remind themselves they were professionals.[103]

A week after the ABA House of Delegates rejected the Ethics 2000 Commission's proposed confidentiality exceptions, Enron CEO Jeffrey Skilling resigned after six months in office. He did so, he said, for family reasons.[104]

Much of the ABA's February 2002 meeting appraised Ethics 2000's remaining proposals. Ethics 2000 was then effectively disbanded. Two events, however, suggested that Fox's victory on exceptions to the client confidentiality rule might be short-lived. First was the seismic shock of the 9/11 terrorist attack. Second, and of immediate concern to lawyers, was Enron's fall.

Enron, Corporate Responsibility, and Lawyer Ethics

The ABA wrapped up its revisions to the Model Rules on February 4, 2002. By then, Enron was in bankruptcy court, and so was Global Crossing. Both were involved in large-scale accounting scandals. In Enron's case, its auditor, the accounting firm Arthur Andersen, was about to be indicted on obstruction of justice charges for shredding documents and deleting electronic files concerning Enron. On February 14 Congressman Michael Oxley introduced a bill related to this scandal. It was intended both to regulate accounting firms and to assess whether the Model Rules sufficiently regulated lawyer conduct. The ABA created a Task Force on Corporate Responsibility to evaluate the Model Rules, including the just-rejected exceptions to the rule on client confidences.[105]

The Enron scandal might have had less impact on lawyers if it had been an outlier. Unfortunately, Enron was at least the third corporate disaster in the last two decades in which lawyers played an important supporting role. The savings and loan debacle of the 1980s had led to recriminations about lawyer conduct and more than $400 million in fines and settlements. In 1992 Washington "superlawyer" Clark Clifford and his partner were indicted for their part in another scandal, this one involving the Bank of Commerce and Credit International. In light of these events, one former partner in a large law firm wrote, "The problem is the corporate and legal culture has lost all sense of right and wrong."[106]

By August, the Arthur Andersen firm had been convicted (later reversed by the Supreme Court), the Sarbanes-Oxley Act had been signed into law, WorldCom and Adelphia had entered bankruptcy, and their CEOs and Tyco's had resigned. All these development appeared to be related to "false or misleading financial statements and alleged misconduct by executive officers."[107]

The Edwards amendment to the Sarbanes-Oxley bill required the Securities and Exchange Commission (SEC) to adopt rules "setting forth minimum standards of professional conduct for attorneys appearing and practicing before the Commission in any way in the representation of public companies." This was a serious threat to the ABA's position as the promulgator of (model) rules of professional conduct. A day after the amendment's adoption, the ABA task force issued its preliminary report. It urged amending Model Rule 1.13 (the organization as a client) and broadening the lawyer's duty to "report up" the corporate ladder (the only requirement of the amendment).[108]

The task force genuflected to congressional (and public) anger by recommending that the ABA adopt the exceptions to client confidences it had rejected eleven months earlier. Surprisingly, it recommended that these be *mandatory* exceptions. Ten states required lawyers to disclose a client confidence to prevent the death of or substantial bodily injury to another person; just four required a lawyer to do so to prevent future financial harm. Only California prohibited a lawyer from disclosing a confidence to prevent another person's death, and eleven applied that prohibition to future financial harms. The task force justified this recommendation by noting that, if Model Rule 1.6 had been out of step a year ago, it was "even more out of step today, when public demand that lawyers play a greater role in promoting corporate responsibility is almost certainly much stronger."[109]

The ABA did not debate these recommendations in 2002. Instead, it awaited SEC action. On November 21 the SEC proposed a rule permitting (but not requiring) a lawyer to disclose a client confidence to prevent substantial harm to another person's financial interests or to rectify the consequences of past fraud in which the lawyer's services had been used. It rejected mandatory disclosure of client confidences because another proposed rule, "noisy withdrawal," was mandatory: if a lawyer reported evidence of a crime or fraud by a corporation to a representative of that corporation, and the violation was ongoing and likely to cause substantial financial injury to another, and if the lawyer did not receive an appropriate response from the representative, the lawyer was required to withdraw "noisily" from representing that client. Noisy withdrawal was permitted in the Model Rules, but making it mandatory was sufficient, the SEC concluded, to otherwise allow discretionary disclosures of client confidences.[110]

The SEC's decision not to mandate disclosure of a client confidence to prevent or rectify fraud causing substantial financial harm opened a door for the ABA. It could concentrate on attacking mandatory noisy withdrawal as impinging on the attorney-client privilege, for the courts could ignore an SEC rule. The ABA's December 18 letter to the SEC also urged it to await congressional approval to mandate noisy withdrawal.[111]

The ABA succeeded. The SEC's final rules eliminated the proposals on noisy withdrawal and kept the other client confidences exceptions permissive. This gave the ABA the opportunity to reassert its ethics-making authority. On March 31, 2003, the task force issued its final report. It continued to urge adoption of the Ethics 2000 exceptions to client confidentiality, but now such exceptions were to be permissive rather than mandatory. Its justifications for this change of mind were not based on empirical data; it constituted another "leap of faith."[112]

The subsequent debate returned ABA delegates to safe ground, arguing that their position best protected the profession's core values. Future ABA president Robert J. Grey Jr. spoke against the recommendations because they would compromise the profession's core values. Future ABA president Dennis W. Archer disagreed, claiming that the core values of "confidentiality, professional integrity, independence, and autonomy" were compromised when a lawyer was barred from disclosing a client confidence related to a financial fraud. Despite support from twelve ABA sections, twelve past ABA presidents, and the Conference of Chief Justices, the proposed amendments were approved by just 52 percent. The impact of these actions was captured in the title of an *ABA Journal* article: "The Non-Revolution."[113]

Ethics 2000 in the Twenty-First Century

The ABA tinkered modestly with the Model Rules after the turn of the millennium. During the Great Recession, the ABA amended Model Rule 1.10 to permit nonconsensual screening, but only after a false start. The CEPR attempted to strong-arm the amendment and was prevented from doing so only by a vote to delay, 192–191.[114]

The CEPR then returned with a broad nonconsensual screening proposal. Proponents argued momentum. Eleven states had adopted screening after 2001; this made twenty-four overall, which was still a minority. Proponents were also affronted because a screening ban unacceptably attacked lawyer integrity. In addition, the CEPR found not "even a handful of instances in which confidentiality was breached," and little evidence of such instances leading to lawyer discipline. This was not rigorous empirical evidence. It did, however, avoid the conflict-of-interest issue.[115]

A substitute amendment appealed to core values. The "fiduciary values of loyalty and confidentiality" were "enduring values" that should not be cast aside. Broad-based screening, Fox argued, would cause the ABA to "lose that role of defining professional responsibility and ethics." He also noted the temptation of permitting screening to protect lawyer income in hard times.[116]

The appeal of Fox's substitute was initially unclear, but it was handily defeated. The vote to adopt a revised Rule 1.10, permitting nonconsensual screening, was much closer, 226–191.[117]

Ethics 20/20

In 2009 ABA president Carolyn B. Lamm created Ethics 20/20. Another review of the Model Rules was necessary to "keep pace with societal change" and the "accelerating pace of technological innovation." Ethics 20/20 possessed the authority to undertake a "plenary review and assessment" of the Model Rules in light of these changes. Its goals were to protect the public interest, preserve "core professional values," and maintain a "strong, independent, and self-regulating profession." Its preliminary outline focused on the multijurisdictional practice of law, the effect of technological innovations on globalization, and ethics issues affected by technology.[118]

The result was both stasis and modest change. The ABA altered some rules and added comments acknowledging the impact of technology on lawyers. It addressed human failure (e.g., "reply all" emails) and human ingenuity (e.g., hacking). Most amendments reflected changes in how attorney-client communications were protected, including information storage and delivery. The more controversial proposals died. Ethics 20/20 announced its decision to continue the ban on most types of multidisciplinary practice structures but left open the possibility "of a very limited form of nonlawyer ownership in a law firm," one that was "more restrictive than" the approach of the District of Columbia. Even the possibility of an alternative law practice structure roused the opposition. The Illinois State Bar Association filed a peremptory resolution asking the House of Delegates to reaffirm its 2000 decision to ban any form of multidisciplinary practice. Its goal was to "shut off the debate." It worked. Even after Ethics 20/20 decided in April not to propose any type of alternative law practice structure, the Illinois State Bar Association pressed its resolution, "defending the core values of our profession against the encroachment of non-lawyers." The cochairs of Ethics 20/20 had already made that promise.[119]

Another Ethics 20/20 amendment was prompted by the Great Recession. Massive layoffs of associates (and some partners) at large firms in 2008 and 2009 increased involuntary lawyer mobility. Law firms wanted to protect themselves from any conflicts of interest brought by newly hired lawyers. This was a more acute problem for associates than partners, as the former's client contacts might be unclear. A law firm's diligent efforts might include asking prospective associates to disclose "information relating to the representation of a client." The breadth of the definition of client information suggested the need for an exception permitting a lawyer to reveal client information when interviewing for a position. Fox futilely objected on the grounds that this harmed the core value of confidentiality and would generate more public mistrust of lawyers. Supporters invoked lawyer integrity; though "the profession changes, the values that make the profession and the values that are embodied in the ABA Model Rules do not change."[120]

Ethics 20/20 cochair Jamie Gorelick attributed its success to the absence of any need for "radical change." That was because "the underlying principles of our profession are sound." This differentiated Ethics 20/20 from the two previous ethics committees, created precisely because society was headed into uncharted territory.[121]

The Great Recession and the Legal Industry

In 1984 Carl Liggio, general counsel of accounting firm Arthur Young (later Ernst and Young), offered a prescient understanding of the future work of lawyers: "Most lawyers think of themselves first and foremost as lawyers, when in reality, they are a very small part of a much larger profession or industry. That industry is the industry of information management." At the time, corporate clients believed they could find a "superior work product" at any good firm. Liggio's insight is one reason why accounting firms became some of the largest law firms in the world. The large, elite New York law firm Milbank Tweed learned that marketing its brains was not "an effective selling point." Milbank's example demonstrates the difficulty of customizing work and is emblematic of a shift in the legal profession's social role.[122]

The perception that lawyers might be a small part of a much larger industry may have worked as a type of Copernican revolution. The lawyer was no longer a central actor in the story of the United States; instead, the lawyer was one instrument among many used by business and government to further their ends. The implicit acknowledgment of this shift can also be demonstrated by a change in the language about lawyers' work. Beginning in the 1990s, commentators began to use the phrase *legal industry*. It became more common by the turn of the millennium as a synonym for *legal profession*. Writers then doubled down on its use after the Great Recession.[123]

Industry is defined as "clever working," "application of skill, cleverness, or craft," and "systematic work or labor." If one emphasizes the cleverness or craft aspect, something distinctive about the work of lawyers remains. If one emphasizes the systematic work aspect, routinization is the lawyer's future.

Used as a synonym, *legal industry* indicates an intentional movement from a profession.[124]

The Great Recession wreaked havoc on the American legal profession. In addition to the thousands of lawyers who were let go, nearly a dozen large law firms went bankrupt. Dewey & LeBoeuf had the dubious distinction of being the largest law firm to file for bankruptcy, and several of its executives were indicted on fraud charges.[125]

One consequence of the Great Recession was a further sorting of "Big Law." Of the many law firms that employed two hundred or more lawyers, only a select few avoided the pitfalls wrought by the recession. The Great Recession's impact on profits per partner focused Big Law's attention on adopting more efficient structures. "Deadweight" partners were culled, and lawyers unable to meet revenue demands were fired. Nearly every action taken by large law firms during and after the Great Recession embraced a winner-take-all approach to the private practice of law. For winners and losers alike, the recession joined lawyers more tightly to their clients.[126]

Alexander Forger was the managing partner of Milbank Tweed during a divisive time in the late 1980s. He declared, "We are not a trade or business. We are a profession." This declaration, he then recognized, was "a hysterical note from the past." The idea of the lawyer as social trustee, as an "officer of the legal system and a public citizen having special responsibility for the quality of justice," had died. If it wasn't dead before, the Great Recession killed it.[127]

Conclusion

Lawyers searching for a solution to the professionalism crisis offered creeds, oaths, civility codes, references to core values, and amendments to the Model Rules. None resulted in a return to professional stability and confidence.

"Working Notes" of the ABA Committee about Research on the Future of the Legal Profession were published on August 31, 2001. The stakes for Americans and their lawyers were immense: "We are in the midst of the biggest transformation of civilization since the caveman began bartering." Successfully adapting to this change required lawyers to "recreate ourselves with a culture and a regulatory structure that preserves our core principles, protects our clients, and maintains our relevance."[128]

What were those core principles? The committee never explained. It noted that the death of law as "an 'industry' and as a profession" would lead to great "risk" to "underlying core principles and the Rule of Law." It also briefly assayed the "Changing Face of Private Law Practice." Changes were coming that risked the profession's core principles. What those changes were and which core principles were at risk were merely hinted at. The committee noted that its work was continuing. The 9/11 attacks occurred less than two weeks later. The committee made no further report.[129]

CONCLUSION

In a 1937 essay, former Harvard Law School dean Roscoe Pound declared, "there is no law without lawyers." Fifty years later, legal ethicist David Luban took Pound's assessment one step further: In the United States, "the lawyers are the law." In a nation that professes to govern based on the rule of law, binding the law to the legal profession heightens the power of lawyers. As power tends to corrupt, the public has often registered its fear that lawyers may abuse their power to the detriment of the people. One way to reduce this threat is to strip lawyers of the power they possess. The few efforts to do so have all failed. A second option is to channel this power, either by stringently regulating lawyers or by creating plausible competitors for the work lawyers do. That has failed as well.[1]

To assuage the public's concern, lawyers have argued that their duty to behave as ethical professionals makes them trustworthy. This duty encompasses faithful service to their clients and to society. The legal profession initially pointed to the oath lawyers swore. Lawyers promised to act faithfully to both the courts and their clients. Additionally, as a body, sworn lawyers were honorable gentlemen; only the actions of a few pettifoggers brought lawyers into disrepute. When references to honor became less common or less useful, lawyers turned to conscience. They were trustworthy because they acted with integrity based on an instructed conscience. When the public found the profession's references to individual conscience less trustworthy, conscience was supplemented and later supplanted by canons and codes of ethics. These standards, and later rules, of proper lawyer conduct were supposed to constrain lawyer behavior. The adoption and subsequent enforcement of these rules were a cost lawyers bore for the public's benefit.

The rub, of course, has always been that most lawyers earn a living from paying clients, not the public. As the folk saying goes, "Whose bread I eat, whose song I sing." Why wouldn't lawyers foster their clients' interests rather than a contrary public interest? This was no more than a minor concern, lawyers argued. Loyalty to client was unlikely to supplant loyalty to the public because wealth from the practice of law was both unusual and un-sought. Further, service to the community included aiding paying clients, and that communal service was the lawyer's foremost mission.

Communal service has always been a hard sell. Yes, practicing lawyers have earned an income premium compared with ordinary workers, but the ordinary lawyer is not and never has been wealthy. Thus, in direct (in courts, legislatures, and administrative agencies) and indirect (as counselors and advisers to clients) ways, ordinary lawyers ordinarily exercise power on behalf of their clients. As a result, the argument of communal service has largely failed to persuade the public. Even so, the public's belief that the members of the legal profession are mostly self-interested has not dislodged lawyers from their position of power. Instead, the public seems to accept (or is resigned to accepting) lawyers as the least-worst governance option.

Making the rules of professional conduct the sole source of what a law-yer may or must do shifts the profession's understanding of its duties. It brings into relief the claim that lawyers owe a duty of faithfulness to the public. The private-practice lawyer's duty to the public was traditionally discussed in qualitative and aspirational terms. The more concerted ef-fort to act like a business may explain the attraction of perceiving the legal profession as a regulated industry, with ethics rules serving as the external (and only) constraints on lawyer behavior. In risk management terms, eth-ics means quantitatively assessing risk to make the law firm (as a business) more economically efficient. Questions about duties based on the lawyer's oath, reputational honor, or instructed conscience are incommensurable. The assertion that lawyers must act in light of a standard moral conception of lawyer ethics becomes incoherent.[2]

In an 1896 talk to ABA members, Boston lawyer Joseph Bangs Warner gave voice to an anxiousness within the legal profession about lawyers' sta-tus and role. Unlike other professionals, Warner began, the duties of lawyers were "unsettled," and the various roles in which the lawyer served led him to conclude that "there is some inherent uncertainty about the function which he has assumed." Not only was the lawyer unable to evade this uncertainty, but the lawyer as advocate was placed in a "paradoxical" position, "demand-ing justice" and also "ready to take any case of any man who will pay him for it, and to do his best to make that case prevail." The advocate's work was not "necessarily of doubtful morality," but it was undertaken "in the sense that it is done only under a strain of conscience."[3]

The American legal profession occasionally idealized the advocate as a "disinterested spokesman" who was "detached from self-interest," as one who laid out the facts and law in a way that left the lawyer "with substantially no responsibility for the decision." This ideal was contradicted in actual practice. In Warner's experience, most advocates sought to vindicate their clients' interests. They were not disinterested, detached technicians; the lawyer-advocate used technical skills to shape the law and the facts for the client's benefit. Warner thus offered this harsh truth to the small, elite membership of the ABA: lawyers could not avoid "responsibility for results." At end of day, the actions taken by a lawyer on behalf of his clients "were unsheltered by any professional immunity, and answerable to public judgment for whatever he does, or tries to do, for his client." The public's judgment of the "unsheltered" lawyer meant that the "moralities of the practice of the law must rest on the individual lawyer." What the lawyer chose to do on the client's behalf was a matter for the lawyer's conscience.[4]

The "strain of conscience" was the weight lawyers bore when trying to serve both their clients and the community. There was no solution; the lawyer's duties to client and public were often (if not always) in irreconcilable conflict, and any effort to serve both client and public was guaranteed to fail.

The ABA's three efforts to state the duties of lawyers tell the story of twentieth-century drift in American lawyer ethics. The Canons of Professional Ethics represented a surprisingly confident profession, possibly a consequence of the elite standing of ABA members. It also represented stasis, for even as the profession was changing, the ABA was uninterested in amending the canons to keep abreast of those changes. The post–World War II economic boom elevated lawyer confidence to its highest level. The adoption of the Code of Professional Responsibility signaled a modicum of positive change but was more indicative of satisfaction with the status quo. States adopted the code quickly, and nearly always as enforceable law. The code's inclusion of ethical considerations was an attempt to guide lawyers in the use of their consciences in the practice of law. The Code of Professional Responsibility and its ethical considerations soon seemed outdated. Lawyers fell from grace as economic prospects dimmed and the Watergate scandal unfolded. The tortuous (and torturous) adoption of the Model Rules of Professional Conduct (1983) exemplified the fractured legal profession. Lawyers were united only in the fact that they all received the same license to practice law.

Law remains king in the United States. Despite the best efforts of many, lawyers still stand kinglike. To suggest that the profession is in danger after

250 years of accumulating and exercising power is foolish. But when declaring law king in *Common Sense*, Thomas Paine was acutely aware that kings may be deposed. The "law *ought* to be king; and there ought to be no other. But lest any ill use should afterwards arise, let the crown, at the conclusion of the ceremony, be demolished, and scattered among the people whose right it is."[5]

NOTES

INTRODUCTION

1. Thomas Paine, *Common Sense* (1776), in *Complete Writings of Thomas Paine*, ed. Philip S. Foner, 2 vols. (New York: Citadel Press, 1945), 1:29; Mass. Const. pt. 1, art. XXX (1780) (separation of powers undertaken "to the end it may be a government of laws and not of men"); Brian Z. Tamanaha, *On the Rule of Law: History, Politics, Theory* (New York: Cambridge University Press, 2004), 59.

2. James Madison, Federalist 51, and Alexander Hamilton, Federalist 78, in *The Federalist Papers*, ed. Clinton Rossiter (New York: New American Library, 1961), 322, 466; Alexis de Tocqueville, *Democracy in America*, ed. J. P. Mayer, trans. George Lawrence (New York: HarperPerennial, 1988), 270 (book I, ch. 8).

3. James Willard Hurst, *Law and the Conditions of Freedom in the Nineteenth-Century United States* (Madison: University of Wisconsin Press, 1956), 11, 6; Charles Sellers, *The Market Revolution: Jacksonian America, 1815–1846* (New York: Oxford University Press, 1991), 47; Christopher Clark, "The Consequences of the Market Revolution in the American North," in *The Market Revolution in America: Political, Social, and Religious Experiences, 1800–1880*, ed. Melvyn Stokes and Stephen Conway (Charlottesville: University Press of Virginia, 1996), 35; Morton J. Horwitz, *The Transformation of American Law, 1780–1860* (Cambridge, MA: Harvard University Press, 1977), 253–266; Neil Duxbury, *Patterns of American Jurisprudence* (Oxford: Oxford University Press, 1995), 9–65.

4. Philip K. Howard, *The Rule of Nobody* (New York: W. W. Norton, 2014).

5. Andie Tucher, *Froth and Scum: Truth, Beauty, Goodness, and the Ax Murder in America's First Mass Medium* (Chapel Hill: University of North Carolina Press, 1994); Amalia D. Kessler, *Inventing American Exceptionalism: The Origins of American Adversarial Legal Culture, 1800–1877* (New Haven, CT: Yale University Press, 2017); Stephan Landsman, *Readings on Adversarial Justice: The American Approach to Adjudication* (St. Paul: West Group, 1988); Stephan Landsman, *The Adversary System: A Description and Defense* (Washington, DC: American Enterprise Institute, 1984); Robert A. Ferguson, *Law and Letters in American Culture* (Cambridge, MA: Harvard University Press, 1984).

6. John Emerich Edward Dalberg-Acton (Lord Acton), *Bartlett's Familiar Quotations*, ed. Geoffrey O'Brien, 18th ed. (New York: Little, Brown, 2012), 528; Daniel J. Boorstin, *The Americans: The Colonial Experience* (New York: Vintage Books, 1958), 205 (noting that twenty-five of fifty-six signatories of the Declaration of Independence and thirty-one of fifty-five delegates to the Constitutional Convention were trained in law).

7. Bellamy Partridge, *Country Lawyer* (New York: Grosset & Dunlap, 1939); Robert

H. Jackson, "The County-Seat Lawyer," *American Bar Association Journal* 36, 6 (June 1950): 497; Charles W. Moores, "The Career of a Country Lawyer—Abraham Lincoln," *Annual Report of the American Bar Association* 35 (1910): 440–447; William L. Ransom, "Abraham Lincoln . . . Profession a Lawyer," *American Bar Association Journal* 22, 3 (March 1936): 155 ("He attained professional distinction without leaving the ranks of those who will always be the great reservoir of strength and stability for our country and our profession—the country lawyer"). Ransom was president of the ABA.

8. Josiah Henry Benton, *The Lawyer's Official Oath and Office* (Boston: Boston Book Company, 1909), 60; Hollis R. Bailey, *Attorneys and Their Admission to the Bar in Massachusetts* (Boston: William J. Nagel, 1907), 16; Charles Warren, *A History of the American Bar* (Boston: Little, Brown, 1911), 77–78; People *ex rel.* Karlin v. Culkin, 162 N.E. 487, 489 (N.Y. 1928) (Chief Judge Benjamin N. Cardozo; when admitted to the bar, a lawyer "became an officer of the court, and, like the court itself, an instrument or agency to advance the ends of justice"); William Howard Taft, *Ethics of the Law: An Address in the Hubbard Course on Legal Ethics* (Albany, NY: Albany Law School, 1914), 5 (lawyers have "a double allegiance, a duty toward one's client, and a duty toward the court").

9. Matt. 6:24 (King James Version); Daniel L. Dreisbach, *Reading the Bible with the Founding Fathers* (New York: Oxford University Press, 2016); Harlan F. Stone, "The Public Influence of the Bar," *Harvard Law Review* 48, 1 (November 1934): 8.

10. *Works of James Wilson*, ed. Robert Green McCloskey, 2 vols. (Cambridge, MA: Belknap Press, 1967), 2:567; Benton, *Lawyer's Official Oath*, 4; Michael Ariens, "Know the Law: A History of Legal Specialization," *South Carolina Law Review* 45, 5 (1994): 1003–1061; Philip Jessup, *Elihu Root*, 2 vols. (New York: Dodd, Mead, 1938), 1:133; Robert W. Platt, "The Decadence of Law as a Profession and Its Growth as a Business," *Yale Law Journal* 12, 7 (May 1903): 441–445.

11. Theophilus Parsons [Jr.], *Memoirs of Theophilus Parsons* (Boston: Ticknor & Fields, 1859), 155; *Dictionary of American Biography* (1934), 14:271, s.v. "Parsons, Theophilus"; *Yale Biographical Dictionary of American Law* (2009), s.v. "Parsons, Theophilus"; Emory Washburn, *The Study and Practice of the Law* (Boston: Little, Brown, 1876), 159 (The lawyer "should spare nothing to vindicate his client's innocence. He should be deaf to the clamor of the masses, and let popular prejudice spend itself.").

12. John Adams, *Diary and Autobiography of John Adams*, ed. L. H. Butterfield, 4 vols. (Cambridge, MA: Belknap Press, 1961), 1:55; Roscoe Pound, "What Is a Profession? The Rise of the Legal Profession in Antiquity," *Notre Dame Law Review* 19, 3 (March 1944): 204; Roscoe Pound, *The Lawyer from Antiquity to Modern Times* (St. Paul: West Publishing, 1953), 5 (slightly modified).

13. Benton, *Lawyer's Official Oath*, 103–104; Anton-Hermann Chroust, *The Rise of the Legal Profession in America*, 2 vols. (Norman: University of Oklahoma Press, 1965), 2:160. Chroust claims that an 1836 revision of the law governing lawyers' admission to practice law in Massachusetts "assumed for the first time in the history of America that the bar was to be regarded not as a learned profession but as a sort of private occupation or business." This may be inaccurate in three respects: in addition to suggesting that lawyers, before such time, were wealthy gentlemen, it suggests that those practicing law were both learned and members of a profession. See Tocqueville, *Democracy*, 264 ("With

lawyers, as with all men, it is particular interest, especially the interest of the moment, which prevails").

14. Evarts Boutelle Greene, *The Revolutionary Generation, 1763–1790* (New York: Macmillan, 1943), 86 ("Anoint the lawyer, grease him in the Fist, / And he will plead for thee, even what thou li[e]st"); Herbert U. Feibelman, "The Passing Independence of the Bar," *Commercial Law Journal* 36, 5 (May 1931): 227–228 ("And for our ills, the finger of blame is pointed at the selfishness and crass materialism and avarice of the bar"); Josiah M. Daniel III, "Am I a 'Licensed Liar'? An Exploration into the Ethic of Honesty in Lawyering . . . and a Reply of 'No!' to the Stranger in the La Fiesta Lounge," *St. Mary's Journal on Legal Malpractice and Legal Ethics* 7, 1 (2016): 32–67.

15. Ambrose Bierce, *The Devil's Dictionary*, in *The Collected Works of Ambrose Bierce*, 12 vols. (New York: Neale Publishing, 1911), 7:187; Marc Galanter, *Lowering the Bar: Lawyer Jokes & Legal Culture* (Madison: University of Wisconsin Press, 2005), 67.

16. Honestus [Benjamin Austin], *Observations on the Pernicious Practice of the Law* (Boston: Adams & Nourse, 1786).

17. *Works of Wilson*, 2:566; T. Walker, "Ways and Means of Professional Success: Being the Substance of a Valedictory Address to the Graduates of the Law Class, in the Cincinnati College," *Western Law Journal* 1, 12 (September 1844): 547. Samuel Johnson wrote in 1773: "A lawyer has no business with the justice or injustice of the cause which he undertakes. . . . The justice or injustice of the cause is to be decided by the judge. . . . If lawyers were to undertake no causes till they were sure they were just, a man might be precluded altogether from a trial of his claim, though were it judicially examined, it might be found a very just claim." Simon James and Chantal Stebbings, eds., *A Dictionary of Legal Quotations* (New York: Macmillan, 1987), 108. On justifications for defending guilty clients in the antebellum United States, see Michael Ariens, "American Legal Ethics in an Age of Anxiety," *St. Mary's Law Journal* 40, 2 (2008): 375–384.

18. Adams, *Diary and Autobiography*, 1:137–138; *Correspondence and Public Papers of John Jay*, ed. Henry P. Johnston (1890; reprint, New York: Da Capo Press, 1971), 1:134–135 (opposing a proposal that would advance the interests of "designing, cheating, litigious pettifoggers, who, like leeches and spiders, will fatten on the spoils of the poor, the ignorant, the feeble, and the unwary"); Noah Webster, *An American Dictionary of the English Language* (1828; reprint, New York: Johnson Reprint, 1970), s.v. "Pettifoggers"; Gerald Leonard Cohen, *Origin of the Word "Shyster"* (Frankfurt: Peter Lang, 1982); Gerald Leonard Cohen, *Origin of the Word "Shyster": Supplementary Information* (Frankfurt: Peter Lang, 1984); Barbara Ann Kipfer and Robert L. Chapman, eds., *American Slang*, 4th ed. (New York: Collins, 2001), 333; Gene Fowler, *The Great Mouthpiece: A Life Story of William J. Fallon* (1931; reprint, New York: Bantam Books, 1962) (Fallon was a prominent 1920s New York criminal defense lawyer); Michael S. Ariens, "Sorting: Legal Specialization and the Privatization of the American Legal Profession," *Georgetown Journal of Legal Ethics* 29, 3 (Summer 2016): 587–589; David Maxwell, "The Public View of the Profession," *Annual Report of the American Bar Association* 82 (1957): 362.

19. Gerard W. Gawalt, *The Promise of Power: The Emergence of the Legal Profession in Massachusetts, 1760–1840* (Westport, CT: Greenwood Press, 1979), 22–23; Frederick Grant Jr., "Observations on the Pernicious Practice of the Law," *American Bar Asso-*

ciation Journal 68, 5 (May 1982): 580–582; Chroust, *Rise of the Legal Profession*, 2:167; Pound, *Lawyer*, 221–249; "Editorial," *Bar Examiner* 1, 8 (June 1932): 211.

20. Chroust, *Rise of the Legal Profession*, 1:90.

21. David Hoffman, *A Course of Legal Study, Addressed to Students and the Profession Generally*, 2nd ed. (Baltimore: Joseph Neal, 1836), 752–775.

22. Burton J. Bledstein, *The Culture of Professionalism: The Middle Class and the Development of Higher Education in America* (New York: W. W. Norton, 1976), 134; D. H. Meyer, *The Instructed Conscience: The Shaping of the American National Elite* (Philadelphia: University of Pennsylvania Press, 1972), 43–50.

23. Chroust, *Rise of the Legal Profession*, 2:165–168; George Sharswood, *A Compend of Lectures on the Aims and Duties of the Profession of the Law* (Philadelphia: T. & J. W. Johnson, 1854), 9; Webster, *American Dictionary*, s.v. "Professional"; Samuel Johnson, *A Dictionary of the English Language*, ed. H. T. Todd (London, 1818), s.v. "Professional" (defined as an adjective); *Black's Law Dictionary*, ed. Bryan A. Garner, 10th ed. (St. Paul: ThomsonReuters, 2014) (dating usage to 1846); *Oxford English Dictionary*, compact ed. (Oxford: Oxford University Press, 1984), s.v. "Professional" (dating usage to 1846); *Black's Law Dictionary*, s.v. "Professionalism"; *Oxford English Dictionary*, s.v. "Professionalism" (both dating usage to 1856).

24. Lon L. Fuller and John D. Randall, "Professional Responsibility: Report of the Joint Conference," *American Bar Association Journal* 44, 12 (December 1958): 1159–1162, 1216–1218; "Professional Responsibility: A Statement," *South Carolina Law Quarterly* 11, 3 (Spring 1959): 306–320.

25. Richard L. Abel, *American Lawyers* (New York: Oxford University Press, 1989), 280; Terence C. Halliday, "Six Score Years and Ten: Demographic Transitions in the American Legal Profession, 1850–1980," *Law & Society Review* 20, 1 (1986): 62.

26. Carol Rose Andrews, Paul M. Pruitt Jr., and David I. Durham, eds., *Gilded Age Legal Ethics: Essays on Thomas Goode Jones' 1887 Code* (Tuscaloosa: Bounds Law Library, University of Alabama Law School, 2003), 45–59 (reprinting 1887 Code); "Transactions," *Annual Report of the American Bar Association* 33 (1908): 86. The canons included an oath, the violation of which was a much more serious issue (see chapter 4).

27. "Proceedings," *Annual Report of the American Bar Association* 94 (1969): 389–392; "Report," *Annual Report of the American Bar Association* 97 (1972): 740–741; Michael Ariens, "The Agony of Modern Legal Ethics, 1970–1985," *St. Mary's Journal on Legal Malpractice and Legal Ethics* 5, 1 (2014): 137–138.

28. Richard B. Allen, "Watergate—A Lawyers' Scandal?" *American Bar Association Journal* 60, 10 (October 1974): 1257–1258; James D. Fellers, "President's Page," *American Bar Association Journal* 61, 5 (May 1975): 529.

1. ORIGINS, 1760–1830

1. John Adams, *Diary and Autobiography of John Adams*, ed. L. H. Butterfield, 4 vols. (Cambridge, MA: Belknap Press, 1961), 1:137–138; John E. Ferling, *John Adams: A Life* (Knoxville: University of Tennessee Press, 1993); *Dictionary of American Biography*

(1928), 1:72, s.v. "Adams, John"; *Yale Biographical Dictionary of American Law* (2009), s.v. "Adams, John."

2. Adams, *Diary and Autobiography*, 1:137–138.

3. *Suffolk County Bar Book, 1770–1805* (Cambridge, MA: John Wilson & Sons, 1882; reprint, 2020); Gerard W. Gawalt, *The Promise of Power: The Emergence of the Legal Profession in Massachusetts, 1760–1840* (Westport, CT: Greenwood Press, 1979), 13–30; Anton-Hermann Chroust, *The Rise of the Legal Profession in America*, 2 vols. (Norman: University of Oklahoma Press, 1965), 1:39–42, 1:52–54.

4. Samuel Haber, *The Quest for Authority and Honor in the American Professions, 1750–1900* (Chicago: University of Chicago Press, 1991), 75; Charles Robert McKirdy, "Lawyers in Crisis: The Massachusetts Legal Profession, 1760–1790" (Ph.D. diss., Northwestern University, 1969), 48–49; Charles R. McKirdy, "Massachusetts Lawyers on the Eve of the American Revolution: The State of the Profession," in *Law in Colonial Massachusetts, 1630–1800*, ed. Daniel R. Coquillette (Boston: Colonial Society of Massachusetts, 1984), 336; John M. Murrin, "The Legal Transformation: The Bench and Bar of Eighteenth-Century Massachusetts," in *Colonial America: Essays in Politics and Social Development*, ed. Stanley N. Katz, 1st ed. (Boston: McGraw Hill, 1971), 415, 431–434, 443–444; Chroust, *Rise of the Legal Profession*, 2:4n4; Daniel J. Boorstin, *The Americans: The Colonial Experience* (New York: Vintage Books, 1958), 205.

5. Honestus [Benjamin Austin Jr.], *Observations on the Pernicious Practice of the Law* (Boston: Adams & Nourse, 1786); Jesse Higgins, *Sampson against the Philistines* (Philadelphia: B. Graves, 1805), 12 (decrying lawyers' "practice of defending right and wrong indifferently, for reward").

6. Adams, *Diary and Autobiography*, 1:78.

7. Adams, 1:189; McKirdy, "Lawyers in Crisis," 48–49; McKirdy, "Massachusetts Lawyers," 336; Gawalt, *Promise of Power*, 27–28.

8. Adams, *Diary and Autobiography*, 3:276; *Black's Law Dictionary*, ed. Bryan A. Garner, 10th ed. (St. Paul: West Group, 2014), s.v. "barrister"; Michael Birks, *Gentlemen of the Law* (London: Stevens & Sons, 1960), 196.

9. Adams, *Diary and Autobiography*, 1:251–252, 1:316; McKirdy, "Lawyers in Crisis," 74–76.

10. Hollis R. Bailey, *Attorneys and Their Admission to the Bar in Massachusetts* (Boston: William J. Nagel, 1907), 16.

11. Geoffrey C. Hazard Jr., "An Historical Perspective on the Attorney-Client Privilege," *California Law Review* 66, 5 (September 1978): 1061–1091; John H. Wigmore, *A Treatise on the System of Evidence in Trials at Common Law*, 4 vols. (Boston: Little, Brown, 1904–1905), 4:§2290.

12. Adams, *Diary and Autobiography*, 2:79 (March 5, 1773), 3:294. Adams's diary is silent during the trials. He allegedly said in 1822, "At the present day, it is impossible to realize the excitement of the populace, and the abuse heaped upon Mr. Quincy and myself for our defence of the British captain and his soldiers: we heard our names execrated in the most opprobrious terms whenever we appeared in the streets of Boston." John Adams, *Legal Papers of John Adams*, ed. L. Kinvin Wroth and Hiller B. Zobel, 3 vols. (Cambridge, MA: Belknap Press, 1965), 3:33n11.

13. Hiller B. Zobel, *The Boston Massacre* (New York: W. W. Norton , 1970), 180, 265

(Preston), 294 (soldiers); Eric Hinderaker, *Boston's Massacre* (Cambridge, MA: Belknap Press, 2019), 187. In the third trial, four civilians were found not guilty. Hinderaker, 213; Serena Zabin, *The Boston Massacre: A Family History* (Boston: Houghton Mifflin Harcourt, 2020), ch. 9, 205. A transcript of the soldiers' trial is in Adams, *Legal Papers*, 3:98–314, 3:312–314 (recording the verdict for each defendant and noting the benefit of clergy granted to those convicted of manslaughter).

14. American Bar Association, "Law Day Celebrates Legacy of President John Adams," May 1, 2011, https://www.americanbar.org/advocacy/governmental_legislative _work/publications/governmental_affairs_periodicals/washingtonletter/2011/may /2011lawday/.

15. William Sullivan, *An Address to the Members of the Bar of Suffolk, Mass. at Their Stated Meeting of the First Tuesday of March, 1824* (Boston: North American Review, 1825), 30; "Sketch of the Professional Life of John Adams," *American Jurist and Law Magazine* 25, 49 (April–July 1841): 65, 67–68; Hinderaker, *Boston's Massacre*, 259–262 (citing David Ramsay's 1789 *History of the American Revolution*: that result "reflected great honour on John Adams, and Josiah Quincy . . . in defiance of popular opinions").

16. Randolph G. Adams, "New Light on the Boston Massacre," *Proceedings of the American Antiquarian Society* 48, 2 (1937): 348–349 (letter of December 3, 1770); Catherine Barton Mayo, ed., "Additions to 'History of Massachusetts Bay,'" *Proceedings of the American Antiquarian Society* 59, 1 (1949): 31–33.

17. Hiller B. Zobel, "Newer Light on the Boston Massacre," *Proceedings of the American Antiquarian Society* 78, 1 (1969): 124; L. Kinvin Wroth and Hiller B. Zobel, "The Boston Massacre Trials," *American Bar Association Journal* 55, 4 (April 1969): 329–333. Wroth and Zobel's essay indirectly responded to Hugh P. Williamson, "John Adams, Counsellor of Courage," *American Bar Association Journal* 54, 2 (February 1968): 148–151.

18. Zobel, *Boston Massacre*, 259–260; Adams, *Legal Papers*, 3:26.

19. Zobel, *Boston Massacre*, 282–283, 289; Mayo, "Additions," 31; Zobel, "Newer Light," 127.

20. Adams, *Legal Papers*, 3:266, 269; Daniel J. Gillen, "Who Shot Patrick Carr?" *Law Society Journal* 12, 1 (February 1946): 48–58.

21. John K. Alexander, "The Fort Wilson Incident of 1779: A Case Study of the Revolutionary Crowd," *William & Mary Quarterly* 31, 4 (October 1974), 589–612; C. Page Smith, "The Attack on Fort Wilson," *Pennsylvania Magazine of History & Biography* 78, 2 (April 1954): 177–188; Charles Page Smith, *James Wilson: Founding Father, 1742–1798* (Chapel Hill: University of North Carolina Press, 1956), ch. 9; Carlton F. W. Larson, *The Trials of Allegiance* (New York: Oxford University Press, 2019), 1–3, 185–189; Carlton F. W. Larson, "The Revolutionary American Jury: A Case Study of the 1778–1789 Philadelphia Treason Trials," *SMU Law Review* 61, 4 (Fall 2008): 1506–1508.

22. Larson, *Trials of Allegiance*, 259–261; *Dictionary of American Biography*, 19:326, s.v. "Wilson, James"; *Yale Biographical Dictionary of American Law*, s.v. "Wilson, James"; Robert R. Bell, *Philadelphia Lawyer: A History, 1735–1945* (Cranbury, NJ: Associated University Presses, 1992), 65–71; Henry J. Young, "Treason and Its Punishment in Revolutionary Pennsylvania," *Pennsylvania Magazine of History & Biography* 90, 3 (July 1966): 287–313.

23. Smith, *James Wilson*, 118; Bell, *Philadelphia Lawyer*, 83–87; Horace Binney, *The Leaders of the Old Bar of Philadelphia* (Philadelphia: C. Sherman & Son, 1859), 9–45. In 2008 Larson wrote that Wilson, Ross, and Lewis, along with Jacob Rush, were employed by the bulk of the defendants. Larson, "Revolutionary American Jury," 1485. He later moderated that statement in Larson, *Trials of Allegiance*, 157.

24. Respublica v. Carlisle, 1 Dall. (1 U.S.) 35 (Pa. O. & Term. 1778); Peter C. Messer, "'A Species of Treason and Not the Least Dangerous Kind': The Treason Trials of Abraham Carlisle and John Roberts," *Pennsylvania Magazine of History & Biography* 123, 4 (October 1999): 303–332; Smith, *James Wilson*, 119–121; Larson, *Trials of Allegiance*, 157. Wilson and Ross represented Joseph Malin in a treason trial in Chester County a week before Carlisle's case and used a number of zealous tactics in their successful defense of him, including procedural and evidentiary challenges. Carlton F. W. Larson, "The 1778–1779 Chester and Philadelphia Treason Trials: The Supreme Court as Trial Court," in *The Supreme Court of Pennsylvania*, ed. John J. Hare (University Park: Pennsylvania State University Press, 2018), 315, 316–319; Respublica v. Malin, 1 Dall. (1 U.S.) 33 (Pa. O. & Term. 1778).

25. Respublica v. Roberts, 1 Dall. (1 U.S.) 50 (Pa. O. & Term. 1778); Smith, *James Wilson*, 121–122.

26. Larson, *Trials of Allegiance*, 164, 188 ("The most significant acquittal").

27. Larson, "Revolutionary American Jury," 1507; Larson, *Trials of Allegiance*, 188.

28. Honestus [Austin], *Observations* (1786), 5–7; Honestus, *Observations on the Pernicious Practice of the Law* (Boston: True & Weston, 1819), in *Sources of the History of the American Law of Lawyering*, ed. Michael H. Hoeflich (Clark, NJ: Lawbook Exchange, 2007), 45–104; *American Journal of Legal History* 13, 3 (July 1969): 244–302; *Dictionary of American Biography*, 1:431, s.v., "Austin, Benjamin"; Frederic Grant Jr., "Benjamin Austin, Jr.'s Struggle with the Lawyers," *Boston Bar Journal* 25, 9 (September 1981): 19–29; Frederic Grant Jr., "Observations on the Pernicious Practice of the Law," *American Bar Association Journal* 68, 5 (May 1982): 580–582; Sidney Kaplan, "'Honestus' and the Annihilation of the Lawyers," *South Atlantic Quarterly* 48, 3 (1948): 401–420; Aaron T. Knapp, "Law's Revolution: Benjamin Austin and the Spirit of '86," *Yale Journal of Law & the Humanities* 25, 2 (Summer 2013): 275 (offering a revisionist interpretation); McKirdy, "Lawyers in Crisis," 116–128. Honestus wrote additional essays for the *Independent Chronicle* published on June 8, 15, and 22, 1786, that were not published in his pamphlet.

29. Honestus [Austin], *Observations* (1786), 18.

30. A Lawyer, "Miscellanies," *Massachusetts Centinel*, April 26, April 29, May 3, 1786; Grant, "Observations," 580; Theophilus Parsons Jr., *Memoir of Theophilus Parsons* (Boston: Ticknor & Fields, 1859), 192–193 (noting misconduct).

31. *Independent Chronicle*, April 27, May 4, May 11, 1786; *Dictionary of American Biography*, 18:190, s.v. "Sullivan, James"; Thomas Amory, *Life of James Sullivan*, 2 vols. (Boston, 1859).

32. Honestus [Austin], *Observations* (1786), 46–47, 50.

33. Grant, "Observations," 580; McKirdy, "Lawyers in Crisis," ch. 5.

34. Grant, "Austin, Jr.'s Struggle," 19; John Bach McMaster, *A History of the People of the United States* (New York: D. Appleton, 1920; reprint, 2012), 254–255, 302, 348–530; Richard E. Ellis, *The Jeffersonian Crisis: Courts and Politics in the Young Republic* (New

York: Oxford University Press, 1971), 112–115; Gawalt, *Promise of Power*, 61–65; Gerard W. Gawalt, "Sources of Anti-Lawyers Sentiment in Massachusetts," *American Journal of Legal History* 14, 3 (July 1970): 283–307.

Adams recorded the following doggerel in his diary (2:132) in 1774:

> You ask me why Lawyers so much are increased
> Tho most of the Country already are fleec'd
> The Reason I'm sure is most strikingly plain
> The Sheep are oft sheered yet the Wool grows again
> And tho you may think e'er so odd of the Matter
> The oft'ner they're fleeced, the Wool grows the better
> Thus downy-chin'd Boys as oft I have heard
> By frequently shaving obtain a large Beard.

35. Grant, "Austin, Jr.'s Struggle," 24; *Dictionary of American Biography*, 1:531–532, s.v. "Austin, Benjamin, Jr."; Ruth G. Matz, "Lawyers and Shays' Rebellion," *Boston Bar Journal* 21, 2 (February 1977): 5–11. A revisionist understanding concluded that the regulators acted in an effort to fight tyranny and a system of governance favoring the rich. Leonard L. Richards, *Shays's Rebellion: The American Revolution's Final Battle* (Philadelphia: University of Pennsylvania Press, 2002), 63–64.

36. Honestus [Austin], "Prefatory Address," in *Observations* (1819), 3–4.

37. Charles Warren, *Jacobin and Junto* (Cambridge, MA: Harvard University Press, 1931), ch. 7, 188–189 ("famous case"); Daniel Breen, "Parson's Charge: The Strange Origins of Stand Your Ground," *Connecticut Public Interest Law Journal* 16, 1 (Winter 2017): 41–78; Grant, "Austin, Jr.'s Struggle," 25–26; Thomas O. Selfridge, *A Correct Statement of the Whole Preliminary Controversy between Tho. O. Selfridge and Benj. Austin* (Charlestown, MA: Samuel Etheridge, 1807), 17, 18; *Trial of Thomas O. Selfridge . . . before the Hon. Isaac Parker . . . for Killing Charles Austin, on the Public Exchange, in Boston, August 4, 1806* (Boston: Russell & Cutler, 1806), 85, 87.

38. Warren, *Jacobin and Junto*, 197; Breen, "Parson's Charge," 72–73, 52; *Trial of Selfridge*; "The Trial of Thomas O. Selfridge for the Killing of Charles Austin, Boston, 1806," in *American State Trials* (Wilmington, DE: Scholarly Resources, 1972), 2:544–702 (summarizing trial testimony and eliminating questions of counsel and Selfridge); Jack Tager, "Politics, Honor, and Self-Defense in Post-Revolutionary Boston: The 1806 Manslaughter Trial of Thomas Selfridge," *Historical Journal of Massachusetts* 37, 2 (Fall 2009): 85–104; Selfridge, *Correct Statement*, 36.

39. *Dictionary of American Biography*, 5:280, s.v. "Dexter, Samuel"; Sigma [Lucius Manlius Sargent], *Reminiscences of Samuel Dexter* (Boston: A. Williams, 1857).

40. *Trial of Selfridge*, 71, 73–95.

41. *Trial of Selfridge*, 124–129; *American State Trials*, 2:647, 653; Selfridge, *Correct Statement*, 44–46.

42. *Trial of Selfridge*, 168, 5, 42–43n*; Breen, "Parson's Charge," 41, 70, 75.

43. Ron Chernow, *Alexander Hamilton* (New York: Penguin Books, 2004), 603. Weeks was "the object of universal abhorrence." Liva Baker, "The Defense of Levi Weeks," *American Bar Association Journal* 63, 6 (June 1977): 821 (unnamed source). Julius Goebel Jr.

noted that Hamilton's cash books lacked any notation of a payment from Weeks. *The Law Practice of Alexander Hamilton*, ed. Julius Goebel Jr., 3 vols. (New York: Columbia University Press, 1964), 1:688; hereafter, cited as *LPAH*.

44. *LPAH*, 1:705, 711–712; Daniel Goleman, *Report of the Trial of Levi Weeks* (New York: John Furman, 1800; Kindle ed.); *LPAH*, 1:704–774 (reprinting Goleman's *Report*); "The Trial of Levi Weeks," in *American State Trials*, 4:1; Estelle Fox Kleiger, *The Trial of Levi Weeks, or the Manhattan Well Mystery* (Chicago: Academy Chicago Publishers, 1989); Paul Collins, *Duel with the Devil: The True Story of How Alexander Hamilton & Aaron Burr Teamed up to Take on America's First Sensational Murder Mystery* (New York: MJF Books, 2014); Chernow, *Hamilton*, 603–606; Nancy Isenberg, *Fallen Founder: The Life of Aaron Burr* (New York: Penguin Books, 2007), 191–196; Milton Lomask, *Aaron Burr: The Years from Princeton to Vice President, 1756–1805* (New York: Farrar, Straus, Giroux, 1979), 90–93. Two other instant summaries of the trial exist; see *LPAH*, 1:693n2. *Dictionary of American Biography*, 11:312, s.v. "Livingston, Henry Brockholst"; *Yale Biographical Dictionary of American Law*, s.v. "Livingston, Henry Brockholst"; Michael B. Dougan, "Livingston, Henry Brockholst," in *Oxford Companion to the Supreme Court of the United States*, ed. Kermit L. Hall, 2nd ed. (New York: Oxford University Press, 2005), 587; Fed. R. Evid. 803(3) (1975); Mut. Life Ins. Co. v. Hillmon, 145 U.S. 285 (1892) (a speaker's statement of the then-existing state of mind can prove future actions).

45. *LPAH*, 1:733–734 (cross-examination), 739 (adjourned), 741 (admonished), 747–750 (Burr), 748, 762–763 (melancholy), 767–769 (character witnesses); Isenberg, *Fallen Founder*, 193 (noting *Daily Advertiser* report that Burr gave the opening statement).

46. *LPAH*, 1:753 (relationship), 756–757 (evening disappearances), 760–762, 770–771 (Croucher). Croucher was later charged with and convicted of raping of his thirteen-year-old stepdaughter. He was defended by Brockholst Livingston. Collins, *Duel with the Devil*, 195–198; Kleiger, *Trial of Weeks*, 197–198.

47. [William Wyche], *Report of the Trial of Henry Bedlow for Committing a Rape on Lanah Sawyer* (New York, 1793), 4; Christine Stansell, *City of Women: Sex and Class in New York, 1789–1860* (Urbana: University of Illinois Press, 1986); Collins, *Duel with the Devil*, 145–146.

48. [Wyche], *Trial of Bedlow*, 3.

49. [Wyche], 19–61.

50. [Wyche], 24–25; Paul A. Gilje, *The Road to Mobocracy: Popular Disorder in New York City, 1763–1834* (Chapel Hill: University of North Carolina Press, 1987), 87–88.

51. Kleiger, *Trial of Weeks*, 201–203; Collins, *Duel with the Devil*, 210–211; Randolph N. Jonakait, "The Origins of the Confrontation Clause: An Alternative History," *Rutgers Law Journal* 27, 1 (Autumn 1995): 155–163 ("*Weeks* was a modern trial"). Michael Millender does not discuss the Weeks trial in his dissertation, but in assessing other trials, he concludes that New York criminal defense lawyers had adopted a "unique style" of zealous adversarial representation by this time. Michael Jonathan Millender, "The Transformation of the American Criminal Trial, 1790–1875" (Ph.D. diss., Princeton University, 1996), 108, ch. 3.

52. *Niles' Weekly Register*, July 15, 1820, 360; Docket Record, *Thomas Bigelow's Case*, Mayor's Court, Philadelphia, Pennsylvania, June 1820 session; Joseph A. Dowling, *The Trial of the Rev. William Hogan, Pastor of St. Mary's Church, for an Assault and Battery*

on Mary Connell (Philadelphia: R. Desilver, 1822), 268; In re Anonymous, 7 N.J. L. Rep. 162, 163 (1824).

53. Historical Society of the New York Courts, "John Van Ness Yates Cases," https://www.nycourts.gov/history/legal-history-new-york/legal-history-eras-02/history-new-york-legal-eras-van-ness-yates.html. A summary of potential value is L. B. Proctor, *Lawyer and Client* (New York: S. S. Peloubet, 1882), 148–159; In re John V. N. Yates, 4 Johns. 317 (N.Y. Sup. Ct. 1809), *rev'd*, 6 Johns. 337 (N.Y. Ct. Corr. Errors 1810).

54. Strother v. State, 1 Mo. 605 (1826); similarly, see State v. Watkins, 3 Mo. 480 (1834), and State v. Foreman, 3 Mo. 602 (1834) (both overturning orders striking lawyers from the roll).

55. William Sampson, *The Case of George W. Niven, Esq.* (Clark, NJ: Lawbook Exchange, 2011), 65 (quoting New York district attorney Hugh Maxwell).

56. Sampson, 3–4. Common-law fraud was narrowly drawn. See Millender, "Transformation," 128–130; Charles Currier Beale, *William Sampson, Lawyer and Stenographer* (Boston: reprinted from Proceedings of New York State Stenographers' Association, 1906, 1907); *Dictionary of American Biography*, 16:321, s.v. "Sampson, William"; *Yale Biographical Dictionary of American Law*, s.v. "Sampson, William"; Maxwell Bloomfield, *American Lawyers in a Changing Society, 1776–1876* (Cambridge, MA: Harvard University Press, 1976), ch. 3.

57. In December 1818 Sampson and John Anthon represented the plaintiff, oil inspector James Maurice, in *Maurice v. Judd*. The issue was: is a whale a fish? Niven was a member of the jury. D. Graham Burnett, *Trying Leviathan: The Nineteenth-Century New York Court Case that Put the Whale on Trial and Challenged the Order of Nature* (Princeton, NJ: Princeton University Press, 2007), 4, 17, 37.

58. Two reports exist of the criminal case against Niven: People v. George Niven, 1 N.Y. Rep. 13 (1820) (Barent Gardenier, reporter; hereafter, cited as Gardenier), and George Niven's Case, 5 N.-Y. City-Hall Rec. 79 (1820) (Daniel Rogers, reporter; hereafter, cited as Rogers). They differ in specificity but report the same events. See Sampson, *Case of Niven*, 12 (printing Latimer's May 22, 1822, affidavit); Rogers, 82. Under the common-law doctrine of coverture, a wife's property was managed by her husband. See *Black's Law Dictionary*, s.v. "Coverture"; Sarah Winsberg, "Attorney 'Mal-practices': An Invisible Ethical Problem in the Early American Republic," *Legal Ethics* 19, 2 (2016): 187–206.

59. *Dictionary of American Biography*, 6:145, s.v. "Emmet, Thomas Addis"; A. Oakey Hall, "Thomas Addis Emmet," *Green Bag* 8, 7 (July 1896): 273–279. John Anthon and William Price are discussed later. The other two lawyers were Josiah Hoffman, who unsuccessfully prosecuted Henry Bedlow, and either Richard or John Riker; the former was a longtime recorder in the Court of Special Sessions, and the latter was a well-respected lawyer.

60. Rogers, 80 (Anthon), and Gardinier, 15 (Price); Rogers, 81, and Gardinier, 15; Gardinier, 16–17, and Rogers, 81–82; Stockton v. Ford, 11 How. (52 U.S.) 232, 247 (1850).

61. Rogers, 82, and Gardinier, 17–18; Rogers, 83–84, and Gardinier, 18–19; Rogers, 84, and Gardinier, 19.

62. Sampson, *Case of Niven*, 3; Harold E. Hammond, "The New York Court of Common Pleas," *New York History* 32, 3 (July 1951): 275–295, 284; John Wilton Brooks,

History of the Court of Common Pleas of the City and County of New York (New York: Werner, Sanford, 1896), 61–63, 23. Maxwell was also well regarded. Brooks, 24. He was "thoroughly learned in the English and American criminal law, with rare elocutionary powers, [and] a pleasing, genial manner." L. B. Proctor, *The Bench and Bar of New York* (New York: Diossy, 1870), 11.

63. Burnett, *Trying Leviathan*, 37; Sampson, *Case of Niven*, 8–9; *Dictionary of American Biography*, 1:314, s.v., "Anthon, John"; Brooks, *History of Court of Common Pleas*, 23, 24; *The United States Attorneys for the Southern District of New York: The First 100 Years (1789-1889)*, comp. Second Circuit Historical Committee and the Federal Bar Council (New York, 1987), 28; *American State Trials*, 5:360–362n4. Price became the "most infamous" of the district's attorneys, fleeing New York for Europe with more than $70,000 in stolen government bonds. He returned to New York but was not prosecuted; at his death, he was deeply in debt. *The Diary of Philip Hone*, ed. Allan Nevins, 2 vols. (New York: Dodd, Mead, 1927), 1:365–366; Jonathan Daniel Wells, *The Kidnapping Club: Wall Street, Slavery, and Resistance on the Eve of the Civil War* (New York: Bold Type Books, 2020), 86–87. On August 11, 1846, "William Price blew out what brains he had left this morning." *The Diary of George Templeton Strong*, ed. Allan Nevins and Milton Halsey Thomas, 4 vols. (New York: Macmillan, 1952), 1:280.

64. Sampson, *Case of Niven*, 18, 20.

65. Sampson, 29–30.

66. Sampson, 48.

67. Sampson, 56, 57.

68. Sampson, 68–69.

69. Sampson, 70, 74.

70. Sampson, 83, 84.

71. Sampson, 90–92.

72. Sampson, 90, 93–94.

73. Winsberg, "Attorney 'Mal-practices,'" 203; "Politics of the Day," *Niles' Weekly Register*, May 28, 1831, 232 (noting a toast by Niven: "Martin Van Buren. He has convinced those who distrusted him, of his political faith; he has given additional evidence of confidence to his friends. Nine cheers.").

74. *Ex parte Burr*, 4 Fed. 791 (No. 2,186), 2 Cranch C.C. 379 (D.C. Cir. 1823), *aff'd on other grounds*, 22 U.S. (9 Wheat.) 529 (1824); "Levi S. Burr," Fold3 Ancestry, https://www.fold3.com/page/630583457/levi-s-burr/photos; Alexander Burton Hagner, "William Cranch," in *Great American Lawyers* (South Hackensack, NJ: Rothman Reprints, 1971), 3:87–119; *Dictionary of American Biography*, 4:502, s.v. "Cranch, William"; *Yale Biographical Dictionary of American Law*, s.v. "Cranch, William."

75. *Burr*, 4 Fed. at 792.

76. *Burr*, 4 Fed. at 794.

77. *Burr*, 4 Fed. at 798–800.

78. *Burr*, 4 Fed. at 800–801.

79. Publisher's advertisement for Col. Levi S. Burr, *A Voice from Sing-Sing, Giving a General Description of the State Prison* (Albany, NY, 1833), 2, 4. "Colonel" was also the honorific by which Aaron Burr, no relation, was known. Levi Burr apparently gave himself a postwar promotion in rank.

80. In re Anonymous, 7 N.J. L. Rep. 162 (N.J. 1824).

81. In re Anonymous, 7 N.J. L. Rep. at 164.

82. Bank of New York v. Stryker, 1 Wheeler's Crim. Cas. 330 (N.Y. Mayor's Ct. 1816) (refusing to disbar a lawyer for writing a bad check).

83. *Burr*, 4 Fed. at 795; United States v. Peacock, 27 Fed. Cas. 479 (No. 16,019) (1805) (forgery); Herty's Case, 12 Fed. Cas. 59 (No. 6,431) (n.d.) ("Cited in Ex parte Burr. . . . Nowhere reported; opinion not now accessible."). Someone named "Thomas Herty," who was engaged in barratry along with Porter, is noted in United States v. Porter, 27 Fed. Cas. 595, 597, 2 Cranch C. C. 60 (No. 16,072) (D.C. Cir. Ct. Dec. term 1812).

84. Ex parte Tillinghast, 4 Pet. (29 U.S.) 108 (1830); Tillinghast v. Conkling, discussed in Ex parte Secombe, 19 How. (60 U.S.) 9, 13 (1856); Harold J. Jonas, "Alfred Conkling, Jurist and Gentleman," *New York History* 20, 3 (July 1939): 295–305.

85. *Dictionary of American Biography*, 4:72, s.v. "Chipman, Daniel"; Alexander Young, *Young against Chipman: Narrative of the Case* (Vergennes, VT: Gamaliel Small, 1827), 88.

86. Young, *Narrative against Chipman*, 4–5, 25 (dated August 10, 1809).

87. Young, 39, 52.

88. Young, 98, 113.

89. Young, 137.

90. Young, 137; Paul S. Gillies, "Daniel Chipman, First Reporter of Decisions," *Vermont Bar Journal & Law Digest* 17, 2 (April 1991): 18n29.

91. Young, *Narrative against Chipman*, 103n*, 78; "Chipman, Daniel, 1765–1850," Biographical Directory of the United States Congress, https://bioguide.congress.gov/search/bio/C000366; "Daniel Chipman," Middlebury History Online, https://middhistory.middlebury.edu/daniel-chipman-middlebury-college-trustee/; *Dictionary of American Biography*, 4:72, s.v. "Chipman, Daniel"; Samuel Swift, *The History of the Town of Middlebury* (Middlebury, VT: A. H. Copeland, 1859).

92. Kenneth A. Degree, "Malfeasance or Theft: What Really Happened to the Middlebury Branch of the Vermont State Bank?" *Vermont History* 68 (Winter 2000): 22, https://vermonthistory.org/journal/68/vt681_202.pdf; Swift, *History of Middlebury*, 325–327. A defense of the directors on the grounds that the loss was caused by theft became the standard history; the sum owed was $28,826. According to Degree, Chipman was Swift's mentor, as Chipman brought Swift in as a lawyer when he passed the bar. Degree, "Malfeasance," 31–32.

93. Degree, "Malfeasance," 25–27.

94. *Letters Written by Alexander Young to the Hon. Robt. B. Bates* (Montreal: Gazette Office, 1829) (accusing Bates of protecting Chipman). Young sued executor Asa Chapman in 1829, but the record does not include an order of judgment.

95. Joseph Jackman, *The Sham-Robbery* (Concord, NH, 1819; reprint, Forgotten Books, 2015); Robert V. Remini, *Daniel Webster: The Man and His Time* (New York: W. W. Norton, 1997); Maurice G. Baxter, *One and Inseparable: Daniel Webster and the Union* (Cambridge, MA: Belknap Press, 1984); *The Papers of Daniel Webster: Legal Papers*, ed. Alfred S. Konefsky and Andrew J. King, 3 vols. (Hanover, NH: University Press of New England, 1983); *Dictionary of American Biography*, 19:585, s.v. "Webster, Daniel"; *Yale Biographical Dictionary of American Law*, s.v. "Webster, Daniel."

96. "No verbatim report of the testimony of witnesses or the arguments of counsel in these trials was ever made." Howard A. Bradley and James A. Winans, *Daniel Webster and the Salem Murder* (Columbia, MO: Aircraft Press, 1956), 10. A confused story of the trials, especially Frank's, can be found in *American State Trials*, 7:395 (Frank), 7:594 (Joe), 7:640 (George). See also Bradley and Winans, *Daniel Webster*, 68; *American State Trials*, 7:454; Benjamin Merrill, "Introductory Note, the Murder of Captain Joseph White," in *Works of Daniel Webster* (Boston: Little, Brown, 1857), 6:41–51; Walker Lewis, "The Murder of Captain Joseph White: Salem, Massachusetts, 1830," *American Bar Association Journal* 54, 5 (May 1968): 460–466; Robert Booth, *Death of an Empire: The Rise and Murderous Fall of Salem, America's Richest City* (New York: St. Martin's Press, 2011); Edward J. Renehan Jr., *Deliberate Evil: Nathaniel Hawthorne, Daniel Webster, and the 1830 Murder of a Salem Slave Trader* (Chicago: Chicago Review Press, 2022).

97. Bradley and Winans, *Daniel Webster*, 90; *American State Trials*, 7:467. Other testimonial evidence included that of witnesses Benjamin Leighton, who reported overhearing a conversation between the brothers detailing their plans to murder White, and John Palmer, who recounted a conversation with the Crowninshield brothers about the conspiracy to murder White. Palmer was a Maine felon, making him an incompetent witness in that state but a competent witness in Massachusetts.

98. Baxter, *One and Inseparable*, 160; Bradley and Winans, *Daniel Webster*, 64–65, 43. Commonwealth v. Knapp, 9 Pick. (26 Mass.) 496, 20 Am. Dec. 491 (Mass. 1830), includes the court's decisions excluding and then admitting Colman's additional testimony about what Frank said, as well as other legal issues.

99. Bradley and Winans, *Daniel Webster*, 64–66, 98; *Commonwealth v. Knapp*, 9 Pick. at 520–21; *American State Trials*, 7:422.

100. Bradley and Winans, *Daniel Webster*, 133; *American State Trials*, 7:503.

101. Bradley and Winans, *Daniel Webster*, 222, 198n33.

102. Bradley and Winans, 201; *American State Trials*, 7:585.

103. Bradley and Winans, *Daniel Webster*, 196, 198.

104. Baxter, *One and Inseparable*, 544n19 (indicating that "moral justice" was done); George Ticknor Curtis, *Life of Daniel Webster*, 2nd ed. (New York: D. Appleton, 1870), 384; Claude M. Fuess, *Daniel Webster*, 2 vols. (Boston: Little, Brown, 1930), 1:297; Bradley and Winans, *Daniel Webster*, 159.

105. Bradley and Winans, *Daniel Webster*, 161, 221–222, 224; Commonwealth v. Knapp, 10 Pick. (27 Mass.) 477, 20 Am. Dec. 534 (Mass. 1830); *American State Trials*, 7:597 (not quoting Webster but indicating his claim that he "appeared solely at the request of the attorney general, and without any pecuniary inducement"). George Crowninshield was found not guilty of being an accessory to murder; he was subsequently charged with misprision of a felony (having knowledge of a felony and failing to properly disclose it) and ultimately found not guilty. Bradley and Winans, *Daniel Webster*, 226–227; *American State Trials*, 7:663.

106. Baxter, *One and Inseparable*, 159.

107. Daniel Webster, "Speech to the Charleston, South Carolina Bar, May 10, 1847," in Thad H. Westbrook, "Daniel Webster's Tribute to the Law and the Legal Profession," *South Carolina Lawyer* 19, 4 (January 2008): 15, 17, and reprinted in many other publications.

108. James D. Rice, "The Criminal Trial before and after the Lawyers: Authority, Law, and Culture in Maryland Jury Trials, 1631–1837," *American Journal of Legal History* 40, 4 (October 1996): 457, 459, 462; George Fisher, *Plea Bargaining's Triumph: A History of Plea Bargaining in America* (Stanford, CA: Stanford University Press, 2003), 100–101 (demonstrating defense counsel's influence on the percentage of cases ending in acquittals or hung juries).

109. Rice, "Criminal Trial," 475; Fisher, *Plea Bargaining's Triumph*, ch. 1 (discussing the use of plea bargains in early-nineteenth-century Massachusetts liquor cases).

2. HONOR AND CONSCIENCE, 1830–1860

1. John Neal, *Wandering Recollections of a Somewhat Busy Life* (Boston: Roberts Bros., 1869), 206; Jeffrey L. Pasley, *"The Tyranny of Printers": Newspaper Politics in the Early American Republic* (Charlottesville: University of Virginia Press, 2001), 241; Frank A. Cassell, "The Great Baltimore Riot of 1812," *Maryland Historical Magazine* 70, 3 (Fall 1975): 244–245.

2. Paul A. Gilje, "The Baltimore Riots of 1812 and the Breakdown of the Anglo-American Mob Tradition," *Journal of Social History* 13, 4 (Summer 1980): 551–552; Neal, *Wandering Recollections*, 206; Frank A. Cassell, "The Structure of Baltimore's Politics in the Age of Jefferson, 1795–1812," in *Law, Society, and Politics in Early Maryland*, ed. Aubrey C. Land, Lois Green Carr, and Edward C. Papenfuse (Baltimore: Johns Hopkins University Press, 1977), 277.

3. Maxwell Bloomfield, "David Hoffman and the Shaping of a Republican Legal Culture," *Maryland Law Review* 38, 4 (1979): 678; David Hoffman, *A Course of Legal Study* (Baltimore: Pomeroy & Toy, 1817); "A Course of Legal Study Respectfully Addressed to the Students of Law in the United States," *North American Review & Miscellaneous Journal* 6, 1 (November 1817): 45–77 (unsigned review by Supreme Court justice Joseph Story); *David Hoffman: Life, Letters and Lectures at the University of Maryland, 1821–1837*, ed. Bill Sleeman (Clark, NJ: Lawbook Exchange, 2011) (reprinting Hoffman's lectures from 1822, 1824, and 1826 and offering a timeline of his law practice).

4. Bill Sleeman, "Biographical Note" and "Timeline," in *David Hoffman*, 20, 34–37, 54; Michael Ariens, "Lost and Found: David Hoffman and the History of American Legal Ethics," *Arkansas Law Review* 67, 3 (2014): 593–598; Robert E. Shalhope, *The Baltimore Bank Riot: Political Upheaval in Antebellum Maryland* (Urbana: University of Illinois Press, 2009). Hoffman's diary for his 1833–1834 travels in Europe is at the New York Public Library.

5. Hoffman, *Course of Legal Study* (1817), 328, 325, "Appendix," 324–334.

6. David Hoffman, *A Course of Legal Study, Addressed to Students and the Profession Generally*, 2nd ed. (Baltimore: Joseph Neal, 1836), 720–775.

7. Hoffman, 720–724.

8. Hoffman, 747–751; *Dictionary of Quotations for Ancient and Modern English and Foreign Sources*, comp. James Wood (London: Frederick Warne, 1893), 170; Howard Schweber, "The 'Science' of Legal Science: The Model of the Natural Sciences in Nineteenth-Century American Legal Education," *Law & History Review* 17, 3 (Fall 1999): 421–466.

9. Hoffman, *Course of Legal Study* (1836), 745–746.

10. Hoffman, 746.

11. George Wilson Pierson, *Tocqueville in America* (Baltimore: Johns Hopkins University Press, 1996), 489–510; John E. Semmes, *John H. B. Latrobe and His Times, 1803–1891* (Baltimore: Norman, Remington, 1916); Alexis de Tocqueville, *Democracy in America*, ed. J. P. Mayer, trans. George Lawrence (New York: HarperPerennial, 1988), 265, 268.

12. Anthony Grumbler, *Miscellaneous Thoughts on Men, Manners and Things* (Baltimore: Coale, 1837), 233–234.

13. Bertram Wyatt-Brown, *Southern Honor: Ethics and Behavior in the Old South*, 25th anniversary ed. (New York: Oxford University Press, 2007), xvi–xvii; Bertram Wyatt-Brown, "Honor," in *A Companion to American Thought*, ed. Richard Wightman Fox and James T. Kloppenberg (Cambridge, MA: Blackwell, 1995), 310–311; Joanne B. Freeman, *Affairs of Honor: National Politics in the New Republic* (New Haven, CT: Yale University Press, 2001), xx; Ariens, "Lost and Found;" Tocqueville, *Democracy in America*, 2:616.

14. Hoffman, *Course of Legal Study* (1836), 760–762.

15. Hoffman, 753, 762–764 (Resolutions VIII, XXV–XXVII, XXX, and XXXV).

16. Hoffman, 759 (Resolution XXII).

17. Hoffman, 758–760, 763 (Resolutions XIX, XX, XXIII, and XXIX).

18. Hoffman, 754 (Resolutions X and XI).

19. Hoffman, 754–755 (Resolutions XII–XV).

20. Hoffman, 764–765, 769–777, 772–775 (Resolutions XXXI, XL, XLI, XLVII, and XLVIII).

21. Hoffman, 775 (Resolution XLIX).

22. Hoffman, 765 (Resolution XXXIII).

23. Hoffman, 754–755, 745; Ratrie v. Sanders, 2 H. & J. 327 (Md. 1808); Davis v. Jacquin, 5 H. & J. 100 (Md. 1820); Clagett v. Salmon, 5 G. & J. 314 (Md. 1833); State Use of Mayor and City Council of Baltimore v. Boyd, 2 G. & J. 365, 366 (Md. 1830).

24. F. J. T., "Hoffman's Course of Legal Study," *American Jurist and Law Magazine* 15, 30 (July 1836): 341; Charles Hodge, "Review, A Course of Legal Study," *Biblical Repertory and Princeton Review* 9, 4 (October 1837): 509–524.

25. "Critical Notices: Grumbler's Miscellaneous Thoughts," *North American Review* 45, 97 (October 1837): 482–484; David Hoffman, *A Course of Legal Study*, 2nd ed. (Philadelphia: Thomas, Cowperthwait, 1846), iii; Grumbler, *Miscellaneous Thoughts*, 3.

26. David Hoffman, "Note to the Reader," in *Hints on the Professional Deportment of Lawyers* (Philadelphia: Thomas, Cowperthwait, 1846).

27. *American Jurist and Law Magazine* and *American Law Magazine* ceased publishing; *New York Legal Observer*, *Monthly Law Reporter*, *Pennsylvania Law Journal*, *Legal Intelligencer*, and *Western Law Journal* began.

28. M. H. Hoeflich, *Legal Publishing in Antebellum America* (New York: Cambridge University Press, 2010), 67; Samuel Warren, *A Popular and Practical Introduction to Law Studies*, 1st American ed. (Philadelphia: J. S. Littell, 1836); Samuel Warren, *A Popular and Practical Introduction to Law Studies*, 2nd ed. (Philadelphia: J. S. Littell, 1845); Samuel Warren, *A Popular and Practical Introduction to Law Studies*, 3rd ed. (Philadelphia:

J. S. Littell, 1863); Timothy Walker, *Introduction to American Law*, 1st ed. (Cincinnati: Derby, Bradley, 1837); Timothy Walker, *Introduction to American Law*, 2nd ed. (Cincinnati: Derby, Bradley, 1846); Timothy Walker, *Introduction to American Law*, 3rd ed. (Cincinnati: Derby, Bradley, 1855).

29. Samuel Warren, *The Moral, Social, and Professional Duties of Attornies and Solicitors* (New York: Harper & Brothers, 1849; 1st British ed., Edinburgh: William Blackwood & Sons, 1848).

30. Conway W. Sams and Elihu S. Riley, *The Bench and Bar of Maryland: A History, 1634 to 1901*, 2 vols. (Chicago: Lewis Publishing, 1901); *Great American Lawyers*, ed. William Draper Lewis, 8 vols. (Philadelphia: J. C. Winston, 1907–1909); *Biographical Cyclopedia of Representative Men of Maryland and District of Columbia* (Baltimore: National Biographical Publishing, 1879); Andrew R. Black, *John Pendleton Kennedy: Early American Novelist, Whig Statesman, and Ardent Nationalist* (Baton Rouge: LSU Press, 2016); Semmes, *Latrobe and His Times*; *Dictionary of American Biography*, 9:111, s.v. "Hoffman, David"; *Yale Biographical Dictionary of American Law*, s.v. "Hoffman, David," 267.

31. John M. Scott, *An Address Delivered to the Law Academy of Philadelphia* (Philadelphia: Mifflin & Parry, 1830), 4, 11, 14; James C. Biddle, *Annual Oration Delivered before the Philomathean Society of the University of Pennsylvania* (Philadelphia: John Young, 1832), 10; Peter McCall, *Discourse Delivered before the Law Academy of Philadelphia* (Philadelphia: William F. Geddes, 1838), 36; Emory Washburn, "On the Legal Profession in New England," *American Jurist and Law Magazine* 19, 37 (April–July 1838): 49, 52; Peter Oxenbridge Thacher, *An Address, Pronounced on the First Tuesday of March, 1831* (Boston: Hilliard, Gray, Little & Wilkins, 1831), 18 ("We belong, gentlemen, to a profession, whose duty it is to keep with vestal purity, and in perpetual flame, this divine science"); Frederick Robinson, *A Letter to the Hon. Rufus Choate, Containing a Brief Exposure of Law Craft, and Some of the Encroachments of the Bar upon the Rights and Liberties of the People* (1832); Ariens, *Lost and Found*, 586–587.

32. "The Good Advocate," *Journal of Law* 1, 4 (August 1830), 58–60; Thomas Fuller, *The Holy State* (1642), quoted in Allison N. May, *The Bar & the Old Bailey, 1750–1850* (Chapel Hill: University of North Carolina Press, 2003), 206.

33. Job Tyson, *Discourse on the Integrity of the Legal Character* (Philadelphia: John C. Clark, 1839), 5, 6, 8, 10, 12; A Member of the Alabama Bar, "Bar Associations," *Southern Literary Messenger* 4, 9 (September 1838): 582 (urging a reduction in the number of pettifoggers to advance "the respectability of the profession").

34. "President Quincy's Address on the Occasion of the Dedication of Dane Law College," *American Jurist and Law Magazine* 9, 17 (January–April 1833): 48, 49–50; Thacher, *Address*, 19; Simon Greenleaf, "A Discourse Pronounced at the Inauguration of the Author as Royall Professor of Law in Harvard University (1834)," in *The Gladsome Light of Jurisprudence: Learning the Law in England and the United States in the 18th and 19th Centuries*, ed. and comp. M. H. Hoeflich (New York: Greenwood Press, 1985), 140; Hoffman, *Course of Legal Study* (1836), 775 (Resolutions XLIX and XXXIII).

35. Hoffman, *Course of Legal Study* (1817), 334; Hoffman, *Course of Legal Study* (1836), 742, 770.

36. Amalia D. Kessler, *Inventing American Exceptionalism: The Origins of American Adversarial Legal Culture, 1800–1877* (New Haven, CT: Yale University Press, 2017),

ch. 4; Stow Persons, *The Decline of American Gentility* (New York: Columbia University Press, 1973), ch. 7.

37. Walker, *Introduction to American Law* (1837), 17.

38. T. Walker, "Ways and Means of Professional Success: Being the Substance of a Valedictory Address to the Graduates of the Law Class, in the Cincinnati College," *Western Law Journal* 1, 12 (September 1844), 547; Scott Rogers Nelson, *A Nation of Deadbeats: An Uncommon History of America's Financial Disasters* (New York: Alfred A. Knopf, 2012), 119–120; Jessica Lepler, *The Many Panics of 1837: People, Politics, and the Creation of a Transatlantic Financial Crisis* (New York: Cambridge University Press, 2013), 128.

39. Walker, *Introduction to American Law* (1846), 661.

40. Peleg Chandler, "Legal Morality," *Monthly Law Reporter* 5, 12 (April 1843): 530; Peleg Chandler, "The Practice of the Bar," *Monthly Law Reporter* 9, 6 (October 1846): 242; *Dictionary of American Biography*, 3:615, s.v. "Chandler, Peleg Whitman."

41. *Dictionary of American Biography*, 3:111, s.v. "Brown, David Paul"; "A Memoir of David Paul Brown," *United States Monthly Law Magazine* 5, 4 (1852): 402–440; "Legal Obituary: David Paul Brown," *Albany Law Journal* 6 (July 1872): 49–50; David Paul Brown, *The Forum: Or, Forty Years Full Practice at the Philadelphia Bar*, 2 vols. (Philadelphia: Robert H. Small, 1856), 1:xxvii–cxxiv.

42. John Dos Passos, *The American Lawyer—as He Was—as He Is—as He Can Be* (New York: Banks Law Publishing, 1907), 29; Brown, *Forum*, 1:211.

43. Lawrence Jenab and M. H. Hoeflich, "Forensic Oratory in Antebellum America," *University of Kansas Law Review* 51, 3 (May 2003): 449–471; Kessler, *Inventing American Exceptionalism*, 161–167; David Paul Brown, *The Forensic Speeches of David Paul Brown*, ed. Robert Eden Brown (Philadelphia: King & Baird, 1873); Hoffman, *Course of Legal Study* (1836), 756.

44. David Paul Brown, "Golden Rules for the Examination of Witnesses," *Pennsylvania Law Journal* 2, 11 (1843): 174–176. The rules for cross-examination were inexplicably printed in a smaller font than the rules for direct examination, but they became the more important rules for postbellum American lawyers. "Memoir of Brown," 425; John Livingston was its publisher. See M. H. Hoeflich, "John Livingston & the Business of Law in Nineteenth-Century America," *American Journal of Legal History* 44, 4 (October 2000): 347–368.

45. David Paul Brown, "Golden Rules for the Examination of Witnesses," *Monthly Law Reporter* 10, 10 (1848): 475–477.

46. James Ram, *A Treatise on Facts as Subjects of Inquiry by a Jury*, ed. John Townshend, 2nd American ed. (New York: Barker, Voorhis, 1870), 309–312; Francis Wellman, *The Art of Cross-Examination* (New York: Macmillan, 1903), 133–142; Francis Wellman, *The Art of Cross-Examination*, enlarged ed. (New York: Macmillan, 1906), 397–404; Brown, *Forum*, 2:ch. 1.

47. Hoffman, *Course of Legal Study* (1836), 755–756, 772–773.

48. "Memoir of Brown," 416; "Biographical Memoir," in Brown, *Forum*, 1:lv.

49. Brown, *Forum*, 2:26, 28, 29, 30, 32, 33, 71–72.

50. Brown, 2:30, 31–32. To "plate sin with gold" is from Shakespeare's *King Lear*, meaning to make sins invisible by covering them with gold.

51. "Memoir of Brown," 418, 421–422; Brown, *Forum*, 2:28.

52. William E. Du Bois, *Trial of Lucretia Chapman* (Philadelphia: G. W. Mentz & Son, 1832); Linda Wolfe, *The Murder of Dr. Chapman: The Legendary Trials of Lucretia Chapman and Her Lover* (New York: HarperCollins, 2004); Brown, *Forensic Speeches*, 135.

53. James C. Mohr, *Doctors and the Law: Medical Jurisprudence in Nineteenth-Century America* (New York: Oxford University Press, 1993), 66, 69.

54. Du Bois, *Trial of Chapman*, 7–8, 12.

55. Du Bois, 181, 200–202, 207.

56. Du Bois, 164, 169; Brown, *Forensic Speeches*, 157–158, 171.

57. *Hansard's Parliamentary Debates* (London: T. C. Hansard, 1821), 3:114; *The Trial of Queen Caroline*, ed. Joseph Nightingale, 2 vols. (London: J. Robins, 1821), 2:8; *The Trial of Queen Caroline*, 2 vols. (Manchester, UK: J. Gleave, 1821), 2:2–3; Henry Brougham, *Opinions of Lord Brougham, on Politics, Theology, Law, Science, Education, Literature, &c.*, 2 vols. (Philadelphia: Lea & Blanchard, 1839), 1:143; Henry Brougham, *Speeches of Henry Lord Brougham*, 2 vols. (Philadelphia: Lea & Blanchard, 1841), 1:63; Henry Brougham, *The Life and Times of Henry Lord Brougham, Written by Himself*, 2 vols. (New York: Harper & Brothers, 1871), 2:308–309n*.

58. Michael Ariens, "Brougham's Ghost," *Northern Illinois University Law Review* 35, 2 (2015): 263–315.

59. Brougham, *Opinions*; Brougham, *Speeches*; "The Lawyer, His Character, &c.," *Pennsylvania Law Journal* 2, 12 (1843): 185–192, continued in 2, 13 (1843): 194–199; Edward O'Brien, *The Lawyer, His Character, and the Rule of Holy Life* (Philadelphia: Carey & Hart, 1843).

60. "The Lawyer, His Character, &c.," 186, 187; David J. A. Cairns, *Advocacy and the Making of the Adversarial Criminal Trial, 1800–1865* (New York: Oxford University Press, 1998), 126, 140 (disagreeing with the reviewer).

61. [David Dudley Field], "The Study and Practice of the Law," *United States Magazine & Democratic Review* 14, 70 (April 1844): 348; David Dudley Field, "The Index of Civilization," in *The Golden Age of American Law*, ed. Charles M. Haar (New York: George Braziller, 1965), 30–37; Daun van Ee, *David Dudley Field and the Reconstruction of the Law* (New York: Garland, 1986); "David Dudley Field," *American Law Review* 28 (May–June 1894): 408–411; Helen K. Hoy, "David Dudley Field," in *Great American Lawyers*, 5:125–174; *Dictionary of American Biography*, 6:360, s.v. "Field, David Dudley"; *Yale Biographical Dictionary of American Law*, s.v. "Field, David Dudley."

62. [Field], "Study and Practice," 348; Brown, *Forum*, 2:28; William Augustus Porter, *The Introductory Address Delivered before the Law Academy of Philadelphia at the Opening of the Session of 1849–50* (Philadelphia: Edmond Barrington & Geo. D. Haswell, 1849), 19; Richard B. Kimball, *The Lawyer: The Dignity, Duties, and Responsibilities of His Profession* (New York: George P. Putnam, 1853), 26.

63. "Lawyers No Witnesses in Their Own Cases," *Pennsylvania Law Journal* 6, 52 (July 1847): 408; Mishler & Herzler v. Baumgardner (Pa. Ct. Com. Pleas 1847), 8 Am. L.J. 289, 307 (1849), 1 West. Leg. Observer 33, 35 (1849).

64. David Mellinkoff, *The Conscience of a Lawyer* (St. Paul: West Publishing, 1973), 132–133, 139–140; Yseult Bridges, *Two Studies in Crime* (New York: Macmillan, 1970), 11–128; Judith Flanders, *The Invention of Murder: How the Victorians Revelled in Death*

and Detection and Created Modern Crime (New York: St. Martin's Press, 2013), 200–209 (questioning guilt); Claire Harman, *Murder by the Book: The Crime that Shocked Dickens's London* (New York: Alfred A. Knopf, 2019).

65. Mellinkoff, *Conscience of a Lawyer*, 126, 141–142.

66. Mellinkoff, 203. The controversy returned in 1849 in England. Charles Phillips and Samuel Warren, *Times* (London), November 20, 1849, reprinted in George Sharswood, "An Essay on Professional Ethics," *Annual Report of the American Bar Association* 32 (1907): 183–196; Samuel Warren, "The Mystery of Murder, and Its Defence," in *Miscellanies: Critical, Imaginative, and Juridical*, 2 vols. (Edinburgh: William Blackwood & Sons, 1855), 2:1–2; "Lawyers, Clients, Witnesses, and the Public," *Littell's Living Age*, January 26, 1850, 179; "What We Have Done, and What Mr. Charles Phillips Has Done," *Littell's Living Age*, February 2, 1850, 230; "Lawyers, Clients, &c.," *Littell's Living Age*, February 16, 1850, 306; "Professional Conduct—The Courvoisier Case," *Monthly Law Reporter* 12, 9 (January 1850): 434–439; "Miscellaneous Intelligence," *Monthly Law Reporter* 12, 9 (January 1850): 481; "Miscellaneous Intelligence," *Monthly Law Reporter* 12, 10 (February 1850): 536–537, 555.

67. "Mr. Charles Phillips and the Courvoisier Case," *Monthly Law Reporter* 12, 11 (March 1850): 553–573.

68. Simon Schama, *Dead Certainties (Unwarranted Speculations)* (New York: Vintage, 1991), 71–318; Robert Sullivan, *The Disappearance of Dr. Parkman* (Boston: Little, Brown, 1971); Helen Thomson, *Murder at Harvard* (Boston: Houghton Mifflin, 1971), 172; Paul Collins, *Blood & Ivy: The 1849 Murder that Scandalized Harvard* (New York: W. W. Norton, 2018); Richard B. Morris, *Fair Trial* (New York: Alfred A. Knopf, 1953), 156–203; Karen Halttunen, *Murder Most Foul: The Killer and the American Gothic Imagination* (Cambridge, MA: Harvard University Press, 1998), 126–132. Older accounts are cited in Leonard W. Levy, *The Law of the Commonwealth and Chief Justice Shaw* (New York: Oxford University Press, 1957), 219n52; George Bemis, *Report of the Case of John W. Webster* (Boston: Little, Brown, 1850).

69. Thomson, *Murder at Harvard*, ch. 7, 138; "The Webster Case," *Monthly Law Reporter* 13, 1 (May 1850): 5 ("Three most distinguished members of the Suffolk bar, who were expected to have led the defence, successively withdrew, and a *piquant* remark, attributed to one of them fully justified by its effect, the *mot* of Mirabeau, that 'words are things'").

70. Sullivan, *Disappearance*, 164.

71. Sullivan, 152–161; "Trial of Professor John W. Webster," in *American State Trials* (Wilmington, DE: Scholarly Resources, 1972), 4:93, 145–146. Littlefield collected the reward money on April 6. Thomson, *Murder at Harvard*, 187.

72. "Trial of Professor Webster" (circa 1850), 36–37, is slightly different from the version in *American State Trials*, 4:181, 183–197, 210; A Member of the New York Bar [A. Oakey Hall], *A Review of the Webster Case* (New York: J. S. Redfield, 1850), 16.

73. *American State Trials*, 4:396. For Merrick's oratory, see Jenab and Hoeflich, "Forensic Oratory," 465–469.

74. "Webster Case," 2, 3, 5, 6, 7, 9, 11, 16. Phillips noted that counsel did not act as an "unscrupulous advocate . . . perverting and distorting evidence, by stormy ejaculations and protestations before 'the Omniscient God' of his client's innocence."

75. Commissioners on Practice and Pleadings, *The Code of Civil Procedure of the State of New-York* (Albany, NY: Weed, Parsons, 1850), 204, 205–209; "Duties of Attorneys and Counsellors," *American Law Journal* 10, 10 (April 1851): 451–457.

76. Claude M. Fuess, *Rufus Choate, the Wizard of the Law* (New York: Milton, Balch, 1928), 268, 135.

77. Edward G. Parker, *Reminiscences of Rufus Choate, the Great American Advocate* (New York: Mason Bros., 1860), 134; George W. Minns, "Some Reminiscences of Rufus Choate," *American Law Review* 11, 1 (October 1876): 8.

78. Fuess, *Rufus Choate*, 141; Jean V. Matthews, *Rufus Choate, the Law and Virtue* (Philadelphia: Temple University Press, 1980), 153; Minns, "Some Reminiscences," 15; Parker, *Reminiscences*, 133; John W. Black, "Rufus Choate," in *A History of Criticism of American Public Address*, ed. William Norwood Brigance, 2 vols. (New York: McGraw Hill, 1943), 1:434, 450.

79. Theophilus Parsons, *Address Commemorative of Rufus Choate* (Boston: Little, Brown, 1859), 23; Daniel Walker Howe, *The Political Culture of the American Whigs* (Chicago: University of Chicago Press, 1979), 226; *Yale Biographical Dictionary of American Law*, s.v. "Choate, Rufus."

80. Parker, *Reminiscences*, 145, 147; Joseph Neilson, *Memories of Rufus Choate* (Boston: Houghton Mifflin, 1884), 11, 6, 8–10.

81. Matthews, *Rufus Choate*, 158; Parker, *Reminiscences*, 155 (emphasis in original). This is recorded in the diary of opposing counsel Richard Henry Dana Jr., whose recollection differed. The case was tried in early December 1854. Its subject was ownership of the goods before the *Missouri* was scuttled and ownership of some of the gold Dixey hid. Pitman testified that Dixey induced him to enter the conspiracy. Choate cross-examined Pitman on those inducements, one of which "he did not know whether he ought to mention. *Choate.* You may keep it secret. *Dana.* No, Capt. Pitman, let us know all about it. *Pitman.* Well, Sir, He said that if we were detected, we would get Mr. Choate to defend us, & he would get us off *if the money was found in our boots.*" Richard Henry Dana, *The Journal of Richard Henry Dana, Jr.*, ed. Robert F. Lucid, 3 vols. (Cambridge, MA: Belknap Press, 1968), 2:666 (emphasis in original); Jeffrey L. Amestoy, *Slavish Shore: The Odyssey of Richard Henry Dana, Jr.* (Cambridge, MA: Harvard University Press, 2015), 77; Samuel Shapiro, *Richard Henry Dana, Jr., 1815–1882* (East Lansing: Michigan State University Press, 1961), 50; The Missouri, 1 Spr. 260, 17 F. Cas. 484, 18 L. Rep. 38 (D. Mass. 1854) (omitting anecdote).

82. Wendell Phillips, "Idols," in *Speeches, Lectures, and Letters* (Boston: Lee & Shepard, 1872), 254 (October 4, 1859). Phillips's speech also attacked Daniel Webster. Fuess, *Rufus Choate*, 271 (quoting undated editorial); Parker, *Reminiscences*, 216; Matthews, *Rufus Choate*, 158 (unnamed newspaper).

83. Parker, *Reminiscences*, 216–228; Samuel Gilman Brown, *The Works of Rufus Choate, with a Memoir of His Life*, 2 vols. (Boston: Little, Brown, 1862), 1:110–117; Fuess, *Rufus Choate*, 142–147; Matthews, *Rufus Choate*, 159; Neilson, *Memories*, 7; Daniel A. Cohen, *Pillars of Salt, Monuments of Grace: New England Crime Literature and the Origins of American Popular Culture, 1674–1870* (Amherst: University of Massachusetts Press, 2006), ch. 9; Parker, *Reminiscences*, 218; Marjorie Carleton, "'Maria Met a Gentleman': The Bickford Case," in *Boston Murders*, ed. John N. Makris (New York: Duell,

Sloan & Pearce, 1948), 15–35; Daniel A. Cohen, "The Murder of Maria Bickford: Fashion, Passion, and the Birth of a Consumer Culture," *American Studies* 31, 2 (Fall 1990): 5–30; Barbara Hobson, "A Murder in the Moral and Religious City of Boston," *Boston Bar Journal* 22, 10 (November 1978): 9–21.

84. Parker, *Reminiscences*, 217–218, 226, 216; Brown, *Works of Choate*, 1:116.

85. Parker, *Reminiscences*, 218, 145; Neilson, *Memories*, 18–20; Matthews, *Rufus Choate*, 161.

86. Peleg Chandler, "Mr. Chandler's Remarks on Mr. Choate," *Proceedings of the Massachusetts Historical Society* 4 (August 1859): 369 (noting that Choate's action "may have been the occasion of grave misconstruction, on the part of a portion of the public," and defending a lawyer's duty to exercise zeal to "the machinery of the social fabric"); "Remarks of Richard Henry Dana Jr., Meeting of the Suffolk Bar," in Brown, *Works of Choate*, 1:254.

87. Chandler, "Remarks on Choate," 371; Amestoy, *Slavish Shore*, 76.

88. Parsons, *Address Commemorative*, 21–23; Parker, *Reminiscences*, 135 ("And, though the case grew even blacker and more desperate under the decisions of the judge, he never wavered[.] I have seen the court rule him down, . . . the judge check him in mid career with the declaration that he was 'all wrong,' but the daring advocate was not at all discomfited.").

89. Parsons, *Address Commemorative*, 23–25; Parker, *Reminiscences*, 145 (agreeing).

90. Parsons, *Address Commemorative*, 25–28.

91. Alexander Volokh, "*n* Guilty Men," *University of Pennsylvania Law Review* 146, 1 (November 1997): 173–216; Parker, *Reminiscences*, 209–210.

92. Dred Scott v. Sandford, 19 How. (60 U.S.) 393 (1857); Carl B. Swisher, *The Taney Period, 1836–1864* (New York: Macmillan, 1974), 244; Don E. Fehrenbacher, *The Dred Scott Case: Its Significance in American Law and Politics* (New York: Oxford University Press, 1978), 319, 670n30; J. Willard Hurst, *The Growth of American Law: The Law Makers* (Boston: Little, Brown, 1958), 311 (estimating that Curtis earned $650,000 in fees from 1857 to 1874); "Address of Hon. Benjamin R. Curtis on Presenting to the Supreme Judicial Court the Resolution of the Suffolk Bar," in Brown, *Works of Choate*, 1:257, 259–260.

93. Brown, *Works of Choate*, 1:273–274; Parker, *Reminiscences*, 127.

94. W. [Timothy Walker], "Letters from Ohio: No.1," *New England Magazine* 1 (July 1831): 34; Walter Stix Glazer, *Cincinnati in 1840* (Columbus: Ohio State University Press, 1999), 5–6; Daniel Aaron, *Cincinnati: Queen City of the West, 1819–1838* (Columbus: Ohio State University Press, 1992), 319n9; Walter Theodore Hitchcock, *Timothy Walker, Antebellum Lawyer* (New York: Garland Press, 1990); *Dictionary of American Biography*, 19:363, s.v. "Walker, Timothy"; *Yale Biographical Dictionary of American Law*, s.v. "Walker, Timothy"; Pierson, *Tocqueville in America*, 552, 554–558, 560–565.

95. Tocqueville, *Democracy in America*, 2:506–507; Gillian Brown, "Individualism," in *Companion to American Thought*, 337; Persons, *Decline of American Gentility*, 24.

96. Daniel Walker Howe, *Making the American Self: Jonathan Edwards to Abraham Lincoln* (New York: Oxford University Press, 1997), 1, 107; Lawrence Frederick Kohl, *The Politics of Individualism* (New York: Oxford University Press, 1989), 7; Daniel Walker Howe, "The Decline of Calvinism: An Approach to Its Study," *Comparative Studies in*

Society & History 14, 3 (June 1972): 306-327; Donald Meyer, "The Dissolution of Calvinism," in *Paths of American Thought*, ed. Arthur M. Schlesinger Jr. and Morton White, Sentry ed. (Boston: Houghton Mifflin, 1970), 71-85; Rush Welter, *The Mind of America, 1820-1860* (New York: Columbia University Press, 1975), 334.

97. D. H. Meyer, *The Instructed Conscience: The Shaping of the American National Elite* (Philadelphia: University of Pennsylvania Press, 1972), 40, 66; Burton J. Bledstein, *The Culture of Professionalism: The Middle Class and the Development of Higher Education in America* (New York: W. W. Norton, 1976), 134; "Inaugural Address of Hon. A. Caruthers," *United States Monthly Law Magazine* 3, 5-6 (May-June 1851): 533, 537; Hon. Geo. W. Woodward, *Law and Lawyers*, vol. 15 (Philadelphia: King & Baird, 1859) ("exalt[ing] reason," "the grand characteristic of our profession"); John Anthon, *The Law Student, or Guides to the Study of the Law in Its Principles* (New York: Geo. S. Appleton, 1850), 14.

98. Bledstein, *Culture of Professionalism*, 134; Emory Washburn, *A Lecture before the Members of the Harvard Law School* (Boston: Harvard Law School, 1861), 8, 10-12, 20.

99. *Webster's American Dictionary*, s.v. "integrity"; Walker, "Ways and Means," 546-547; Walker, *Introduction to American Law* (1846), 662-663; Rush v. Cavenaugh, 2 Pa. 187, 189 (1845); Fred C. Zacharias and Bruce A. Green, "Reconceptualizing Advocacy Ethics," *George Washington Law Review* 74, 1 (November 2005): 1-67.

100. Perry Miller, *The Life of the Mind in America from the Revolution to the Civil War* (New York: Harcourt, Brace, & World, 1965), 204; Maxwell Bloomfield, *American Lawyers in a Changing Society, 1776-1876* (Cambridge, MA: Harvard University Press, 1976), 136-190; Philip Gaines, "The 'True Lawyer' in America: Discursive Construction of the Legal Profession in the Nineteenth Century," *American Journal of Legal History* 45, 2 (April 2001): 132-153; Kimball, *Lawyer*, 21-22; Hon. A. O. P. Nicholson, *Address Delivered before the Two Literary Societies of the University of North-Carolina, June 1, 1853* (Raleigh, NC: W. W. Holden, 1853), 9.

101. Terence C. Halliday, "Six Score and Ten: Demographic Transitions in the American Legal Profession, 1850-1980," *Law & Society Review* 20, 1 (1986): 62; "The Legal Profession in the United States," *United States Monthly Law Magazine* 3, 1 (January 1851): 28 (listing 22,500 "practicing lawyers"); Edward J. Balleisen, *Navigating Failure: Bankruptcy and Commercial Society in Antebellum America* (Chapel Hill: University of North Carolina Press, 2001), 135-146, 61-62; Gary B. Nash, "The Philadelphia Bench and Bar, 1800-1861," *Comparative Studies in Society & History* 7, 2 (January 1965): 218; Brown, *Forum*, 1:558-559, 568-569.

102. "Christianity in the Legal Profession," *Southern Literary Messenger* 27, 1 (July 1858): 72; Parsons, *Address Commemorative*, 31.

103. Shapiro, *Dana*, 46-48, ch. 4; Amestoy, *Slavish Shore*, 78-79, 121-122. Slave catchers initially sought and failed to render the Crafts, a husband and wife who were well-known fugitive slaves, from Boston. Steven Lubet, *Fugitive Justice: Runaways, Rescuers, and Slavery on Trial* (Cambridge, MA: Harvard University Press, 2010), 47-49, 137-141; Charles Francis Adams, *Richard Henry Dana: A Biography*, 2 vols. (Boston: Houghton Mifflin, 1890); Robert A. Ferguson, *Law and Letters in American Culture* (Cambridge, MA: Harvard University Press, 1984), ch. 9; *Yale Biographical Dictionary of American Law*, s.v. "Dana, Richard Henry, Jr."; Dana, *Journal*, 2:410-412; *Dictionary of American*

Biography, 17:42, s.v. "Shaw, Lemuel"; *Yale Biographical Dictionary of American Law*, s.v. "Shaw, Lemuel."

104. Amestoy, *Slavish Shore*, ch. 10; Lubet, *Fugitive Justice*, 141; Gary Collison, "'This Flagitious Offense': Daniel Webster and the Shadrach Rescue Cases, 1851–1852," *New England Quarterly* 68, 4 (December 1995): 610–611; John D. Gordan III, *The Fugitive Slave Rescue Trial of Robert Morris* (2013; Kindle ed.); Gary Collison, *Shadrach Minkins: From Fugitive Slave to Citizen* (Cambridge, MA: Harvard University Press, 1997).

105. Amestoy, *Slavish Shore*, 126–128; Robert V. Remini, *Daniel Webster: The Man and His Time* (New York: W. W. Norton, 1997), 696–697; Maurice G. Baxter, *One and Inseparable: Daniel Webster and the Union* (Cambridge, MA: Belknap Press,1984), 477–481; Shapiro, *Dana*, 48–49; Amestoy, *Slavish Shore*, ch. 12, 1, 149; Adams, *Dana: A Biography*, 1:128–129, 212–213.

106. Dana, *Journal*, 2:625–627; Albert J. von Frank, *The Trials of Anthony Burns* (Cambridge, MA: Harvard University Press, 1998).

107. Dana, *Journal*, 2:636; Amestoy, *Slavish Shore*, 195–196; Shapiro, *Dana*, 92; Adams, *Dana: A Biography*, 1:282–283; Samuel Shapiro, "The Rendition of Anthony Burns," *Journal of Negro History* 44, 1 (January 1959): 34–51; Shapiro, *Dana*, ch. 7; Paul Finkelman, "Legal Ethics and Fugitive Slaves: The Anthony Burns Case," *Cardozo Law Review* 17, 6 (May 1996): 1793–1858.

108. Finkelman, "Legal Ethics," 1806.

109. Dana, *Journal*, 2:552n55; *Dictionary of American Biography*, 9:49, s.v. "Hillard, George Stillman."

110. Michael S. Ariens, "American Lawyers in an Age of Anxiety," *St. Mary's Law Journal* 40, 2 (2008): 390–391; Margaret Center Klingelsmith, "History of the Department of Law," in *University of Pennsylvania, the Proceedings at the Dedication of the New Building of the Department of Law, February 21st and February 22nd* (Philadelphia: Press of International Print Co., 1901), 221; George Sharswood, *Lectures Introductory to the Study of Law* (Philadelphia: T. & J. W. Johnson, 1870), 10; Samuel Dickson, "George Sharswood— Teacher and Friend," *American Law Register Original Series* 55, 7 (October 1907): 401–427; Samuel Dickson, "George Sharswood," in *Great American Lawyers*, 6:121; Brown, *Forum*, 2:154–159; Edwin R. Keedy, "George Sharswood—Professor of Law," *University of Pennsylvania Law Review* 98, 5 (April 1950): 685–694; *Dictionary of American Biography*, 17:28, s.v. "Sharswood, George"; *Yale Biographical Dictionary of American Law*, s.v. "Sharswood, George."

111. George Sharswood, *A Compend of Lectures on the Aims and Duties of the Profession of the Law* (Philadelphia: T. & J. W. Johnson, 1854), 25–26; Sharswood, *Lectures Introductory*, 17; Michael Feldberg, *The Philadelphia Riots of 1844* (Westport, CT: Greenwood Press, 1975); Allen Steinberg, *The Transformation of Criminal Justice* (Chapel Hill: University of North Carolina Press, 1989), 147–148, 163–164; Charles R. Barker, "Philadelphia in the Late Forties," *Philadelphia History* 2 (1931): 262.

112. Sharswood, *Compend of Lectures*, 23–26, 28–30, 31–34, 40–44, 80, 98; Porter, *Introductory Address*, 19.

113. Sharswood, *Compend of Lectures*, 50.

114. Sharswood, 27, 30, 54, 55, 95, 98; George Sharswood, *An Essay on Professional Ethics*, 2nd ed. (Philadelphia: T. & J. W. Johnson, 1860), 111, 115.

115. Kohl, *Politics of Individualism*, 15; John C. Lord, *"The Higher Law," in Its Applica-tion to the Fugitive Slave Bill* (New York: Union Safety Comm., 1851); Samuel T. Spear, *The Law-Abiding Conscience, and the Higher Law Conscience* (New York: Lambert & Lane, 1850); Ichabod S. Spencer, *Fugitive Slave Law: The Religious Duty of Obedience to Law* (New York: M. W. Dodd, 1850); Hitchcock, *Timothy Walker*, 138.

116. Sharswood, *Compend of Lectures*, 54, 55, 95, 98, 91; Sharswood, *Essay* (1860), 106, 111, 115; Nash, "Philadelphia Bench and Bar," 214–220.

117. George Sharswood, *An Essay on Professional Ethics*, 3rd ed. (Philadelphia: T. & J. W. Johnson, 1869); George Sharswood, *An Essay on Professional Ethics*, 4th ed. (Phila-delphia: T. & J. W. Johnson, 1876); George Sharswood, *An Essay on Professional Ethics*, 5th ed. (Philadelphia: T. & J. W. Johnson, 1896).

3. CLIENTS, ZEAL, AND CONSCIENCE, 1868–1905

1. George F. Shelton, "Law as a Business," *Yale Law Journal* 10, 7 (May 1901): 276; George Sharswood, *An Essay on Professional Ethics*, 3rd ed. (Philadelphia: T. & J. W. John-son, 1869), 84, 145; D. Bethune Duffield, *The Lawyers' Oath* (Ann Arbor, MI: Dr. Chase's Steam Printing House, 1867), 18–24; William Allen Butler, *Lawyer and Client: Their Re-lation, Rights & Duties* (New York: D. Appleton, 1871), 74 ("the legal laborer is worthy of his hire, [but] it should not be forgotten for a moment that the true motive and spur of effort on the part of the lawyer is something far beyond the pecuniary result of his ef-forts"); Samuel H. Wandell, *"You Should Not": A Book for Lawyers, Old and Young, Con-taining the Elements of Legal Ethics* (Albany, NY: Matthew Bender, 1896), 3 ("*You should not* practice law with the idea that your profession is only designed as a means of money getting. . . . Yours is a calling of dignity and honor."); In re Badger, 35 P. 839 (Idaho 1894); M. H. Hoeflich, "Ethics and the 'Root of All Evil' in Nineteenth Century American Law Practice," *St. Mary's Journal on Legal Malpractice and Legal Ethics* 7, 2 (2017): 160–183.

2. Robert J. Gordon, *The Rise and Fall of American Growth: The U.S. Standard of Living since the Civil War* (Princeton, NJ: Princeton University Press, 2016), pt. I; John Higham, *Strangers in the Land: Patterns of American Nativism, 1860–1925*, 2nd ed. (New Brunswick, NJ: Rutgers University Press, 1988); Mark Twain, *The Gilded Age* (1873; Kin-dle ed.); Alan Trachtenberg, *The Incorporation of America: Culture and Society in the Gilded Age* (New York: Hill & Wang, 1982); Terence C. Halliday, "Six Score and Ten: Demographic Transitions in the American Legal Profession, 1850–1980," *Law & Society Review* 20, 1 (1986): 62; *Law Notes* 4, 6 (September 1900): 103; Horace W. Fuller, "Over-crowding the Profession," *Green Bag* 3, 4 (April 1891): 198–199.

3. To avoid confusion with the individuals, I refer to the law firm as "Field & Shear-man," even though it used "and" in its official name, rather than "&." George Martin, *Causes and Conflicts: The Centennial History of the Association of the Bar of the City of New York, 1870–1970* (Boston: Houghton Mifflin, 1970), 55–60, 88–103; Alvan S. Southworth, "A Generation of the New York Bar," *American Lawyer* 2, 5 (1894): 199–200.

4. Paul Collins, *The Murder of the Century: The Gilded Age Crime that Scandalized a City & Sparked the Tabloid Wars* (New York: Crown, 2011), 107–109; Cait Murphy, *Scoundrels in Law: The Trials of Howe and Hummel* (New York: Smithsonian Books,

2010); Richard Wightman Fox, *Trials of Intimacy: Love and Loss in the Beecher-Tilton Scandal* (Chicago: University of Chicago Press, 1999), 1; *The Annals of Murder*, comp. Thomas M. McDade (Norman: University of Oklahoma Press, 1961).

5. E. Parmalee Prentice, "The Speculation in Damage Claims for Personal Injury," *North American Review* 164, 483 (February 1897): 199–208; Edwin A. Parker, "Anti-Railroad Personal Injury Litigation in Texas," *Proceedings of the Texas Bar Association* 19 (1900): 165–192; Robert A. Silverman, *Law and Urban Growth: Civil Litigation in the Boston Trial Courts, 1880–1900* (Princeton, NJ: Princeton University Press, 1981), 99–121; Randolph E. Bergstrom, *Courting Danger: Injury and Law in New York City, 1870–1910* (Ithaca, NY: Cornell University Press, 1992), 20; William G. Thomas, *Lawyering for the Railroad: Business, Law, and Power in the New South* (Baton Rouge: LSU Press, 1999); "Winnow the Bar," *American Lawyer* 1, 4 (April 1893): 5; John Fabian Witt, *The Accidental Republic: Crippled Working Men, Destitute Widows, and the Remaking of American Law* (Cambridge, MA: Harvard University Press, 2004), 60.

6. Theron G. Strong, *Landmarks of a Lawyer's Lifetime* (New York: Dodd, Mead, 1914), 354; James Bryce, *The American Commonwealth*, 2 vols. (Birmingham, AL: Legal Classics Library, 1987), 2:492; John Dos Passos, *The American Lawyer—as He Was—as He Is—as He Can Be* (New York: Banks Law Publishing, 1907).

7. Carol Rose Andrews, Paul M. Pruitt Jr., and David I. Durham, eds., *Gilded Age Legal Ethics: Essays on Thomas Goode Jones' 1887 Code* (Tuscaloosa: Bounds Law Library, University of Alabama Law School, 2003) (hereafter, cited as *GALE*); Edson Sunderland, *History of the American Bar Association and Its Work* (1953); John Austin Matzko, *Best Men of the Bar: The Early Years of the American Bar Association, 1878–1928* (Clark, NJ: Lawbook Exchange, 2019), ch. 7.

8. George Templeton Strong, *Diary of George Templeton Strong*, ed. Allen Nevins and Milton Halsey, 4 vols. (New York: Macmillan, 1952), 4:404–405; Daun van Ee, *David Dudley Field and the Reconstruction of the Law* (New York: Garland, 1986), 293–294.

9. John Steele Gordon, *The Scarlet Woman of Wall Street: Jay Gould, Jim Fisk, Cornelius Vanderbilt, the Erie Railway Wars, and the Birth of Wall Street* (New York: Weidenfeld & Nicolson, 1988); Charles F. Adams Jr., "The Erie Railroad Row," *American Law Review* 3, 1 (October 1868): 41–86; Charles F. Adams Jr., "A Chapter of Erie," *North American Review* 109, 224 (July 1869): 30–106; Charles F. Adams Jr., "An Erie Raid," *North American Review* 112, 231 (April 1871): 241–291; Albert Stickney, "Art. V—The Lawyer and His Clients," *North American Review* 112, 231 (April 1871): 392–421; Charles F. Adams Jr. and Henry Adams, *Chapters of Erie and Other Essays* (Boston: James R. Osgood, 1871); Frederick C. Hicks, ed., *High Finance in the Sixties* (New Haven, CT: Yale University Press, 1929); Martin, *Causes and Conflicts*, 66–67, 92–98.

10. Strong, *Diary*, 4:202.

11. Commissioners on Practice and Pleadings, *The Code of Civil Procedure of the State of New-York* (Albany, NY: Weed, Parsons, 1850), 205; [David Dudley Field], "The Study and Practice of the Law," *United States Magazine & Democratic Review* 14, 70 (April 1844): 345–351.

12. Van Ee, *David Dudley Field*, 218–220; Chester L. Barrows, *William M. Evarts: Lawyer, Diplomat, Statesman* (Chapel Hill: University of North Carolina Press, 1941), 191 (noting a "corrupt alliance between the judiciary and the grafters").

13. Adams, "Erie Railroad Row"; Adams, "Chapter of Erie"; Gordon, *Scarlet Woman*, 165; [Thomas G. Shearman], "The Judiciary of New York City," *North American Review* 105, 216 (July 1867): 148–176 (Barnard, unnamed but identifiable, as corrupt).

14. Adams, "Erie Railroad Row," 49–52; van Ee, *David Dudley Field*, 223–224 (arguing it was Field's son Dudley who went to Brooklyn).

15. Adams, "Erie Railroad Row," 57, 59, 60.

16. Adams, 63–64 (alleging it was $50,000); Martin, *Causes and Conflicts*, 9. Matthew P. Breen, *Thirty Years of New York Politics, Up-to-Date* (New York, 1899), 319–323, references a similar confrontation during which Brady all but accused Haskin and Barnard of corruption, but he writes that it concerned Barnard's appointment of Haskin as receiver of the Washington Life Insurance Company, not Erie-related matters. Brady was cross-examining Haskin about his conduct as receiver, Haskin "answered evasively and impudently," and Barnard "flippantly sustained Mr. Haskin in every instance." At long last, Brady "boldly asked questions directly inculpating Judge Barnard and his favorite Receiver." Breen apparently links this to 1868. It is doubtful Brady twice accused Barnard and Haskin of corrupt behavior. Though much cited, no one has clarified whether these were separate events. *In Memoriam: James T. Brady* (New York, 1869); L. B. Proctor, *The Bench and Bar of New York* (New York: Diossy, 1870), 238–276; "Brady, James Topham," in *History of the Bench and Bar of New York*, ed. David McAdam et al., 2 vols. (New York: New York History Co., 1897), 1:266–267; "James Topham Brady," *American Law Review* 3, 4 (July 1869): 779–781; *Dictionary of American Biography*, 2:583, s.v. "Brady, James T."

17. Adams, "Erie Railroad Row," 65–69; Strong, *Diary*, 4:202.

18. Adams, "Erie Railroad Row," 71–73; *Dictionary of American Biography*, 4:132, s.v. "Clark, Horace Francis."

19. "The Erie Contempt Case," *New York Herald*, May 1, 1868, 5; Adams, "Chapter of Erie," 57–58.

20. Adams, "Erie Railroad Row," 84; "Legal News," *Albany Law Journal* 3 (January 28, 1871): 80; "The Erie Counsel Fees," *Albany Law Journal* 3 (February 25, 1871): 158; Adams, "Chapter of Erie," 59.

21. Adams, "Chapter of Erie," 74, 78; van Ee, *David Dudley Field*, 228; Gordon, *Scarlet Woman*, 190–194, 307–308.

22. Adams, "Chapter of Erie," 85; W. A. Swanberg, *Jim Fisk: The Career of an Impossible Rascal* (New York: Charles Scribner's Sons, 1959), 90; Gordon, *Scarlet Woman*, 196, 203, 226–227; Walter K. Earle, *Mr. Shearman and Mr. Sterling and How They Grew* (New Haven, CT: Yale University Press, 1963), 77.

23. Van Ee, *David Dudley Field*, 232; Adams, "Chapter of Erie," 101; George S. Merriam, *The Life and Times of Samuel Bowles*, 2 vols. (New York: Century, 1885), 2:94–95; Swanberg, *Jim Fisk*, 81–84; David Dudley Field, Dudley Field, and Samuel Bowles, *The Lawyer and His Client* (Springfield, MA: Republican Office, 1871), 13 (letter of January 13, 1871, from Bowles to Dudley Field chastising him for denying or failing to remember that his firm and his father represented Fisk in the defamation suit).

24. Stickney, "Art. V—Lawyer and His Clients"; Francis C. Barlow, *Facts for Mr. Field* (Albany, NY: Weed, Parsons, 1871), 13–24.

25. Shearman represented Gould in more than three hundred lawsuits related to the failed effort to corner the gold market; still, Gould profited greatly. Kenneth D. Acker-

man, *The Gold Ring: Jim Fisk, Jay Gould, and Black Friday, 1869* (New York: Harper & Row, 1988), 277–279; Earle, *Mr. Shearman and Mr. Sterling*, 77–78; "The New York Gold Conspiracy," in Adams and Adams, *Chapters of Erie*, 100–134; Hicks, *High Finance*, 120–155; Gordon, *Scarlet Woman*, 299–301, 343–346.

26. "James Fisk's Lawyers," *New York Times*, December 16, 1870, 4; "James Fisk's Lawyers," *New York Times*, December 26, 1870, 2; Barlow, *Facts for Mr. Field*, 45 (Field's March 13 reply in the *Tribune*).

27. Timothy Walker, *Introduction to American Law*, 2nd ed. (Cincinnati: Derby, Bradley, 1846), 662.

28. Field, Field, and Bowles, *Lawyer and His Client*, 7–9; "The Bar and the Press," *New York Times*, January 30, 1871, 1; Andrew L. Kaufman, *Problems in Professional Responsibility*, 2nd ed. (Boston: Little, Brown, 1984), 434; "The Duties and Rights of Counsel," *Albany Law Journal* 3 (February 4, 1871): 81–85; Michael Schudson, "Public, Private, and Professional Lives: The Correspondence of David Dudley Field and Samuel Bowles," *American Journal of Legal History* 21, 3 (1977): 191–211; Thomas L. Shaffer, *American Legal Ethics: Text, Readings, and Discussion Topics* (New York: Matthew Bender, 1985), 315–329 (discussing debate); [Field], "Study and Practice," 347–348.

29. Merriam, *Life and Times of Bowles*, 2:98–100; "More about Legal Morality," *Nation*, February 2, 1871, 71 ("And it must, it would seem, be admitted that Mr. Bowles does not make a very strong case"); Stickney, "Art. V—Lawyer and His Clients," 396.

30. "Forensic Ethics," *Nation*, January 26, 1871, 56; "Bench and Bar of New York," *Nation*, February 9, 1871, 91; "Our 'Upright Judiciary,'" *Nation*, March 2, 1871, 140; Barlow, *Facts for Mr. Field* (reprinting letters); "Local Miscellany," *New York Tribune*, February 4, 1871, 8; *Dictionary of American Biography*, 7:347, s.v. "Godkin, Edwin Lawrence." Godkin apprenticed in Field's office in 1857–1858.

31. Barlow, *Facts for Mr. Field*, 5, 24, 25, 29; *Dictionary of American Biography*, 1:608, s.v. "Barlow, Francis Channing"; Albert Stickney, "Memorial of Francis C. Barlow," in *The "Memorial Book" and Mortuary Roll of the Association of the Bar of the City of New York* (1896), 96–107; *In Memoriam: Francis Channing Barlow* (Albany, NY: J. B. Lyon, 1923); McAdam, *History of Bench and Bar*, 2:35.

32. Stickney, "Art. V—Lawyer and His Clients," 394–395, 397, 418; Edmund Wetmore, "Memorial of Albert Stickney," in *Association of the Bar of the City of New York Yearbook* (1909), 139.

33. "Erie Raid," in Adams and Adams, *Chapters of Erie*, 135; Hicks, *High Finance*, 156.

34. "Bar Association," *American Law Review* 5, 3 (April 1871): 556–558; "The Bar Association of the City of New York," *American Law Review* 5, 3 (April 1871): 448–449, 455; *Dictionary of American Biography*, 16:546, s.v. "Sedgwick, Arthur George"; G. Edward White, *Justice Oliver Wendell Holmes: Law and the Inner Self* (New York: Oxford University Press, 1993).

35. Field, Field, and Bowles, *Lawyer and His Client*, 3; Barlow, *Facts for Mr. Field*, 35 (reprinting Field's March 13 letter published in the *New York Tribune*); George Sharswood, "Legal Ethics," *Albany Law Journal* 3 (February 25, 1871): 158; Thomas G. Shearman, "Some Facts for the Nation," *Albany Law Journal* 3 (March 18, 1871): 217–218; "'The Nation' and the Corrupt Judges," *Albany Law Journal* 3 (March 18, 1871): 206–207; Adams and Adams, *Chapters of Erie*, 110; Hicks, *High Finance*, 129; David Dudley Field,

"To the Editor of the Westminster Review," *Westminster Review* 95 (April 1871): 590 ("I have no relations with any of the judges of this State, and no power over them"), responding to [Henry Adams], "The New York Gold Conspiracy," *Westminster Review* 94 (1870): 411, in Adams and Adams, *Chapters of Erie*, 100–134.

36. George Ticknor Curtis, "An Inquiry into the Albany and Susquehanna Railroad Litigations of 1869, and Mr. David Dudley Field's Connection Therewith," in Hicks, *High Finance*, 345. When Barnard was investigated in early 1872, Field testified that the arrest of Smith and others "was the mode, and only mode" to obtain the railroad's missing books. Thus, the arrest was intentional, not an accident. *Charges against George G. Barnard, and Testimony Thereunder, before the Judiciary Committee of the Assembly* (New York: Weed, Parsons, 1872), 39; *Dictionary of American Biography*, 4:613, s.v. "Curtis, George Ticknor."

37. "Mr. Curtis' Defence of Mr. Field," *American Law Review* 5, 4 (July 1871): 759–760; "Mr. George Ticknor Curtis on the Field Controversy," *Albany Law Journal* 3 (May 27, 1871): 335–337.

38. Albert J. Stickney, "The Erie Railway and the English Stock," *American Law Review* 6, 2 (January 1871): 230–254.

39. Martin, *Causes and Conflicts*, 74–75. *Charges against George Barnard* provides a full exposition.

40. *Impeachment Proceeding against George G. Barnard*, 3 vols. (Albany, NY: Weed & Parsons, 1872), 3:2041 (recording votes and lengthy discussions); Martin, *Causes and Conflicts*, 75–84.

41. *Impeachment Proceeding*, 3:1420–1473.

42. Jeremiah S. Black, "A Great Lawsuit and a Field Fight," *Galaxy* 14 (March 1872): 376, 390–391; Hicks, *High Finance*, 383; *Dictionary of American Biography*, 2:310, s.v. "Black, Jeremiah Sullivan"; Margaret Center Klingelsmith, "Jeremiah Sullivan Black," in *Great American Lawyers*, ed. William Draper Lewis (South Hackensack, NJ: Rothman Reprints, 1971), 6:1–73.

43. Albert Stickney, "The Truth of a 'Great Fight,'" *Galaxy* 14 (October 1872): 578; Hicks, *High Finance*, 393. Stickney made a more vicious analogy: "To which may be added the 'opinions' of Mr. Field and Judge Barnard, delivered of each other, to the same effect. And it will be remembered that Mr. Fagin had a very deep admiration for Mr. Jack Dawkins." Stickney, "Truth," 576; Hicks, *High Finance*, 388–389. Stickney refers, of course, to the criminal characters Fagin and the Artful Dodger in Charles Dickens's *Oliver Twist*.

44. Martin, *Causes and Conflicts*, 91–98; van Ee, *David Dudley Field*, 271–280.

45. "A Field Day," *New York Herald*, December 11, 1872, 10; "Purifying the Bar," *Albany Law Journal* 7 (February 8, 1873): 83–85 (substantially republished in Martin, *Causes and Conflicts*, 92–100); "Field (D. D.), Letters to, March 18, 1871–December 31, 1872," *Tributes to Lawyers* 25, 9 (n.d.); a thirteenth letter, from Reverdy Johnson to Field, is included but was written after the December 1872 meeting.

46. "Letter of Montgomery Blair to Field," November 26, 1872, *Tributes to Lawyers* 14; William Fullerton, *Tributes to Lawyers* 6; Thomas W. Clerke, *Tributes to Lawyers* 16.

47. Martin, *Causes and Conflicts*, 404n5; "Purifying the Bar," 84–85. A second effort to expel Field failed the following month. Martin, 100–101.

48. "Purifying the Bar," 85.

49. [Field], "Study and Practice," 346.

50. Van Ee, *David Dudley Field*, 292n43 (van Ee does not clarify that two sections were eliminated); [Field], "Study and Practice," 346, 347; *Speeches, Arguments, and Miscellaneous Papers of David Dudley Field*, ed. A. P. Sprague, 2 vols. (New York: D. Appleton, 1884), 1:484–494, 487.

51. "Purifying the Bar," 85.

52. "South Carolina Bar Association," *Southern Law Times* 2, 19 (August 1886): 449; George McCrary, "The True Lawyer," *Columbia Jurist* 2, 38 (1886): 462; William N. Ashman, *The Profession of the Law: Address Delivered before the Law Academy of Philadelphia* (Philadelphia, 1889).

53. "Columbia College Law School," *Albany Law Journal* 1 (May 28, 1870): 419–420; *Dictionary of American Biography*, 5:571, s.v. "Dwight, Theodore"; Julius Goebel, *A History of the School of Law, Columbia University* (New York: Columbia University Press, 1955), 32–120; Butler, *Lawyer and Client*, 41–42; George C. Holt, *Memorial of William Allen Butler* (New York, 1903), "William Allen Butler," *Annual Report of the American Bar Association* 25 (1902): 781–785; McAdam, *History of Bench and Bar*, 2:71.

54. Dorman B. Eaton, *The Public Relations and Duties of the Legal Profession* (New Haven, CT: Hodgson & Robinson, 1882), 322–323; Martin, *Causes and Conflicts*, 40–42; *Dictionary of American Biography*, 5:607, s.v. "Eaton, Dorman Bridgman"; Henry D. Sedgwick, *The Relation and Duty of the Lawyer to the State, Lecture before the Law School of the University of the City of New York, February 9th, 1872* (New York: Baker & Godwin, 1872); Edward M. Paxson, *The Road to Success, or Practical Hints to the Junior Bar* (Philadelphia: Law Academy, 1888), 9; Richard Harris, *Hints on Advocacy in Civil and Criminal Courts*, rev. William L. Murfree Sr., 2nd American ed. from 6th English ed. (St. Louis: William H. Stevenson, 1884), 163; Henry Wade Rogers, *Address to the Law Class of Michigan University, June 17, 1886* (Ann Arbor, 1886), 24; John Wesley Donovan, *Modern Jury Trials and Advocates* (Albany, NY: Banks & Bros., 1881), 181; George F. Hoar, *The Function of the American Lawyer in the Founding of States* (New Haven, CT: Tuttle Morehouse & Taylor, 1881), 21 (rejecting Brougham); Asa Iglehart, "Is the Bar Unpopular?" *American Law Register* 26, 11 (1878): 684 (criticizing lawyers who "always tell the young men that there is a manifest decline in the American bar, and it is their destiny to lift it up") (also published in *Southern Law Journal* 2, 3 [March 1879]: 129); *Dictionary of American Biography*, 16:97, s.v. "Rogers, Henry Wade"; "Henry Wade Rogers," *Yale Law Journal* 36, 1 (November 1926): 112–114; *Dictionary of American Biography*, 9:87, s.v. "Hoar, George Frisbie"; Edward P. Weeks, *Treatise on Attorneys and Counsellors at Law* (San Francisco: Sumner Whitney, 1878) (ignoring the issue); George Warvelle, *Essays in Legal Ethics* (Chicago: Callaghan, 1902), 160, 211–216 (following Sharswood); A. Oakey Hall, "Ogden Hoffman," *Green Bag* 5, 7 (July 1893): 297–300; A. Oakey Hall, "Cross-Examination as an Art," *Green Bag* 5, 9 (September 1893): 423–426; A. Oakey Hall, "John Van Buren," *Green Bag* 7, 5 (May 1895): 209–217; A. Oakey Hall, "Thomas Addis Emmet," *Green Bag* 8, 7 (July 1896): 273–279; A. Oakey Hall, "Daniel Dougherty and the Philadelphia Bar," *Green Bag* 9, 4 (April 1897): 143 (noting the Philadelphia bar rejected Brougham's ethic and "has always equaled, if it did not surpass, all other bars, in freedom from pettifoggers and from chicanery"); Croswell Bowen, *The Elegant Oakey*

(New York: Oxford University Press, 1956); *Dictionary of American Biography*, 8:114, s.v. "Hall, Abraham Oakey."

55. Candace Millard, *Destiny of the Republic: A Tale of Madness, Medicine and the Murder of a President* (New York: Anchor Books, 2011), 275; Kenneth D. Ackerman, *The Dark Horse: The Surprise Election and Political Murder of President James A. Garfield* (New York: Carroll & Graf, 2003); *Report of the United States vs. Charles J. Guiteau* (Washington, DC: Government Printing Office, 1882).

56. Peter Kaufman, *Skull in the Ashes: Murder, a Gold Rush Hunt, and the Birth of Circumstantial Evidence in America* (Iowa City: University of Iowa Press, 2013), 145, 147, 150; Harold Schechter, *The Devil's Gentleman: Privilege, Poison, and the Trial that Ushered in the Twentieth Century* (New York: Ballantine Books, 2007); Robert Loerzel, *Alchemy of Bones: Chicago's Luetgert Murder Case of 1897* (Urbana: University of Illinois Press, 2004); Elizabeth Dale, *The Chicago Trunk Murder: Law and Justice at the Turn of the Century* (De Kalb: Northern Illinois University Press, 2011); Timothy Messer-Kruse, *The Trial of the Haymarket Anarchists: Terrorism and Justice in the Gilded Age* (New York: Palgrave Macmillan, 2011); Newman Levy, *The Nan Patterson Case* (New York: Simon & Schuster, 1959); D. H. Chamberlain, *Some of the Present Needs and Duties of Our Profession* (New York: G. P. Putnam's Sons, 1888), 11 (criticizing "undiscriminating readiness and unrestrained zeal with which many members of our profession accept any service and serve any cause which offers pecuniary compensation").

57. Commonwealth v. Hill, 39 A. 1055 (Pa. 1898). See also Commonwealth v. Jongrass, 37 A. 207 (Pa. 1897) ("There is no code of professional ethics which is peculiar to the criminal courts. There are no methods of practice to be tolerated there that are not equally entitled to recognition in the civil courts.").

58. "The Profession's Duty," *American Lawyer* 1, 5 (May 1893): 4–5; "Professional Duty," *American Lawyer* 1, 7 (July 1893): 4–5; Cara Robertson, *The Trial of Lizzie Borden: A True Story* (New York: Simon & Schuster, 2019).

59. Theron G. Strong, *Joseph H. Choate* (New York: Dodd, Mead, 1917), 201–220; Paul Sarnoff, *Russell Sage, the Money King* (New York: Ivan Obolensky, 1965), 290–302; "Laidlaw v. Sage," *Harvard Law Review* 7, 5 (1893): 302–304; "Laidlaw v. Russell Sage," *Harvard Law Review* 8, 4 (1895): 225–226; Jacob A. Stein, "Laidlaw, Sage, Prosser and Joseph Choate," *Green Bag 2d* 8, 2 (Winter 2005): 173–176; Laidlaw v. Sage, 30 N.Y.S. 496 (N.Y. S. Ct. 1894), *rev'd*, 52 N.E. 679 (N.Y. 1899); "Wants Russell Sage to Pay," *New York Times*, July 6, 1899, 1; Charles F. Amidon, "The Quest for Error and the Doing of Justice," *American Law Review* 40, 5 (September–October 1906): 681–693.

60. Richard H. Underwood, *Gaslight Lawyers: Criminal Trials & Exploits in Gilded Age New York* (Lexington, KY: Shadelandhouse Modern Press, 2017), 145. Abraham Levy was the highly respected primary lawyer for Nan Patterson. Levy, *Nan Patterson Case*, 67–69; Richard O'Connor, *Courtroom Warrior: The Combative Career of William Travers Jerome* (Boston: Little, Brown, 1963), 143, 156; Murphy, *Scoundrels in Law*, 247; Arthur Train, *The Confessions of Artemas Quibble* (New York: Charles Scribner's Sons, 1923) (fictional retelling); Arthur Train, *True Stories of Crime* (1908; reprint, Coppell, TX, 2020), ch. 10 (nonfiction retelling); Molly A. Guptill, "The More Things Change the More They Stay the Same: Mr. Tutt and the Distrust of Lawyers in the Early Twentieth Century," *Cardozo Public Law, Policy & Ethics Journal* 3, 1 (December 2004): 305–352;

"Decadence of New York's Criminal Bar," *New York Times*, September 7, 1902, 34; "The Repentance of Jerome," *New York Times*, May 14, 1905, 8.

61. *Report of the Organization and of the First, Second, and Third Annual Meeting of the Alabama State Bar Association* (Montgomery, AL: Smith & Armstrong, 1882), 235–236, 250, 263; "Proceedings," *Annual Report of the American Bar Association* 1 (1878): 16, 26; Iglehart, "Is the Bar Unpopular?" 681–688; Bradwell v. Illinois, 16 Wall. (83 U.S.) 165 (1873); Herman Kogan, *The First Century: The Chicago Bar Association, 1875–1974* (Rand McNally, 1974), 15; "Jurist—Advocate—Toiler—Shyster," *Southern Law Times* 1, 3 (October 1885): 31 ("he steals the seamless mantle of justice to cover his gross enormities"); "Address of Prof. Theo. W. Dwight," *Columbia Jurist* 1, 19–20 (June 1885): 144; "Some Energetic Remarks on 'Shyster' Judges," *Southern Law Times* 1, 18 (January 1886): 393–395 (reprinting remarks from a judge in a newspaper); "A Shyster Convicted," *New York Times*, April 2, 1871, 6; "What a Shyster Is," *New York Times*, April 2, 1874, 9; "Shyster: An Explanation of the Origin of the Word Attributed to Hon. John Wentworth," *New York Times*, April 22, 1874, 5 (inaccurate history). The first published use of *shyster* was in New York in "The Pettifogger," *Subterranean*, July 22, 1843, 12. See Gerald Leonard Cohen, *Origin of the Word "Shyster"* (Frankfurt: Peter Lang, 1982); Gerald Leonard Cohen, *Origin of the Word "Shyster": Supplementary Information* (Frankfurt: Peter Lang, 1984); Simeon E. Baldwin, "The Ideals of the American Advocate—a Symposium," *Central Law Journal* 58 (1904): 423–424.

62. David I. Durham, "An Improbable Journey," in *GALE*, 37–43; Brent J. Aucoin, *Thomas Goode Jones: Race, Politics, and Justice in the New South* (Tuscaloosa: University of Alabama Press, 2016); Paul M. Pruitt Jr., *Taming Alabama: Lawyers and Reformers, 1804–1929* (Tuscaloosa: University of Alabama Press, 2010); "Code of Ethics, Alabama State Bar Association," in *GALE*, 45–59.

63. George W. McCrary, "Address of Hon. Geo. W. McCrary," *Western Jurist* 14, 5 (May 1880): 193–194, 200, 203; George W. McCrary, *The True Lawyer* (Kansas City, MO: H. N. Farey, 1885); McCrary, "True Lawyer," 459–463; Hoar, *Function of the American Lawyer*, 21; Theodore Bacon, "Professional Ethics," *Journal of Social Science* 17 (1882): 37–46; Edward B. Merrill, "A Plea for Professional Ethics," *New York State Bar Association Report* 6 (1883): 148; Eaton, *Public Relations*, 8–9, 13, 15, 19–20; "Report," *Annual Report of the American Bar Association* 2 (1879): 233; Homer Greene, "Can Lawyers Be Honest?" *North American Review* 152, 411 (February 1891): 202–203 (rejecting the idea of an ethics code as utopian).

64. Alfred Zantzinger Reed, *Training for the Public Profession of the Law* (New York: Charles Scribner's Sons, 1921), 206n4; Roscoe Pound, *The Lawyer from Antiquity to Modern Times* (St. Paul: West Publishing, 1953), 273; "Code of Ethics," *Virginia State Bar Association Proceedings* 1 (1888): 61; *Report of the Committee on Legal Ethics to the Georgia Bar Association, May 1889*, 1.

65. Aucoin, *Thomas Goode Jones*, 50, 80, 104, 119, 126; David I. Durham, "A Call for Regulation of the Profession," in *GALE*, 1; Paul M. Pruitt Jr., "Thomas Goode Jones: Personal Code of a Public Man," in *GALE*, 75; Pruitt, *Taming Alabama*, 66–69; Walter Burgwyn Jones, "First Code of Ethics Adopted in the United States," *American Bar Association Journal* 8, 2 (February 1922): 111–113.

66. "Code of Ethics," in *GALE*, 46–47.

67. "Code of Ethics," 50–52, 58–59 (Rules 50, 57, 53, 14, 20, 51, 12).

68. "Code of Ethics," 50–51 (Rules 10, 13).

69. "Code of Ethics," 50; "Report," *Annual Report of the American Bar Association* 31 (1907): 695 (item 14, "all fair and honorable means").

70. Valmaer, *Lawyer's Code of Ethics: A Satire* (St. Louis: F. H. Thomas Law Book Co., 1887), 8, 12, 13, 15, 16. The title page of the copy I have indicates in handwriting that the author is Michael V. Ream, about whom I could find no information; there is no book review in any law journal, although it was referred to favorably in Eugene Wambaugh, "Light Reading for Law Students," *Law Bulletin of the State University of Iowa* 2 (1893): 29; republished in part in Valmaer, "Code of Ethics for Lawyers (a Satire)," *American Law School Review* 2, 8 (February 1910): 366–376.

71. Merrill, "A Plea," 154.

72. John D. Works, "Open Letters," *Century* 37 (January 1889): 475–477 (responding to "Lawyers' Morals," *Century* 29 [November 1884]: 145–146); J. Edward Johnson, *History of the Supreme Court Justices of California, 1850–1900*, 2 vols. (San Francisco: Bender-Moss, 1963), 1:156–161.

73. Greene, "Can Lawyers Be Honest?" 200–201, 203. A lawyer responded to Greene by blaming the jury system. Frederic J. Swift, "Honest Lawyers and Capable Juries," *Columbia Law Times* 5, 3 (December 1891): 77.

74. Silverman, *Law and Urban Growth*, 35; Halliday, "Six Score and Ten," 62; John M. Shirley, "The Future of Our Profession," *Annual Report of the American Bar Association* 6 (1883): 200–202 (noting that of 3,795 foreign-born lawyers, just 400 were born outside of the British Isles, British America, Germany, and Scandinavia); "Obituaries: John M. Shirley," *Annual Report of the American Bar Association* 10 (1887): 418–421.

75. Witt, *Accidental Republic*, 60–61; "Winnow the Bar"; "Editorial," *American Law Review* 25, 4 (July–August 1891): 611–612 (reprinting John J. Wickham, "How to Prevent the Overcrowding of the Profession," *Pittsburgh Legal Journal*); "Current Topics," *Albany Law Journal* 55 (June 12, 1897): 389–390 ("profession is overcrowded"); Reed, *Training for the Public Profession*, 266, 103; Fuller, "Overcrowding the Profession"; Southworth, "Generation of the New York Bar," 199; "Proceedings," *Annual Report of the American Bar Association* 15 (1892): 9; "Proceedings," *Annual Report of the American Bar Association* 22 (1899): 518–564; Cowley v. O'Connell, 54 N.E. 558 (Mass. 1899); In re Randel, 52 N.E. 1106 (N.Y. 1899).

76. Melville Davisson Post, *The Strange Schemes of Randolph Mason* (1896; reprint, New York: Open Road, 2014; Kindle ed.); Melville Davisson Post, *Man of Last Resort (The Clients of Randolph Mason)* (1897; reprint, New York: Open Road, 2014; Kindle ed.); *Dictionary of American Biography*, 15:119, s.v. "Post, Melville Davisson"; "Getting into Practice in New York," *American Law Review* 33, 2 (March–April 1899): 314; Walter L. Miller, "The Legal Profession in the South," *American Law Review* 33, 1 (January–February 1899): 87; Gribble v. Pioneer Press Co., 25 N.W. 710 (Minn. 1885) (calling a lawyer "shyster" is defamatory per se).

77. T. Fletcher Dennis, "The Lawyer from a Moral Standpoint," *American Journal of Politics* 5 (1894): 76, 77; *Albany Law Journal* 50 (July 14, 1894): 26–29; *Minnesota Law Journal* 2, 7 (July 1894): 179–183; Isaac Miller Hamilton, "Monstrosities of the Law," *American Lawyer* 2, 7 (July 1894): 295; L. G. Smith, "The Evolution of the Ambulance

Chaser," *Green Bag* 14, 6 (June 1902): 263; "Current Topics," *Albany Law Journal* 54 (July 11, 1896): 23; H. M. Wiltse, "Who Is the Shyster?" *American Lawyer* 5, 10 (October 1897): 490–491; Robert L. Harmon, "The Lawyer and the Shyster," *American Lawyer* 5, 9 (September 1897): 445.

78. "Editorial," *Virginia Law Register* (old series) 4, 11 (March 1899): 768; "Current Topics," *Albany Law Journal* 60 (October 28, 1899): 257; *Black's Law Dictionary*, s.v. "ambulance chaser"; Ken Dornstein, *Accidentally, on Purpose: The Making of a Personal Injury Underworld in America* (New York: St. Martin's Press, 1996), 41–46, 55–57; John B. Lewis and Charles C. Bombaugh, *Strategems and Conspiracies to Defraud Life Insurance Companies* (Baltimore: James H. McClellan, 1896); Edward J. Balleisen, *Fraud: An American History from Barnum to Madoff* (Princeton, NJ: Princeton University Press, 2017), 143; "A New Subject for Bar Associations to Attend To," *American Lawyer* 9, 6 (June 1901): 268–269 ("trickster").

79. Wm. C. P. Breckinridge, "The Lawyer; His Influence in Creating Public Opinion," *Virginia State Bar Association Proceedings* 3 (1891): 167–168; Strong, *Landmarks*, 354; Michael Ariens, "Know the Law: A History of Legal Specialization," *South Carolina Law Review* 45, 5 (1994): 1003–1061; John Anthony Moretta, *William Pitt Ballinger: Texas Lawyer, Southern Statesman, 1825–1888* (Austin, TX: Center for American History, 2000), 239–245, 249–253; Thomas, *Lawyering for the Railroad*, 51–52; *Law Notes* 4, 6 (September 1900): 103.

80. "The Contingent Fee Business," *Albany Law Journal* 24 (July 9, 1881): 25; Sharswood, *Essay on Professional Ethics*, 2nd ed. (1860), 103–107; 3rd ed. (1869), 163–165; 4th ed. (1876), 160–162; Samuel Hand, "Address," in *Proceedings of the New York State Bar Association* (Albany, NY: Argus, 1880), 79; Tracy C. Becker, "Contingent Compensation for Legal Services—Their Legal Status and Ethical Relations," in *Proceedings of the New York State Bar Association* (Albany, NY: Argus, 1880), 143; Jeffries v. Mutual Life Ins. Co., 110 U.S. 305 (1884); Taylor v. Bemiss, 110 U.S. 42 (1884).

81. Eli Shelby Hammond, "Personal Injury Litigation," *Yale Law Journal* 6, 6 (June 1897): 328–332; Irving G. Vann, *Contingent Fees: An Address in the Hubbard Course on Legal Ethics* (Albany, NY: Albany Law School, 1905); Clarence A. Lightner et al., "The Abuse of Personal Injury Litigation," *Green Bag* 18, 4 (April 1906): 193–215; "Report," *Annual Report of the American Bar Association* 31 (1907): 710 (Maryland exception); Parker, "Anti-Railroad Personal Injury Litigation," 171–172; Moretta, *William Pitt Ballinger*, 233 (contrary view); Michael Ariens, *Lone Star Law: A Legal History of Texas* (Lubbock: Texas Tech University Press, 2011), 264.

82. "List of Bar Associations in the United States," *Annual Report of the American Bar Association* 10 (1887): 439–447 (omitting New Hampshire and including District of Columbia); Pound, *Lawyer from Antiquity to Modern Times*, 274–275. The only states or territories lacking a bar association in 1900 were Delaware (established in 1901), Idaho (1901), Arizona (1906), Massachusetts (1909), and Wyoming (1915). "Report," *Annual Report of the American Bar Association* 31 (1907): 67; *Memorandum for Use of American Bar Association's Committee to Draft Canons of Professional Ethics*, comp. Lucien Alexander (1908), 5 (hereafter, cited as *Red Book*).

83. *Proceedings of the Michigan State Bar Association* 7 (1896): xiii ("It was the recommendation of the American Bar Association at its last meeting that State Bar As-

sociations follow the example of the Alabama and Virginia Associations and formulate and adopt a Code of Legal Ethics"); *Proceedings of the Michigan State Bar Association* 8 (1897): 10; "Report," *Annual Report of the American Bar Association* 18 (1895): 325; David L. Erickson, *Early Justice and the Formation of the Colorado Bar* (Denver: Continuing Legal Education in Colorado, 2008), 149; People ex rel. Colorado Bar Ass'n v. Weeber, 57 P. 1079 (Colo. 1899).

84. *Red Book*, 5 (listing New York, Pennsylvania, Ohio, Vermont, Oklahoma, Nebraska, Utah, Kansas, South Dakota, "and doubtless a number of others not yet heard from"); Bertram Wyatt-Brown, *Southern Honor: Ethics and Behavior in the Old South*, 25th anniversary ed. (New York: Oxford University Press, 2007); James Bowman, *Honor: A History* (New York: Encounter Books, 2006); Henry Ward Rogers, "The Ideals of the American Advocate—A Symposium," *Central Law Journal* 58 (May 1904): 424.

85. Henry St. George Tucker, "Address of the President," *Annual Report of the American Bar Association* 28 (1905): 384; Theodore Roosevelt, "*Address at Harvard University* (June 28, 1905)," in Theodore Roosevelt, *Presidential Addresses and State Papers*, 4 vols. (New York: P. F. Collier, 1910), 4:419–420.

86. Charles F. Chamberlayne, "The Soul of the Profession," *Green Bag* 18, 7 (July 1906): 396–398, 400–401. Chamberlayne was the author of the five-volume *A Treatise on the Modern Law of Evidence* (Albany, NY: M. Bender, 1911–1916), three of which were published after his death in 1913. William Twining, *Rethinking Evidence: Exploratory Essays*, 2nd ed. (Cambridge: Cambridge University Press, 2006), 65–69 (brief biography of Chamberlayne); "Notice of Current Topics," *American Law Review* 42, 5 (September–October 1908): 755–757; "Book Reviews," *American Law Review* 48, 2 (March–April 1914): 309–311.

87. Martin, *Causes and Conflicts*, 389, 110–114; Breen, *Thirty Years*, 484–485; Strong, *Landmarks*, 85–86; Strong, *Diary*, 4:504 ("Judge Davis has justly earned much praise by his vigorous action against the crew").

88. Breen, *Thirty Years*, 485; Philip C. Jessup, *Elihu Root*, 2 vols. (New York: Dodd, Mead, 1938), 1:89, 93 ("no substantiation . . . has been found"); Burton J. Hendrick, "How Should a Lawyer Behave?" *World's Work* 33 (January 1917): 328–335. Jessup believed Root was criticized for representing Tweed because he later opposed William Hearst's run for New York governor. John Oller, *White Shoe: How a New Breed of Wall Street Lawyers Changed Big Business and the American Century* (New York: Dutton, 2019), 79.

89. Martin, *Causes and Conflicts*, 157.

90. Joseph G. Allegretti, *The Lawyer's Calling: Christian Faith and Legal Practice* (New York: Paulist Press, 1996), ch. 2; Matt. 16:26 (King James Version).

4. LEGAL ETHICS, LEGAL ELITES, AND THE BUSINESS OF LAW, 1905–1945

1. Charles F. Chamberlayne, "The Soul of the Profession," *Green Bag* 18, 7 (July 1906): 396; Edmund Wetmore, "Address of the President," *Annual Report of the American Bar Association* 24 (1901): 203–240; Alfred Hemenway, "The American Lawyer," *Annual Report of the American Bar Association* 28 (1905): 390–406; Henry St. George Tucker,

"Address of the President," *Annual Report of the American Bar Association* 28 (1905): 299–389; John F. Dillon, "The True Professional Ideal," *American Lawyer* 3, 2 (February 1895): 59–61; Theodore Roosevelt, "*Address at Harvard University* (June 28, 1905)," in Theodore Roosevelt, *Presidential Addresses and State Papers*, 4 vols. (New York: P. F. Collier, 1910), 4:419–420; Louis D. Brandeis, "The Opportunity in the Law," *American Law Review* 39, 4 (July–August 1905): 555–563; Robert Treat Platt, "The Decadence of Law as a Profession and Its Growth as a Business," *Yale Law Journal* 12, 7 (May 1903): 441–445; T. H. Marshall, "The Lawyer's Conscience," *American Lawyer* 14, 6 (June 1906): 245 (noting that lawyers who aid "the money-getter" are not "of low degree" but "the man who is above reproach in the community in which he lives"); John Dos Passos, *The American Lawyer—as He Was—as He Is—as He Can Be* (New York: Banks Law Publishing, 1907), 46; Champ S. Andrews, "The Law—A Business or a Profession?" *Yale Law Journal* 17, 8 (June 1908): 602–610.

2. Tucker, "Address," 383–384.

3. "Report," *Annual Report of the American Bar Association* 28 (1905): 132; "Report," *Annual Report of the American Bar Association* 29 (1906): 600–604; "Final Report," *Annual Report of the American Bar Association* 33 (1908): 55–86 (approved); Charles F. Chamberlayne, "Legal Idealism," *Green Bag* 21, 9 (September 1909): 437; Duane Mowry, "Commercialism in the Practice of Law," *Albany Law Journal* 64, 9 (September 1902): 359–360. Although the oath and the canons were separated, I refer to the 1908 ABA Code as the ABA Canons to distinguish it from the 1969 ABA Code of Professional Responsibility (see chapter 5).

4. "Transactions," *Annual Report of the American Bar Association* 35 (1910): 53 (this list incorrectly omitted Texas); "Report," *Annual Report of the American Bar Association* 39 (1914): 560n3 (hereafter, cited as *1914 Report*); "Report," *Annual Report of the American Bar Association* 49 (1924): 467.

5. Michael Ariens, *Lone Star Law: A Legal History of Texas* (Lubbock: Texas Tech University Press, 2011), 185, 315n15; In re Cohen, 159 N.E. 495 (Mass. 1928); Henry S. Drinker, *Legal Ethics* (New York: Columbia University Press, 1953), 26–30; Julius Henry Cohen, *The Law—Business or Profession?* (New York: Banks Law Publishing, 1916), ch. 1 (voluntary bars possess some disciplinary authority); George Martin, *Causes and Conflicts: The Centennial History of the Association of the Bar of the City of New York, 1870–1970* (Boston: Houghton Mifflin, 1970), 364; Michael J. Powell, *From Patrician to Professional Elite: The Transformation of the New York City Bar Association* (New York: Russell Sage Foundation, 1988), 18–21; Michael Ariens, "Brougham's Ghost," *Northern Illinois University Law Review* 35, 2 (2015): 293n184; *1914 Report*, 565–566.

6. Harlan Fiske Stone, "The Public Influence of the Bar," *Harvard Law Review* 48, 1 (November 1934): 10.

7. Dos Passos, *American Lawyer*, 175; "Editorial," *Bar Examiner* 1, 8 (June 1932): 211; Philip J. Wickser, "Ideals and Problems for a National Conference of Bar Examiners," *Bar Examiner* 1, 1 (November 1931): 7; "Overcrowded Occupations," *Saturday Evening Post*, July 15, 1933, in *Bar Examiner* 2, 10 (August 1933): 267–268; "The Law as a Learned Profession: A Recent Episode Considered," *New York Law Review* 5, 1 (January 1927): 1–4; *1914 Report*, 566–567; Robert Stevens, *Law School: Legal Education in America from the 1850s to the 1980s* (Chapel Hill: University of North Carolina Press, 1983), 96; "Report,"

Annual Report of the American Bar Association 46 (1921): 683; "Should Candidates for Admission to the Bar Be Examined on the Subject of Legal Ethics and Professional Deportment," *American Law School Review* 2, 6 (May–June 1909): 251–256.

8. Chamberlayne, *Soul*, 396; Dos Passos, *American Lawyer*, 45–49; Theron G. Strong, *Landmarks of a Lawyer's Lifetime* (New York: Dodd, Mead, 1914), 354; Jerold Auerbach, *Unequal Justice: Lawyers and Social Change in Modern America* (New York: Oxford University Press, 1976), 99–101; "Report," *Annual Report of the American Bar Association* 29 (1906): 601.

9. Terence C. Halliday, "Six Score and Ten: Demographic Transitions in the American Legal Profession, 1850–1980," *Law & Society Review* 20, 1 (1986): 62, 77. Less reliable is the very different count of licensed lawyers in "ABA National Lawyer Population Survey, Historical Trend in Total National Lawyer Population, 1878–2020," *American Bar Association*, https://www.americanbar.org/content/dam/aba/administrative/market_research/total-national-lawyer-population-1878-2020.pdf.

10. Michael Ariens, "American Lawyers in an Age of Anxiety," *St. Mary's Law Journal* 40, 2 (2008): 415–417; "Report," *Annual Report of the American Bar Association* 55 (1930): 624–625 (hereafter, cited as *1930 Report*); Michael Ariens, "The Ethics of Copyrighting Ethics Rules," *University of Toledo Law Review* 36, 2 (Winter 2005): 249; *1930 Report*, 479, 94–95; K. N. Llewellyn, "Book Review," *Columbia Law Review* 31, 7 (November 1931): 1217 ("Let this be written large, for senior partners in law-factories to ponder on: Law does not exist for corporation executives alone"); Ferdinand Lundberg, *"The Law Factories: Brains of the Status Quo,"* *Harper's* 179 (June 1939): 180–192.

11. "Transactions," *Annual Report of the American Bar Association* 31 (1907): 62–64; "Report," *Annual Report of the American Bar Association* 31 (1907): 685; "Final Report," *Annual Report of the American Bar Association* 33 (1909): 570; "Code of Ethics Adopted by the Alabama Bar Association, Dec. 14, 1887," in *Gilded Age Legal Ethics: Essays on Thomas Goode Jones' 1887 Code*, ed. Carol Rose Andrews, Paul M. Pruitt Jr., and David I. Durham (Tuscaloosa: Bounds Law Library, University of Alabama Law School, 2003), 46–47 (hereafter, cited as *GALE*).

12. "Report," *Annual Report of the American Bar Association* 31 (1907): 62, 685; Walter Burgwyn Jones, "Canons of Professional Ethics: Their Genesis and History," *Notre Dame Law Review* 7, 4 (May 1932): 493; James M. Altman, "Considering the ABA's 1908 Canons of Ethics," *Fordham Law Review* 71, 6 (May 2003): 2440–2441; *Memorandum for Use of American Bar Association's Committee to Draft Canons of Professional Ethics*, comp. Lucien Alexander (1908) (hereafter, cited as *Red Book*). I have relied on James Altman and M. Louise Rutherford, *The Influence of the American Bar Association on Public Opinion and Legislation* (Clark, NJ: Lawbook Exchange, 2005), 87–90; "Final Report," *Annual Report of the American Bar Association* 33 (1908): 567–572.

13. "Transactions," *Annual Report of the American Bar Association* 33 (1908): 61–80, 571; Peter Karsten, "Enabling the Poor to Have Their Day in Court: The Sanctioning of Contingency Fee Contracts: A History to 1940," *DePaul Law Review* 47, 2 (Winter 1998): 231.

14. Irving G. Vann, *Contingent Fees: An Address in the Hubbard Course on Legal Ethics* (Albany, NY: Albany Law School, 1905); Percy Werner, "The Abuse of Personal Injury Litigation," *Green Bag* 18, 4 (April 1906): 202; Cohen, *Law*, 205–206 (noting that the

Boston Bar Association was an exception); Andrewes v. Haas, 108 N.E. 423 (N.Y. 1915); *Red Book*, 71; "Report of the Special Committee on Contingent Fees," *Proceedings of the New York State Bar Association* 31 (1908): 103.

15. *Red Book*, 43; Robert A. Silverman, *Law and Urban Growth: Civil Litigation in the Boston Trial Courts, 1880–1900* (Princeton, NJ: Princeton University Press, 1981), 99–121; Randolph E. Bergstrom, *Courting Danger: Injury and Law in New York City, 1870–1910* (Ithaca, NY: Cornell University Press, 1992), 20.

16. *Annual Report of the American Bar Association* 31 (1907): 686; George Costigan, "The Proposed American Code of Legal Ethics," *Green Bag* 20, 2 (February 1908): 57–59; *Red Book*, 33–34; Auerbach, *Unequal Justice*, 41–50; Altman, "Considering," 2489.

17. Roscoe Pound, "The Causes of Popular Dissatisfaction with the Administration of Justice," *Annual Report of the American Bar Association* 29 (1906): 404–405 ("sporting theory" was John Henry Wigmore's phrase); David Wigdor, *Roscoe Pound: Philosopher of Law* (Westport, CT: Greenwood Press, 1974), 129; Paul Sayre, *The Life of Roscoe Pound* (Iowa City: University of Iowa, 1948); *Yale Biographical Dictionary of American Law*, s.v. "Pound, Roscoe"; Richard S. Harvey, "Correct Ideals in the Prosecution of Criminal Cases," *American Lawyer* 16, 2 (February 1908): 112–117.

18. Edwin M. Borchard, *Convicting the Innocent: Errors of Criminal Justice* (1932; reprint, New York: Da Capo Press, 1970), xxxi n. 20, xv; Francis L. Wellman, *Gentlemen of the Jury* (New York: Macmillan, 1931), 95; William McAdoo, "Criminal Procedure and Crime and a Foreword about the Magistrates' Courts," *New York University Law Review* 5, 2 (April 1928): 114; Arthur Train, *Courts, Criminals and the Camorra* (1912; Kindle ed.), loc. 487; *Dictionary of American Biography Supp.*, 3:773, s.v. "Train, Arthur Cheney"; Arthur Train, *My Day in Court* (New York: Charles Scribner's Sons, 1939); *Yale Biographical Dictionary of American Law*, s.v. "Train, Arthur Cheney"; Charles A. Boston, *Address of Charles A. Boston upon Legal Ethics* (1915), 19.

19. *GALE*, 49–50; *Annual Report of the American Bar Association* 32 (1907): 183.

20. *GALE*, 53 ("The client can not be made the keeper of the attorney's conscience in professional matters").

21. Geoffrey Cowan, *The People v. Clarence Darrow: The Bribery Trial of America's Greatest Lawyer* (New York: Notable Trials Library, 1995), 51–52, 434; John A. Farrell, *Clarence Darrow: Attorney for the Damned* (New York: Doubleday, 2011), chs. 12, 13; Adela Rogers St. Johns, *Final Verdict* (New York: Bantam Books, 1964), 402–507.

22. *Red Book*, 114; Charles A. Boston, "A Code of Legal Ethics," *Green Bag* 20, 5 (May 1908): 225, 230–231; Charles A. Boston, *Address of Charles A. Boston, Esq. on the Proposed Code of Professional Ethics* (1910), 33 ("It is not sufficient that the code should be a mere catalogue of specific offences") (hereafter, cited as *Boston Address*); Lyon Boston, "Memorial of Charles Anderson Boston," in *Association of the Bar of the City of New York Yearbook: 1935*, 278; William W. Miller, "Charles A. Boston, 1863–1935," *American Bar Association Journal* 21, 5 (May 1935): 281–282; "Charles A. Boston, Bar Leader, Dead," *New York Times*, March 9, 1935, 15; *Dictionary of American Biography Supp.*, 1:98, s.v. "Boston, Charles Anderson."

23. Boston, "Code of Legal Ethics," 229–230; *Boston Address*, 69, 74–83; Powell, *From Patrician*, 19–21, 144; John C. Myers, "Boards of Legal Discipline," *Law Notes* 13, 5 (August 1909): 85–87.

24. The Pennsylvania Bar Association committee charged with drafting ethics rules ignored the canons in favor of more specific provisions. Its approach was rejected by the membership for reasons of uniformity. "Report of the Special Committee on Legal Ethics," in *Report of the 16th Annual Meeting of the Pennsylvania Bar Association* (Philadelphia, 1910), 159, 292; "The Code of Legal Ethics of the Bar Association of San Francisco," *Green Bag* 23, 1 (January 1911): 16–21; "The Connecticut Code of Professional Ethics," *Green Bag* 22, 4 (April 1910): 252–254; "ABA Special Committee on Supplementing the Canons of Professional Ethics," in *Annotated Canons*, comp. Charles A. Boston (1926) (reprinting the rules); Elmer E. Rogers, "The Etiquette of the Lawyer," *Chicago Legal News* 41, 17 (December 5, 1908): 140.

25. *Boston Address*, 12–14; *A Comparison between the Code of Ethics Suggested by Charles A. Boston for the New York County Lawyers' Association and the Code of the American Bar Association* (1908), 2; *Code of Ethics Suggested to the Committee on Professional Ethics of the New York County Lawyers Association by Charles A. Boston, Esq., Including Therein the Statement of Professional Ideals Compiled by Henry W. Jessup, Esq.* (1908).

26. *Code of Ethics Suggested*, 1–8 (Legal Duties), 12–16 (Professional Ideals), 16–30 (Professional Ideals of the Lawyer). The history of the NYCLA ignores this debate. Edwin David Robertson, *Brethren and Sisters of the Bar: A Centennial History of the New York County Lawyers' Association* (New York: Fordham University Press, 2008); Charles A. Boston, "Work of the Committee on Professional Ethics of the New York County Lawyers' Association," *Bench & Bar* 3, 2 (December 1912): 66–67 (noting the NYCLA did not publish materials for financial reasons).

27. Robertson, *Brethren*, 29, 32; *Boston Address*, 65–68.

28. *Boston Address*, 36–38, 50, 51, 60–62; Boston, "Code of Legal Ethics," 230; *Code of Ethics Suggested*, 27; *Opinions of the Committees on Professional Ethics of the Association of the Bar of the City of New York and the New York County Lawyers' Association* (New York: Columbia University Press, 1956), 533–539 (NYCLA Opinion 47); Charles A. Boston, "Legal Ethics," *Bulletin of the Commercial Law League of America* 18, 9 (September 1913): 113.

29. Robertson, *Brethren*, 52, 54–55, 70n19; Charles A. Boston, "The Recent Movement toward the Realization of High Ideals in the Legal Profession," *Annual Report of the American Bar Association* 37 (1912): 772; "The Legal Ethics Clinic of the New York County Lawyers Association," *Illinois Law Review* 7, 9 (April 1913): 554–571; *1914 Report*, 568–569; "Report," *American Bar Association Journal* 2, 3 (July 1916): 552–553; "Report," *American Bar Association Journal* 3, 3 (July 1917): 487; "Report," *Annual Report of the American Bar Association* 47 (1922): 286–287, 50–51; Martin, *Causes and Conflicts*, 372–374; Cohen, *Law*, 333; William Cyrus Sprague, *The Commercial Lawyer and His Work*, 2nd ed. (Chicago, 1918), 109–138; Henry Wynans Jessup, *The Professional Ideals of the Lawyer* (New York: G. A. Jennings, 1925); Drinker, *Legal Ethics*, 31–32.

30. "NYCLA, Number 1 (January 1912)," in *Opinions of the Committees*, 505; Charles A. Boston, "Practical Activities in Legal Ethics," *University of Pennsylvania Law Review* 62, 2 (December 1914): 118; Boston, *Address of Charles A. Boston upon Legal Ethics*, 22–23.

31. *Opinions of the Committees*, 533–539; Charles A. Boston, "Legal Ethics," *American*

Legal News 23, 8 (August 1913): 15–21 (reprinting speech to Commercial Law League); Julius Henry Cohen, "Co-operation vs. Solicitation in Bankruptcy," *American Legal News* 23 (December 1912): 5–15.

32. Robertson, *Brethren*, 52, 61, 68n6; Cohen, *Law*, 253–254; *Bulletin of the Commercial Law League of America* 18, 9 (September 1913): 105; Morris Weisman, *A History of the Commercial Law League of America* (Chicago: Morris Weisman Educational Foundation, 1976), 63–64; Julius Henry Cohen, *They Builded Better than They Knew* (New York: Julian Messner, 1946); Samuel J. Levine, "The Law: Business or Profession? The Continuing Relevance of Julius Henry Cohen for the Practice of Law in the Twenty-First Century," *Fordham Urban Law Journal* 40, 1 (November 2012): 2n2 (listing numerous biographical sources); *Yale Biographical Dictionary of American Law*, s.v. "Cohen, Julius Henry"; Samuel J. Levine, "Rediscovering Julius Henry Cohen and the Origins of the Business/Profession Dichotomy: A Study in the Discourse of Early Twentieth Century Legal Professionalism," *American Journal of Legal History* 47, 1 (January 2005): 3–15; Rebecca Roiphe, "A History of Professionalism: Julius Henry Cohen and the Professions as a Route to Citizenship," *Fordham Urban Law Journal* 40, 1 (November 2012): 51–61.

33. Cohen, *Law*, 243, 313.

34. Cohen, *They Builded Better*, 37–38; Cohen, *Law*, 158; Felix Adler, *Life and Destiny* (1903; reprint, Prabhat Books, 2008; Kindle ed.); Horace L. Friess, *Felix Adler and Ethical Culture: Memories and Studies*, ed. Fannia Weingartner (New York: Columbia University Press, 1981); *Boston Address*, 30 (acknowledging the influence of the group and Adler); Boston, "Practical Activities," 111.

35. Boston, "Recent Movement toward High Ideals," 792; "Proceedings," *Annual Report of the American Bar Association* 38 (1913): 12.

36. *1914 Report*, 559, 561–563, 565–569.

37. Cohen, *Law*, 176, 309–310. Tregoe also wrote to NACM members in early January 1916 urging them to seek out the attorney "equipped to give the most efficient service and who cannot be induced to do that which is contrary to the ethics of his profession." Cohen, 313; Sprague, *Commercial Lawyer*, 62–63; "Report," *Annual Report of the American Bar Association* 41 (1916): 455.

38. "Transactions," *Annual Report of the American Bar Association* 41 (1916): 30–31; "Report," *American Bar Association Journal* 3, 7 (July 1917): 484–486; In re Schwarz, 175 A.D. 335, 161 N.Y.S. 1079 (App. Div. 1916); In re Neuman, 169 A.D. 638, 155 N.Y.S. 428 (App. Div. 1915).

39. In re Schwarz, 195 A.D. 194, 186 N.Y.S. 535, *aff'd* 231 N.Y. 642, 132 N.E. 931 (1921). Schwarz had also come before the Appellate Division the year before in Matter of Rowe Co., Inc. v. Schwarz, 191 A.D. 179, 181 N.Y.S. 87 (A.D. 1920).

40. "Report," *Annual Report of the American Bar Association* 45 (1920): 279, 287; Charles A. Boston, "Some Problems of Legal Ethics, Particularly Ambulance-Chasing and the Disciplining of Attorneys," *Proceedings of the Minnesota State Bar Association* 15 (1915): 23.

41. Thomas Francis Howe, "The Proposed Amendment to the By-laws," *American Bar Association Journal* 8, 7 (July 1922): 436–437; "Transactions," *Annual Report of the American Bar Association* 47 (1922): 50–51.

42. *Annual Report of the American Bar Association* 38 (1913): 70, 152; John Austin

Matzko, *Best Men of the Bar: The Early Years of the American Bar Association, 1878–1928* (Clark, NJ: Lawbook Exchange, 2019), 53; Gene Carney, *Burying the Black Sox: How Baseball's Cover-up of the 1919 World Series Fix Almost Succeeded* (Potomac Books, 2007), ch. 4.

43. Carney, *Burying the Black Sox*, ch. 3. The players were acquitted but banned for life from major league baseball. Carney, 148–150.

44. David Pietrusza, *Judge and Jury: The Life and Times of Kenesaw Mountain Landis* (1998; Kindle ed., 2011), chs. 11–13; *Dictionary of American Biography Supp.*, 3:437, s.v. "Landis, Kenesaw Mountain."

45. "Transactions," *Annual Report of the American Bar Association* 46 (1921): 61–67; Pietrusza, *Judge and Jury*, ch. 13.

46. Letter from Charles A. Boston to ABA Executive Committee, September 24, 1921, *William H. Taft Papers, series 3, General Correspondence and Related Material, 1877–1941, Sept. 24–Oct. 20* 1921, Manuscript/Mixed Material, 1, 4, https://www.loc.gov/item/mss4223400236/; John P. MacKenzie, *The Appearance of Justice* (New York: Charles Scribner's Sons, 1974), 181–187; Edward J. Schoenbaum, "A Historical Look at Judicial Discipline," *Chicago-Kent Law Review* 54, 1 (1977): 8 (noting the adoption of judicial recall in Oregon in 1908, California in 1911, and Arizona, Colorado, and Nevada in 1912); Matzko, *Best Men of the Bar*, 221–225 (discussing the ABA's worry about judicial recall); Henry W. Jessup, "The Ethics of the Legal Profession," *Annals of the American Academy of Political & Social Science* 101, 190 (May 1922): 28–29; Edward A. Harriman, "The Need for Standards of Ethics for Judges," *Annals of the American Academy of Political & Social Science* 101, 190 (May 1922): 29–32; "Transactions," *Annual Report of the American Bar Association* 34 (1909): 88; "The Proposed Canons of Judicial Ethics," *American Bar Association Journal* 9, 2 (February 1923): 73–76; Michael Ariens, "The Appearance of Appearances," *University of Kansas Law Review* 70, 4 (2022): 645–647.

47. "Final Report and Proposed Canons of Judicial Ethics," *American Bar Association Journal* 9, 7 (July 1923): 449–453; "Final Report," *Annual Report of the American Bar Association* 48 (1923): 452–460.

48. "Transactions," *Annual Report of the American Bar Association* 48 (1923): 74–76.

49. Letter from Robert von Moschzisker to William Howard Taft, July 10, 1924, *Taft Papers, series 3, General Correspondence and Related Material, 1877 to 1941; June 18–Aug. 11,* 1924, Manuscript/Mixed Material, https://www.loc.gov/item/mss4223400268/; Ariens, "Appearance of Appearances," 648–651; MacKenzie, *Appearance of Justice*, 187.

50. "Proceedings," *Annual Report of the American Bar Association* 49 (1924): 65–71; MacKenzie, *Appearance of Justice*, 186–187.

51. "Final Report and Proposed Canons of Judicial Ethics," *American Bar Association Journal* 9, 7 (July 1923): 449; Ariens, "Appearance of Appearances," 648–649; MacKenzie, *Appearance of Justice*, 191.

52. Susan A. Henderson, "The Origin and Adoption of the American Bar Association's Canons of Judicial Ethics," *Judicature* 52, 9 (April 1969): 387–388.

53. *Annual Report of the American Bar Association* 49 (1924): 26.

54. "Proceedings," *Annual Report of the American Bar Association* 38 (1913): 12, 169; *1914 Report*, 559–570; "Report," *American Bar Association Journal* 5, 3 (March 1919): 447–453; "Report," *Annual Report of the American Bar Association* 45 (1920): 283–297;

Howe, "Proposed Amendment," 436–437; "Draft Amendment," *American Bar Association Journal* 8, 6 (June 1922): 379.

55. J. H. Tregoe, "The Canons of Commercial Ethics," *Annals of the American Academy of Political & Social Science* 101, 190 (May 1922): 209. The NACM adopted canons of commercial ethics in 1912 and 1913. Cohen, *Law*, xiv, 312–313.

56. "'Bankruptcy Rings' Laid to Lawyers," *New York Times*, September 1, 1922, 13. The circular letter is not mentioned in J. Harry Tregoe, "Pioneers and Traditions of the National Association of Credit Men," in *NACM, Golden Anniversary Credit Congress Souvenir Program* (New York, May 11–15, 1947), 7, discussed in Weisman, *History of Commercial Law League*, 89. "Corrupt 'Bankruptcy Ring' Newest Business Brigand," *New York Times*, December 23, 1922, 10; "Call Bankrupts Lawyers' Victims," *New York Times*, December 3, 1922, 33; National Association of Credit Management, "J. Harry Tregoe," http://history.nacm.org/j-harry-tregoe.shtml.

57. Everett V. Abbot, "Some Actual Problems of Professional Ethics," *Harvard Law Review* 15, 9 (May 1902): 719–721; "Report," *Bulletin of the Commercial Law League of America* 17, 6 (June 1912): 4–5.

58. "Transactions," *Annual Report of the American Bar Association* 48 (1923): 46–51. The ABA, the NACM, and the Commercial Law League met to discuss proposals for reform of abuses, and the Supreme Court issued general orders regarding bankruptcy practice. Weisman, *History of Commercial Law League*, 90–92; "Report," *Annual Report of the American Bar Association* 50 (1925): 478–502 (hereafter, cited as *1925 Report*); *Annual Report of the American Bar Association* 50 (1925): 95–100.

59. *Annual Report of the American Bar Association* 48 (1923): 51.

60. *Annual Report of the American Bar Association* 49 (1924): 26, 48–50, 467.

61. *1925 Report*, 536; Robertson, *Brethren*, 29, 36; Jessup, "Ethics of the Legal Profession," 21.

62. *1925 Report*, 537; "Canons of Professional Ethics," *Bulletin of the Commercial Law League of America* 17, 10 (October 1912): 8–13; Weisman, *History of Commercial Law League*, 61–62, 94–95; "Report," *Commercial Law League Journal* 30, 9 (September 1925): 502–503.

63. *1925 Report*, 507; Weisman, *History of Commercial Law League*, 97.

64. "Proposed Supplements to Canons of Professional Ethics," *American Bar Association Journal* 13, 5 (1927): 269; *Annotated Canons*; "ABA Committee on Supplements to Canons of Professional Ethics," in *Comments of Walter F. Taylor, Jr. on Mr. Boston's Proposed Supplemental Canons* (n.d.). Taylor died before the last meeting of the Boston Committee. "Report," *Annual Report of the American Bar Association* 52 (1927): 374.

65. Weisman, *History of Commercial Law League*, 98; Maurice P. Davidson, "A Report of the Conference," *Commercial Law League Journal* 31, 5 (May 1926): 206–207; "Report," *Commercial Law League Journal* 31, 5 (May 1926): 253–254.

66. "Report," *Commercial Law League Journal* 32, 7 (July 1927): 343–344; Weisman, *History of Commercial Law League*, 101; "Proceedings," *Commercial Law League Journal* 32, 10 (October 1927): 540–543.

67. Weisman, *History of Commercial Law League*, 101–103.

68. Weisman, 102; "Supplemental Report," *Commercial Law League Journal* 32, 10 (October 1927): 540–541; "Memorial of the Commercial Law League of America," *Com-*

mercial Law League Journal 32, 9 (September 1927): 505–509; James B. Ryan, "Certain Proposed Canons of Ethics," *Commercial Law League Journal* 32, 8 (August 1927): 376–381.

69. Weisman, *History of Commercial Law League*, 104; "In re Proposed Additional Canons of Ethics," *Commercial Law League Journal* 32, 9 (September 1927): 505; "Proceedings," *Commercial Law League Journal* 32, 10 (October 1927): 543.

70. "Proceedings," *Annual Report of the American Bar Association* 52 (1927): 108–109; "Report," *Annual Report of the American Bar Association* 52 (1927): 372; "Supplemental Report," *Annual Report of the American Bar Association* 52 (1927): 386.

71. "Proposed Supplements," 273; "Minority Report," *Annual Report of the American Bar Association* 52 (1927): 387–395.

72. Jessup, "Ethics of the Legal Profession," 25–26; Jessup, *Professional Ideals*, 11–14; "H. W. Jessup Is Dead: Noted as Lawyer," *New York Times*, December 10, 1934, 21.

73. "Summary Ideals," *American Bar Association Journal* 13, 5 (May 1927): 271–273; *Annual Report of the American Bar Association* 52 (1927): 382–385; "Minority Report," *American Bar Association Journal* 13, 5 (May 1927): 274–275; *Comments of Taylor*, 38–43.

74. Weisman, *History of Commercial Law League*, 110. Because the ABA so resolved, Boston believed the committee was duty-bound to include a canon on banning lawyer bonds, despite the controversy. "Report," *Annual Report of the American Bar Association* 53 (1928): 315–316.

75. "Important Supplemental Canons of Professional Ethics," *American Bar Association Journal* 14, 5 (May 1928): 292–294; "Report," *Annual Report of the American Bar Association* 53 (1928): 495–499.

76. Weisman, *History of Commercial Law League*, 111.

77. Cohen, *Law*, 226–233; "Proceedings," *Annual Report of the American Bar Association* 53 (1928): 120–131; *Annual Report of the American Bar Association* 52 (1927): 7 (listing members of the executive committee).

78. Cohen, *Law*, 179, 314.

79. Weisman, *History of Commercial Law League*, 114–115.

80. Weisman, 116; "Report," *Annual Report of the American Bar Association* 54 (1929): 513.

81. *Annual Report of the American Bar Association* 55 (1930): ix, 89–90.

82. John L. Cortelyou, "In Memoriam: Francis Xavier Busch (1879–1975)," *DePaul Law Review* 25, 1 (Fall 1975): xv–xvii; "Francis X. Busch, Trim Lawyer," *New York Times*, November 29, 1975, 30; Weisman, *History of Commercial Law League*, 123.

83. Weisman, *History of Commercial Law League*, 124–125; "Report," *Annual Report of the American Bar Association* 56 (1931): 469; "Proceedings," *Annual Report of the American Bar Association* 56 (1931): 115–116; "Report," *Annual Report of the American Bar Association* 56 (1931): 307–308.

84. Weisman, *History of Commercial Law League*, 129, 131; *Annual Report of the American Bar Association* 57 (1932): 35.

85. "Report," *Annual Report of the American Bar Association* 57 (1932): 558–560.

86. Weisman, *History of Commercial Law League*, 133.

87. "Report," *Annual Report of the American Bar Association* 58 (1933): 428 (propos-

ing two judicial ethics amendments); "Proceedings," *Annual Report of the American Bar Association* 58 (1933): 154.

88. *Annual Report of the American Bar Association* 58 (1933): 154–161, 177–180.

89. "Proceedings," *Annual Report of the American Bar Association* 58 (1933): 161–163.

90. "Proceedings," 165, 172–173. The last sentence of Canon 35, declaring that lawyers customarily received commercial collections from lay forwarders, was deleted. "Proceedings," 176–177.

91. Weisman, *History of Commercial Law League*, 138.

92. Albert P. Blaustein and Charles O. Porter, *The American Lawyer: A Summary of the Survey of the Legal Profession* (Chicago: University of Chicago Press, 1954), 258. In 1935 the ABA held a national conference to consider the "serious problem" of a "volume of misconduct." H. W. Arant, "Some Observations on the Washington Conference on Disciplinary Procedures," *American Bar Association Journal* 21, 7 (July 1935): 410–412.

93. *Annual Report of the American Bar Association* 55 (1930): 476, 94–95; Mitchell Dawson, "Frankenstein, Inc.," *American Mercury* 19, 75 (March 1930): 274–280 (corporate law practice); Ariens, "American Lawyers in Age of Anxiety," 413–415 (the pass rate for the New York bar exam was 32 percent in 1932).

94. In re Richards, 63 S.W.2d 672 (Mo. 1933); James R. Devine, "Lawyer Discipline in Missouri: Is a New Ethics Code Necessary?" *Missouri Law Review* 46, 4 (Fall 1981): 733–736; "An Important Recent Decision," *American Bar Association Journal* 19, 12 (December 1933): 711; "Aftermath of Richards Case Decision in Missouri," *American Bar Association Journal* 20, 1 (January 1934): 1.

95. State ex inf. Miller v. St. Louis Union Trust Co., 74 S.W.2d 348 (Mo. 1934); "Report," *Annual Report of the American Bar Association* 58 (1933): 477; *Annual Report of the American Bar Association* 59 (1934): 531 ("It is not an evil because it takes away business from lawyers"); John D. Jackson, "The Unauthorized Practice of the Law," *Missouri Bar Journal* 5, 1 (January 1934): 5–7; *Annual Report of the American Bar Association* 58 (1933): 498; Jacob M. Lashly, "Better Organization of the Bar," *Missouri Bar Journal* 6, 10 (October 1935): 206.

96. *Missouri Bar Journal* 5, 12 (December 1934): 323–327; "Report," *Missouri Bar Journal* 5, 5 (May 1934): 67–77; "Supreme Court Adopts Commission's Report," *Missouri Bar Journal* 5, 6 (June 1934): 83; *Missouri Bar Journal* 5, 12 (December 1934): 310; "Missouri Supreme Court Adopts Recommendations of Commission with Regard to Discipline and Bar Admissions," *American Bar Association Journal* 20, 7 (July 1934): 391–392; Carl H. Langknecht, "Judicial Regulation of Law Practice in Missouri," *Commercial Law Journal* 39, 11 (November 1934): 582–586; Frank E. Atwood, "Objectives and Methods of Bar Integration," *American Bar Association Journal* 20, 4 (April 1934): 203–206; "Advisory Committee Invites Answers to Questions on Legal Ethics," *Missouri Bar Journal* 6, 5 (May 1935): 74.

97. Boyle G. Clark, "The Commercial Lawyer in an Independent Bar," *Missouri Bar Journal* 6, 8 (August 1935): 116–118, reprinted in *Commercial Law Journal* 40, 10 (October 1935): 551–554; Boyle G. Clark, "Missouri's Accomplishments and Program for Eliminating the Unlawful Practice of Law," *Missouri Bar Journal* 6, 10 (October 1935): 172–177; "St. Louis Bar Association Begins Drive against Unauthorized Practice of Law," *Missouri Bar Journal* 6, 4 (April 1935): 55.

98. "Canon 43 Amended and New Section Added to Rule 36 by Supreme Court," *Missouri Bar Journal* 6, 10 (October 1935): 194; Weisman, *History of Commercial Law League*, 144 (noting Clark "vitriolically" attacked the league and spoke with "mounting vehemence").

99. Weisman, *History of Commercial Law League*, 143; *Annual Report of the American Bar Association* 60 (1935): 26.

100. "Rules as to Law Directories and Law Lists," *Missouri Bar Journal* 7, 3 (March 1936): 47–48; "The Supreme Court Denies Petitions to Postpone Effective Date of Rules Affecting the Bar's Relations and Dealings with Lists and Directories," *Missouri Bar Journal* 7, 7 (July 1936): 125–126; Tyree G. Newbill, "Reputable Law Lists," *Missouri Bar Journal* 7, 9 (September 1936): 161–162.

101. Clark v. Austin, 101 S.W.2d 977 (Mo. 1937).

102. State ex rel. McKittrick v. C. S. Dudley & Co., Inc., 102 S.W.2d 895 (Mo. 1937). See also Clark v. Reardon, 104 S.W.2d 942 (Mo. App. 1937); Richmond Ass'n of Credit Men v. Bar Ass'n of Richmond, 189 S.E. 153 (Va. 1937).

103. Liberty Mut. Ins. Co. v. Jones, 104 S.W.2d 407 (Mo. 1937).

104. Donald S. Lamm, "Legal Ethics—Where Are We Now?" *Missouri Bar Journal* 9, 6 (June 1939): 116–117.

105. "Report," *Annual Report of the American Bar Association* 59 (1934): 588; "Report," *Annual Report of the American Bar Association* 60 (1935): 548–551.

106. "Notice of Proposed Amendments to the Constitution and By-laws of the American Bar Association," *American Bar Association Journal* 22, 8 (August 1936): 578; "Proceedings," *Annual Report of the American Bar Association* 61 (1936): 78–79; Edson Sunderland, *History of the American Bar Association and Its Work* (1953), 173–182; "Report," *Annual Report of the American Bar Association* 61 (1936): 797, 993–994, 699.

107. "Report," *Annual Report of the American Bar Association* 62 (1937): 758–759; "Supplementary Report," *Annual Report of the American Bar Association* 62 (1937): 761–767.

108. "Statements of Principles and Agreements between the American Bar Association and Various Other Groups," *Annual Report of the American Bar Association* 75 (1950): 571. An agreement with life insurance underwriters was reached in 1941–1942. I. Maurice Wormser, *Frankenstein, Incorporated* (New York: McGraw-Hill, 1931), 165, 173–178.

109. "Proceedings," *Annual Report of the American Bar Association* 62 (1937): 351–352; "Report," *Annual Report of the American Bar Association* 65 (1940): 252 ("Only a single agency," i.e., the ABA, could solve the law list problem); Weisman, *History of Commercial Law League*, 147–155; "Proceedings," *Annual Report of the American Bar Association* 68 (1943): 145.

110. "Special Committee on Law Lists Prepares for Effective Action," *American Bar Association Journal* 24, 1 (January 1938): 61–62; Frank E. Atwood, "Progress of American Bar Association Special Committee on Law Lists," *Missouri Bar Journal* 9, 1 (January 1938): 7–8; "Rules and Standards as to Law Lists," *Annual Report of the American Bar Association* 63 (1938): 838; "Proceedings," *Annual Report of the American Bar Association* 67 (1942): 126–127; "Proceedings," *Annual Report of the American Bar Association* 68 (1943): 144–145.

111. "Milwaukee Ambulance Chasing Quiz," *Bulletin of the Wisconsin State Bar Association* 1, 3 (April 1928): 66–68; "Milwaukee Ambulance Chasers Disciplined," *Journal of the American Judicature Society* 11, 3 (October 1927): 83–85; Paul A. Holmes, "The Circuit Court Inquisition into Legal Abuses," *Marquette Law Review* 11, 4 (June 1927): 183–188; State ex rel. Reynolds v. Circuit Court of Milwaukee Cty., 214 N.W. 396 (Wis. 1927); Rubin v. State, 216 N.W. 513 (Wis. 1927); State v. Rubin, 229 N.W. 36 (Wis. 1930) (declining to disbar); Paul A. Holmes, "The Ambulance Chasing Panacea," *Marquette Law Review* 12, 3 (April 1928): 193–205; Charles L. Aarons, "The Practice of Law by Non-Lawyers," *Marquette Law Review* 14, 1 (December 1929): 1–9; Ken Dornstein, *Accidentally, on Purpose: The Making of a Personal Injury Underworld in America* (New York: St. Martin's Press, 1996), 135–142.

112. In re Association of the Bar of the City of New York, 222 A.D. 580, 227 N.Y.S. 1 (App. Div. 1927) (the petition was joined by the NYCLA and the Bronx Bar Association); In re Brooklyn Bar Association, 223 A.D. 149, 227 N.Y.S. 666 (App. Div. 1927); "Mr. Justice Wasservogel's Report in the Judicial Investigation of 'Ambulance Chasing' in New York," *Massachusetts Law Quarterly* 14, 1 (November 1928): 4, 5, 11, 21; Isidor J. Kresel, "Ambulance Chasing, Its Evils and Remedies Therefor," *Proceedings of the New York State Bar Association* 52 (1929): 323; Sidney Handler, *The Results of the Ambulance Chasing Disbarment Proceedings in the Appellate Division, First Department* (1931), 3–5; People ex rel. Karlin v. Culkin, 223 A.D. 822, 248 N.Y.S. 465 (App. Div. 1928); Kenneth de Ville, "New York City Attorneys and Ambulance Chasing in the 1920s," *Historian* 59, 2 (Winter 1997): 290–310; Julius Henry Cohen, "Buccaneer Lawyers of New York Routed," *Journal of the American Judicature Society* 12, 4 (December 1928): 101–103; Dornstein, *Accidentally*, 125–134; Alexander L. Schlosser, *"Lawyers Must Eat"* (New York: Vanguard Press, 1933), 129–138; "Personal Injury Litigation Report Was Adopted at State Bar Meeting," *New York State Bar Association Bulletin* 2 (1930): 93; Herbert Mitgang, *The Man Who Rode the Tiger* (New York: Fordham University Press, 1996), chs. 9–10, 172 (Samuel Seabury's 1930 investigation of magistrates' courts found "corrupt, fraudulent, unlawful or unprofessional" behavior among lawyers).

113. Dornstein, *Accidentally*, 143–146; Auerbach, *Unequal Justice*, 127; "Nationwide War on 'Ambulance Chasers,'" *American Bar Association Journal* 14, 11 (November 1928): 561–564; Robert R. Bell, *The Philadelphia Lawyer: A History, 1735–1945* (Cranbury, NJ: Associated University Presses, 1992), 237, 241–242 (Drinker's anti-Semitic comments).

114. I. Maurice Wormser, "Legal Ethics in Theory and in Practice," *Annals of the American Academy of Political & Social Science* 167, 1 (May 1933): 195 (quoting December 3, 1932, *New York Times* article that "there is more ambulance chasing in New York City today than there was five years ago"); Bernard Botein, *Accident Fraud Investigation* (1937); Dornstein, *Accidentally*, 178–191; Robert Monaghan, "The Liability Claims Racket," *Law & Contemporary Problems* 3, 4 (October 1936): 491–504.

115. Thomas Clifford Billig, "What Price Bankruptcy: A Plea for 'Friendly Adjustment,'" *Cornell Law Review* 14, 4 (June 1929): 414–446; "David Steinhardt Hunted on Shortage in His Receiverships," *New York Times*, January 8, 1929, 1; "Steinhardt Kills Himself with Poison as He Surrenders," *New York Times*, April 20, 1929, 1; Schlosser, *"Lawyers Must Eat,"* 74–93; *Yale Biographical Dictionary of American Law*, s.v. "Dono-

van, William J. (Wild Bill)"; Anthony Cave Brown, *The Last Hero: Wild Bill Donovan* (New York: New York Times Books, 1982); David J. Skeel Jr., *Debt's Dominion: A History of Bankruptcy in America* (Princeton, NJ: Princeton University Press, 2001), 76–77 (quoting Donovan in a 1930 issue of *Credit Monthly*, the NACM's magazine).

116. William Donovan, *Administration of Bankruptcy Estates*, reprinted in House Judiciary Committee Report, 71st Cong. (Comm. Print 1931), 1–3, 7; "Report," *Annual Report of the American Bar Association* 55 (1930): 338, 80; *Strengthening of Procedure in the Judicial System: The Report of the Attorney General on Bankruptcy Law and Practice* (December 5, 1931), Sen. Doc. No. 72-65 (1932), 16.

117. Julius Henry Cohen, "Bankruptcy Practice—A Diagnosis and a Remedy," *New York University Law Review* 6, 4 (May 1929): 366, 376.

118. Homer Cummings, "The Lawyer Criminal," *American Bar Association Journal* 20, 2 (February 1934): 82–85; K. N. Llewellyn, "Must a Lawyer Believe in His Cause?" *New York Times Magazine*, September 9, 1934, SM6 (contrary view).

119. Joseph Borkin, *The Corrupt Judge: An Inquiry into Bribery and Other High Crimes and Misdemeanors in the Federal Courts* (New York: Clarkson N. Potter, 1962), 139–186; John T. Noonan Jr., *Bribes: The Intellectual History of a Moral Idea* (New York: Macmillan, 1984), 574. Memolo refused to repeat his congressional testimony at trial, and Johnson was acquitted. Two of Johnson's sons were convicted; both convictions were reversed on appeal.

120. William E. Harbaugh, *Lawyers' Lawyer: The Life of John W. Davis* (New York: Oxford University Press, 1973), 251–255; Nancy Lisagor and Frank Lipsius, *A Law unto Itself: The Untold Story of the Law Firm Sullivan and Cromwell* (New York: William Morrow, 1988), 100–101; Walter K. Earle, *Mr. Shearman and Mr. Sterling and How They Grew* (New Haven, CT: Yale University Press, 1963), 205–207; Martin Mayer, *Emory Buckner* (New York: Harper & Row, 1968), 126; Wayne K. Hobson, "Symbol of the New Profession: Emergence of the Large Law Firm, 1870–1915," in *The New High Priests: Lawyers in Post–Civil War America*, ed. Gerard W. Gawalt (Westport, CT: Greenwood Press, 1984), 5.

121. Newman Levy, "Lawyers and Morals," *Harper's Monthly* 154 (February 1927): 288; Henry W. Jessup, "Ethical Constraints on Professional Endeavors," *New York Law Review* 5, 5 (May 1927): 165–168; Newman Levy, *My Double Life: Adventures in Law and Life* (New York: Doubleday, 1958); "Newman Levy Is Dead at 77; Lawyer Noted for Light Verse," *New York Times*, March 23, 1966, 47.

122. Ferdinand Lundberg, "The Legal Profession: A Social Phenomenon," *Harper's* 178 (December 1938): 4; Lundberg, "Law Factories"; Ferdinand Lundberg, "The Priesthood of the Law," *Harper's* 178 (April 1939): 526.

123. Stone, "Public Influence," 2, 6, 7, 10; Wormser, "Legal Ethics," 196.

124. Stone, "Public Influence," 8–10.

5. PROSPERITY, PROFESSIONALISM, AND PREJUDICE, 1945–1969

1. Manley O. Hudson, "The World Court—The Next Step," *American Bar Association Journal* 31, 9 (September 1945): 443–445.

2. David A. Simmons, "Leadership—A Responsibility of the Bar," *American Bar Association Journal* 31, 4 (April 1945): 170; E. J. Dimock, "Factual Outline of the Indictment of War Criminals," *American Bar Association Journal* 31, 12 (December 1945): 638; Robert H. Jackson, "The Rule of Law among Nations," *American Bar Association Journal* 31, 6 (June 1945): 290–294; "Charter of the International Military Tribunal," *American Bar Association Journal* 31, 9 (September 1945): 454–457; Robert H. Jackson Center, "Nuremberg Trial," https://www.roberthjackson.org/nuremberg-timeline/.

3. Studs Terkel, *"The Good War": An Oral History of World War Two* (New York: Pantheon Books, 1984); Simmons, "Leadership," 170; Albert P. Blaustein, "The 1949 Lawyer Count: A Preliminary Statement," *American Bar Association Journal* 36, 5 (May 1950): 370–375; Albert P. Blaustein and Charles O. Porter, *The American Lawyer: A Summary of the Survey of the Legal Profession* (Chicago: University of Chicago Press, 1954), 3; Terence C. Halliday, "Six Score and Ten: Demographic Transitions in the American Legal Profession, 1850–1980," *Law & Society Review* 20, 1 (1986): 62, 77.

4. James T. Patterson, *Grand Expectations: The United States, 1945–1974* (New York: Oxford University Press, 1996), 61; Marc Levinson, *An Extraordinary Time: The End of the Postwar Boom and the Return of the Ordinary Economy* (New York: Basic Books, 2016), 9–13, chs. 1–2; Judith Stein, *Pivotal Decade: How the United States Traded Factories for Finance in the Seventies* (New Haven, CT: Yale University Press, 2010), ch. 1.

5. Marc Galanter and Thomas Palay, *Tournament of Lawyers: The Transformation of the Big Law Firm* (Chicago: University of Chicago Press, 1991), 20, 25; Mary Ann Glendon, *A Nation under Lawyers: How the Crisis in the Legal Profession Is Transforming American Society* (Cambridge, MA: Harvard University Press, 1994), 22; Richard H. Sander and E. Douglass Williams, "Why Are There so Many Lawyers? Perspectives on a Turbulent Market," *Law & Social Inquiry* 14, 3 (Summer 1989): 448; B. Peter Pashigian, "The Number and Earnings of Lawyers: Some Recent Findings," *American Bar Foundation Research Journal* 1 (Winter 1978): 63–64; Harry T. Edwards, "A New Role for the Black Law Graduate—A Reality or an Illusion?" *Michigan Law Review* 69, 8 (August 1971): 1410; Edward J. Littlejohn and Leonard S. Rubinowitz, "Black Enrollment in Law Schools: Forward to the Past?" *Thurgood Marshall Law Review* 12, 2 (Spring 1986): 428; William T. Coleman with Donald T. Bliss, *Counsel for the Situation: Shaping the Law to Realize America's Promise* (Washington, DC: Brookings Institution Press, 2010), 97–99 (discussing how racial discrimination made it difficult for Coleman to find a job with large law firms in his hometown of Philadelphia and in Boston, Washington, DC, and New York, despite finishing first in his class at Harvard Law School, serving as a commissioned officer in World War II, and clerking for Justice Felix Frankfurter); Erwin O. Smigel, *The Wall Street Lawyer: Professional Organization Man* (New York: Free Press of Glencoe, 1964), 45; Clara N. Carson with Jeeyoon Park, *The Lawyer Statistical Report: The U.S. Legal Profession in 2005* (Chicago: American Bar Foundation, 2012), 3, table 2; Blaustein and Porter, *American Lawyer*, 29–32; Terence C. Halliday, "The Idiom of Legalism in Bar Politics: Lawyers, McCarthyism, and the Civil Rights Era," *American Bar Foundation Research Journal* 1982, 4 (Fall 1982): 913–988; Michael Ariens, "The Rise and Fall of Social Trustee Professionalism," *Professional Lawyer* (2016): 54–63.

6. "Proceedings," *Annual Report of the American Bar Association* 69 (1944): 456; "Proceedings," *Annual Report of the American Bar Association* 71 (1946): 310; Reginald He-

ber Smith, "Survey of the Legal Profession: Its Scope, Methods and Objectives," *American Bar Association Journal* 39, 7 (July 1953): 548–555; *Yale Biographical Dictionary of American Law*, s.v. "Smith, Reginald Heber."

7. "Proceedings," *Annual Report of the American Bar Association* 76 (1951): 544–545; Arthur T. Vanderbilt, "The Survey of the Legal Profession," *Annual Report of the American Bar Association* 72 (1947): 350; "Survey of the Profession: Council and Director Announce Definitive Plans," *American Bar Association Journal* 33, 11 (November 1947): 1075–1079 (a sixth part was later added to the survey); Reginald Heber Smith, "Survey of Our Profession: 'Progress Report' as to Organization and Work," *American Bar Association Journal* 34, 9 (September 1948): 771–775, 848–850; "Reginald Heber Smith Succeeds Vanderbilt as Director of Survey," *American Bar Association Journal* 34, 1 (January 1948): 18.

8. Smith, "Survey of Our Profession," 771.

9. Robert T. McCracken, "Report on Observance by the Bar of Stated Professional Standards," *Virginia Law Review* 37, 3 (April 1951): 400, 423, 425; Henry S. Drinker, *Legal Ethics* (New York: Columbia University Press, 1953), 7 (agreeing with McCracken).

10. Blaustein and Porter, *American Lawyer*, ch. 9, 248–250.

11. Henry S. Drinker, "Laymen on the Competency and Integrity of Lawyers," *Tennessee Law Review* 22, 3 (April 1952): 372–374, 378.

12. Orie L. Phillips and Philbrick McCoy, *Conduct of Judges and Lawyers* (Los Angeles: Parker, 1952), 83–84, 126, 198–200, 203, 205.

13. Phillips and McCoy, viii; Charles P. Curtis Jr., "The Ethics of Advocacy," *Stanford Law Review* 4, 1 (December 1951): 3–23; Charles P. Curtis, *It's Your Law* (Cambridge, MA: Harvard University Press, 1954), ch. 1; *Dictionary of American Biography Supp.*, 6:142, s.v. "Curtis, Charles Pelham"; *Yale Biographical Dictionary of American Law*, s.v. "Curtis, Charles Pelham, Jr."; Smith, "Survey of Our Profession," 774; Henry S. Drinker, "Some Remarks on Mr. Curtis' 'The Ethics of Advocacy,'" *Stanford Law Review* 4, 3 (April 1952): 349–357; *Yale Biographical Dictionary of American Law*, s.v. "Drinker, Henry Sandwith"; Deborah S. Gardner and Christine G. McKay, *Building a Law Firm, 1849–1999* (Philadelphia: Drinker Biddle & Reath, 1999), 24–25, 41–42.

14. Curtis, "Ethics of Advocacy," 3, 4, 9, 18, 19, 20–22.

15. Drinker, "Some Remarks," 349, 352–353; Drinker, *Legal Ethics*, 5–6, 145n32; "Report," *Annual Report of the American Bar Association* 77 (1952): 257 ("We see no evidence that competitive or commercial practices threaten to break down the high standard of our profession").

16. "Opinion 146 (July 17, 1935)," in *American Bar Association Opinions of the Committee on Professional Ethics and Grievances*, rev. ed. (American Bar Association, 1957), 306–307; Robert B. Tunstall, "Ethics in Citation: A Plea for Re-interpretation of a Canon," *American Bar Association Journal* 35, 1 (January 1949): 5; "Opinion 280 (June 18, 1949)," in *American Bar Association Opinions*, 589–590.

17. Curtis, "Ethics of Advocacy," 11; Drinker, "Some Remarks," 353.

18. Drinker, "Laymen," 377.

19. Michal R. Belknap, *Cold War Political Justice: The Smith Act, the Communist Party, and American Civil Liberties* (Westport, CT: Greenwood Press, 1977); Michal R. Belknap, "Cold War in the Courtroom: The Foley Square Communist Trial," in *American*

Political Trials, ed. Michal R. Belknap (Westport, CT: Greenwood Press, 1981), 233–262; United States v. Sacher, 182 F.2d 416 (2d Cir. 1950). Frank initially concluded the lawyers were owed due process before the contempt citation was imposed, but he changed his mind. Marvin Schick, *Learned Hand's Court* (Baltimore: Johns Hopkins Press, 1970), 291; Sacher v. United States, 343 U.S. 1 (1949).

20. Felix Frankfurter, "A Lawyer's Duty as to a Retainer in an Unpopular Case," *American Bar Association Journal* 34, 1 (January 1948): 22; Louis Joughin and Edmund M. Morgan, *The Legacy of Sacco & Vanzetti* (1948; reprint, Princeton, NJ: Princeton University Press, 1978), 377, 319.

21. Reginald Heber Smith, Memorandum Concerning Complaints against Lawyers, February 11, 1949, 14–16; Smith, "Survey of the Legal Profession," 553 (indicating a published version forthcoming, which never occurred).

22. Curtis, "Ethics of Advocacy," 14–17. Curtis suggested that Sacco and Vanzetti were guilty, to which Hill replied, "I have never said, and I cannot say, what I think on that subject because, you see, Charlie, I was their counsel." Curtis, 18; Curtis, *It's Your Law*, 29–31; Moshik Temkin, *The Sacco-Vanzetti Affair: America on Trial* (New Haven, CT: Yale University Press, 2009), 1; Joughin and Morgan, *Legacy of Sacco & Vanzetti*, 319.

23. Belknap, *Cold War*, 220, 232–233n15; Stanley I. Kutler, *The American Inquisition: Justice and Injustice in the Cold War* (New York: Hill & Wang, 1982), ch. 6; Jerold Auerbach, *Unequal Justice: Lawyers and Social Change in Modern America* (New York: Oxford University Press, 1976), 240–246.

24. *Sacher*, 343 U.S. at 13; *Sacher*, 182 F.2d at 454.

25. Philip L. Graham, "A Publisher Looks at the Law," *Record* 7, 1 (January 1952): 20, 27–28.

26. George Martin, *Causes and Conflicts: The Centennial History of the Association of the Bar of the City of New York, 1870–1970* (Boston: Houghton Mifflin, 1970), 277; "Sessions," *Annual Report of the American Bar Association* 75 (1950): 94.

27. "The Proposed Anti-Communist Oath: Opposition Expressed to Association's Policy," *American Bar Association Journal* 37, 2 (February 1951): 123–126; Zechariah Chafee Jr., *The Blessings of Liberty* (Philadelphia: J. B. Lippincott, 1956), ch. 6, 159; Ralph S. Brown Jr. and John D. Fassett, "Loyalty Tests for Admission to the Bar," *University of Chicago Law Review* 20, 3 (Spring 1953): 497.

28. Tom C. Clark, "Civil Rights: The Boundless Responsibility of Lawyers," *American Bar Association Journal* 32, 8 (August 1946): 457; Kutler, *American Inquisition*, 154 (quoting August 30, 1949, *Look* magazine article by Clark); John P. Frank, "The United States Supreme Court: 1950–51," *University of Chicago Law Review* 19, 2 (Winter 1952): 199; "The Independence of the Bar," *Lawyers Guild Review* 13, 4 (Winter 1953): 164–165. The elite Philadelphia law firm Drinker, Biddle & Reath, with the support of politically conservative Henry Drinker, represented persons called to testify before the House Un-American Activities Committee and several of the nine officers of the Communist Party of Pennsylvania, as did other major firms in the city. Gardner and McKay, *Building a Law Firm*, 41–42.

29. "Report," *Annual Report of the American Bar Association* 76 (1951): 586–600; "Proceedings," *Annual Report of the American Bar Association* 76 (1951): 531–533, 545–548; "Report," *Annual Report of the American Bar Association* 77 (1952): 463.

30. *Yale Biographical Dictionary of American Law*, s.v. "Seymour, Whitney North"; *American Bar Association Journal* 45, 4 (April 1959): 369; "Report," *Annual Report of the American Bar Association* 78 (1953): 304; "Proceedings," *Annual Report of the American Bar Association* 78 (1953): 132.

31. "Report," *Annual Report of the American Bar Association* 78 (1953): 307; Irving R. Kaufman, "Representation by Counsel: A Threatened Right," *American Bar Association Journal* 40, 4 (April 1954): 299–302.

32. *Annual Report of the American Bar Association* 78 (1953): 294, 439.

33. "Lawyers and the Fifth Amendment," *American Bar Association Journal* 39, 12 (December 1953): 1084; Ralph S. Brown Jr., "Lawyers and the Fifth Amendment: A Dissent," *American Bar Association Journal* 40, 5 (May 1954): 404–407; Erwin N. Griswold, *The 5th Amendment Today* (Cambridge, MA: Harvard University Press, 1955), 14–19; Telford Taylor, *Grand Inquest* (New York: Simon & Schuster, 1955), 196–199; Daniel H. Pollitt, "Fifth Amendment Plea before Congressional Committees Investigating Subversion: Motives and Justifiable Presumptions—A Survey of 120 Witnesses," *University of Pennsylvania Law Review* 106, 8 (June 1958): 1117–1137 (explaining why innocent persons invoke the privilege); John Charles Boger, "Daniel H. Pollitt: In Memoriam," *North Carolina Law Review* 89, 1 (December 2010): 9–16; Hoffman v. United States, 341 U.S. 479, 486 (1951) (explaining the breadth of the privilege); Halliday, "Idiom of Legalism," 938–940 (Chicago Bar Association's opposition to relaxing the privilege).

34. Larry Tye, *Demagogue: The Life and Long Shadow of Senator Joe McCarthy* (Boston: Houghton Mifflin Harcourt, 2020); "'I Am Happy to Plead Guilty,'" *Newsweek*, January 25, 1954, 30; "Letters," *Newsweek*, March 1, 1954, 2–3; *Record* 8, 2 (February 1953): 57 (printing January 1953 ABCNY resolution).

35. "Report," *Annual Report of the American Bar Association* 79 (1954): 319; Tye, *Demagogue*, ch. 9.

36. Tye, *Demagogue*, ch. 9. Shamefully, the *ABA Journal* did not publish a review of Taylor's *Grand Inquest*. Kutler, *American Inquisition*, 182.

37. David F. Maxwell, "The Public View of the Profession," *Annual Report of the American Bar Association* 82 (1957): 364; Lucas A. Powe Jr., *The Warren Court and American Politics* (Cambridge, MA: Harvard University Press, 2000), 135–178; Schware v. Board of Law Examiners, 353 U.S. 232 (1957); Konigsberg v. State Bar of California, 353 U.S. 252 (1957).

38. "Sessions," *Annual Report of the American Bar Association* 82 (1957): 127; "The President's Proclamation," *American Bar Association Journal* 44, 4 (April 1958): 343; Charles S. Rhyne, "'Law Day—U.S.A.': Emphasizing the Supremacy of Law," *American Bar Association Journal* 44, 4 (April 1958): 313–316; Jason Krause, "Charlie Rhyne's Big Idea," *American Bar Association Journal* 94, 5 (May 2008): 65; David Ray Papke, "Law Day," in *Oxford Companion to American Law*, ed. Kermit L. Hall et al. (New York: Oxford University Press, 2002), 491.

39. *Lawyers in the United States: Distribution and Income: Part II Income* (1958), 3; Robert M. Segal and John Fei, "The Economics of the Legal Profession: An Analysis by States," *American Bar Association Journal* 39, 2 (February 1953): 113; National Conference of Accountants and Lawyers, "Statements of Principles in the Field of Federal Income Taxation," *Annual Report of the American Bar Association* 76 (1951): 699; "Report,"

Annual Report of the American Bar Association 82 (1957): 316; "Sessions," *Annual Report of the American Bar Association* 82 (1958): 127; "Report," *Annual Report of the American Bar Association* 83 (1958): 435; John C. Satterfield, "The American Bar Association Takes a Look at the Economic Status of the Legal Profession," *American Bar Association Journal* 44, 2 (February 1958): 156–157.

40. *Annual Report of the American Bar Association* 83 (1958): 436–437; American Bar Association Special Committee on Economics of Law Practice, *The 1958 Lawyer and His 1938 Dollar* (American Bar Association, 1958).

41. "Report," *Annual Report of the American Bar Association* 83 (1958): 399; *1958 Lawyer*, 3; Reginald Heber Smith, foreword to Segal and Fei, "Economics of the Legal Profession," 111 ("The brutal fact is that the lawyers of the United States have been as indifferent to their own interests as they have been jealous of, and faithful to, the interests of their clients").

42. *Lawyers' Economic Problems and Some Bar Association Solutions* (n.d.), 15, 26. Satterfield established a minimum fee schedule for Mississippi lawyers. John C. Satterfield Collection, University of Mississippi, http://www.olemiss.edu/depts/general_library/archives/finding_aids/MUM00685.html#ref4. In the early 1960s the accounting firm Price Waterhouse studied billable hours for the Special Committee on Economics, which generated law firms' rush to adopt the billable hour. William G. Ross, *The Honest Hour: The Ethics of Time-Based Billing by Attorneys* (Durham, NC: Carolina Academic Press, 1996), 2.

43. Ariens, "Rise and Fall," 67–68. ABA Informal Opinions 506 (May 31, 1962) and 238 (March 28, 1963) followed ABA Formal Opinions 297 and 305.

44. John D. Conner and N. S. Clifton, "Income of Lawyers, 1961–1962," *American Bar Association Journal* 51, 8 (August 1965): 753–755; Cullen Smith and N. S. Clifton, "Income of Lawyers, 1965," *American Bar Association Journal* 55, 6 (June 1969): 562–564; "Report," *Annual Report of the American Bar Association* 87 (1962): 599.

45. *The American Bar Foundation Annual Report, 1957–1958* (Chicago: American Bar Foundation, 1958), 7–8, 18; Philbrick McCoy, "The Canons of Ethics: A Reappraisal by the Organized Bar," *American Bar Association Journal* 43, 1 (January 1957): 38–42; "Report," *Annual Report of the American Bar Association* 82 (1957): 300–301; *Report of the Special Committee of the American Bar Foundation on Canons of Ethics (June 30, 1958)* (Chicago: American Bar Foundation, 1958), 92, 100; Robert T. McCracken, "The Canons of Ethics: Some Observations on a Reappraisal," *American Bar Association Journal* 43, 12 (December 1957): 1098–1100.

46. *American Bar Foundation Annual Report, 1957–1958*, 18; *Report of Special Committee of American Bar Foundation*, ch. 5. The McCoy Committee's report was not discussed in detail in the ABF's *1958 Annual Report* either.

47. Letter from Ja[me]s L. Shepherd Jr., Chairman, Standing Committee on Professional Ethics, to William P. Roberts, December 31, 1959, A. James Casner Papers, box 3, folder 8, Harvard Law School Library.

48. "Formal Op. 270 (November 30, 1945)," in *American Bar Association Opinions*, 560; Blaustein and Porter, *American Lawyer*, 249–250; Drinker, *Legal Ethics*, 159–169, ch. 4; *Report of Special Committee of American Bar Foundation*, 89–90; Brotherhood of Railroad Trainmen v. Virginia State Bar, 377 U.S. 1 (1964).

49. Drinker, *Legal Ethics*, 4–5.

50. Lon L. Fuller and John D. Randall, "Professional Responsibility: A Statement," *South Carolina Law Quarterly* 11, 3 (Spring 1959): 306–320; "Professional Responsibility: Report of the Joint Conference," *American Bar Association Journal* 44, 12 (December 1958): 1159–1162, 1216–1218; *Annual Report of the American Bar Association* 77 (1952): 437, 41.

51. Michael Ariens, "American Legal Ethics in an Age of Anxiety," *St. Mary's Law Journal* 40, 2 (2008): 427–428; "State Delegates Nominate New Officers and Governors," *American Bar Association Journal* 45, 4 (April 1959): 368–369; Erwin N. Griswold, "In Memoriam: A. James Casner," *Harvard Law Review* 104, 5 (March 1991): 981–988; "A. James Casner, ALI's Senior Reporter, Dies at Age of 83," *ALI Reporter* 13, 1 (October 1990): 1–2; Robert S. Summers, *Lon L. Fuller* (Stanford, CA: Stanford University Press, 1984); *Yale Biographical Dictionary of American Law*, s.v. "Fuller, Lon L."

52. Letter from Elliott E. Cheatham to Lon L. Fuller and Harry W. Jones, September 21, 1953, Lon L. Fuller Papers, box 2, folder 8, Harvard Law School Library; Elliott E. Cheatham, *Cases and Materials on the Legal Profession*, 2nd ed. (Brooklyn, NY: Foundation Press, 1955); Lon L. Fuller, "Professional Responsibility: A Statement (Aug. 5, 1954)," Fuller Papers, box 1, folder 1; Fuller and Randall, "Professional Responsibility," 1216.

53. Fuller and Randall, "Professional Responsibility," 1216–1217.

54. Lon L. Fuller, "Professional Responsibility: A Statement (May 2, 1955)," 1, Casner Papers, box 37, folder 5; Fuller and Randall, "Professional Responsibility," 1159; Lon L. Fuller, "Professional Responsibility: A Statement (October 1, 1957)," Fuller Papers, box 1, folder 1.

55. Robert P. Lawry, "The Central Moral Tradition of Lawyering," *Hofstra Law Review* 19, 2 (Winter 1991): 311–363.

56. L. L. Fuller, "The Philosophy of Codes of Ethics," *Electrical Engineering* 73 (October 1955): 917; Lon L. Fuller, "The Forms and Limits of Adjudication," *Harvard Law Review* 92, 2 (December 1978): 353–409 (parts of which echo in the statement); Lon L. Fuller, "What the Law School Can Contribute to the Making of Lawyers," in *Education for Professional Responsibility* (Pittsburgh: Carnegie Press, 1948), 32–35.

57. Fuller and Randall, "Professional Responsibility," 1160; David Luban, "Rediscovering Fuller's Legal Ethics," *Georgetown Journal of Legal Ethics* 11, 4 (Summer 1988): 820–827; David Luban, *Legal Ethics and Human Dignity* (New York: Cambridge University Press, 2007), 130 (critiquing Fuller).

58. Letter from Lon L. Fuller to John D. Randall, July 10, 1958, Casner Papers, box 37, folder 10; "Proceedings," *Annual Report of the American Bar Association* 83 (1958): 167–168; "Proceedings," *Annual Report of the American Bar Association* 84 (1959): 541–542.

59. John C. Satterfield, "Address of the President," *Annual Report of the American Bar Association* 87 (1962): 516–542; John C. Satterfield, "Law and Lawyers in a Changing World: The President's Annual Address," *American Bar Association Journal* 48, 10 (October 1962): 922–935; "Report," *Annual Report of the American Bar Association* 87 (1962): 726–729.

60. Eugene V. Rostow, "The Lawyer and His Client (Part I)," *American Bar Association Journal* 48, 1 (January 1962): 27; Eugene V. Rostow, "The Lawyer and His Client (Part

II)," *American Bar Association Journal* 48, 2 (February 1962): 146–151; *Yale Biographical Dictionary of American Law*, s.v. "Rostow, Eugene Victor"; "Tributes," *Yale Law Journal* 113, 1 (November 2003): 1–25.

61. "Report," *Annual Report of the American Bar Association* 86 (1961): 476, 478. Rush H. Limbaugh was the committee chairman, and the language indicates disagreement with the substantive aims of those active in the civil rights movement.

62. Rostow, *"Lawyer and His Client (*Part II)," 150.

63. "Report," *Annual Report of the American Bar Association* 87 (1962): 578–580.

64. Leon Jaworski, "The Unpopular Cause," *American Bar Association Journal* 47, 7 (July 1961): 714–717; John Edgar Hoover, "Shall It Be Law or Tyranny," *American Bar Association Journal* 48, 2 (February 1962): 119 ("The Communist Party has every right to legitimate legal counsel"); "Symposium: The Right to Counsel and the 'Unpopular Cause,'" *University of Pittsburgh Law Review* 20, 4 (June 1959): 725–753; Joseph E. Downs and Alvin L. Goldman, "The Obligation of Lawyers to Represent Unpopular Defendants," *Howard Law Journal* 9, 1 (Winter 1963): 49–67; Minor Alexander, "The Right to Counsel for the Politically Unpopular," *Law in Transition* 22, 1 (Spring 1962): 19–45.

65. Gideon v. Wainwright, 372 U.S. 335 (1963); NAACP v. Virginia ex rel. Button, 371 U.S. 45 (1963). *Gideon* did not apply to misdemeanors, allowing authorities flexibility in charging and holding arrested protesters; in 1964 the Mississippi legislature broadened the penalties for breach of the peace and "increased maximum penalties for violation of municipal ordinances." John Dittmer, *Local People: The Struggle for Civil Rights in Mississippi* (Urbana: University of Illinois Press, 1994), 229.

66. Ann Garity Connell, *The Lawyers' Committee for Civil Rights under Law: The Making of a Public Interest Group* (Chicago: Lawyers' Committee for Civil Rights under Law, 2003), 77n128, 80; "Report," *Annual Report of the American Bar Association* 88 (1963): 614–618; "Proceedings," *Annual Report of the American Bar Association* 88 (1963): 424.

67. Connell, *Lawyers' Committee*, 114; "Report," *Annual Report of the American Bar Association* 88 (1963): 496–504.

68. Daniel H. Pollitt, "Counsel for the Unpopular Cause: The 'Hazard of Being Undone,'" *North Carolina Law Review* 43, 1 (December 1964): 11–15 (reprinting in part Daniel H. Pollitt, "Lawyers and Neglected Clients," *Harper's*, August 1964, 81); Howard R. Sacks, ed., *Defending the Unpopular Client* (National Council on Legal Clinics, 1961), 1 (this guide was made into a film hosted by elite criminal defense lawyer Edward Bennett Williams).

69. Bruce Watson, *Freedom Summer: The Savage Season of 1964 that Made Mississippi Burn and Made America a Democracy* (New York: Penguin Random House, 2011); Dittmer, *Local People*, chs. 10, 11. Less than three weeks later, the bodies of civil rights workers James Chaney, Michael Schwerner, and Andrew Goodman were found near Philadelphia, Mississippi. Watson, 205–211; Jack Oppenheim, "The Abdication of the Southern Bar," in *Southern Justice*, ed. Leon Friedman (Westport, CT: Greenwood Press, 1975), 128–129; Pollitt, "Counsel for the Unpopular Cause," 13; *The Mississippi Bar's Centennial: "A Legacy of Service"* (LEXIS-NEXIS, 2006), 139–140; Sanders v. Russell, 401 F.2d 241, 245 (5th Cir. 1968); Connell, *Lawyers' Committee*, 131. The Mississippi Bar Association's authorized history omits this resolution but indicates that "322 members"

joined a Special Liaison Committee "to provide attorneys for those who sought legal assistance in civil rights cases," which is misleading. *Mississippi Bar's Centennial*, 240.

70. Connell, *Lawyers' Committee*, 131–132; Pollitt, "Counsel for the Unpopular Cause," 24n73 (noting that a white civil rights defendant wrote to forty white Mississippi lawyers requesting representation, all of whom declined).

71. Connell, *Lawyers' Committee*, 132–134; William L. Marbury, "New Responsibilities for the Bar," *American Bar Association Journal* 53, 4 (April 1967): 319; Oppenheim, "Abdication," 127–135.

72. Connell, *Lawyers' Committee*, 157–159. National Lawyers Guild lawyers also represented Mississippians during Freedom Summer. Dittmer, *Local People*, 230. Efforts in federal district courts in Mississippi to limit the appearances of unlicensed lawyers were overturned by the Fifth Circuit. Sanders v. Russell, 401 F.2d 241 (5th Cir. 1968).

73. Marbury, "New Responsibilities," 318–319.

74. George Lewis, *Massive Resistance: The White Response to the Civil Rights Movement* (New York: Oxford University Press, 2006), 177; Earl Johnson Jr., *Justice and Reform: The Formative Years of the American Legal Services Program*, 2nd ed. (New Brunswick, NJ: Transaction Books, 1978), 39–43, 49–70.

75. Randall B. Woods, *Prisoners of Hope: Lyndon B. Johnson, the Great Society, and the Limits of Liberalism* (New York: Basic Books, 2016); Steven M. Teles, *The Rise of the Conservative Legal Movement: The Battle for Control of the Law* (Princeton, NJ: Princeton University Press, 2008), 32–34; John C. Jeffries Jr., *Justice Lewis F. Powell, Jr.* (New York: Charles Scribner's Sons, 1994), 197–201; "Proceedings," *Annual Report of the American Bar Association* 90 (1965): 110–111.

76. Marion A. Ellis and Howard E. Covington Jr., *Sages of Their Craft: The First Fifty Years of the American College of Trial Lawyers* (West Group, 2000), 7–23, 66; "A Code of Trial Conduct, Promulgated by the American College of Trial Lawyers," *American Bar Association Journal* 43, 3 (March 1957): 223–226, 283.

77. "Code of Trial Conduct," 224; "Opinion 280 (June 18, 1949)," in *American Bar Association Opinions*, 588–590.

78. "Code of Trial Conduct," 224; Michael Ariens, "Brougham's Ghost," *Northern Illinois University Law Review* 35, 2 (Spring 2015): 301–302.

79. Edward H. Levi, *Four Talks on Legal Education* (Chicago: University of Chicago Law School, 1952), 31–32; Robert G. Storey, "The Legal Profession and Criminal Justice," *Journal of the American Judicature Society* 36, 6 (April 1953): 166–173; Daniel T. O'Connell, "Problems Confronting Trial Courts," *Journal of the American Judicature Society* 37, 3 (October 1953): 73 ("Why do those who have started practice within the last two score years, or perhaps a little earlier, regard practice of the criminal law as unworthy of their time and minds?"); Samuel Dash, "The Emerging Role and Function of the Criminal Defense Lawyer," *North Carolina Law Review* 47, 3 (1968–1969): 598n1; Arthur Lewis Wood, *Criminal Lawyer* (New Haven, CT: College & University Press, 1967), 48–49, 57.

80. Lunce v. Overlade, 244 F.2d 108, 109–110 (7th Cir. 1957).

81. W. M. Moldoff, "Incompetency of Counsel Chosen by Accused as Affecting Validity of Conviction," *American Law Reports 2d* 74 (1960): 1397.

82. Wood, *Criminal Lawyer*, 28–30, 63–67, 256, 109, 131.

83. Ralph Slovenko, "Attitudes on Legal Representation of Accused Persons," *American Criminal Law Quarterly* 2, 3 (Spring 1964): 105.

84. J. Skelly Wright, "The Renaissance of the Criminal Law: The Responsibility of the Trial Lawyer," *Duquesne University Law Review* 4, 2 (1965–1966): 211–223; B. J. George Jr., "A New Approach to Criminal Law," *Harper's* 228 (April 1964): 183–188; Henry H. Foster Jr., "Lawmen, Medicine Men and Good Samaritans," *American Bar Association Journal* 52, 3 (March 1966): 225; Andrew S. Watson, "On the Low Status of the Criminal Bar: Psychological Contributions of the Law School," *Texas Law Review* 43, 3 (February 1965): 289–311; Abraham S. Blumberg, "The Practice of Law as a Confidence Game," *Law & Society Review* 1, 2 (June 1967): 24, 31; Abraham S. Blumberg, "Lawyers with Convictions," in *The Scales of Justice*, ed. Abraham S. Blumberg, 2nd ed. (New Brunswick, NJ: Transaction Books, 1973), 67–83; Jonathan D. Casper, *American Criminal Justice: The Defendant's Perspective* (Englewood Cliffs, NJ: Prentice-Hall, 1972), 123 ("For the bulk of the defendants—represented by public defenders—their attorney appeared to be at best a middleman and at worst an enemy agent"); "The Lawyer for the Defense," *American Bar Association Journal* 50, 10 (October 1964): 944.

85. "Report," *Annual Report of the American Bar Association* 90 (1965): 229–231; Jeffries, *Justice Powell*, 196–197; McMann v. Richardson, 397 U.S. 759, 771 (1970); Powe, *Warren Court*, chs. 15, 16; William J. Stuntz, *The Collapse of American Criminal Justice* (Cambridge, MA: Harvard University Press, 2011), 216–243; "Report," 41 F.R.D. 389 (1966).

86. Monroe Freedman, "Professional Responsibility of the Criminal Defense Lawyer: The Three Hardest Questions," *Michigan Law Review* 64, 8 (June 1966): 1469–1484; Monroe Freedman, *Lawyers' Ethics in an Adversary System* (Indianapolis: Bobbs-Merrill, 1975), 75; John T. Noonan Jr., "The Purposes of Advocacy and the Limits of Confidentiality," *Michigan Law Review* 64, 8 (June 1966): 1486; *Yale Biographical Dictionary of American Law*, s.v. "Noonan, John T., Jr."

87. Freedman, "Professional Responsibility," 1482–1484; Lon L. Fuller, "The Adversary System," in *Talks on American Law: A Series of Broadcast to Foreign Audiences*, ed. Harold S. Berman (New York: Vintage, 1961), 38.

88. David G. Bress, "Professional Ethics in Criminal Trials: A View of Defense Counsel's Responsibility," *Michigan Law Review* 64, 8 (June 1966): 1493–1498; Noonan, "Purposes of Advocacy," 1487–1489; Monroe H. Freedman, "Getting Honest about Perjury," *Georgetown Journal of Legal Ethics* 21, 1 (Winter 2008): 133n1.

89. Dash, "Emerging Role," 630–632; "Standards of Conduct for Prosecution and Defense Personnel: A Symposium," *American Criminal Law Quarterly* 5, 1 (Fall 1966): 8–10; Warren E. Burger, "Standards of Conduct for Prosecution and Defense Personnel: A Judge's Viewpoint," *American Criminal Law Quarterly* 5, 1 (Fall 1966): 12; Addison M. Bowman, "Standards of Conduct for Prosecution and Defense Personnel: An Attorney's Viewpoint," *American Criminal Law Quarterly* 5, 1 (Fall 1966): 30.

90. "Report," *Annual Report of the American Bar Association* 96 (1971): 289–309; "Proceedings," *Midyear Report of the American Bar Association* 96 (1971): 138; American Bar Association Project on Standards for Criminal Justice, "Standards Relating to the Prosecution Function and the Defense Function" (approved draft, 1971), 141.

91. ABA, "Standards," 145–146; Robert Lefcourt, introduction to *Law against the*

People: Essays to Demystify Law, Order and the Courts, ed. Robert Lefcourt (New York: Vintage Books, 1971), 4; Jonathan Black, introduction to *Radical Lawyers: Their Role in the Movement and in the Courts*, ed. Jonathan Black (New York: Avon Books, 1971), 12.

92. Paul A. Teschner, "Lawyer Morality," *George Washington Law Review* 38, 5 (July 1970): 834–835.

93. Jerome E. Carlin, *Lawyers on Their Own* (New Brunswick, NJ: Rutgers University Press, 1962), 158–159, 211; "Books for Lawyers," *American Bar Association Journal* 49, 3 (March 1963): 277 (Leonard S. Zubrensky).

94. Smigel, *Wall Street Lawyer*, 265, 305; "Books for Lawyers," *American Bar Association Journal* 50, 9 (September 1964): 863 (George D. Hornstein); Louis Auchincloss, *The Great World and Timothy Colt* (Boston: Houghton Mifflin, 1956).

95. Jerome E. Carlin, *Lawyers' Ethics: A Survey of the New York City Bar* (New York: Russell Sage Foundation, 1966), 52–53, 66–67, 71–76.

96. Carlin, chs. 6, 8, 148; Geoffrey C. Hazard Jr., foreword to Carlin, xx.

97. Quintin Johnstone and Dan Hopson Jr., *Lawyers and Their Work* (Indianapolis: Bobbs-Merrill, 1967), 561–563; "Books for Lawyers," *American Bar Association Journal* 53, 11 (November 1967): 1054–1055 (Roy E. Willy).

98. Joel F. Handler, *The Lawyer and His Community: The Practicing Bar in a Middle-Sized City* (Madison: University of Wisconsin Press, 1967), 112, 155; "Books for Lawyers," *American Bar Association Journal* 53, 12 (December 1967): 1142–1143 (Ray D. Henson).

99. "Proceedings," *Annual Report of the American Bar Association* 89 (1964): 381–383; Jeffries, *Justice Powell*, 195–196; letter from Lewis J. Powell Jr. to Edward L. Wright, September 9, 1964, Casner Papers, box 25, folder 1.

100. "Henry Drinker Receives American Bar Association Medal," *American Bar Association Journal* 50, 10 (October 1964): 942–943; Sherman S. Welpton Jr., "Genesis of the Code of Trial Conduct," *American Bar Association Journal* 58, 7 (July 1972): 709–711; American College of Trial Lawyers, *Code of Trial Conduct* (American College of Trial Lawyers, 1963); John F. Sutton Jr., "The Proposed Amendments to the Texas Canons of Ethics," *Texas Bar Journal* 26, 11 (December 1963): 996–1003; Gilbert I. Low, "Proposed Amendments to the Texas Canons of Ethics," *Texas Bar Journal* 27, 11 (December 1964): 984–987; "December 10, 1963—San Francisco Lawyer Melvin Belli Takes over Jack Ruby Case in Dallas, Texas," YouTube, https://www.youtube.com/watch?v=ffP2Wzh34_g; Melvin Belli with Maurice C. Carroll, *Dallas Justice: The Real Story of Jack Ruby and His Trial* (New York: David McKay, 1964), 34–35; "Casus Belli," *Time*, March 27, 1964, 34; "Proceedings," *Annual Report of the American Bar Association* 89 (1964): 381.

101. Sherman S. Welpton Jr., interview by Olavi Maru, Los Angeles, November 3, 1976, American Bar Foundation Program on Oral History, 7.

102. Walter E. Craig, "The Challenges of Professional Responsibility," *American Bar Association Journal* 50, 9 (September 1964): 828.

103. *Brotherhood of Railroad Trainmen*, 377 U.S. at 8.

104. "Proceedings," *Annual Report of the American Bar Association* 89 (1964): 381–383; Edward L. Wright, "Study of the Canons of Ethics," *Catholic Lawyer* 11, 4 (Autumn 1965): 323–326.

105. "Memorandum Regarding Work of Special Committee on Evaluation of Ethical

Standards (Nov. 16, 1964)," Casner Papers, box 25, folder 1; Carrie Sharlow, "Michigan Lawyers in History: Glenn M. Coulter," *Michigan Bar Journal* 91, 11 (November 2012): 44–45; "Former Treasurer Coulter Dies," *American Bar Association Journal* 61, 3 (March 1975): 380; John Floyd Sutton Jr., interview by Olavi Maru, Houston, TX, December 20, 1976, American Bar Foundation Program on Oral History, 5; letter from Edward L. Wright, Chairman, to All Committee Members, January 5, 1965, Casner Papers, box 25, folder 2.

106. "Memorandum (Nov. 16, 1964)," 3–4, Casner Papers, box 102; "Meeting of Special Committee on Evaluation of Ethical Standards, American Bar Association (Dec. 3–4, 1964)," 5, Casner Papers, box 102; Canon 3, Code of Professional Responsibility (1969); United Mine Workers v. Illinois St. B. Ass'n, 389 U.S. 217 (1967) (extending holding).

107. "Memorandum (Nov. 16, 1964)," 2–5; letter from Geoffrey C. Hazard Jr. to Edward L. Wright, February 26, 1965, 2, Casner Papers, box 25, folder 3; letter from John F. Sutton Jr., Reporter, to Wright Committee Members, October 14, 1965, 2, Casner Papers, box 25, folder 5; Sutton interview, 4–5, 13; Wright, "Study of the Canons of Ethics," 325.

108. Wright interview, 10; Welpton interview, 16; "Report," *Annual Report of the American Bar Association* 91 (1966): 604.

109. Preamble to Code of Professional Responsibility of the American Bar Association (tentative draft, October 1968); Sutton interview, 14; *Annual Report of the American Bar Association* 94 (1969): 731–732; Welpton interview, 13–14 ("I recall that Ed Wright and John Sutton were all in favor, initially, of putting the ethical considerations over into a separate document. . . . I was very much in favor of putting the whole thing into one composite picture because I thought if you took the ethical considerations away and just had the disciplinary rules alone it just wouldn't be a good format at all."); Sutton interview, 4 ("My third point was that the Code should not be reduced to a mere set of criminal rules, but it should contain ethical guidance for the lawyer").

110. "Report," *Annual Report of the American Bar Association* 94 (1969): 728. For example, draft Disciplinary Rule (DR) 1–102(A)(6) states, "persistently engages in any illegal conduct," and adopted DR 1–102(A)(4) states, "engage in conduct involving dishonesty, fraud, deceit, or misrepresentation." Code of Professional Responsibility Preliminary Draft (January 15, 1969), v–vi.

111. "Preliminary Statement of the Code of Professional Responsibility," *Annual Report of the American Bar Association* 94 (1969): 731–732. The preamble to the preliminary draft declared that footnotes were informative only and "will be deleted from the final report." But they remained.

112. Ariens, "American Legal Ethics," 439n489; John M. A. DiPippa, "Lon Fuller, the Model Code, and the Model Rules," *South Texas Law Review* 37, 2 (March 1996): 327; Lon L. Fuller, *The Morality of Law*, rev. ed. (New Haven, CT: Yale University Press, 1969), 5 ("Where the morality of aspiration starts at the top of human achievement, the morality of duty starts at the bottom"); Luban, "Rediscovering Fuller's Legal Ethics," 806–807, nn. 30, 32; "Preamble and Preliminary Statement," *Annual Report of the American Bar Association* 94 (1969): 731–732.

113. "Code of Professional Responsibility," *Annual Report of the American Bar Association* 94 (1969): 783n5; Fuller and Randall, "Professional Responsibility," 1160.

114. "Report," *Annual Report of the American Bar Association* 97 (1972): 741; William B. Spann Jr., "The Legal Profession Needs a New Code of Ethics," *Bar Leader* 3, 3 (November–December 1977): 2–3; John F. Sutton Jr., "How Vulnerable Is the Code of Professional Responsibility?" *North Carolina Law Review* 57, 4 (May 1979): 497–517.

115. "Proceedings," *Annual Report of the American Bar Association* 94 (1969): 389–392; *Annual Report of the American Bar Association* 94 (1969): 739, 741; "Report," *Annual Report of the American Bar Association* 97 (1972): 740; R. W. Nahstoll, "Limitations on Group Legal Services Arrangements under the Code of Professional Responsibility, DR 2–103(D)(5): Stale Wine in New Bottles," *Texas Law Review* 48, 2 (January 1970): 334–350; Judith L. Maute, "Pre-paid and Group Legal Services: Thirty Years after the Storm," *Fordham Law Review* 70, 3 (December 2001): 915–943; Judith L. Maute, "Changing Conceptions of Lawyers' Pro Bono Responsibilities: From Chance Noblesse Oblige to Stated Expectations," *Tulane Law Review* 77, 1 (November 2002): 123–124.

116. Com. on Pro. Ethics and Cond. of the Iowa B. Ass'n v. Randall, 285 N.W.2d 161 (Iowa 1979), *cert. denied*, 446 U.S. 946 (1980); Michael Ariens, "The Fall of an American Lawyer," *Journal of the Legal Profession* 46, 2 (Spring 2022): 195–243.

117. *Randall*, 285 N.W.2d at 165, quoting Com. on Pro. Ethics v. Behnke, 276 N.W.2d 838, 844 (Iowa 1979).

118. In re Randall, 640 F.2d 898 (8th Cir.), *cert. denied*, 454 U.S. 880 (1981).

119. "Preamble to Code," *Annual Report of the American Bar Association* 94 (1969): 731.

120. "Obituary," *Cedar Rapids [IA] Gazette*, December 30, 1983, 10A; "Preamble to Code," 731; "Happenings," *American Bar Association Journal* 70, 4 (April 1984): 146.

6. BEGINNING AND ENDING, 1970–1983

1. Whitney North Seymour, foreword to *Is Law Dead?* ed. Eugene V. Rostow (New York: Simon & Schuster, 1971), 7 (nodding to "Is God Dead?" *Time*, April 1966, cover story); Jeffrey B. Morris, *"Making Sure We Are True to Our Founders": The Association of the Bar of the City of New York, 1970–1995* (New York: Fordham University Press, 1997), 22–25.

2. "The President's Proclamation," *American Bar Association Journal* 44, 4 (April 1958): 343; Philip S. Foner, *May Day: A Short History of the International Workers' Holiday, 1886–1986* (New York: International Publishers, 1986).

3. Rick Perlstein, *Nixonland: The Rise of a President and the Fracturing of America* (New York: Simon & Schuster, 2008), 477–489. Hundreds of ABCNY lawyers traveled to Washington on May 20, 1970, to protest the invasion of Cambodia. Morris, *"Making Sure,"* 1–2, 25–29; Francis T. Plimpton, "Report of the President, 1969–1970," *Record* 25, 7 (October 1970): 459 ("galvanic shock to the New York legal community").

4. Gerald B. Lefcourt, "The Radical Lawyer under Attack," in *Law against the People: Essays to Demystify Law, Order and the Courts*, ed. Robert Lefcourt (New York: Vintage Books, 1971), 254, 258; Donald T. Weckstein, "Maintaining the Integrity and Competence of the Legal Profession," *Texas Law Review* 48, 2 (January 1970): 267–284; Don-

ald T. Weckstein, "Training for Professionalism," *Connecticut Law Review* 4, 3 (Winter 1971–1972): 409–436.

5. Richard Abel, *American Lawyers* (New York: Oxford University Press, 1989), 160; "Report," *Annual Report of the American Bar Association* 97 (1972): 818–838; "Special Report: The Job Gap for College Graduates in the '70s," *Business Week*, September 23, 1972, 51; Marc S. Galanter, "Planet of the APs: Reflections on the Scale of Law and Its Users," *Buffalo Law Review* 53, 5 (Winter 2006): 1379, fig. 2 (charting increase in legal services from 1967 to 2002); Richard H. Sander and E. Douglass Williams, "Why Are There so Many Lawyers? Perspectives on a Turbulent Market," *Law & Social Inquiry* 14, 3 (Summer 1989): 448; American Bar Association, "Statistics Archives" (historical data 1963–2013), https://www.americanbar.org/groups/legal_education/resources/sta tistics/statistics-archives/; ABA National Lawyer Population Survey, "Historical Trend 1878–2021," https://www.americanbar.org/content/dam/aba/administrative/market_re search/2021-national-lawyer-population-survey.pdf; Barbara A. Curran, "American Lawyers in the 1980s: A Profession in Transition," *Law & Society Review* 20, 1 (1986): 20, table 1.

6. David R. Brink, "President's Page: Change and Challenge," *American Bar Association Journal* 67, 9 (September 1981): 1080; foreword to *Report of the Task Force on the Role of the Lawyer in the 1980s* (American Bar Association, 1981), v; Murray L. Schwartz, "The Death and Regeneration of Legal Ethics," *American Bar Foundation Research Journal* 4 (Fall 1980): 962; Sander and Williams, "Why Are There so Many Lawyers?" 448.

7. Abel, *American Lawyers*, 290.

8. John Griffiths, "Ideology in Criminal Procedure, or a Third 'Model' of the Criminal Process," *Yale Law Journal* 79, 3 (January 1970): 369n42; In re Griffiths, 413 U.S. 717, 732 (1973) (Burger, C.J., dissenting); Marvin Frankel, "The Search for the Truth: An Umpireal View," *University of Pennsylvania Law Review* 123, 5 (May 1975): 1055–1059; Michael S. Ariens, "Sorting: Legal Specialization and the Privatization of the American Legal Profession," *Georgetown Journal of Legal Ethics* 29, 3 (Summer 2016): 587–589n62.

9. *Griffiths*, 413 U.S. at 732 (Burger, C.J., dissenting); *Black's Law Dictionary*, s.v. "officer of the court" ("a lawyer, who is obliged to obey court rules and who owes a duty of candor to the court"); Barbara Ann Kipfer and Robert L. Chapman, eds., *American Slang*, 4th abr. ed. (New York: Collins, 2001), 333 (defining "mouthpiece" as "a lawyer").

10. David Langum, *William M. Kunstler, The Most Hated Lawyer in America* (New York: New York University Press, 1999); William M. Kunstler and Sheila Isenberg, *My Life as a Radical Lawyer* (New York: Carol Publishing, 1994); "'The Blackest White Man I Know,'" *Life*, July 25, 1969, 50; Victor Navasky, "Right On! With Lawyer William Kunstler," *New York Times Magazine*, April 19, 1970, 92; John Schultz, *The Chicago Conspiracy Trial*, rev. ed. (Chicago: University of Chicago Press, 1993); James W. Ely Jr., "The Chicago Conspiracy Case," in *American Political Trials*, ed. Michal R. Belknap (Westport, CT: Greenwood Press, 1981), 263–285; Michal R. Belknap, "Chicago Conspiracy Case," in *Oxford Companion to American Law*, ed. Kermit L. Hall et al. (New York: Oxford University Press, 2002), 92.

11. Preamble to Code of Professional Responsibility, *Annual Report of the American Bar Association* 94 (1969): 731.

12. "A Lawyer for Hire," *American Bar Association Journal* 56, 6 (June 1970): 552;

introduction to *Standards Relating to the Defense Function* (American Bar Association, 1971), 147.

13. "Views of Our Readers: Kunstler and the Lawyer's Role," *American Bar Association Journal* 56, 8 (August 1970): 716, 722.

14. Florynce Kennedy, "The Whorehouse Theory of Law," in Lefcourt, *Law against the People*, 81; Michael Ariens, "The Agony of Modern Legal Ethics, 1970–1985," *St. Mary's Journal on Legal Malpractice and Legal Ethics* 5, 1 (2014): 164, nn. 229–230.

15. In re Dellinger, 461 F.2d 389 (7th Cir. 1972); In re Dellinger, 370 F. Supp. 1304, 1315 (N.D. Ill. 1973), *aff'd*, 502 F.2d 813 (7th Cir. 1974); John C. Tucker, *Trial and Error: The Education of a Courtroom Lawyer* (New York: Basic Books, 2003), 150–163 (interpreting events).

16. *Disorder in the Court* (New York: Pantheon Books, 1973), 337; Louis Nizer, "What to Do When the Judge Is Put up against the Wall," *New York Times Magazine*, April 5, 1970, 210; Louis Nizer, *My Life in Court* (New York: Doubleday, 1961); American Bar Association, "Standards Relating to the Judge's Role in Dealing with Trial Disruption (1971)," in *Disorder*, 343–348; Geoffrey C. Hazard Jr., "Securing Courtroom Decorum," *Yale Law Journal* 80, 2 (December 1970): 433–450; Edward H. Levi, *The Crisis in the Nature of Law* (New York: Association of the Bar of the City of New York, 1970).

17. "Views of Our Readers," 716, 722; Canon 5, Code of Professional Responsibility ("A lawyer should exercise independent professional judgment on behalf of a client").

18. Bill Bishop with Robert G. Cushing, *The Big Sort: Why the Clustering of Like-Minded America Is Tearing Us Apart* (Boston: Houghton Mifflin, 2014), 214n*; Marc Levinson, *An Extraordinary Time: The End of the Postwar Boom and the Return of the Ordinary Economy* (New York: Basic Books, 2016), 1–13; Robert J. Gordon, *The Rise and Fall of American Growth: The U.S. Standard of Living since the Civil War* (Princeton, NJ: Princeton University Press, 2016), 7, 522–531; Allen J. Matusow, *Nixon's Economy: Booms, Busts, Dollars, and Votes* (Lawrence: University Press of Kansas, 1998), 214–240; W. Carl Biven, *Jimmy Carter's Economy: Policy in an Age of Limits* (Chapel Hill: University of North Carolina Press, 2002); Judith Stein, *Pivotal Decade: How the United States Traded Factories for Finance in the Seventies* (New Haven, CT: Yale University Press, 2010); Table P-8: Age—People: All Races, by Median Income and Sex: 1947–2018, https://www.census.gov/data/tables/time-series/demo/income-poverty/historical-income-people.html (in 2018 dollars, median income for males was $40,810 in 1973 and $41,615 in 2018; inflation fell to 4.9 percent in December 1976 but rose to over 13 percent in December 1979 [https://www.bls.gov/opub/mlr/2014/article/one-hundred-years-of-price-change-the-consumer-price-index-and-the-american-inflation-experience.htm]; unemployment trended down from 7.5 percent in January 1977 to 6 percent in December 1979 [Bureau of Labor Statistics, Monthly Unemployment Rate, 1948–2020, https://data.bls.gov/timeseries/LNS14000000?years_option=all_years]); Michael Ariens, "Know the Law: A History of Legal Specialization," *South Carolina Law Review* 45, 5 (1994): 1054–1058; John P. Heinz and Edward O. Laumann, *Chicago Lawyers: The Social Structure of the Bar*, rev. ed. (Chicago: Northwestern University Press, 1994), 130–136; John P. Heinz et al., *Urban Lawyers: The New Social Structure of the Bar* (Chicago: University of Chicago Press, 2005), 37; Clara N. Carson with Jeeyoon Park, *The Lawyer Statistical Report: The U.S. Legal Profession in 2005* (Chicago: American Bar Foundation,

2012), 2, table 1; Benjamin H. Barton, *Glass Half Full: The Decline and Rebirth of the Legal Profession* (New York: Oxford University Press, 2014), 5, fig. 1.1; Sander and Williams, "Why Are There so Many Lawyers?" 448, table 9.

19. Archibald Cox, "The Loss of Mystical Qualities Makes It Harder to Revere the Law," *Student Lawyer* 3, 6 (February 1975): 10; Archibald Cox, "The Lawyer's Public Responsibilities," *Human Rights* 4, 1 (Fall 1974): 3; Peter Megargee Brown, "The Decline of the Lawyer's Professional Independence," in *The Lawyer's Professional Independence: Present Threats, Future Challenges*, ed. John B. Davidson (Chicago: ABA Press, 1984), 24; Michael Ariens, "The Rise and Fall of Social Trustee Professionalism," *Professional Lawyer* (2016): 52; Steven Brint, *In an Age of Experts: The Changing Roles of Professionals in Politics and Professional Life* (Princeton, NJ: Princeton University Press, 1994); Special Committee, New Jersey State Bar Association, Comments to Model Rules Discussion Draft (January 1980) (criticizing the preamble as marking a "significant departure from the traditional concept that the 'duty of the lawyer to his client and his duty to the legal system are the same'").

20. *Griffiths*, 413 U.S. at 732; Frankel, "Search for the Truth," 1055.

21. "Report," *Annual Report of the American Bar Association* 95 (1970): 783–989 (hereafter, cited as Clark Report); Vincent R. Johnson, "Justice Tom C. Clark's Legacy in the Field of Legal Ethics," *Journal of the Legal Profession* 29 (2004–2005): 33–70; Michael Franck, "New Life for Lawyer Self-Discipline: The Disciplinary Report of the Clark Committee," *Judicature* 54, 9 (April 1971): 383–389 (the author was the committee's reporter).

22. Clark Report, 797, 798, 804.

23. David F. Maxwell, "The Public View of the Profession," *Annual Report of the American Bar Association* 82 (1957): 362.

24. Clark Report, 799–805.

25. "Report," *Annual Report of the American Bar Association* 96 (1971): 714; "Report," *Annual Report of the American Bar Association* 97 (1972): 793–802; Michael C. Dorf, "Disbarment in the United States: Who Shall Do the Noisome Work?" *Columbia Journal of Law & Social Problems* 12, 1 (Fall 1975): 14n90.

26. "Report," *Annual Report of the American Bar Association* 98 (1973): 687.

27. "Report," *Annual Report of the American Bar Association* 99 (1974): 742; "Report," *Annual Report of the American Bar Association* 100 (1975): 818; "Report," *Annual Report of the American Bar Association* 103 (1978): 454–477; *Annual Report of the American Bar Association* 103 (1978): 233; "Report," *Annual Report of the American Bar Association* 104 (1979): 373–415; *Annual Report of the American Bar Association* 104 (1979): 258.

28. "Standards for Lawyer Discipline and Disability Proceedings Proposed Draft December 1978," *Annual Report of the American Bar Association* 104 (1979): 381, 387, 405; Jeanne Gray and Mark I. Harrison, "Standards of Lawyer Discipline and Disability Proceedings and the Evaluation of Lawyer Discipline Systems," *Capital University Law Review* 11, 3 (1982): 549n82 (the last duty was largely ignored); F. Raymond Marks and Darlene Cathcart, "Discipline within the Legal Profession: Is It Self-Regulation?" *University of Illinois Law Forum* 2 (1974): 209.

29. Gray and Harrison, "Standards," 545n66.

30. "Report," *Annual Report of the American Bar Association* 109 (1984): 386; Curran, "American Lawyers," 20, table 1; Abel, *American Lawyers*, 291, table 33; Sharon Tisher

and Lynn Bernabei, *Bringing the Bar to Justice* (Public Citizen, 1977), 93, ch. 5; Marks and Cathcart, "Discipline," 235.

31. William J. Stuntz, *The Collapse of American Criminal Justice* (Cambridge, MA: Harvard University Press, 2011), 247–249; Abraham S. Blumberg, "The Practice of Law as a Confidence Game," *Law & Society Review* 1, 2 (June 1967): 31; Jackson B. Battle, "In Search of the Adversary System—The Cooperative Practices of Private Criminal Defense Attorneys," *Texas Law Review* 50, 1 (December 1971): 61; Lynn M. Mather, *Plea Bargaining or Trial? The Process of Criminal Case Disposition* (Lexington, MA: Lexington Books, 1979), 23.

32. Canon 5, EC–13, and DR 7–103, Code of Professional Responsibility; Jerome H. Skolnick, "Social Control in the Adversary System," *Journal of Conflict Resolution* 11, 1 (March 1967): 57.

33. *Annual Report of the American Bar Association* 96 (1971): 289, 138; Standards Related to the Prosecution and Defense Function (approved draft, American Bar Association, 1971), 10; introduction to Standards Related to the Prosecution Function (American Bar Association, 1971), 23 ("the conduct of lawyers involved in the administration of criminal justice is neither supervised nor disciplined adequately in this country").

34. Standard 5.7(b), Prosecution Function, 39; introduction to Defense Function, 141–142.

35. Defense Function, 145–147; Standard 3.1(b), 157; Standard 5.2(a), 162–163.

36. Standard 5.7, Prosecution Function, 39, differs from Standard 7.6, Defense Function, 166–167; "Commentary," Defense Function, 272.

37. Standard 5.2(b), Defense Function, 163; Standard 7.7(c), Defense Function, 167.

38. Lauren A. Arn, "Implementation of the ABA Standards for Criminal Justice: A Progress Report," *American Criminal Law Review* 12, 3 (Winter 1975): 477–492; Martin Marcus, "The Making of the ABA Criminal Justice Standards: Forty Years of Success," *Criminal Justice* 23, 4 (Winter 2009): 10.

39. *The Other Face of Justice* (National Legal Aid and Defender Association, 1973), 70; Albert W. Alschuler, "The Defense Attorney's Role in Plea Bargaining," *Yale Law Journal* 84, 6 (May 1975): 1182–1188, 1200–1202, 1313; Skolnick, "Social Control," 58.

40. "Report," *Annual Report of the American Bar Association* 104 (1979): 320.

41. Standard 4–7.6(b), in *Standards for Criminal Justice*, 2nd ed. (American Bar Association, 1980), 4–92; the third edition (1991) stated: "Defense counsel's belief or knowledge that the witness is telling the truth does not preclude cross-examination." Robert P. Lawry, "Cross-Examining the Truthful Witness: The Ideal within the Central Moral Tradition of Lawyering," *Dickinson Law Review* 100, 3 (Spring 1995): 580 ("Appeals to honor and conscience are gone").

42. "Report," *Annual Report of the American Bar Association* 104 (1979): 320.

43. Warren's unusual "retirement" letters are discussed in G. Edward White, *Earl Warren: A Public Life* (New York: Oxford University Press, 1982), 307–313, 414n23; Laura Kalman, *Abe Fortas: A Biography* (New Haven, CT: Yale University Press, 1990), 327–356.

44. Robert Shogan, *A Question of Judgment: The Fortas Case and the Struggle for the Supreme Court* (Indianapolis: Bobbs-Merrill, 1971), 192.

45. William Lambert, "Fortas of the Supreme Court: A Question of Ethics," *Life*, May

9, 1969, 32; "ABA Formal Op. 322 (May 18, 1969)," *American Bar Association Journal* 55, 7 (July 1969): 666–668.

46. Bruce H. Kalk, "The Making of 'Mr. Justice Haynsworth'? The Rise, Fall, and Revival of Judge Clement F. Haynsworth Jr.," *South Carolina Historical Magazine* 117, 1 (January 2016): 16–18, 21–22; Shogan, *Question of Judgment*, 271–272 (positing that the ethics "controversy" provided cover to those substantively opposed to Haynsworth); John P. Frank, *Clement Haynsworth, the Senate, and the Supreme Court* (Charlottesville: University Press of Virginia, 1991), 64.

47. "Report," *Annual Report of the American Bar Association* 95 (1970): 1049–1051; Bruce Allen Murphy, *Wild Bill: The Legend and Life of William O. Douglas* (New York: Random House, 2003), 432–434.

48. "Report," *Annual Report of the American Bar Association* 96 (1971): 733; *Annual Report of the American Bar Association* 97 (1972): 351, 858, 556.

49. Preface to *Code of Judicial Conduct* (American Bar Association, 1972); E. Wayne Thode, *Reporter's Notes to Code of Judicial Conduct* (American Bar Association, 1973).

50. "Report," *Annual Report of the American Bar Association* 100 (1975): 860.

51. Raymond J. McKoski, "Judicial Discipline and the Appearance of Impropriety: What the Public Sees Is What the Judge Gets," *Minnesota Law Review* 94, 6 (June 2010): 1928; Raymond J. McKoski, "Disqualifying Judges When Their Impartiality Might Reasonably Be Questioned," *Arizona Law Review* 56, 2 (2014): 411–478; Leslie W. Abramson, "What Every Judge Should Know about the Appearance of Impropriety," *Albany Law Review* 79, 4 (2015–2016): 1579–1615.

52. "Commentary, Canon 2," *Code of Judicial Conduct*, 9.

53. Thode, *Reporter's Notes*, 8–9, 61; "Canon 3(C)(1)," *Code of Judicial Conduct*, 14; McKoski, "Judicial Discipline," 1930.

54. Stanley I. Kutler, *The Wars of Watergate: The Last Crisis of Richard Nixon* (New York: W. W. Norton, 1992), 272 (quoting an April 2, 1973, editorial in the *Rockford [IL] Morning Star*, a Republican paper); Jake Garn and Lincoln C. Oliphant, "Disqualification of Federal Judges under 28 U.S.C. 455(a): Some Observations on and Objections to an Attempt by the United States Department of Justice to Disqualify a Judge on the Basis of His Religion and Church Position," *Harvard Journal of Law & Public Policy* 4, 1 (Summer 1981): 28–46; Pub. L. 93-512, 88 Stat. 1609 (December 5, 1974); 28 U.S.C. §455.

55. McKoski, "Disqualifying Judges," 437–438.

56. McKoski, 416; Richard E. Flamm, "The History of Judicial Disqualification in America," *Judges' Journal* 52, 3 (Summer 2013): 14.

57. EC 6-1, Code of Professional Responsibility.

58. McMann v. Richardson, 397 U.S. 759, 771 (1970); Argersinger v. Hamlin, 407 U.S. 25 (1972); David L. Bazelon, "The Defective Assistance of Counsel," *University of Cincinnati Law Review* 42, 1 (1973): 2.

59. Joel Jay Finer, "The Ineffective Assistance of Counsel," *Cornell Law Review* 58, 6 (July 1973): 1077–1120; Davis v. State, 486 S.W.2d 904 (Ark. 1972); Scott v. United States, 427 F.2d 609 (D.C. Cir. 1970); Moore v. United States, 432 F.2d 730 (3d Cir. 1970); State v. Merchant, 271 A.2d 752 (Md. 1970); Caraway v. Beto, 421 F.2d 636, 637 (5th Cir. 1970).

60. Strickland v. Washington, 466 U.S. 668, 687–689, 693, 696 (1984).

61. Stephen F. Smith, "Taking Strickland Claims Seriously," *Marquette Law Review* 93,

2 (Winter 2009): 516; Richard Klein, "The Emperor Gideon Has No Clothes: The Empty Promise of the Constitutional Right to Effective Assistance of Counsel," *Hastings Constitutional Law Quarterly* 13, 4 (Summer 1986): 632; Jeffrey L. Kirchmeier, "Drink, Drugs, and Drowsiness: The Constitutional Right to Effective Assistance of Counsel and the Strickland Prejudice Standard," *Nebraska Law Review* 75, 3 (1996): 426–427, 455–463; Stephanos Bibas, "The Psychology of Hindsight and After-the-Fact Review of Ineffective Assistance of Counsel," *Utah Law Review* 1 (2004): 1–11.

62. Warren E. Burger, "The Special Skills of Advocacy: Are Specialized Training and Certification of Advocates Essential to Our System of Justice?" *Fordham Law Review* 42, 2 (December 1973): 234, 227, 238; Michael S. Ariens, "A Uniform Rule Governing Admission and Practice of Attorneys before United States District Courts," *DePaul Law Review* 35, 3 (Spring 1986): 649–674.

63. Ariens, "Know the Law," 1042–1060; "Final Report," *California State Bar Journal* 44, 4 (July–August 1969): 493–517; "Standards for Specialization Announced," *California State Bar Journal* 48, 1 (January–February 1973): 80–87; William J. Derrick, "Specialization in the Law: Texas Develops Pilot Plan for Specialization in Criminal Law, Labor Law, Family Law," *Texas Bar Journal* 36, 5 (May 1973): 393–400; Richard Wells, "Certification in Texas: Increasing Lawyer Competence and Aiding the Public in Lawyer Selection," *Baylor Law Review* 30, 4 (Fall 1978): 689–691.

64. *Annual Report of the American Bar Association* 104 (1979): 982, 847.

65. Jerome Hochberg, "The Drive to Specialization," in *Verdicts on Lawyers*, ed. Ralph Nader and Mark Green (New York: Thomas Y. Crowell, 1976), 121; Marvin W. Mindes, "Lawyer Specialty Certification: The Monopoly Game," *American Bar Association Journal* 61, 1 (January 1975): 42–46; Marvin W. Mindes, "Specialization and Certification: The Splitting of the Bar," *University of Toledo Law Review* 11, 2 (Winter 1980): 273–301; Bates v. State Bar of Ariz., 433 U.S. 350 (1977); "State Status Report on Lawyer Specialty Certification," *Commercial Law Bulletin* 7, 6 (November–December 1992): 13.

66. Michael S. Ariens, "Modern Legal Times: Making a Professional Legal Culture," *Journal of American Culture* 15, 1 (March 1992): 33–34.

67. "Final Report," 67 F.R.D. 159, 164 (1975); "Report and Tentative Recommendations of the Committee to Consider Standards for Admission to Practice in the Federal Courts to the Judicial Conference of the United States," 79 F.R.D. 187, 191 (1978); "Final Report of the Committee to Consider Standards for Admission to Practice in the Federal Courts to the Judicial Conference of the United States," 83 F.R.D. 215, 221 (1979).

68. Christen R. Blair, "Trial Lawyer Incompetence: What the Studies Suggest about the Problem, the Causes and the Cure," *Capital University Law Review* 11, 3 (1982): 419–443; "Lawscope; Just How Good (or Bad) Are Federal Trial Lawyers?" *American Bar Association Journal* 63, 11 (November 1977): 1525, 1540; Adrian A. Spears, "Federal Court Admission Standards—A 45-Year Success Story," 85 F.R.D. 235, 236n6 (1979); "Report and Tentative Recommendations," 79 F.R.D. 187, 193–194 (1978); Anthony Partridge and Gordon Bermant, *The Quality of Advocacy in the Federal Courts* (Federal Judicial Center, 1978), 5, 15; Dorothy Linder Maddi, "Trial Lawyer Competence: The Judicial Perspective," *American Bar Foundation Research Journal* 1 (1978): 117–118.

69. Partridge and Bermant, *Quality of Advocacy*, 13, 7; Linder Maddi, "Trial Lawyer Competence," 144.

70. Warren E. Burger, "Some Further Reflections on the Problem of Adequacy of Counsel," *Fordham Law Review* 49, 1 (October 1980): 1–25; "Lawscope: Enhancing Lawyer Competence: ALI-ABA Confab on Issue," *American Bar Association Journal* 67, 3 (March 1981): 265–267; David R. Brink, "Let's Take Specialization Apart," *American Bar Association Journal* 62, 2 (February 1976): 191–196; *Report and Recommendations of the Task Force on Lawyer Competency: The Role of the Law Schools* (American Bar Association, 1979), 3–7.

71. *Report with Findings and Recommendations to the Conference of Chief Justices from Its Task Force on Lawyer Competence* (May 26, 1982), Pub. No. NCSC-021, https://cdm16501.contentdm.oclc.org/digital/collection/legserv/id/10; *Final Report and Recommendations of the Task Force on Professional Competence* (American Bar Association, 1983); "Report," *Annual Report of the American Bar Association* 111, 2 (1986): 366–368; Bryant G. Garth, "Rethinking the Legal Profession's Approach to Collective Self-Improvement: Competence and the Consumer Perspective," *Wisconsin Law Review* 3 (1983): 639–687.

72. "Report," *Annual Report of the American Bar Association* 101 (1976): 884, 639.

73. Scott Stossel, *Sarge: The Life and Times of Sargent Shriver* (Washington, DC: Smithsonian Books, 2004), 442–443; Legal Services Corporation, "History: The Founding of LSC," https://www.lsc.gov/about-lsc/who-we-are/history; 42 U.S.C. §2996b(a); Lawrence J. Fox, "Legal Services and the Organized Bar: A Reminiscence and a Renewed Call for Cooperation," *Yale Law & Policy Review* 17, 1 (1998): 310.

74. Burton A. Weisbrod, ed., *Public Interest Law: An Economic and Institutional Analysis* (Berkeley: University of California Press, 1978), 50–51; Ann Southworth, *Lawyers of the Right: Professionalizing the Conservative Coalition* (Chicago: University of Chicago Press, 2008), 12; Steven Teles, *The Rise of the Conservative Legal Movement: The Battle for Control of the Law* (Princeton, NJ: Princeton University Press, 2008), 62; Jefferson Decker, *The Other Rights Revolution: Conservative Lawyers and the Remaking of American Government* (New York: Oxford University Press, 2016), 8.

75. "Proceedings," *Annual Report of the American Bar Association* 90 (1965): 110–111; Earl Johnson Jr., *Justice and Reform: The Formative Years of the American Legal Services Program*, 2nd ed. (New Brunswick, NJ: Transaction Books, 1978), 39–43, 49–70; Ariens, "Rise and Fall," 75; "Address of Chesterfield Smith," *Administrative Law Review* 26, 4 (Fall 1974): 381; "Report," *Annual Report of the American Bar Association* 98 (1973): 831; *Annual Report of the American Bar Association* 99 (1974): 377, 895; *Annual Report of the American Bar Association* 100 (1975): 966, 684–685.

76. "Report," *Annual Report of the American Bar Association* 100 (1975): 966; "Implementing the Lawyer's Public Interest Practice Obligation," *American Bar Association Journal* 63, 5 (May 1977): 679; David L. Shapiro, "The Enigma of the Lawyer's Duty to Serve," *New York University Law Review* 55, 5 (November 1980): 735–792; Judith L. Maute, "Changing Conceptions of Lawyers' Pro Bono Responsibilities: From Chance Noblesse Oblige to Stated Expectations," *Tulane Law Review* 77, 1 (November 2002): 91–162.

77. Kutak, Rock and Huie lawyer Daniel Reynolds compiled a summary of the commission's discussions, and the firm printed copies; I received a copy. *Journals* (privately printed summaries of the Kutak Commission's discussions, identified by location), Re-

search Triangle, NC, February 23–24, 1979, 24; *Journals*, Atlanta, GA, April 7–8, 1979, 13; *Journals*, Seattle, WA, June 29–30, 1979, 7 (each discussing an issue); Jonathan M. Winer, "Ethics Draft Ignites Uproar," *National Law Journal*, August 27, 1979, 12; *"The Record: Text of Initial Draft of Ethics Code Rewrite Committee,"* *Legal Times*, August 27, 1979, 45; Michael Ariens, "The Last Hurrah: The Kutak Commission and the End of Optimism," *Creighton Law Review* 49, 4 (September 2016): 731.

78. *Journals*, Salt Lake City, UT, August 24–26, 1979, 30–31.

79. *Compilation of Comments on Model Rules of Professional Conduct*, comp. Geoffrey C. Hazard Jr., 4 vols. (1980) (comments on Rule 8.1 are found in vols. 2–4); Ariens, "Last Hurrah," 715.

80. Rule 6.1, Proposed Final Draft (American Bar Association, 1981), 179; "Report," *Annual Report of the American Bar Association* 107 (1982): 833–920 (final draft); "Rule 6.1," *Annual Report of the American Bar Association* 107 (1982): 887–88.

81. *Watergate and Related Activities Phase I: Watergate Investigation: Hearings before the Select Comm. on Presidential Campaign Activities of the U.S. Senate*, 93rd Cong. 1053–1054, 1312 (1973); Mark Curriden, "The Lawyers of Watergate," *American Bar Association Journal* 98, 6 (June 2012): 38; Marion A. Ellis and Howard E. Covington Jr., *Sages of Their Craft: The First Fifty Years of the American College of Trial Lawyers* (West Group, 2000), 123; Kathleen Clark, "The Legacy of Watergate for Legal Ethics Instruction," *Hastings Law Journal* 51, 4 (April 2000): 673–682; Donald T. Weckstein, "Watergate and the Law Schools," *San Diego Law Review* 12, 2 (March 1975): 261–278; Ariens, "Agony of Modern Legal Ethics," 174–175; John W. Dean III, "Watergate: What Was It?" *Hastings Law Journal* 51, 4 (April 2000): 611–659; John W. Dean III and James Robenalt, "The Legacy of Watergate," *Litigation* 38, 3 (Spring 2012): 20–21 (reporting the exchange); John W. Dean, *Blind Ambition: The White House Years* (1976; reprint, New York: Open Road, 2016), 274 (quoting himself: "You know, what is incredible is the number of lawyers on the list").

82. Rick Perlstein, *The Invisible Bridge: The Fall of Nixon and the Rise of Reagan* (New York: Simon & Schuster, 2014), 140; Michael Asimow, "Lawyers, Popular Perception of," in Hall et al., *Oxford Companion*, 495; *The Organized Bar: Self-Serving or Serving the Public? Hearing before the Subcomm. on Representation of Citizen Interests of the S. Comm. on the Judiciary*, 93rd Cong. 7 (1974) (noting that lawyers' approval rating was better than Congress's); Gallup, "Honesty/Ethics in Professions," https://news.gallup .com/poll/1654/honesty-ethics-professions.aspx.

83. Stanley I. Kutler, *The American Inquisition: Justice and Injustice in the Cold War* (New York: Hill & Wang, 1982), 212–213; Dean, *Blind Ambition*, 128–132, 199.

84. Kutler, *American Inquisition*, ch. 10, 288, 291, 297, 300, 315.

85. James P. White, "Is that Burgeoning Law School Enrollment Ending?" *American Bar Association Journal* 61, 2 (February 1975): 202–204; Nixon v. Sirica, 487 F.2d 700 (D.C. Cir. 1973); United States v. Nixon, 418 U.S. 683 (1974).

86. "N.O.B.C. Reports on Results of Watergate-Related Charges against Twenty-Nine Lawyers," *American Bar Association Journal* 62, 10 (October 1976): 1337; Clark, "Legacy of Watergate," 678–679 (nine disbarred, six suspended, one not disciplined); James D. Fellers, "President's Page," *American Bar Association Journal* 61, 5 (May 1975): 529; Richard B. Allen, *"Watergate—A* Lawyers' Scandal," *American Bar Association Journal*

60, 10 (October 1974): 1257–1258; Robert W. Meserve, "President's Page," *American Bar Association Journal* 59, 7 (July 1973): 681; Weckstein, "Watergate and Law Schools," 261; David R. Brink, "Who Will Regulate the Bar?" *American Bar Association Journal* 61, 8 (August 1975): 937.

87. "Report," *Annual Report of the American Bar Association* 99 (1974): 1107; Michael Ariens, "The Ethics of Copyrighting Ethics Rules," *University of Toledo Law Review* 36, 2 (Winter 2005): 246–247; Victor Li, "Watergate's Whistleblower," *American Bar Association Journal* 101, 6 (June 2014): 31–32; Lynne Reaves, "Ethics in Action: Two Recall Watergate Lessons," *American Bar Association Journal* 70, 8 (August 1984): 35.

88. Michael Ariens, "'Playing Chicken': An Instant History of the Battle over Exceptions to Client Confidences," *Journal of the Legal Profession* 33, 2 (Spring 2009): 247; "Proceedings," *Annual Report of the American Bar Association* 99 (1974): 166.

89. SEC v. Nat'l Student Mktg. Corp., 457 F. Supp. 682 (D.D.C. 1978); SEC v. Nat'l Student Mktg. Corp., 430 F. Supp. 639 (D.D.C. 1977); SEC v. Nat'l Student Mktg. Corp., 73 F.R.D. 444 (D.D.C. 1977); SEC v. Nat'l Student Mktg. Corp., 402 F. Supp. 641 (D.D.C. 1975); SEC v. Nat'l Student Mktg. Corp., 68 F.R.D. 157 (D.D.C. 1975), aff'd, 538 F.2d 404 (D.C. Cir. 1976), cert. denied, 429 U.S. 107 (1977); SEC v. Nat'l Student Mktg. Corp., 59 F.R.D. 305 (D.D.C. 1973); SEC v. Nat'l Student Mktg. Corp., 360 F. Supp. 284 (D.D.C. 1973).

90. *SEC v. Nat'l Student Mktg. Corp.*, 457 F. Supp. at 713; James M. McCauley, "Corporate Responsibility and the Regulation of Corporate Lawyers," *Richmond Journal of Global Law & Business* 3 (2003): 24.

91. Junius Hoffman, "On Learning of a Corporate Client's Crime or Fraud—The Lawyer's Dilemma," *Business Lawyer* 33, 4 (March 1978): 1404–1405n38; "Report," *Annual Report of the American Bar Association* 98 (1973): 759; "The Code of Professional Responsibility and the Responsibility of Lawyers Engaged in Securities Law Practice—A Report of the Committee on Counsel Responsibility and Liability," *Business Lawyer* 30, 4 (July 1975): 1289–1301; "Federal Criminal Code, Amnesty, Gun Control, Bank Secrecy Are Debated by the House of Delegates," *American Bar Association Journal* 61, 9 (September 1975): 1085–1086; "Proceedings," *Annual Report of the American Bar Association* 100 (1975): 666–668.

92. DR 4–101(A), Code of Professional Responsibility; David J. Fried, "Too High a Price: The Exception to the Attorney-Client Privilege for Contemplated Crimes and Frauds," *North Carolina Law Review* 64, 3 (March 1986): 446–462.

93. Hoffman, "On Learning," 1406–1408n47.

94. Richard Zitrin and Carol M. Langford, *The Moral Compass of the American Lawyer: Truth, Justice, Power, and Greed* (New York: Ballantine Books, 1999), 7–26; Tom Alibrandi and Frank H. Armani, *Privileged Information* (New York: Dodd, Mead, 1984), 100–103; Mark Hanson, "The Toughest Call," *American Bar Association Journal* 93, 8 (August 2007): 28–29; *Sworn to Silence* (1987; fictionalized television movie).

95. People v. Belge, 372 N.Y.S.2d 798 (Onondaga Cty. Ct. 1975), aff'd, 376 N.Y.S.2d 771 (App. Div. 1975), aff'd, 359 N.E.2d 377 (N.Y. 1976).

96. Zitrin and Langford, *Moral Compass*, 23.

97. "Justice Department and Other Views on Prepaid Legal Services Plans Get an Airing before the Tunney Subcommittee," *American Bar Association Journal* 60, 7 (July

1974): 792–793; "Justice Department Continues Its Contentions that the Houston Amendments Raise Serious Antitrust Problems," *American Bar Association Journal* 60, 11 (November 1974): 1410; "House of Delegates Redefines Death, Urges Redefinition of Rape, and Undoes the Houston Amendments," *American Bar Association Journal* 61, 4 (April 1975): 465–466; "Justice Department Charges Code Advertising Provisions Violate Federal Antitrust Laws," *American Bar Association Journal* 62, 8 (August 1976): 979; "Association Files Answer in Civil Antitrust Suit Brought by the United States," *American Bar Association Journal* 62, 9 (September 1976): 1179–1180; "Justice Department Dismisses Antitrust Suit against American Bar Association," *American Bar Association Journal* 64, 10 (October 1978): 1538; Goldfarb v. Va. St. Bar, 421 U.S. 773, 777–778, 785–788 (1975); Richard J. Arnould and Robert N. Corley, "Fee Schedules Should Be Abolished," *American Bar Association Journal* 57, 7 (July 1971): 655–662; John M. Ferran and Allen R. Snyder, "Antitrust and Ethical Aspects of Lawyers' Minimum Fee Schedules," *Real Property, Probate & Trust Journal* 7, 4 (Winter 1972): 726–727; Bates v. State Bar of Ariz., 433 U.S. 350 (1977); "F.T.C. Goes Public on Lawyer Probe," *American Bar Association Journal* 64, 7 (July 1978): 959–960.

98. "Proceedings," *Annual Report of the American Bar Association* 94 (1969): 389–392; United Transportation Union v. State Bar of Michigan, 401 U.S. 576 (1971); J. Robert Kramer II, "Group Legal Services: From Houston to Chicago," *Dickinson Law Review* 79, 4 (Summer 1975): 621–649; Judith L. Maute, "Pre-paid and Group Legal Services: Thirty Years after the Storm," *Fordham Law Review* 70, 3 (December 2001): 915–943; "Proceedings," *Annual Report of the American Bar Association* 99 (1974): 166–174; "Proceedings," *American Bar Association Journal* 100 (1975): 246–251; "Justice Department and Other Views," 793.

99. "House Broadens Code's Publicity in General Rules," *American Bar Association Journal* 62, 4 (April 1976): 472; "Proceedings," *Annual Report of the American Bar Association* 101 (1976): 227–235; "Code Amendments Broaden Information Lawyers May Provide," *American Bar Association Journal* 62, 3 (March 1976): 309–310.

100. "Proceedings," *Annual Report of the American Bar Association* 101 (1976): 663–664; "Association Files Answer," 1179–1180; Lawrence E. Walsh, "The Annual Report of the President of the American Bar Association," *American Bar Association Journal* 62, 9 (September 1976): 1120.

101. "Report," *Annual Report of the American Bar Association* 97 (1972): 742.

102. "Justice Department Dismisses Antitrust Suit," 1538, 1540; "Antitrust Chief Jabs Bar on Response to Bates," *American Bar Association Journal* 63, 12 (December 1978): 1703; "Proceedings," *Annual Report of the American Bar Association* 102 (1977): 542–547, 595–600; "Proceedings," *Annual Report of the American Bar Association* 103 (1978): 606–608; *Annual Report of the American Bar Association* 102 (1977): 989 (renamed Model Code).

103. "F.T.C. Goes Public," 959; Terry Calvani, "An FTC Commissioner's View of Regulating Lawyers," *American Bar Association Journal* 70, 8 (August 1984): 70–72.

104. "Trade or Professional? Bars Must Choose," *American Bar Association Journal* 64, 7 (July 1978): 959.

105. Ariens, "Rise and Fall," 63–68; John D. Conner and N. S. Clifton, "Income of Lawyers, 1961–1962," *American Bar Association Journal* 51, 8 (August 1965): 753–755;

Reuben E. Slesinger, "1971: Back on the Track," *American Bar Association Journal* 57, 3 (March 1971): 248–250.

106. Brink, "Who Will Regulate the Bar?" 937.

107. Robert J. Kutak, "The Adversary System and the Practice of Law," in *The Good Lawyer: Lawyers' Roles and Lawyers' Ethics*, ed. David Luban (Totowa, NJ: Rowman & Allenheld, 1984), 173, 177–178.

108. 70 F.R.D. 79 (1976); Roscoe Pound, "The Causes of Popular Dissatisfaction with the Administration of Justice," *Annual Report of the American Bar Association* 29 (1906): 395–417; William H. Erickson, "The Pound Conference Recommendations: A Blueprint for the Justice System in the Twenty-First Century," 76 F.R.D. 277, 288 (1977); Milton Pollack, "Discovery—Its Abuse and Correction," 80 F.R.D. 219, 222 (1978).

109. "Discovery Reform Pushed by A.B.A. Committee," *American Bar Association Journal* 63, 12 (December 1977): 1691–1692; William B. Spann Jr., "President's Page," *American Bar Association Journal* 64, 2 (February 1978): 157; John F. Grady, "Trial Lawyers, Litigators, and Clients' Costs," *Litigation* 4, 3 (Spring 1978): 58; Philip H. Corboy, "Second Report of the Special Committee for the Study of Discovery Abuse (January 1980)," *Litigation News* 5, 3 (April 1980): 10; Weyman I. Lundquist, "Trial Lawyer or Litigator," *Litigation* 7, 4 (Summer 1981): 3–4, 60; Timothy S. Robinson, "'Discovery' Cases Abuse Due Process," *Washington Post*, May 19, 1980, 4.

110. Paul Hoffman, *Lions in the Street: The Inside Story of the Great Wall Street Law Firms* (Saturday Review Press, 1973), 227; Paul Hoffman, *Lions of the Eighties: The Inside Story of the Powerhouse Law Firms* (Garden City, NY: Doubleday, 1982), 38.

111. Steven K. Brill, "Building a Law Firm—Fast," *Esquire*, May 23, 1978, 11; Steven K. Harper, *The Lawyer Bubble: A Profession in Crisis* (New York: Basic Books, 2013), 71; Dan Rottenberg, "The Pinstripe Revolution," *Chicago*, July 1979, 125.

112. Alexis de Tocqueville, "Money Talks: Why It Shouts to Some Lawyers and Whispers to Others," *Juris Doctor* 2, 4 (January 1972): 55; Abel, *American Lawyers*, 311; Gerard J. Clark, "Fear and Loathing in New Orleans: The Sorry Fate of the Kutak Commission's Rules," *Suffolk University Law Review* 17, 1 (Spring 1983): 82; Roger C. Cramton, "The Lawyer's Professional Independence: Memories, Aspirations, and Realities," *in The Lawyer's Professional Independence: An Ideal Revisited*, ed. John B. Davidson (Chicago: ABA Press, 1985), 46; Richard Sander and E. Douglass Williams, "A Little Theorizing about the Big Law Firm: Galanter, Palay, and the Economics of Growth," *Law & Social Inquiry* 17, 3 (Summer 1992): 392n4; Peter W. Bernstein, "Profit Pressures on the Big Law Firms," *Forbes*, April 19, 1982, 84; "The Big-Law Business," *Newsweek*, April 16, 1984, 87; Marc Galanter and Thomas Palay, *Tournament of Lawyers: The Transformation of the Big Law Firm* (Chicago: University of Chicago Press, 1991), 41.

113. Rottenberg, "Pinstripe Revolution," 98; Peter Megargee Brown, *Rascals: The Selling of the Legal Profession* (New York: Benchmark Press, 1989), 110–119.

114. L. Ray Patterson, "Wanted: A New Code of Professional Responsibility," *American Bar Association Journal* 63, 5 (May 1977): 639–642; Ariens, "Last Hurrah"; Ted Schneyer, "Professionalism as Bar Politics: The Making of the Model Rules of Professional Conduct," *Law & Social Inquiry* 14, 4 (Fall 1989): 677–737.

115. Thomas D. Morgan, "The Evolving Concept of Professional Responsibility," *Harvard Law Review* 90, 4 (February 1977): 702–743; Frankel, "Search for the Truth";

Monroe Freedman, *Lawyer's Ethics in an Adversary System* (Indianapolis: Bobbs-Merrill, 1975); Ariens, "Agony of Modern Legal Ethics," 176, nn. 325, 327 (citing others); William B. Spann Jr., "The Legal Profession Needs a New Code of Ethics," *Bar Leader* 3, 3 (November–December 1977): 2; Ariens, "Last Hurrah," 696.

116. "Proceedings," *Annual Report of the American Bar Association* 108 (1983): 778; Ariens, "Last Hurrah," 692; Ariens, "Rise and Fall," 77–80.

117. *Journals*, Aspen, CO, September 29–October 1, 1977, 4; *Journals*, New York City, December 16–17, 1977, 16.

118. *Journals*, New York City, 14.

119. *Journals*, Seattle, June 29–30, 1979, 16 (quoting reporter Geoffrey Hazard); Preliminary Working Draft Code of Professional Standards, February 6, 1978, 1; L. Ray Patterson, "Legal Ethics and the Lawyer's Duty of Loyalty," *Emory Law Journal* 29, 4 (Fall 1980): 918; *Yale Biographical Dictionary of American Law*, s.v. "Hazard, Geoffrey C., Jr."; "In Memoriam: Geoffrey C. Hazard, Jr.," *ALI Reporter* 40, 2 (Spring 2018): 1, 4–5.

120. *Journals*, San Francisco, December 14–16, 1978, 3; *Journals*, Research Triangle, NC, February 23–24, 1979, 12, 19–20.

121. Winer, "Ethics Draft Ignites Uproar," 1; "Trial Lawyers Group Parts Company with ABA on Ethics Code," *American Bar Association Journal* 65, 9 (September 1979): 1299; "The Record," *Legal Times*, August 27, 1979, 26; Mark H. Aultman, "Legal Fiction Becomes Legal Fantasy," *Journal of the Legal Profession* 7 (1982): 39; Richard S. Jacobson and Jeffrey R. White, *David v. Goliath: ATLA and the Fight for Everyday Justice* (Baltimore: ATLA, 2004), 248 (noting the ATLA code "was not adopted by any state").

122. "The Record," 28, 36.

123. *Journals*, Salt Lake City, August 24–26, 1979, 1; *Journals*, New Orleans, October 26–27, 1979, 15.

124. "ABA Ethics Revision Criticized: Could Destroy Judicial System," *Daily Record*, January 17, 1980, 6; "A License to Squeal?" *Wall Street Journal*, February 11, 1980, 20; "The Proposed New Code," *National Law Journal*, February 25, 1980, 16; *Journals*, Research Triangle, NC, February 23–24, 1979, 12.

125. Discussion Draft, January 30, 1980, Rules 1.7(b), 3.1(a)(3), 1.7(c)(2).

126. Preface to Discussion Draft; NOBC, Report and Recommendations on Study of the Model Rules of Professional Conduct (Discussion Draft of January 30, 1980), 2.

127. Cover letter for Discussion Draft; "Chairman's Introduction," Proposed Final Draft; *Compilation of Comments*, 3:O-40, 2, 26–27; Ariens, "Last Hurrah," 712–713.

128. *Compilation of Comments*, 1:8, 10, 11, 4:2; Walter P. Armstrong Jr., "The Kutak Commission Report: Retrospect and Prospect," *Capital University Law Review* 11, 3 (1982): 490.

129. "The American Lawyer's Code of Conduct Discussion Draft—June 1980," *Trial* 16, 8 (August 1980): 44–63; NOBC, Report and Recommendations, 33, 76; "Section Council Opposes Kutak Model Rules," *Litigation News* 6, 2 (January 1981): 1, 4; letter from Robert J. Kutak to Dear Colleagues, October 9, 1980.

130. Proposed Final Draft, May 30, 1981, Rules 1.6(b)(2), 4.1(b) comment, 4.4 comment, 3.3 comment.

131. "Proposed Final Draft (as Revised through June 30, 1982)," *Annual Report of the*

American Bar Association 107 (1982): 833–921; "Report," *Annual Report of the American Bar Association* 107 (1982): 832, 829.

132. "Report," *Annual Report of the American Bar Association* 107 (1982): 830.

133. "Proceedings," *Annual Report of the American Bar Association* 107 (1982): 614–629.

134. Ariens, "Last Hurrah," 691; Stuart Taylor Jr., "Ethics and the Law: A Case History," *New York Times Magazine*, January 9, 1983, SM31; Geoffrey C. Hazard Jr., "Rectification of Client Fraud: Death and Revival of a Professional Norm," *Emory Law Journal* 33, 2 (Spring 1984): 302; "Report," *Annual Report of the American Bar Association* 108 (1983): 728–739; "Proceedings," *Annual Report of the American Bar Association* 108 (1983): 291–369; Clark, "Fear and Loathing," 79–91 (discussing the debate).

135. Art Garwin, ed., *A Legislative History: The Development of the ABA Model Rules of Professional Conduct, 1982–2013*, 4th ed. (ABA Center for Professional Responsibility, 2013), 105, 113; Robert P. Gandossy, *Bad Business: The OPM Scandal and the Seduction of the Establishment* (New York: Basic Books, 1985), 7, 117–119, 125–135; Hazard, "Rectification," 306; Susan P. Koniak, "When the Hurlyburly's Done: The Bar's Struggle with the SEC," *Columbia Law Review* 103, 5 (June 2003): 1236–1280.

136. "Report," *Annual Report of the American Bar Association* 108 (1983): 1136–1184; "Proceedings," *Annual Report of the American Bar Association* 108 (1983): 766–778.

137. Stein, preface to *Pivotal Decade*; Daniel T. Rodgers, *Age of Fracture* (Cambridge, MA: Belknap Press, 2011), 9; Edward O. Laumann and John P. Heinz, "Specialization and Prestige in the Legal Profession: The Structure of Deference," *American Bar Foundation Research Journal* 1 (Winter 1977): 166–167, 177, 180–181; Heinz and Laumann, *Chicago Lawyers*, ch. 4.

138. "Proceedings," *Annual Report of the American Bar Association* 108 (1983): 767; preamble to Model Rules of Professional Conduct; "'. . . In the Spirit of Public Service': A Blueprint for the Rekindling of Lawyer Professionalism," 112 F.R.D. 243, 259 (1986).

7. THE PROFESSIONALISM CRISIS AND LEGAL ETHICS IN A TIME OF RAPID CHANGE, 1983–2015

1. *Black's Law Dictionary*, ed. Bryan A. Garner, 8th ed. (St. Paul: West Group, 2004), s.v. "professionalism." Its definition was expanded, explained, and given a date of first use in the tenth edition (2014).

2. John B. Davidson, ed., *The Lawyer's Professional Independence: Present Threats/Future Challenges* (Chicago: ABA Books, 1984).

3. Peter Megargee Brown, *Rascals: The Selling of the Legal Profession* (New York: Benchmark Press, 1989), 113–119; Peter Megargee Brown, "The Decline of the Lawyers' Independence," in Davidson, *Lawyer's Professional Independence: Present Threats*, 25; Peter Megargee Brown, *Flights of Memory, Days before Yesterday: A Memoir* (New York: Benchmark Press, 1989).

4. Michael Ariens, "The Rise and Fall of Social Trustee Professionalism," *Journal of the Professional Lawyer* (2016): 50n9; Steven Brint, *In an Age of Experts: The Changing Role of Professionals in Politics and Public Life* (Princeton, NJ: Princeton University Press,

1994); Morris Harrell, "Preserving Professionalism," *American Bar Association Journal* 69, 7 (July 1983): 864; John B. Davidson, ed., *The Lawyer's Professional Independence: An Ideal Revisited* (Chicago: ABA Books, 1985).

5. Warren E. Burger, "The State of Justice," *American Bar Association Journal* 70, 4 (April 1984): 62-66; "Report," *Annual Report of the American Bar Association* 111, 2 (1986): 371; "'. . . In the Spirit of Public Service.'"

6. "Informational Report," *Annual Report of the American Bar Association* 112, 2 (1987): 240; "Report," *Annual Report of the American Bar Association* 117, 2 (1992): 1178; "Informational Report," *Annual Report of the American Bar Association* 115, 2 (1990): 1641; "Informational Report," *Annual Report of the American Bar Association* 118, 2 (1993): 261-263.

7. Preface to *Lawyers' Ideals/Lawyers' Practices: Transformations in the American Legal Profession*, ed. Robert L. Nelson, David Trubek, and Rayman Solomon (Ithaca, NY: Cornell University Press, 1992); "Professionalism in the Practice of Law: A Symposium on Civility and Judicial Ethics in the 1990's," *Valparaiso University Law Review* 28, 2 (Winter 1989): 513-741; "Essays," *Emory Law Journal* 41, 2 (Spring 1992): 403-513; "The Future of the Legal Profession," *Case Western Law Review* 44, 2 (Winter 1994): 333-870; "Conference on the Commercialization of the Legal Profession," *South Carolina Law Review* 45, 5 (1994): 883-1002; Sol Linowitz, *The Betrayed Profession: Lawyering at the End of the Twentieth Century* (New York: Scribner Book Co., 1993); Mary Ann Glendon, *A Nation under Lawyers* (Cambridge, MA: Harvard University Press, 1994), 20-21; Anthony T. Kronman, *The Lost Lawyer: Failing Ideals of the Legal Profession* (Cambridge, MA: Harvard University Press, 1994); Marc Galanter, "Lawyers in the Mist: The Golden Age of Legal Nostalgia," *Dickinson Law Review* 100, 3 (Spring 1996): 549-562; Marc Galanter and Thomas Palay, *Tournament of Lawyers: The Transformation of the Big Law Firm* (Chicago: University of Chicago Press, 1991), ch. 3; Michael Ariens, "American Legal Ethics in an Age of Anxiety," *St. Mary's Law Journal* 40, 2 (2008): 420-421.

8. *Annual Report of the American Bar Association* 113, 2 (1988): 591-592 (sample creed).

9. *Annual Report of the American Bar Association* 113, 2 (1988): 612, 614, 25.

10. Gallup, "Honesty/Ethics in the Professions," https://news.gallup.com/poll/1654 /honesty-ethics-professions.aspx (noting that the favorable opinion of lawyers dropped from 25 percent in 1976 to 18 percent in 1988, accompanied by a higher negative opinion of lawyers: 26 percent in 1976 and 33 percent in 1988).

11. Special Committee on Professionalism, Illinois State Bar Association, "The Bar, the Bench and Professionalism in Illinois," *Illinois Bar Journal* 76, 8 (April 1988): 441-452; "The Texas Lawyer's Creed—A Mandate for Professionalism," in Thomas M. Reavley, "Rambo Litigators: Pitting Aggressive Tactics against Legal Ethics," *Pepperdine Law Review* 17, 3 (1990): 659-662; Chief Justice's Commission on Professionalism, "About Us," http://cjcpga.org/aboutus/; ABA Standing Committee on Professionalism, introduction to *A Guide to Professionalism Commissions* (American Bar Association, 2011); Justin A. Stanley, "The ABA Commission and Its Sequel," *Bar Examiner* 59, 2 (May 1990): 31; Catherine Therese Clarke, "Missed Manners in Courtroom Decorum," *Maryland Law Review* 50, 4 (1991): 949n10, 1012n320; Rob Atkinson, "Dissenter's Commentary on the Professionalism Crusade," *Texas Law Review* 74, 2 (December 1995): 261n3;

Ariens, "Rise and Fall," 51n17; Cheryl B. Preston and Hillary Lawrence, "Incentivizing Lawyers to Play Nice: A National Survey of Civility Standards and Options for Enforcement," *University of Michigan Journal of Law Reform* 48, 3 (Spring 2015): 701–744; *Interim Report of the Committee on Civility of the Seventh Federal Judicial Circuit* (1991), 10; *Final Report of the Committee on Civility of the Seventh Federal Judicial Circuit* (1992), 4; *Report of the Task Force on Law Schools and the Profession: Narrowing the Gap, Legal Education and Professional Development—An Educational Continuum* (American Bar Association, 1992), 207–221; *Teaching and Learning Professionalism* (American Bar Association, 1996); *Teaching and Learning Professionalism: Symposium Proceedings* (American Bar Association, 1997); In re Code for Resolving Professionalism Complaints, 116 So.2d 280 (Fla. 2013); Ariz. Sup. Ct. R. 31 (West 2014); In re Anonymous Member of the South Carolina Bar, 709 S.E.2d 633 (S.C. 2011).

12. Conference of Chief Justices, *A National Action Plan on Lawyer Conduct and Professionalism* (1999), viii, 94–95.

13. Warren E. Burger, "The Decline of Professionalism," *Tennessee Law Review* 61, 1 (Fall 1993): 4–7; Warren E. Burger, "The Decline of Professionalism," *Fordham Law Review* 63, 4 (March 1995): 952–953.

14. Richard H. Sander and E. Douglass Williams, "Why Are There so Many Lawyers? Perspectives on a Turbulent Market," *Law & Social Inquiry* 14, 3 (Summer 1989): 448–449; Barbara A. Curran, ed., *The Lawyer Statistical Report: A Statistical Profile of the U.S. Legal Profession in the 1980s* (Chicago: American Bar Foundation, 1985), 4; Barbara A. Curran, "American Lawyers in the 1980s: A Profession in Transition," *Law & Society Review* 20, 1 (1986): 19–52; American Bar Association, "ABA National Lawyer Population Survey" (1955–2019), https://www.americanbar.org/about_the_aba/profession_statistics/.

15. Morris Harrell, "Introductory Remarks," in Davidson, *Lawyer's Professional Independence: Present Threats*, x; Burger, "State of Justice," 62; Robert J. Kutak, "The Rules of Professional Conduct in an Era of Change," *Emory Law Journal* 29, 4 (Fall 1980): 889; Bill Bishop with Robert G. Cushing, *The Big Sort: Why the Clustering of Like-Minded America Is Tearing Us Apart* (Boston: Houghton Mifflin, 2014); Daniel Bell, *The Coming of Post-Industrial Society: A Venture in Social Forecasting* (1973; reprint, New York: Basic Books, 1999).

16. Burger, "State of Justice," 65.

17. Michael Ariens, "Know the Law: A History of Legal Specialization," *South Carolina Law Review* 45, 5 (1994): 1054; Michael Ariens "Sorting: Legal Specialization and the Privatization of the American Legal Profession," *Georgetown Journal of Legal Ethics* 29, 3 (Summer 2016): 579–599; John P. Heinz et al., *Urban Lawyers: The New Social Structure of the Bar* (Chicago: University of Chicago Press, 2005); John P. Heinz and Edward O. Laumann, *Chicago Lawyers: The Social Structure of the Bar*, rev. ed. (Chicago: Northwestern University Press, 1994); Robert H. Jackson, "The County-Seat Lawyer," *American Bar Association Journal* 36, 6 (June 1950): 497.

18. Rule 7.4, Model Rules of Professional Conduct; "Report," *Annual Report of the American Bar Association* 113, 2 (1988): 592.

19. Michael S. Ariens, "Modern Legal Times: Making a Professional Legal Culture," *Journal of American Culture* 15, 1 (March 1992): 34.

20. Marc S. Galanter, "Planet of the APs: Reflections on the Scale of Law and Its Users," *Buffalo Law Review* 53, 5 (Winter 2006): 1382–1383; Richard Sander and E. Douglass Williams, "A Little Theorizing about the Big Law Firm: Galanter, Palay, and the Economics of Growth," *Law & Social Inquiry* 17, 3 (Summer 1992): 392n4; Benjamin H. Barton, *Glass Half Full: The Decline and Rebirth of the Legal Profession* (New York: Oxford University Press, 2014), 4–5; Galanter and Palay, *Tournament of Lawyers*, 40–41; Sander and Williams, "Why Are There so Many Lawyers?" 434–440.

21. William G. Ross, *The Honest Hour: The Ethics of Time-Based Billing by Lawyers* (Durham, NC: Carolina Academic Press, 1996), 2–3; Michael H. Trotter, *Profit and the Practice of Law: What's Happened to the Legal Profession* (2012), ch. 4; Michael H. Trotter, *Declining Prospects: How Extraordinary Competition and Compensation Are Changing America's Major Law Firms* (North Charleston, SC: CreateSpace, 2012), ch. 1; Galanter and Palay, *Tournament of Lawyers*, 57, 65; Bernard A. Burk and David McGowan, "Big but Brittle: Economic Perspectives on the Future of the Law Firm in the New Economy," *Columbia Business Law Review* 1 (2011): 29; Arthur D. Austin, "Book Review," *Harvard Journal of Law & Public Policy* 11, 2 (Spring 1988): 528n10.

22. Steven K. Harper, *The Lawyer Bubble: A Profession in Crisis* (New York: Basic Books, 2013), 73; "The Best-Paid Trial Lawyers," *Forbes*, October 16, 1989, 204 (noting a subset of personal injury lawyers is the highest paid).

23. William D. Henderson, "Rise and Fall," *American Lawyer* 35, 6 (June 2014): 56; Ellen Joan Pollock, *Turks and Brahmins: Upheaval at Milbank, Tweed; Wall Street's Gentlemen Take off Their Gloves* (New York: American Lawyer Books, 1990), 187–240; William H. Rehnquist, "The Legal Profession Today," *Indiana Law Journal* 62, 2 (1987): 155; William H. Rehnquist, "The State of the Legal Profession," *Legal Economics* 14, 2 (March 1988): 46 (attributing "eat what you kill" to Roger C. Cramton, "Ethical Dilemmas Facing Today's Lawyer—Obligation to the Client—To the Public," *Bar Leader* 10, 4 [January–February 1985]: 16, which quoted "one entrepreneurial lawyer" as saying, "You eat only what you kill"); Milton C. Regan Jr., *Eat What You Kill: The Fall of a Wall Street Lawyer* (Ann Arbor: University of Michigan Press, 2004), ch. 1; Ronald J. Gilson and Robert H. Mnookin, "Sharing among the Human Capitalists: An Economic Inquiry into the Corporate Law Firm and How Partners Split Profits," *Stanford Law Review* 37, 2 (January 1985): 339–353; William Winter, "The Fine Art of Rainmaking," *American Bar Association Journal* 70, 10 (October 1984): 54–58; *Black's Law Dictionary*, ed. Bryan Garner, 7th ed. (St. Paul: West Group, 1999), s.v. "rainmaker" (first defined).

24. Heinz and Laumann, *Chicago Lawyers*, xvii (noting a pay gap "larger in the legal profession" than any other).

25. Robert L. Nelson, "Ideology, Practice, and Professional Autonomy: Social Values and Client Relationships in the Large Law Firm," *Stanford Law Review* 37, 2 (January 1985): 530.

26. Pollock, *Turks and Brahmins*, 264.

27. *First Blood* (1982) starred Sylvester Stallone as John Rambo, a Vietnam War veteran evading capture by whatever means necessary. John J. Curtin Jr., "A Message from the President: Civil Matters," *American Bar Association Journal* 77, 8 (August 1991): 8; Georgene Vairo, "Rule 11 and the Profession," *Fordham Law Review* 67, 2 (November 1998): 627–628.

28. *Annual Report of the American Bar Association* 113, 2 (1988): 592.

29. *Teaching and Learning Professionalism*, 6–7 (italics omitted).

30. "Report," *Annual Report of the American Bar Association* 117, 1 (1992): 527–528, 537; *Lawyer Regulation for a New Century* (American Bar Association, 1992); National Organization of Bar Counsel, Report and Recommendations on Study of the Model Rules of Professional Conduct (Discussion Draft of January 30, 1980), 2; Mary M. Devlin, "The Development of Lawyer Disciplinary Procedures in the United States," *Georgetown Journal of Legal Ethics* 7, 4 (Spring 1994): 930–933.

31. "Report," *Annual Report of the American Bar Association* 117, 1 (1992): 538.

32. *Annual Report of the American Bar Association* 118, 2 (1993): 180, 29; *Annual Report of the American Bar Association* 114, 2 (1989): 297, 302–362, 58; *Annual Report of the American Bar Association* 117, 1 (1992): 49–56.

33. "Proceedings," *Annual Report of the American Bar Association* 120, 1 (1995): 3–4; *Annual Report of the American Bar Association* 121, 2 (1996): 499–510, 4.

34. Debra Moss Curtis and Billie Jo Kaufman, "A Public View of Attorney Discipline in Florida: Statistics, Commentary, and Analysis of Disciplinary Actions against Licensed Attorneys in the State of Florida from 1988–2002," *Nova Law Review* 28, 3 (Spring 2004): 689, 691–695. These authors found some tantalizing evidence that female lawyers were underrepresented in disciplinary cases, indicating that the addition of female lawyers may lead to a decline in disciplinary actions. Michael Ariens, *Lone Star Law: A Legal History of Texas* (Lubbock: Texas Tech University Press, 2011), 186.

35. Kyle Rozema, "Lawyer Misconduct in America" (January 2, 2020 draft), 11, https://www.law.umich.edu/centersandprograms/lawandeconomics/workshops/Docu ments/Paper%202.%20Kyle%20Rozema.Lawyer%20Misconduct%20in%20America .pdf; Richard L. Abel, *American Lawyers* (New York: Oxford University Press, 1989), 145, 148; Leslie C. Levin, "The Emperor's Clothes and Other Tales about the Standards for Imposing Lawyer Discipline Sanctions," *American University Law Review* 48, 1 (October 1998): 1–83.

36. Ronald E. Mallen, *Legal Malpractice: 2019 Edition* (St. Paul: West Publishing, 2019), 24; Tom Baker and Rick Swedloff, "Liability Insurer Data as a Window on Lawyers' Professional Liability," *UC Irvine Law Review* 5, 6 (2015): 1304; Herbert M. Kritzer and Neil Vidmar, *When Lawyers Screw Up: Improving Access to Justice for Legal Malpractice Victims* (Lawrence: University Press of Kansas, 2018), 66–68, 71.

37. "Report," *Annual Report of the American Bar Association* 101 (1976): 884–886; "Proceedings," *Annual Report of the American Bar Association* 101 (1976): 639; *Profile of Legal Malpractice: A Statistical Study of Determinative Characteristics of Claims Asserted against Attorneys* (American Bar Association, 1986), 6.

38. *Profile of Malpractice Claims, 2012–2015* (American Bar Association, 2016), 11, 18; Kritzer and Vidmar, *When Lawyers Screw Up*, 73–74, 85.

39. Kritzer and Vidmar, *When Lawyers Screw Up*, 78–80, 82.

40. Kritzer and Vidmar, 4–6, 76–85, 147, 168–169; Baker and Swedloff, "Liability Insurer Data," 1294–1295; Susan Saab Fortney, "A Tort in Search of a Remedy: Prying Open the Courthouse Doors for Legal Malpractice Victims," *Fordham Law Review* 85, 5 (April 2017): 2039.

41. Geoffrey C. Hazard Jr., foreword to *Restatement (Third) of the Law Governing*

Lawyers, 2 vols. (St. Paul: American Law Institute Publishers, 2000), 1:xxi; *Profile of Mal-practice Claims*, 17.

42. *Profile of Malpractice Claims*, 17; Kritzer and Vidmar, *When Lawyers Screw Up*, 100–101, 108–109.

43. Federal Rules of Civil Procedure, 97 F.R.D. 165, 167 (1983); Amendments to the Federal Rules of Civil Procedure, 146 F.R.D. 401, 420 (1993); D. Michael Risinger, "Honesty in Pleading and Its Enforcement: Some 'Striking' Problems with Federal Rule of Civil Procedure 11," *Minnesota Law Review* 61, 1 (1976): 35–37; Vairo, "Rule 11," 590; Melissa L. Nelken, "Has the Chancellor Shot Himself in the Foot? Looking for a Middle Ground on Rule 11 Sanctions," *Hastings Law Journal* 41, 2 (January 1990): 384.

44. Fed. R. Civ. P. 11 Advisory Committee's Note to 1983 Amendment, 97 F.R.D. 165, 191 (1983); Vairo, "Rule 11," 625–626; Lawrence C. Marshall, Herbert M. Kritzer, and Frances Kahn Zemans, "Use and Impact of Rule 11," *Northwestern University Law Review* 86, 4 (1992): 958–965.

45. Marshall et al., "Use and Impact," 945, 960–961, 964–975; Melissa L. Nelken, "The Impact of Federal Rule 11 on Lawyers and Judges in the Northern District of California," *Judicature* 74, 3 (October–November 1990): 149–150; Nelken, "Has the Chancellor Shot Himself," 394; Vairo, "Rule 11," 590, 621, 623, 625–630.

46. 97 F.R.D. at 173–174; Michael Ariens, "The Last Hurrah: The Kutak Commission and the End of Optimism," *Creighton Law Review* 49, 4 (September 2016): 721–723; Vairo, "Rule 11," 590; Peter Joy, "The Relationship between Civil Rule 11 and Lawyer Discipline: An Empirical Analysis Suggesting Institutional Choices in the Regulation of Lawyers," *Loyola of Los Angeles Law Review* 37, 3 (Winter 2004): 807; Jeffrey A. Parness, "Disciplinary Referrals under New Federal Civil Rule 11," *Tennessee Law Review* 61, 1 (Fall 1993): 51, 55; Interim Report on the Joint Project of the American College of Trial Lawyers Task Force on Discovery and Civil Justice and IAALS (2008), 3.

47. Fed. R. Civ. Proc. 11(C)(2) (1993).

48. Joy, "Relationship," 789–791.

49. *The Judicial Response to Lawyer Misconduct* (American Bar Association, 1984); Canon 3(D)(2), ABA Model Code of Judicial Conduct (1990); Rule 2.15(B), ABA Model Code of Judicial Conduct (2007); Arthur F. Greenbaum, "Judicial Reporting of Lawyer Misconduct," *UMKC Law Review* 77, 3 (Spring 2009): 537–568; Arthur F. Greenbaum, "The Automatic Reporting of Lawyer Misconduct to Disciplinary Authorities: Filling the Reporting Gap," *Ohio State Law Journal* 73, 3 (2012): 437–506; James Lindgren, "Toward a New Standard of Attorney Disqualification," *American Bar Foundation Research Journal* 2 (Spring 1982): 436–437; American Bar Association, https://www.americanbar.org/groups/professional_responsibility/resources/judicial_ethics_regulation/map/.

50. Attorney Grievance Comm'n of Maryland v. Stein, 819 A.2d 372, 379 (Md. App. 2003).

51. Charles W. Wolfram, *Modern Legal Ethics* (St. Paul: West Publishing, 1986), 329; Richard E. Flamm, *Lawyer Disqualification: Disqualification of Attorneys and Law Firms*, 2nd ed. (Berkeley, CA: Banks & Jordan Law Publishing, 2014), §1.3, ch. 30; Kenneth L. Penegar, "The Loss of Innocence: A Brief History of Law Firm Disqualification in the Courts," *Georgetown Journal of Legal Ethics* 8, 4 (Summer 1995): 831–832, 889–890;

Keith Swisher, "The Practice and Theory of Lawyer Disqualification," *Georgetown Journal of Legal Ethics* 27, 1 (Winter 2014): 71–161.

52. Swisher, "Practice and Theory of Lawyer Disqualification," 138, 75.

53. Swisher, 73, 128–137; Firestone Tire & Rubber Co. v. Risjord, 449 U.S. 368, 370 (1981); Flanagan v. United States, 465 U.S. 259 (1984); Richardson-Merrell, Inc. v. Koller, 472 U.S. 424 (1985).

54. American Bar Association, "Alphabetical Listing of Jurisdictions Adopting Model Rules," https://www.americanbar.org/groups/professional_responsibility/publications /model_rules_of_professional_conduct/alpha_list_state_adopting_model_rules/. After 2009, only California had not adopted some part of the Model Rules, which it did effective November 1, 2018.

55. "Introduction to Report," *Annual Report of the American Bar Association* 126, 2 (2001): 257; *Annual Report of the American Bar Association* 112, 1 (1987): 627, 47; Shapero v. Kentucky B. Ass'n, 486 U.S. 466 (1988); Shapero v. Kentucky B. Ass'n, 726 S.W.2d 299 (Ky. 1987); "Report," *Annual Report of the American Bar Association* 114, 1 (1989): 129, 49.

56. "Report," *Annual Report of the American Bar Association* 114, 1 (1989): 643, 58.

57. Peel v. Attorney Registration and Disciplinary Committee, 496 U.S. 91 (1990); In re Peel, 534 N.W.2d 980, 985–986 (Ill. 1989); "Report," *Annual Report of the American Bar Association* 117, 3 (1992): 493–494, 36.

58. *Annual Report of the American Bar Association* 119, 2 (1994): 652–653, 50.

59. *Annual Report of the American Bar Association* 115, 3 (1990): 873–878, 732–757; *Annual Report of the American Bar Association* 116, 2 (1991): 41–45, 91–107, 411–453; Ted Schneyer, "Policymaking and the Perils of Professionalism: The ABA's Ancillary Business Debate as a Case Study," *Arizona Law Review* 35, 2 (1993): 363–396; Dennis J. Block, Irwin H. Warren, and George F. Meierhofer Jr., "Model Rule of Professional Conduct 5.7: Its Origin and Interpretation," *Georgetown Journal of Legal Ethics* 5, 4 (1992): 739–821 (justifying a ban); Art Garwin, ed., *A Legislative History: The Development of the ABA Model Rules of Professional Conduct, 1982–2013*, 4th ed. (ABA Center for Professional Responsibility, 2013), 671–691.

60. "Report," *Annual Report of the American Bar Association* 119, 1 (1994): 185, 5–9.

61. "Report No. 2," *Annual Report of the American Bar Association* 116, 2 (1991): 108; "Proceedings," *Annual Report of the American Bar Association* 116, 2 (1991): 12–16.

62. John P. Frank, "The American Law Institute, 1923–1998," *Hofstra Law Review* 26, 3 (Spring 1998): 625; *The American Law Institute: Seventy-Fifth Anniversary, 1923–1998* (Philadelphia: American Law Institute, 1998), 7; William P. LaPiana, "'A Task of No Common Magnitude': The Founding of the American Law Institute," *Nova Law Review* 11, 3 (Spring 1987): 1085–1126; G. Edward White, "The American Law Institute and the Triumph of Modernist Jurisprudence," *Law & History Review* 15, 1 (Spring 1997): 1–47; "Bibliography," in *American Law Institute: Seventy-Fifth Anniversary*, 348–351; American Bar Association, "ABA National Lawyer Population Survey: Historical Trend in Total National Lawyer Population, 1878–2019," https://www.americanbar.org/content/dam /aba/administrative/market_research/total-national-lawyer-population-1878-2019.pdf. For purposes of full disclosure, I am an ALI member.

63. Geoffrey C. Hazard Jr., "Report of the Director," *ALI Proceedings* 63 (1986): 42;

Geoffrey C. Hazard Jr., "Report of the Director," *ALI Proceedings* 67 (1990): 503, 505. Linda Mullenix became assistant reporter in 1990.

64. Hazard, foreword to *Restatement*, 1:xxi.

65. William Draper Lewis, introduction to *Model Code of Evidence* (Philadelphia: American Law Institute, 1942), vii–xi; Michael Ariens, "Progress Is Our Only Product: Legal Reform and the Codification of Evidence," *Law & Social Inquiry* 17, 2 (Spring 1992): 213–255.

66. Charles W. Wolfram, "The Concept of a Restatement of the Law Governing Lawyers," *Georgetown Journal of Legal Ethics* 1, 1 (1987): 195–196, 199–200; Herbert Wechsler, "Restatements and Legal Change: Problems of Policy in the Restatement Work of the American Law Institute," *Saint Louis University Law Journal* 13, 2 (Winter 1968): 190; Richard L. Revesz, "The Debate over the Role of Restatements," *ALI Reporter* 41, 3 (Summer 2019): 1, 4; Herbert Wechsler, "The Course of the Restatements," *American Bar Association Journal* 55, 2 (February 1969): 147–151.

67. *ALI Proceedings* 75 (1998): 154–155; "Actions Taken with Respect to Drafts Submitted at 1998 Annual Meeting," *ALI Reporter* 21, 1 (Fall 1998): 10; Geoffrey C. Hazard Jr., "Foreword," *ALI Proceedings* 75 (1998): v; "Final Meetings on Law Governing Lawyers Postponed until February," *ALI Reporter* 21, 1 (Fall 1998): 5. A restatement begins with a preliminary draft, which is reviewed by advisers and then sent to the council as a council draft; after review and approval, the council draft is sent to the members as a tentative draft. If the council and members agree, the provisions of the tentative draft are included in a proposed final draft, which must also be approved by both the members and the council. The approved proposed final draft is subject to a later process to ensure the internal integrity of the entire document. Lawrence J. Latto, "The Restatement of the Law Governing Lawyers: A View from the Trenches," *Hofstra Law Review* 26, 3 (Spring 1998): 700–701.

68. Council Draft No. 2 (September 15, 1988), 105; Council Draft No. 2A (November 15, 1988), 105, revising Preliminary Draft No. 3 (May 25, 1988), 106; *ALI Proceedings* 73 (1996): 307–321; Fred C. Zacharias, "The Restatement and Confidentiality," *Oklahoma Law Review* 46, 1 (Spring 1993): 73–86; Fred C. Zacharias, "Fact and Fiction in the Restatement of the Law Governing Lawyers: Should the Confidentiality Provisions Restate the Law," *Georgetown Journal of Legal Ethics* 6, 4 (Spring 1993): 903–932; Proposed Final Draft No. 2 (April 6, 1998), 192–193; Proposed Final Draft No. 1 (March 29, 1996), 332–333 (including a chart of exceptions to the client confidence rule); *Restatement*, §§66–67. The *Restatement*'s language improved the law by avoiding some traps of Rule 1.6(b)(1); Wolfram did not favor this limitation. Proposed Final Draft No. 1, 319n1; "Reporter's Note," lii. This was Hazard's preferred solution. Zacharias, "Fact and Fiction," 909–910n41; Ariens, "Last Hurrah," 740–741.

69. Zacharias, "Fact and Fiction," 914–917; Zacharias, "Restatement and Confidentiality," 76–77; *Restatement*, §66, illustration 3 at 498.

70. Lee A. Pizzimenti, "Screen Verite: Do Rules about Ethical Screens Reflect the Truth about Real-Life Law Firm Practice," *University of Miami Law Review* 52, 1 (October 1997): 315; Robert W. Hillman, "Law Firms and Their Partners: The Law and Ethics of Grabbing and Leaving," *Texas Law Review* 67, 1 (November 1988): 1–61.

71. Susan R. Martyn, "Conflict about Conflicts: The Controversy Concerning Law

Firm Screens," *Oklahoma Law Review* 46, 1 (Spring 1993): 54–56, nn. 11–15; *ALI Proceedings* 67 (1990): 282 (statement of associate reporter Thomas Morgan), 287, 289; *Restatement*, §124(2)(a–c); Neil W. Hamilton and Kevin R. Coan, "Are We a Profession or Merely a Business? The Erosion of the Conflicts Rules through the Increased Use of Ethical Walls," *Hofstra Law Review* 27, 1 (Fall 1999): 60–61, nn. 11–12.

72. Preliminary Draft No. 3 (May 25, 1988), §204, 410; Preliminary Draft No. 4 (January 25, 1989), 87 (no screening); *ALI Proceedings* 68 (1990): 282, 286–287, 289 (noting that the council, "in its wisdom," supported screening); Council Draft No. 3 (September 14, 1989), 95; Council Draft No. 3A (December 15, 1989), 107 (screening permitted); Martyn, "Conflict about Conflicts," 56; Preliminary Draft No. 4A (June 1, 1989), 96; *ALI Proceedings* 68 (1991): 422, 426 (Wolfram stating, "I am now persuaded that our present version of [screening] does make good practical and theoretical sense").

73. Preliminary Draft No. 4A (June 1, 1989), §204, 96; Council Draft No. 3 (September 14, 1989), §204, 95; Council Draft No. 3A, §204, 107; Tentative Draft No. 3 (April 10, 1990), §204, 135–136.

74. *ALI Proceedings* 67 (1990): 293–294.

75. Tentative Draft No. 4 (April 10, 1991), §204(2), 64, 71, Comment (d)(ii).

76. *ALI Proceedings* 68 (1991): 416, 421, 426–427, 448; a third motion to amend was rejected in a voice vote (439). Compare Preliminary Revisions, §204(2)(a), 8–48 ("not likely to be significant in the later case") with Preliminary Draft No. 11, §204, 8–53 ("unlikely to be significant in the subsequent matter").

77. Martyn, "Conflict about Conflicts," 56, 61; Hamilton and Coan, "Are We a Profession," 92, 94.

78. Pizzimenti, "Screen Verite," 321 ("law firms do vigorously attempt to avoid conflicts" but are "hampered" by both "insufficient legal and factual information" and a bias due to the adversarial approach taken to legal problems and to "their personal conflicting interests"), 323; Abel, *American Lawyers*, 311–312, tables 45c, 46; Michael Ariens, "Ethics in the Legal Industry," *Creighton Law Review* 51, 4 (September 2018): 698–699.

79. *ALI Proceedings* 73 (1996): 374–383.

80. Wolfram, "Concept of a Restatement," 197.

81. Jonathan R. Macey, "The Transformation of the American Law Institute," *George Washington Law Review* 61, 4 (April 1993): 1229; Stephen M. Bainbridge, "Independent Directors and the ALI Corporate Governance Project," *George Washington Law Review* 61, 4 (April 1993): 1044 (noting "the process by which the Principles took shape most closely resembled the rough-and-tumble politics of a state legislature"); Alex Elson, "The Case for an In-Depth Study of the American Law Institute," *Law & Social Inquiry* 23, 3 (Summer 1998): 625–640; Alex Elson and Michael L. Shakman, "The ALI Principles of Corporate Governance: A Tainted Process and a Flawed Product," *Business Lawyer* 49, 4 (August 1993): 1761–1792; *ALI Proceedings* 68 (1991): 10; Roswell Perkins, "The President's Letter," *ALI Reporter* 13, 3 (April 1991): 1; Charles Alan Wright, "The President's Page," *ALI Reporter* 16, 4 (Summer 1994): 1.

82. Alan Schwartz and Robert E. Scott, "The Political Economy of Private Legislatures," *University of Pennsylvania Law Review* 143, 3 (January 1995): 597; Macey, "Transformation," 1231.

83. Charles W. Wolfram, "Bismarck's Sausages and the ALI's Restatements," *Hofstra*

Law Review 26, 4 (Spring 1998): 824–825; William T. Barker, "Lobbying and the American Law Institute: The Example of Insurance Defense," *Hofstra Law Review* 26, 3 (Spring 1998): 573–593 (defending his lobbying); Charles Alan Wright, "The President's Page," *ALI Reporter* 19, 2 (Winter 1997): 2.

84. Monroe Freedman, "Caveat Lector: Conflicts of Interest of ALI Members in Drafting the Restatements," *Hofstra Law Review* 26, 3 (Spring 1998): 646, 654–666, 657–658.

85. Freedman, 660; Heinonline, American Law Institute case citations.

86. *Restatement*, §9(3), Comment i; *Meehan v. Shaughnessy*, 533 N.E.2d 1255 (Mass. 1989); *Restatement*, §10 (barring nonlawyers from owning any interest in a law firm or any business that includes the practice of law); Robert W. Hillman, "Law Firms and Their Partners Revisited: Reflections on Three Decades of Lawyer Mobility," *Texas Law Review* 96, 4 (March 2018): 787–809.

87. Laurel S. Terry, "A Primer on MDPS: Should the 'No' Rule Become a New Rule?" *Temple Law Review* 72, 4 (Winter 1999): 878–879.

88. "Report," *Annual Report of the American Bar Association* 124, 2 (1999): 225.

89. *Annual Report of the American Bar Association* 124, 2 (1999): 10–14, 223, 753; "Report," *Annual Report of the American Bar Association* 125, 2 (2000): 25, 183.

90. George C. Nnona, "Situating Multidisciplinary Practice within Social History: A Systemic Analysis of Inter-Professional Competition," *St. John's Law Review* 80, 3 (Summer 2006): 857n21.

91. Bethany McLean and Peter Elkind, *The Smartest Guys in the Room: The Amazing Rise and Scandalous Fall of Enron*, 10th anniversary ed. (New York: Portfolio/Penguin, 2013), 143–144, 405; Michael Ariens, "'Playing Chicken': An Instant History of the Battle over Disclosure of Client Confidences," *Journal of the Legal Profession* 33 (Spring 2009): 296–297; Lawrence J. Fox, "MDPs Done Gone: The Silver Lining in the Very Black Enron Cloud," *Arizona Law Review* 44, 3–4 (2002): 548; D.C. R. Pro. Conduct 5.4(b) (1996).

92. Michael M. Boone and Terry W. Conner, "Change, Change, and More Change: The Challenge Facing Law Firms," *Texas Bar Journal* 63, 1 (January 2000): 18 ("*Change has become the norm in business, and the legal industry is not immune to it*" [emphasis in original]); Fred C. Zacharias, "The Quest for a Perfect Code," *Georgetown Journal of Legal Ethics* 11, 4 (Summer 1998): 787–800.

93. W., "Notes on the Early Jurisprudence of Maine: Number Three," *Law Reporter* 3, 4 (August 1840): 126; Thomas Francis Howe, "The Proposed Amendment to the By-laws," *American Bar Association Journal* 8, 7 (July 1922): 436; Robert J. Kutak, "The Rules of Professional Conduct in an Era of Change," *Emory Law Journal* 29, 4 (Fall 1980): 889 ("in these times of rapid change, when technology no longer advances but 'leaps'"); Terry Carter, "Law at the Crossroads," *American Bar Association Journal* 88, 1 (January 2002): 30 (noting "seismic shifts to come").

94. James Podgers, "Model Rules Get the Once-over," *American Bar Association Journal* 83, 12 (December 1997): 90.

95. Podgers, 90.

96. E. Norman Veasey, "Introduction to Report," *Annual Report of the American Bar Association* 126, 2 (2001): 257–259.

97. "Minority Report," *Annual Report of the American Bar Association* 126, 2 (2001): 268–276; Veasey, "Introduction to Report," 262–263; Margaret C. Love, "Screening Law-

yers from Conflicts," *American Bar Association Journal* 87, 5 (May 2001): 61; Andrew L. Kaufman, "Ethics 2000—Some Heretical Thoughts," *Professional Lawyer Symposium* (2001): 1–2; Susan P. Shapiro, "If It Ain't Broke: An Empirical Perspective on Ethics 2000, Screening, and the Conflict-of-Interest Rules," *University of Illinois Law Review* 5 (2003): 1299–1329; Susan P. Shapiro, *Tangled Loyalties: Conflict of Interest in Legal Practice* (Ann Arbor: University of Michigan Press, 2002).

98. *Annual Report of the American Bar Association* 126, 2 (2001): 58–59; "Minority Report," 269–272; Garwin, *Legislative History*, 265–274; *Annual Report of the American Bar Association* 134, 1 (2009): 29–30, 302.

99. "Proceedings," *Annual Report of the American Bar Association* 126, 2 (2001): 13, 37, 308, 314–315; "Minority Report," 273; Mark Hansen, "Let the Debate Begin: Report on ABA Ethics Rules Is Read for the House," *American Bar Association Journal* 87, 8 (August 2001): 80; Irma S. Russell, "Client Confidences and Public Confidence in the Legal Profession: Observations on the ABA House of Delegates Deliberations on the Duty of Confidentiality," *Professional Lawyer* 13, 3 (Spring 2002): 21 (noting that some members are "radically out of step with the tradition of confidentiality in the American legal profession").

100. *Annual Report of the American Bar Association* 126, 2 (2001): 34–37, 308, 315; "Minority Report," 273; *ALI Proceedings* 73 (1996): 311; *Restatement*, §§66(3), 67(4), and Comment g (declaring a lawyer was not liable in such a situation); Hansen, "Let the Debate Begin," 80.

101. *Annual Report of the American Bar Association* 126, 2 (2001): 35, 314; *Annual Report of the American Bar Association* 116, 2 (1991): 16, 108.

102. "Proceedings," *Annual Report of the American Bar Association* 125, 2 (2001): 22–26 (mentioning "core values" nine times in the 2000 debate on multidisciplinary firms); "Proceedings," *Annual Report of the American Bar Association* 126, 2 (2002): 7, 36–38, 59 (mentioning "core values" nine times in the Ethics 2000 debate).

103. Nathan M. Crystal, "Core Values: False and True," *Fordham Law Review* 70, 3 (December 2001): 750–762.

104. Kurt Eichenwald, *Conspiracy of Fools: A True Story* (New York: Broadway Books, 2005), 73–85.

105. "Proceedings," *Annual Report of the American Bar Association* 127, 1 (2002): 37; "Informational Report," *Annual Report of the American Bar Association* 127, 2 (2002): 206–207; "Report No. 2," *Annual Report of the American Bar Association* 127, 2 (2002): 273; "Proceedings," *Annual Report of the American Bar Association* 127, 2 (2002): 16–17; Ariens, "'Playing Chicken,'" 296.

106. Steve France, "Unhappy Pioneers: S&L Lawyers Discover a 'New World' of Liability," *Georgetown Journal of Legal Ethics* 7, 3 (Winter 1994): 726 ("At least twenty-two of the largest 200 law firms in the country . . . have been sued for malpractice by the federal banking agencies in connection with services provided to failed banks and thrifts"); Roger C. Cramton, "Enron and the Corporate Lawyer: A Primer on Legal and Ethical Issues," *Business Lawyer* 58, 1 (November 2002): 143n3; Harris Weinstein, "Attorney Liability in the Savings and Loan Crisis," *University of Illinois Law Review* 1 (1993): 53 (noting there have been "over 1000 criminal cases and nearly 2000 civil suits arising from the savings and loan crisis," including "more than ninety civil cases brought against law-

yers"); James M. McCauley, "Corporate Responsibility and the Regulation of Corporate Lawyers," *Richmond Journal of Global Law & Business* 3 (2003): 22–25, nn. 30–34 (listing scandals); William H. Widen, "Enron at the Margins," *Business Lawyer* 58, 3 (May 2003): 962–963.

107. Arthur Andersen LLP v. United States, 544 U.S. 696 (2005); Sarbanes-Oxley Act, Pub. L. 107-204, 116 Stat. 745 (2002); Ariens, "'Playing Chicken,'" 297; "Preliminary Report of the Task Force on Corporate Responsibility," *Business Lawyer* 58, 1 (November 2002): 190; Jenny B. Davis, "The Enron Factor," *American Bar Association Journal* 88, 4 (April 2002): 45, 61.

108. 148 Cong. Rec. S6778–79 (July 15, 2002); "Preliminary Report of the Task Force," 203–204; Ariens, "'Playing Chicken,'" 272–273.

109. "Preliminary Report of the Task Force," 205–207, nn. 39–40; Proposed Final Draft No. 2 (April 6, 1998), 192–193.

110. "Implementation of Standards of Professional Conduct for Attorneys," 67 Fed. Reg. 71620, 71688–71689, 71693 (December 2, 2002); "Report of the American Bar Association Task Force on Corporate Responsibility," *Business Lawyer* 59, 1 (November 2003): 172–173.

111. Ariens, "'Playing Chicken,'" 278–279n258.

112. "Report No. 1," *Annual Report of the American Bar Association* 128, 2 (2003): 499–500, 513n38 (noting the initial "proposal engendered strong criticism").

113. "Proceedings," *Annual Report of the American Bar Association* 128, 2 (2003): 14, 16, 18 (218–201); James Podgers, "The Non-Revolution," *American Bar Association Journal* 89, 10 (October 2003): 80.

114. "Informational Report," *Annual Report of the American Bar Association* 133, 2 (2008): 98; "Proceedings," *Annual Report of the American Bar Association* 133, 2 (2008): 43–44; Garwin, *Legislative History*, 267.

115. *Annual Report of the American Bar Association* 134, 1 (2009): 309; Garwin, *Legislative History*, 268; Erik Wittman, "A Discussion of Nonconsensual Screens as the ABA Votes to Amend Model Rule 1.10," *Georgetown Journal of Legal Ethics* 22, 3 (Summer 2009): 1220n68.

116. "Proceedings," *Annual Report of the American Bar Association* 134, 1 (2009): 26.

117. "Proceedings," 28; Garwin, *Legislative History*, 268.

118. Memorandum from Jamie S. Gorelick and Michael Traynor, "Preliminary Issues Outline (Restated)," June 1, 2010, https://www.americanbar.org/content/dam/aba/ad ministrative/professional_responsibility/2011build/ethics2020/inbound_foreign_law yer_memo_templates.pdf.

119. "Proceedings," *Annual Report of the American Bar Association* 137, 2 (2012): 4–6, 13–20; "Reports," *Annual Report of the American Bar Association* 137, 2 (2012): 175–243; *Annual Report of the American Bar Association* 138, 1 (2013): 20–23, 159–209; memorandum, "Summary of Actions," December 28, 2011, https://www.americanbar.org /content/dam/aba/administrative/ethics_2020/20111228_summary_of_ethics_20_20 _commission_actions_december_2011_final.pdf; memorandum on alternative business structures, December, 2, 2011, https://www.americanbar.org/content/dam/aba /administrative/ethics_2020/20111202-ethics2020-discussion_draft-alps.pdf; https://www .americanbar.org/groups/professional_responsibility/committees_commissions/stand

ingcommitteeonprofessionalism2/resources/ethics2020hompeage/; James Podgers, "Summer Job," *American Bar Association Journal* 98, 6 (June 2012): 27–29; James E. Moliterno, "Ethics 20/20 Successfully Achieved Its Mission: It Protected, Preserved, and Maintained," *Akron Law Review* 47, 1 (2014): 158.

120. *Annual Report of the American Bar Association* 137, 2 (2012): 18–20, 234; ABA Formal Op. 09-455 (2009).

121. James Podgers, "Clean Sweep," *American Bar Association Journal* 98, 9 (September 2012): 59–60.

122. Galanter and Palay, *Tournament of Lawyers*, 67n187; Pollock, *Turks and Brahmins*, 264; Mitchell Kowalski, *The Great Legal Reformation: Notes from the Field* (iUniverse, 2017), 111–112 ("quality legal expertise is fast becoming nothing more than table stakes").

123. Ariens, "Ethics in the Legal Industry," 673–677; Google Books Ngram Viewer, "legal profession, knowledge industry, legal industry," https://perma.cc.ES6H-48DC. "Legal industry" is not in *Black's Law Dictionary* (2019) or *Bouvier Law Dictionary*, ed. Stephen Michael Sheppard, compact ed. (New York: Wolters Kluwer Law & Business, 2011).

124. *Oxford English Dictionary*, s.v. "industry."

125. Ariens, "Ethics in the Legal Industry," 678, nn. 28–31. One Dewey & LeBoeuf executive was convicted, a second was acquitted, and charges against a third were dropped.

126. Aric Press, "The Super Rich Get Richer," *American Lawyer* 36, 5 (May 2014): 130–135; Michael D. Goldhaber, "The Great Class Divide," *American Lawyer* 36, 5 (May 2014): 150 (in 1994 "most AmLaw 100 firms were equity-only partnerships"; twenty years later, just seventeen remained so); Chris Johnson, "Rich and Richer," *American Lawyer* 37, 5 (May 2015): 98–101, 122–123; Harper, *Lawyer Bubble*, 97; *2013 Report on the State of the Legal Market* (Georgetown University Law Center, Center for the Study of the Legal Profession), 10 (reporting that 169 of the AmLaw 200 have two-tiered partnerships).

127. Pollock, *Turks and Brahmins*, 266.

128. ABA Committee about Research on the Future of the Legal Profession, "Working Notes: Deliberations on the Current Status of the Legal Profession" (August 31, 2001), 2; "Informational Report," *Annual Report of the American Bar Association* 127, 1 (2002): 362–363.

129. ABA Committee, "Working Notes," 4, 36.

CONCLUSION

1. Roscoe Pound, "A Century of American Law," in *Law: A Century of Progress, 1835–1935*, ed. Allison Reppy, 3 vols. (New York: New York University Press, 1937), 1:8; David Luban, *Lawyers and Justice: An Ethical Study* (Princeton, NJ: Princeton University Press, 1988), xvii.

2. Anthony V. Alfieri, "The Fall of Legal Ethics and the Rise of Risk Management," *Georgetown Law Journal* 94, 6 (August 2006): 1909–1955.

3. Joseph B. Warner, "The Responsibilities of the Lawyer," *Annual Report of the Ameri-*

can Bar Association 19 (1896): 319–320; Moorfield Storey, "Joseph Bangs Warner," in *Later Years of the Saturday Club, 1870–1920*, ed. M. A. DeWolfe Howe (Boston: Houghton Mifflin, 1927), 295–299; Philip P. Wiener, *Evolution and the Founders of Pragmatism* (1949; reprint, Philadelphia: University of Pennsylvania Press, 1972), 235–242. Warner was one of the founding members of the Metaphysical Club, along with Oliver Wendell Holmes Jr. See Louis Menand, *The Metaphysical Club* (New York: Farrar, Straus & Giroux, 2001), 201. Warner's speech is echoed in Holmes's famous address to the graduates of Boston University School of Law a year later. O. W. Holmes Jr., "The Path of the Law," *Harvard Law Review* 10, 8 (March 1897): 457–478.

4. Warner, "Responsibilities of the Lawyer," 323–324, 328, 336.

5. Thomas Paine, *Common Sense* (1776), in *Complete Writings of Thomas Paine*, ed. Philip S. Foner, 2 vols. (New York: Citadel Press, 1945), 1:29.

INDEX

AALS (Association of American Law Schools), 9, 182
ABA (American Bar Association). *See specific references*
ABA Advisory Committee on the Prosecution and Defense Function, 195
ABA Annual Report, 181, 234
ABA Canons. *See* Canons of Professional Ethics, ABA
ABA Code of Professional Responsibility. *See* Code of Professional Responsibility, ABA
ABA Criminal Justice Standards for the Prosecution Function and Defense Function, 195, 207, 215–216, 221
ABA House of Delegates, 159, 166, 176, 182, 189, 200–203, 240, 242, 259, 261, 274–275, 279
ABA Model Rules of Professional Conduct. *See* Model Rules of Professional Conduct, ABA
Abbot, Everett V., 137, 144
ABCNY. *See* Association of the Bar of the City of New York
ABF (American Bar Foundation), 180–182, 200, 224, 246
accounting firms, 248, 269–271, 276, 280. *See also* Arthur Andersen; Big Five
Adams, Charles Francis, Jr., 85, 95, 99–100, 106
Adams, John, 5, 7, 12, 14–15, 51, 78
and Boston Massacre trials, 5, 16–19, 78

Adler, Felix, 137
adversary system, 2–3, 6, 48–49, 74, 76, 131, 170–173, 192–194, 203, 235, 242
advertising, 130, 135–136, 139–140, 203, 223, 233. *See also* Canon 27; commercialism
Agnew, Spiro T., 228
Airlie Conference on Legal Manpower Needs of Criminal Law, 193
Alabama Code of Ethics, 91, 112–115, 121–122, 129–130, 135
Alabama Rule 10, 115, 132
Alabama State Bar Association, 9, 91, 112–115, 118
"A Lawyer," 21–22
Albany and Susquehanna Railroad (A&S), 96, 99–101, 103–104
Albany Law Journal, 101–102, 104, 120
Alexander, Lucien, 129
ALI. *See* American Law Institute
ambulance chasing, 7, 91, 118–119, 128, 130, 160–162
American Bankers Association Trust Division, 159
American Bar Association (ABA). *See specific references*
American Bar Endowment, 205
American Bar Foundation (ABF), 180–182, 200, 224, 246
American College of Trial Lawyers, 190, 199, 210
American Institute of Electrical Engineers, 184
American Jurist & Law Magazine, 17, 56

Printed in the USA
CPSIA information can be obtained
at www.ICGtesting.com
LVHW082057021223
765382LV00005B/570